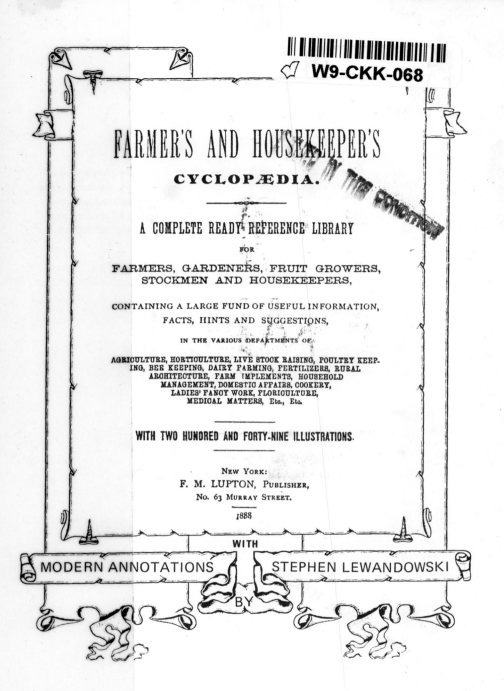

FARMER'S AND HOUSEKEEPER'S
CYCLOPÆDIA.

A COMPLETE READY REFERENCE LIBRARY

FOR

FARMERS, GARDENERS, FRUIT GROWERS, STOCKMEN AND HOUSEKEEPERS,

CONTAINING A LARGE FUND OF USEFUL INFORMATION, FACTS, HINTS AND SUGGESTIONS,

IN THE VARIOUS DEPARTMENTS OF

AGRICULTURE, HORTICULTURE, LIVE STOCK RAISING, POULTRY KEEP-
ING, BEE KEEPING, DAIRY FARMING, FERTILIZERS, RURAL
ARCHITECTURE, FARM IMPLEMENTS, HOUSEHOLD
MANAGEMENT, DOMESTIC AFFAIRS, COOKERY,
LADIES' FANCY WORK, FLORICULTURE,
MEDICAL MATTERS, Etc., Etc.

WITH TWO HUNDRED AND FORTY-NINE ILLUSTRATIONS.

NEW YORK:
F. M. LUPTON, PUBLISHER,
No. 63 MURRAY STREET.

1888

WITH

MODERN ANNOTATIONS

STEPHEN LEWANDOWSKI

BY

—THE COMPLETE 1888 EDITION—

Published by The Crossing Press, Trumansburg, N.Y.

Graphics--
Front Cover, Tom Parker
Back Cover, Karl Wolff & Tom Parker
Title Page, Karl Wolff

The remedies and advice recommended in the Home Physician chapter and elsewhere in this book are not those of the publisher, but they are considered to be of social and cultural interest. They are not to be considered prescriptions or advice for specific or general ailments, or in any way to replace or substitute for the guidance and services of a qualified medical practitioner.

2nd Printing, March 1978

Copyright ⓒ 1977 The Crossing Press

Library of Congress Cataloging in Publication Data

[Lupton, Frank M   ] 1854-1910.
    Farmer's and housekeeper's cyclopaedia.

    Reprint of the ed. published by Lupton, New York, under title: The national farmer's and housekeeper's cyclopaedia; first published under title: The farm and household cyclopaedia.
    Includes index.
    1. Agriculture--Handbooks, manuals, etc.
2.   Home economics--Handbooks, manuals, etc.
I.   Lewandowski, Stephen. II. Title.
S501.L964   1977   630   77-23827
ISBN 0-912278-90-0
ISBN 0-912278-91-9 pbk.

Publisher's Preface

One day last fall, a friend of ours, John Baisley, who does butchering for a living, came to the house carrying a glossy, white piece of fur. He explained that it was a goatskin which he had just tanned, using a recipe from an old book he had found lying in pieces in an abandoned house. He remarked it was hard to come by a good method for tanning a skin with the fur on. This book, he went on, had proven useful on other occasions-- many old-time ways of doing things were still the best.

We asked to see the old book, which turned out to be *The Farmer's & Housekeeper's Cyclopaedia.* When we opened it, we found, next to a handwritten recipe for cold cream, a statement by a previous owner, "This book is worth its weight in gold." After reading the book, we agreed that the material in it was too valuable to let die. There is much modest wisdom here that we, in all our sophistication, can learn from.

To make the book even more useful, we asked another friend, Stephen Lewandowski, a poet who works for the County Soil Conservation Department, to write an extensive introduction for the book as well as notes preceding each chapter. We have reprinted the Cyclopaedia intact. In order to distinguish the Lewandowski update from the body of the Cyclopaedia, we tinted the pages of the Lewandowski notes a light grey color.

We wish to thank everyone who labored on this book, particularly Mel Ankeny, who lent us an undamaged copy from his personal library so we could reproduce the edition you are now reading.

Elaine and John Gill

—The recipe for tanning hides which John Baisley referred to may be found on page 259.

INTRODUCTION — By Stephen Lewandowski

Why This Book?

American agricultural newspapers of the 19th century often jeered at "book farmers," those people who approached farming through manuals and handbooks rather than through direct personal experience on the land. Certainly, it would be best for farmers to have both direct experience as well as book knowledge, but this combination is not always possible.

Usually, it is the experience directly on the land that is lacking for new farmers. Valuable farm methods can be lost in a single generation and, once lost, are gone for good unless they are recorded in a book. The practical know-how of the farmer in 1888 was set down in this *Farmer's & Housekeeper's Cyclopaedia*. We have reprinted it in the hope it will prove useful to small farmers today. When certain chapters were deficient in information, I have suggested other books to look at.

Agriculture has changed a great deal in the 90 odd years since this book was first issued. Farming has become more of an industry. Small, independent farmers have been unable to compete and have been driven out. There are far fewer farms now than then, and the amount of land under cultivation has decreased substantially. However, the last agricultural census indicates that there may be some reversing of this trend. Younger men are becoming attracted to farming (the average age of farmers has gone down) and the average size of land holdings has decreased a bit. Perhaps there is some life and hope for the small farmer yet. This book is intended to further that hope.

Farming is not a simple life. It is a way of making a richer life with a small outlay of money. It is also a way of unplugging as many of society's offers and demands as can conveniently be discarded. We will always be connected to society, but we can take responsibility for our energy consumption, the making of a comfortable shelter for ourselves, and the production of our food.

Robert Rodale in his book *Organic Gardening* defines the organic gardener as a "living, contributing part of the cycle of life itself. He does not merely take. He is a giver, a sharer, a restorer." This definition fits very well with a conservation principle that humans were given stewardship over the land, not dominion.

The *Farmer's & Housekeeper's Cyclopaedia* respects all forms of life and the land itself. The author tries to work with and through natural forces. He encourages wild birds in the orchard, he lets chickens range freely, he trains a colt to the bit by letting the colt train itself. He always favors the most natural approach to farm methods. The *Cyclopaedia* is organic in spirit.

Judging Land

Walk over the land. Observe the natural vegetation. Dig a hole. Dig several holes. The soils may change within a hundred yards or the soil may be consistent throughout. To learn the general tendencies of soils in the area you're looking at, visit the local offices of the Soil Conservation Service. Often the soils will have been mapped, and, if you can locate your property, the technicians will give you ideas of what to look for and what generally can be done with the land.

Soils are judged on a variety of characteristics. Texture is very important. The soil may be sandy and coarse, loamy with clods that break easily, or clayey with clods that are plastic and sticky when wet and hard to break when dry. Texture is important in how the soil holds water; a medium, loamy soil with some sand and some clay is best. Texture also relates to how the land may be worked or what's called "tilth." Sandy and clayey soils require quite different preparations before they're fitted to crops. A clay soil may need fall plowing to be arable at all and rollers, harrows and clod-crushers may have to be widely used to form a surface even enough for most planting.

The color and mottling of the topsoil and subsoil furnish good indications of how the soil will drain. Colors are best observed when the soil is wet. Well-drained land is most often a uniform shade of brown through topsoil and subsoil. Moderately well drained land has a gray or mottled zone about a foot or foot and a half below the surface. Poorly drained lands present a dense gray or yellow subsoil within a foot of the surface.

Stoniness may be a problem on some land. Small rocks may be a nuisance but won't impede machinery; large boulders and outcroppings will.

The subsoil is important to the total drainage of the land. If the subsoil is granular in texture and breaks up easily into crumbs, it will drain excess water very well. If it breaks into irregular blocks, the subsoil is heavy and less pervious. The worst subsoil for drainage is that which arranges itself in plates like shingles. It is very heavy, made of fine materials and almost impervious.

The slope of the land is important in what sort of activities may be carried out there. Some lands may be dangerous to work with a tractor; they may have been worked a hundred years ago with animal power, but they no longer are. Also, fields with strong and long slopes may erode considerably if they are brought into cultivation.

The usefulness of the land is directly effected by its physical features. In the Northeast, farmers are most concerned with the land's drainage; in the Midwest, they want land that will hold what little moisture can be supplied by rain or irrigation. One can estimate a field's drainage possibilities by checking it for springs, observing the texture and color and tilth of the topsoil, the color and texture of the subsoil, the slope of the land, and by making such considerations as: is it possible to drain this land? Can the water be gotten to an outlet in a ditch or stream? Some fields have hollows that are nearly impossible to economically drain with modern equipment.

The depth of the soil is very important. Many plants will send down roots to two feet if they can. Deeply rooted plants will resist drought. Normal summer rainfall often doesn't supply enough water for continued crop growth. Thus the depth of the soil and the degree to which it will hold water is important to regular plant growth and maturation.

Much soil can be lost from a severely sloping field of erodable materials. Some soils will resist erosion very well by their firm and binding consistency. Others must be used for crops only with the greatest care. Erosion can be slowed down by contour plowing, diversion ditches, terraces and strip cropping. Sometimes the Soil Conservation Service will suggest that a field not be worked at all but be kept in grass for pastureland.

The ease with which a field may be cultivated is determined by its slope, stoniness, wetness, past erosion, and physical characteristics such as hedgerows, stone walls, knolls and creeks. A farmer can adjust his mechanical treatment of the land and his choice of crops and use to the physical necessities of the land.

The local office of the Soil Conservation Service or the Soil & Water Conservation District will have technicians who'll be glad to talk with you about the soil and its capabilities. They sometimes get used to talking with large-scale, professional farmers and it's hard to get them to explain specifics, but it's up to the landowner to keep after them for information. Tenacity counts for a lot. The agent of the Cooperative Extension can test your land for lime and can obtain a more complete test of your soil from a state university or testing station. Make use of these public servants.

Work

Work is the single largest ingredient that the small farmer can apply to his capital investment in the land. Lacking money to invest in machines or animals, the small farmer may be able to put his energy to use to overcome part of this lack. This is not to say that work by itself will overcome all deficiencies nor that one should court work. One will have enough to do without looking for more. Old-timers in the neighborhood can tell you this. They are your major source of information and advice, and I encourage every young farmer to listen to what the old people have to say. Take the time to listen first. You may save yourself a great deal of work.

The *Michigan Farmer* of April 15, 1849 contains a short essay on "Productive Farming" which it would be worthwhile to repeat here:

> *A great error in farmers is to undertake more work than they can perform well. The consequence is that much of the labor they perform is worse than useless, because the productive qualities of the soil are exhausted, without yielding such a return as the same amount of labor would if properly applied. . .Were the labor expended in cultivating large fields expended in husbanding manure and cultivating a small quantity of land, the aggregate crops would be much larger than they are. . .In this country, farming, in too many cases, reminds us of the fable of the man and the goose that laid a golden egg every day. The prospect of the future is often blasted by attempting too much at present. Every farmer should recollect that his land is his capital, and a great part of his wealth depends upon the productiveness of his farm. If, by injudicious farming, land is worn out, a great part of the farmer's capital is sunk. We would therefore recommend every farmer to husband everything which, by application to the soil, will increase its productive qualities, and in spring*

to sow part of his tillable land in clover. These
means will, if the other departments are properly
tended to, insure success. (p. 117)

This good advice asks that the farmer keep in mind not just the season's crop but the whole future of the land. It encourages the farmer to think not only of work that will improve crops but which will build the land up for better crops in future years. Careful attention to the whole spectrum of farm activities, what the essay calls "husbanding," will bring about this long-term enrichment of the land and advancement of the farmer.

The farmer's condition is a sort of marriage to the land. As the land goes, so he or she will go. Farmers must develop a hind-sight and a fore-sight that many other kinds of lives do not demand. The land moves so slowly, so deliberately that the farmer, to tune his work with its cycles, must be able to see much further ahead. And he must also be attached to principles that disappear into the human past. How can we ask a person to think in terms of processes that so far outstrip his own life span? An idea of the many generations of men on the land will help stretch his vision. If fertility is exhausted or damaged in one lifetime, it will take many future generations to re-establish. For the person interested in understanding the web of relations between man and the cultivated plants, I recommend Edgar Anderson's *Plants, Life and Man* (Berkeley: University of California Press 1971) as good reading.

The small farmer will have to be more in tune with the cycles of land, plants and animals. He cannot afford, even if he wished to, to make the alterations on the face of the land that agribusiness with its chemicals, huge machines and storage and processing plants can. His object is continued survival and satisfaction, not maximum profit. It's a way of life, not just a business.

The small farmer must expect to work. To make a go of it on the farm, hard and long work is absolutely necessary. The only other choice is to find a cash-producing, relatively undemanding job and run the farm on the side.

To find meaningful work, whatever its form, is a great gift. So many people work at jobs they consider useless. What opinions shall these people hold of their lives spent in doing such work? The right form of work will vary from person to person. It's easy enough to feel righteous about your own work and scornful of another person's, but the satisfaction is what counts. If you want to work the land, to live close to it, and see the direct results of your labor in what you can produce to eat, wear and feed to others, the small farm is the place for you.

Water

To begin speaking of water, I'll quote from Dr. W.W. Hall's article "Farmers' Houses" in the *Report of the Commissioner of Agriculture for the Year of 1863* (Washington: Government Printing Office, 1863):

> *The first consideration is pure, soft water. That from a spring is most to be desired, and can be easily procured by means of pipes when the spring is located above the residence. If the spring is on a level with or below the house, and is copious, with some fall, a portion can be thrown up into the reservoir at the dwelling by means of a water-ram or some sort of simple and inexpensive equipment.*
>
> *If no sufficient spring is convenient, a well (with an old fashioned pump in it) where soft water can be obtained by digging, is probably the next best supply, as it, too, is always cool and lively. Every part of the kitchen, the wash and the bake house, the dairy and barn can be supplied from a pump by aid of pipes, saving much labor at small cost.*
>
> *But in limestone and other sections where pure soft water cannot be obtained from a spring or by digging, by all means provide a capacious cistern for the dwelling and another for the farm buildings. By means of properly constructed filters attached to the cisterns, and by keeping the roofs free from pigeons and other poultry, clean pure soft water can always be provided in great abundance.*
>
> *Whether spring, well, or cistern be employed, examine them often and carefully, and especially each spring and fall, and have them thoroughly cleansed when needed. (pp321-2)*

To have clean, pure water brought directly into the house was a great convenience, one that we now take for granted. Windmills were often used to pump water to a tank at an elevation from which it might flow into the house. A house was frequently equipped with both a cistern and a well. Well water was used for drinking and cooking, and the cistern water for washing and cleaning. Now, with well-drilling equipment that can drill a shaft hundreds of feet deep, if need be, there's no excuse for not having good water in the house.

An equally great convenience was the development of an indoor privy. Scarcely any of the 19th century agricultural writers would have thought of disposing of human excrement as offensive. "Night soil," the outhouse contents, was considered a highly potent fertilizer, and it never occurred to them to use it otherwise or throw it away. The source quoted above states that "the faeces of one individual will fertilize an acre of ground every year to a greater extent than any ordinary compost." (p. 330) Human waste was composted with lime, whether it was dug out of the outdoor privy yearly or cleaned out of earth-toilet chambers in the house every week. It was spread on the fields like all other manure.

A plan for a house in the 1871 *American Agriculturalist* shows a pipe system for filtering and channeling liquid wastes of the household and finally allowing their absorption by a grid system in the lawn. Solid waste was put into earth-toilets, covered with dry absorbent dirt and lime, and these toilet receptacles below the house were emptied frequently into the compost heap for garden use.

Keep in mind that water runs downhill when positioning your barns and waste heap in relation to the supply of your water. Water contaminated by sewage is very unhealthy.

Heat

People have been concerned about having enough wood to use for a long time. Around 1790 Boston and Philadelphia offered rewards for tree-planting; they were concerned with a shortage of timber and firewood near the cities. Unfortunately the population's concern with forest reserves has been more evident on paper and less in the forests themselves. In 1831 a federal law was passed against cutting live oak on naval reservations, and this law stood for almost sixty years as the only law protecting government lands from logging.

In 1865 an article published by Rev. Frederick Starr in the *Report of the Department of Agriculture* forecast a timber famine in the United States within thirty years. True or not, this prediction began to stir up some interest in protecting forests. New York and Maine followed suit with a few years. In 1872, Arbor Day was celebrated in Nebraska, and the Timber Culture Act of

1873 provided 160 acres of land in the Midwest in return for planting forty (later ten) acres of trees.

In the 1870's the American Forestry Congress and the American Forestry Association were formed and began to lobby not only for planting forest trees on public land and replanting trees on areas that had been clear cut, but for more careful management of cutting procedures to improve existing forests.

In 1881 the Division of Forestry was established in the Department of Agriculture and staffed with four men at an appropriation of $10,000. In 1883, forestry education began to be offered in state land grant colleges.

In 1885, forest commissions were formed in Colorado, California and New York. 1891 marked the beginning of the National Park system with the setting aside of a forest reserve at Yellowstone.

Where does this leave us now? It leaves us, as anyone can tell you who's tried to build with wood in the last ten years, with a very small store of very costly timber. The problem is less marked in the Southeast and Northwest, areas with considerable timber supplies, but it still exists. The crux of the problem is that we've allowed our forest growing stock to shrink and deteriorate. By the last two decades of the 19th century the greatest forests of white pine and hemlock had been used up. It's true that a larger percentage of the Northeastern states is in forest now than in 1888, but the forests are just not capable of producing the quality wood that the virgin forests of the region were.

We are in somewhat better shape for wood-burning. With other fuel prices going sky-high and the call on for personal conservation, it's fitting that we look to our burnable wood resources. Thinking about burning more wood doesn't mean a further depletion of our forests. Wood, as forestry agents are fond of pointing out, is a renewable resource. Thus, when we think about burning wood for fuel, we are asking that the existing supplies be managed and cut more knowledgeably.

Yearly growth of a managed woodlot should yield at least half a standard cord (4'x4'x8') per year. It has been estimated than an average family using wood for heating and cooking will use about fifty face cords (4'x8'x12-18") per year. Thus the average growth on thirty acres of woodlot should supply a family's needs. This wood supply would come from fall wood or culling, not from depleting the standing timber. Culling actually improves the woodlot—the straightest, most valuable trees are encouraged by cutting out trees which crowd and distort their forms.

It's estimated that a cord of seasoned hardwood is equal in heating value to a ton of anthracite coal or two hundred and forty gallons of fuel oil. At current fuel oil prices this makes a cord of seasoned hardwood burned in an efficient stove worth at least $100! Supposing that you can cut and prepare a cord of wood for the fire in six to ten hours work, it's work that's well paid in savings.

As a further benefit, burning a cord of hardwood produces about sixty pounds of ashes. These ashes should be spread on garden plots as they are of great advantage in sweetening the land with their calcium carbonate (lime) and fertilizing the land with their potash and phosphoric acid.

It's best to burn what's most directly available in the woodlot as culls or scrap. If you have a choice of woods, black birch, hickory, ironwood, black and honey locust, swamp white and white oaks, shadbush and dogwood are the best burning. White ash, beech, fruitwoods, sugar maple and red oak are also well worth burning. Whatever the variety of wood, it will benefit from seasoning. Placing the split up wood under shelter and off the ground for several months will increase its heating value and decrease the risk of fires from the build-up of creosote in the chimney.

At least yearly cleaning of the chimney, burning seasoned wood, making sure combustion's clean, and insulating the short pipe which connects your stove to the chimney will decrease the danger of fires.

A wide variety of woodstoves are being produced in the U.S. and Europe. I suspect the manufacture of wood stoves has doubled or tripled in the last five years, and formerly moribund companies have found themselves again doing a good business. The choice of the kind of stove will depend on the size of the house to be heated, the other uses of the stove, and the buyer's suspicions about its efficiency. Ashley stoves and wood space heaters have a very good reputation.

A relatively new publication will be of interest to woodburners. The *Woodburning Quarterly & Home Energy Digest* (8009 34th. Ave. S., Minneapolis, Mn. 55420, $5.00/year) publishes articles about how to get the maximum heat out of your stove or fireplace with the maximum safety. The many woodstove ads will give you a notion of what's available.

Alternative Power Sources

We've seen a dramatic rise in energy costs in the last ten years. Woodburning is one way to by-pass the need for costly energy sources. Other energy collection systems in which the technology is sufficiently advanced to merit greater attention are solar energy systems and windmills. Few people are prepared to claim that our whole energy dependence can be alleviated by such systems, but they do make it possible for specific, inventive individuals to become more energy independent.

The technology for collecting and storing the sun's energy is daily being refined and improved. A house which is built or converted to take advantage of solar energy, even such as can be collected on its own roof-space, will be substantially reduced in its dependence on other forms of energy.

Thirty or forty years ago, wind-driven generators were in common use in rural areas. At that time, an average windmill could contribute about 3, 000 watts of power for the basic needs of a household. Two things have happened since then—power lines were brought into rural areas with government assistance, and homes in rural areas began to expand their collections of energy-using devices. A study in 1975 showed that electric power supplied by a commercially designed and constructed windmill would cost five to eight times more than the power delivered by the local utility company, based on a fifteen year period of operation. However, there is no reason to believe that utility power will remain this cheap, and there's no reason why a person shouldn't cut out a large part of the capital investment on a windmill by building it him or herself. With the long winter months and a barn to work in, a farmer could make a good start on a windmill.

Several leaflets now available would be of help in constructing a windmill: *How to Construct a Cheap Wind Machine* (Do-It-Yourself Leaflet L-5, Brace Research Institute, Quebec, Canada, 1973) or *Windmills and Wind Generators* (Agricultural Engineering Leaflet 2001, Cooperative Extension, University of California, 1974). Larger books worth looking into for wind and other forms of power are: *The Mother Earth News Handbook of Homemade Power* (NY: Bantam Books, 1974, $1.95), *Windmills and Millwrighting* by Stanley Freeze (NY: Great Albion Books, 1973, $7.95) or *Producing Your Own Power* edited by Carol H. Stoner (NY: Vintage Books [Rodale], 1975, $3.95).

Windmills come in two main forms; the choice depends on the

consistency of prevailing winds and the use to which they'll be put. Windmills have been used in pumping water, grinding grain and churning; they are easily hooked to a generator to produce electric power. One form of windmill is the light weight, high speed, three or four bladed propeller. The other design is closer to what we're familiar with from pictures of windmills on the plains in the 30's, a heavy, many bladed turbine. Both designs work on a horizontal axis, which means that the power must be converted to a vertical axis. Both designs must include a means of turning the blades into the changing wind and of feathering the propeller in too high a wind. Other designs such as the Savonius rotor and the Darrieus rotor which operate on a vertical axis and accept wind from any direction are being tested.

It's been estimated that the average electricity consumption for a household without electric heat would be 400-600 kilowatt hours per month. Half of the power needs of such a household could be met by a 30% efficient windmill generator with a ten foot blade diameter operating in an average of 14 m.p.h. winds.

Letter From A Young Farmer

Hearing of my work on this book, my correspondent, friend and 40 acre farmer, John Sillick of Royalton, N.Y. wrote me:

Dear Steve,

There is a misconception that the rural life is simple. There is nothing simple about it. Everything depends on everything else. You are too close to the raw materials and spend your time & energy processing them into other forms. The manure becomes corn (weather permitting) becomes cow becomes meat becomes you. One could, perhaps should, lead the Thoreauvian life, but that's not farming. "Walden" is clear about that. Henry stayed, very deliberately, clear of farms. Farming, as opposed to gardening, demands a level of mechanization. When you raise your first crop you learn an important lesson: food is too cheap. That hundred bushels of corn that you nursed through the hot sun is worth $250. That's all. While food is cheap, considering the things that go into producing it, equipment is very expensive. A stainless steel milking pail costs $40 and you must have one to avoid spoiling your milk. The cost of tractor parts leaves you stand-

ing at the counter with your mouth open.

Money. The idea of money must be on the farmer's mind. Unless there is some profitable outcome to his projects, he will eventually realize he is a fool to work so hard when he can live better another way. However, one should not overlook the higher quality of home produced and prepared foods and the money saved by not having to go to the grocery store.

A friend of mine raised some chickens through the fall and winter and found when he tallied the bills that the birds cost him about ten dollars apiece. That sounds incredible; but it illustrates the idea well: don't plan to make money on animals if you don't raise your own feeds. It becomes an expensive hobby and not a real way of life. At some point you'll feel silly.

The machinery to grow your own grain and make hay costs a lot too. An old tractor, plow, and disc harrow costs a minimum of $1500 and a lot of repair time. It will, in other terms, require the gross income on five beef animals before you can turn over the sod to grow the corn to feed them. For cattle or horses you will also need a haywagon ($200) and a mower ($200) if you can find a decent one.

Auctions are one way of acquiring equipment, but perhaps not the best for two reasons. It is hard to judge the condition of the stuff, and everyone else who wants it is there to bid against you. I think the best way to get equipment is to see it sitting unused somewhere and just go up to the house and make an offer. If they don't want to sell it, maybe they'll know someone else who would sell you what you want. Or advertise for what you need. I've gotten amazing results by putting a sign in front of my house stating what I needed to buy or had for sale. People see it every day and it costs nothing. In fact, we bought our farm at a time when the real estate agents said the market was dry; we ran an ad in the classified section of the paper.

Old farm equipment has gone up in price in the last ten years. A lot of people are interested in small farming again. The equipment is a long term investment, and a person has to be committed to small farming for a long time to justify the money it takes just to get started.

Growing grain isn't a simple thing. Before you plow, get a soil test! The test will tell you what you need to add to get a crop. Without it you're only guessing and will probably lose. Heavy applications of manure will not bring on a good crop. In fact manures will inhibit a crop for up to a year as the soil tries to digest all the material. Recently concentrated natural fertilizers have become available in both soluble and granular form.

A cultivator is also necessary if you want to avoid herbicides. Cultivate as early as you can to keep the weeds from getting a toe hold on the field.

Making good hay takes experience and luck. The hay's at its best in June, but June's the month you're most likely to get rained on. Despite the fact that almost all hay's baled, the small farmer doesn't have to do this. In fact, the hay is better if it is not baled. Cattle prefer it. Also it is practical to stack hay outdoors if you put a cap on it. The new woven plastic bags can be sewn together to make a fine cap and little hay will go to waste.

The chief problem with growing small grains is weed growth during the last stages of grain growth. Usually ragweed. Weeds don't effect the yield but the green seed makes it hard to keep the grain from spoiling unless you dry the grain specially. To combat this, sow clover heavily with the seed grain. The clover will crowd out the weeds and give you a late hay crop or pasture, and improve your soil in the process.

Here's some considerations about raising animals to make money: if you're raising your own grain, the only additional cost in raising chickens is that of a protein concentrate, usually soy meal. You can sell roasting chickens but it's preferable to sell them live since cleaning chickens is time consuming and government standards are prohibitively expensive to meet. Although the market price on eggs fluctuates a lot, good farm fresh eggs can be sold at a profit; they're noticeably better than their supermarket counterparts. Marketing around the neighborhood is easy. But this market is limited and people won't drive much out of their way for eggs.

A weaned piglet costs anywhere from $10 to $30 depending on the price of pork. To get the hog to market weight (200 lbs.) takes 1,000 lbs. of grain which costs $50-60. The price of pork ranges from 30 cents to 50 cents a pound so with luck you might make $10 for your six months work. Some books advertise methods of replacing grains with greens, but then tell you the fraction saved is very small. You can't replace much of the grain and get hogs up to adult weight quickly.

Fattening steers for slaughter involves the same problems. You can make money if you raise your own feeds. You can increase profits by selling animals directly to the consumer instead of at cattle auction. You arrange to deliver the beef to a butcher who cuts it according to the customer's wishes. For a good animal you can charge a few cents more per pound than the auction would bring you, and the customer will save a good deal of money and get more dependable quality meat than is normally available. It's not hard to get solid and steady customers this way.

Since selling milk requires a fantastic amount of specialized equipment, I can recommend only one way of making money with dairy cattle: feeding the milk to other meat producing animals, especially veal calves. Veal market prices are currently very high, and a good dairy animal like a Holstein can nurse three calves at a time. In a three week span she can produce 600 lbs. of meat which sells for between 30 cents and 70 cents a pound. If she raises four batches of calves a year, she makes you about $1700, before you deduct the cost of the calves. She'll contribute one herself, and calves cost about $25 apiece at a week old. A drawback in this scheme is that calves demand close attention. But the small farmer is able to supply this. In fact, he should be able to avoid the losses that large operations incur due to calf mortality. Calves fed on real milk are more naturally resistant to disease than calves raised on formulas. Milk feeding is an old idea that is once again practical for the small farmer.

There are a lot of easier and faster ways to make money than small farming but for people who love the land and want to live near it and crave independence that life on the land alone can provide—is there any other life?

John Sillick

Concluding Remarks

The sum of my advice in this introduction would be to listen to the old people. Be humble in the face of their experience, persistence and luck. Listen carefully and don't ask 'smart' questions. Ask about what you need to know. Country life is a mixture of directness and waiting. Country people enjoy getting to know you but it'll take time and talk about the weather. Their advice is worth waiting for. Be direct. Be patient.

This book represents one man's understanding and opinions, the views of his friends, and what he could glean from the period's agricultural journals. Much of the material is borrowed from other sources, and just as freely passed into other publications. What counted was not novelty but utility. From reading other encyclopedias, almanacs, handbooks, journals and newspapers, I get the sense of a pool of common information which circulated among the people. Frank M. Lupton, the author and publisher of the *Farmer's & Housekeeper's Cyclopaedia,* assembled what seemed to him pertinent and put it into this form in 1888. Later he published an *American Domestic Cyclopaedia,* a poultry book, and a *Book of Dreams* which borrowed liberally from other sources.

This book's advice leaps several generations. If you can't go to your grandparents, listen to what we set down here. Many people will find advice from their grandparents' generation, and the principles underlying it, more useful and to their taste than what's modern and 'easier.' As my own grandmother said of the modern age: "Many changes, few improvements."

If you find this book useful, please let us know. I've compiled a list of sources of information:

Sources of General Information are your County Cooperative Extension Agent. The Department of Agriculture employs agricultural experts to advise you. Unfortunately, their advice is linked to the use of chemical fertilizers, pesticides, and herbicides and is oriented toward the large-scale and expanding farmer. They do have important information, however, and it will benefit you to bear with them and use what you can of their experience. Don't give up on them; hope that you can show them advantages to your way of doing things.

Excellent yearbooks of state agricultural associations, farmer's organizations, or the Department of Agriculture, old-fashioned handbooks, and bound volumes of agricultural newspapers often can be obtained at flea markets and antiquarian bookstores. They aren't very expensive especially when you consider the wealth of practical information they contain.

Consumer Information Center, Pueblo, Colorado, 81009 supplies pamphlets on subjects such as plumbing, auto repair and building rehabilitation.

The Complete Homesteading Book by David Robinson (Charlotte, Vt.: Garden Way Publishing Co., 1976) ranges from buying land to helpful advice on crops and animals to personal testimony about the advantages of living on the land.

Country Women by Jeanne Tetrault & Sherry Thomas (Garden City, NY: Doubleday & Co., 1976).

The Manual of Practical Homesteading by John Vivian (Emmaus, Pa., The Rodale Press, 1975). One expects good practical books from Rodale Press and this is no exception.

A History of Agriculture in the State of New York by Ulysses Prentiss Hedrick (NY: Hill & Wang, 1966 [1933]. Plug into whatever history of agriculture you can find for your state. If you live in New York, you're lucky in having this excellent and readable history of agriculture.

These magazines have been recommended as worthwhile subscriptions:

The Coevolution Quarterly, Box 428, Sausalito, CA. 94965

Countryside Magazine, 312 Portland Rd. Highway 19 East, Waterloo, Wis. 53594

The Natural Farmer, Box 247, Plainfield, Vt., 05667

Organic Gardening and Farming, 33 East Minor St., Emmaus Pa., 18049

Rain, 2270 N.W. Irving, Portland, Or., 97210

Well-Being, 833 W. Fir St. San Diego, Ca. 92101

† † †

My thanks for their help and cooperation to--

Rodney Lightfoote, Agricultural Agent, Cooperative Extension, Ontario County, New York

John Sillick, Royalton, New York

Sally Mills, Mendon, New York

Bill Pruitt, Genesee Co-Op, Rochester, New York

Sherwood Pierce, Ontario County Soil & Water Conservation District

Rundell Library, Science & Technology Division, Rochester, New York

Cooperative Extension, Ontario County, New York

PREFACE.

THE purpose of this volume is to supply a ready reference library of useful facts and suggestions for farmers and housekeepers. Within the prescribed limits of the work it would be impossible to present the fullest details of agricultural and kindred sciences, hence the author has deemed it politic to deal mainly with the more practical relations of agriculture and domestic affairs. Such matters as are self-evident and well understood by every practical agriculturist—as for instance the details of the cultivation of the commoner farm products—it has been thought wise to treat upon but meagerly, in order that full scope might be given to practical hints and useful suggestions in all branches of agriculture. The object of the work is not to tell the farmer and the housewife that which they already know, but to present to them valuable information which it is believed cannot fail to be of material assistance in rural homes.

In the preparation of the work great care has been taken and no pains have been spared to make it complete in every detail. Consultation of the best authorities insures its reliability, and it is believed that it will be found invaluable by all who become possessed of it, and that it will prove one of those exceptional books which are prized more highly by reason of age and constant association; for it will doubtless be consulted almost daily in the course of rural and household affairs. There is hardly a day in a farmer's life but that some problem arises not easy of solution without a reliable treatise of this kind to consult. Such a want it is the purpose of this volume to supply. The author is well aware that the masses of agriculturists have but little money to waste upon luxuries of any kind, and he is equally confident that the purchase of this book, far from being a waste of his hard earnings, will prove one of the most profitable of investments. Its perusal will develop new ideas, new methods and new theories in every branch of farm labor of incalculable value, and the household department will be found equally as serviceable to the farmer's wife as will the agricultural department to the farmer.

In the compilation of the work we have been largely indebted to the leading agricultural journals of this country and Europe, as well as to many standard works upon agricultural and household topics. Access to extensive files of the former could alone insure completeness in a work of this kind. Entire originality, therefore, we do not claim. We maintain, however, that we have succeeded in producing a work of far greater value than any exclusively original production could possibly be, for we present her in the views of nearly all the ablest writers in the country upon the various topics treated, giving to the people at large the benefits of their extensive experiment and research. It would be possible for a farmer, by subscribing for all the leading agricultural periodicals of the country for a number of years and by purchasing a considerable library of standard works upon the subject, and carefully culling therefrom such items and articles as he considered of the greatest interest and value, and pasting them in a scrap-book, to collect a mass of matter equivalent to that portion of this book allotted to "The Farm," and his wife, possessing herself of authorities upon the subjects in which she is interested and pursuing a like course, might produce a partial duplicate of the matter contained in the department of "The Household"; but the cost would have been as three hundred to a unit, and the result would be a clumsy, voluminous scrap-book with no method of arrangement, in comparison with a neat, handy and convenient volume arranged with every facility for reference. From this indisputable argument the value of the work to all interested in the subjects of which it treats may be computed; but we would not be misunderstood as claiming that the possession of the work by a farmer and housekeeper will obviate the necessity of subscribing for the agricultural paper as usual, for, while the book is the more valuable for reference, especially in cases of emergency, the agricultural paper is indispensable as enlightening the farmer upon the new theories constantly being promulgated and the new discoveries at all times being made, without which knowledge he would fail to keep pace with the age in which he lives, and therefore be unable to compete with his more progressive neighbors in the prosecution of his calling.

The term "Cyclopædia" as applied to the work is a misnomer according to the lexicographer's definition, inasmuch as the alphabetical arrangement of titles, as required for works thus designated, has not been preserved, the compiler being convinced that the arrangement of the subject-matter in departments would be more acceptable to the public. As by common usage applied to any work covering all subjects embraced in a certain field of knowledge, however, the title is entirely in keeping with the character of the book, for as a treatise upon all matters pertaining to the farm and the household it is complete. It is a book for each of the heads of the rural household, being equally as valuable and interesting to the farmer's wife as to the farmer himself, and may be truthfully said to embrace the cream of more than a dozen ordinary volumes, for it combines a book on Rural Architecture, on Crops, on Fertilizers, on Gardening, on Fruit Culture, on Live Stock, on Poultry, on Dairy Farming, on Bee Keeping, on Implements, on Farm Management, on Cookery, on Medical Matters, on Fancy Work, on Floriculture, on the Toilet, on Domestic Economy and Household Management—in fact, it embraces all subjects in which farmers and housekeepers are most directly interested.

The arrangement of the work in departments will, we think, commend itself to all, while the copious index at the end will render it extremely easy of consultation. The book is a permanent storehouse of useful facts, hints and suggestions for farmers and housekeepers. It may be consulted upon any problem or in any emergency that may arise, and will rarely fail to elicit the information desired. We believe it to be the very book that every farmer and housewife needs, and that it will repay its small cost many times over each month in the year.

CONTENTS.

---

vi CONTENTS.

LIST OF ILLUSTRATIONS.

The *Cyclopaedia* provides house plans in the latest 1888 styles, Georgian cottages with Gothic woodwork. They seem to me more likely houses for the city than the country. Luckily their interiors are more practically arranged than their ornamental exteriors. We presume that few modern builders would be much concerned with a parlor 'for special occasions.' No dining rooms are provided in the plans so we presume the eating was done, as it should be on the farm, in the kitchen.

Heating, of course, is a central concern in the house. The houseplans seem to be adapted to central heating. Different arrangements would be wanted in a house heated by coal, wood or oil, depending on the placing of stoves, furnace or fireplaces. A house fitted for a fair-sized wood stove and provided with a seasoned supply of hardwood fuel can be kept quite comfortable through the winter.

For the landowner interested in building a house, we suggest *The Owner Built Home* by Ken Kern (NYC: Scribners, 1975) or *Low-cost, Energy-efficient Shelter for the Owner and Builder* edited by Eugene Eccli (Emmaus, Pa.: Rodale Press, 1976) as books that provide specific practical plans for the house.

For the person interested in styles of houses and particularly in understanding 'folk' architecture in the U.S., we recommend Henry Glassie's *Pattern in the Material Folk Culture of the Eastern U.S. (*Philadelphia: Pa. U. of Pa. Press, 1968). This book provides photographs and floor plans of the main styles of buildings constructed prior to 1860. If you want a 'dog-trot,' a 'salt-box,' an 'I' or a 'Cape Cod,' look at this book.

We are given a wide choice of barn styles. The octagonal or round barn style is said to be one of the many inventions of the Shakers. It is reputed to be handy and economical. The *Cyclopaedia* provides plans for a two-level, side-opening English style barn (p. 17), for a transverse crib barn (p. 19) and for a two-level, end-opening barn (p. 21). Other plans for cribs and barns, such as the Dutch barn, can be found in Glassie's *Patterns. . .* For more specific instructions on the construction of practical barns, we suggest the reader consult James Boyd's *Practical Farm Buildings* (Dansville, Il.: Interstate Publishers & Printers, 1973) or R. Lyttle's *Farm Builder's Handbook* (Farmington, Michigan: Structures Pub. Co., 1973).

THE FARM.

RURAL ARCHITECTURE.

AN INEXPENSIVE COTTAGE.—ELEVATION.

An Inexpensive Cottage.—We give the plan of a neat and beautiful country cottage, the low cost of construction of which adapts it to the wants of those in moderate circumstances, while, in attractive appearance and general convenience, it rivals those of a much higher cost.

This cottage is designed in the rural Gothic or English manner, but much modified, so as to adapt it to almost any site. The light, open porch may be omitted without injuring the design. In the plan, *A* is the porch, from which we enter the hall or entry, 8 feet wide, with the two best rooms, each 16x18 feet, on either side of it. Connected with the living-room, in its rear, is a good pantry. *B* is the back entry, communicating with the kitchen. *C* is the back porch, which may be left open in summer, and inclosed in winter, when it will serve as a place for coal and wood. On one side of the kitchen fire-place is a closet, and on the other a sink, into which, if possible, a water-pipe should be brought. The first story of this cottage is 10 feet, and the second story 5 feet, on the sides, and 8 feet in the middle of the rooms. The pitch of the roof is a right angle. The cost of this cottage, with the interior neatly finished and painted in oil color, and the two principal rooms grained and varnished like oak, and their walls papered with suitable paper—all the other rooms having brown walls whitewashed—would be about $800.

An Ornamental Country Cottage.—We give on pages 13 and 14 illustrations of a plan and elevation of a cheap, but very ornamental, country cottage, which will be found both convenient and comfortable for a small family. If this plan is not extensive enough to meet your wants, it can be easily enlarged upon by making additions, or by enlarging the size of the whole plan, and thus increasing the dimensions of the rooms. This, however, would necessarily add to the cost of construction. The cottage, as shown in our illustration, presents a very aristocratic appearance, and, considering the small amount of money required for its construction, is, we think, a very desirable plan for a cheap and good dwelling-house. The dimensions of the rooms on the ground floor are plainly given in our second illustration. The porch, with its seat, is large and roomy; the living-room is of good size, well lighted by a square bay-window. The kitchen is well supplied with closets. The first floor could be very much im-

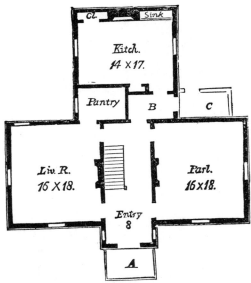

AN INEXPENSIVE COTTAGE.—GROUND PLAN.

proved by adding a one-story kitchen at the rear, making the living-room into a parlor, and the kitchen into a dining and sitting-room; the additional cost would be very small. The second floor contains three bedrooms, very conveniently arranged, and each provided with a closet. The two downstairs rooms and the large front bedroom are supplied with open fire-places, the value of which for ventilation is so often overlooked in cheap houses. Besides this, there should be ventilating tubes or shafts in the chimney sides, with registers opening from each room, thus insuring a good system of ventilation. The roof should be ventilated by openings under the projected eaves. The estimated cost of this building is from $1,200 to $1,800, according to locality and style of finish.

General Suggestions to Those Intending to Build.—The following excellent recommendations are from the *American Home and Farm Cyclopædia:* Farmers can afford to leave cellar-kitchens, basements, third stories, and all other unnecessary stair-climbing devices to their city cousins, who have to count the cost of every square foot they build upon. The only advantage of second stories in the country is that they are more healthful for sleeping apartments.

If every fire has a separate flue, and each flue terminates in its own particular chimney-top, there will never be any trouble over smoking fires, if the chimney is high enough.

Proper care in the arrangement of various rooms will save those who have to do the housework a thousand needless steps. Kitchen and dining-

AN ORNAMENTAL COUNTRY COTTAGE.—ELEVATION.

room should always be adjoining apartments. The china closet best opens into the dining-room. A trap-door connecting the pantry with the dining-room is a great convenience. It is well to have the wood-shed very near the kitchen, and connected with it by a covered way, avoiding exposure in inclement weather.

An attic over the entire house, with a window at each end, will be found of signal utility for drying clothes in bad weather.

Provide plenty of closets and cupboards in all of the rooms. The lady of the house, who is the one most vitally interested in this matter, should not

be allowed to insist upon this in vain.   Varnishing wood will make the paint
last longer, and saves incalculable elbow grease in house-cleaning.

Shingles of cedar will last from thirty to forty years, and those of pine
from twelve to twenty years.

In the arrangement of out-buildings, the following relative proximity will
be found convenient: First, the house; attached to that the kitchen-wing,
with wood-house appended; then, at a little distance, the privy, carriage-
house, and workshop, with pig-sty and poultry-house adjoined.

Stone and brick walls should always be furred off, leaving an air space
between the stonework and plastering throughout the entire wall, and open-

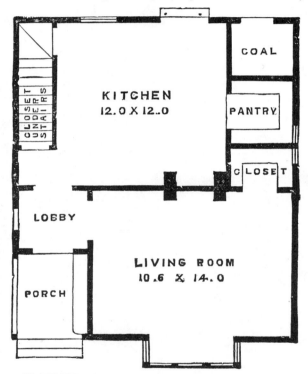

AN ORNAMENTAL COUNTRY COTTAGE.—GROUND PLAN

ing into the attic.   This prevents dampness, and insures an equable temperature.   Brick houses must have a slate, sheet-copper, or tarred paper
cut-off inserted in the foundation just below the water-shed, as otherwise
the moisture of the ground is worked up by the brick, keeping the walls constantly damp.

Frame houses may be made much warmer and more comfortable than
they usually are by covering the studding with tongued and grooved
sheathing, and this in turn by tarred building paper, placing the weather
boarding over the whole.   Fit the sheathing and weather boarding closely
around door and window-frames, and let the tarred paper lap over a little
where there is likely to be a crack.

Where ingrain carpets are to be used, it favors their economical cutting to have either the length or breadth of each room some multiple of their usual width—one yard—as twelve feet, fifteen feet, etc.

Construction of an Octagonal Barn.—There are various plans for laying out and building barns of this shape, in all of which the principles are the same. There is a concrete or stone foundation wall, which may be either below ground for a cellar or partially below it for a basement, or wholly above it for a stable, an inclined way being built on two opposite sides to give access to the barn floor. Upon this foundation the sills are laid, the corners being made at an angle of 135 degrees, instead of 90 degrees, as in the square building. There are no cross-beams necessary except upon the floor, there being eight bents in the building, all on the outside, the plates

FIG. 1.—ELEVATION OF AN OCTAGONAL BARN.

being mortised exactly as the sills are, and the posts placed with regard to the necessary doors and windows, and the strength necessary to support the roof and stiffen the building. As many braces as may be thought needful may be used, but the braces must all be on the lines of the walls, and none of them cross-braces. The roof is an eight-sided cone, strengthened with purlin plates, and may be open at the center for a cupola or ventilator. The joints of all the plates and the sills will be at an angle of 62 1-2 degrees, instead of 45 degrees, as in a square building. This form of the frame will give a roof of the strongest kind—one that cannot spread, if well put together, and one that offers less resistance to the wind than any other form of elevated roof. Inside of the barn there is nothing to interfere with the piling of grain or hay to the roof, and a wagon may be driven anywhere upon the floor. The plan of the basement is shown at Fig. 2, *a* being a passage for the cows, and a drive-way for removing the manure; *b, b,* are the stalls for the cows, of which there are fifty-two, having the feed-trough toward the center, and all reached by an inner drive-way. There are six stalls, and a

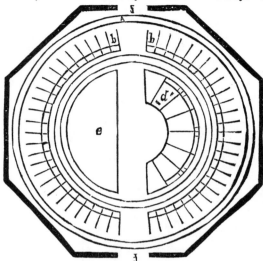

room at each end of the stalls for harness. At *e* is a place for storing plows, carriages, wagons, or machines. A drive-way *(f, f)* passes through the basement from east to west. As many windows as needed may be built in the wall. The sills of the barn are laid upon the wall, as already mentioned; the posts are 28 feet high, and the plates upon these support the rafters. The plates are fastened together at the ends by being halved, and the corners fastened by half-inch iron bolts, as shown at Fig. 3. At each corner is a brace of 8x8 timber,

FIG. 2.—PLAN OF BASEMENT.

bolted to and through the plates by three-quarter-inch bolts, and strengthened by an iron plate on the inside, through which the bolts pass. The shoulders of the corner rafters rest upon these braces and plates, as shown at Fig. 4. These rafters are of 6x12 timber. Purlin plates of 8x10 inch timber are bolted under the rafters, and are fastened together at the corners in the same manner as the plates. The intermediate rafters rest upon these purlins. Iron tie-rods may be used to strengthen the rafters and hold them together, if thought necessary. Fig. 1 shows the elevation, with a portion of the roof removed to show the manner of laying the rafters and bridging them. A crown rim is bolted to the rafters at the point of the roof —or, rather, the rafters are bolted to the crown rim—which supports a cupola. The cupola is fifty feet from the floor of the barn, the roof rising twenty-two feet, and the post being twenty-eight feet high. The floor of the barn is laid upon beams, supported by brick piers or timber posts in the basement.

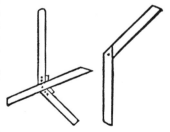

FIG. 3.—CORNER JOINT.

FIG. 4.—CORNER BRACE.

A line of beams may be laid above the floor on either side, above which floors may be laid; the space thus made may be used for granaries, or storage of farm tools or machines, or other cumbrous property.

Plan for a Barn.—We present herewith a plan for a new and improved barn. For convenience, neatness of appearance, and practical utility, it will be found most excellent, and should any of our readers contemplate build⸗ing, they would do well to give this article a careful study; and should they not desire to follow out the plan to the letter, they might still be able to gain from it some valuable hints in planning a barn of a different style. The following is the description of the plan we have illustrated:

A, stables, 8x28, for nine cows, earth floor; B, man's room; C, carriages: D, harness room; E, meal or shorts; F, shelled corn; G, oats; H, passage-way; I, passage-way, 4 feet wide, platform floor, with pump; L, box for mixing feed; M, stairs; N, O, stalls, 5 feet wide; P, Q, R, stables, 6 feet wide; S, feed-bin for cattle; V, feed-box for horses; W, wagon shed, earth floor, 18x21; X, wagon shed, open at south and east, 9x17; Y, tool room, 9x10; Z, feed-bin; W, T, water-trough.

Main barn, 30x42 feet; posts, 18 feet in the clear; shed wing, 26x30 feet; posts, 12 feet in clear; lean-to shed, 14 feet wide, 42 feet long— all to have roof at one-third angle of rise.

There will be 230 feet in length of wall underground, to be built of rough stone 1 foot high and 18 inches thick. Upon this is to be laid, in courses, quarried stone, in blocks, not less than 8x12 inches, 1 foot high and 1 foot thick, and all pointed. There will be required twelve piers, each 18 inches square and 2 feet high; these to be built of stone, and four of them to have the upper stone 12x18 inches. All to be laid in good strong lime mortar, and in a workman-like and

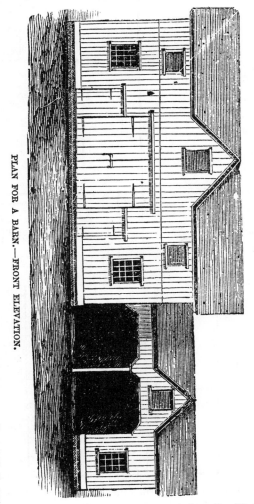

PLAN FOR A BARN.—FRONT ELEVATION.

substantial manner. There will be required for sills 334 feet in length of 8x8 timber, and 42 feet in length, 6x8; this last for the sill in front of cones in lean-to shed. For posts, girts of main beams, plates, etc., etc., there will be required 913 feet in length, of 6x6. For purlin beams, girts, etc., there will be required 454 feet of length, 4x6; and for intermediate girts, braces, etc., 394 feet of length, of 3x4 stuff. The sides should all be of oak or white pine.

The main beams, purlins, posts, girts, etc., may be of oak, ash, red birch, white pine, or white wood. The joists are to be of oak or white pine, and these will be required as follows: 103 pieces, each 14 feet long, 2x8; 20 pieces, each 9 feet long, 2x8; 20 pieces, each 10 1-2 feet long, 2x8; and 11 pieces, each 8 feet long, 2x8. The rafters will be as follows: 42, each 19 feet long, 2x4 at

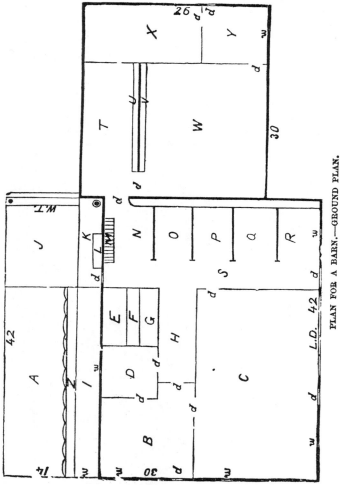

PLAN FOR A BARN.—GROUND PLAN.

one end and 4x6 at the other, for the main beam; 21, each 17 feet long, 3x4, for the lean-to shed; and 30, each 16 feet long, 2x4 at one end and 3x5 at the junction of the first with the second stories (as shown from outside). There should be a strip inserted of 2x2. The frieze board to be 8 inches wide and 2 inches thick. The boards all to be straight edge, and the whole to be battened with strips one inch thick and three inches wide, having the edges beveled half an inch, exhibiting a face of two inches. The whole to be of good, merchantable, dry pine timber. The roof boards may be of any light and durable timber, and shall be laid so that no space of over two inches may be found. That portion of the roof which projects beyond the upright portion of the building shall be of double thickness. The shingles are to be of the best quality, and laid only 4 inches to the weather. The windows are to be made as per plan, all frames to be of seasoned pine, free from knots. The sash windows of 12 lights, each 9 x 12 inches, except two, viz., one in south end of main barn, and one in east side of same; these to be as shown in plan. The blind windows to be hung with butt hinges, and fastened with hasp hooks, both outside and inside. They are to swing outward.

The doors are all to be formed to present an appearance outside same as balance of barn. They are to be jack-planed sufficiently to render them free of splinters in handling. They are to be placed and formed of height, width, etc., as shown in plan. They are all to be hung with wrought-iron strap hinges, and secured by latches and hasp hook staples.

A Complete Stock Barn.—We present herewith an illustrated plan, with careful description, of a complete stock barn, embracing many good and sensible points in its construction, from which we trust our friends may gather some valuable suggestions.

The body of the main barn is 100 feet long by 50 feet wide, the posts 18 feet high above the sill, making 9 bents. The beams are 14 feet above the sills, which is the height of the inner posts. The position of the floor and bays is readily understood from the plan. The floor, for a grain barn, is 14 feet wide, but may be contracted to 12 feet for one exclusively for hay. The area in front of the bays is occupied with a stationary horse-power and with machinery for various farm operations, such as threshing, shelling corn, cutting straw, crushing grain, etc., all of which is driven by bands from drums on the horizontal shaft overhead, which runs across the floor from the horse-power on the other side; this shaft being driven by a cog-wheel on the perpendicular shaft round which the horses travel.

A COMPLETE STOCK BARN.—ELEVATION.

A passage four feet wide extends between the bays and the stables, which occupy the two wings. This extends up to the top of the bays, down which the hay is thrown for feeding, which renders this work as easy and convenient as possible.

A one-sided roof is given to the sheds (instead of a double-sided), to throw all the water on the outside, in order to keep the interior of the yards dry. Eave-troughs take the water from the roofs to cisterns. The cisterns, if connected by an underground pipe, may be all drawn from by a single pump if necessary.

The floor of the main barn is three feet higher than that of the stables. This will allow a cellar under it, if desired—or a deeper extension of the bays—and it allows storage lofts over the cattle, with sufficient slope of roof. A short flight of steps at the ends of each passage, admits easy access from the level of the barn floor.

The sheds, which extend on the three sides of the barn, and touch it at the rear end, are on a level with the stables. An inclined plane, from the main floor through the middle of the back shed, forms a rear egress for wagons and carts, descending three feet from the floor. The two rooms, one on each side of this rear passage, 16 by 34 feet, may be used for housing sick animals, cows about to calve, or any other purpose required. The stables at the front ends of the sheds are convenient for teams of horses or oxen, or they may be fitted for wagon houses, tool houses, or other purposes. The rooms, 16 feet square at the inner corners of the sheds, may be used for weak ewes, lambs, or for a bull stable.

Racks or mangers may be fitted up in the open sheds for feeding sheep

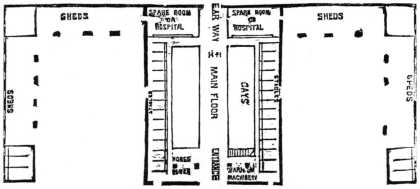

A COMPLETE STOCK BARN.—GROUND PLAN.

or young cattle, and yards may be built adjoining, on the rear, six or eight in number, into which they may run and be kept separate. Barred partitions may separate the different flocks. Bars may also enclose the opening in front, or they may, if required, be boarded up tight. Step ladders are placed at convenient intervals, for ascending the shed lofts.

A granary over the machine room is entered by a flight of stairs. Poles extending from bay to bay, over the floor, will admit the storage of much additional hay or grain.

A Convenient Barn.—A recent inquiry about how to build a barn, writes a correspondent of an agricultural periodical, tempts me to describe mine, which I think very handy. My barn is situated on a side hill with an incline of about seven feet in forty to the west. There is a bridge at each end for a driveway, only one of which is shown in our illustration, Fig. 1.

On the right, as you enter the main door, the bays extend down to the ground nine feet. Under the main floorway I keep my sheep. Under the bridge each end is open, to give the sheep plenty of light and air, as it will not do to keep them too warm. In stormy weather I close the doors. On the left of the main floorway is the cow linter, and, beneath, the pig pen. The arrangement will be more readily understood from the illustration, Fig. 2.

1. Sheep pen; 2. Barn floorway; 3. Standing floor in the linter; 4. Cows' manger; 5. Iron strap used instead of stanchion; 6. Tie chain; 7. A trough filled with dirt or sawdust for the animals' front feet to stand on, thus preventing slipping; 8. Cows' feed door; 9. Sheeps' feed door; 10. Sheep rack; 11. Pig pen; 12. Windows used for cleaning sheep pens and pig pens; 13. Tight partition; 14. Walk behind the cows; 15. Scuttle for cleaning out manure.

A CONVENIENT BARN.—FIG. 1.

It will be noticed that the door through which the sheep are fed opens downward, and does not conflict with the cows' feed door, which lifts upward. By having these doors the linter can be closed up tight in cold weather, and the cattle will keep warm. The main part of the barn need not be clap-boarded. So long as the roof is tight and the hay does not get wet, it is no injury to the fodder to have it well ventilated. This ventilation is indeed beneficial and necessary to carry off from the fodder the effluvia from the manure in the cellar.

Cheap Barn Cellar.—But comparatively few farmers (as compared to the masses) have yet been convinced that it will pay to construct a root-cellar, and then to raise the roots to fill it with, but for all that, those who have provided themselves with cellars find they pay. As it is not always convenient to have one beneath the barn, it may be built above ground as follows: Dig down three feet the size desired; twelve by twenty feet makes a good large cellar; and ten by sixteen feet will do for six or eight hundred bushels. Get on hand a lot of small logs or poles from six to ten inches in diameter, with which to build the portion above ground. Cut the poles for each side three feet longer than the width or length of the excavation. Place the first two poles on flat stones or blocks

A CONVENIENT BARN.—FIG. 2.

back a foot from the edge of the hole dug, and upon opposite sides. Flatten the ends with the ax and lay two cross poles as you would in starting a log house. In these end pieces one foot from the end cut notches for the next side poles to lie in. With each round, set the side poles in a foot, which will give a regular slant to the roof, and make a very strong frame for the weight that is to come upon it. The end that is to contain the door should be carried up straight, while the other may be slanted up, as the sides.

Cover this frame with cull or common lumber, laying the boards on up and down. Next put on a heavy layer of marsh hay or straw to keep the dirt from coming in contact with and rotting the lumber; over this put a foot of earth. A shute should be provided for filling the house, and a small ventilation flue for winter. The end where the door is located should be

AN OLD BARN IMPROVED.—ELEVATION.

double boarded and filled in between with saw-dust or cut straw; there should also be a double door. A storing house of this kind, if well made, will last eight or ten years, and give as good satisfaction as one costing $200.

How an old Barn was Improved.—We present herewith a brief description of how an old barn was remodeled and greatly improved without much expense, and furnish illustrations showing the barn after the changes had been made, and the plan of the basement underneath in detail. By a careful study of this plan, our readers may be able to gather some valuable hints and suggestions. The original building was the common 32x42 feet barn, with fourteen posts, a fourteen-feet floor in the middle, with bay on one side and stable on the other, with a lean-to of thirteen feet in the rear, the building standing on the line of the road and facing the west, the grounds descending say one foot in thirty to northeast. It was first raised so that the northeast corner would clear six feet, dug out to a level of one foot below that of the lowest corner; then a ditch was dug one and a half feet below that under the outside sills, all around which was filled with

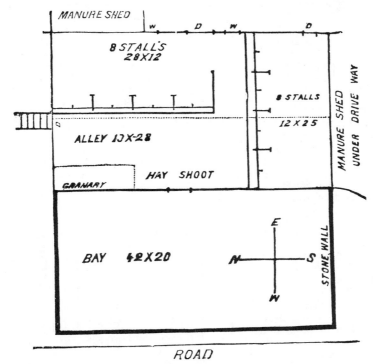

AN OLD BARN IMPROVED.—PLAN OF BASEMENT.

small stone. A substantial stone wall was laid on the west side, and twenty feet on both north and south ends; the rest of the building was double-boarded save where protected by other buildings. The front doors were then closed, the floor taken up, cut out the bay girts, and laid off a floor of twenty feet on the west side (space reaching from the ground to roof), made a floor twelve feet wide in upright and all of lean-to—in all twenty-five feet, and cut a door in south end. The bay now would hold more than the whole barn before; a large floor, 25x42, thirteen feet of which can be used to store grain, and a space of 25x42 feet for stable. A good idea of the interior construction may be obtained from the illustrated plan of the basement.

Hanging Barn Doors on Rollers.—The great convenience of sliding or rolling doors on the farm outbuildings is well known, and as every farmer with a little ingenuity can construct them himself, there is no reason why they should not be generally adopted. Our illustration, Fig. 1, represents the sliding doors, completed, as applied to the barn; Fig. 2, the manner of applying the rollers to the doors and track. The rollers, track and other trimmings may be obtained at any hardware store. The track is first

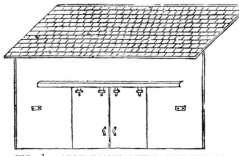

FIG. 1.—APPEARANCE AFTER COMPLETION.

securely fastened to the edge of an inch or two-inch board, about four or five inches wide. This is then firmly nailed or spiked to the building, parallel to and even with the top of the doorway, and should extend the width of the door on each side. In order that the doors may run easily, the track should be laid as level as possible, and upon one board. The manner of fastening the rollers of the doors is clearly shown in the engraving Fig. 2. The doors are placed upon the tracks at the ends of the latter, and are prevented from running off by placing a block at the end of the track or upon the side of the door. The track should be protected from the weather by some kind of covering. Two narrow boards nailed together similar to an eaves-trough, and fastened to the building above the track and rollers, form the best kind of protection from snow or rain.

Model Carriage-House and Stable.—Our engraving of the elevation, on the following page, shows doors of the rectangular, carriage-house portion of the building; also door to hayloft. The carriage-house doors are folding, and open outward, as they can be made closer when hung on hinges than when hung on rollers; and as it is desirable that all doors and windows should be as close as practicable, that they may not affect the

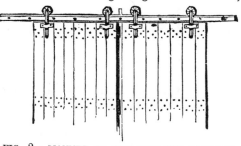

FIG. 2.—MANNER OF APPLYING THE ROLLERS.

ventilation, the ingress of which is provided for by a subterraneous air duct, seen at A, in the ground plan.

The posts are sixteen feet in length; the ceiling of the stable is nine feet in the clear, with storage in the loft for twelve tons of hay.

The oat bin is a cylinder of one hundred bushels capacity, around which circular stairs are built. Its location could not be more convenient, as six horses can be fed grain with walking but fourteen feet, on account of the six stalls being with the head end around a semicircle of sixteen feet diameter. This circular area is open to the cupola, and being supplied with air through the floor, under the stairs, and the animals all breathing into a common center directly under the egress, the air is constantly changed without a perceptible current, and it is nearly at the temperature of the earth below the frost and solar influence; no doors nor windows need be opened.

By reference to our illustration of the ground plan, it will be seen that the stall partitions are radial. The stalls are five feet in width in front, and eleven feet at the rear end. The stalls V and VI are arranged with strong gates hung to the wall of the building, in a line with the stall partitions, which, when closed, as seen in stall VI, form spacious, convenient box stalls. There is no partition between the carriage-house, VII, and the stable por-

MODEL CARRIAGE-HOUSE AND STABLE.—ELEVATION.

tion of the building, except that formed by the stall partitions and the gates closed, as seen in stall VI.

The ventilation is so effectual that the air of the stable does not effect the carriage-house; and it being arranged with three drive doors, three pairs of horses to carriages may all be driven into the carriage-house at once, and the doors closed behind them, and the horses taken to their respective stalls. There are two harness closets, H, H.

The rectangular figures in each stable floor, are cast-iron drip grates, each covering a sink, or pit, into which the urine falls. These are all connected by pipes, which all connect with a main inner conduit, laid in the ground by way of the stable door. This conduit discharges into the manure house. The quadrant-shaped figures at the head of the stalls, are hinged iron mangers, which may be turned into the feeding passages for conven-

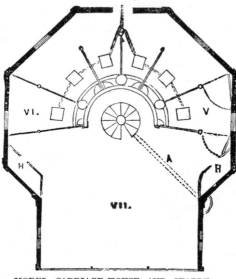

ience in feeding, and the mangers may be unhinged and removed from the building when cleansed.

The circular figure in the line of the stall partitions, is the base of a sheet-iron hay tube, which is supported at the height of the manger, and extends to the upper surface of the loft floor, where it is supplied with hay. These tubes have an opening to each stall, so that one tube supplies two horses, the tube being covered at the top, and close, except the feeding openings, and the lattice bottom to them protects the hay from air and dust, and is the most perfect and durable hay-feeding arrangement yet discovered.

MODEL CARRIAGE-HOUSE AND STABLE.—
GROUND PLAN.

The object of the lattice bottom to the hay tubes, is to preserve the hay seed which sheds. It falls into a drawer for the purpose, and the seed thus saved is of excellent quality, and the quantity thus collected well remunerates for the cost of the arrangement. The cupola is octangular, and has four openings, with stationary blinds, and four with glazed sash, which thoroughly light the hay-loft and feeding passage.

The building is perfectly lighted and ventilated, and exhibits a pretty elevation from any point of view.

FENCES AND GATES--Update

The sort of fence and gate we construct depends on what we wish to protect and whether we're fencing in or fencing out. In most sections, farmers are held legally responsible for their animals and must fence them in. They are not responsible for keeping others' animals out. Pigs, cattle, horses, sheep and poultry require different sorts of fencing for their confinement and safety. Beyond these concerns, the choice of fencing becomes an aesthetic matter.

In this chapter we're introduced to several sorts of post and rail fences, durable gates, fancy gates and some of the tools needed for putting a fence up.

Fencing will last as long as the posts remain sound in the ground. A method for preserving wood posts not mentioned here is to soak the ends of the posts in creosote, a coal tar derivative. Posts should be cut in the spring, when the bark slips away most easily. They must be completely debarked and seasoned for six months for the preservative to work its best. The posts are boiled in creosote 10-12 hours.

Equally important with preservatives is the choice of wood for the posts. The *Cyclopaedia* suggests black walnut posts, but the value of that tree, large and healthy, in the veneer market is too great. American chestnut was a favorite wood for fencing for many years, but that tree is nearly extinct. The longest lasting posts now are furnished by red and white cedar, osage orange, black or honey locust, and white oak.

If fences are not strictly needed, the landowner might consider a hedgerow. Hedges of osage orange, buckthorn and honey locust grow thick and fast, are not easily penetrated, and provide good cover for wildlife.

The *Cyclopaedia* by no means exhausts the range of materials nor the means of constructing fences from wood. Persons interested in fencing a parcel of land should also consult the recently reprinted *Fences, Gates and Bridges* by George Martin (Brattleboro, Vt.: The Stephen Greene Press, 1974 [1887] for a wider variety of fences made from stone, sod, board, picket, barbed wire, and rails, hedges, and portable fencing and hurdles.

FENCES AND GATES.

Farm Fences.—In the following list of farm fences we have endeavored to illustrate and describe only those that are of practical value and in actual use by many farmers. They illustrate the various modes of arranging rails for the turning of stock and indicating the boundary line of farms. In many sections of the country the common crooked, zig-zag (sometimes called the Virginia or worm) rail fence is extensively used, and, in consequence of the scarcity of the desired material, cannot be immediately replaced by the improved board, post and rail, iron or stone fence. As commonly constructed, with wide-spreading stakes at each corner, it occupies a strip of ground nearly a rod in width, which is far worse than useless, affording a harboring place for noxious weeds, etc.

Fig. 1 represents a section of a straight rail fence. The stakes are first driven in the soil from four to six inches asunder, sufficient to admit of a rail of medium size; a stone or block of wood a few inches in height is placed between the stakes, upon which are properly placed two or three

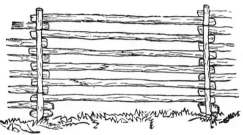

FARM FENCES.—FIG. 1.

rails; a piece of annealed wire is then placed around both stakes. the ends being well twisted together, upon which are placed rails until within a few inches of the top, when another bit of wire, a wooden pin, or a wooden cap, as most convenient, is attached.

In building this class of fence, it will be necessary to cut away with an axe a portion of each end of many rails, that they may fit closely within the stakes. In this, as well as other rail fences, the largest and heaviest rails should be reserved for the top, rendering their removal by unruly stock and high winds less easy. Keep the crooked ones in a panel by themselves, and if they are very crooked it is policy to use them for stakes, or consign them to the flames; for to have a fence to please and not to provoke the intrusion of stock, use none but *straight* rails.

When economy of rails is desired, immediately after setting the stakes cast up a ridge of earth by plowing two furrows on each side, throwing up the second furrow with a shovel, making a ridge a foot or more in height, and not less than a foot in breadth at the top; proceed as above in the construction of the fence; sow grass seed upon the ridge. This plan saves two rails to a panel, renders the stakes more firm and less liable to heave by the action of the frost, and unruly cattle do not have the same advantage in attempting to get through or over it. In situations not liable to the prevalence of high winds, this is the fence that should be used, occupying less ground than many other kinds; and, when properly constructed, it is a substantial and neat fence.

Fig. 2, though in appearance somewhat resembling the previous one, is

FARM FENCES.—FIG. 2.

more expensive, and is designed especially for the use of poles or slender rails that it would be impossible to properly arrange in a fence by any other plan. To the stakes are nailed cleats, as shown, from four to seven at every set of stakes. Size of rails and purpose of fence will decide this point. A ridge of earth can be thrown up as in the previous plan, with a corresponding economy of timber.

Fig. 3 exhibits a mode of staking a zig-zag fence. After the foundation has been laid, the stakes should be driven; holes should be made with a crowbar to the depth of twenty inches at least. One man, standing on a box or bench, drives them with a sledge-hammer or common wooden beetle, while an assistant keeps them upright. Make all the holes before you commence driving the stakes, which should be all sharpened, and the top end reduced to a size admitting the caps to pass over them readily before they are brought to the field.

When the fence is made four or more rails high (the size of rails, etc., will govern), the caps are put upon, and the fence finished by the addition of two or three more rails.

In localities where caps are expensive or difficult to obtain, good annealed wire, size 10, will answer all purposes. It should be drawn tightly up around the stakes; it will bury into them, and the weight of the rails above the wires will rest upon the stakes, having a tendency to keep them in the ground when acted upon by the frost.

The most expeditious manner in which to sharpen stakes is to have a large, flat block of wood for the stake to stand on, which is held upright with one hand and sharpened with an axe held in the other; a hollow cut in the upper surface of the block will considerably expedite the operation. Hop poles, stakes for grape-vines, etc., are best sharpened in the above manner.

In Fig. 4 is shown the best plan known for staking the common rail fence. It dispenses with stakes at the corners, and in consequence of their central position, they are not liable to be broken or loosened while plowing; nor does the fence occupy as much land as by the old mode. In consequence of the central point at which the stakes cross the upper

FARM FENCES.—FIG. 3.

rail of fence, it is required to sustain the weight of the stakes and riders; therefore, this part should be made strong and durable, of well-seasoned material.

Fig. 5 represents a plan of bracing a rail fence, whether it be staked and ridered, staked and capped, locked and ridered, staked and wired, or wired and pinned, all of which kinds of fence are easily blown down by a heavy wind, rails broken, stock let into fields of valuable grain, time spent, and patience exhausted in rebuilding them. The manner of using the arrangement is clearly shown in the figure. It consists in placing on the inside leeward corner a piece of rail, one end resting upon the ground, the other placed underneath the third rail from the top. A fence braced as

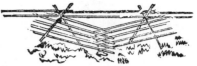

FARM FENCES.—FIG. 4.

shown has stood five years without repairing, while a locked, staked and ridered fence by the side of it has been prostrated three times, although in a less exposed situation, thus demonstrating the value of this attachment when used in connection with the common rail fence.

FARM FENCES.—FIG. 5.

Straight Rail Fence.— We present a section of straight rail fence, which will be found easy and cheap to construct, and economical in saving timber and occupying space on the land.

In constructing this fence good posts should be firmly set at such distances apart as will admit of the rails reaching from the center of one post to the center of the other. If necessary, straighten the face of the posts with an axe, and hew down the ends of the rails to a uniform thickness. These rails are fastened to the posts by means of a stake, which rests on a stone or block of wood, and is firmly wired at the top and bottom to the post. In constructing the fence it is better to wire the bottom of the stake first—at the proper distance—and the top rather loosely, so as to admit the rails easily. When the rails are laid up draw the top wire tight, and if proper care has been taken in straightening the face of the post, hewing the ends of the rails, etc., the work will bind together very tightly.

SECTION OF STRAIGHT RAIL FENCE.

The fence will last as long as the posts; it is strong, requires no nails, nor any more wire than to stake an ordinary crooked fence, and it takes but little over half the posts necessary for an ordinary board fence.

Durable Fence Posts.—We give herewith a drawing and description of a fence post which we think will last one's life-time. The bottom of the post is formed of a stone—some kind that will drill easily—about eight inches thick and twenty long. In this stone two holes are drilled, one an inch and a quarter in diameter and three inches deep, and the other, half an inch in diameter and two inches deep; the holes should be about one foot apart. Bed the stone in the ground nearly level with the surface, with the small hole on the inside of the fence. Next take a scantling four inches square and three feet long, and put a bar of inch and a quarter iron into one end, lengthwise, about six inches. The end of the bar should project four or five inches. Place this into the largest hole in the stone, hold it plumb, turn in melted brimstone, and you have a post. Bend the end of a rod of half inch iron, and fasten in the other hole in the same way; the other end should be flattened and attached to the scantling with a stout screw. The bar should set tight in the post, and about one inch space for air should be left between the scantling and stone.

DURABLE FENCE POSTS.

Always-Ready Gate.—We give an illustrated plan of an always-ready gate—a small gate for a barnyard or elsewhere, where a passageway is much used. It is very convenient. This gate swings in a V-shaped inclosure, or in two sides of a triangle. Having the top hinge the longest and the post plumb, the gate, at rest, always hangs in the center, and rightly constructed will always leave a passageway of two feet. Cattle cannot get through it, nor do we think

ALWAYS-READY GATE.

sheep will pass it. It is always shut and always open. It requires no watching to keep it closed, and will be found convenient in many ways.

A Good Farm Gate.—We present herewith an engraving of a good and serviceable farm gate, which may be easily and cheaply constructed as follows:

Four posts are set firmly in line, so that the front will be true. Measure fourteen feet, on line with those already set, and set the post the gate shuts against. Then place the sill for the gate to run on, fourteen or sixteen feet long, put down solid. The sill for the gate to run back on can be made of any light material that will sustain the weight of the gate. The sill should have about one inch down grade toward the shutting post, and be spiked fast to

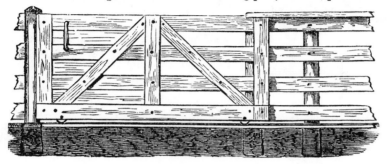

A GOOD FARM GATE.

the posts. The gate is made of any width lumber, and long enough to lap four inches on the shutting posts, and about two feet on the groove post, to keep it shady. At the bottom, the gate must have two boards to support the bolts that the rollers turn on. These rollers should be six inches in diameter, an inch thick, to run on half-round iron, placed at a proper distance from the bottom board of the fence, so as to let the gate pass without rubbing. The iron rod should have holes punched so as to let twelve-penny nails through to nail to the sill, about two feet apart. Nail down the rod and it is ready for the gate. The gate is put together with *sixteen* two and one-half inch bolts and eight three and one-half inch bolts; the three and one-half inch bolts go through three boards at the bottom. The rollers (as per drawing) go between the bottom boards close under the brace, so as to get the bearing; the bolts should fit the rollers as tight as possible. These rollers in their place, put up the gate on the rod, and run it back on the fence; mark the four posts one inch above the top of the gate; saw

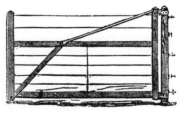

A CHEAP GATE.

them off square, in line; place on top of the posts a joist twelve inches wide, two inches thick; let it project over in front of the gate far enough to clear it; now nail a six-inch strip on the edge of the joist, so that the top edge will be even with the top side of the joist; the four inches projecting down will serve as a groove for the gate to run in and keep it in its place; now spike the joist to the top of the post firmly; let the gate lap on the shutting post about four inches on half the posts; then nail the ends of the boards to the post occupying the other half, so that the gate will shut against the butts, which will help sustain the post; now nail a board solid in line with the butts, and thick enough to project a quarter to a half inch from the gate; nail a stout board on the previous one, and let it project over about three inches toward the gate, and in line with the post, so as to make a groove for the gate to stand in. If it is properly shaped the gate will jam in it and remain solid until it is removed back.

A Cheap Gate.—This gate, illustrated on preceding page, is designed merely for farm use. Wood and metal or wire are combined in a novel manner in its construction. It may be cheaply made by unskilled labor, and combines lightness with durability. The gate is composed of two wooden uprights, one at the hinge end and the other at the free end, two horizontal rails and an oblique brace connecting the rods. An iron brace connects the upper end of the inner upright, and is provided with an eye which receives the pintle of upper hinge. Wires are stretched between the uprights, forming a complete panel. This gate is very light, and at the same time simple and strong.

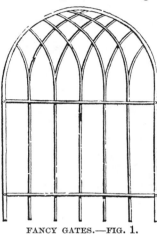

FANCY GATES.—FIG. 1.

Some Fancy Gates.—For the benefit of such readers as may be contemplating the luxury of a new front yard or garden fence, or, in fact, an ornamental fence of any description, we present on this and the following page four neat and ornamental designs of cheap, fancy framed gates, which any carpenter can make, and which may be used appropriately with almost any style of picket or even with iron fences. These gates are usually made three feet six or eight inches wide. The space between the posts for an ordinary door yard gate should be three feet ten inches. That is, however, a matter to be decided by convenience, and the use to which it is to be put. A wide gate is more convenient than a narrow one, especially where baby carriages and wheelbarrows are much used, and the gate is employed as a common and general entrance and exit by the family for all purposes.

FANCY GATES.—FIG. 2.

To Preserve Fence Posts.—A correspondent at Benton Harbor, Mich., sends us the following statement by Parker Earle (a widely known horticulturist), in the Chicago *Times*, and requests our opinion of his mode for preserving fence posts. In answer, it may be stated that no single experiment, or no single series of experiments under like circumstances, can be adopted as a rule for unlike conditions. For general application, we would recommend first impregnating the whole of the post with crude petroleum as a general preservative, and when dry apply hot tar to the portion going into the ground, but none above. The petroleum will penetrate the pores, and the tar coating will hold it there. The following is

Mr. Earle's statement: "In building a fence around our young orchard, several years ago, we tried many plans for preserving the posts. Having occasion to remove the fence this winter, we noted the condition of the posts as follows: Those set with no preparation were decayed an inch or more in thickness; those coated with a thick wash of lime were better preserved, but were quite seriously attacked by worms; those posts coated with hot tar were perfectly sound as when first put into the ground; those painted with petroleum and kerosene were equally sound, and as good as new. In future we shall treat all posts in the following manner before setting: Let the posts get thoroughly dry, and then, with a pan of cheap kerosene and a white-wash brush, give the lower third of the post, the part to go into the ground, two or three good applications of the oil, letting it soak in well each time. Posts so treated will not be troubled by worms or insects of any kind,

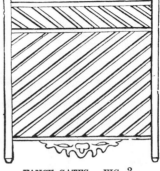

FANCY GATES.—FIG. 3.

but will resist decay to a remarkable degree. This we find to be the simplest, easiest, cheapest, and best method of preservation."—*Country Gentleman.*

Easy Method of Taking Up Posts.—Wishing to take up fence posts, which were sound, and standing solid in heavy clay soil baked hard by drouth, a correspondent made his head save his muscle: "I found that by pouring a pail of water around the post it may be very readily loosened by the hand. Then by hooking a chain about it loosely, slipping the noose down as far as possible below the surface of the ground, and hooking the other end of the chain around a piece of light scantling, near the center, to act as a lever, the post may be lifted out of its bed very easily."

FANCY GATES.—FI~

A Good Fence.—Raise black walnut posts on the lot where they are wanted. If they grow fast they will do in from five to seven years. Use the barb wire. Black walnut injures crops less than almost any other tree. No stock will gnaw or hurt it. The roots run straight down, so you can plow against the trunk. It grows straight and tall, and has but few limbs. The working of the tree will not break the wire. Black walnut will pay all expenses in a few years in fruit.

Post and Rail Fences.—We give herewith plain directions, with appropriate sketches, which we think will enable any ordinarily skillful farm-hand to make the simple machinery necessary for boring the holes in the posts, mortising them out, pointing the rails, digging the holes in the earth, and putting up a good and substantial rail fence. The posts are 7 1-2 feet long for a six-rail fence, which is the best and most generally used, and 3 to 4 inches thick by 7 to 8 inches wide. These posts are hewn out. The holes in the posts are oblong (up and down the post), and in size are 2 1-2 x 6 inches.

The rails are 9 1-2 feet long, and 5 to 6 inches wide by 2 to 3 inches thick on the bark edge, and a quarter to a half inch thick on the other edge.

In building the fence the bark edge is placed *down*, as the thin edge sheds rain or snow more readily, which prevents rotting so rapidly. The rails lap in the holes about five or six inches, as shown in the section, Fig. 4.

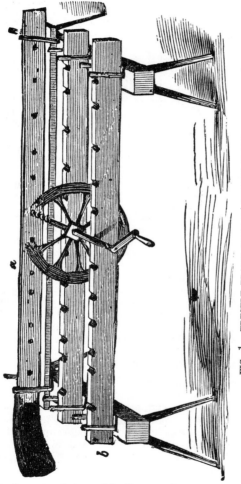

FIG. 1.—TRESTLE FRAME USED IN BORING THE POSTS.

In making the posts the timber is cut into proper lengths, and then split in proper size and hewn, leaving the ground end for two feet rough and unhewn, giving a stout base. This part of the work is done in the forest, after which they are hauled home, and put in piles ready for boring. The mode of making the oblong holes in the post is shown in the cut (Fig. 1), *a* representing the post, *thin edge up*. Two holes are bored with a two-and-a-quarter-inch auger at the points shown by the holes in the post on the trestle at *a*. The auger holes are six inches apart *from outside to outside*. The trestle frame is made of stout timber and planks, as shown in the figure. The planks are put on the benches edgewise, and fastened with stout pins. A plank is placed from one bench to the other for the post to rest on, and these benches are eleven and a half feet apart. In the two planks it will be seen that notches are sawed at points to correspond with the holes to be made by the auger. These notched planks are placed thirteen or fourteen inches apart, to enable the round or square wheel (see Figs. 1 and 5) to run easily in between them. The post is held on the plank firmly by stout wooden pins and wedges. The bottom hole in the post is made two inches above the ground level. The next hole is three inches from the top of the bottom hole; the next four inches above that; the next is five above that; and the top hole is six inches above the one below it. In boring the holes the auger, which is firmly fastened in the wheel, must be moved (wheel and all, of course) into the proper notches, and in this way every post is bored alike, **and** all the holes in the post are the proper distance apart. After your posts are bored, the next step is to have a narrow-blade axe, with a short handle, as shown at *c*, Fig. 2 (a common axe, would do, however), and with this mortise out the holes, which is done by laying the post flat-

wise on the ground, or on a stout, low trestle, similar to the " pointer " shown at Fig. 3. When one side is mortised half out, turn the post and finish. A good hand will bore and mortise fifteen posts a day with these tools. The rails for this kind of a fence are split out in the woods, 9 1-2 feet long, all of the same length. A good hand can cut down the timber and split out one hundred of them in a day, in fair timber. They are hauled home generally before being pointed. The ends of the rails should fill the holes as nearly as possible, so as to exclude moisture, the tighter the better. Pointing the rails is simple work. Two short-legged, stout trestles of a n y rough logs are placed a b o u t eight feet apart, as shown at Fig. 3, in each of

FIG. 2.—SHOVEL, AXE AND DIGGER.

which two large wooden pegs are driven to receive the rail, and between these pegs the rail is placed, *thin edge up*, and fastened in between the pegs with wedges of wood. They are now sharpened off to about an inch thick for six to eight inches, the corners slightly nipped, and the work is done. A man will point over two hundred in a day.

To make holes in the earth, a digger (see Fig. 2) is used. It is about ten

FIG. 3.—TRESTLE FOR POINTING THE RAILS.

inches long by five wide, made perfectly s t r a i g h t, and to weigh, handle and all, about twelve pounds. It is made of good iron, laid with the best steel. Any blacksmith can make one. They cost about $1.50, w i t h o u t handle. T h e handle should be six feet long, and heavy. A club at one end would do for a ram-

mer ˙to run the dirt in the holes. In making the fence, set the first post firmly, and slip in one end of the rails, as shown at *a*, in Fig. 4. After the next hole is dug set the next post in, and before you put in the dirt place the other end of the rails in on both sides, and drive; then fill up and ram firmly, and so on to the end. Drive the rails with a wooden maul. Never use an axe. When you come to a corner, you must have a large post with holes in the sides—the other holes only half way through the post—to re-

FIG. 4.—SECTION OF THE SIX RAIL FENCE.

ceive the turn rails. In digging the holes, a little practice will enable you to throw out over half of the dirt with the digger (see Fig. 2), especially if the earth is tenacious. After that a long-handled, small scoop shovel, as shown at *d*, Fig. 2, will be found serviceable.

We neglected to say that the handle to the auger is about 3 1-2 feet long, and can be, as it usually is, fastened on by a blacksmith. The square wheel shown in Fig. 5 is easily made, and is about 5 feet in diameter. The trestle (Fig. 1) is 3 1-2 feet high. The auger is put in the wheel and hung on the trestle precisely like an ordinary grindstone. As to the best materials for this fence, black locust is the best for posts, mulberry next, then white oak. For rails, white oak, ash, walnut, and cotton-wood, in the order named.

Fence for Marsh or Soft Soil.—T h e improvement we herewith illustrate is designed for bracing the common board fences built across low, marshy ground, that is overflowed at every fall of rain. The work, or face side, of

FIG. 5.—AUGER WHEEL.

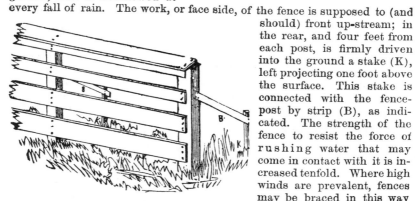

FENCE FOR MARSH OR SOFT SOIL.

the fence is supposed to (and should) front up-stream; in the rear, and four feet from each post, is firmly driven into the ground a stake (K), left projecting one foot above the surface. This stake is connected with the fence-post by strip (B), as indicated. The strength of the fence to resist the force of rushing water that may come in contact with it is increased tenfold. Where high winds are prevalent, fences may be braced in this way upon the leeward side.

FIELD CROPS--Update

Much of the material provided in this chapter remains as good general advice now as it was in 1888. But the orientation and scope of agriculture have changed considerably. Any discussion of field crops must include more plants and more varieties of plants than were available in 1888. Buckwheat, sunflowers, soybeans, sorghum, rye, ryegrass, millet and barley are field crops not even mentioned. There are many varieties of clover and alfalfa, and hundreds of hybrids of corn. Some hybrids will mature in nearly half the time it takes others.

And of course the system of ensilage which was just being introduced in 1888 has had a tremendous effect on American farms. Indeed, it would be hard to find a dairy farm now without huge complexes of silos whose function is to store the chopped corn mixture. Cribs (see illustration p. 41) have almost disappeared from use.

As corn has become the main field crop for fodder, so its culture has been mechanized for greater efficiency. To suggest to a farmer that cabbage might be planted among the rows of corn is almost ridiculous. Farmers do currently plant sudan-grass and sorghum in their corn rows or as borders to corn fields, but these crops may be mechanically harvested and fed into the siloes. If a farmer determined not to mechanically cultivate or harvest his corn, he might wish to plant vine crops such as squash, cucumbers and pumpkins among the corn rows. They will grow excellently in the relative shade, and pumpkins have been used quite successfully as fodder.

The debate between advocates of root crops and advocates of cereals as fodder has since 1888 been settled in favor of cereals. Roots such as potatoes, mangel-wurtzel beets, carrots, turnips and rutabagas, though continuing as a main source of fodder in Eastern Europe, are now thought by American farmers to lack nutrients that cereals contain. American farmers are most concerned with proteins in their fodder and these are best supplied by such cereals as soybeans. Some nutritionists have advised that plant proteins would be better used by direct human consumption than in building meat on beef cattle.

Subsoiling (pp. 51-2) is currently very popular. Large machines or repeated passes are necessary to plow to a level of two feet. Care must be taken not to disturb drainage systems, which may be only buried a foot and a half in old fields. Fields which do not have tile drainage systems will benefit considerably by subsoiling. Recent research has shown that years of heavy equipment use, or simply heavy subsoil, may cause compaction at the plow sole and this layer will stop root growth. Subsoiling leads to better aeration of the soil with less risk of fungal diseases and aids drainage of the ground's excess water.

Varieties of field crops are fitted to different soils and climatic conditions. A beginner deciding what field crops to plant is well advised to contact the County Extension Agent who can provide him with current information published by the state agricultural universities and experimental stations and arrange for his soil to be tested. A standard, though highly technical text for field crops is H.C. Rather's *Field Crops* (NY: McGraw-Hill Book Co. 1942). Gene Logsdon's *Small-Scale Grain Raising* (Emmaus, Pa.: Rodale Press, 1977) is a fine book for the small-scale farmer.

FIELD CROPS.

Wheat Shocks.—The illustrations portray the various methods practiced for securing wheat, rye, oats, etc., in shocks, in which position they should be arranged. Wheat should be cut from five to ten days before maturity—that is, when about one-third of the chaff is yet green, or while many of the berries can be mashed between the thumb and finger. The points gained thereby are: By thus early reaping the grain is not as liable to be prostrated by rain or high winds, and is not as liable to shell during the process of gathering. The grain secured by this process, and at the time indicated, is heavier, and the flour is better.

Fig. 1 delineates a large, oblong shock which is made by placing ten sheaves in a double row, the bottom of each pair being a foot asunder, set bracing and meeting at the top, the whole covered by two sheaves, whose ends, each side of band, are so spread that when in position they will afford a more secure protection from rain, and render the liability to derangement in high winds much less.

In Fig. 2 is shown a very good plan for securing a dozen or more sheaves in a round shock. Two caps are used, crossing at right angles above the center of the shock.

WHEAT SHOCKS.—FIG. **1.**

Fig. 3 illustrates another mode of capping a round shock. But six sheaves should be placed upright in each shock, unless the straw be of extra length, as in the case of rye. Bind the caps securely near the butts, breaking down all around before placing in proper position. The latter is a mode seldom practiced, yet highly recommended by many farmers. Should the sheaves be damp or contain slowly drying weeds, shock in the manner shown in Fig. 1, which exposes a greater area of each sheaf to the combined influence of sun and air than by any other known process.

Harvesting Wheat.—Wheat, when cut before the grain has passed from the milk to the dough state, will shrivel and give small measure and light weight. The straw will be more valuable for fodder, however, than if harvested later. On the other hand, if left to become over-ripe, the grains grow harsh and rough, and the bran will be so thick and brittle that no after manipulation of the kernels will bring the wheat in condition to make the best quality of flour without carrying a large proportion of flour off with the bran.

The cultivator's safety lies, therefore, between the extremes of early and late cutting. In a word, harvest the crop when the grain has passed from the milky stage to a doughy one. If the wheat be cut when the grain reaches the dough state, the bran will be thin and elastic, and can be separated more readily from the flour than when dead ripe. In addition to the flour being finer, it will also be increased in quantity in consequence of the bran being lighter than when ripe. A saving of wheat is likewise gained, which otherwise would be lost by shelling in the field.

WHEAT SHOCKS.—FIG. 2.

The novice can ascertain the exact time when wheat and other small grain ought to be cut by opening heads in different portions of the field, and examining the kernels carefully. The straw near the ground will also proclaim the time for harvest by its yellow hue.

Wheat cut in the dough state ought not to be dried suddenly. It may be bound and stacked at once, or, if there is only a small quantity, drawn to the barn. Some farmers put it into small stacks. If stacked so that the wind and sun will not dry up all the juices in the plant, enough of these will be slowly concentrated in the seed to accomplish the maturity of the grain in perfection.

If by rapid ripening in the sun the kernels are shrivelled, more bran is formed in proportion to the flour.

A large class of farmers practice threshing from the shock and hauling grain direct to market. The advantages of this plan vary with the season. When the wheat has been bleached out by hot suns and repeated rains, it should be stacked and go through the "sweat." During this process the straw and grain become damp and heat is evolved. At such times the grain cannot readily be threshed, therefore it is not advisable to attempt it until both straw and grain are dry. Then it will be found that the berry

WHEAT SHOCKS.—FIG. 3.

has been restored to color and exhibits a plump appearance, having absorbed nutritive matter from the stalk. The grain has not only undergone a change for the better, but the straw is also improved in quality.

It is suggested that farmers take time to look about for extra fine heads of wheat for future seed. It will also be wise to carefully note the results of the several varieties grown, with a view to comparing their respective merits, and selecting for another year's crop those sorts which promise best returns. When fertilizers have been used, it will also be well to mark the results. It is only by a careful comparison of different plants under different treatments that a farmer surely arrives at conclusions which best suit the special requirements of his land and his location.

How to Stack Straw.—We give an illustration showing how straw can be stacked so that it will be preserved from spoiling, and at the same time answer for a shelter to protect stock from the storms. The pen should be two or three logs high (or higher, if the logs are small), and large enough to correspond with the quantity of straw. Then set fence rails or poles all around inside of the pen, as represented. It can be built at the tail end of the threshing machine, so that the straw can fall in it. It will require less hands to stack.

Draining Wheat Fields.—If no other method has been devised for draining wheat fields, which are sometimes too wet, it will pay to plow furrows from the lowest spot to some lower point outside. Every experienced wheat grower knows that if water is allowed to stand upon the ground late in the fall, the crop will not only be directly injured thereby, but will also be liable to be severely damaged by "winter killing," and it should be the aim to prevent, as far as possible, both of these evils.

HOW TO STACK STRAW.

A heavy rain will do little damage to a wheat field if provision is made for the prompt removal of the surplus water, while a moderate rainfall upon undrained land which is already too wet will cause the destruction of many of the plants, and largely reduce the possible yield of the crop. While thorough drainage is much better than any makeshift which can be invented, it is much better to adopt the very imperfect plan recommended above than it is to make no provision for the protection of the crop from injury by an excess of moisture in the soil.

Weevil in Wheat.—A correspondent of an agricultural paper says: "Some years ago, hearing complaint of weevil in wheat about the close of harvest, when I was ricking my wheat, I got fresh slaked lime and threw over the rick in building it—laying two courses of sheaves, then lime sufficient to whiten the stack. A neighbor who threshed his wheat from the shock came to me a few days after, and said he should lose his wheat, for it was alive with weevil. I told him to throw lime over it, and shovel it through his wheat, which he did. Two days later there was not a weevil seen in it."

Wheat Maxims in Small Compass.—The following information about wheat growing has been condensed: 1. The best soil for wheat is rich clay

loam; 2. Wheat likes a good, deep, soft bed; 3. Clover turned under makes just such a bed; 4. The best seed is oily, heavy, plump, and clean; 5. About two inches is the best depth for sowing the seed; 6. The drill puts in the seed better and cheaper than broadcasting; 7. From the middle of September to the last of October is the best time for sowing; 8. Drilled, one bushel of seed per acre; if sown broadcast, two bushels per acre; 9. One heavy rolling after sowing does much good; 10. For flour, cut when the grain begins to harden; for seed, not until it has hardened.

FIG. 1.

An Ohio Corn Crib.—
We give an illustration (Fig. 1) of a very convenient and substantial double corn crib, with a wagon shed between. Such a crib can be built any size, and filled with grain, without the least sign of weakness. One is a brace for the other, and the more grain you have in it the firmer it will be. It is use-
less to explain how the timbers should be put together, and where every door should be cut out, when one glance at the illustration will answer. Fig. 2 represents the double doors made to correspond with the entrance of the shed. The doors, when shut, are fastened to a piece of scantling, standing perpendicular—one entering the beam, the other entering a block put in the ground. The foundation can be of wood or stone, as suits best. This is what we call the "Ohio Dutch Yankee corn crib."

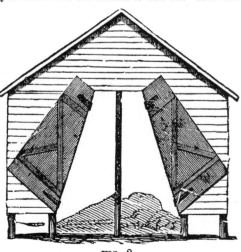

FIG. 2.

Hilling Injurious to Corn.—Careful experiments have proved that corn which is hilled will blow down more readily than that which has level culture. This can be accounted for by the fact that corn roots run very near the surface, and when hills are made they are confined to the small space covered by the hill; while in level culture the roots run from one row to the other, thus enabling the corn to stand strong, as nature intended, and in no way liable to be blown down, except by winds of unusual violence.

A Convenient Corn Crib.—We illustrate a very convenient style of corn crib, which, while costing but a mere trifle more than an ordinary crib, possesses some of the main advantages of a corn house; namely, a space protected from the weather sufficient to accommodate a team with a wagon load of corn. At the proper season the grain may be shelled therein, and it is an excellent place to shelter a lumber wagon. The plan needs but little explanation. It is simply two cribs placed side by side, and facing each other. The cribs and space between them are covered by one roof. The cribs should be about four feet wide at the bottom, and grow broader as they rise, the taper being on the outside; the projecting roof throws the water clear of

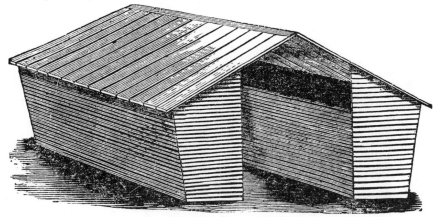

A CONVENIENT CORN CRIB.

the crib. The height should be sufficient to allow easy shoveling of the corn from the wagon into the top of the crib. If one wishes to make it rat-proof, it may be elevated on posts, capped with inverted tin pans; but in that case it would hardly do to store tools in it. Some would suggest a floor and doors, which can easily be added to the plan, if desired. The best material is sawed scantlings for a frame, and three or four-inch-wide strips for siding. The roof may be made of matched boards. In case it should be determined to floor and hang doors, it would be well to board up the inside of the crib with matched stuff to the height of the eaves.

Seed Corn.—No one will deny that great care should be observed in selecting seed corn to plant, and yet numbers of farmers never see their seed corn until it is carried to the field at planting-time. We think the best plan is to place a barrel in a corner of the crib, and throw in it every large and vigorous ear. Shell off about two inches of the large ends, in order to get the largest and most prolific grains. This produces a large and healthy plant, that grows much faster than small ones do. Many farmers may think it quite a tedious job to select every ear of corn planted in this way; but they will not find it so after giving it a trial, and selecting as much as possible on rainy days. This plan, once adopted, will ever be adhered to afterward. Try it; you will not regret it, but find it remunerative.

CORN CRIBS.—FIG. **1.**

Cheap Corn Cribs.— There are many farmers who follow a mixed husbandry, and who raise comparatively small quantities of corn, who cannot afford to pay much for structures used for this purpose. For such we herewith give directions, accompanied with drawings, showing how a cheap and yet suitable crib may be made.

The elevation (Fig. 1) is an excellent crib. The sills are four by six inches, framed; if only a small crib is needed, it will only be necessary to bore two-inch holes at each corner, and one intermediate, and insert sharpened sticks three inches square, to which secure slats horizontally, three-quarters of an

CORN CRIBS.—FIG. **2.**

inch apart. As this structure has but one door, it is best to divide the room in two parts, the best or sound corn to be put in the near compartment, and the poor corn in front, where it may be first fed out. A still cheaper plan

CORN CRIBS.—FIG. **3.**

of construction is to use poles or small logs, secured together in the form shown in Fig. 2. This is an exceedingly cheap and expeditious manner of constructing a corn crib. If properly done, it will last for years, is easy of access, and, with a good cover, corn will keep in it as well as in those more expensive.

Fig. 3 gives a side view of a crib constructed of poles or logs, showing the manner of splicing at A, A, the logs midway between the supports. Pin or nail the logs at the point of joining. In this way log cribs several hundred feet in length are often constructed.

The Enemies of Corn.—Its enemies in the field, the bin, and the mill are numerous. Among its bird foes the crow is most dreaded by the farmer. He is a bold, saucy fellow, well endowed with bird sense, and soon sees a scare-crow is a humbug. The common devices used for this purpose —an open newspaper, bright tin, a clapping wind-mill, an effigy, etc., are effective only for a short time, when something new must be found. A practical farmer suggests that early planting will circumvent him, since he is not particularly an early bird. Another claims that the use of a planter which covers the seed and presses down the earth upon it has been a perfect defense for him. He has seen twenty crows pulling away after the corn had got above the ground, and found they had nipped the tops off, yet could not get the kernel up.

Great damage is often done to the corn crop by a corn-worm *(Heliothus Armiga)*, identical with the boll-worm, so injurious to the cotton crop. The parent of the worm is a moth of brownish-yellow color, with dark brown or black markings. The caterpillar is green with black stripes and dark spots, and is covered with hairs. When full grown it measures about one and one-half inches. It is extremely voracious, though not particularly dainty, since it eats whatever comes in its way. Peas, stringed beans, tomatoes, pumpkins, cotton or corn are all one to his greedy appetite. The moth deposits its eggs upon the corn silk, and the young caterpillars soon work their way down to the tender kernel. When the caterpillar attains its full size it descends into the soil a few inches and there weaves its cocoon. Two or more broods are produced each year. Birds and parasites destroy this insect both as worm and moth. Men destroy it by means of torches, lamps and lanterns, sometimes arranged over dishes of oil or water, into which it falls and drowns. Plates of vinegar and molasses put among the corn will entrap many of them.

Aphis Maidis, a little plant louse, infests corn and lives upon its juices. The eggs, which are laid in the ground, hatch in May, when the lice gather upon the roots, and here remain until the roots harden so that they are driven to the stem and tassels, where they are found in great numbers about July. Their presence can be easily detected by an army of red ants dancing attendance upon them, since they wear two black honey-tubes standing up like horns on the upper and hinder part of the abdomen, which secrete a saccharine fluid, of which the ants are very fond. They have a curious history of reproduction. The female deposits her eggs in the ground and dies. The brood are wingless females, and without the intervention of the male bring forth alive another female brood.

These do likewise, and so continue for five or six or more generations. The last brood are both males and females. These pair again, and deposit their eggs, which remain over winter in the ground, and the next spring begin the same round over again. It is claimed that nothing but cropping against them is of any avail.

The corn-stalk borer is a comparatively new enemy, or, at any rate, has been only lately described. The moth is of an ashy-gray color, and probable lays her eggs near the base of the leaf where the leaf is sheathed around the stalk. The worm is orange yellow, with rows of reddish warts, and a flat, black head, with which it bores its way into the stalk. It sheds its skin four times before it attains full growth. The cocoon is woven within the stalk, and the moth makes its exit through the holes bored by the worm. Three or more broods are produced each year. It hibernates in stalks and stubble. The stalks not eaten by stock should be burned early in February, and the stubble should be plowed up and burned, or plowed under very deeply.

Curing Corn Fodder.—Much corn fodder is spoiled while being cured. A good way to prevent this is to set firmly in the ground a small stake or large-sized bean-pole, around which a few armfuls of corn is set, and bound securely near the top. This makes a firm center around which to build. Then set up more corn, placing it evenly all around, and leaning it no more than is necessary to have it stand. When enough is placed to make a large stock, all that can cure, draw a rope, with a slip noose in one end, around the stock as tight as convenient, using a step-ladder to stand upon if the corn is very tall. An assistant can now bind with a straw band or with selected stalks, after which the rope may be removed. If doing the work alone, the rope can be tied while the band is being put on. Corn fodder well put up in this way may be kept, if desired, in the field till winter.

Saving Seed Corn.—To save seed corn successfully in a cold climate, you should not keep it in a warm place, or especially where it is warm but a part of the time, as there is danger that the changes of temperature may destroy the germinative power. Continued warmth is also conducive to decomposition, which will destroy the life of the seed. Corn and similar seeds are best kept in a dry, cool room, where the temperature is uniform. When your seed from the "small pile over the living-room" failed to germinate, the cause was probably due to both dampness and warmth, which incited incipient decay. Seeds differ greatly in the degree of cold they will endure without losing vitality. Corn has germinated after having been subjected to the most intense cold of the polar regions, and an experiment is reported in which other seeds germinated after having been frozen into a cake of ice.

Corn Culture.—"The suckers," says H. M. Engle, in a prize essay, "should, under all circumstances, be taken off before they appropriate too much substance which the main stalks should receive, but under no circumstances allow suckers to tassel, for, whatever pains may be taken to bring or keep corn at its greatest perfection by selection of seed, the pollen from the sucker may undo what has been gained by years of careful selection. I would as soon think of breeding from a scrub male to a thoroughbred animal as to have the pollen from suckers cast upon an excellent variety of corn. It is also well known that the pollen from a neighboring field is ofttimes carried to an almost incredible distance, and consequently may cause more mixture than is desirable."

Points on Corn.—Deep plowing among growing corn after the roots have met in the rows is disastrous; "root pruning" is a mistake; to break the roots checks the growth, and in hot, dry weather deep cultivation will surely cause the corn to curl, showing injuring and suffering, while shallow working will keep it fresh and green. As soon as a crust is formed on the soil, it should be broken up to admit both moisture and air, for the one dissolves the fertilizing matter which is in the soil, and the latter effects its decomposition and renders it soluble. So that after a rain, which has crusted the surface, the cultivator should be started as soon as the soil is dry enough; this tends to hold the moisture and prevent speedy evaporation.

Raising Good Corn in a Dry Season.—"Some Yankee," says a practical farmer, "will ask, 'How do you raise good corn in a drouth?' I'll tell. I plowed and rolled my ground, spread my manure on, and harrowed it in; put a handful of hen manure and fine bone composted in the hill; cultivated it flat; did not hill any. When the drouth came, cultivated, but very shallow; the result was a good crop. On another plot the manure was spread on the sod and turned under without any fertilizer in the hill, and was almost a failure. My neighbors report that they have very fair corn on land that the manure was spread on after plowing and fertilizing in the hill."

Husking.—Some people who husk corn throw the shock upon the ground, spread it out, and go to work on their knees. They know no better. If they will make a frame four feet wide and long enough to hold a shock after it is spread out, with a board in the middle running lengthways to sit on, they will find they have done a sensible thing. The frame may be eighteen inches high, or any other height they may like better.

Cabbages with Corn.—A writer in the *Fruit Recorder* says that one of his neighbors planted some cabbage among his corn where the corn missed, and the butterflies did not find them. He has therefore come to the conclusion that if the cabbage patch were in the middle of the corn patch, the butterflies would not find them, as they fly low and like plain sailing.

Potato Culture.—Destroying the potato beetle, says the *American Cultivator*, and its even more destructive larvæ, has come to be the most important point in the successful growing of potatoes. Paris green is the common agent employed, though London purple is cheaper, equally effective, and has the advantage, when used with water, of being soluble, while Paris green, under similar conditions, is insoluble. It does not follow, however, because these poisons will do the work, that every grower can make them equally effective. In their indiscriminate use the inexperienced cultivator is liable to do more harm than good. The young potato shoot is very tender, and either Paris green or London purple applied in too strong doses will burn the vines. If the vines be injured at this early stage of their growth from any cause, the resultant crop will be greatly diminished.

For nearly all early planted potatoes, when the vine grows slowly, hand picking to destroy the first crop of beetles is very important. It should be performed as soon as the shoots are up, and, if possible, before any eggs are laid. In a potato-growing section, where old beetles from last year's hatch appear by the thousands, this indeed involves considerable labor. In fact, in such a locality it is not easy to grow early potatoes on a large scale. From a few short rows in a garden we have picked up by count between eight hundred and nine hundred beetles on a warm, sunshiny half-day, just as the potatoes were coming up. The next day the process was repeated, with nearly half as many beetles secured, while more or less in number were gathered every subsequent day for a week. It was just at the time the beetles were coming out of the ground, and the garden potatoes being early planted, attracted all the beetles in the neighborhood. It is of little avail to attempt to poison these beetles in the spring. Occasionally one will eat as expected, but the majority are too busy propagating and laying eggs to attend to anything else. It is the fact that beetles are very numerous in spring, together with the difficulty in destroying them by poison, which frightens so many from the business. The inexperienced grower is apt, as soon as he finds his vines infested, to prepare a dose of poison, making it of very great strength, so as to make certain of killing the enemy. In nine cases out of ten the tender vines are injured, and the beetles are seldom appreciably diminished in numbers. With close hand picking at first, and a reserving of the poison until the larvæ make their appearance, the result is very different and much more satisfactory.

The main crop of potatoes should be planted late—that is, if large quantities are to be grown. Planting a few in the garden or somewhere else, as a bait to draw the first beetles, greatly lessens the subsequent work. Even in the same field the potato beetle is more destructive on some varieties than on others. Those who have grown the Magnum Bonum say it is especially liable to attack. Grown alongside other varieties, the bugs singled out this, while the others largely escaped. It has been suggested that one or two rows of this kind be planted around the potato field as a protection to the main crop. On the other hand, it is said the Early Gem is especially distasteful to the bugs. There is probably some difference in the comparative liability of different varieties to this insect attack. We have generally found, however, that the larger growing varieties and the strongest hills of the same variety are least injured. It is possible to plant on highly-manured ground, with seed so vigorous that its rapid growth will largely reduce the cost of fighting the bugs. The female beetle instinctively chooses a vine that is a feeble grower on which to deposit her eggs. Where the vine is full of sap, either the eggs will not be laid or many of them will fail to hatch. We hope very much, from the results of recent experiments, in discovering the true way to cut potato seed. If the proper cutting of potato seed will insure greater vigor or growth, many of the difficulties in fighting the potato beetle will be overcome.

It should not be forgotten that the potato grower has insect friends as well as enemies. All kinds of lady-bugs eat the eggs of the potato beetle. It is the abundance of these lady-bugs about old apple orchards that often makes potato growing successful near an orchard when the field crop will be entirely destroyed. There are several varieties of insects that prey on the potato larvæ. Farmers who use no poison sometimes find dead potato bug larvæ on their vines. These dead specimens should always be left undisturbed, as in all probability they are filled with eggs of the parasite that has destroyed them, only needing opportunity to hatch and continue the good work. On general principles, if any insect is found in the potato field whose habits are not known, it is best to leave it undisturbed, since it is quite probably a friend engaged in destroying the farmer's enemies. Entomologists have discovered thirty or more insect enemies of the potato bug in its various stages of growth, and there are probably others not yet known. But for these friendly insects difficulties in growing potatoes would be much greater than those which now prevail.

Phosphate for Potatoes.—Wm. T. Woerner, of New Brunswick, N. J., writes: "In planting potatoes I have used no other manure than phosphate of some reliable brand, for the last ten years, and in that time I have not had a grub-eaten potato where I put the phosphate. All my potatoes grow as smooth as a bottle, and of a large, salable size. I never use stable manure of any kind on potatoes now. I would not put it on if it was given to me, and I had to pay fifty dollars per ton for phosphate. My neighbors have tried it with a like result. It is a very cheap fertilizer; on good ground I only use about two bags per acre (400 lbs.), which is a good manuring on ordinary soil. I have raised four hundred bushels to the acre with nothing but phosphate, applied in the row."

A Handy "Bug-Catcher."—Although it is now the custom of most of our farmers to rid their crops of that terrible pest, the potato bug, by Paris green poisoning, still we think the following illustrated sketch of a bug-catcher, sent by a gentleman who has used the contrivance with great success, will prove interesting and profitable to our readers. He says: "With the pan I use for catching Colorado beetles, any one can do as much work as three or four people collecting the pests, according to the ordinary method

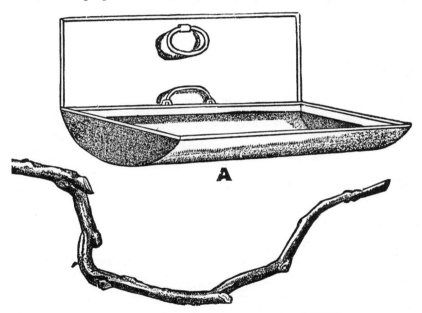

CONTRIVANCE FOR CATCHING THE POTATO BEETLE.

of hand picking. The pan is made of tin, and any tinman can fashion it. It is a box or pan, two feet long, one foot wide, and six inches deep. The bottom should be round, or cylindrical, so that the rim of the pan can be got close to the ground when the vines are small. Stiffen the edge with wire. On the inside, at the top, solder a rim or flange about three-quarters of an inch wide. This should slant downward somewhat, as its object is to prevent the 'bugs' from crawling out when once they have gone in. On one side of the pan solder or rivet a handle, such as those on common tin milk-pails. On the same side as the handle solder a shield of tin eighteen inches high, and of the same length as the pan, slanting backward a little. The edges should be stiffened with wire. About four inches from the top of the shield, and in the center, solder a loop or ring large enough to admit the arm to the shoulder. In using, insert the left arm through the loop, and grasp the lower handle with the hand, then, holding the pan close up to the vines and near the ground, with a crooked stick, like the one represented, gather the vines over the pan, giving them a smart shake against the shield and over the pan. A good, active man, with this contrivance, can ' bug ' an acre of potatoes effectively in two hours."

The Potato Disease.—There are many devices suggested for avoiding the disease known as potato rot. There is one made by an English writer, who says it has been found that " by hilling the plants up very high as soon as the blight appears, the spores are prevented in a great measure from being washed down by the rains, and the rot consequently much diminished. It was found that although the spores were readily washed downward through one or two inches of earth, they very rarely reached a depth of five inches. The experiment was repeated many times with the uniform result that where the plants were not hilled up, and the tubers lay but one or two inches deep, the percentage of rot was very large. But where the tubers were covered to the depth of five inches, the damage from the disease was inconsiderable." If a physician were to say to a patient having the small-pox that if the lower part of the body were swathed in wet sheets the disease would not get down to the legs and feet, it would be a parallel suggestion to this. The rot is a disease which infects the whole plant. It has been found that when the disease began in the tops at a late stage of the growth, mowing off the diseased tops saved the tubers. This is something like amputating a gangrened limb to save the body, and is a reasonable remedy. But the spores are not always, and are in fact rarely, ripe at the season of growth, and are generally in the soil and infect the plant from the roots. The tubers are not roots, but stems, and receive the infection from the roots when the source of it is in the soil. When the leaves are infected by spores, carried in the air from distant fields, where they have remained during the resting season, the disease spreads through the tissues of the plant and reaches the tubers in that way, from within, and not from without. The spores are not free until the plant decays, being set free by the decomposition of the diseased tissues. This being distinctly known, it becomes of the greatest importance to destroy the infected vines by burning them, and thus preventing the soil from infection by the matured spores in the leaves and stems. Earthing up the potatoes might possibly have helped to preserve the tubers from the disease by removing the water from the saturated soil; this water being injurious to the plant and producing all the conditions favorable to the spread of the disease. A more healthful condition of the plants would tend to prevent this unhealthful condition and confine the disease to the leaves and stems, and save the tubers. But every one who has had diseased potatoes, knows that tubers, apparently sound when dug, will rot in the cellar. This is because the disease is already in them when they are dug, and develops in them in the course of time from the infection. Earthing up cannot save them then, nor can it at any other time, excepting through its influence in the way we have pointed out. But here, where our seasons are not so wet, it would not avail us as it might the farmers of sodden England or Scotland or Ireland, where " the rain it raineth every day," more or less. This difference of climate is very important to be remembered when considering such matters as this from an English view.

Methods of Raising Potatoes.—There is, writes a practical farmer, a great variety of opinion in regard to raising potatoes, size of seed, and cultivation. Some advocate large, while others prefer small potatoes for seed, thinking that they are as good or better than large ones. They may raise good crops from small seed for one or two years, but if they do not obtain their seed from those that do take pains to select large seed, I think they will soon find their potatoes run out and become small. Why do we select a nice, well-shaped ear of corn for seed, not always the largest, but the best developed? Also, why screen wheat, oats, etc., to secure the plumpest and best seed to plant or sow? (At least we should if we do not.) We thereby raise a better quality of grain, and more of it, from year to year. I do not wish any one to infer that we should take the largest potatoes for seed, but those of a good marketable size, of nice shape, free from warts, scabs or other deformity.

Having my seed selected, I cut them to single eyes, or at most two, and plant them in drills three feet apart, and fifteen inches apart in the drills, having the drills deep, in well-plowed and thoroughly pulverized soil. I prefer a piece that had corn on the previous year, well manured and plowed in for that crop, and kept under good cultivation during the season. On potatoes I use some good commercial fertilizer that has plenty of potash in it, and use it liberally—400 to 500 pounds per acre. This will help keep the wire-worms away, and will increase the potatoes in size and quality, I am quite certain. I harrow, as soon as I see the first plants breaking the ground, with a smoothing harrow, to kill all the weeds that may have started. I cultivate often, whether there are any weeds or not, until they are in blossom. I have never failed to raise a good crop of nice smooth potatoes, and there was always a ready market for them. I often get considerable more than market price for them, which is quite an advantage in a plentiful season. My crop averaged about 500 bushels per acre last season.

How to Keep Sweet Potatoes.—A Texas writer says: I would like to give my plan for keeping sweet potatoes. I think the most essential thing is to dig them at the proper time, and I think that time is about the full moon in October (that is, in Texas). No matter about the weather, unless the ground is too wet. I never wait for frost; but if frost comes before the full moon, dig as soon as possible, or at least before any rain. I dig with a bull-tongue plow; but any way, so they are not cut or bruised too much, will do. In gathering them, sort out the cut ones; but before putting up let them have at least one day's sun. If the ground is wet, two days is better; but in no case let them take the dew of the night. I put them in a shallow cellar under some house, say from three to four feet deep. After they are put away, throw a little fine, dry dirt over them, just enough to dust over the cuts. That will cause them to dry and not commence rotting. Let them lay that way till the weather begins to turn cool. Then begin to cover up as the weather gets colder, till they are from ten to twelve inches deep; in all cases cover with dry dirt. I differ with those who want straw or leaves under potatoes; I want them on the ground.

When they are banked outdoors they should be on an elevated place, or throw up the dirt so water will not stand about them. Put the potatoes on the naked ground, about twenty-five or thirty bushels in a bank; set up corn stalks around them; then throw some grass or leaves on the stalks; bank up enough of dirt against the stalks to hold them. Let them stand that way till the weather begins to get cool; then begin to cover. When the weather gets very cold they should be covered at least twelve inches; but in warm weather they should have a little air at the top. In all cases have them well sheltered; a very small leak will ruin a bank of potatoes.

Points About Potatoes.—In the judgment of the South Deerfield (Mass.) Farmers' Club, potatoes, when properly cared for, are, next to tobacco, the best paying crop a farmer can raise. The trouble is, potatoes are too often neglected and receive attention only when other crops are cared for. Turf land is the best, except in very dry seasons. Plow in the fall and harrow in a good coat of manure in the spring. Furrow out, and in the hills apply ashes and tobacco stalks cut about six inches long, at the rate of sixteen loads per acre. Twelve hundred pounds of fish and potash to the acre, harrowed in, with a little phosphate in the hill, produced a good crop.

More attention should be given to selecting good seed potatoes. Use good-sized smooth tuber cut into four pieces. Change the seed every year or two. The Early Rose is the best kind for home use. Peerless, Beauty of Hebron, and Burbank Seedling give larger yields, but are inferior in quality. The Snowflake bakes well. Early Vermont resembles Early Rose, and is better in yield and quality.

Hoeing potatoes is best done with a horse-hoe or tobacco-ridger. Go through the piece three times with a horse-hoe, and you wouldn't need to put a hoe into it; that is, on smooth land free of stones. To get ahead of the bugs, cover the potato tops about an inch deep as soon as they are up; in about a week cut a lot of small potatoes into four or more pieces and wet them and sprinkle Paris green on them, stirring well until the pieces are covered with it; scatter these pieces over the field, and the beetle will eat them and die. If all do not partake of this wholesome diet and slugs appear, apply Paris green mixed with plaster. Potatoes are a paying crop at fifty or sixty cents a bushel, and the small ones are excellent to feed hogs, stock, and horses.

Getting Potatoes Early.—Some years ago, writes a correspondent of the *Gardener's Monthly*, I conceived the idea of planting my potatoes with shoots to them. Probably the sprouts suggested the idea; at any rate I carried out the plan, and have been so well pleased with it that I have followed it out for three years. A few weeks before planting time I select my seed potatoes, and set them in a warm place to sprout. By the time my ground is ready the shoots are about three inches in length. The potatoes are handled carefully, so as not to break the growth, and cut up in suitable sizes, as in the ordinary way. One strong shoot is left to each piece. The sets must be put into the ground carefully, of course, or the shoots will be broken off. As growth commences at once, the green tops show in a few days. There is easily a saving of two weeks time at the start. Those who have rather a low ground, which cannot be worked very early in spring, as I have, will find this method will enable them to compete with their neighbors on higher ground, with success. By July 10th, I was using fine Beauty of Hebrons (an excellent early sort by the way), planted April 25th. They were not then fully ripe, though the yellow tint in the leaves was getting quite perceptible. Generally the tops are dead at this date, but an unusually fine potato season kept them growing later this year.

Raising Potatoes.—The following suggestions are from a practical farmer: I select a piece of suitable ground in the fall. Sod is best. Manure it heavily with good barnyard manure, and plow under so as to let the sod rot before cold weather; then in the spring I manure with well-rotted manure on the surface, and harrow thoroughly till the manure is completely incorporated with the soil; then I mark one way three feet apart and plant two pieces in a place about one foot apart, about four inches deep. Then, just as the potatoes begin to break ground, I harrow thoroughly, then cultivate till it is time to lay by; then I use a single-shovel plow to hill them with; keep all weeds down—they are death to potatoes. I have raised from 450 to 500 bushels to the acre in favorable seasons.

Now, as to the seed: I cut to a single eye; I would as soon think of planting a whole ear of corn in a hill as a whole potato. I have often, in case of a new kind, cut the eye cluster into three or four pieces, and had a good hill from each piece. As to time of planting, I always try to get my whole crop in for early potatoes. I believe the earlier they can be got in the more certainty of a good crop. As to kinds, I have raised legions of them, but for early, the Beauty of Hebron; for medium, the Burbank's Seedling and the Mammoth Pearl; and for late, the Belle and the Late Rose. Of course, others are good and may do better in other places.

New Remedy for Potato Bugs.—A farmer successfully tried a remedy for potato bugs, as follows: He procured a number of boards and placed them here and there among his potatoes, and on these boards were placed raw potatoes sliced. At noon on the first day of the experiment he and his hired men found every piece of potato covered with bugs. The men killed this crop, and at night another crop was killed, though not so large, and in a week not a bug could be seen, and his trouble with bugs after this was comparatively small. He thinks it would be a good plan to dip the pieces of potato in Paris green, as it would save the work of killing the bugs.

Potatoes in Winter.—Potatoes stored in cellars, in some cases, rot. To check or prevent this, keep the cellar as cool as possible without freezing. Then scatter quick-lime over them. This is of threefold benefit. It keeps them from rotting, makes the potatoes dryer and better, and disinfects the atmosphere, preserving the family from malarial fevers.

Experiments in Plowing.—Mr. Knox, a veteran plow-maker, has called our attention to the effect of deep plowing of some soils to offset the danger from lack of rains in dry seasons. Some years ago an experiment was made by a Western Massachusetts farmer in plowing portions of a large field at varying depths. One part was turned over seven inches deep, another ten inches, and a third, after being plowed ten inches, was subsoiled to the depth of ten inches more, making a soil comparatively loose to the depth of twenty inches. The next year, which was a dry one during the summer, corn was grown upon the whole field, which was treated uniformly throughout, and the yield of the three divisions carefully measured. The seven-inch plowing yielded as well as the ordinary fields in the vicinity. That part plowed ten inches deep was greener all through the season, and gave decidedly better yield, but that which was plowed ten inches, and subsoiled ten inches in addition, produced just one-third more corn than that plowed in the usual way, seven inches deep. The next year the whole field was by agreement sowed to oats, as a continuation of the experiment, the season proving even drier than the preceding one, when corn was grown. When the oats were about ready to cut, Mr. Knox, being in the neighborhood, called to see them. Before reaching the farm, the field came in view from the car windows, and Mr. Knox, who was on the lookout, said to a companion, that the gentleman had not done as he agreed, for he could see that he had sown different kinds of grain upon the different plots, the size and color of the growth both marking the lines, dividing the land plowed at three different depths. But on arriving at the field he found nothing but oats, and as stated by the owner, all sown on the same day, and treated precisely alike in every respect.

On the shallow plowed section, the growth was short and the straw yellow; on the ten-inch plowing the oats were taller and less yellow, while on the sub-soiled portion they were green and very heavy. The final tests showed full one-third more grain on the sub-soiled part than on that which was plowed only seven inches deep.

Now, it will not do for farmers to calculate that deeply stirring every kind of soils would alone add fifty per cent. in the yield of crops grown upon them the following two years, for they would doubtless be disappointed in very many cases. Yet, as a rule, a deep, mellow soil from which surplus water can readily settle without making the land into mortar, and through which the same moisture can again freely rise by capillary attraction, other things being equal, will always bring a farmer the better results.

There are soils which naturally are never too wet, and rarely too dry, and it will usually be found on examination, that they are in the same mechanical condition for a considerable depth, say two feet or more, that one likes to have his surface soil, light, friable, and containing a due proportion of vegetable matter. They will also be found to contain sand and clay in about the right proportion to keep the soil both mellow and moist through the varying climatic conditions. Deep plowing of stiff clays is often dangerous at first; but a good dry soil suits all kinds of crops in all kinds of weather. Deep plowing tends to make such a soil, but this alone will not always be sufficient. Draining and manuring must accompany deep plowing.

Early or Late Fall Plowing.—There is this against early fall plowing, that it favors the springing up of grass and weeds, which necessitates replowing in the spring. The fall rains, should they be heavy, will pack the surface of clay soil, which the frost that follows does not always relieve, and never if pressed during the winter by a deep snow. This not only compels plowing in the spring, but the soil then turns up rough, and generally too wet and sticky, and also it is necessarily done late in the season, so that fall plowing, instead of benefiting, hurts it, and the crop for the season is lost or seriously affected—the land showing it for a year or two more. But as the season is now advanced, there is little danger from the rains; the land would rather be benefited by them. Late plowing, therefore, is in order. Land ordinarily the wettest can now be plowed to the greatest advantage. It requires more power to break it, but the improved condition in the spring will more than pay the expense. This is a point not sufficiently considered.

If late fall plowing is an advantage, better still if it can be done in winter or early in spring, so as to be followed by freezing and thawing. My best success has been obtained by winter and early spring plowing. Yet there is hardly a year in which one of the three seasons—either late in the fall, during the winter or early in the spring—is not available. To make as sure as possible, do the work in the fall, if the ground will admit, but avoid making mortar. The same applies to winter and early spring.

Other soils, especially the sand and leachy shales, have less to fear from water; they are also less benefited by the frost. They are the soils, therefore, that may be left unplowed till spring. One of the difficulties with spring plowing is that it does not allow of the winter application of manure, should it be required, though with an early spring and favorable weather, this may be done without interfering much with the work which usually requires all the time. The aim should be always to get the plowing done near to winter (or in it) as possible, so as to get the benefit of the freezing and thawing, and avoid the packing of the heavy rains.

The Philosophy of Hoeing.—It may be overdone or underdone. There is reason in everything, "even in roasting eggs," as the saying is. So in hoeing crops. If we hoe up the soil in large lumps, as we are apt to do with the very serviceable modern prong-hoes, we let the keen, dry air into contact with the starting but enfeebled roots, and, by their parching, an irreparable injury is done. Such lumps should be crushed down so as to be permeable to air throughout, and yet serve to protect the roots from its free sweep. But, as in avoiding Scylla we may run to wreck on Charybdis, so, in crushing the soil, we may make it too fine, in which case the first heavy rain will run the surface together in a crust impervious to the air, and, for want of enough of air, essential to active root action, growth will be checked until the hoe or its equivalent is used.

Quantity of Seed to an Acre.—The following should be kept for reference: "Barley, broadcast, two to three bushels; bean, pole, in hills, ten to twelve quarts; beets, in drills, five to six pounds; broom corn, in hills, eight to ten quarts; buckwheat, one bushel; cabbage, in beds, to transplant, half pound; carrots, in drills, three to four pounds; Chinese sugar cane, twelve quarts; clover, red, alone, fifteen to twenty pounds; clover, alsike, alone, eight to ten pounds; clover, lucerne or alfalfa, twenty pounds; corn, in hills, eight to ten quarts; corn for soiling, three bushels; cucumber, in hills, two pounds; flax, broadcast, one and one-half bushels; grass, Kentucky blue, three bushels; grass, orchard, three bushels; grass, English rye, two bushels; grass, red top, three bushels; grass, timothy, one-half bushel; grass, Hungarian, one bushel; grass, mixed lawn, four bushels; hemp, one and one-half bushels; mustard, broadcast, half bushel; melon, musk, in hills, two to three pounds; melon, water, in hills, four to five pounds; millet, common, broadcast, one bushel; oats, broadcast, two to three bushels; onion, in drills, five to six pounds; onion for sets, in drills, thirty pounds; onion, sets, in drills, six to twelve bushels; parsnips, in drills, four to six pounds; peas, in drills, one and one-half bushels; peas, broadcast, three bushels; potatoes (cut tubers), ten bushels; pumpkin, in hills, four to six pounds; radish, in drills, eight to ten pounds; rye, broadcast, one and one-half to two bushels; salsify, in drills, eight to ten pounds; spinach, in drills, twelve to fifteen pounds; sage, in drills, eight to ten pounds; squash, bush varieties, in hills, four to six pounds; squash, running varieties, hills, three to four pounds; tomatoes, to transplant, quarter pound; turnip, in drills, one pound; turnip, broadcast, half pound; vetches, broadcast, two to three bushels; and wheat broadcast, one and one-half to two bushels."

Soaking Seeds.—I am often asked, writes a New England agriculturist, whether it does any good to soak seeds before sowing them? In general I believe it does more harm than good, and if done at all, a good deal of judgment should be used to prevent mischief. Thus peas, beans and corn are often soaked to hasten germination with the belief that they will come a day or two earlier, but in case the weather is cold and wet for some time after sowing the seed, it will be more likely to suffer injury from the weather than if sown dry. Especially is this true of the McLean pea and other delicate green peas, and of the various kinds of sweet corn. When the weather is dry and hot, however, it may be an advantage to steep the seeds before using them, and especially so in the case of seeds that are slow to germinate, such as celery and parsnips and carrots. To steep these seeds for a few days until germination has started and then dry them just enough to make them pass readily through the seed drill, will hasten their coming up, so that weeding will be less difficult in case the land is foul; but such seed should not be sown upon foul land if it can be avoided. Care is required in steeping seed that fermentation does not occur, which will frequently kill the seed. It may be arrested by turning off the water and spreading out the seed thinly upon a piece of sheeting and partially drying it. To steep seeds in chemical solutions with the belief that this will answer in place of fertilizing the land, I believe, is sheer humbug and imposition upon common sense. The only chemical stuffs that have proved useful, so far as I know, are the blue vitriol to destroy germs of smut, strychnine to destroy crows and blackbirds and a smearing of tar on corn seed for protection from these birds.

Raising Roots.—The average farmer is now devoting all his energies to the production of the greatest possible number of bushels of grain. Concentration of effort is generally commendable, but when applied to one particular branch of agriculture to the exclusion of others just as important, or to the detriment of the whole enterprise, it is not commendable. In other words, it is very bad management, and the evil effects of such a course will, sooner or later, become manifest in the exhausted condition of the soil, where this system of indiscriminate grain raising has been pursued.

The true policy of farming is to produce good crops and feed them out, so far as practicable, upon the farm. The larger the stock carried on the farm the greater will be the amount of fertilizing material produced.

In this case, good management would consist in growing those crops from which we could realize the greatest return per acre, thereby enabling us to carry more stock upon a given area.

Considered in this way, the root crop is an important factor in stock raising, as it yields largely to the acre, and is a most nutritious and wholesome diet, when stock is deprived of other green food during the feeding months. Aside from their nutritious qualities, roots possess a mechanical value of no less importance, as they materially aid in the assimilation of dry food, which too often forms the exclusive diet of stall-fed stock.

Of all roots, carrots are the most nutritious, and when the soil is deep, rich, and mellow, they will yield enormously, sometimes as high as ten or twelve tons to the acre. They keep well and can be fed all the year round if properly cared for. They are not so easily harvested as the beet and mangold, as the roots penetrate deeply into the soil, necessitating the use of the spade or plow when harvesting. Probably, for this reason, they are not so extensively raised as they should be.

The mangold seems to be the favorite at present, as, perhaps, all things considered, it should be. Under the most favorable circumstances it will yield even heavier than the carrot, and it also keeps well for spring feeding. Rutabagas and turnips come last in the order when considered as to their respective values. The greatest argument in their favor is, that they can be raised with the least labor and can be raised as a second crop, sown late in the season. This is particularly the case with the turnip, which may be sown as late as August 1st.

To raise roots profitably, we must, of course, do away as far as possible, with all hand labor. The garden or field should be long and narrow, with the drills running lengthwise, so that horse-power may be used to advantage when cultivating them. For sowing, the garden seeder, run by hand, is the best implement. When rightly managed this work need not interfere with other farm work. Many farmers have an idea that such crops must be in the ground the very first of the season, before the other field crops are sown; but such is not the case. Those calculated for feeding out to stock should not be started out before the first of June. By leaving them until this time, the seeds will germinate more surely and rapidly, and the weeds will not have three or four weeks the start of the plants, as is the case when sown early in the spring.

Let us have acres of roots this year instead of rods. I am confident that the farmer who sows and properly cares for an acre of roots this year, will want two acres or more next year.

Storing Roots.—A writer in the *Nebraska Farmer* says: "We always find turnips put in the cellar become pithy and worthless. My method is to obviate this, and I do it in this way: When I pull my turnips I cut off the top way down into the turnip, cut deep enough to cut all the eye out; then cut the root off smooth and nice, and you have them in a condition to place in a cool part of the cellar, or to bury out in open ground, and you need have no fear of pithy turnips. Beets should be buried out of doors, with manure over the dirt, so the ground will not freeze. In this way you can get at them any time in the winter. A part of the parsnip crop should be in the fall; they may be put in the cellar; no matter if they do wilt, they are so much the sweeter."

Cutting Clover Hay.—Clover hay is greatly improved by curing in the cock. The method is as follows: The clover cut in the forenoon is left to wilt in the swath until evening. Before the dew begins to fall it is raked into winrows, and is thus left until noon the next day. Then it is spread, and is exposed for an hour or two to the sun. It is then raked and heaped into cocks, about four feet wide and five feet high, and then left until the whole crop is ready to carry off the field, or at least twenty-four hours. In the cock it ferments, heats and sweats, but takes no injury, because the heated vapor passes off freely, as may be noticed by walking in the field at night. During this curing process, some of the woody fiber is changed to starch and sugar, and the quality of the hay thereby improved. Before the hay is hauled the cocks are thrown over, and the insides are aired for a short time, to evaporate any moisture. It is then drawn to the barn, and although it may heat again, it will suffer no injury. Generally it will not heat after the first fermentation, and will go into the barn green, sweet and without any loss of leaf by over-drying. Sometimes immature buds have bloomed in the mow when the clover has been thus cured, and the hay has preserved even the color of the fresh blossoms.

Making Hay—A Good Suggestion.—Farmers who have cut grass for hay should let it alone during the continuance of wet weather. There is no greater mistake than to break the swath, as grass never takes less harm and throws off more wet than just as it is left by the scythe or machine. Every blade of grass is provided by nature with a waterproof mantle in the shape of an impenetrable glassy covering of silica. This envelope is perfectly able to keep out the rain; but tedding and turning breaks it and opens joints into which the wet enters. It is then that the mischief begins, the external wet mingling with the internal sap and causing fermentation. How long grass will resist the bad effects of rain we hardly venture to state, but we are confident that a week or ten days' bad weather will be best met by the passive system here indicated.

To Banish Crows From a Field.—Machinery of various kinds, such as wind-mills in miniature, horse rattles, etc., to be put in motion by the wind, are often employed to frighten crows; but with all these they soon become familiar, when they cease to be any use at all. The most effectual method of banishing them from a field, as far as experience goes, is to combine with one or the other of the scare-crows in vogue the frequent use of the musket. Nothing strikes such terror into these sagacious animals as the sight of a fowling-piece and the explosion of gunpowder, which they have known so often to be fatal to their race. Such is their dread of a fowling-piece that if one is placed on a dyke or other eminence, it will for a long time prevent them from alighting on the adjacent grounds. Many persons now, however, believe that crows, like most other birds, do more by destroying insects and worms, etc., than harm by eating grain.

About Tobacco Growing.—The ground for tobacco should be plowed in the fall or early in spring, six to eight inches deep, and just before planting plow it again, this time more shallow. Pulverize and level the surface soil, then mark out in checks or drills. If White Burley tobacco is to be grown make the rows three and a half feet one way by twenty inches the other. Always procure well matured, pure seed, and be sure that it is true to name. Some kinds are better adapted to certain soils than are others, and you may labor under a disadvantage if seeds are not true to name. When the plants appear above the ground, after being transplanted, begin using the hoe and continue until they are too large to work in.

Seed Corn.—In an address on the subject of corn, Professor Beal remarked that the top-most ear was the best for seed; of two fields, one planted with seed taken at random and the other selected in the field, the latter yielded as much again as the former. Manure and cultivation may be thrown away on poor seed. The best time to cultivate corn is before planting. A shallow cultivation was recommended. Twenty-three ears of corn can be produced from one kernel: by proper cultivation and the use of the best seed as high as twenty-five ears. Smut is a great damage to corn, and smutty corn is very injurious to cattle.

Weeds.—There is no surer or better way to perpetuate weeds, than to pull or mow them and cart to the barn yard or pig pen. The seeds will ripen perfectly, and when carted out to the field again with the manure, they will find plant food just where they would put it were they, instead of us, lords over creation. If one finds a weed that he is choice of, with its thousands of seeds just ripening, and fears that pulling and leaving it on the ground will cause the seeds to rot from dampness, it is well to deposit such weed on a rock or fence, where it will dry, and the seeds ripen in safety.

Improving Pasture Lands.—A few years since, says a writer, I had an old pasture that had almost run out, covered with weeds and patched with moss. I mixed a few barrels of salt and wood ashes, and applied about two barrels of the mixture per acre, covering about half of the lot. The result surprised me. Before fall the moss had nearly all disappeared, and the weeds were rapidly following suit, while the grass came in thick, assuming a dark-green color, and made fine pasturage. The balance of the lot remained unproductive as before, but the following year it was salted with like results.

Blue Grass and Timothy.—A writer on blue grass says: "Prepare the ground late the previous autumn, so that it may have a mellow, fresh surface in the spring, and very early sow timothy, clover, and blue grass at the same time. About two crops of clover and timothy are obtained before the blue grass gets full possession. After that it chokes them out. The land is not pastured in less than two years from sowing."

Combining Different Varieties of Potatoes.—It is said that the qualities of two different varieties of potatoes may be combined in one new variety in the following manner: Cut an eye, with some of the flesh, from one kind and insert it in a corresponding cut in another with which you desire to mix. When the sprout starts it will feed for a time upon the potato and partake of its qualities.

Killing Canada Thistles.—The best way is to let them grow until they blossom, then cut them off near the top of the ground; the stalk will then be hollow; the water will get in the hollow and rot them, so they will never sprout again. If they are cut off with a hoe or plow, the ground will close over them, and there will come two sprouts for one.

Late Weeds.—In the old wheat fields, where the weeds have started up, turn in the sheep. They are not dainty in the choice of food, and weeds that are pushed forward by the late rains might as well be converted into mutton as to remain and make the field foul.

FERTILIZERS--Update

Before putting anything on the ground the farmer would do well to contact his County Extension Agent for a soil test. Soils can be tested at minimal charges at state land-grant universities. Current methods can specify exactly what nutrients should be added for good plant growth. Also, the farmer should contact his local unit of the Soil Conservation Service to ask for material on the texture and drainage of soil on his farm. Technicians of the SCS furnish advice on planting and land use, from a conservation point of view.

Reading this chapter, one will notice that whether eggs or meat are wanted for consumption, it will be advisable to keep animals for the manure they produce. Although current agricultural methods relegate manure to "a soil structure conditioner," if the farmer determines to use no inorganic fertilizers, he or she is left with various manures, wood ashes, mined phosphates, nitrates and potash, lime, salt and bone dust. Green manure may also be used, by planting and then plowing under rye, ryegrass, sudan-grass, clover or peas. All of these sorts of manures are discussed in this chapter.

Liming is a process that will benefit many lands too acid in their content. Most plants (except potatoes, strawberries and blueberries) thrive in alkaline soils produced by liming.

Salt's effect on plant life is still unknown. Hearsay bears out some of this chapter's remarks on salting. Currently large amounts of salt (1000 lbs. per acre) are used only on fields sown to table beets as it preserves the greenness of their tops. Salt is also used to prepare land for asparagus.

Current methods of manure-handling pool it in large semi-liquid or liquid amounts and apply it any time it can be quickly incorporated. Many large dairy farms are constructing huge manure holding pits which will also accomodate waste water from the milking parlor. This practice will conserve wastes, make them easily applicable, and satisfy stricter environmental laws.

Most of what's said in this chapter about better feeding as a way of producing better manures is viewed as too costly a process. But these economics are based on the availability of man-made fertilizers which require oil and natural gas for their production. If resource costs and fertilizer costs were to rise, perhaps manure from well-fed pigs, cattle and chickens would be in greater demand. Flax seed oil cake is very good for manure and is still used as special feed for lambs and meat animals. It is too expensive for everyday use. Wheat bran and coarse middlings, both by-products of wheat-milling, are used to augment diets.

The special needs of specific plants which the author points out have since been confirmed by research, i.e. corn, requires large amounts of phosphates and potash, and farmers are well-advised to meet these specific needs if they would have good crops.

The soil's texture can be as important to crops as its fertility. All sorts of vegetable matter help the texture and increase the soil's ability to hold moisture. Land that is too rich in vegetable material is rare and, when encountered, often used in intensive, highly specialized vegetable farming. Muck lands, which are rich in vegetable matter, are used for carrots, potatoes, onions, celery and lettuce. Drainage and, once drained, erosion are greater problems on muck land than fertility.

Though organic farmers currently operate on a relatively limited scale, the new farmer would do well to examine their methods of organizing wastes to produce the greatest amounts of manure. He will find that their methods are much like those recommended in this book. Rodale's *Complete Book of Composting* is a classic in the field. Also F. Billington's *Compost for the Garden Plot or Thousand-acre Farm* (Boston: C.T. Branford Co., 1956) provides much useful information.

FERTILIZERS.

A Few Words About Lime.—Professor Puryear, who is recognized as a skillful chemist, gives in a recent paper the following succinct suggestions on the uses and misuses of lime:

What are the uses of lime in agriculture?

1. Lime is always one of the nine substances found in the ash of plants. The grasses and forest trees particularly take it up from the soil in great abundance. When lime is not present in the soil in sufficient abundance to meet this demand, it should be added.

2. Lime is needed to hasten the decomposition of vegetable matter, and so make it available as plant food. If we wrap up a piece of lime in a cloth, in a short time the cloth is so decomposed that it will fall into shreds from its own weight. Tanners use lime in their vats to rot the hair from the hides. Now, lime behaves exactly in this way in the soil. The vegetable matter in the soil is useless until it decomposes, and lime hastens the process of decomposition.

3. Lime is frequently necessary to correct acidity in the soil. Soils charged with vegetable acids are never productive. On such soils we put lime, which, combining with these acids, forms neutral salts of lime. A person takes a little lime-water for the same reason when he suffers from acidity of the stomach. When lands have been freshly drained, they are always acid. The excess of water, with which the land was saturated, had excluded the atmosphere, and so had prevented the complete decomposition of vegetable matter. This vegetable matter, if the air had not been excluded, would have been converted by atmospheric oxygen into carbonic acid, ammonia, etc., but, without oxygen, its elements rearrange themselves, and form those injurious compounds, ulmic, humic, and geic acids. When the soil is drained, the atmosphere strikes through and destroys these acids, but not entirely in a single season. The process, of necessity, is slow. The soil to the depth of several feet, it may be, is sour, and it will be some time before the atmosphere can thoroughly permeate this soil and burn out these hurtful acids. Lime, then, comes to help the slow operation of natural causes. When it is spread upon the soil, it is carried downward by the rains, and combines with and neutralizes speedily and effectually the vegetable acids. We cannot possibly err, then, when we put lime on freshly-drained lands. In such lands there are not only free acids, but a large amount of organic matter, which has not been decomposed because of the exclusion of atmospheric oxygen. The application of lime to such soils corrects this acidity, and, by decomposing, renders immediately available this large amount of vegetable matter.

The ash of the grasses contains twenty-two per cent. of lime. Hence the practice of top-dressing the grasses with gypsum, which is the sulphate of lime.

Lime may be injuriously applied. If the soil contain but little vegetable matter, the application of lime, particularly heavy applications, will cause this vegetable matter to decompose too quickly. When the crop approaches maturity it finds that its quantum of vegetable matter has already been decomposed and used up. The result will be conspicuously disastrous if the soil was not deficient in lime. The lime has supplied no want, but has only inflicted an injury,

1. Lime is known as caustic or quick lime. This is the article as we obtain it from the kiln. Heat has expelled carbonic acid from the carbonate of lime, and caustic lime is the result.

2. Hydrated or slaked lime. When we add to lumps of caustic lime about twenty-five per cent. of water, the lumps fall down into a perfectly *dry* powder, giving us slaked lime.

3. Upon exposure to the atmosphere, this slaked lime loses its properties. It becomes the carbonate of lime, or mild lime—the very compound chemically from which the lime was originally obtained. This mild lime, or carbonate of lime, has no caustic or disorganizing properties whatsoever. It may be asked, then, why we do not use lime in its natural state, namely the carbonate of lime, if it gets into that condition when we spread it on the soil? We answer:

1. Although lime goes back to carbonate of lime, it does not do so all at once, and, in the process of returning to that condition, it decomposes vegetable matter, and so makes it plant food.

2. The natural limestone rock—the carbonate—is very hard, and its reduction to a powder by mechanical means would be difficult and expensive. Now, when lime slakes in the air, it falls down into a dry powder. No mechanical reduction, therefore, is necessary. It requires less expenditure of force to burn the limestone, and let the lime fall to powder of itself, than to reduce the natural rock by mechanical power.

Trees, like grasses, contain lime largely. The indication is to apply old mortar, or lime in any form, to fruit or shade trees, and this should be don in the fall.

Home-Made Fertilizers for the " Common Farmer."—The following is from the *Ohio Farmer:* Let us look at an *average* barnyard—one that may be met with most anywhere. Here we see a large pile of horse manure steaming away as though on fire. Here a pile of cow manure all frozen so it cannot rot its own litter before summer. There a pile of dry corn-stalks, as they have been thrown out of the feeding-room. In one part of the yard stands a straw stack that the cattle run around and pull down, but the scatterings are left close around the stack, and are tramped two feet deep, while a few feet from the stack the ground may be seen. The corner of the yard where the out-door feeding is done is the only portion that is in any order for manure.

Now I will leave it to my readers if I have not described an average barnyard. This is where farmers are to blame. It is but little trouble to keep our barnyards in proper shape if we only will. Let us ask the proprietor of our sample barnyard if he has so much work during winter that he cannot attend to his yard. His answer will be: " No, but I thought the barnyard could take care of itself." With most of farmers there is a great deal of spare time during the winter. Their work, aside from stock feeding, is not very pushing, and a day's time now and then would not be missed. Let us have that day once in a while to straighten up that yard, and I will see to it that you are paid for it next fall. Let us take a fork every few days and go around that straw stack, taking the loose straw that is under foot and cover up that bare spot of ground. Throw it wherever the manure is thin, and the cattle will tramp it more, making better manure of the straw, while it helps the quality of what is already there. Take a horse and sled every week or so, and move that pile of horse manure and that pile of corn-stalks. Put them around in thin spots in your yard, like you did that straw, and then see what a difference it makes in your yard. Above that cow manure pile just have a few stock hogs where they can get at it, and I dare say it will be taken care of. Two or three hogs are the best aids you can find to assist about the yards, but in justice to the hogs I will say that it is not the best thing for them. But every farmer has a few stock hogs that he is carrying over winter, and I am sure he cannot keep them cheaper than in his barnyard, where they get most of their living out of the cattle droppings and what is left after feeding. If your cattle are fed on corn in the stable, the hogs will thoroughly scatter the manure pile to secure the corn.

But now let us look a little to the bedding of our cows and horses. You read of A.'s or B.'s plan of securing liquid manure by troughs and pits, but you say you cannot do that way. I will tell you what you *can* do. Go to that straw stack and take largely of straw to bed your stock with. Don't be afraid of it, but make their bedding deep, especially behind them, where it will catch all the droppings. Then in cleaning your stables don't sort the straw too close, but throw out all that is dirty and fill up again with clean straw. The result will be that you are saving nearly all the liquid manure as well as brother A. or B. does it, and you have not had any of the trouble you were so afraid of. Moreover, your cows have had the benefit of a nice bed to sleep on, and they come out of the stable looking clean, instead of reminding you of a walking manure pile, as we often see cattle that are poorly bedded. There are some who have not got this extra amount of straw to lavish on their stock. To all such I say, go to your nearest saw-mill and get sawdust, and use freely for bedding, as this is as nearly as good an absorbent as straw, and makes good bedding.

Now, my brother farmers, such of you as *will not* give heed to the subject of foreign fertilizers and articles pertaining thereto, just try my plan for your own home-made fertilizers, and see how much you can increase them, and just that much will you increase your profits of the farm. Let us keep our eyes open through the winter, and at every opportunity turn a hand toward the barnyard, and manage carefully until we turn our stock out in the spring, and then we will counsel together again as to how we will handle what we have already saved, so as to improve the quality, and reduce the quantity, thus lessening the expense of removing to the field.

Something in Regard to Fertilizers.—Different soils and different crops require very much different treatment and different elements of plant food. A judicious cultivation of the soil adds to its producing capacity. The elements of plant growth contained in soils are unlocked and made available to some extent by proper working of the soil. It was formerly believed that it was necessary to add all the constituents of plant growth to the soil before plants could be produced. That if we wished to raise wheat we must add the constituents of wheat. If we wished to raise potatoes add the constituents of potatoes. This is not now considered absolutely necessary. If we use a fertilizer rich in nitrogen, phosphoric acid, and potash, with judicious rotation of crops, we may not only raise good crops indefinitely, but bring the land up to a higher state of productiveness every year.

On some soils we could safely leave out the potash, enough being yielded annually by decomposing particles of soil—unlocking the sand grains, as it were, to get their treasures. On some soils nitrogen perhaps would not be called for at first, and on others, rarer still, phosphoric acid might for a time be found sufficient in the soil.

Cereal crops are especially benefited by nitrogen and nitrogenous manures. Usually from forty to eighty pounds per acre are required for full crops or largest crops. Clover is the best medium to use in charging soils with nitrogen. It is a nitrogen trap that is easily set and sure to catch. Clover may be specially fertilized with plaster. Potash is of little value in cereal growing, and phosphoric acid not greatly called for. In connection with nitrogen, phosphoric acid and potash are both useful in small quantities.

For Indian corn phosphoric acid is perhaps the best special fertilizing element. Land plaster often does good service. On some soils potash also proves valuable.

Grass requires all the elements of plant food. Well-rotted manure is perhaps the best special manure for it. Bone-dust comes next. Either of these can be used at seeding, or afterward as top dressing. Clover requires nitrogen and phosphoric acid in small quantities. Potash and lime are its most valuable manures. Turnips require nitrogen and phosphoric acid, the latter in soluble form. Superphosphates are specials for the turnip crop. Mangels want more nitrogen and less phosphoric acid than turnips. Potatoes are similar to turnips in their likes, and on most soils they need a supply of potash furnished. There is usually potash enough in our common barnyard manure for potatoes.

One hundred pounds of good bone, thirty-five pounds sulphuric acid, and thirteen pounds of water, mixed in a wooden vat or tub, will make one hundred and forty-eight pounds superphosphate dry. In mixing, however, much more water will be found necessary to possibly properly mix the mass, and when properly mixed, if after standing a day or two it is too damp, may be dried by adding ground plaster, or other material. The bone-dust should be wet with the water first, then the acid added, a little at a time; by so doing the vessel in which the mixture is made is less acted upon, and the incorporation with and action upon the bone is better. Stir with a wooden hoe or mixer. Never attempt to reduce whole bones with the sulphuric acid.

The advantage of reducing bones or rock phosphate with sulphuric acid is to render the solubility in water the greater when applied to the soils. Liming soils really adds no plant food to the soil, but has a tendency to develop it in the soil by the caustic, dissolving, breaking-down effect that the action of the lime has upon the particles of the soil, unlocking them, making them give up their hidden stores of plant food. It not only acts upon the mineral constituents in the soil, but upon the vegetable constituent parts.

Variation in Manures.—The subject of manures is of the highest importance in practical farming, for it is the basis of every effort at improvement. It is much better understood than formerly, thanks to the effort of agricultural scientists, combined with the experiments of practical workers. There are, however, some points which, though fully established, are too often overlooked. One of the most important of these is that bulk counts for little in fertilization as compared with quality. The introduction of guano and similar concentrated fertilizers, as superphosphate, nitrates of

potash or soda, has had a wonderfully educating influence in this respect
Farmers have marveled to see the large results from application of a few
hundred pounds per acre of these fertilizers, and in some quarters these results have led to an undervaluation of the home-made manures. The fact
that the concentrated fertilizer, being deposited generally with the seed, is
more immediately available, does not demonstrate its superiority except for
the single crop to which it is applied. The farmer who owns the land he
tills, as most American farmers do, is interested not only in immediate profits, but in maintaining, if not increasing, the fertility of his soil. It behooves
such a farmer to make himself thoroughly posted as to the comparative
value of stable and barnyard manures made from different feeds and by different animals.

There is a much greater variation in the value of stable manure than is
usually supposed, and this not depending on the amount or quality of the
litter used as an absorbent, but rather on the excrement itself. A well-fed
horse standing idle in the stable passes more of the manurial value of what
he eats in his excreta than the same horse fed on the same material and
hard at work. The nitrogenous and phosphatic materials that are of greatest value for all crops are precisely those which are retained in the working
animal to repair the waste of sinew and bone from labor. There is an equal
and invariable difference in manure, depending on the kind and value of the
food used. It does not follow that food of highly fattening qualities will
make rich manure. Few materials are more fattening than sugar, but as
sugar is only carbon, though it will lay on fat rapidly, it adds little of value
to the manure pile. Oil-meal makes a valuable fertilizer, for while the oil
in the meal is fattening, it is also rich in phosphates. English farmers have
grown rich, or, what is the same thing, made their farms rich, by feeding
oil-cake to fattening animals. The oil, of little value manurially, went into
the fat cattle and sheep, while the principal part of the most valuable fertilizing material was returned to their farms. We have other feeds costing
much less than oil-meal, which for the resulting manure are nearly or quite
as valuable. Among the least understood of these feeds is wheat-bran and
coarse middlings. These are rich in the phosphates, comparatively poor in
fattening qualities, but of more value for working animals than is generally
supposed. It has been found by experiment that a mixture of wheat-bran
with corn-meal makes a much better feed for work-horses than corn alone.
It is not only in diluting the corn, which by itself is of too heating a nature,
that such a seed is valuable, but the bran is absolutely richer in nitrogen
and greatly richer in phosphates than the corn-meal.

The time will undoubtedly come when progressive farmers in the older
sections of the country will feed for the purpose of making the most valuable
manures with as much carefulness as they now feed for growth, milk, wool,
or fat. In large sections of the country most of the profit of feeding must be
found in the manure pile. As this fact becomes better recognized, the manurial value of certain feeds and the difference in the resultant manures will
receive that attention which its importance in the farm economy deserves

How to Enrich the Soil.—The *Farm and Fireside* says: The production of paying crops on old, upland clay soils depends largely upon restoring
to it, in the most economical way, the plant-food most needed by the crop to
be grown. If corn is to be grown, manures containing a liberal amount of
phosphoric acid and potash will be required. As these substances are valuable, constant cropping with corn will soon greatly diminish the value of the

land. If wheat is to be grown care must be taken to supply the necessary amount of phosphates. Wheat, oats, barley, and rye each require a large per cent. of ammonia, which accounts in part for the excellent results that follow the use of ammoniated superphosphates. If a crop of seven hundred and fifty pounds of seed cotton is grown upon an acre of land, about six and one-third pounds of phosphoric acid and seven and a half of potash will be taken from the soil. In growing tobacco the soil is quickly exhausted of potash; for this reason excellent results follow the planting of this crop on newly cleared lands. Manures of all kinds should be carefully saved and applied to suit the needs of the crop to be grown. Cabbage grows luxuriantly when supplied with green manure. The bean plant, on the contrary, requires that which is thoroughly rotted. Nitrogenous manures greatly increase the yield of wheat and other grains, and when used with phosphates on soils of average fertility, give a visible increase of root crops also. Another important factor in enriching the soil is a judicious rotation of crops, to be determined to some extent by the soil, climate, and the leading crops to be grown. In the North clover is indispensable, but in the South the cornfield pea answers an excellent purpose, especially for green manuring. In this section, where the soil is clay, and wheat and corn are the leading crops, red clover is indispensable. Soil exhaustion may be measurably prevented by even the simplest of all rotations, that of wheat, followed by clover, and this by corn. Such a rotation may be begun by sowing red clover in March upon the fields now seeded with wheat. Sow three pecks of red clover and one peck of mammoth clover, and one peck of timothy seed upon each six acres. The clover should not be pastured for the first year, except for a sufficient time for the hogs to pick up the scattered grain after harvest. After the 1st of June of the second year the clover can be pastured, but a sufficient quantity of that in which the most timothy grows should be reserved to cut for hay. This system provides for the accumulation of manure in a level yard with raised sides, so that the liquids will keep the entire crop of wheat straw and refuse cornstalks and other matter in a moist condition, and the decomposition of these materials is much hastened. After the haying and harvesting season is over, twenty-two horse loads of manure are applied to the acre on the clover field; that is to be plowed to a depth of eight to ten inches very early the following spring, where the corn corp is to be planted. Each load is divided into eight piles, placed five and one-half yards apart. Before seeding to wheat the corn is cut and shocked, and a heavy, sharp-toothed harrow precedes the drill. The high-cut stalks, when harrowed down, act as a mulch for the wheat plants during the winter, and measurably prevent washing even upon high ridges. A great advantage in this method of rotation is that the labor required to bring up the land in April is not half as great as in midsummer, and the corn, by being planted fully a week earlier than it can be on similar soils where there is no sod, yields abundantly and matures early, so that there is no delay in seeding with wheat early in the fall. As may be inferred from what has already been said, the prime factors for cheaply enriching the soil and increasing its fertility annually, are the liberal application of properly-cared-for barnyard manure, and a systematic rotation of crops, of which red clover is the basis.

Composting Manure.—Mixing manure or fertilizers is laborious work, and if nothing is gained by it, it is labor lost. But something may be gained by it when the condition of the material can be changed for the better, and at the same time something may be lost when anything can be changed for the worse. In composting, for instance, such raw substances as swamp muck, leaves, tannery wastes, with manure, or in mixing various manures, as from the horse stable, cow sheds, pig pens, and poultry house, valuable results may be obtained; while in mixing lime or wood ashes with manure, and especially in mixing the common fertilizer with poultry manure and wood ashes, harm may be done and valuable fertilizing matter may be wasted. In the one case the more actively fermenting horse or pig manure will serve to decompose more readily the colder cow manure, and to produce decomposition in the abundant litter or raw matter that may have been used. Besides, when the whole manure heap has been reduced to an even and homogeneous condition and quality, it is made more valuable for use in the field, and neither unduly or wastefully enriches one portion of it while inadequately fertilizing another portion. It is, therefore, a judicious and useful practice to mix these manures or these substances in the heap, either in the yard or the field, and so add considerably to the value of a part without detracting from the value other portions. But in the other case much harm may be done by mixing any substances in the heap which may exert an injurious action upon the others. This may happen when lime or wood ashes are mixed with the manure or with the poultry manure; and the more harm is done, the richer in ammonia the manure may be. Lime and potash are alkalies, and when fresh are in a caustic condition. That is, they are free from carbonic acid, which, when combined with an alkali, renders it neutral, or mild and inert. When fresh lime or wood ashes are mixed with manure they at once seek to combine with carbonic acid, from whatever source they can procure it. Ammonia is an alkali, and in manure is generally in combination with carbonic acid as carbonate of ammonia. The lime or wood ashes take the carbonic acid from the carbonate of ammonia, and the ammonia escapes as gas into the air, and so far as the owner of the manure is concerned this ammonia is lost, and as ammonia is the most valuable and costly fertilizing element in existence, the loss is very serious. It is easy, however, to avoid this loss by using the lime or the ashes by themselves on the soil, and not with the manure directly, in which way they will do as much good.

But sometimes it is advisable to mix lime or wood ashes in a compost heap, and this may be done safely when the special behavior of these three indispensable substances are understood. If the manure is quite fresh there is very little ammonia in it, and if there is more, a large proportion of absorbent matter, as swamp muck in the heap will absorb and hold it, and carbonic acid will be produced by its decomposition in sufficient quantity to saturate the alkali of the lime or ashes or to take up the ammonia as fast as it is formed or set free. In fact, a farmer who understands the chemical decompositions and combinations which go on in a heap of decaying manure or compost may use lime and wood ashes with safety and with advantage. With regard to the common mixture of ashes, hen manure, and plaster, too, this may be safely and beneficially made at the time it is to be used, but not if it is to remain mixed for any considerable time previously.

Salt as a Manure.—Since soda, if essential in plant growth, is only required in small amounts, and chlorine, though essential for most plants, is still required in only small amounts, and common salt is found in minute quantity in most soda, chemists have asked why salt should be of any benefit as a manure, and from theoretical grounds have been disposed to deny that salt has any value as a manure. Yet practical farmers, not having the fear of science before their eyes, have pointed to the increased crops, and asked, " How is that ? "

There can be no conflict between practice and science, because science is the classified explanation of practice. I have said enough to show that it is not enough to cause the rejection of a substance as manure to say that it is not " essential " to plant growth.

Let us see what explanation can be made of the use of salt in agriculture beyond the small amount required for the ash element.

Professor May showed that solution of salt would render soluble the ammonia which had entered into insoluble condition in the soil.

Professor Atwater, in a recent report says: " Something has been said about the use of ordinary salt as a fertilizer. One important office of the salt is to make soluble, and consequently useful in the plant, the materials already locked up, as it were, in the soil. Supposing you have been putting on barnyard manure and other fertilizers. Some of the nutritive materials, as, for instance, potash and phosphoric acid, may perhaps have been taken up by the soil, and remain there in a difficult soluble condition. Furthermore, there are in the soil some of these ingredients that were in the original rock of which the soil is made up, and are still, so to say, locked up, or, in other words, still remain in an insoluble form therein. One effect of salt, as is the case oftentimes with gypsum and lime, is to set loose that potash as phosphoric acid. You must expect, therefore, in putting on salt, that its chief use will be, not as a direct nutriment to the plant, but rather as a means of setting other materials loose; and salt is very useful on this account, because it is not readily observed in the upper layers of the soil, but often leaches through into the layers; and it will have the effect of setting these materials free all the way down.

" The German farmers say, however, that you must be careful in the use of salt. If you put on too much it injures the vegetation. Further, it will not do to put on loose soil. A very loose, sandy soil is not ordinarily benefited by the application of salt. Again, it is best applied to soils which contain considerable humus. And, finally, it should be used on soils which are in pretty fair condition as regards the contest of fertilizing elements. On soils which are not too loose, which have a good amount of humus, and which are in pretty fair condition as regards the amount of fertilizing material, organic and inorganic, contained in them, it is oftentimes a good thing to apply salt."

Refuse Salt as a Fertilizer.—A Wisconsin farmer writes: I have used salt as a fertilizer for the last three years with good success, and I also find that where I have sown 200 pounds per acre the previous year my crops are much better than where I sowed salt in the spring of the same year. We have better crops in this county than in any other county in the State of Wisconsin, and produced by the use of salt. Farmers who at first could not believe that salt is good for anything are the most firm believers in it to-day. Those who sowed salt last year will sow double, and those who did not sow are going to sow next spring.

I sow the refuse salt from the packing houses. I have just finished drawing 22,000 pounds home to sow on my own farm. I shall try it on my winter wheat this week at the rate of 300 pounds to the acre. I have spread 2 1-2 tons on an acre, but plowed and worked it up with the soil for a turnip crop or for barley. It cost only 50 cents per ton, which made it a cheap fertilizer. It is used very liberally in England, where I came from. Many people have a wrong impression about salt. They think when they salt cattle and sheep that salt kills the grass, but this is not so. The stock kills it by eating the ground where the salt was put down. I will admit that salt will kill most plants, and would like to find some one who would pay for enough for me to try the experiment.

I hold that in the West land needs salt as much as cattle do. The first time I tried it was on a twenty-acre lot sowed with spring wheat. In two weeks I could see the difference between what I sowed with salt and that which had received no salt, and I could also see the difference when harvested. The part sowed with salt had no chinch bugs, while on the other, which had no salt, I could gather up a quart to every sheaf the reaper threw off. I have never seen any damage done by chinch bugs where there had been two hundred pounds of salt sowed broadcast on the crop. The time for sowing is when the grain is about four inches high. I have sowed salt when the grain was coming out in head, and with good results, but would prefer to sow it earlier.

I prefer packing salt because it contains more or less grease and fat, besides blood from the meat, which is the essence of manure. Let farmers try the experiment, if only on a small piece, and not wait for some one else. Wheat yielded from twenty to thirty-five bushels per acre where salt was sowed, and where it was not sowed the wheat was not worth the cutting. Most of those who did cut it got nothing but No. 4 wheat, weighing fifty-one and fifty-two pounds to the bushel.

Formulas for Commercial Fertilizers.—A writer in the *Fruit Recorder* says: To produce a crop of wheat over what the natural yield would be without manure, I use about two hundred pounds sulphate of ammonia, one hundred pounds ground bones, forty pounds oil of vitriol, fifty pounds of muriate of potash, forty pounds sulphate of soda, one hundred and seventy pounds land plaster.

For Indian corn, to produce about thirty bushels shelled per acre, over natural yield: one hundred pounds of ground bones, forty pounds oil of vitriol, one hundred and fifty pounds sulphate of ammonia, one hundred and twenty-five pounds muriate of potash, high grade or eighty per cent., thirty-five pounds sulphate of soda, one hundred and twenty pounds land plaster.

For oats, to produce about thirty bushels over natural yield; One hundred and fifty pounds sulphate of ammonia, fifty pounds ground bones, twenty pounds oil of vitriol, fifty pounds muriate of potash (high grade), thirty pounds sulphate of soda, one hundred pounds land plaster.

For cabbage, to produce fourteen or fifteen tons over natural yield: Three hundred and fifty pounds muriate of potash (high grade), four hundred pounds sulphate of ammonia, two hundred and fifty pounds ground bones, one hundred pounds oil of vitriol, fifty pounds sulphate of soda, two hundred pounds of land plaster.

For potatoes, to produce over two hundred bushels over natural yield: Five hundred and fifty pounds sulphate of potash, two hundred pounds sulphate of ammonia, one hundred pounds ground bones, forty pounds oil of vitriol, one hundred and twenty pounds land plaster, forty pounds sulphate of soda.

For onions, to produce about four hundred bushels over natural yield: Two hundred and twenty pounds sulphate of ammonia, one hundred and fifty pounds ground bones, sixty pounds oil of vitriol, two hundred and fifty pounds sulphate of potash, one hundred and twenty pounds land plaster.

For rutabagas, to produce ten to eleven tons over the natural yield: One hundred pounds ground bones, forty pounds oil of vitriol, two hundred and seventy-five pounds sulphate of ammonia, six hundred pounds sulphate of potash, one hundred and fifty pounds land plaster, thirty-five pounds sulphate of soda.

The above formulas are given in quantities for one acre of each kind of crops.

It requires one hundred pounds oil of vitriol to dissolve forty pounds ground bones. Put the ground bones into a water-tight plank box and soak the bone with water for two or three days, turning on about twenty-five pounds of water to each one hundred pounds of bone; then turn on your oil of vitriol and stir it thoroughly with a wooden stick, two or three times a day for five or six days, then mix in the sulphate of ammonia, next the muriate of potash and sulphate of soda, and lastly the land plaster; thoroughly mix the whole mass together. To dry it off and make it fit to handle, incorporate dry muck, fine charcoal or sawdust, but do not use lime or wood ashes as a dryer. Sometimes farmers can collect bones on their own or neighboring farms, or get them very cheap from a butcher, in this case they want to mash them up fine with a sledge, and about sixty pounds oil of vitriol used to one hundred pounds of coarse bones.

Fertilizers vs. Plant Food.—The *Farmer's Magazine and Patron's Guide* says: Experiments are becoming continually reported by farmers that are misunderstood, and lead to conclusions, on the part of the experimenters at least, that are detrimental to agricultural progress. Take an example now before us, that of a farmer who used lime, superphosphate, guano, salt, a chemical fertilizer, and no manure, on as many plots of wheat. The yield in each case was good, varying from twelve bushels on the unmanured to twenty-six to thirty-five bushels for the manured plots. The lime gave the greatest apparent *profit* per acre, though the yield was not so large as where guano, chemical and superphosphates were used. Reasoning from the figures alone, this experimenter thinks he has a guide for future practice in wheat farming, and accordingly has now put seventy acres in winter wheat manured only with lime.

We shall be interested to learn the result of several years of this practice, but predict that it will prove an unprofitable venture. The soil on which this experiment was tried is naturally fertile clay wheat soil. Lime on such land always has a good effect for one or two applications—not as plant food, however, but in acting upon the soil chemically to make available that fertility which is contained in the soil, but in an unavailable condition. Lime *adds* no element to the soil, but forces it to yield up its stores of fertility. It should not be understood from this that lime is not plant food, for it is; but the great majority of soils, if not all, contain so much of it already that there is no necessity for supplying more. This lime, however, is in such a form that it does not have the effect upon the soil of newly applied freshly slaked lime.

It is a wise economy to utilize whatever of fertility the soil contains, but it must be done judiciously and not wastefully. So soon as it is found that the application of lime no longer produces adequate crops, the true reason should be assigned to the result, and that reason is that the supply of plant food is being exhausted, and outside sources must be called upon to make up the deficiency.

It is legitimate and proper to draw upon our bank account, but we must also deposit, or there will soon be nothing in the bank to draw from.

Making Our Own Fertilizers.—A Virginia farmer writes: Having studied the subject of fertilizing our lands when it is impossible to manure with stable manure, and watched the effects on different kinds of land, I have come to the conclusion that when commercial fertilizers are honestly made it pays, even at the low price of grain, to buy and use them on grain lands, especially when being seeded down to grass, and when the land is too thin to make a set of grass a certainty. My experience has been that the money will be returned out of the gain. The set of grass will be always improved; the benefit will be felt while the land is in grass, and there will be a much heavier sod to turn under when the land is broken up. Now if it pays to purchase these fertilizers at from $25 to $90 per ton, besides paying freight on them and hauling them from the depot, how much better it would be for us if we could manufacture our fertilizers at home at one-fourth the cost! I once heard a gentleman, who had had years of experience in this line, say that pure Peruvian guano, even at $90 to $100 per ton, is the cheapest of all fertilizers. Now, unless I am mistaken, Peruvian guano is simply rotted bird manure, and must have lost some of its strength by being exposed to the air and sun. I suppose the birds that made this guano fed on bugs, fish, wild seeds, etc. We thus have one ingredient at least equal to the best fertilizer known, right on our farms, and one that can be vastly increased with very small additional expense. It is certainly of vast importance to the farmer to see that the flock of fowls is kept up, and see that not one ounce of manure is wasted.

Another thing is the hog manure. This is certainly a splendid fertilizer, and should be saved with the utmost care. I have known farmers to build their hog pens on a hillside leading to a branch to let the hogs get water, and thereby lose nearly all their manure. It may not be equal to Peruvian guano, but it is certainly half as good. Another valuable fertilizer is wasted on nine-tenths of all the farms in the country. This is the night soil, and everything that comes from the house—the liquid manures are as strong as the solids. My plan is to save all these things; pulverizing and making them into a real genuine fertilizer that can be drilled, handled, or used as are commercial fertilizers. Sink in your yard a vat that will hold two hundred bushels. (If one is not enough, you can sink another.) It should be well made out of two-inch oak planks, and have a lid with a good handle, so the wash-woman can lift the lid and pour her soap suds into it as easy as pouring it elsewhere, and where the chamber-maid should be required always to put into it everything in her line. Now add all the hen manure you can get; all the night soil, and a load or two of the best hog manure. Then add muck, loam or plaster enough to absorb all gases and stop all smell, so as to make it perfectly inoffensive. When the box is nearly full, add (if there is not enough already) enough liquid to make the mass mix easily, and with a long pole thoroughly mix, and keep stirring for several days, so as to reduce all lumps. You can then remove all sticks, cobs, etc., that may have found their way into it, with a coarse sieve fastened on a long pole. When thoroughly mixed and sifted, allow it to dry out, and if not dry enough when you want to use, spread it on boards and dry thoroughly. This fertilizer can be made at a small cost per ton, and will be found to do good work.

Home-Made vs. Commercial Manures.—A correspondent of the *New England Homestead* writes: The great body of common farmers will never profitably develop their agricultural resources or to any great extent increase the fertility of their farms until they keep or fatten more cattle and sheep. And the way to keep more stock is, to keep it without more ado –just as our wise financier remarked that the way to resume specie payments was to resume.

Notwithstanding the legislation for the protection of the honest manufacturer as well as the purchaser, the common farmer feels that in buying many varieties of commercial manures he is not master of the situation. This is why I advise farmers to keep stock or make their fertilizers upon their own farms as much as possible—to buy animal food rather than plant food. For horned cattle as a rule, buy firm cotton-seed meal, corn meal, fodder corn or corn fodder and swale hay. In purchasing food for other kinds of stock, we must be guided by their varied conditions, always feeding such kinds and quantities as will be kindly relished and thoroughly digested.

For several years I have bought twenty-five cords of stable manure annually. A large proportion comes from Boston and costs me eight dollars per cord delivered on my farm. Yet I consider it as cheap as any fertilizer in the market. In a cord of good manure free from foreign substances, we get the results of about two tons of hay together with the grain fed, less the animal waste or growth. If judiciously applied, the ground that receives the manure will in a number of years yield its full equivalent with interest. If plant food is to be bought, buy first good stable manure, fine ground bone, good hard wood ashes, and muriate of potash. When the honest manufacturer will sell these elements compounded as cheaply as the farmer can purchase and compound them himself, it may do to buy still more largely of commercial or chemical fertilizers. And in their application we must no longer work blindly.

Use of Plaster and Ashes.—Henry Ives, one of the best farmers in far-famed Western New York, writes thus sensibly to the *Tribune:* "To use plaster on any of our growing crops requires so slight a cast and so often proves beneficial, that one can hardly afford to neglect its application, although occasionally no perceptible advantage is derived from it, and, at best, we scarcely look for benefit except for the one season and the one crop. But in using ashes we are more sure of benefit, and its good effects are so lasting that after one liberal application, say of from 50 to 100 bushels per acre (though if leached ashes are used one could safely apply three to six times this quantity), the effect will show for five, ten, or even fifteen years, by increasing fertility. When applying plaster to corn, or plaster and guano, phosphate or hen manure, or even with a small quantity of ashes (in all cases from 100 to 200 weight to the acre is enough of the plaster), the ingredients should be prepared and well mixed on the barn floor, loaded into an open wagon, so as to have it along convenient to the work, and almost any time in the early growth of the corn apply a small handful to each hill, not as some do, by throwing it carelessly in a compact heap near to the hill, but as it is thrown sift through the fingers, giving it an even distribution all about the hill. But after the corn is a little more advanced I believe it would do it more good, and without costing much if any more, to use two or three times as much of the fertilizing mixture, sowing it broadcast over the field. If, instead, the farmer could apply 60 or 80 bushels of ashes to the acre, it should be done before planting or seeding, so as to be well mixed with the soil when preparing it for the seed-bed. This, I believe, is the most lasting of any kind of fertilizer, and one of the cheapest, too, when the ashes can be obtained without costing more than 25 or 30 cents a bushel. After such an application of ashes, or other fertilizer, or manure, it is still just as desirable as ever to plaster the corn growing on such fertilized land.''

Experience with Muck.—A correspondent of the *Country Gentleman* gives his experience with muck as follows: As the attention of farmers is drawn to the necessity of enriching their farms, I will give the result of several years' experience with muck. My practice has been as follows: In the fall, when the muck beds are dry, I throw out into piles as much as I think I need for the coming year. At some convenient time I draw a quantity near the house, where I can throw on it the soap suds from washing, night soil, scrapings from the hen house, and leached or unleached ashes. I generally commence this compost heap in the fall, but if any one would commence in the spring he would make a much larger amount.

In the spring I shovel over the pile once or twice; then it is ready for use. This manure I use in the hill for all hoed crops, as phosphate is used. I consider it far ahead of barnyard manure in the hill, and equal to phosphates, for the nature of manure is to dry up, while the nature of muck is to attract moisture. It is about one day's work for a man to put this into one acre of corn or potatoes, putting a good handful in each hill. I have found that this manure contains an alkali, or something, so that birds and crows will not pull corn, and wire-worms will not eat the roots of corn. White grubs will not gnaw potatoes that are planted in it. It makes a corn crop ripen about one week or ten days earlier than without it. I have known farmers to pay 50 cents a load for muck to make compost from to be used on tobacco, and they thought it paid them well.

I have noticed that the first crop does not use up all the strength of one application. It can be seen in the next crop. It does not hurt seed corn or potatoes to be dropped into this compost, they will grow better than in common earth. This compost heap has some advantages over phosphate. It does not cost any money if one has a muck bed, and it will keep insects away from the roots of crops. I have drawn and mixed barnyard manure and muck in piles during the winter, in the proportion of two of manure to one of muck, and I consider it better than raw manure from the yard for any crop.

What a Pint of Manure Did.—A Wisconsin farmer sends this experience to the *American Agriculturist:* "Last year, in hauling yard manure across a field afterwards planted to corn, some of it scattered off in driblets, from a handful to a pint or so in a place. When planting the corn, I found portions of these droppings, and where noticed, drew them into the hills, and with the hoe mixed them a little with the soil as the seed was dropped. In three instances, where a large handful or about a pint of the manure was thus put in, a stick was driven down to mark the hills. When hoeing, we noticed that in these hills the corn plants had started off more vigorously, were greener, and at the third hoeing they were six to twelve inches higher than the other hills adjoining. Our curiosity being awakened, we followed up the observations, and when gathering the crop each of the three stalks in all the three hills had on it two large plump ears, while the surrounding corn did not average one good ear to the stalk.

"This set us to thinking and figuring. That bit of manure had given the young corn roots a vigorous start, just as good feed starts off a young calf, or pig, or lamb, and the roots penetrated further in every direction and gathered more food and moisture. These stalks being better nourished from below, ran far away from the poorly fed neighbors. As to the figures, the rows were three and one-half feet apart, and the hills three feet distant in the rows, say four thousand hills on an acre, and four thousand pints of manure is about sixty-two and one-half bushels, or two large wagon loads. Anybody can reckon the difference between six large, well-filled ears of corn on each hill, and less three per hill, and the cost of the manure as compared with the total value of the final crop. The plowing, and the seed, and the hoeing, amount to the same in each case. All I have to say is, that every corn-hill planted on my farm this year will have at least a pint of manure in it."

How to Double the Usual Quantity of Manure on the Farm.— Provide a good supply of black swamp mold or loam from the woods, within easy reach of your stable, and place a layer of this, one foot thick, under each horse, with litter as usual on top of the loam or mold. Remove the droppings of the animals every day, but let the loam remain for two weeks, then remove it, mixing it with the other manure, and replace with fresh mold. By this simple means any farmer can double not only the quantity but also the quality of his manure, and never feel himself one penny the poorer by the trouble or expense incurred, while the fertilizing value of the ingredients absorbed and saved by the loam can scarcely be estimated.

Josiah Quincy, Jr., has been very successful in keeping cattle in stables the year through, and feeding them by means of soiling. The amount of manure thus made had enabled him to improve the fertility of a poor farm of one hundred acres, so that in twenty years the hay crop had increased from twenty to three hundred tons. The cattle are kept in a well-arranged stable, and are let out into the yard an hour or two mornings and afternoons, but they generally appear glad to return to their quarters. By this process, one acre enables him to support three or four cows. They are fed on grass, green oats, corn fodder, barley, etc., which are sown at intervals through the spring and summer months, to be cut as required; but he remarks that his most valuable crop is his manure crop. Each cow produces three and a half cords of solid, and three cords of liquid manure, or six and a half cords in all. Five to eight miles from Boston, such manure is worth from five to eight dollars a cord. From this estimate, he has come to the conclusion that a cow's manure may be made as valuable as her milk.

Advantages of Sheltering Manure.—Many farmers allow the manure made by their stock of cattle to be thrown out doors, where it remains exposed in heaps or in the yard for several months. The rains fall upon it, and streams of black water laden with the soluble and valuable elements of the manure run away from the manure heap during every heavy rain, the sun burns it, and the winds dry it, the volatile gases escape and are lost. In this way a large part of the plant food contained in the manure is lost. That a serious loss is thus occasioned has been proved by experiment. A Scotch farmer and land-owner showed by experiment that covered manure increased the productiveness of his land enough the first year he used it to pay the cost of rough sheds put up to protect it. Four acres of good land were measured off; two of them were manured with ordinary barnyard manure, and the other two with an equal quantity of manure from the covered shed. The whole was planted to potatoes. The two acres manured with barnyard manure, which had been exposed to the weather, yielded five hundred and sixty-four bushels of potatoes, while the other two acres manured with covered manure, yielded nine hundred and thirteen bushels, or four hundred and fifty-one bushels more than the other. The increased effect of the covered manure did not cease with the first year. The next year both plots were sown with wheat, and from the two acres dressed with the barnyard manure ninety bushels of wheat were harvested, while from the two acres dressed with the covered manure, one hundred and eight bushels of wheat were obtained. These facts show the importance of protecting the barn manure from the weather.

The Fertility of Soils.—The fertility of a soil depends not alone on its composition. A proper mechanical texture is essential. On the texture of soils depends not only their suitableness for the growth of different crops, but likewise the rapidity of their growth. It is the texture, also, which regulates to a just extent the soil's power of absorbing and retaining heat, moisture and manure.

To be fertile the soil must be firm enough to afford a proper degree of support to the growing plants, and yet loose enough to allow the delicate fibres of the rootlets to extend themselves in all directions. It must be loose enough to allow free access of air and suitable drainage, and at the same time close enough to retain sufficient moisture.

Unless there be a sufficiently free passage for the rain throughout the substance of the soil the plant food will not be properly prepared, nor the stationary roots of plants be fed.

The fertility of a soil is also dependent on the climate in which it lies. Local conditions as to rainfall, temperature, etc., must be considered in estimating the value of soils. They may be the same in composition and texture and yet differ widely in value. The amount of rain, the season of its descent determine largely the value of the soil of localities for agriculture.

The temperature of the air in any given locality has an important bearing upon the productiveness of the soil, whatever may be its composition and texture and the amount of rainfall.

Green Manures.—I have never yet been able to make as much barnyard manure as I wanted, writes a Southern farmer, and commercial fertilizers are dangerous things to come in contact with a farmer's pocket, so I touch them lightly; then what is the next best resort? Green manures. In the fall of 1882, I determined to try rye as a fall crop, and I sowed a twenty-five acre lot in it, and the following May I plowed it under, when fully headed, and sowed black peas, one bushel per acre (having used the same quantity of rye). We had a nice pea fallow, and plowed them under about the first of October, and sowed wheat in the latter part of October, 1883. Last year we cut the wheat, and though it had the rust very badly, we made between twelve and fifteen bushels per acre. The growth of the straw was very fine, and I am confident we would have made from twenty to thirty bushels per acre but for the rust, on land that would not, before these green fallows, have made ten bushels of wheat. I now believe you may grow wheat on the same lands every year by following each crop with a pea-fallow, along with ten bushels of lime per acre, applied when the peas are fallowed in. We did not apply any lime on our fallow, as the land had been limed a few years before with fifty bushels per acre. I verily believe the lands can be cropped, as above stated, and constantly improved. We should never buy peas to sow but once, and thus save our seed each year, even if you have to sow a separate lot for that purpose. I have tried peas as a fallow crop for the past three years, and find them the best and cheapest substitute for barn-yard manures that the poor land farmer can find. They are good to sow on the corn lands, at the last working in June, and fallow in when the corn is cut off in October; and I have been told, by some old farmers, that they will improve the land just as much if left until the frost kill them, and then fallow, as when fallowed under green. If all farmers would use every means in their power to feed and improve their lands, we would soon have a different country from the present.

Bone Dust for Top Dressing.—In reply to a correspondent who asks if bone dust would not make a good dressing for grass land to be applied in the fall, the *American Agriculturist* says: " We think it would be better to compost the bone dust with yard manure and then apply the compost. If six or eight cords of this fine compost were applied to the acre it would only furnish a good dressing of itself, which the land would be the better for, would act as a sort of mulch or protection for grass roots, and if the soil was at all inclined to 'heave,' it would be a positive benefit. But our correspondent must remember that the disadvantage of using bone dust or ground bone alone, as a fertilizer, is the fact of its slow action. The nitrogen and phosphoric acid which the bones contain is very slowly rendered available for plants, on account of their insoluble nature; but where the bone dust is added to yard or barn manure as a compost, the bones cause the mass to ferment somewhat, and the heat engendered liberates the phosphoric acid and nitrogen, which is absorbed by the manure and given out more quickly to plants when brought in contact with them. Good practice and the last scientific authorities have united in recommending this as the best treatment for ground bone and the best manner of its application to plants. Fifty pounds of ground bone to a cord of manure would be sufficient."

Liquid Manure for Gardening.—It is well known that the liquid manure of animals is more valuable than the solids. In all densely populated countries all these are carefully saved and carried direct to the fields, or stored in tanks for future use.

In the West, and indeed all over the United States, but little attention is paid to the liquid wastes of the stables and yards. This has given rise to the saying that " the leaks in the stable are not in the roof." The point is, that it costs but little more in building a stable to provide drainage through which the liquid manure may safely be carried to a tank or a tight-bottomed pond in the yard, than it does to leave the whole without drainage, to rot the foundations and saturate the soil beneath. Once conveyed to the place of deposit, it may be pumped to the manure pile, or carried direct to the garden, the meadow, or fields, where it will pay for the labor expended, ten-fold.

For the garden it is especially valuable, for here the chief expense is in the cultivation. It costs no more to cultivate an acre of thoroughly enriched land than an acre of poor land; in fact, not so much, for on rich soil the vegetation will quickly cover the ground, and thus smother the weeds, while on poorer soil the weeds continue to grow during the whole summer. If no other convenience be at hand, a hogshead may be placed in the wagon, having an orifice at the bottom, to which a hose may be attached, and thus the land may be watered on either side as the team passes through the central drive, which every garden should have for convenience in hauling in and hauling out manure, trash and produce. If this be not feasible, on account of the small size of the garden, a can with a flat spout, or even large buckets to which a flat pouring place is added, will be speedy and efficient.

Gardeners well know the value of manure, and especially of liquid manure. They spare no pains or price to get all they can, and often apply from 20 to 40 loads of compost or decomposed manure per acre, annually. It is what makes or mars the profit in gardening. The result of the gardener's experience may be easily learned by any farmer who reads, if indeed, it be not so devoted to impractical matter that the proper talent in this direction is not retained. It is just this that makes the difference in the value of any technical journal. If it spread over too much ground, it is efficient in nothing. Just so with the individual. If he engage in three or four separate callings, some of them must suffer. The field of agriculture is broad enough, and in this field there is none more important than the proper saving and application of manure, and especially so in the vegetable garden which no farmer, however few his acres, can afford to be without, especially if he have due regard for the health of his family.

Application of Fertilizers.—Recent experiments have demonstrated that where the application of superphosphates to the soil has produced no effect, the cause was to be attributed to a sufficiency of those salts already existing therein. Where 2 cwts. soil contain less than 3 1-2 ounces of phosphoric acid, the superphosphate will prove beneficial. When it contains 5 ounces of phosphoric acid, the addition of the salt will turn out to be useless. It follows from this that, contrary to the received opinion, it is not necessary to apply nitrates mixed with the phosphates, when the latter are present in the soil. M. Pagnoul continues his interesting experiments as to the solubility of phosphates by diverse agents. He conclusively proves that stable, indeed, we may add barn-yard manure, will dissolve natural phosphates in the powdered state, and thus economize the expensive superphosphates.

A Patent Fertilizer Which Anybody May Use.—This invention relates to a combination of chemicals to be used in connection with dry peat, or muck and unleached ashes, or with any refuse matter having fertilizing properties, to form a fertilizing compound; and it consists in combining dissolved bone, ground plaster, nitrate of soda, sulphate of soda and sulphate of ammonia, in proportion substantially as follows:

Dissolved bone, three bushels; ground plaster, three bushels; nitrate of soda, forty pounds; sulphate of soda, forty pounds; and sulphate of ammonia, thirty-three pounds. This mixture is incorporated with, say, twenty bushels of dry peat or muck, and three bushels of unleached ashes.

The manner of preparing a fertilizing compound from the above ingredients is as follows: The peat or muck and ashes, if such matter be used as the base of the mixture, are thoroughly mixed with the dissolved bone, and the nitrate of soda, sulphate of soda, and sulphate of ammonia, after being dissolved in water, added thereto. The ingredients are next incorporated with the ground plaster, after which the compound is allowed to stand for, say, thirty or forty days, when it becomes ready for use.

The Work of Potash.—Potash is a fertilizing element whose restoration to the soil is indispensable, as it is carried off by crops in considerable proportions. This restitution becomes the more imperative when plants of the leguminous family, such as clover, disappear, to be replaced by mass. Unwashed wood ashes, containing six to eight per cent. of potash, and three to four of phosphoric acid, often produce marvelous effects; the mass disappears, and the clover and similar plants take its place.

M. Rimpeau, at Schlanstedt, Saxony, and Prince William, at Schaumbourg, have been occupied with the influence of potash on the production of sugar in beets. After the bedding was cleaned in the morning, the boards were strewn with one cwt. of kainite and one-half cwt. of gypsum, per two tons of soiled bedding; the latter, on being removed, was allowed to steep in putrid wine, and in time applied at the rate of eleven tons per acre, to a marly soil. The manure, enriched with kainite, produced a slight augmentation in yield of roots, over the gypsum combination. The salient fact elucidated by Prince William on his estate in Bohemia is, that chloride of potassium exercises no essential action in humid years, while in dry seasons one and a half cwt. per acre secures an increase of three tons of roots per acre; that the salt of potash acts less by furnishing that element to vegetation, than by its absorbing and retaining humidity for the plant.

Ashes in the Compost.—When ashes are used in combination with stable manure, the latter is decomposed too rapidly, but if immediately applied to the land there is no waste, or if covered with loam, the component parts are rendered more soluble and the manure acts with greater rapidity. If the liquid excrement from the cows is mixed with the manure, sufficient soluble matter is thereby supplied for a first crop, and while the crop is growing and maturing, the solid manure has been decomposing and preparing for another crop; or, it may be said, the liquid manure will give the young plant a quick start, while afterwards the solid part will aid in finishing the crop. Ashes do not act so quickly on hen manure as on stable manure, since the former is much dryer; consequently decomposition does not take place immediately. If applied soon after composting, the compound will give good results, but if allowed to remain too long after composting, the ammonia will be lost to some extent. If the compost be covered with fresh loam, there will be no loss, since the loam will absorb the ammonia.

How to Keep and Spread Manures.—It seems to be conclusively settled in Europe that by far the best way to keep manure is to let it remain under the animals all winter, accumulating to a depth of several feet under them, and absorbing all the urine. When thus tramped down firmly it never heats, and is fully one-fourth stronger than when piled out doors exposed to the sun and rain, both of which injure it greatly. The animals are kept clean by abundant applications of leaves, loose straw, etc., for beds.

Mr. Gregory, the great Marblehead seedsman, pronounces night soil or privy manure to be fully fifty per cent. stronger than that of animals. It is too strong to apply separately and requires to be decomposed with stable manure to get the best results. In China, Japan and East, all human manure is carefully saved. There it is carried about in buckets, and is very highly prized as a valuable article. In this country it is recklessly thrown away and wasted, being treated as a nuisance. In no possible manner can the fertility of lands be so kept up as by saving all the excrement from men and animals, voided after eating their food, and returning it to the soil from which it came.

Value of Home-Made Manure.—Of manures, that of the cow is the poorest, that of the horse being double in value, and that of the hog five times that of the horse. Hen manure, mixed with two or three times its own bulk of muck, or even loam, is as good as most guano kept for sale. Ashes, leached or unleached, are excellent. The contents of the closet may be kept inodorous, and in an easily workable condition, by casting plaster on them frequently until removed, and then by adding four times as much more of muck or loam, you will have a fertilizer·equal to poudrette. Bones, old boots and shoes, hogs' bristles, and all old scraps, which would otherwise lie about as nuisances and eyesores to all who see them, may be made soluble and fit for fertilizing by burying them in unleached ashes, with an occasional slight watering and stirring of the heap, and addition of ashes, until reduced to a proper state for pulverizing. The pig should be supplied with all the weeds you can gather before they seed, and peat, muck, turf, etc., if thrown into his yard, he will work over, and pay for his keeping by largely increasing the amount of manure. He will work over ten or twelve loads if given to him.

Clover as a Fertilizer.—A stick of wood burned on the surface mostly passes off in gas, leaving only the ashes; but the same stick if burned in a coal-pit, excluded from the air, forms a mass of carbon of nearly or quite its original size. Now all decay of vegetable matter is a slow combustion, and when this is done under the soil, not only the gases retained in the soil, but more carbon is formed, and this carbon has the power to appropriate the valuable gases always present in the atmosphere. The great value of clover as a fertilizer is due, first to the carbon furnished by the decay of the plant, and second to the fine mechanical effect on the soil, which renders it porous, so that the atmosphere penetrates it and deposits plant food. It is clear that better fertilizing effects will result from the plowing down of the crop to decay in the soil. Ordinarily more can be made out of the tops than they are worth for manure, and if rightly managed, the roots will supply the needed fertility.

Home-made Superphosphate.—A Western journal remarks that almost every farmer has upon his own premises one of the best superphosphate manures known. The elements are found in the old bones, scattered carelessly over yard, garden and farm, and common wood ashes, generally allowed to go to waste. If the bones are gathered, placed under shelter, thoroughly mixed with three or four times their bulk of ashes, kept moist with water enough to make a good lye and occasionally stirred and mixed, they will, in a few months, become so tender and friable that they may be pounded into powder, and in this state they form a valuable manure, better than the average of the commercial fertilizers that seem so expensive. The ashes, of course, should be mixed with the bones. The fertilizer thus made should be applied by the handful in the hill of corn, and its effects may be early seen in the deep, rich green of the growing plant. This may seem like small business to a farmer who has but little spare time, but it is by just such economy that our best farms become so profitable, and it is by lack of such economy that so many farms fail to yield even a comfortable living.

Soap Suds.—The value of this article as a stimulant of vegetable life cannot be too highly appreciated. It contains the aliment of plants in a state of ready solution, and when applied, acts not only with immediate and obvious effect, but with a sustained energy which pertains to few even of the most concentrated manures. When it is not convenient—the most economical method, perhaps, of using it—it should be absorbed by materials which may be used as an ingredient in the compost heap. Suds, muck, and other similar articles, should be deposited where the suds from the sink and laundry can find its way to them and be absorbed for the benefit of the crops. In this way several loads of manure, suitable for the support and sustenance of any crop, may be made at comparatively small expense. The highly putrescent character of this fermentable liquid qualifies it admirably for the irrigation of compost heaps of whatever material composed. Being a potent fertilizer, it must of course impart additional richness to almost any material to which it may be added. Try it, and mark the result.

Manure for Almost Nothing.—If you have any dead animal—say, for instance, the body of a dead horse—do not suffer it to pollute the atmosphere by drawing it away to the woods or any other out-of-the-way place, but remove it a short distance only from your premises, and put down four or five loads of muck or sods, place the carcass thereon, and sprinkle it over with quicklime, and cover over immediately with sods or mold sufficient to make, with what had been previously added, twenty good wagonloads, and you will have within twelve months a pile of manure worth twenty dollars for any crop you choose to put it upon. Use a proportionate quantity of mold for smaller animals, but never less than twenty good wagon-loads for a horse; and if any dogs manifest too great a regard for the enclosed carcass, shoot them on the spot.

Poultry Manure.—Fifty fowls will make, in their roosting house alone, ten cwt. per annum of the best manure in the world. Hence fifty fowls will make more than enough manure for an acre of land, seven cwt. of guano being the usual quantity applied per acre, and poultry manure being even richer than guano in ammonia and fertilizing salts. No other stock will give an equal return in this way; and these figures demand careful attention from the large farmer. The manure, before using, should be mixed with twice its bulk of earth, and then allowed to stand in a heap, covered with a few inches of earth, till decomposed throughout, when it makes the very best manure which can be had.

An Experiment with Ashes.—An experiment made with five wagon loads of coal ashes on twenty square rods of ground may be cited as an instance of beneficial mechanical effects. The amount of ashes was about two hundred bushels, that is to say, ten bushels to the rod. They were drawn on late in the fall, the ground having been recently plowed. In the spring, the ground was plowed again, thus mixing the ashes with the soil. It was then planted with garden stuffs. All the plants made more growth than in the previous year, when the ground, after being liberally manured, was planted to the same crops. But the favorable change was not attributable to manurial properties in the coal ashes. Before the application the soil was compact and heavy, a fault that the ashes corrected, and without doubt this was practically the sole effect.

Peter Henderson on Fertilizers.—Peter Henderson says that the best known fertilizers of commerce are Peruvian guano and bone dust. Whatever kind of concentrated fertilizer is used, he finds it well repays the labor to prepare it as follows before it is applied to the land: To every bushel of guano or bone dust add three bushels of leaf mold, well pulverized dry muck, yard scrapings, well decomposed stable matter, or, if neither of these can be obtained, any loamy soil, but in every case the material mixed with the fertilizer must be fairly dry, as it is used as a temporary absorbent for the fertilizer.

Top-Dressing.—Some farmers think that top-dressing with manure is best done during the winter. In the fall the manure, unless very fine and evenly spread, will cover up injuriously much of the plant. When spread in winter, on the contrary, it acts as a mulch and a protection while the plant is dormant, neutralizing the effects of freezing and thawing. An authority on the subject advises that artificial fertilizers be spread on grain lands in the fall, and barnyard manure after the snow comes.

Improving Light Soil.—The best way to improve a light sandy soil is to put on all the vegetable matter you can, either in the form of muck from swamps, or by turning under peas, buckwheat, clover, or some similar crop. If the land is very porous, more or less of the fertilizing materials applied will sink out of the reach of ordinary crops. Your main point is to get the land full of vegetable matter, not only to increase its fertility, but to make it hold moisture in summer.

Liquid Manure.—The liquid voidings of animals are worth more (good authorities say one-sixth more), pound for pound, than the solid excrements, and are saved with greater care by the best European farmers and gardeners. All the leaks in the stable are not in the roof; those often in the floor are quite as objectionable, and are the cause of a great deal of wastage. Make the stable floor tight, with a gutter at the heels of the stock to carry it off to an adjacent tank, or into a heap of muck or other absorbent.

Saving Fertilizers.—One of the most prevalent errors among average farmers is the neglect of making and preserving manure, and also its improper application to the ground. Collect all the refuse material you can, use your chip dirt from the wood pile in absorbing liquids. Apply it to the flat lands at any time during winter. It can then be thrown on broadcast and plowed in as soon as the ground opens. The necessity of returning as much vegetable nutriment to the ground as has been taken off by the crop cannot be too strongly impressed upon the attention of our farmers.

How to Apply Manure.—The old plan of plowing under manure has pretty much been abandoned by many farmers as wasteful. Advanced farming believes and teaches that the intimate and thorough incorporation of the fertilizing principle, into that portion of the soil which is to be occupied immediately by roots of the growing crop, is a truth taught by experience on all soils, and in all climates, and the more evenly and thoroughly this is done the more surely will the crop be satisfactory.

Spreading Manure.—An English writer says: " The wasteful practice of spreading manure on surface of the soil, and allowing it to lie bleaching for weeks, and even months before being plowed in, is still carried on in some counties in England, and stoutly defended by hosts of clay land farmers," and he expresses the opinion that " if the perpetrators of such an enormity be right, science is at fault, analysis is an illusion, and ammonia and all its kindred a family of impostors."

Mixing Manure in Winter.—When teams are not otherwise employed in the winter it is a good plan to draw the pile of horse manure around horse stables and spread it over the heaps of cattle and sheep excrement. The manure of the horse and the cow especially are admirable supplements each to the other, that from the horse being naturally too active and that from the cow too slow. Enough bedding should be placed under horses to absorb all their liquid excrement, so that none be wasted.

Home-Made Guano.—Save all your fowl manure from sun and rain. To prepare it for use, spread a layer of dry swamp muck (the blacker it is the better) on your barn floor, and dump on it the whole of your fowl manure; beat it into a fine powder with the back of your spade; this done, add hard wood ashes and plaster of Paris, so that the compound shall be composed of the following proportions: Dried muck, four bushels; fowl manure, two bushels; ashes, one bushel; plaster, one and one-half bushels. Mix thoroughly, and spare no labor; for, in this matter, the effort expended will be well paid for. A little before planting, moisten the heap with water, or, better still, with urine; cover well over with old mats, and let it lie till wanted for use. Apply it to beans, corn, or potatoes, at the rate of a handful to a hill; and mix with the soil before dropping the seed. This will be found the best substitute for guano ever invented, and may be depended on for bringing great crops of turnips, corn, potatoes, etc.

Materials for Compost.—In several of the States compost heap may be made of muck or earth for a basis; to this may be added leaves, cotton-seed, ashes, gympsum, night soil, stable manure, trash from the fields (except weeds in seed), and all the slops from the houses and cabins. If desired, bone-dust may be added, but the fine artificial fertilizers will be better, if used by themselves.

Value of Vegetable Substances.—The tops of turnips, potatoes, beets, carrots and parsnips are very valuable and should not go to waste. Those of the beets are rich in nitrogen, while potato tops contain a large proportion of potash. All of them contain both in more or less quantity. They rot quickly, and should be added to the compost heap when unfit for other purposes.

Facts Regarding Fertilizers.—The raising of thirty bushels of wheat to the acre will remove from the land fifty-one pounds of nitrogen, twenty-four pounds of phosphoric acid and thirty-nine pounds of potash. This can be replaced by sixty pounds of sulphate of ammonia, 171 pounds of superphosphate of lime, and seventy-seven pounds of chloride of potassium.

Alternating Manure.—Market gardeners find it profitable to alternate stable with other manures rather than use the same kind continuously on the same land. Farmers can take a hint from this. Perhaps one reason why phosphates have been so largely successful has been because the stable manures previously used have been deficient in phosphoric acid.

How to Use Hen Manure.—The manure from the poultry house is valuable for any crop. It may be spread on grass very thinly, about two barrels per acre being enough. One way to get it fine is to spread it on the barn floor and thrash it with a flail, but a wet cloth should be tied around the mouth or nose while this is being done.

Nitrogen for Potatoes.—Potatoes need nitrogen and potash. Fresh manures applied in spring increase the liability of disease. We believe potatoes can be raised profitably with chemicals, when farmers will experiment at home and learn how to buy just what is needed and nothing more.

Nitrate of Soda for Wheat.—An authority avers that an application of 100 pounds of nitrate of soda to an acre of wheat, when the crop looks weak, will show its benefit in a few days, not only improving it in growth, but largely increasing the yield.

Combining Ashes and Bones.—Doctor Nichols gives the following exact figures of the quantities used in reducing bones with ashes: Break one hundred pounds of bones into small fragments and pack them in a tight cask or box with one hundred pounds of good wood ashes, which have been previously mixed with twenty-five pounds of dry, water-slaked lime, and twelve pounds of powdered sal soda. Twenty gallons of water will saturate the mass, and more may be added as required. In two or three weeks the bones will be soft enough to turn out on the barn floor and be mixed with two bushels of good soil. We should prefer road dust to the soil.

Fertilizers a Good Investment.—Farmers who have money at command cannot easily put it in a more profitable investment than judicious outlay on their land. A careful use of good manure repays the expenditure, even during the course of many years, and draining wet land is estimated to return from forty to eighty per cent. on the yearly cost. In the same way good stock pays far better than poor; good fencing, well selected fruit trees, carefully looked-after homesteads, all repay the money laid out, and, besides all that, add immensely to the comfort of the occupier.

Top-Dressing in Winter.—Some farmers think that top-dressing with manure is best done during the winter. In the fall the manure, unless very fine and evenly spread, will cover up injuriously much of the plant. When spread in winter, on the contrary, it acts as a mulch and a protection while the plant is dormant, neutralizing the effects of freezing and thawing. An authority on the subject advises that artificial fertilizers be spread on grain lands in the fall, and barnyard manure after the snow comes.

A Good Garden Manure.—The manure produced by sawdust when used as a bedding for horses, is said to be a better fertilizer for certain garden crops than any other. When mixed with the soil in which celery is grown it is said to greatly benefit those plants.

A Useful Hint.—Coal ashes, scattered on the stable floor, will absorb the liquid manure, prevent the cattle from slipping and falling, afford an excellent addition to the pickings of poultry around the place, and can afterwards be spread on the soil.

Salt and Plaster on Lawns.—A dressing of salt and plaster on newly made lawns will result in great benefit to the young grass roots, making them strong and hardy for wintering over.

Bran as a Fertilizer.—It is said by those who have tried it, that bran is as good as the best commercial fertilizers for potatoes and corn, and much cheaper.

THE GARDEN--Update

When this book was printed in 1888, few man-made fertilizers, herbicides or pesticides were available. Most of the methods of controlling pests and weeds mentioned in this chapter are in accord with the principles of organic gardening.

As well as the manure and lime this book so often recommends, the gardener may wish to apply bloodmeal, bone dust, compost, granite dust, saw dust, wood ashes or seaweed and kelp to the garden. These substances supply different nutrients and their use should be preceded by a soil test to determine what's needed.

Mulching is recommended as a good means of raising watermelons (p. 93). The practice of mulching, covering the ground around plants with straw, shredded paper, or plastics, is particularly practical in crops such as viney plants, which cannot be easily weeded. Pumpkins, cucumbers, melons and squashes will benefit from careful mulching. Mulch may be used on other kinds of plants as well, where it will control weed growth and maintain the soil's moisture.

This book notes that tomato stems, potato stems, tobacco, hellebore, saltpeter, sulphur, lime and pyrethrum may be used to control insects in various plants. Organic gardeners continue to use pyrethrum as well as ryania and rotenone for pest control. They are plant extracts, commercially available, but care should be exercised in their use in that they will kill beneficial as well as harmful insects.

Plants can be protected simply by choosing resistant varieties (i.e. the Badger Shipper cabbage resists club root). Quantities of natural insect predators such as mantis and ladybugs can be purchased for release in the garden.

Some plants are unpleasant in smell and taste to insects and will protect their neighbors. A border of garlic, onions, chives, tansy, mint, catnip, horseradish, marigold, rue, geraniums or nasturiums will repel many insect pests.

Once plants are attacked by insects, they may be treated with soapy water, brews of elder leaves, tomato stems, tobacco, garlic, onions, red peppers or wormwood. The taste and smell of these preparations will not only drive away pests but keep them away.

A good supplement to this chapter would be any one of the organic gardening books published by the Rodale Press in Emmaus, Pa. I've found their magazine "Organic Gardening" and *Organic Plant Protection* particularly interesting. For the gardener who wants to raise mushrooms, I recommend Roy Genders' very complete and helpful *Mushroom Growing for Everyone* (London: Faber & Faber, 1970).

THE GARDEN.

Saving Seeds.—In saving seeds only the best specimens of each kind should be saved, and all inferior ones rejected; this is easy enough with such plants as squashes, cucumbers, tomatoes, melons, etc., care being used to save only the earliest, fairest, and most perfect specimens. The seed should be allowed to ripen thoroughly before taking it from the fruit, which will require some weeks with squashes, after gathering from the vine; tomatoes are placed in the sun for a few days, and melon-seeds may be taken directly when the melon is fit to eat; seeds of this nature having a fleshy pulp are usually cleaned by allowing them to ferment in water for a day or two, when the pulp will easily wash off, after which the seed is spread upon a sheet in the sunshine to dry. Seeds of vines keep longer if not allowed to freeze; they will preserve their vitality five or six years if kept in a warm, dry place. A closet near a chimney is a good place, and, since mice and rats are fond of such tidbits as melon-seeds, it will be advisable to lock them up in a tin chest or other rat-proof arrangement. When saving seeds of beets, cabbage, turnip, etc., those who are most particular reject all but the seed grown on the leading stem. Beet-seed is cleaned by threshing, sifting, and picking over to get out the sticks; it varies much in size, and should be separated by a sieve, in order to have it run evenly through the seed drill, for it is the most troublesome of all seed to sow evenly. Perhaps some inventor will discover a method of shelling out best seeds, so that they can be sown evenly; if this could be done, one of the chief items of labor in raising beets would be greatly lightened, and a saving of more than half the seed would be effected also; for the beet-seed as now sown is a pod containing two to five seeds each, and is so rough and uneven in shape as to give much trouble to sow it evenly with a drill; in fact, to insure a good stand, very heavy seeding and laborious thinning are essential. If the pod could be crushed and the seed shelled out, it could then be drilled in as evenly as any other seed. Seeds of all kinds keep best in a dry, even temperature. When to be kept in large lots, they may be put in bags and hung from the ceiling of the room, to keep them from the mice. Most seeds are good from two to five years, if carefully kept; onion-seed, however, is very inferior after the first year, and worthless after the second. When old seed is to be used, it should be previously tested by sowing a counted lot in a hot-bed or other suitable place, and counting the number of plants that come up, and noting the vigor of the plants; the plants from old seed are usually less vigorous than from fresh seed, and sometimes are so weak as to be worthless.

The Best Garden Vegetables.—The following is an extract from an essay on "Market Gardening," read before the American Nurserymen's Association, at Dayton, O.: Within the past dozen years many important advances have been made in earliness and in quality of vegetables. Among beets we have the Egyptian, which matures at least five days ahead of any other variety, except the Old Bassano, which was too light in color to suit; in cabbages, the Early Summer; and in cauliflower, the Snowball; in celery,

the Golden Dwarf; and the next season is likely to develop a great improvement in the New White Walnut celery—a stout, solid kind, having a rich,
walnut-like flavor, and graceful feather-like foliage. In lettuce, the black-
seeded Simpson and the White Summer Cabbage lettuce now lead all the
out-door varieties. In muskmelons, the Hackensack, of which many thousand acres are grown for the New York market, is almost exclusively planted.
In peas, a great improvement is developed in the dwarf variety known as
American Wonder, though for general early crop the improved Dan O'Rourke
is best. Potatoes vary so much in different localities that it is difficult to
say which of the new sorts are most valued; we find, however, that in our
general trade more of Beauty of Hebron is planted than any other of the new
sorts. In radishes, the Round Dark Red is now the main favorite, while
next in order comes White Tipped Turnip. In spinach, the Savoy and the
new Thick-Leaved are the best for general crop, though we find that the
Savoy should not be sown in spring, as it runs too quickly to seed. Though
every year brings out new claimants for favor in tomatoes, it is my convic-
tion that we have not advanced one day in earliness, unless in such varieties
as Key's Prolific and Little Gem (which are of poor quality), in twenty-five
years, although we have now many varieties somewhat improved in quality.
The varieties now most popular with New York market gardeners are Acme
and Paragon, though, from the unusual advertising given to Trophy, the
general cultivation of that is greater than any other; but, as it is usually
found now, it is far inferior to many others, besides being one of the latest.

Rotation of Garden Crops.—Have you not frequently noticed that
some men change their garden spots every few years? If you ask them why
they do so, they will tell you that vegetables don't seem to do well there
after a few years' cropping.

In starting a garden on an ordinary piece of ground, which has not before
been used for this purpose, two or three years are required to get it pulverized and enriched sufficiently to produce a first-class crop, hence the
necessity for retaining the same piece of ground for garden purposes. This can
be done by adopting a proper system of rotation. It is a good plan to make
a diagram of the plot used for a garden, and have it marked off into divisions
of suitable proportions for the vegetables required. Each division should be
numbered, or, what is just as good, the name of the vegetable raised there
written upon it. These diagrams drawn each year should be carefully preserved, so that, by referring to them, one could ascertain just what had been
raised on each particular division for years back, and by this means keep up
a systematic rotation.

For convenience, the garden-plot should be long and narrow, thus
enabling a horse cultivator to be used to advantage. I have noticed that
most gardens are nearly square in form, but have never yet been given a
good reason for this.

A garden 8x20 rods in size can be cultivated with a horse at less expense
and with less work than a garden 3x4 rods can be worked by hand, as gardens of this size usually are.

Such garden vegetables as rhubarb, asparagus, and others of a like kind,
requiring two or more years to reach the proper bearing condition, should,
of course, be given a permanent place for several seasons; but they, too,
need removing about once in four years, in order to get the best possible results. They should never be so located as to interfere with the cultivation
of other vegetables.

Many gardeners put these plants among their small fruits, but they are as much in the way there as anywhere in the vegetable garden. They will not do so well, and are also a heavy drain on the soil, causing an injury to the bushes about them. The best way is to give them one of the long, narrow divisions, above referred to, clear through the length of the garden.

How to Make a Good Garden.—The soil must be well drained, either naturally or artificially. It must be rich; and the manure should be thoroughly worked into the soil. Plow the land in the autumn, and plow it again as early as possible in the spring. If there is any rubbish, remove it or dig holes and bury it below the reach of the plow. Then plow again, or work the land with a cultivator. I take off some of the inside teeth of the cultivator, so that the horse can draw the cultivator as deep, or nearly as deep, as the land has been plowed. This work should be done when the soil is dry and the weather warm. You cannot possibly stir the soil too much while the sun is shining. It lets in the sun's rays and warms and mellows the soil. On light, sandy soil, thoroughly and deeply plowed and manured the fall previous, there are many crops which can be sown to advantage without again plowing in the spring. It often happens in this latitude that five or six inches of the surface soil in the spring is thawed out and dry enough to work, while underneath the ground is frozen solid. If we wait till this frozen soil can be plowed, we frequently lose a good opportunity for putting in early crops of peas, potatoes, onions, cabbage, lettuce, radish, spinach, etc. And besides, the soil that we turn up with the plow, and which comes to the surface, and in which we sow the seed, is cold and damp, while the sub-surface soil which we turn under is warm and dry.

Transplanting.—Inexperienced gardeners are apt to think that a rainy day is the only fit time for setting out plants, and will often delay a week or two longer than is necessary waiting for it, and finally plant when the ground is soaked and when they sink to their ankles in the soil. That is the worst time that could possibly be chosen, excepting when the ground is congealed with cold. For it is impossible that the mold, sticky and clammy while wet, can filter among the roots, or remain of suitable texture for them to spread themselves in, permeable to them and equally pervious to the air in every part without anywhere exposing their tender parts to actual contact in chambers of corrosive oxygen. A rainy day is an advantage if the plants are set before the ground has become wet, but the safe and sure way is to go for the plants as soon as the ground is fully prepared, no matter how dry the weather. A pail or bucket should always be taken to carry the plants in, having a little water in the bottom. The roots being set in this will absorb until the plant is so gorged that it will endure a drying air after being set in place. If the ground is very dry, water should be poured in before planting, which is very much better than pouring upon the surface, because of no injurious crust being formed, for a continually open surface during the growing season, to admit of free circulation of air and capillary action from below, is absolutely essential to free, profitable growth.

Mushroom Culture.—Of all the edible mushrooms, the common Meadow Mushroom *(Agaricus edulis)* is the only one adapted for culture, and, with proper care and management, it can be grown almost anywhere and at all seasons. Nowhere has the cultivation of this delicacy reached so high a state of perfection as in the vicinity of Paris, in France, and the following description of the methods practiced there, given by Messrs. Vilmorin-Andrieux, will, therefore, be of interest to those who contemplate mushroom culture:

The chief conditions to obtain a satisfactory result consist in growing mushrooms in a very rich soil and under a genial, as nearly as possible even, temperature. To secure this latter condition, the culture is often carried on in cellars; but any other locality, such as sheds, out-houses, stables, railway arches, etc., will suit as well, provided that either naturally or by artificial means the temperature does not exceed 86 degrees, nor fall lower than 50 degrees Fahr.

TUB.

The first thing to be considered after the choice of a convenient locality is the preparation of the mushroom bed. The most essential material being horse droppings, preference to be given to those of well-nourished animals, collected as dry and as free from straw as possible. This fermenting material would be too hot to be used by itself at once; to reduce the strength it should be well mixed with one-fourth or one-fifth of its bulk of good garden soil, when the bed may be prepared immediately, the fermentation being slow and the heat produced only moderate and even. Care should be taken to construct the bed in a dry place, and to make the sides firm and tidy. If it is intended to use the horse-dung by itself, as the mushroom growers around Paris do, it is necessary to allow the first heat to evaporate, which is done by piling the droppings as they come from the stable in successive layers to the height of about three feet, in a dry spot, removing all foreign matter from it and pressing it into a compact mass, sprinkling with water such portions as are very dry. In this state it is to be left till the most violent fermentation has passed, which is generally the case in six to ten days, when the heap is to be re-made, taking care that those portions which were *outside*, and consequently less fermented, are placed *inside*, to insure an equal temperature. It should be well mixed and firmly placed, so that the whole may be of a similar texture.

MOVABLE BEDS AGAINST A WALL.

Generally, a few days after being remade, the fermentation is so strong as to render it necessary to be made up a third time.

Sometimes, after the second operation, it is ready for the beds being made, which may be seen when the heating material has become brown, the straw which is mixed with it has lost almost entirely its consistence, when it has become greasy, and the smell is not longer the same as when fresh. It is difficult to obtain a good material without preparing a heap of at least three feet each way; and if that quantity is not required for making the beds, the surplus may with advantage be used in the kitchen-garden.

The material is now brought to the place where the beds are to be made, which may be of any form and size; but experience has shown that the best way to make use of space and material is to raise the beds to a height of from twenty to twenty-four inches, with a width of about the same at the foundation. An excessive rise of the temperature, in consequence of renewed fermen-

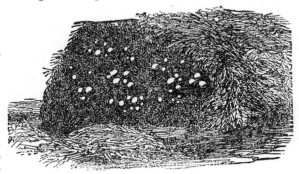

BED WITH TWO SIDES PARTIALLY UNCOVERED.

tation, is to be less feared than when the beds are of larger dimensions. When a large place is at disposal, preference is given to beds with two slanting sides; when the beds are resting against a wall, and consequently present but one available side, the width ought to be less than the height.

Barrels sawn in two, so that each part forms a tub, are well adapted to form beds, as well as simple shelves on which sugar-loaf-shaped beds may be raised, which, already formed, may be carried into cellars, etc., where the introduction of the raw materials would be objectionable.

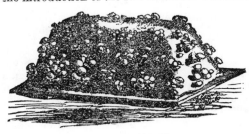

MOVABLE SHELF.

The beds thus established should be left for a few days before spawning, to see whether the fermentation will not be renewed with excessive vigor, which may be ascertained by the touch of the hand, but it is safer to use the thermometer; as long as the temperature exceeds 86 degrees Fahr. the bed is too hot, and it should be allowed to cool by itself, or by making openings with a stick to allow the heat to escape.

When the temperature remains at 76 degrees, it is time for spawning. Prepared spawn is found in the seed stores at all times, which may be kept without trouble from year to year. The spawn sold in France is not in bricks or solid lumps, as in England, but in light masses of scarcely half-decomposed loose and dry litter.

A few days before spawning, it is advisable to expose the spawn ·to a moderately warm moisture, which will insure a safer and more rapid growth; it should be broken up in pieces about the length and thickness of the hand by half that width, and inserted into the bed at a distance of ten to twelve inches each way; on beds twenty to twenty-four inches in height, which are mostly in use, it should be inserted in two rows, dove-tail fashion.

Where the bed is situated in a place under cover and of an even temperature, nothing else is to be done but to wait for the growth; if, however, the bed is placed in the open air and exposed to change of the weather, it must be covered with long litter or hay to keep a uniform temperature all around the bed.

Under favorable circumstances, and if the work has been done well, the spawn ought to show activity in seven or eight days; it is advisable to look to it, and to replace such spawn as might not thrive, which can be seen by the absence of white filaments in the surrounding materials.

Fifteen to twenty days later the spawn ought to have taken possession of the whole bed and should come to the surface; the top and sides of the bed should then be covered with soil, for which a light mold in preference to a heavy one should be used, slightly moistening it, without making it too wet. If it does not naturally contain saltpetre, it would be good to administer a small quantity of salt or saltpetre, or to give it a watering of liquid manure.

The covering with soil should not exceed more than an inch in depth, and be pressed strongly so as to adhere firmly; watering should only be done where the soil becomes very dry. Where a covering has been removed for some purpose it must be replaced at once.

A few weeks after, according to the state of temperature, more or less, the mushrooms will appear. In gathering them care should be taken to fill the empty spaces with the same soil as used for the covering. Leaving the bed to itself, it will produce from two to three months; but its fertility may be prolonged by careful waterings at a temperature of 68 degrees to 86 degrees Fahr., with an admixture of guano or saltpetre.

By establishing under cover three or four beds annually in succession, a continued supply may be reckoned upon; besides, during the summer months, beds may be raised out-of-doors at very little expense, securing an abundant supply. Frames in which vegetables are forced may in the intervals be used for mushroom culture with very good results, providing the temperature be congenial, and that the young mushrooms are slightly protected with soil as soon as they appear.—*The American Garden.*

Asparagus.—A writer in the *Massachusetts Ploughman* says: I desire to impress upon the attention of our farmers the importance of using asparagus more largely as a luxury of the table. It is more rarely to be found in country gardens than any other esculent, and when found hard to take note of, as the plat is scarcely bigger than a door mat and furnishes about enough shoots for one square meal. When an expenditure of two or three dollars will provide a bed which will last twenty or twenty-five years, and annually furnish one of the earliest and most delicious vegetables, it seems almost impossible to account for its being so much neglected by the farming community. It is not only an appetizer and a luxury but a very valuable diuretic, and especially beneficial to sedentary persons and all who are troubled with symptoms of gravel. Our best growers make a bunch of sixteen stalks weigh four pounds. Almost every one who cultivates vegetables knows how to make an asparagus bed, but the opinions as to its after treatment are very discordant. For a private family the bed should not be less than five feet wide and twenty feet long. Dig out the ground two, or better, three feet deep, and fill up with chips, sawdust or sticks of wood packed close together five or six inches from the bottom. Put on this six inches of the strongest stable manure, and fill up to the top with manure and dirt, about half and half. The whole space need not be dug out at once, but the bed can be made in the usual mode of trenching. The roots may now be put in over the entire bed ten inches apart, or in single rows two feet apart, and ten inches plant from plant, and then covered with rich soil about three inches deep, and over the whole a peck of salt and a peck of ashes mixed together, sown.

Asparagus, being a marine plant requiring salt and alkalies for fertilizers, needs in most localities an annual supply of these materials, though cultivators living within the influence of the sea-coast say they can find no benefit in using salt. The beds, of course, are to be kept clean at all times, and an abundant supply of liquid manure from the stable or washroom during the summer will be found the best method of manuring. The ordinary method of after culture in this country is to let the stalks grow until November, then cut them down. Cover the bed with coarse manure, and in the spring fork it in. In France the stems are cut down to about thirteen inches. In England they do as we, cutting down to the ground, but uncovering the stools, so as to leave on only a very slight covering of soil. Now, for small gardens in which asparagus is grown for family use, I doubt the propriety of cutting down the stalks in the fall, and consider it the best plan to let them stand until spring, and then put on the bed all the old pea-brush or other loose dry material, and burn them and the stalks together, and the ashes will furnish all the manure required, and the bed go on improving indefinitely. The practice of the Romans was to "burn the haulm in its own place." And later authorities say, "Cut the dry tops close early in the spring, spread and burn them evenly on the ground, hoe and rake the beds over, and you will have large crops for twenty-five years." Not far from my residence is an asparagus-bed which the present owner, now an octogenarian, helped make more than half a century ago. The only manuring it has received for the latter half that period is the annual spring burning of the stalks and refuse material on the bed, and it is not only vigorous, but improving, sending up new shoots to fill the vacant places occasioned by too late cutting. If this practice works well in Berkshire, where the frost descends to the depth of several feet, and asparagus-beds are not injured, though covered with nothing but the haulms, during such a winter as last, when the white mantle of snow was wanting, it would seem to be adapted to any climate.

The greatest injury to beds of asparagus is cutting too late. Cut all the shoots at a suitable age up to the 20th of June. Always cut below the surface. In Spain, previously to the cutting, the bed is covered lightly with dead leaves to the depth of about six or eight inches, and the cutting does not commence till the plants peep through this covering. In France the cultivators form over each stool a conical lump of soil, like a large mole-hill, ten to twelve inches high, in early spring or soon as the ground is dry, and the asparagus is gathered when it pushes an inch or two above the hills. In the climate of Paris the cutting is never prolonged beyond the middle of June. The experience of nearly all who grow this vegetable is, that if some shoots are not allowed to go to seed, the plants will soon become weakened, and die.

Celery.—Our manner of treating the celery crop of late years is very much simplified, says Mr. Peter Henderson. Instead of sowing the seed in a hot-bed or cold frame, as practiced in Europe, it is sown in the open ground, as soon as it is fit to work, in April, and kept carefully clear of weeds until the time of planting, in June and July. In our warmer climate, if raised in hot-beds, as in England, a majority of the plants would run to seed. The tops are shorn off once or twice before planting, so as to insure "stocky" plants, which suffer less on being transplanted.

After the ground has been nicely prepared, lines are struck out on the level surface, three feet apart, and the plants set six inches apart in rows. If the weather is dry at the time of planting, great care should be taken that the roots are properly "firmed." Our custom is to turn back on the row, and press by the side of each plant gently with the foot. This compacts the soil, and partially excludes the air from the roots until new rootlets are formed, which will usually be in forty-eight hours, after which all danger is over. This practice of pressing the soil closely around the roots is essential in planting of all kinds, and millions of plants are annually destroyed by its omission. After the planting of the celery is completed, nothing further is to be done for six or seven weeks, except running through between the rows with the cultivator or hoe, and freeing the plants of weeds, until they get strong enough to crowd them down. This will bring us to about the middle of August, by which time we have usually that moist and cold atmosphere essential to the growth of celery. Then we begin the "earthing up" necessary for the blanching and whitening of that which is wanted for use during the months of September, October, and November. The first operation is that of "handling," as we term it; that is, after all the soil has been drawn up against the plant with the hoe, it is further drawn close around each plant by the hand, firm enough to keep the leaves in an upright position and prevent them from spreading. This being done, more soil is drawn against the row (either by the plow or hoe, as circumstances require), so as to keep the plant in this upright position. The blanching process must, however, be finished by the spade, which is done by digging the soil from between the rows, and banking it up clear to the top on each side of the row of celery. Three feet is ample distance between the dwarf varieties, but when larger sorts are used the width of the rows must be at least four and a half or five feet.

An Easy Method of Blanching Celery.—The common and laborious process of earthing up and winter storage of celery is doubtless a great obstacle in the way of its culture by many busy farmers. The *Country Gentleman* suggests this easy method of blanching, which does away altogether with the necessity of trenches or banking, at least for moderate supplies: "If intended for winter blanching, about the middle of November they are taken up on a dry day and placed in water-tight troughs or other vessels in a quite dark cellar, the plants standing erect and closely together. Enough water is poured on the roots to cover them, and the supply is continued through the winter as it evaporates. This constitutes the entire labor. The stalks are gradually and handsomely blanched in the darkness, and many new ones spring up during the winter months, especially if the apartment is not very cold, and these new shoots are remarkable for their delicacy and perfect freedom from any particle of rust, appearing like polished ivory. A small separate apartment in the cellar, without windows, answers well for this purpose. Boxes, tubs, or any vessels which will hold a few inches of water may be employed. The plants, as grown in the open ground, need not be earthed up at all, or they may be slightly earthed to bring them into a more compact form, if desired. Probably the best way would be to adopt the course which is sometimes employed of setting out the plants in summer on the level surface of deep, rich soil, eight or ten inches or a foot apart each way, in order that their close growth may tend to give them a more upright form. They are merely kept clean by hoeing through the season.

Cauliflower.—The growing of cauliflowers is receiving more attention than formerly, particularly so the earlier varieties. The crops of Dwarf Erfurt and Snowball begin to come forward in June, and these, with the later sorts, are in market almost without intermission until November. Cauliflowers require very high cultivation, even more so than cabbages, and plenty of moisture. Whether grown in the kitchen garden or upon a large scale, the crop is a paying one. The demand is evidently rapidly increasing, and there is no more delicious vegetable grown.

Cold-frame plants are probably the best and hardiest for early crops; the frames, however, need rather more protection during cold nights than is required for cabbage plants. Seeds sown in hot-beds in February will produce plants that are not much, if any, inferior to cold-frame plants. They should be transplanted out once before setting in the open ground, and also should be gradually hardened by exposure; in this way they may be in condition to set out as early in April as the ground will permit. Set the early sorts about two feet by fifteen inches, and cultivate the same as cabbages. Where irrigation is practicable, great advantage is thus obtained during a drought.

For late cauliflowers, sow seed in open ground, from the middle of May till the middle of June, in hills, the same as directed for late cabbages. Thin to one plant in each hill; this avoids the drawbacks resulting from transplanting in a dry time. When the plants first appear, they are liable to the attacks of a small black fly; guard against this by frequent dusting with plaster, which apply in the morning, while the dew is on. When the heads are forming, tie the leaves together at the top, thus avoiding discoloration by exposure to the sun.

Tomato Culture.—Perhaps no other garden vegetable, says a competent authority, has grown more or faster in public favor than the tomato. It is one of the most profitable garden crops, if cultivated right and got into the market early. I have made tomato culture a special study for the last six or seven years, endeavoring to grow the best and earliest tomatoes. I would get all the new varieties I could to test, cultivating them in the best way according to my knowledge and judgment to make the vines produce the earliest and nearest perfect fruit. I will give the mode of cultivating that I have found to be the best and most profitable way as yet.

Start the plants in a hot-bed; sow the seeds in a box large enough to hold the required number of plants wanted; sow in this box in rows one or two inches apart the seeds thick, and insert in the hot-bed up to the top. When the plants have four or six leaves, transplant in another hot-bed four inches apart. Notice that the beds are the same or near the same temperature. The transplanting is done to give the plants more room and give them abundance of roots. The plants should be hardened by taking off all cover, or if sash is used raise them of a warm, clear day. When all danger of frost is past, transplant to the open ground. Break the ground deep and work it mellow, mixing with the soil all the manure that can be spared from other crops, for the richer the soil, if it is warm, the better. Mark off the rows five feet apart; put one or two shovelfuls of rich, well-rotted manure every three feet in the rows, working it well with the soil, and set the plant some deeper than it was in the bed. Before taking the plants up, wet the bed thoroughly, and take up as much soil with the plant as you can. Set in cloudy weather, if you can, if the weather is warm. The least check the plants receive the better. As soon as they start to grow, begin to cultivate them. Cultivate the balk or space between the rows, deep and thoroughly, raking the ground level. Cultivate every three days, if the weather will admit. Remember, tillage is *earliness!* Tillage is *manure.*

As soon as the laterals or suckers appear keep them off. At the second or third cultivation top-dress the ground with hen manure and work it in the soil. If you have but little hen manure, just put it around the hills. Keep the vines nicely and well tied up to stakes. As soon as the fruit begins to form, go through the vines and keep all imperfect, deformed fruit off and all laterals. Sell by the number, three to five cents each. Sell to the consumer; they are the ones to appreciate nice fruit, and will pay for it too.

As soon as the fruit is grown let the suckers alone; they will give you fruit later. Varieties—Perfection, Paragon; or Acme is very nice, but I prefer the two first.

Training Tomato Plants.—There is no doubt that a greater quantity of desirable fruit is obtained when the branches of each tomato plant are elevated on brush or frames, as the fruit is by this means exposed to sun and air; oftentimes only one stake is employed; any arrangement that brings about the required exposure and keeps the fruit from the ground will serve a good purpose.

The maturity of the first fruit that sets may be greatly accelerated by pinching off the extremities of the tops and the surrounding shoots that appear. A good rule is to stop side shoots at the first blossom.

A novel method of training the tomato plant appeared in a report of the Maine Pomological Society. Stakes seven or eight feet long were inserted in the ground the last of May, three feet apart, in a warm, sheltered location, and strong tomato plants were procured, which had been started under a glass and contained one or two blossom buds. These were planted near the stakes. The plant was then tied to the stake with listing, and all the side branches which had pushed at the axillar or angles formed by the separation of the leaves, were pinched or cut out with scissors, so as to compel the plant to grow on a single stem; and every week during the season, these branches were removed, and the stems, from time to time, were tied to the stake. When a sufficient number of clusters had been formed, the remainder were removed, so as to concentrate the whole energies of the plant to the growth and ripening of the remaining tomatoes; and the heavier branches were supported by tying them to the stakes. It was claimed for this method that the ripening of the fruit was not only hastened, but its size increased.

Late Tomatoes.—To raise late tomatoes a good plan is to stick into each watermelon hill a tomato plant. They do not interfere with the former, and come in after the garden crop gives out. Those coming in late are the best for canning and putting up for winter use.

Onion Growing.—A successful gardener writes: Let me say to those who, by reason of repeated failures, have become discouraged, and abandoned the growing of onions, that if they will put the following directions in practice they will be astonished at the result. One of the most important and first considerations is the soil, for it is of no more use to try on unsuitable soil than it is to "spit against the wind," and if you attempt it you will only "get your labor for your pains." The soil must be clean, rich, and light, not a gravelly kind, or one so dry as to suffer from drouth—sandy loam is the best. Next, the ground should be heavily salted, and this well worked in before sowing. The sowing should be done in April, and as early in the month as possible; "delay is dangerous." With a heavy roller, or the feet, or in some way, the ground in which the seeds lie should be pressed down quite hard. Weeding should be attended to as soon as you can safely do so, and as often as the grass (which is the only weed that will be likely to appear if the ground has been heavily salted) appears and is large enough to pull (the smaller the better), being careful not to throw earth upon the onions in any way or at any time during their growth. Follow these rules, and if weather favors, success is certain, and the weather must be quite unusual to cause failure. The tops should be left on the bed or field to rot, or to spade or plow in; and onions improve by being grown on the same ground year after year. While I believe it to be better to work the soil up fine for the reception of the seed, and after sowing to press the ground down hard upon the seed, yet I have known very good crops grown by making a groove or furrow with a sharp instrument in unplowed ground, covering the seed with the earth thrown out by the process, pressing it down, a heavy coat of manure having been applied as a top dressing the fall before, and raked or burnt off before sowing. Top dressing is a good practice for onions, whether the land is plowed or not. Plow shallow if you plow at all.

A New Method of Raising Onions.—A new method of onion-growing is strongly recommended by a French horticulturist. Some of the seedlings in the original bed should be left standing at intervals of about a couple of inches, and the spaces between them caused by the removal of the rest, filled in with good garden mold mixed with pigeon's dung, or ordinary fæces. The beds must be kept well watered, and it is said the resulting crop will astonish the grower.

Keeping Winter Squashes.—Many farmers are at a loss to know how some are successful in keeping their squashes in good condition, until May or June, while they lose most of theirs before the end of February; they usually attribute their want of success to causes beyond their control, when a careful investigation would show that mismanagement was the principal cause. Squashes to keep well must, first, be well ripened; second, they should be gathered before heavy frosts come; third, should be well dried; fourth, the shell should be well glazed over, and while it need not be thick it should be hard; fifth, they should be kept where the temperature is very even, never very cold, or very hot; sixth, in handling, great care should be taken not to bruise them; this is of the highest importance. Many farmers leave their squashes out until the frost kills the vines; the squashes are thus left exposed to the cold winds, and they are frequently left until it is cold enough to freeze water, and change the color of the tops of the squashes; this is fatal to their good keeping. Others, when they find that cold weather has come, hurry them in just as night sets in, and in their haste to get them under cover, they load them into the wagon as though they were stones; thus bruising nine out of every ten to a degree that causes them to rot by Thanksgiving time.

Squashes are often stored in the barn, in one heap, until they get chilled, when they are carried into a warm, damp cellar, where they soon rot, and the owner is at a loss to know the reason. When stored in heaps, if the storehouse be dry, the under squashes will send out moisture in such quantities as to keep the whole heap surrounded by moisture. Squashes to keep well, should not only be kept in a dry atmosphere with a very even temperature, but they should be spread on the floor, or on shelves, so that the air can easily pass between them.

All of the soft shell and unripe squashes should be disposed of as soon as possible after they are harvested, and only the hard shell and perfectly ripe ones should be kept for winter; crookneck squashes keep best with most people; the reason probably is, they are ripe and are handled with care, and are usually hung up in a dry place. The same treatment of marrow squashes would no doubt secure very satisfactory results.

Squash Culture.—A successful raiser of squashes says he manages in this way: I dig holes as deep as I conveniently can with a hoe, six feet apart, close by the side of early peas or potatoes. As soon as the weather will permit I stamp a wheelbarrow of unfermented manure in each hole, pour in a pail of water, and haul over the manure six inches of earth, being careful that the hill is no higher than the surrounding surface. Plant ten or twelve seeds in each hill; when they begin to run, thin to two vines in each hill. The potatoes will be fit for family use before the squashes begin to run, and can be dug ahead of them, leaving the ground mellow, so that the squash vines will root at every joint. This is a great saving of ground in a small garden. Train them all one way.

Experiments in Melon and Squash Culture.—A practical gardener makes the following statement: "Last year, as a test of a frequent practice among growers of melons and squashes, I pinched the ends of the long main shoots of the melons, squashes, and cucumbers, and left some to run at their own will. One squash-plant sent out a single stem reaching more than forty feet, but did not bear any fruit. Another plant was pinched until it formed a compact mass of intermingling side-shoots eight feet square, and it bore sixteen squashes. The present year a muskmelon-plant thus pinched in, covered the space allotted to it, and it set twenty-three specimens of fruit; the most of them were pinched off. The pinching causes many lateral branches, which latter produce the female or fertile blossoms, while the main vines produce only the male blossoms. The difference in favor of the yield of an acre of melons treated by this pinching process may easily amount to 100 barrels."

Hints on Melon Culture.—A correspondent at Brighton, Ill., writes to an agricultural paper: "Of course everybody who knows anything at all about melon culture understands that melons do best on warm sandy land, but everybody, perhaps, don't know that I have raised fine melons on heavy clay soil. I put the land in first-rate condition and fertilize in the hill with well-rotted barnyard manure. I also raise the hills a few inches above the level to make the ground warmer and dryer. I never put seed in the ground until the weather is settled and the soil is dry and warm. I use plenty of seed, so as to insure a good stand. The very day the vines begin to show green above ground I begin sprinkling the hills with bone-dust, which operation I repeat every day until they are out of reach of the striped bug, that foe to melon patches. Now I don't say that sprinkling with bone-dust is a sure preventive in all cases to the bug, but it has proved a paying application to me. I have had fewer bugs in my melon patch since I began using it, and it also acts as a tonic to the vines, making them more vigorous. I do not confine the applications of bone dust to melon vines, but use it wherever I fear the striped bugs."

A New Method of Watermelon Culture.—A correspondent of the *Rural New Yorker* describes the following method by which an extraordinary crop of watermelons was raised: Holes were dug ten feet apart each way, eighteen inches square and fifteen inches deep. These holes were filled with well-rotted manure, which was thoroughly incorporated with the soil. A low, flat hill was then made and seed planted. When the vines were large enough to begin to run, the whole surface was covered to the depth of a foot or fifteen inches with wheat straw. The straw was placed close up around the vines. No cultivation whatever was given afterward; no weeds or grass grew. The vines spread over the straw, and the melons matured clean and nice. The yield was abundant, and the experiment an entire success. This is surely worth trying.

Boxes for Melons and Cucumbers.—It is a good plan to make boxes, say twelve inches square and eight inches high, without bottom or top; these, placed over the cucumber or melon hills, and covered with grass, give an impetus to the plants early in the season that nothing short of a hot-bed will effect. If very early, place a little fresh manure around these boxes to keep the contents warm. It is astonishing what an effect this simple contrivance will produce; and not only is it valuable for protection from the cold weather, but it is equally valuable as a protection from melon bugs and other predatory insects that seem to watch for our choicest esculents.

Cucumbers on Trellises.—No one who has not tried it can have any idea of the luxurious growth of a cucumber when trained on a stake, which has a set of stubby side branches left along its length, and the crop on some so trained was enormous. By this the vines occupy less space, and it is the natural habit of the cucumber to climb instead of trailing on the ground.

How to Grow Early Cabbages.—A successful gardener writes: I sow the seeds of the kinds I wish to grow in February or first of March, in small or shallow boxes, in forcing-pit, hot-bed, or if these are not to be had, a sunny window of the house will do. The boxes I use are eighteen by twenty-four inches, three inches deep, made of one-half inch boards. The kinds of early cabbage I generally raise are Early Jersey Wakefield (best if pure), Winningstadt, Early Summer and Fottler's Early Drumhead. The first two for early, the others for second early. I only treated the first two as above stated; the second early I sow in common hot-beds from the 1st to the 15th of March. After the seeds sown in boxes are up and about three inches high, it is necessary to transplant them in other boxes, like those they were sown in, about one and a half to two inches apart every way; or put one plant in each pot, and pots close together in boxes, treating the same as if planted in boxes. Pots are better than boxes, and I use them largely. About one week or ten days before planting in garden, they must be hardened off by exposing gradually, night and day, in the open air. I set my plants the end of April or beginning of May. The plants which are in boxes are taken in the boxes to the part of the garden where the ground is ready to plant. Plant Wakefield twenty inches in rows and Early Summer the same; the other kinds twenty-four inches. The rows should be thirty inches apart, so that a cultivator can be used. Early radish, lettuce, spinach, etc., can be sown between the cabbage rows, and be out before the cabbage needs all the room. After cabbage, celery can be sown, on the same ground. In this way other vegetable plants can be raised to advantage. In fact, I have raised all the following with success: Early cauliflower, early lettuce, early kohlrabi, early savoy, early celery, early beet, early tomatoes, early cucumbers and early squashes.

Fertilizer for Cabbage.—"I find," says a writer in the *New England Homestead*, "that cabbage needs more hoeing and stirring of the soil than almost any other crop. Neither do I approve of too much stable manure, except for an early crop, for it has a tendency to dry the soil and does not furnish potash enough. I had much rather have tobacco stems or stalks, cut up fine and plowed under broadcast, with some chemicals in the drill, for a medium or late crop. As to chemicals, whether to be used alone or in combination with other manures, I recommend this formula as being best and cheapest, which every farmer must make for himself: Two hundred pounds of dry ground fish, two hundred pounds of bone meal dissolved in sulphuric acid, two hundred pounds castor pomace and one hundred pounds of muriate potash, or more if the potash salts (kainit) are used. The fish and castor pomace furnish ammonia in quick and slow forms; the bone, phosphoric acid; while the potash is very necessary to a cabbage crop. A ton of this mixture costs about $40, and is sufficient for an acre with light manuring, or half the quantity if manure is used liberally. This is the best cabbage grower I have found. With it and tobacco stalks, used as described, I raised cabbages that weighed over twenty pounds. One dozen, as they were taken to market, weighed over two hundred pounds."

Novel Method of Growing Cabbages.—A novel plan for setting celery and cabbage plants which has several desirable points to recommend it, is to place them between the rows of your potatoes or sweet corn after the last hoeing. The growing corn or potatoes will afford a partial shade which is very desirable at the time of setting the young plants and until they get fully established, and yet ripen and can be removed in time for them to occupy the ground as a second crop. Two crops on one piece of ground with ten dollars' worth of labor and manure will afford more profit than one crop on which five dollars are expended.

Parsley.—No garden is complete without a parsley bed, and nothing looks prettier or more ornamental. It is not only useful in soups, but for garnishing dishes of meats and vegetables it cannot be surpassed. The only objection to it is its slow germination. As a small bed of parsley is sufficient for a family garden, the labor necessary to its cultivation is trifling, as the attention to a few square yards of ground can hardly be considered an encroachment upon regular work. It is a native of Sardinia and loves warm weather, but owing to the length of time required for the seeds to germinate, it should be sown very early. It the seed is soaked for twenty-four hours in warm water, previous to sowing, they will sprout in shorter time, or, what is better, mix them with earth dampened with warm water, and keep near the stove in a box until the seeds burst. The earth in the box should not be allowed to become dry from evaporation, but the moisture should be kept by frequent additions of warm water, care being observed not to have it too wet. The ground should be very rich, with well-rotted manure if any is used, spaded deep and fine, and well raked, in order that not the smallest lump or stone may remain. Then sow the seed in rows, mixed with radish, and cover lightly. As the radish will soon push through and show the rows, the grass can be kept down with the hand.

Spinach.—Spinach; though an aristocratic crop on some accounts, may become also the one crop of the masses for early use, if they will only grow it. And this is the way: Wheel some manure upon the patch where your early garden peas were, spade the ground thoroughly, mark it off in drills eighteen inches apart and an inch or so deep, and sow to spinach. That is all there is to it. Sow the seed thickly in the rows, and when it has attained sufficient size to thin out, what a delicious dish of " greens " you will have this fall, at a season, too, when, although green things are generally no rarity, yet, because of their extreme delicacy and lusciousness, you will esteem them a great and rare treat. Then with the on-coming of freezing ground, cover with straw or litter of any kind. Let this remain till after the frost is out of the ground in the spring, when it may be taken off, and, with the first tulips of your flower garden, you will also have spinach greens for your dinner—a most delicious and healthy dish. Moreover, if you do happen to have more than you want, just take them to the village market, and see how readily you can sell the surplus. Perhaps, indeed, you may thus establish quite a profitable local trade in this delicious crop. Try it.

Poles for Beans and Other Climbers.—White birches and alders so commonly used for bean poles, are about the poorest, for they last only one season at the best, and sometimes break off at the surface of the ground, and let down the beautiful pyramid of green before the pods are ripe. White cedar from the swamps is durable, and the rough bark enables the vines to climb without any help from strings, but these are not always accessible. Red cedar is much more widely distributed, and on the whole makes the best bean pole. The wood is as durable as the white cedar, and young trees, from which poles are made, grow quite stout at the ground, and, if well set, will resist very strong winds. A set of these poles will last for a generation. For bean poles, all the side branches are trimmed off, but for a support for ornamental climbers, these may be left on. A cedar, six or eight feet high, with the branches gradually shortened from below, upwards, makes an excellent support for ornamental vines. One of these, covered with a clematis, or other showy climber, makes a pyramid of great beauty. It is well to prepare a supply of poles for beans and other plants before the work is pressing.

Beets.—For beets the soil should be rich, mellow and deep. Plant in drills about two inches deep and the rows about twelve or fifteen inches apart. Set the seeds in the drills about two inches apart. For field culture the rows should be wide enough to admit the horse cultivator and the roots not nearer than one foot in the rows. The mangel-wurzel beets grow to a very large size, are coarse and wonderfully productive, making excellent food for cattle. Those who have never tried the mangels for stock have yet to learn of their great value for cattle, both for milk and meat. Then, they are juicy and refreshing, and add to the health and comfort of the animals. In no way can so much good food be grown as cheaply as in mangels.

The Melon Worm.—The melon worm (*Phakellura hyalinatalis*) is about an inch and a quarter in length when mature, of a light yellowish-green color, and nearly translucent. The moth is remarkable for its beauty, its wings being pearly-white bordered with a narrow band of black, its legs and body white, and the abdomen terminated with a feather-like tuft tipped with white and black. In our accompanying illustration, the chrysalis, worm, and moth are shown. This worm belongs to the same genus as the pickle worm *(Phakellura nitidalis)*, the moth of the latter differing from that of the former in having the ground-work of the wings a bronze-yellow, and the black border a little broader.

The melon worm is proving to be, in many parts of the country, a most destructive enemy to melons, cucumbers, pumpkins, and other cucurbitaceous plants. It goes to work in an exceedingly business-like way, making

skeletons of the plant leaves or excavating numerous cavities in the fruit where it appears. Sometimes it forces its way into the melon until out of sight, though more frequently it makes a shallow cavity an eighth of an inch or more in depth, and in this pursues its work.

Efficient remedies for this pest are still wanting. Paris green and London purple would probably prove effective, but it is not safe to use these on account of their liability to poison those who eat the fruit. *Pyrethrum*, or Persian Insect Powder, might prove as effective in ridding the plants of the worms, and it has the advantage of being entirely harmless

THE MELON WORM.

to human beings. Whatever poison is used, it should be applied to both foliage and fruit, inasmuch as the destruction of the former will prevent the latter from coming to maturity. Early planting, so that the fruit may be picked early, or before the destructive brood appears, is a preventive, and if the worms be destroyed on their first appearance on the foliage before the fruit begins to form, there will be much less danger to the fruit crop.

Insects on Garden Vegetables.—The most common of these are the caterpillars of medium-sized butterflies, the wings of which are white, with a few black spots; there are three distinct species, but all are similar in their habits. Wherever these butterflies are seen flitting about over the cabbage and cauliflower plants, trouble from "worms" may soon be expected. Safety consists in attacking them early. Some worms eat into the forming head, and when they have thus hidden, nothing can be done. In small gardens, hand-picking will answer, but where there are many cabbages, this is not practicable. The Persian Insect Powder, the *Pyrethrum*, is the best, and a safe application. There are in some localities cabbage worms which come from other butterflies, but they are to be treated in the same manner. The large green caterpillar, of the five-spotted Sphinx, known as the "Tomato Worm," is most destructive; it will soon leave nothing but bare stems upon a tomato plant, eating the green fruit as well as the leaves. When the tomatoes are supported by some kind of a trellis, as they always should be in a garden, worms may be detected by the quantity of large pellets of droppings found upon the ground. Where these are seen, the worm should be sought for. Stems without leaves also indicate its presence. When not eating, it will be found close to the stems, on their underside, and as it is of nearly the same color, may escape notice. The "worms" are never very numerous, and hand-picking is the best way to deal with them. In spite of the horn at the tail-end, they can neither sting nor bite. Frequently one of these will be found with its body nearly covered with small egg-shaped white cocoons, often mistaken for eggs. Worms with these should not be destroyed, as they are too weak to do much damage, and the parasitic insect should have time to leave these cocoons, as they are our friends, and should be encouraged. The tomato-worm may sometimes be found on potatoes.—*American Agriculturist.*

Hot Water on the Garden.—Insecticides are in demand. The farmer's first interest is to gain an insecticide that is effective. The next important point is that it be sufficiently cheap in cost to permit of free use. Hot water some of the English gardeners accept as a cheap insecticide not sufficiently appreciated, and capable of more extended employment than is usually believed. Hot water judiciously applied has been found effective among American farmers for cabbage worms. In careful hands its application, after the cabbage heads begin to form, has not injured the plants, but has destroyed the bugs. Experiments with hot water on the aphis at Stoke Newington and reported in the English journals, made it appear that aphides perish immediately if immersed in water heated to 120 degrees Fahrenheit. In order to ascertain the degree of heat infested plants could endure in the dipping process, a number of herbaceous and soft-wooded plants were immersed in water heated to various degrees above 120. Fuchsias were unharmed at 140 degrees and injured at 150 degrees. Pelargoniums were unhurt up to 150 degrees, but the slightest rise above that figure killed the soft wood and young leaves. Ferns, heliotropes, petunias, begonias, mignonette and many other plants of soft texture were unhurt by being dipped in water at 140 degrees, but the slightest rise above that point proves detrimental. Roses grown in pots for market were kept clean by dipping in water at 120 degrees without injury to the plants and every aphis destroyed.

Gas Tar as a Remedy for Bugs.—A correspondent of the Chicago *Tribune* says: "For the last five years I have not lost a cucumber or a melon vine or a cabbage plant. Get a barrel with a few gallons of gas tar in it; pour water on the tar; always have it ready when needed, and, when the bugs appear, give them a liberal drink of the tar water from a garden sprinkler or otherwise, and, if the rain washes it off and they return, repeat the dose. It will also destroy the Colorado potato beetle, and frighten the old long potato bug worse than a threshing with a brush. Five years ago this summer both kinds appeared on my late potatoes, and I watered with the tar water. The next day all Colorados that had not been protected from the sprinkler were dead, and the others, their name was legion, were all gone, and I have never seen one on the farm since. I am aware that many will look upon this with indifference, because it is so simple and cheap a remedy. Such should always feed their own and their neighbors' bugs, as they frequently do."

Remedy for the Green Fly.—A writer in the *Deutsche Zeitung* states that he last year had an opportunity of trying a remedy for destroying green fly and other insects which infest plants. It was not his own discovery, but he found it among other recipes in some provincial paper. The stems and leaves of the tomato are well boiled in water, and when the liquid is cold it is syringed over plants attacked by insects. It at once destroys black or green fly, caterpillars, etc.; and it leaves behind a peculiar odor, which prevents insects from coming again for a long time. The author states that he found this remedy more effectual than fumigating, washing, etc. Through neglect a house of camelias had become almost hopelessly infested with black lice, but two syringings with tomato plant decoction thoroughly cleansed them.

To Destroy Bugs on Vines.—To destroy bugs on squash and cucumber vines, dissolve a tablespoonful of saltpetre in a pailful of water; put one pint of this around each hill, shaping the earth so that it will not spread much, and the thing is done. Use more saltpetre if you can afford it—it is good for vegetable, but death to animal life. The bugs burrow in the earth at night and fail to rise in the morning. It is also good to kill the "grub" in peach trees—only use twice as much, say a quart to each tree. There was not a yellow or blistered leaf on twelve or fifteen trees to which it was applied last season. No danger of killing any vegetable with it—a concentrated solution applied to beans makes them grow wonderfully.

Protecting Young Plants.—The striped bug is very destructive to young plants, especially of vines. It is almost impossible to get a stand of early cucumbers, on account of this pest. A writer in one of our exchanges states that a good protection is secured by cutting a sheet of cotton wadding into nine equal pieces, and then spliting them, making eighteen, at a cost for all of only four cents. These are placed over the hills before the plants are up, the corners held down with small stones. They are elastic and stretch as the plants grow. The bug cannot get through them. They are also some protection against frost.

A Valuable Mixture.—A valuable mixture to keep on hand is one of coal ashes, sulphur and hellebore. The ashes should be very fine. It is best after passing them through the ordinary coal-ash sieve. To one pailful of ashes thus sifted, add a quart each of flour of sulphur and hellebore, and mix together. For currant worms, plant lice, cabbage fleas, slugs on pear trees, melon bugs, we found this so effectual that we confidently recommend it. It is always best to use it in the cool of the morning while the dew is upon the leaf.

To Get Rid of Grubs.—The carrot crop is rendered useless in many gardens by grubs eating into the roots. This takes place in many well-managed gardens. The best remedy is to scatter a quantity of soot and lime over the surface of the ground before forking it over for the carrots. This works it into the ground, and keeps the soil free from all sorts of grubs for the whole season. The next best way is to sow the lime and soot between the rows and hoe it into the ground.

Coal Ash Walks for the Garden.—Good, sound, dry walks are a necessity in all garden grounds, in order that the work in them may be carried on with comfort during all weathers, and although there is nothing like good gravel for walks in pleasure grounds, it frequently happens that, from the difficulty of getting gravel in quantity within a reasonable distance, the kitchen garden walks have to be made of what is most abundant. After trying all sorts of materials in different counties, it was found that nothing makes a better path than ashes. The way in which we use them is to form grass verges one foot wide and about one foot deep. In the bottom of the walk are put brickbats, stones, or other rubbish. On these a good layer of clinkers is spread, and broken down tolerably fine, when a good coating of ashes is spread evenly over the surface, and rolled down. These form one of the pleasantest paths on which to walk, wheel, or cart that it is possible to have. Weeds are not troublesome, for the material has been cleaned by passing through the furnace, and if a few seeds blow on to the surface and germinate they can be easily removed.

Club Root in Cabbage.—The beet requires a deep, permeable soil, for M. Waronin, an authoritative microscopic botanist of Europe, who has given particular attention to destructive insects, and especially to those predatory in the cabbage, finds that the abnormal growth on the roots, which he denominates club root, but which is known in the United States as club foot, is caused by a minute fungus, to which he has given the name of *Plasmodiophora brassicæ.* Thin sections of the diseased portions reveal the fungus with its spores, under the higher powers of the microscope. As the spores are exceedingly numerous, the soil becomes infested with them, and communicates the trouble to plants upon the same soil next year. A diseased crop should not be followed by cabbage again. Only healthy plants should be set. An application of lime to the soil has proved of benefit, and from the nature of the trouble, he thinks, the use of sulphur would be useful.

Soil for Sugar Beets.—The beet requires a deep, permeable soil, for its roots penetrate deeply into the ground and are abundantly supplied with fine fibers through which it receives its nourishment. If the soil does not permit the root to grow down deeply the top will be forced to grow above the ground, and the crown which grows out of ground is nearly worthless for sugar purposes. A deep, sandy loam is the best soil to produce beets rich in sugar. They will, however, grow on a variety of soils, and any soil which will plow and subsoil to the depth of twelve or fifteen inches is a good beet soil. Avoid all wet lands and muck bottoms as unsuitable. Beets will not flourish on wet lands, and what grow are not sweet. Muck bottoms produce large tops but small roots with little sugar in them.

Sulphur and Tobacco.—A mixture of sulphur and finely ground tobacco, two parts of the former to one of the latter, has been found an excellent preventive of the ravages of insects on squash and other vines, as well as for keeping lice from cattle, dogs and poultry. It is also recommended for sprinkling trees and bushes that are eaten by canker worms or currant worms,

Cultivation of Tobacco.—To raise tobacco, select a sheltered situation, where the young plants can receive the full force of the sun; burn over the surface of the ground early in spring (new land is best), rake it well, and sow the seeds; have a dry, mellow, rich soil, and after a shower, when the plants have got leaves the size of a quarter-dollar, transplant as you would cabbage plants, three and one-half feet apart, and weed out carefully afterward. Break off the suckers from the foot-stalks, as they appear; also the tops of the plants when they are well advanced, say about three feet high, except those designed for seed, which should be the largest and best plants. The ripeness of tobacco is known by small dusky spots appearing on the leaves. The plants should then be cut near the roots, on the morning of a day of sunshine, and should lie singly to wither. When sufficiently withered, gather them carefully together, and hang them up under cover to cure and prepare for market.

Starting Plants Early.—A writer on gardening gives the following hints on starting tender seeds, such as tomatoes, squashes, melons, and the like: " It is desirable in transplanting not to check the growth by disturbing the roots. A good way to avoid this is to scrape out turnips, fill them with good soil and plant in two or three seeds, setting them in a warm, light place, and keeping them moist. When the weather is suitable, place these out in the garden at the proper depth. The turnip will decay and the plant will thrive unchecked if properly cared for. Do not use potatoes instead of turnips. Another method is to get squares of sod, say six inches wide, from good, mellow soil, turn them bottom up, and put such seeds as squash, melon or sweet corn, and treat them in the same way, not putting out till the weather is quite warm, and then protecting against bugs. For more delicate plants, flowers, etc., make little square paper boxes out of thin writing paper, or thick newspaper, merely folding them at the corners as you would the paper in covering a book, and tacking them with a needle and thread; make them about three inches square and two deep. Fill with good soil; start the seeds and put them out at the proper time, boxes and all, without disturbing the roots. If you fear the paper is too strong for the roots to penetrate, cut carefully on the bottom of the box the shape of a cross, and all will be well."

Seeds for Small Gardens.—People who grow largely for market know, as a part of their business, how many garden seeds to sow, but this is not always the case with the man or woman who has but a small garden. For these we give the following: Asparagus, bed of 15 square yards, 1 pint. Beet, row 50 feet, 2 ounces. Cabbage, bed of 8 square yards, 1 ounce. Carrots, drill of 120 feet, 2 ounces. Carrots, bed of 12 square yards, 2 ounces. Celery, 4 square yards, 1 ounce. Endive, 4 square yards, 1 ounce. Bush beans, row 80 feet, 1 pint. Leek, 2 square yards, 1 ounce. Lettuce, 4 square yards, 1 ounce. Onions, 9 square yards, 2 ounces. Parsley, row 80 feet, one and a half ounces. Parsnip, drill of 200 feet, 2 ounces. Peas, early, row 60 feet, one and a half pints. Peas, large, late, row 80 feet, one and a half pints. Potatoes, row 30 feet, half peck. Radishes, 4 square yards, one and a half ounces. Spinach, 10 square yards, 2 ounces. Spinach, drill of 120 feet, 2 ounces. Turnip, 4 square yards, 1 ounce.

Asparagus as a Lawn Plant.—A friend suggests a very good idea as to asparagus: " Of course the old plan of sticking the plants in close beds is all wrong. There are many bits of fine soil in gardens, even the so-called pleasure grounds and hardy plant borders, where a strong clump of the common asparagus would be a great ornament, as well as of use. I shall plant a hundred or more good clumps of asparagus in our borders here, partly for its tender shoots in spring, partly for its spray for cutting during the summer and autumn months, but mainly for its feathery grace as a beautiful, hardy plant. In many a villa garden, even where good asparagus may never be seen raised in the ordinary way, a capital supply could be obtained by simply dotting a few plants here and there in borders, and on the margins of shrubberies, not only as single specimens, but as groups and masses—never, however, nearer to each other than four feet."

Training Tomatoes.—A housewife, who vouches for the success of her plan, makes these suggestions for tomato training: "When the plants are ready for the garden, make a considerable hill of good compost. Chip manure is excellent, and a quantity of chicken manure is good. After the hill is made, drive a long stake through it. This may be six feet high. Set the plant near it. The training will require attention. The plant will immediately begin to sucker, or throw outside shoots, just above each leaf. These must be cut off, and then the plant will run up vigorously. Tie it to the stake, and do not be afraid to use the knife. Keep on cutting each stem that appears in the axil of a leaf, and keep on tying. The first bearing branches come directly from the body of the plant. Remember that this trimming must be continued as long as the plant bears. Thus trained, the fruit is superior in size, quantity, and flavor, besides being less liable to rot or drop off."

Bending Down Onions.—Many old truck farmers have caused surprise to lookers-on at their work, to see them bending over their onion tops. The time to do this is when some begin to show signs of flowering. The method is thus explained: "This operation may be done by the hand, but time is saved by two persons each holding one of the ends of a pole in such a manner as to strike the stems an inch or two above the bulbs. This is called 'laying over,' and is of great benefit to all crops of onions, as the growth of the stems is thereby much checked, and the whole nourishment thrown into the bulbs. It is an old practice in family gardens, and has never failed to give satisfactory results."

Early Cucumbers and Melons.—For early melons or cucumbers many plant the seeds on inverted sods cut about four inches square. The sods are placed in a frame of any kind, and covered to the depth of half an inch with mellow, rich earth. The plants root firmly in these sods the same as they would in small flower-pots, and may safely be transplanted as soon as the weather becomes settled and warm. For melons this is an excellent plan, since our seasons are scarcely long enough to ripen them before the cool nights of autumn, when the seeds are planted in the ground in the usual way.

Benefits of Hoeing.—Any one passing along where there are gardens can nearly always find evidences of the benefits of a constant stirring of the soil. The man who cultivates continually has always a better crop than has the one who is satisfied with a hard surface. The benefits from a loose soil are, in fact, so great as what many a load of manure gives. Those who have flower-beds know how much better plants grow when the ground is stirred. In the growing season all the rain that falls is needed by the crops, and a loose soil keeps the rain which the hard ground allows to run off.

New Ideas in Asparagus Culture.—Gardeners generally are beginning to adopt the practice of giving at least one yard distance between the plants in making new plantations of asparagus. They have found that the roots run horizontally, and not directly downward, and, therefore, that it is not advisable to continue the old practice of digging down two or three feet for a narrow bed, to be filled with manure mixed with soil, on which plants are to be set only a foot apart. Large shoots of asparagus an inch in diameter cannot be had by such treatment.

Substitute for Bean Poles.—A New England farmer says: "In my own gardening I have found a most satisfactory substitute for bean poles, which latter are not only expensive, but a source of trouble and care. I plant a sunflower seed by each hill of beans, the stock answering the same purpose as the ordinary bean pole, besides providing an excellent feed for my poultry. I have been using for this purpose a mammoth variety of sunflower seed, many of the flowers of which measured fifteen inches across the seed bed."

Potato Juice as an Insect Destroyer.—As an insect destroyer the juice of the potato plant is said to be of great value; the leaves and stems are well boiled in water, and when the liquid is cold it is sprinkled over plants attacked with insects, when it at once destroys caterpillars, black and green flies, gnats, and other enemies to vegetables, and in no way impairs the growth of the plants. A peculiar odor remains, and prevents insects from coming again for a long time.

To Force Radishes.—Radishes may be grown in a few days by the following method: Let some good radish seed soak in water for twenty-four hours, and then put them in a bag and expose to the sun. In the course of the day germination will commence. The seed must then be sown in a well-manured hot-bed, and watered from time to time in lukewarm water. By this treatment the radishes will, in a very short time, acquire quite a large bulk, and be very good to eat.

Culture of Sugar-Beets.—The best sugar-beet, when properly grown, should be conical, and with a single tap-root. To grow such beets the soil should be deep, mellow, free from stones, and abundantly rich. A deep, sandy loam, with plenty of vegetable matter, may be expected to produce, with clean culture, a profitable crop of sugar-beets. A strong clay is not suitable, neither is a soil that is low and naturally wet and cold.

Weeds on Gravel Walks.—Weeds on gravel walks may be destroyed and prevented from growing again by a copious dressing of the cheapest salt. This is a better method than hand-pulling, which disturbs the gravel and renders constant raking and rolling necessary. One application early in the season, and others as may be needed, while the weeds are small, will keep the walks clean and bright.

Water Necessary to Cauliflower.—A gentleman in Colorado informs us that by irrigation he grew cauliflower-heads four feet three inches in circumference. Cauliflower is fond of water, and we have seen large plantations on the continent of Europe that were regularly watered every evening except during rainy weather.

ORCHARDS AND VINEYARDS--Update

Whether a few well-chosen trees to supply a family or thousands of trees whose fruit may be sold from a roadside stand, made into cider and vinegar, or carried to processors or storage, orchards take great care. As pesticides have been increasingly and widely used, insects and birds which served as natural controls to damaging pests have been killed off. Orchardists find their back against the wall, spraying toxic chemicals with great frequency.

The *Cyclopaedia* gives some advice which may short-circuit the pesticide cycle. Highly resistant fruit trees have been bred by State Experimental Stations such as the NYS station at Geneva, NY. Proper drainage of orchard soils, fertilization of trees within the area of their outspread branches, sprays such as tobacco stem or garlic concoctions, and mechanical measures such as wrapping young trunks against sunburn and rabbits and encouraging chickens and birds to forage among the trees will make the trees healthier and reduce risks of insect or fungal pests. Healthy trees are more resistant to attack than unhealthy ones.

As chemical controls of orchards have increased, the variety of fruits being raised has decreased. Because of problems in storage and processing, only about five or six varieties of apples are readily available, where there were hundreds in 1888.

Fruit trees come in two sizes: standard and dwarf. Dwarf trees have been bred to reach only 10-15 feet in height and to bear fruit for about 10 years. Dwarf trees yield good apples. In the espalier system, they are trained to grow like vines upon wire supports. Dwarves are heavily pruned to keep them short, with little leafage and resting on the supports. Those who expect shade from their trees and who don't mind using a ladder to pick will continue to plant standard trees. Standards also need good pruning.

Pruning helps to keep the tree healthy, growing, and producing the maximum amount of good quality fruit each year without exhaustion. A good general maxim to follow in pruning is to cut out branches which cross, to keep off suckers which will grow straight up from the crown, and to allow the greatest number of limbs the most light. Trees are trained to grow wide but not tall.

Good nurseries will be able to provide the prospective orchardist with information about planting practical varieties. J.E. Miller Nurseries in Canandaigua, NY is a reputable family nursery which does a large mail-order business. Miller's is one of the few nurseries in the country which supplies old varieties of apples.

Books may help. I recommend Roger Yepsen, Jr.'s *Trees for the Yard, Orchard and Woodlot* (Emmaus, Pa.: Rodale Press, 1974) or *Fruits for the Home Garden* by Ken & Pat Kraft (NY: William Morrow, Inc., 1968) as points to begin. County Extension agents will supply technical leaflets for large-scale or family-size orchards.

Grapes may be either European varieties (grown mostly in California) or hybrids of European and native stock. The hybrids are more capable of withstanding Northeastern winters without being lowered from their supports.

Varieties of grapes planted will depend on the climate, insect and fungus pests, and the use to which they'll be put. Table grapes, wine grapes and raisin grapes are different varieties, though there is some overlap.

I suggest people contemplating a vineyard have a look at A.J. Winkler's *General Viticulture* (Berkeley: U of California Press, 1962) in their local libraries. It is an exhaustive and scholarly approach to grapes but will repay study. Coming at grapes from quite a different point of view is the pleasant *Home Winemakers' Handbook* by Walter S. Taylor and Richard Vine (NY: Harper & Row, 1968) which traces wine from choosing varieties of vines to savouring the result.

ORCHARD AND VINEYARD.

Pruning—Making the Cut.—In pruning branches from trees with the knife, the method of making the cut is a matter of some importance. We have had some illustrations made, showing several ways, often followed, which are wrong, and the one which is right; *a* shows the right method of making the cut, at an angle of about forty-five degrees, and having the bud at the back in the best position for throwing new bark and wood quickly over the wound; *b* shows too much of the wood cut away, leaving the bud exposed and liable to die by drying or freezing; *c*, this cut was started right, but, owing to a dull knife or want of firmness in the hand, the cut was made too sloping. This

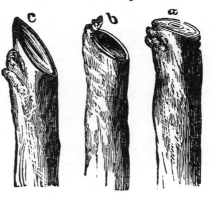

will not heal over so quickly as the cut at *a; d, e,* and *f* are all wrong; the wood above the bud dying will cause knots and perhaps decay. Crooked limbs will also result from these ways of cutting.

Pruning Deciduous Trees.—As a general rule, the less shade trees are

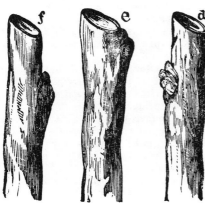

pruned the better. Nature will form a better top and a more harmonious tree in all its parts than art. Severe pruning is no longer practiced, even in fruit orchards, by our best horticulturists. The custom that formerly prevailed of pruning evergreens and other trees, so as to make top-shaped, ovate, and other fantastic tops, is no longer regarded as good taste. If you want a tree with a low-spreading top, plant one that grows that way. If you want an ovate or pyramidal top, plant a tree that will make such a top, but do not attempt to force trees to assume different forms from those which nature gives them. Each tree treated in this way is a standing lie, and proclaims to every passer-by the folly of its owner.

The true idea is to make each species assume, as nearly as possible, the typical form of that species. To do this, some pruning is sometimes necessary. If the trees are not crowded—if each one has room enough for the air and sunlight to have free access to it on all sides, it will round out and develop its full proportions, and if it does not actually attain it, will approximate its typical form. Where the lower limbs are in the way, of course they must be sacrificed; but where they are not, leave them, and you will have a finer and more thrifty tree. If a limb, as is often the case with the elm in our dry soil, extends beyond the rest, absorbing the strength and destroying the symmetry of the tree, it should be cut back while yet small.

The soft maple often throws out limbs that have no firm attachments to the body, and they will sooner or later split off; these should be removed while small. The idea of cutting back the top of a soft maple, or any other tree, to prevent it from becoming top heavy, is fallacious; it relieves for the time, but makes it worse afterward. If a soft maple, as some of them will do, breaks bodily, and continues to do so, it is better to remove it and plant another in its place. Severe pruning lowers the vitality of any ordinary tree, making it less able to bear the drouth and heat of summer and the cold of winter, and leaving it an easy prey to borers and other noxious insects.

As a strong man is able to resist disease, so a vigorous tree is able to resist the attacks of its enemies, while a feeble one succumbs.

So far as possible all limbs should be removed while small. It is rarely necessary to cut a large limb from a tree that has been properly cared for.

The Best Time to Prune Fruit Trees.— The correct principles which underlie the pruning of fruit trees are probably as imperfectly understood as any other point in fruit-growing. Most people prune in the spring, some through the winter, others in the summer. Now, after carefully observing the effects of pruning done at different seasons, I have come to the conclusion that the best time to prune is in early summer, after the first rush of sap is past, and before the trees have made much growth of new wood.

When trees are pruned in winter, a considerable time must elapse before the wounds made begin to heal over. During this time the combined action of the frost and sun are injurious to the newly-cut and exposed wood and bark, and it will take a longer time to heal over than if the wound was made at the time when the tree was beginning to make new growth.

When trees are pruned in early spring, the sap is then in a thin, watery state; it oozes out of the cut, causing premature decay and permanent injury to the tree.

When trees are pruned in early summer, after the rush of thin, watery sap is past and the tree has fairly commenced to make a new growth, the wounds will commence at once to heal over. The exposed wood will remain sound for a longer period than if cut in early spring.

Another very important point in early summer pruning is, it does not check the growth of the tree, as when it is done later in the season.

Some advocate pruning in July and August, but I would only prune then in cases where the tree was making too much wood growth, which I wanted to check and throw the tree into a bearing state.

Another very important point in pruning, and yet one which is very much neglected, is to cover the cuts with some substance to protect them from the influence of the weather. Common grafting wax, or a mixture of clay and cow manure, is beneficial; but perhaps the best thing, when it can be got pure and good, is gum shellac dissolved in alcohol to the consistency of paint. A protection of this kind is always beneficial to newly-pruned trees; it neutralizes to a great extent the injurious effects arising from pruning trees at an improper season.

Pruning Versus Mutilation.—There is, perhaps, no one item in horticulture about which so little is really understood as the principle which should govern in the pruning away of limbs and branches from trees. The following illustration will serve, perhaps, better than a long homily, to show how we would prune a tree and keep it in condition from year to year, healthy and productive. Fig. 1 exhibits a tree which has had little or no pruning; its top branches have become rather crowded, and some seasons the fruit is not well colored. We take our long stepladder and a pair of good, strong pruning shears, set our ladder just outside, underneath the limbs, and with our sharp shears cut away the small spray and limbs that cross one another and crowd the extremities, so as to prevent the sun's rays penetrating to the center of the tree. The dark, short marks indicate some of the cuts that we should make in pruning the tree. Fig. 2, shown on next page, exhibits the tree as it is often found after the mutilator, not pruner, has operated upon it. Vandals roam the country every spring claiming to know how to prune trees. We hope what we have here said and illustrated may save at least one good orchard from this system of murderous pruning.

PRUNING.—FIG. 1.

Pruning for Fruit. — By arresting or removing the little faults of his children as soon as they are shown, the wise father prevents their attaining such inveteracy as will not submit to correction, but burst out immediately with fresh misdeeds. So with orchard trees. It is a great mistake to let growth run on without restraint for two or three years, and to suppose that a pruning then will set all to rights. The fundamental rule of the art is to take away all young shoots that are not fitted to make permanent bearing branches. Remove these, the sooner the better, but remove no others. Cut out and suppress all wild shoots that issue below the graft, and whose growth would rob or smother it. Cut out all shoots in the interior of the trees that will not have light enough in summer for the leaves of any fruit buds that might form on them, and which could, therefore, not mature into fruitage. Thin the new growth all over top so that no shoot will shade another or be shaded; those that are left being such as extend the main bearing branches, which gardeners call "leaders." Often a crowding branch can be propped or braced out into open light, and so two branches be relieved with little or no pruning of either, with a gain of large fruit-producing area. One other case must be noted: that of a tree exhausted so much as to be covered with fruit buds and making no new shoots. A tree in health should make new shoots every year all over the top, at least eight inches long. If it does less, the soil is poor, or the roots are robbed or dried, or the stem is injured and cannot carry the sap, or the wood of the top has become unsound. The thing to be done then is to cut back the top, reducing it largely, to give the exhausted system less to do and more chance to recover. The vexed question of even and odd years, or fruitful and barren ones in alternation, which is so important to growers of Baldwins, Greenings, and some other winter sorts is solved most easily by a resolute thinning in the winter preceding the fruitful years, so as to reduce the bearing, and increase the wood and bud forming for the next year.

Pruning Peach Trees.—A fruit tree overloaded with fruit is very unsatisfactory to its owner. The fruit itself is of no more value than half the quantity of a better size. Then, too, the tree is often injured, so much

PRUNING.—FIG. 2.

so as to cause it to lose a year or two recovering. It is better to be satisfied with a small quantity of fruit, and this judicious pruning brings about. The *Prairie Farmer* advocates the following system of pruning peach trees: "The main branches of a young tree should be, early in spring, cut back to eighteen inches, being careful to leave on t h e m any sub-branches near their base. The next spring the resulting, or next c r o p of branches, should be cut back in about the same way, and sub-branches half of them cut clear away, leaving every other one, and those not cut away cut back one-third or one-half. The summer after this the trees should give a splendid crop of fine fruit that will need no thinning. The after cutting back and pruning should be after the same general plan, thinning out and cutting back the upper and outer branches, but never thinning out the small branches near the base of the large branches, except as above. As the trees grow older it will be necessary to cut back and thin out more, year by year, and, eventually, it will be necessary to cut back half the main branches near their base at some point just above where a thrifty young twig is growing, so as to form a vigorous head."

Necessary Precautions After Pruning.—After pruning the orchard, care should be taken to clean up and burn all the brush before the embryo insects harboring in it have time to mature. The loose bark should also be scraped off and burned, and every cluster of the eggs of the tent caterpillar be removed betimes and cast into the fire. Attention to these matters will save a great deal of vexation and loss.

Grafting Apple Trees.—Apple trees may be grafted in spring, any time after severe cold weather is past, until the leaves are fully formed. There are many different methods of grafting in vogue among nurserymen and orchardists, but for large trees in the orchard, what is called cleft grafting is the one usually practiced. In performing the operation, the main stem, if not more than an inch or two in diameter, or a branch, or any number of them on a large tree, is sawed off, and the portion remaining is split downward two inches or more with a large knife or chisel, being careful not to bruise or break the bark. Then a cion from a tree which we desire to propagate is cut, with two or three buds upon it, as shown in Fig. 1, the lower end being cut on each side, forming a long, slender wedge. The cleft in the stock may be held open with a small hard wood or iron wedge, driven in the center. When the cions are prepared, insert one on each side of the cleft, as is shown in Fig. 2, being careful to have the outside of the wood of both cion and stock exactly even, and then withdraw the wedge, and the stock will grasp and hold the cions firmly in place. The end of the stock and the side clefts should then be carefully covered with grafting wax, for the purpose of excluding air and water. To prevent the grafting wax sticking to the fingers of the operator, a little piece of tallow or other kind of grease may be applied to the hand and fingers each time, before taking hold of the wax.

When cions are to be taken from trees in the same orchard or neighborhood, they may be cut and inserted the same day, even if somewhat advanced in growth of buds; but, as a rule, the cions should be taken from the trees before the buds begin to swell in spring, and then put in a cool cellar and rolled in damp moss cloth, or buried in earth, where their growth

FIG 1.

FIG. 2.

will be retarded. Grafting trees is a very simple operation, and almost any boy who can whittle a stick can readily learn how to perform it successfully. Make a clean smooth cleft in the stock, and use a sharp knife in preparing the cion, and then see that the two join as we have directed, and there is little danger of failure if the cions are healthy and in proper condition. Strong, firm one-year-old wood should be used for this purpose; that which is about one-quarter to three-quarters of an inch in diameter is the most suitable.

The apple, pear, plum, and cherry may be grafted in the manner we have described, and by almost any one who will try.

Grafting Wax.—There are a great many recipes given for making grafting wax, but the following is, in our opinion, the best: To four pounds of resin and one of beeswax add one pint of linseed oil; put in an iron pot, heat slowly, and mix well. Pour into cold water, and pull by hand until it assumes a light color; work into sticks, and put into a cool place until wanted. In using, oil the hands, work the wax until soft, and press it tightly around the graft and over the cracks. If the day be warm, it is better to occasionally moisten the hands with water.

TRANSPLANTING LARGE TREES.—FIG. 1.

Grafting the Wild Cherry.—The common black cherry regarded as " wild " can be grafted with other and best varieties as easily as cherries usually are. Many of these trees, which produce the poorest kind of fruit, can all be top grafted, and may be made to yield an abundance of excellent fruit. Only healthy trees should be selected for grafting, and the cions should be in the best condition.

Transplanting Large Trees.—Many and various are the reasons for transplanting large trees. Many persons desire to remove from the forest to their own grounds trees of twenty or more feet in height for farming, new ornamenting, screens, or shade. Trees of more than four inches in diameter should be removed with a ball of earth attached. This operation is easily and safely performed in two different ways, as the accompanying figures indicate. When the trees are to be removed long distances, the plan used in Fig. 1 should be adopted. First dig around and loosen the tree, care being taken not to injure the roots by digging too near the tree. Place the connecting pieces (M) of the standards (R R) against the tree, to which fasten by ropes winding cloths or matting about the tree, to prevent breaking the bark. One horse attached to the rope (B) will easily raise the tree and ball of earth and place it upon the stone boat or drag (P), upon which it may be transplanted long distances without injury. It may be removed from this vehicle to the hole prepared for its reception by the same process.

Another quite common method is to use the rear wheel and axle of a farm wagon. Firmly secure on top of the center of axle a pole (S) twelve feet in length, the short end projecting from the axle two feet, to which is secured a short chain with hooks. Loosen the tree as before described; wind about the tree, close to the ground, matting or old carpet, pass around a small chain a number of times, into which catch in the hook, and by lowering the lever (S) to the ground the tree will assume the position shown in Fig. 2. The heavy ball of earth keeps the tree in an upright position, and one man holding the lever, and the other leading the horse, the tree is carried to the place for its reception, and there deposited by raising the lever.

Care of Trees After Transplanting.—Newly transplanted trees that are not starting properly should receive attention. The first suggestion is always to pour water on the surface. But little, if any, of this moisture ever reaches the roots, where it could be beneficial. Experience of late years has taught our tree planters that when the soil is firmly pressed, so as to come into immediate contact with all the roots, and of course stop all air passages among them, but little water after planting is needed. During an excessively dry spell, however, several deep holes may be made in the soil by means of an iron bar, and water poured in several times; but in ordinary seasons a liberal mulch over the surface will answer. The best restorative for a weakly tree after transplanting is to shade the bark, and this may be done by wrapping the body loosely with newspapers, allowing them to extend even to the main

TRANSPLANTING LARGE TREES.—FIG. 2.

branches, if large. Moisture over the tops is quite as helpful as at the roots, so that a thorough syringing among the branches every evening until active growth sets in will answer an excellent purpose.

Points on Pear Culture.—The cultivation, until the trees have come into their second or third year of bearing, may consist in growing corn the first year, as it affords considerable protection to the young trees from the heat of the first summer. After this some hoed crop, like potatoes, peas or beans, may be grown; and it should be fertilized with well-rotted stable manure and thoroughly cultivated. This keeps the trees supplied with food and the soil loose and friable. Hot, violent manures should never be applied to an orchard, and especially to one of pears. Use an ordinary one-horse cultivator, and a good one-horse plow. A good workman will go deep enough with such a plow, and not injure the roots as he would with a large one. By all means be sure of the efficiency and carefulness of a man before admitting him into the orchard with a horse and cultivator or plow. The damage a poor man did in one of our orchards in less than half a day would not have been covered by two or three months of his wages. A five-year-old pear tree in vigorous health is worth fully $10, and when a dozen such are injured the aggregate loss is quite an item. The horse should be a careful one, accustomed to such work.

Owing to other pressing duties, it occasionally happens that a heavy growth of fall grass is permitted in the orchard, after the vegetable crops do not longer need cultivation. It should not remain all winter, especially around the trees, as it affords snug retreats for rabbits, field mice, etc., which too frequently gnaw the bark of the young trees, sometimes completely girdling them, and causing death. To prevent this, in the late fall, with a hoe or strong iron rake, remove the grass from around each tree for two or three feet, and to make a further protection, ridge up around the trees with the plow, this ridge can be easily plowed or cultivated down in the spring to give a level surface to the orchard.

Planting hoed and well-manured crops between the trees supplies them with all the matter needed during the first few years. When the trees get too large to make it either desirable or profitable to grow such crops, manure in some form must be specially applied to make up the deficiency. Bone-dust makes a valuable dressing, as does well-rotted stable manure, which, no doubt, is the most easily obtainable on the farm. There is nothing which equals wood-ashes, and we attribute much of our success in raising heavy crops and splendid specimens of pears to the liberal use of this fertilizer. Not only did we use all that we could save on the place, but bought liberally at good prices. If enough cannot be secured to put over the whole surface spread the ashes around each tree. The best time to apply the manure is in late fall or early spring, after the plowing and before the harrowing. If there is an undue growth of wood and foliage diminish the supply of manure; and it is sometimes well to put the land down to clover (never to timothy, wheat, rye or other uncultivated grain), and let it remain one or two years in sod. It can then be plowed and planted with corn to break the sod, and the ground either used for vegetables or kept fallow.—*Agriculturist.*

Waste Bones for Trees and Vines.—The bones of fish, fowls, and the large and small pieces of bones which are purchased with beefsteak and mutton, constitute the very best food for fruit trees and grape vines, if the fragments are only placed where the roots can lay hold of them. Instead of allowing pieces of bones to be cast into the backyard, as food for stray dogs and cats, domestics should be directed to deposit everything of the sort in a small tub provided with a cover. As soon as a few pounds have accumulated, take the tub to some grape vine or fruit tree, dig a hole three or more feet long, a foot or two wide, and not less than a foot deep, into which the bones are dumped, spread over the bottom of the excavation, and covered with the soil. The more the fragments can be spread around, the better, but they should be buried so deep that a plow or spade will not reach them. The roots of growing vines or fruit trees will soon find the valuable mine of rich fertility, and will feed on the elements that will greatly promote the growth of healthy wood, and the development of fair and luscious fruit.

Many horticulturists and farmers purchase bone-dust costing not less than two cents a pound, simply to enrich the soil around and beneath their trees and vines. Fragments of bones are just as valuable as ground bone, although their elements of fertility will not be found available in so short a time as if the large pieces were reduced to atoms. Nevertheless, if large bones be buried three or four feet from a grape vine, the countless numbers of mouths at the ends of roots will soon dissolve, take up, and appropriate every particle. When cast out of the kitchen door, bones are a nuisance; whereas, if properly buried, they become a source of valuable fertility. Let every person who owns a grape vine or fruit tree save all the bones that pass through the kitchen, and bury them where they will be turned to some profit.

Orchard Management.—In three years, says a writer, I improved the production of my fruit trees from fifteen to two hundred bushels, by treating them in the following manner: I first reduced the top one-fourth, then in the fall I plowed the soil as well as I could, it being quite rocky, and turned a short furrow toward the tree. As I worked from them I let the plow fall a little lower, and when between the trees I allowed the plow to run deep, so that the water would settle away from them in the spring. I hauled a fair quantity of coarse manure, pulverized it well, and marked out the hills, measuring each hill. I planted corn and beans, and harvested a nice crop of corn, beans, and pumpkins. The following spring I repeated the same form of cultivation, and harvested the second crop of corn, beans, and pumpkins, which paid me to satisfaction. My trees began to grow very fast; and that fall I harvested seventy bushels of very good apples. The following spring I manured for the third time, planted it to potatoes, which grew very large, but rotted very badly. I made up the loss, however, by harvesting 200 bushels of large and natural fruit. I changed the production of a yellow bellflower tree from three-fourths of a bushel to seven bushels, and sold them for $1.25 per barrel, which I think a very good return for my labor. From my experience I am of the opinion that most trees have too much top for the amount of roots and a deficiency of nourishment for producing a developed fruit. I like fall or winter pruning. Always cover the cut with grafting wax or a thick paint. After removing the limbs by thinning out the center of the tree, it has a tendency to make it grow broad. Too many varieties are bad, and hardy stock is all that is needed.

The Roots of Fruit Trees.—While fruit growers are aware now that the roots of trees and plants extend to a great distance, still it is difficult to break away from the old habit of manuring about the trunks, trusting that somehow or other the fertilizer will be appropriated, and fearing that if spread broadcast it may some way become lost. It will be found difficult to place manure in an orchard or vineyard where the plants will not reach it, and if properly spread it will not be lost. Should it sink into the subsoil the roots will follow it and bring it back by the ear, as a teacher would a truant school-boy. We have observed the roots of apple trees in sand pits extending downwards ten feet. We recently followed the roots of an old grape vine twenty feet under the location of a defunct building. When we stopped digging, the roots were as large as a little finger, were four feet beneath the surface, and probably extended ten feet farther. A pile of manure about the base of this vine would have done but little good. Knowing the extent and habit of root growth, it is apparent that cultivation close about the trunks of the trees or vines is not necessary; and is often productive of more harm than good in marring and breaking, besides tempting profanity on the part of the plowman.

How to Fertilize Fruit Trees.—Here and there on all farms and in most fruit gardens will be seen an occasional tree or grape vine which seems to lack vigor—does not grow well, and yet seems to have no particular disease. The probabilities are that the tree is dying of starvation and needs a liberal supply of food. When you give it this ration do not pile a load of manure around the trunk of the tree or the body of a grape vine. That is just the place where it will do the least good. Nearest the trunk of the tree the roots are all large; the fibrous roots—the feeders—are farther off, near the ends of the roots. These only can take up the nutriment. It is always safe to assume that the roots extend as far from the trunk in every direction as do the limbs of the trees, and to properly fertilize, spread the manure all over that area. Then fork it in, and you have done a good work and·done it well. If some disease has begun its work on the tree, you will put the tree in a healthy, vigorous condition, the better enabling it to successfully contend against its enemies. We have seen numerous old pear and apple trees, bearing poor and gnarled fruit, which the owners consider of no value, which such treatment as we have outlined above would restore to their original usefulness.

A Belgian Fruit Gatherer.—We illustrate a novel little invention for gathering fruit as used by the Belgians. It is made as follows: Take a pole ten or twelve feet long, and on top of this attach a thin disk, as shown by the illustration, about six inches in diameter, set with wooden teeth, just like the teeth of a hayrake. Carefully placing this under a pear so that the pear rests on the disk, and giving a slight twist, it will at once detach and bring down the fruit without marring or injuring it in any way.

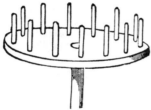

BELGIAN FRUIT GATHERER.

How to Renew an Orchard.—We would plow the orchard in the fall, and then either cross-plow it in the spring or cultivate it thoroughly, according to its condition. Thorough working the ground will help the orchard and also the crop. It should be plowed shallow, especially under the trees, and care should be taken not to break off or mutilate the roots. Much damage is done to orchards by careless plowing. Corn is the best hoed crop for an orchard, and beans the next best. Potatoes should never be planted in an orchard, as they exhaust the potash from the soil, and this is just what the apple trees require. Barley, or spring rye, is the best adapted to be sown for the seeding. Under the apple trees the grain should be thinly scattered, for much seed would only be wasted on account of the shade, but the grass seed should be put on thickly. The least exhaustive crop should always be grown in an orchard, or else the trees will be robbed of needed sustenance; hence it is always best to pasture the ground rather than mow it: nothing will run an orchard down so fast as to make it a meadow, as it is a double robbery. The ground may be plowed in the spring, but for an orchard, we would prefer turning it over in the early autumn, in order that the trees may have the full benefit of the decayed sod and the more mellow soil.

Errors in Fruit Tree Culture.—Deep planting is one error—to plant a tree rather shallower than it formerly stood is really the right way, while many plant a tree as they would a post. Roots are of two kinds—the young and tender rootlets, composed entirely of cells, the feeders of the trees, always found near the surface getting air and moisture; and roots of over one year old, which serve only as supporters of the trees, and as conductors of its food. Hence the injury that ensues when the delicate rootlets are so deeply buried in earth. Placing fresh or green manure in contact with the young roots is another great error; the place to put manure is on the surface, where the elements disintegrate, dissolve, and carry it downward. Numerous forms of fungi are generated and reproduced by the application of such manures directly to the roots, and they immediately attack the tree. It is very well to enrich the soil at transplanting the tree, but the manure, if it be in contact with or very near the roots, should be thoroughly decomposed.

Fruit Tree Culture.—A writer in the *Western Agriculturist* gives these rules, which are of wide application: 1. Instead of "trimming up" trees according to the old fashion, to make them long-legged and long-armed, trim them down, so as to make them even, snug and symmetrical. 2. Instead of manuring heavily in a small circle at the foot of the tree, spread the manure, if needed at all, broadcast over the whole surface. 3. Instead of spading a small circle about the stem, cultivate the whole surface broadcast. 4. Prefer a well pulverized, clean surface in an orchard, with a moderately rich soil, to heavy manuring and a surface covered with a hard crust and weeds and grass. 5. Remember that it is better to set out ten trees with all the necessary care to make them live and flourish, than to set out a hundred trees, and have them all die from carelessness. 6. Remember that tobacco is a poison, and will kill insects rapidly if properly applied to them, and is one of the best drugs for freeing fruit trees rapidly of small vermin.

Protection of Trees.—Mr. A. M. Daniels, in an address before the Chenango County Farmers' Club, in relation to the protection of trees, stated as the result of his observation that, "when the fruit is stimulated to rapid growth by an abundance of juices in the tree, it is affected by the hot sun and drying wind. In the disease called the frozen sap blight, so disastrous to young orchards when it affects the trunk, the tree dies. This occurs more frequently after severe winters, by inactive or arrested circulation. Young orchards should be protected from the hot sun or cold of winter by the use of straw, cloth, or board boxes. The scorching rays of the sun should never be allowed to come on the body of a tree, and Nature by the foliage provides against it. No fruit tree can stand freezing and thawing in spring without being injured by it. The great object to be attained in raising a young orchard is ripened and mature growth. When that is attained we are on the road to success. Late growth should not be stimulated."

Fruit Cellars.—Fruit cellars need careful oversight; for the late sorts to come to proper perfection, and to keep well, they must be in a temperature as low as may be without freezing; it must not be forgotten that fruit in ripening gives off heat, and this must be regulated by the admission of cold air from without. In ripening, a considerable amount of carbonic acid is given off, which would be of use in retarding the ripening, but very dangerous if allowed to accumulate in the cellar of a dwelling, hence ventilation by means of a chimney, or in some other manner, is a matter that must be attended to.

Thinning Fruit.—An orchardist who makes his trees bear a moderate crop every year, of larger and finer fruit than when crowded, gives the following directions for doing the work: A light ladder is used to give ready access to any part of the tree. The branch is held in the left hand, while with sheep shears in the right, every bunch of apples is cut off, leaving a part of the stem of each fruit. This is done as soon as the blossoms have fallen, and before the young fruit has attained any size. When this branch is entirely cleaned, the next branch is skipped, and the third cleaned of the fruit like the first, and so on until every alternate branch is divested of its fruit. This work is not done on the small limbs here and there over the tree, but on main branches, and equally on both sides of the tree. Of medium-sized trees, an active man will go over fifteen or twenty in a day

Destroying the Plum Curculio.—A great deal of useless advice has been given out concerning easy methods of destroying the plum and peach curculio. In most parts of the country it is impossible to raise plums unless one exercises a daily warfare against the insects. Persons who have two or three plum trees about the yard should succeed in raising fruit enough for their own use, but this they are seldom able to accomplish. The less trees one has, the greater will be the proportionate number of insects to attack them.

Such methods as burning coal tar under the trees, hanging cobs, saturated with molasses, among the limbs, are usually of no avail in saving a crop of plums or peaches. The only sure method is persistent catching. The curculios spend their nights near the base of the tree, under chips and barks. Early in the morning they ascend the trees, to lay their eggs in the young fruit.

There are two modes of catching them. The one devised by Mr. Ransom, of Benton Harbor, Mich., is to nicely smooth the earth about the base of the trees, and to lay a few small blocks of wood or chips on the surface. The beetles crawl under these for shelter, and can be taken very early in the morning before they ascend the trees. The chips should be examined as soon as one can see in the morning. This is the method most practiced in the extensive peach belt of Michigan.

The other method is to spread a large sheet under the tree, and jar the beetles off on to it by means of one or two quick blows with a long-handled mallet or bumper. Each of the large branches should be struck, and the mallet should be wound with cloth to prevent injury to the trees. This practice should be followed early in the morning also, as when the days get warm the beetles are too lively to be caught. Many of the best peach and plum growers practice both these methods. In the case of a few trees about a yard both should be used, and there will be little doubt as to a good reward in fruit. The practice should be followed up every morning for a couple of weeks after the blossoms fall, and at wider intervals until the insects disappear. A sheet may be stretched over a large wooden frame for convenience in handling.

A Suggestion to Growers of Plums.—If you want a good crop of plums or damsons, as soon as your trees are out of blossom, and the fruit formed, keep a hen with a brood of young chickens tied beneath the tree, and give her a range as wide as the boughs of the tree, and she and her brood will destroy every curculio, and reward your care and forethought with a crop of luscious plums. Keep the chickens there until the fruit be half or more than half grown.

Manure for Fruit Trees.—It is best to abstain from the use of stimulating animal manures, unless decomposed, and previously composted with mellow soil. Nothing is better than wood ashes to induce a sound, healthy growth and good yield. The scrapings of the wood pile mixed with ashes, decayed leaves, and road washings, are all of value as manures. Salt sprinkled around the trees, or applied in the form of brine, is frequently beneficial, especially where the fruit falls before ripening.

Maxims for Fruit Growers.—All fruit trees like a rather dry, rich soil. On a cold clayey bottom diseases are usually frequent. Do not plant deep; cut off tap roots, and encourage surface fibres. Surface manuring is the best mode of doing this after the tree is planted. Do not allow anything to grow vigorously around your trees the first year of planting, nor allow the soil to become hard or dry.

Insects Injurious to Fruit Trees.—To keep the insects from the trees requires the closest observance, and, soon as found, destruction must commence. Their habits should be learned as much as possible. When the insects are in the winged state is the time they lay their eggs. They multiply with astonishing rapidity, one insect often hatching thousands in a single season. June is the time most of the insects lay their eggs, and at that time bonfires should be built at night, when the insects will fly into them and be destroyed; or, if you have only a few trees in the garden, get some bottles with wide mouths, and fill half full with a mixture of water, molasses, and vinegar, and tie up in the trees; empty in a week, and fill again. And at that time (June) the bark should be washed with soft soap, the trunk and the limbs as far as can be reached; also sprinkle a handful of coarse salt around the roots of the tree—we have found it valuable. Put coal ashes, about a peck, around the base of each tree, as it not only drives away the grubs, but acts as a fertilizer. The best way to kill insects on the tree is to dust air-slaked lime over it when the dew is on the tree; or, steep tobacco stems in boiling water, and, when cool, syringe the tree.

Birds are of great value in destroying insects, and they should have the best of care given them, to encourage their building and living on the place, especially our common sparrow (not the English sparrow), wrens, bluebirds, robins, quails, etc. Don't allow them to be frightened or shot at, and they will pay well.

Toads and bats destroy a great many insects in the spring. As the green fruit drops it should be gathered up and fed to the hogs, for it contains a worm which burrows in the ground. Where small quantities of trees are grown, as in the garden, it is a good plan to fence in the trees, and let the hogs or chickens eat the green, wormy fruit as it falls; we have known plum trees to bear enormous and paying crops when treated in this way.

Pear Blight and Peach Yellows.—Pear blight and peach yellows are subjects of prolific and dissenting discussion at every horticultural meeting. Mr. Satterthwait, in a report on the diseases of fruit trees to the Pennsylvania State Horticultural Society, points out the great difference between the two diseases; namely, that while the yellows is extremely contagious, no one need fear to plant a pear tree where a blighted one has been removed. He stated that he had thousands of trees, vigorous and entirely healthy, that were planted beside the stumps of trees killed by the pear blight, and not one was ever affected. He regards it as proved to a certainty that pear blight is an entirely different disease in its nature from the peach yellows, and he mentioned, as additional proof, that it is a usual occurrence for pear trees to be locally affected, or in a single branch, without the disease spreading, and the tree entirely recovering its health and vigor.

Mr. Satterthwait reported favorably of the Kieffer pear, about which opinions are so variable   With him it has proven not only wonderfully productive, but handsome in appearance and gaining high prices in market.   He believes the quality of this much-disputed pear depends largely on properly ripening the fruit.   His plan consists in packing the pears in wooden boxes, containing about one bushel each, and placing them in a cool, dry cellar, one on top of the other.   In this connection it may be well to state that C. M. Hovey, of Boston, is credited with saying that the Kieffer is the least satisfactory of all his eight hundred varieties of the pear—another indication that the Kieffer gives different results in different localities under varying circumstances.

Tomato Leaves a Remedy for the Curculio.

"I planted a peach orchard," writes M. Story, of the Society of Horticulture of France, "and the trees grew well and strongly.   They just commenced to bud when they were invaded by the curculio (pulyon), which insects were followed, as frequently happens, by ants.   Having cut some tomatoes, the idea occurred to me that, by placing some of the leaves around the trunk and branches of the peach trees, I might preserve them from the rays of the sun, which are very powerful.   My surprise was great, upon the following day, to find the trees entirely free from their enemies, not one remaining, except here and there where a curled leaf prevented the tomato from exercising its influence.   These leaves I carefully unrolled, placing upon them fresh ones from the tomato vine, with the result of banishing the last insect and enabling the trees to grow with luxuriance.   Wishing to carry still further my experiment, I steeped in water some leaves of the tomato, and sprinkled with this infusion other plants, roses, and oranges.   In two days these were also free from the innumerable insects which covered them, and I felt sure that, had I used the same means with my melon patch, I should have met with the same result.   I therefore deem it a duty I owe to the Society of Horticulture to make known this singular and useful property of the tomato leaves, which I discovered by the merest accident."

The Codling Moth and Other Enemies of the Apple.

This old enemy of the farmer is now getting in his work upon the growing apples. Where an orchard is infested with them, we know of no reliable method of getting rid of them and saving the crop.   The curculio, which is so destructive to the plum crop, is of late quite as damaging to the apples, in some sections doing much more harm than the former; and there is still anothe pest which is working a terrible harm to the crop—the apple maggot (*Tri peta Pomonella*).   This burrows in the apple, often several maggots bein found in the same apple.   The eggs are laid by a small fly, somewhat reser bling the common house-fly, but much smaller, through a small opening the skin, made with its ovipositor.

The best guard against these pests is for every farmer who has an orchard to keep sheep or swine running in it all the season through.   These will eat up every infected apple and thus destroy the larvæ, which, if left unmolested, will bring forth a crop of pests for next year's crop.   If every one would do this, it is safe to assume that the ravages of these pests would be materially decreased.

Diseased Cherry Trees.

Many of our neighbors' cherry trees are becoming knotty, and dying, writes a correspondent of *The Rural New Yorker*. A lady narrated in our hearing, a few evenings since, her experience with a tree of the same description. A large tree, of the common red variety, stood by the kitchen door. The body and limbs were knotty and rough, the fruit scanty and worthless; the dead leaves in fall were continually drifting over the porch and walk; in fact, in the good housewife's eyes, the tree was simply a nuisance, and she importuned her husband to remove it. He refused to do this, however, and she determined to kill the tree. First, a barrel of beef brine was poured about the roots, and this was followed by boiling suds, every wash day. The result was satisfactory, but far from that anticipated. The following season the tree was loaded with superior fruit, and was free from all knots and other defects. The enormous crop and changed appearance of the tree might not have been attributable to the application of brine and soap-suds, yet we believe the experiment to be worthy of trial.

Kerosene as an Insect Destroyer.—Kerosene is a cheap and effective insecticide where it can be applied without injury to the growing tree or plant, but to what extent it can be safely used has not been fully determined, the results obtained not being uniform. Spraying kerosene upon the leaves of cotton killed the plant. The bark of elm-trees, around which bands of felt saturated with kerosene had been applied, was destroyed wherever the oil reached it. The trunks of orange-trees which had been wet with kerosene to destroy scale insects were denuded of the greater part of the bark to which the oil had been applied. On the other hand, a bark louse, which was very abundant upon some ivy, was destroyed by the application of pure kerosene, with no apparent bad results to the vine.

Protection Against Pear Blight.—The *Gardener's Monthly* gives a statement from G. R. Dykeman, of Shippensburg, Pa., of his experiments in applying oil to the trunks of fruit trees—a practice which has been strongly recommended for its beneficial effects, among other things as a protection against pear blight. Mr. D. applied oil last year to 600 peach trees, 200 apple, several pear and plum trees, and 100 quince. All the peach trees, five years planted, were killed; the other trees were not injured. Other peach trees were painted with refuse lard and linseed oil, and these are all dead. The object in greasing was to keep the rabbits off. Oil is sometimes applied for the white scale.

Injuries to Trees.—Injuries to trees should be repaired as soon as discovered. Limbs broken by snow and ice must be sawed off to make a smooth wound, and this covered with paint, varnish, or wax. Barking by mice or rabbits often looks more serious than it really is. The majority of cases will recover if the wound is protected by a thick poultice of cow-dung and clayey loam, bound on with a piece of coarse material. In very severe cases the tree may be saved by connecting the bark above and below the wound, by means of twigs of the same tree; the ends are chamfered, and inserted under the bark above and below, to bridge over the wound, covering the exposed parts with grafting wax.

Protection Against the Plum Curculio.—A fruit grower states that he kept a plum tree from curculios by sprinkling the ground under the tree with corn meal. This induced the chickens to scratch and search. The meal was strewn every morning from the time the trees blossomed until the fruit was large enough to be out of danger. The consequence was that the fowls picked up the curculios with the meal, and the tree, being saved from the presence of the insect, was wonderfully fruitful.

Suggestions to Fruit Growers.—I find that lime, wood ashes and old iron put around the roots of declining fruit trees have a very beneficial effect, writes a fruit grower of many years' experience. These fertilizers restore the tree to a healthy condition, and also greatly improve the fruit in quality and quantity. I made the application on a Windsap and Never Fail, about half a bushel of mixed lime and ashes to each, and dug it in with a hoe some six feet around the trunk, and put the old iron immediately around the base of each.

The trees put forth with renewed vigor, bloomed abundantly, and yielded a good crop of fruit. An excellent wash for trees may be made thus: Heat an ounce of salsoda to redness in an iron pot, and dissolve it in one gallon of water, and while warm apply it to the trunk. After one application the moss and old bark will drop off and the trunk will be quite smooth. The wash has highly recuperative properties, making old trees bear anew.

I have tried soft soap as a wash with good results, and also a coating of lime in the spring season, which is a fine specific for old trees. The question is often asked, is it best to manure trees in the fall or spring? I have found the summer season to be a good time; I have much faith in mulching, especially young trees, for several seasons after they are planted. Apple trees are said to have two growths during the season—the secondary growth takes place after midsummer, hence it is that a top-dressing of good manure, and also coarse litter, facilitates the late growth, and often produces very marked results in the habit and formation of the tree.

The good effect that mulching has to young trees is, that it wards off the intense heat of the sun from the tender roots, and also has a tendency to hold moisture. A good top-dressing of stable manure in the fall, around young trees, with a good many corn cobs cast over the surface of the soil, give satisfactory results.

Ants on Young Trees.—An authority says that ants do not destroy trees. The ants are after the lice which are hurting the trees. These lice exude a sweet substance which attracts the ants, and the ants do no harm. To get rid of the lice make a solution of whale-oil soap, and add to a pailful one drachm of carbolic acid. Syringe or spray this on the under side of the leaves and it will either kill or drive away the lice, and the ants will be seen no more.

Diseased Peach Trees.—The following is said to be a sure remedy for the yellows in peach trees: " One part of saltpetre to two of salt, placed close to the body of a tree before a rain. It seems not only to destroy any fungoid growth of vermin which may be infesting the roots, but to act as an excellent fertilizer."

Suggestion Regarding Apple Trees.—It is a good idea to wrap the trunks of apple trees with burlap sacks, and to examine the wrappings every few days, or at least every week, to ascertain if any of the grubs or worms of the codling moth have found their way into them, that they may be destroyed.

The Peach Borer.—A fruit-grower placed tobacco-stems around the trunks of peach trees, and there is not the slightest sign of a borer in any of the trees so treated. He set the stems around the butts of the trees, and tied them at the top. It keeps off rabbits as well in winter.

Fruit Growing Jottings.—"Line upon line, precept upon precept," says a Southern fruit grower, must be written regarding the proper manner of planting out fruit trees; not that there exists a great diversity of opinion, but because so little heed is paid to the plain teachings of nature and common sense. "The way father or grandfather did it" is authority for the majority, and they seek no further knowledge.

Now the world moves, and many new and valuable methods have been devised which insure the desired kind and quality of fruit, hasten maturity and prevent decay. The non-progressive orchardist sells his fruit for a nominal figure, whenever he has any to sell, which is not often, and is continually complaining because his orchard "doesn't pay." It *does* pay for all the labor bestowed upon it, but it will not pay for what it does not receive.

Any kind of a fruit tree is an enormous feeder if it produces any amount of fruit. Who can reasonably expect to receive barrel upon barrel from any given tree, year after year, when nothing is fed to it? As well might the owner expect to work a week on the memory of a Sunday dinner.

Trees should be fed, therefore, and liberally, too, if large crops of fine fruit are expected from them.

The old-fashioned way of crowding trees in the space devoted to orchard purposes is still persisted in, notwithstanding the teachings of nature to the contrary. Trees are crowded in the rows like lodgers in a tenement house, and the results are as disastrous in one case as in the other. Trees, like human beings, need air and light. They *must* have these, or their lives do not reach three score years and ten. Fruit *will not* grow in the shade, and it is beyond the power of any man to cause it to do so.

'Tis true, when trees are young, a proper space seems unreasonably large—there seems to be a waste, but there really is none. It is questionable if planting small crops, like strawberries, melons, tomatoes, etc., is advisable, even in the earlier stages of growth, and it certainly is not unless a liberal quantity of some proper fertilizer is applied. As the tree enlarges and reaches out its arm-like branches, it asks for more food; it also asks that God's sunlight may be permitted to kiss it from topmost branch to root, and unless this request is granted it shoots skyward, bearing no fruit except upon its highest branches, and becomes liable to be attacked by numerous diseases.

Who has not noticed that a tree, standing solitary and alone, *always* bears a liberal quantity of fruit? Who has not noticed that such trees are invariably healthy? Who has not remarked that if the entire orchard was like this or that solitary tree, there would be money in fruit growing? Must so plain a lesson be unheeded? Can we not learn so simple a lesson without paying the immense price we do for tuition? The number of trees upon a given area does not determine the value of the orchard. If they are in excess of the proper number, they certainly are, comparatively, of little worth.

One argument used by those who favor close planting is that the shade thereby produced kills the grass and weeds which would steal the life-blood of the tree. This argument is born of pure laziness, and if carried into effect, as it too often is, the tree is deprived of its means of thrift, that its loafing owner may not blister his hands or burn his neck in his efforts to keep grass and weeds from choking his trees.

We have often walked through the orange groves on the lower Mississippi and been amazed at the imbecility so extensively displayed. A dense forest instead of an orchard, dead limbs and clinging moss, close thorny tops with small, sour, gnarly, diseased fruit on the extremities, is the rule. Occasionally we find an orchard owned by a man who uses his brains for some useful purpose, and there we find fine trees, with sunshine all around them, with light, open branches, clean and smooth; large, perfect fruit on every twig and branch from top to bottom, far better in quality than his neighbor produces. In the first instance the fruit is difficult to dispose of, and prices are ruinous. The owner is always in debt and always will be. In the other case the fruit finds eager purchasers at remunerative figures. The owner "gets ahead" in the world by using a small modicum of brains with his muscle.

In raising fruit trees for profit, the following general principles should not be overlooked: 1. Effective drainage; 2. Thorough preparation; 3. Liberal fertilization; 4. Procuring best varieties; 5. Intelligent cultivation; and each of these general principles may be sub-divided, and each will afford the owner a theme for constant study.

That fruit growing, as now practiced, is non-paying, we are ready to admit; that it may be made immensely profitable, we confidently assert. To attain this desired object something must be done besides blindly treading in the footsteps of old ways and expecting nature to perform impossibilities.

The whole Southern country can be made a vast fruit-field. Any and every man may literally "sit under his own vine and fig tree." Millions can be annually added to our material wealth. There need be no poverty in such a country, and there will be none in the near future, when our almost boundless resources are more fully developed.

What Pears Shall I Grow ?—What is said regarding the growing of apples, pears, field crops, flowers, or any plant or crop having a place in our agricultural or gardening operations, must be said with reference to certain wants, conditions, circumstances, or localities, if the directions would possess any value. No rule suits every case; no crop or plant is applicable to every locality; no advice meets every condition. Still, there are certain well-understood principles which are of value, because embodying the accumulated results of the best practice, under varying conditions and circumstances.

Now, as regards pears, a farmer or gardener who is to set a number of trees in spring would naturally ask, shall I set Dwarfs or Standards ? To this there might be given several answers, and they would take shape something after this form: For profit, for permanency, for market purposes, the Standard; for quick returns at the expense of short life, for grounds of small extent, for family uses, the Dwarf. The Standards are long-lived, grow larger, and produce more fruit (one or two varieties excepted) than the Dwarfs. Besides, the trees seem to have the habit of growing wood for future use—a good quality where one is planting for profit and permanency. The Dwarfs, on the other hand, come into bearing young, are well adapted for garden culture, or where a few pears are wanted for family use, but at ten or a dozen years old have seen their best days.

The tree is most at home in a rather heavy loam, but it must be warm and rich, kept clean and mellow by frequent culture—something the trees delight in during the growing season. Animal manure, wood ashes, and farm compost are the best fertilizers, and these, as is well understood, should be applied in the fall. The best pear-growers are united in the belief that thorough and systematic pruning—not with saw and knife, on the butchering principle, but the pinching off all surplus young shoots, when not over four to six inches long—regulates the growth and welfare of the trees, and has a tendency to induce the maturity of the fruit spurs, by which means an earlier and better quality of fruit is obtained, while the tree itself is kept uniform, well balanced and handsome. If those not experienced in pear culture are to set out trees, they certainly cannot have a better guide than to ascertain from growers in their own localities the varieties best adapted to their soil, situation, local circumstances, rather than to learn these points by their own, perhaps expensive, experience. A day spent in obtaining this information among one's neighbors will be time well used.

After all, one likes to see varieties. So here is one, made up after much study and inquiry, which it is believed will not vary greatly from the list which a hundred of the best growers in the best pear sections of New England would recommend. It is true some we have placed high on the list might be put down a peg or two, and others brought to the top which we have placed further down; but a list of the best eight varieties would be very likely to include these sorts, in about these positions: 1. Bartlett, a general favorite, of admirable quality and always salable at the highest price. 2. Seckel, high flavor, productive, uniformly bringing a good price in market. 3. Sheldon, a fine grower and good bearer, selling for the highest price. 4. Beurre d'Anjou, an excellent, productive and profitable sort. 5. Duchesse d'Angouleme, very popular and of the highest quality. 6. Beurre Bosc, an esteemed late sort, high flavored and much in demand as a market pear. 7. Lawrence, a good bearing sort, one of the best winter pears. 8. Vicar of Wakefield, very productive, and, as it ripens out of season of most others, finds a ready market at good prices.

Girdling Fruit Trees.—Some years ago, on an Iowa farm, a span of spirited horses, hitched to a wagon, got away from the driver and ran through the orchard, running over and badly barking some dozen trees. This was early in June. The next year those trees, and especially the limbs most barked and scarred, were full of fruit, while there was a very limited quantity on the balance of the orchard.

But what is the philosophy of this girdling trees or vines to make them bear fruit? Trees and vines do not grow merely by the absorption of moisture and material direct from the earth. It is true the roots take up from the earth the water and mineral matter necessary for plant growth, but it does not go directly to the part where it is to stay. But these go up, not between the bark and wood, but in the body of the tree or vine to the leaves, where it is combined with the carbon which is absorbed by the leaves, and goes through Nature's secret laboratory of combining water, mineral and carbon, until they are sufficiently digested to be used as wood growth, when it passes downward and is deposited in the infinitesimal cells beneath the bark. So that the growth is made by the downward flow of this prepared material for wood growth.

Now, if the tree or vine be girdled on the body or limbs, this prepared sap cannot pass below where the bark is taken off, and consequently that part above the girdle receives more than its share of sap, while none is supplied to the body below the girdle. Thus the limbs are crowded with growth food, which causes the development of fruit buds—makes the limbs grow faster and the fruit larger. But this process, if the main body of the tree is operated on, will in the end ruin the tree. The body and roots must have nourishment as well as the branches, and this girdling deprives them of this support. If this system is practiced at all, it should be only a part, leaving the ungirdled limbs to supply nourishment to the balance of the tree. June is the time girdling is done, which is only intended as preparatory to the next year's crop. It is claimed, however, that girdling in June makes a more perfect development of the fruit then on the limbs.

Girdling is done by taking out a rim of bark entirely around the tree, limb or vine, not over one-fourth of an inch wide. Sometimes this space is healed up the first year, but certainly the second year, if the tree be not too feeble and sickly. We advise all to go slowly and carefully in this matter, but it is worthy of an experiment by all.

But yet there are many things which need studying, and diverse matters should be reconciled. One contends that girdling stops the rapid growth of the tree, and causes a more abundant fruitage. Another that girdling causes an abnormal growth of the limb, and the largely-increased production of fruit. Great are the mysteries of Nature.

Covering for Wounds of Trees.—It often happens that, either by intention, as in pruning, or by accident, trees are wounded in various ways. A common practice is to cover large wounds with coal tar; but this is objected to by some as injurious to the tree. Experiments made in the orchards and gardens of the Pomological Institute, at Ruthlegen, in Germany, go to show, however, that its true use is not injurious; but that, on the contrary, a callous readily forms under the tar, on the edges of the wound, and that the wounded part is thus protected from decay. There is, nevertheless, another objection: for if the tar is applied a little too thick, the sun melts it, and it runs down on the bark of the tree. This can be obviated by mixing and stirring and thus incorporating with the tar about three or four times its weight of powdered slate, known as slate-flour—the mixture being also known as plastic slate and used for roofing purposes. It is easily applied with an old knife or flat stick, and though it hardens on the surface, it remains soft and elastic underneath. The heat of the sun does not melt it, nor does the coldest winter weather cause it to crack—neither does it peel off.

The same mixture is also useful for other purposes in the garden. Leaky water-pots, barrels, pails, gutters, sashes, etc., can be easily repaired with it, and much annoyance and loss of time be thus avoided. It will stick to any surface, provided it be not oily; and as it does not harden when kept in a mass, it is always ready for use. A gallon will last for a long time.

A most excellent preparation for small wounds and for grafting, is thus prepared: Melt a pound of rosin over a slow fire. When melted, take it from the fire and add two ounces of balsam of fir (Canada Lalsam), or two ounces of Venice turpentine (not spirits of turpentine), stirring it constantly. As soon as it is cool enough, mix in four to six ounces of alcohol of 95 degrees strength—according to the season—until it is as thick as molasses. It keeps well in close-corked bottles for a long time. Should it become too thick, by the gradual evaporation of the alcohol, it is easily thinned by putting the bottle in warm water and stirring in sufficient alcohol to bring it to a proper fluidity. It is applied with a brush.

This preparation is much better than liquid grafting wax composed of resin, beef-tallow and spirits of turpentine, which often granulates. If there be any danger that the cions will dry up by evaporation, they may, beneficially, be brushed over with this composition, it being first made more fluid by adding alcohol. By this means I succeeded, in February of last year, in grafting a single eye of Ægle Sepinaria upon a lemon tree, in a dry fitting-room, without the use of any glass covering.

Preserving Fruit.—Light and heat are the agents in ripening fruits. The sagacious pomologist, therefore, keeps them in a dark place and at as low a temperature as possible short of freezing. Heat and moisture cause decay. Hence the fruit room, in addition to being kept cool, is also kept dry. These three conditions were observed by Professor Myce in his system of preservations, ice being used for cooling, and proper dryers for taking up the superabundant moisture. We have had ripe tomatoes kept for three months in such a house, and in the most perfect manner. Fruit-growers may arrive sufficiently near the mark, so that fruit may be kept perfectly during the cold months, by means of frost-proof walls, and a careful system of ventilation, avoiding a thorough draft.

Since fruit is easily affected by odors, care should be taken that the air of any fruit house should be kept clean and sweet. To this end nothing but fruit should be kept in the fruit house— at least nothing that will give off unpleasant odors. So particular are some in this respect that they will not keep apples and pears in the same room. To insure perfect cleanliness, the walls and floors should be frequently whitewashed with lime. We see no reason why the sub-earth air duct system may not be one of the best means for winter ventilation, as it certainly must be for summer ventilation.

With care fruits may be retarded in their ripening for long periods. When wanted for use they are removed to a warm and light place, where they quickly mature. When extra fine specimens are to be preserved, they are carefully packed in some dry odorless substance, as cotton-wool, bran, buckwheat hulls, dry oak leaves, or pure sand. Land plaster is said to be an excellent means for saving apples through the winter intact. A thin layer of plaster is placed in the bottom of the barrel, then a layer of apples, and so alternately layer of plaster and apples until the barrel is filled, when the barrel is headed and kept in a cool place until spring, coming out sound and intact. This plan should keep russets, and other varieties liable to shrivel, and those wishing to keep apples as late as possible, and having no fruit house, may find this plan valuable. There will be no loss in the plaster, for it will be worth all it costs, and more, for sowing on the land after the apples are used

Bark Lice on Apple Trees.—Judicious pruning of the branches, draining the land where the trees stand, manuring the soil and keeping it free from grass and weeds, all have the effect to promote vigorous growth, and are therefore useful in preventing the depredations of bark lice. Unless a vigorous growth of a tree can be insured, it is of little use to apply substances to kill the lice. The lady-bird, whose presence should always be welcomed on farms, is the mortal enemy of the bark louse, as it is of many other sorts of insects. But hurtful insects increase so much faster than useful birds do that we may never expect to see the latter exterminate the former. Indeed, no amount of cultivation and no number of birds ever collected in an orchard will be sufficient to clear it of the scale bark lice, if they are generally distributed among the trees. If but a few trees have bark lice on them, and they are well covered with them, it is best to cut them up. This heroic treatment will prevent their spreading to other trees. The time to kill the insects is when they begin to hatch. They are most readily killed by applying some wash to the bark with a stiff brush or swab. The articles most highly recommended for killing the lice are strong lye made of wood ashes, a solution of caustic soda of potash, diluted soft soap, and a mixture of lime whitewash and kerosene oil. If the latter is employed, the proportions of the mixture should be one pint of kerosene to a gallon of the white-wash. Whatever substances are chosen, they should be applied thoroughly. To insure complete destruction of the insect, a second application should be made some days after the first.

Top Grafting Trees.—A practical fruit grower gives the following as his mode of top grafting: I have in a measure discarded the old system of cleft grafting, for a cheap, safer and easier way. I save the cions by cutting them in the fall or early winter, pack in sand or sawdust and keep in a cool cellar. After the trees have come out in leaf, during May and June, cut a bud from the cion and insert under the bark well tied and waxed to keep out the air and water, setting one bud in each leading limb all over the tree. In the course of two or three weeks these buds will have connected or else have died. For all that have connected saw the limbs off above the bud and throw the growth into them. Those that have died set again in July or August with buds taken from the new growth of wood, and cut them off the next spring. I set tops in that way in twenty seedling apple trees twelve years old in June, 1878, putting in on an average twelve to the tree. In 1884, six years from setting, they have forty bushels of Stark apples, worth one dollar per bushel. The expense of budding was ten dollars. If the same trees had been changed by cleft grafting the change would have cost two or three times that amount.

Hints on Marketing Pears.—Pears, whether early or late, should never remain on the tree until they become mellow. Whenever they have made their growth they should be gathered. It is easy to tell the proper condition by observing the ease with which the stem parts from the tree. If, on taking hold of the pear and lifting it, the stem readily breaks away from the spur to which it is attached, the fruit has received all the nourishment it can get from the tree, and the sooner it is gathered the better. Pears are sent to market in crates and half barrels; especially fine specimens are sent in shallow boxes, only deep enough for a single layer of fruit, and each pear is wrapped in thin white paper. Extra specimens of any of the standard kinds will bring enough more to pay for this extra care in packing. The early varieties mature quicker after gathering than the later kinds, but all should reach the market in a firm and hard condition. As with all other fruits, it will pay to carefully assort pears. Make three lots, firsts and seconds for market, and the third for keeping at home—for the pigs, if need be; there is positively no sale for poor pears.

Ants in the Orchard.—Many of the leading orchard proprietors in northern Italy and southern Germany are cultivators of the common black ant, an insect they hold in high esteem as the fruit grower's best friend. They establish ant-hills in their orchards, and leave the police service of their fruit trees entirely to the colonists, which pass all their time in climbing up the stems of the fruit trees, cleansing their boughs and leaves of malefactors, mature as well as embryotic, and descending laden with spoils to the ground, where they comfortably consume or prudently store away their booty. They never meddle with sound fruit, but only invade such apples, pears and plums as have already been penetrated by the canker, which they remorselessly pursue to its fastness within the very heart of the fruit. Nowhere are apple and pear trees so free from blight and destructive insects as in the immediate neighborhood of a large ant-hill five or six years old. The favorite food of ants would appear to be the larvæ and pupæ of those creatures which spend the whole of their brief existence in devouring the tender shoots and juvenile leaves of fruit trees.

Cultivating the Orchard.— A successful fruit grower pursues the following plan: He plows his orchard one way, leaving strips close to the trees about eight feet wide, and plants potatoes, covering them with straw. In the fall, when he digs his potatoes, he piles the straw, and the next spring he plows the ground crosswise and plants again, using the same straw. After the straw has been used two years, it is turned under in the fall, to manure the ground. In this way his orchard is manured with very little trouble, and he cultivates his orchard at the same time. He says that he does not believe, from his own experience, that it is good for fruit trees to have the plow run any closer than four feet on each side, but thinks it better to cultivate in this way between the rows than to seed down to grass and pasture.

Hints on Gathering Apples and Pears.—Most people are disposed to gather the autumn fruits too soon. A rule is generally adopted by gardeners, that if the pips of the apples or pears are turning brown, the crop may be taken; but a decidedly dark and settled hue of the seed is a safer criterion. As to the objection that waiting late into the autumn causes a loss of the fruit by falling, it has little weight, because it is by this process that the weaker and least sound fruit is got rid of, while the best remains. Taking the crop too early will not only injure the good fruit by causing it to shrivel, but will also render frequent removals necessary in order to separate from the stock the rotten ones, which would, of themselves, have fallen from the tree if more time had been given.

To Preserve Pear Trees From Blight.—A New Hampshire fruit grower preserves his pear trees from blight by winding a rope of straw around the trunks so as to completely cover them from the ground to the limbs, keeping it on, moderately tight, through the season. His theory is that the blight is caused by the rays of the hot sun coming in contact with the body of the tree, heating the sap and causing it to dry up and the bark to grow to the wood of the tree.

Iron for Fruit Trees.— The scales which fly off from iron being worked at forges, iron trimming, filings, or other ferruginous material, if worked into the soil about fruit trees, or the more minute particles spread thinly on the lawn, mixed with the earth of flower beds or in pots, are most valuable to the peach or pear, and, in fact, supply necessary ingredients to the soil. For colored flowers they heighten the bloom and increase the brilliancy of white or nearly white flowers of all the rose family.

Secret of Raising Quinces.—Purchase the orange variety, and set the trees from six to eight feet apart in rich soil. Bandage the stem with two or three wrappings of old cloth as far down in the ground as possible, as the root starts from near the surface. Let the bandages run six or eight inches above the ground, then pack the soil a couple of inches around the bandages. This should be renewed every spring.

Fruit Pests.—At the time when fruit trees are blossoming, and when sparrows have commenced their annual raids upon them, a good way of driving away these diminutive plagues, consists of lime-washing the trees. When thus whitened, the birds disappear.

In the Vineyard.—We present herewith a brief illustrated article, from the pen of a successful grape grower, giving some hints and suggestions on the planting and culture of grape vines, which we think will be found interesting:

"I have been looking over my former years' work, have been reading back, or rather over again the views of others, and after studying all I took my spade and digging fork and went to an Isabella vine, planted some ten

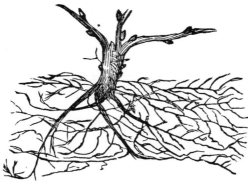

years or more since, and which has never shown any disease, but yearly ripened its fruit regularly and evenly. It was on clay soil. I dug carefully all around it a distance of four feet each way from the vine, or eight feet diameter, took out a trench with the spade, then with my fork I commenced to shake out roots, which I found much as here represented (Fig. 1). Of course the length of the roots is not here shown,

IN THE VINEYARD.—FIG. 1.

for some I broke off in digging; but there was no direct tap root of any size, and altogether the larger portion of the roots were within ten inches of the surface. Small roots as large as a goose quill, it is true, were apparently down below. Some of them pulled upon lifting the vine, others broke off, but there was not a large or main root so situated. It may not be that this is any guide showing the general habit of roots of the vine, when grown in vineyards of clay soils and yearly pruned; but for the present I will so consider it, and when I plant avoid, as I have generally heretofore, setting the roots too deep. Most workers on the grape tell us that the roots must be planted deep, at least, they must have ten inches of soil over and above the upper root of the plant; and they tell us that if the plants are too small for such purpose, then we must excavate a basin, set the plant, and as it grows fill up around the stem. The accompanying figure shows this mode of planting as I understand it

IN THE VINEYARD.—FIG. 2.

(Fig. 2). A straight line drawn across from the ends of the dotted line would show the level of the ground; the dotted line the excavation, with the plant having two eyes, and set in just deep enough to cover the lower eye or bud with soil. The roots are shortened as here shown to about eighteen inches in length and spread out regularly, setting the base of the main stem on a little mound or rise, not a sharp cone, but a broad mound.

The next manner of planting, highly recommended by a good cultivator, I have followed with good results. It is to prepare the ground where this plant is to stand by finely pulverizing it, then excavate a breadth or circle sufficiently wide to admit of straightening out the entire roots of the vine without cutting away a single inch; make the excavation about six inches deep at the outside of the circle and rising so that the center is four inches below the level of the surrounding ground. Fig. 3 shows this method, the straight line being the surface of the mound on which the plant is placed before filling in the earth. This depth for planting I believe a good one."

Winter Care of Grape Vines.—All varieties of grape vines not thoroughly hardy should receive some winter protection to secure best results, and it is claimed by many that it pays to give protection to the hardiest kinds even. Some growers attribute their success with Delaware, Duchess, Roger's Hybrids, etc., simply to covering, while their neighbors signally fail with the same varieties. As the treatment in both cases is exactly alike, the different results can only be attributed to the protection given in one case and its omission in the other. The process is simple, and depends on the extent of the operation. After the vines have shed their leaves and matured their wood, they should be pruned, and on the approach of cold weather, loosened from the trellis, bent down on the ground, and held there with stakes, rails, or something similar. This is sometimes found sufficient, especially when snow lies till late in the spring. If not satisfied with this dependence, a slight covering with leaves, straw, cornstalks, limbs of evergreens, will prove effectual. If danger is to be apprehended from the depredations of mice, which in some sections are very troublesome, a slight covering of earth on the top is all that is necessary. It should be remembered that it is the young wood of the present season's growth that

IN THE VINEYARD.—FIG. 3.

is to be protected—this contains the buds in which are the embryo fruit cluster for next year's crop. Of course, similar protection would not hurt the old wood, but it is not always feasible to provide it. But the main question necessarily preceding all this, on which depends the success or entire failure of the whole operation, is the maturity and thorough ripening of the wood.

Keeping Grapes.—In Europe a method of preserving grapes is now very generally followed. The cluster is cut with a piece of the cane still attached, and the lower end of the cane is inserted in the neck of a bottle containing water. Grapes thus treated are kept in a perfect manner for a long time. European journals have figured racks and other devices for holding the bottles in such a manner that they may sustain the weight of the fruit, and also to allow the clusters to hang free, and much as they would upon the vine. We are not aware that this method has been tried with our native grapes. These, even at the holidays, when the price is the highest, sell for too little to make this method of keeping profitable, but for home use, the experiment seems to be worth trying.

Keeping Grapes in Cellars.—If grapes mature perfectly they may be kept for a considerable length of time if cut without bruising, and hung up in a dry, cool, and rather dark cellar. The stem should be covered, when cut, with wax, and hung with the stem up. Immature grapes will not keep in this way or any other.

Keeping Grapes in Winter.—Perhaps among the many methods and devices employed in keeping grapes in their natural state for winter use, there will be found none better than the simple ones we here illustrate and

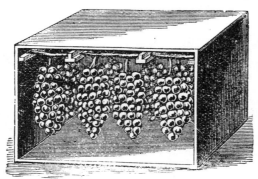

describe. The first method is to take new soap boxes, or any other box of about that size, and nail cleats on the inside of the ends or sides about one inch from the top, and between them bars at various distances, as required by the varying length of the bearing shoot cuttings. The bars are made by nailing a small strip on top of each, as shown in our illustration, Fig. 1. As late as possible cut off the bearing shoots containing the bunches, with

FIG. 1.—KEEPING GRAPES IN WINTER.

pruning shears, and shorten them so they will crowd between the end of the box and the top part of the bar, resting on the bottom part, thus hanging the bunches in their natural position. By this method the boxes can be handled without shaking the shoots off the bars, carried to the light. each bunch examined as winter advances, decaying berries or bunches removed, and the best kept without any moldy taste, as is so common when they are packed solid.

Another method of preserving grapes for winter, is in the first place to have the bunches as perfect as possible. Cut away all green, decayed or imperfect berries. Air them sufficiently to slightly dry or cure the stem, then keep the grapes cool, dry and in the dark. Shallow boxes, of about five inches in depth, are well adapted to keeping grapes, but the wood should not be of a resinous character but wholly odorless, that the fruit may not be tainted. Our illustration, Fig. 2, represents a plan adopted by the French, which is to suspend the bunches from hoops in a warm room or dry cellar. In this position they may be readily examined at any time. It is said that grapes will keep well treated in this manner.

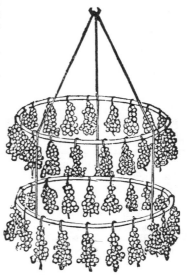

FIG. 2.—KEEPING GRAPES IN WINTER.

How to Prune the Grape.—The custom has usually been to prune in February, but we believe it would be better if done earlier. The excised portions should be cut up in pieces from one to two feet in length, as the buds might be best adapted to planting, tied in bundles of, say, one or two dozen, and buried a few inches under the soil in a location whence the water would drain off, or under an open shed. There they would keep fresh and in full life until planting in the spring. The vines should be cut loose from the trellis and left to sprawl over the ground, in which position they will stand the winter much better.

A Cheap Trellis.—Our illustration upon this page gives a good idea of a permanent and quite cheap grape-vine trellis. The posts rest on stones sunk a little into the ground. The posts may be of any desired size of timber. A capping piece connects them along each side, and cross pieces join the opposite posts. Wire is used for the lattice work. Such a trellis costs about fifty cents a running foot, and is not at all unsightly.

A CHEAP TRELLIS.

Culture of Hardy Grapes.—J. T. Lovett, of Little Silver, the well-known New Jersey fruit grower, says in regard to the culture of hardy grapes: Plant in rows six feet apart, and the vines eight feet apart in the rows. Dig holes twelve to fifteen inches deep, and of a size amply large to accommodate the vines. They should then be filled to within six or eight inches of the top with fine, rich soil, throwing in while doing so a few bones or some wood ashes, if to be had. Cut back one-year vines to two eyes, placing the lower one below the surface; two-year vines to three or four eyes, and putting two or three eyes below the surface. Spread out the roots (which should have previously had one-third their length cut off), place the stock of the vine at one side of the hole, and fill with fine soil, pressing it firmly. When planted, set a stake at the stock (to which the vine should be kept tied), which will be all the support required for two years. Keep old wood trimmed off, growing fruit on new canes. Any manner of pruning that will admit the sun to the fruit will insure a crop; and laying the vines on the ground, even without covering, will increase both the quality of the fruit and the size of the bunches, besides insuring safety from injury by frost. For mildew dust with flower of sulphur while the vines are wet.

Bleeding Grape Vines.—It is stated that an English grape grower stopped the profuse bleeding of a thrifty grape vine by forming a sort of hard cement over the cut ends by repeated dustings at short intervals with Portland cement.

SMALL FRUITS--Update

The type and amount of small fruits you raise will depend on what you can eat, what you can sell, and what you can put away.

The *Cyclopaedia's* advice on raspberries, strawberries, blackberries and currants is pertinent. (Because they are secondary hosts to white pine blister rust, planting currants in New York is discouraged). Raspberries, blackberries and currants need little care once established. Strawberries, however, require much care and hand labor since they are fragile and prone to freeze. They repay the grower with an extremely salable crop, if the care is taken.

Most varieties mentioned here have been replaced by newer varieties. Stark Red Giant, Surecrop, Dunlap and Geneva are varieties of strawberries well-adapted to the Northeast. Raspberry varieties being raised are Latham, Newburgh, September (all red) and Sodus (purple). El Dorado, Bailey and Darrow are blackberry varieties currently popular.

Recommendations of the *Cyclopaedia* to the contrary, cranberries have never been raised in much quantity except in the boggy areas of Maine and Northwest. They must be completely covered with water at some time of year.

Blueberries may be raised in areas with extremely acid soil conditions or in barrels sunk in the ground whose soil acidity has been raised by the application of acid fertilizer and acid peat.

Beyond the small fruits mentioned by the *Cyclopaedia*, I'd like to propose the planting of nut trees. Butternuts, pecans, hazelnuts, hickories and walnuts will bear well with a minimum of care, and their nuts will keep well and contain high concentrations of oil and protein.

Putting Food By by Ruth Hertzberg, Beatrice Vaughan and Janet Greene (Brattleboro, Vt., Stephen Greene Press, 1973) is an excellent guide to preserving fruits. It deals with freezing, drying, canning, and making preserves in the most specific detail and includes everything the novice needs to know. It is also an excellent guide to preserving foods other than fruit.

Nurseries such as Kelly Brothers of Dansville, NY will be able to furnish information on varieties of small fruit to suit your plans and taste; their catalogue is beautiful and informative.

SMALL FRUITS.

Cranberry Culture.—The constantly increasing price of the cranberry, and the great numbers of marshes with alluvium soil free from clay or loam that one meets almost everywhere, prompts the question why cranberries are not more generally cultivated. Of all the self-supporting crops, none needs less care than the cranberry, if the conditions that govern its culture are first complied with, and none certainly shows greater financial results. The first essential is the marsh and its soil, with reference also to the ability to control the water supply. A soil having any proportion of clay should be avoided, and selection made of a combined decaying vegetable mass, with natural sand, and the less loam there is in this the better. Eastern growers cover their marshes with sand, but in the West, if the swamp, upon examination, seems to have a fair amount of sand or silex, it is quite probable that success may be attained in putting out the plants without this sand mulch. As a rule, it is a greater guarantee of success to have a stream of water crossing the marsh, for then in dry weather the gates can be closed and the marsh saturated, and if insect pests make their appearance the vines can be submerged for a day, which will make the worms loosen their hold, but the chances may be taken on a common "dry" patch of swamp. It is supposed that any one who attempts the culture of cranberries will make the dams and embankments of the most solid and substantial character, with gates that will not only work, but be water-tight, else failure will come with the first freshet. Ditching should next be seen to, and rapid drainage secured. This is done by a broad central channel and lateral ditches, which should not be at right angles to it, but approaching it in diagonal lines. The amount of water will have to be taken into consideration—the more water, the more ditches—a fact that will determine also the width of the main outlet. If the swamp is of some extent, it is to be presumed that a ditch at least six or eight feet in width will be needed. These ditches should not be over two feet in depth, and unless there are very heavy discharges of water from the uplands, or natural water courses, the side ditches need not be nearer than one hundred feet from each other. One ditch should always run parallel with and about six feet, or even more, from the dam; the soil thrown out can be utilized in building the dam. The planting requires some discernment. If the muck is covered with alders, reeds, and the like, a great amount of labor will have to be performed in advance, but the experience of a great many has been, where the muck was only covered with a growth of wild grass, that the ditching and consequent dry soil will so hinder its growth that the berry vines will thrive and soon force it into subjection, and, upon the whole, it will, in the first year of the growth of the cranberry, prove a source of profit in the way of protection from exposure and the like. By this method the labor of setting the vines will only be one of thrusting a narrow spade into the soil, pushing the handle over to one side, insert the plants, three or four in number, and press the soil firmly about the plants with the foot. Where weeds and wild sage have a strong hold upon the swamp, the removal of the turf is the only way to succeed with the cranberries. To pay $50 and $75 an acre to clear the ground, in addition to the expense of ditching, seems a large outlay, but when the plants have established themselves and you find that the acre has produced one hundred to one hundred and fifty bushels of berries, worth $4 per bushel, the "light shines from an entirely different quarter." Planting these hills three feet apart each way gives both ample room and chance for cultivation, and in a couple of years the plants will occupy the entire ground, and if no chance is given to seed the ground with weeds, the care of the vines will be quite a small item for several years.

Preparing Soil for Strawberries.—Upon this subject E. P. Roe writes as follows: In the garden, light soils can be given a much more stable and productive character, covering them with clay to the depth of one or two inches every fall. The winter's frost and rain mix the two diverse soils to their mutual benefit. Carting sand on clay is rarely remunerative; the reverse is decidedly so, and top-dressing of clay on light land is often more beneficial than equal amounts of manure.

As practically employed, I regard quick stimulating manures, like guano, very injurious to light soils. I believe them to be the curse of the South. They are used "to make a crop," as it is termed; and they do make it for a few years, but to the utter impoverishment of the land.

And yet, by the aid of these stimulating commercial fertilizers, the poorest and thinnest soil can be made to produce good strawberries if sufficient moisture can be maintained. Just as a physician can rally an exhausted man to a condition in which he can take and be strengthened by food, so land, too poor and light to sprout a pea; can be stimulated into producing a meagre green crop of some kind, which plowed under, will enable the land to produce a second and heavier burden. This, in turn, placed in the soil, will begin to give a suggestion of fertility. Thus poor or exhausted soil can be made by several years of skillful management, to convalesce slowly into strength.

Coarse, gravelly soils are usually even worse. If we must grow our strawberries on them give the same general treatment that I have suggested.

On some peat soils the strawberry thrives abundantly; on others it burns and dwindles. With a soil, I should experiment with bone dust, ashes. etc until I found just what was lacking.

No written directions can take the place of common sense judgment, and above all, experience. Soils vary like individual character. I have yet to learn of a system of rules that will teach us how to deal with every man we meet. It is ever wise, however, to deal justly and liberally. He that expects much from his land must give it much.

I have dwelt at length upon the preparation and enrichment of the land, since it is the corner stone of all subsequent success. Let me close by emphasizing again the principle which was made prominent at first. Though we give our strawberry plants everything else they need, our crop of fruit will still be good or bad in proportion as we are able to maintain abundant moisture during the blossoming and fruiting season. If provision can be made for irrigation, it may increase the yield tenfold.

When to Plant Strawberries.—The above question is often asked, and its answer must depend upon circumstances. One fact about the strawberry plant should be known, and this will enable each one to decide for himself. The plants that are sent out by nurserymen are those that were formed last year by the runners from old plants taking root in the soil of the bed. If these are taken up in the usual way and planted in a new bed—it may be after the lapse of several days—they require a whole season to get established and become sufficiently strong to bear a crop. If these plants are set this spring, they will bear a crop next spring; if such plants are set next autumn, they will require all of next season to grow in, and while they may produce here and there a few berries, they will give no real crop until the following year. Growers of fruit for market set a share of their plants in the fall, because then they have leisure and the ground is in excellent condition. If the plants are made to strike root in pots, these in early autumn may be planted in beds without any disturbance of their roots, and will give a fair crop next spring. Such plants are more expensive than others, and if a crop of fruit is wanted next spring, it is better to set out the plants now. Making the rows two feet apart, and setting the plants one foot apart in the row, as a general rule is best.

With regard to protecting strawberry plants, if some light material can be put over the plants that will not smother and rot them, and yet will be just enough to make shade from the winter sun and a screen from frosty winds, it will be doing a good turn to the strawberry plant. Manure is bad. There is salt in it, especially when fresh, which is destructive to foliage; but clean straw, or swamp, or marsh hay that is free from weeds, answers the purpose very well. But it must not be put on very thick. The idea is, just enough to make a thin screen, and yet enough to hold the moisture long. Shade without damp is the idea. Such light protection is good for the plant.

Covering Strawberries.—The strawberry endures cold well, writes a successful small fruit grower, but not the great sudden changes of temperature, and cold, drying winds. If the situation is such that the plants are not exposed to the winds, and the stools are large and thick with foliage, this foliage will be a sufficient protection; doubtful, however, should the snow be very deep and close packed, and lie long, or ice form on the surface of the ground, locking it for a long time. It is worse still if the frost extends deep into the ground. Under such circumstances the smothering influence may either kill the plant or seriously injure it. The plants without covering are safe where the winter is mild and the soil has perfect drainage. But the safe thing is to cover the plants. For perfect protection I find nothing so good as hemlock brush, or straw kept in place by a hemlock bough, with the concave side under, thus preventing the fatal pressure of the snow. I put on the covering at the beginning of winter, and keep it on until spring frosts are over. The plant will then come out fresh, strong and unharmed, and immediately push its growth.

This answers for a small plot of ground. For field culture, light stable manure with three or four parts of sawdust, or other fine vegetable absorbent, to one of manure, succeeds well as a covering, but should be used only where the soil requires the fertility, as too high manuring produces foliage rather than fruit.

Vegetable material worked into the soil is one of the best elements in the strawberry culture, as also in the culture of other berries. It loosens clay and improves the character of sandy soil, seeming also to form the right pabulum for the fruit. I also get the best crops and the finest berries in this way. Two weeks ago I gave the plants a sprinkling of liquid manure (diluted urine), and they are brightening up and invigorated so as to withstand the winter better, and put out strong and early in the spring. This attention is only a trifle, but it helps a good deal. The strawberry, like the grape, is very susceptible to treatment, and can be made to do much more than we usually see.

Cultivation of Strawberries.—An Illinois journal says that the preparation of the ground for strawberries, and, indeed, for all berry fruits raised in the garden, is exceedingly simple. Any land rich enough to bring forty to fifty bushels of corn per acre, under good cultivation, will do. The ground should be plowed deeply and thoroughly well pulverized. Mark the land if for field culture, the distance as for corn. If for garden culture, the field may be marked both ways, and one good plant placed at each intersection, spreading the roots naturally, placing the plants so the crowns will not be above the surface, giving a little water to the roots if the soil be not fairly moist, and after the water has settled away, drawing the dry earth over all. For garden culture, one plant to three feet of space will be sufficient, unless the plants are to be raised in stools, and the runners kept cut out, when a plant to each two feet will be about right, if you want extra large berries. The cultivation is simple. The spaces between the rows, about two feet wide, may be kept clean with the cultivator. In the rows the weeds may be kept, early in the season, clean with the cultivator; later, when the runners have encroached on the rows, the weeds must be pulled out if necessary, but on fairly clean soil, the cultivation will not be difficult. Beds of the previous year, and which should be in full fruit this season, may be kept clean between the rows with the cultivator. The weeds will not trouble much until the crop is gathered.

About Raspberries.—Not one-half the people grow raspberries that should. To say nothing of the excellence of this fruit freshly taken from the vines, with cream or without, it is really the best there is for canning, and either raw or canned it finds a ready market. It is easily cultivated, produces large crops, and has few insect enemies.

In starting a bed the best time is in the fall, but if neglected then, plant early in the spring, pressing the earth firmly about the roots and cutting the canes off six inches high. Count all suckers as weeds except three to five to the hill. The hills may be four feet apart each way, so they can be worked with the plow and cultivator. No stakes are needed, for the canes are kept stocky by being pinched off when about a yard high.

As to varieties, of course there is none better for this locality than the Brandywine. It is true and tried. It carries well to market, and its bright red color makes it the most salable berry in the catalogue. For home use alone it is no better than the Herstine, but this is not solid, and the plants need covering in winter north of this latitude. The Herstine is a splendid berry—good enough for anybody. The Philadelphia is a valuable old standard, but is soft and too dark in color. The Reliance is nearly of the same color, but we believe every way better than the Philadelphia.

The Cuthbert is immensely praised just now, and so many unite in commending it, that it certainly must have merit. It is perfectly hardy, and thrives North and South. It is said to be very productive, the berries are immense, and the bearing time holds on a long time. The Queen of the Market is quite similar to the Cuthbert, in fact so nearly alike are the two berries, that many consider them identical.

The above are all red varieties. Of the black caps the Mammoth Cluster is the old popular variety, but the new Gregg is said to be greatly superior to it.

The Blackberry and Whortleberry.—Those who find it difficult to get good ripe blackberries and whortleberries may be glad to know that they can be grown in their own gardens as well as the strawberry, and that with the right treatment they will surpass in flavor and size any which may have grown in their grandfather's day. The low-bush or running blackberry grows best on a warm soil of either sandy loam or gravel, and when properly grown and well ripened is much better than any of the high bush varieties. The plants should be set in May, in rows three feet apart and two feet in the rows. Care should be taken to select good strong young roots, and those which bear large sweet berries, avoiding those which bear the sour berries that ripen later in the season; it is best to mark the plants when the fruit is ripening, or secure the assistance of one who knows where the right variety grows. For garden culture the ground should be well hoed the first part of the season, and mulched with leaves or hay about the first of August. If properly cared for the first year, but little needs to be done the next spring; the crop will be large if the vines are well supplied with water during the ripening season; during this time they require quite as much water as the strawberry. The berries should not be picked until fully ripe, and to be in the best condition for sauce should be picked but a short time before eaten; when thus picked, they surpass in richness and flavor the strawberry; as it cannot be transported when fully ripe, any better, if so well as the strawberry, its good qualities are known only to those who cultivate it in their own garden, and understand the right time to pick it. But few dishes can be placed upon the table so acceptable as a dish of good, well-ripened blackberries of the variety which grow on the low running vines. To keep the garden clean, new vines should be set every year, and the old ones removed as soon as the berries are picked. The whortleberry, both the high and the low-bush, requires a different treatment from the blackberry; it will grow on almost any soil. Bushes should be selected that are known to produce large-sized and good flavored berries; they should be set near enough together to shade the ground; a large portion of the top should be cut off; the ground be mulched with a heavy coat of leaves, and should not be disturbed by cultivation, but should be kept well mulched until the bushes are thick enough and large enough to shade the ground, and thus they protect themselves; when once established they require but little care. When the bushes seem to have too much old wood to bear well, they should be cut down to the ground in the autumn; the next year they will make a vigorous growth, and the year after bear some very large berries, but not a full crop until the following year.

Gooseberries and Currants.—There is no reason why both these very useful fruits should not be found abundantly in every garden. They are no trouble to raise. They grow readily from cuttings. Take the wood of last year, from six to ten inches in length; prepare the bed or place where they are to stand permanently; force them into the ground not less than four inches, press the dirt firmly around them, mulch them, and let them alone. If a brush is desired let the buds on the cuttings remain; but if a tree or single stem be preferred, remove all the buds that would go beneath the surface. Let them stand about three feet in the row; and if there is more than one row, let the rows be four feet apart.

In the spring the dead wood of both the gooseberries and currants should be cut out, and the new growth should be thinned where there is too much, as it will interfere with the product. The best red currant is the Dutch, and the best gooseberries are Downing's Prolific and Houghton's Seedling.

Advantages of Mulching.—The Germantown *Telegraph* says: " Although we have suggested many times in the past the great advantage of mulching raspberry and blackberry beds, it cannot be suggested too often. But this mulching should not be done or rather renewed in the season until the heat of the sun or drought requires it; neither should it be done until after the suckers or new plants show themselves and are of sufficient height not to be injured by the application of the mulch, which, if too thick and applied too soon, will in a great measure prevent the sprouting, and where it does not will cause the sprouts to be weak and spindling. Currant bushes also delight in a moist, cool soil, and mulching provides this if applied in sufficient quantity. Anything in the way of weeds, small branches of trees, grass from lawn cuttings, etc., will answer. The mulching of tomato plants, egg plants, etc., will prove very beneficial. We know that some persons have not our faith in mulching, and prefer beds of plants, young trees, etc., to have the soil stirred up about them frequently. This, we are aware, is excellent, but it does not hinder the mulching also. Let the old mulch be removed, the soil well loosened, and then apply fresh mulch."

Fall Setting of Small Fruits.—It is urged that those contemplating setting small fruits should give one trial at least to fall setting. All that is necessary is to either back up over the roots with earth, or throw a forkful of litter over each plant, before the ground freezes up, and in the spring haul this away. First, because they get settled in their place, and getting the benefit of early spring rains, start early, and make a full growth next season, while if set next spring, it cannot be done properly until the ground is settled and the heavy spring rains have ceased. Second, all fruit growers know how pressed they are for time in the spring. Third, raspberries and blackberries have very tender germs that start very early in the spring, and these are likely to be broken off if set then, while if set in the fall, they have not started enough to damage them in transplanting. And fourth, but not least, a much larger proportion of them live when set in the fall—a fact abundant in itself to show the superior merits of fall planting, especially of blackberries, raspberries, currants, grapes, and such sorts.

Red Raspberry.—There is no fruit that is in greater demand at such paying prices, and with which the market is so poorly supplied, as the red raspberry, and one reason why the market is so poorly supplied is because there has been sent over the country so many tender sorts that have so easily winter killed, but now with such hardy and productive sorts as the Brandywine, Philadelphia, Turner, Highland Hardy, Thwack and Cuthbert, and that succeed so well wherever tried, there is no excuse for not having this delicious fruit in abundance. Another reason why they pay so poorly is that they have been allowed to grow helter skelter all over the ground. If you would have fruit in abundance, and of larger size, the suckers must be kept down same as weeds, and the same cultivation that will keep the ground in proper plight and keep weeds down will keep suckers down.

Easy Method of Cultivating Small Fruits.—A writer in the New York *Tribune* says: " It is a source of constant regret with farmers that small fruits require so much care and attention, and that, too, in the season when they are hardest at work at something else. Field work must be done at all events, and the 'berry patch' struggles on single handed with the weeds and grass, till it submits to the inevitable sward. Some years ago coming into possession of a patch of black cap raspberries that had received the usual shiftless culture, I treated them in the following way: After carefully plowing and hoeing them, I covered the ground with a heavy layer of very strawy manure, and the work was done, not only for that year but for the two years following, only renewing the mulch each spring. Only a few struggling Canada thistles will ever grow through such mulch; the soil is always rich and moist, and the berries can ask no better treatment. Since that time I have tried the same plan without removing the sod, and find the result is quite as satisfactory. Farmers, try it, and you will not need to complain that berries cost more than they are worth.

Winter Protection of Strawberry Vines.—A good strawberry protector is a cheap baked-clay saucer, twelve to thirteen inches in diameter, with a hole in the center. The advantages claimed by its use are: a much larger crop; much finer berries; cleaner, and free from sand and dirt; mulching the ground; the retention of the rains to the roots of the vines; killing the weeds; early ripening; easier picking. They are turned over as a winter protection to the vines. Persons who have used it pronounce it the most important invention ever made in connection with strawberry raising.

Setting a Strawberry Bed.—The old plan of spading under a portion of the old strawberry bed, so as to leave the plants in rows, will not pay. Better reset clean land with vigorous plants, arranging to grow a crop of potatoes every third year to clean the land and mellow it. The picking of berries on heavy clay lands causes it to become so packed as to require cultivating at least one season in every four with some hoed crop. Strawberry plants may be set in May or in August; in fact, at almost any time during the spring, summer or fall season.

Easy Method of Disposing of the Currant Worm.—A successful small fruit grower circumvents the ravaging currant worm by allowing no sprouts to grow. He allows but three main stems to a bush, and rubs off all root sprouts when about six inches long. The worms begin with the new growth first; hence, he says, no sprouts, no worms. The fruit also is far finer on plants thus treated, the common red Dutch being nearly as large as the Cherry currant, and a better bearer.

An Easy Method of Irrigation.—An old fruit can may be pierced with one or more pin holes, and then sunk in the earth near the roots of the strawberry or tomato, or other plants, the pin holes to be made of such size that when the can is filled with water the fluid can only escape into the ground very slowly. Practical trials of this method of irrigation leave no doubt of its success. Plants thus watered yield bounteous returns throughout the longest droughts.

Trellises for Blackberries and Raspberries.—The fruit canes of the blackberries and raspberries should be tied up to stakes or trellises. The young growing canes form the fruiting ones for next year; cut away all except three to five to each stool, and when large enough tie them up; they should be pinched off at four feet for raspberries and six feet for blackberries.

LIVE STOCK--Update

Because horses aren't as important now for farming as they were in 1888, I'll omit discussion of them. If one wants horses either for recreation or working I recommend Jeanne K. Posey's *The Horsekeeper's Handbook* (NY: Winchester Press, 1974) as a good manual for stabling, feeding, and handling healthy horses.

Raising beef cattle is a huge industry, especially in the Midwestern states. In numerical order, Herefords, Angus, Polled Herefords, Shorthorns, Charlois, and Brahmans are the favorite breeds of beef cattle. Beef cattle are distinguished from dairy cattle by their ability to thrive on roughage grazed from the range. They build up meat, feeding off pasture lands more than twice as much as dairy cows. Only in the last stages when they're being fattened for slaughter are they fed much grain. Good text books are *Beef Cattle* by A.L. Neumann & Roscoe Snapp (NY: John Wiley & Sons, Inc., 1969) and *Approved Practices in Beef Production* by Elwood Jeurgensen (Danville, Il.: Interstate Printers & Publishers, 1974). A lot of land is needed for beef cattle; even in areas with good grass, ten to thirty acres may be needed for each animal for a year's grazing.

If you raise corn, you can raise pigs. Pigs will forage to a considerable extent and, like chickens and goats, will eat anything, but to build sound flesh need plenty of grains in their diet. *Swine Production* by C. Bundy, R.V. Diggins, & V. Christensen (Englewood Cliffs, NJ: Prentice-Hall, 1976) is a good handbook. Though pig manure is quite "hot" it's very good for the land.

Sheep are excellent animals for the small farmer because, apart from re-quiring good pasture and attention at special times of the year, they care for themselves very well. Good fences are necessary for raising sheep, more to keep dogs out than to keep sheep in. Walter M. Teller in his *Starting Right with Sheep* (Charlotte, Vt.: Garden Way Publishing Co., 1973) recommends Cheviot as a good breed to raise. They have medium-length wool, are good foragers and are very hardy. Southdowns are noted for their meat, Shropshires are prolific, Hampshires are large, and Oxfords and Suffolks are large, heavy, and very fast growing. Teller estimates that it takes about one acre of Northeastern grass land to keep one sheep and her lambs.

A very popular animal among small farmers is the goat. My neighbor has Browns and French Alpines. A freshened goat will give about a gallon of milk a day. As well as being quite palatable as a drink, goat's milk can be made into excellent cheese. Goats are hardy, self-sufficient and capable of obtaining most of their food from pasture. A pamphlet which would be of great help in choosing and caring for goats is *Dairy Goats--Why? What? How?* available from the American Dairy Goat Association, P.O. Box 186, Spindale, NC, 28160.

LIVE STOCK.

How to Judge a Horse.—1. Never take the seller's word. If disposed to be fair, he may have been the dupe of another, and will deceive you through representations which cannot be relied upon.

2. Never trust a horse's mouth as a sure index of his age.

3. Never buy a horse while in motion; watch him while he stands at rest and you will discover his weak points. If sound, he will stand firmly and squarely on his limbs without moving any of them, feet planted flat upon the ground, with legs plump and naturally poised. If one foot is thrown forward with the toe pointing to the ground and the heel raised, or if the foot is lifted from the ground and the weight taken from it, disease of the navicular bone may be suspected, or at least tenderness, which is a precursor of disease. If the foot is thrown out, the toe raised, and the heel brought down, the horse has suffered from lamnitis, founder, or the back sinews have sprained, and he is of little future value. When the feet are all drawn together beneath the horse, if there has been no disease, there is a misplacement of the limb at least, and weak disposition of the muscles. If the horse stands with his feet spread apart, or straddles with his hind legs, there is weakness of the loins, and the kidneys are disordered. When the knees are bent, and totter and tremble, the beast has been ruined by heavy pulling, and will never be right again, whatever rest and treatment he may have. Contracted or ill-formed hoofs speak for themselves.

4. Never buy a horse with a bluish or milky coat in his eyes. They indicate a constitutional tendency to ophthalmia, moon-blindness, etc.

5. Never have anything to do with a horse who keeps his ears thrown backward. This is an invariable indication of bad temper.

6. If the horse's hind legs are scarred, the fact denotes that he is a kicker.

7. If the knees are blemished, the horse is apt to stumble.

8. When the skin is rough and harsh, and does not move easily and smoothly to the touch, the horse is a heavy eater, and digestion is bad.

9. Avoid a horse whose respiratory organs are at all impaired. If the ear is placed to the heart and a wheezing sound is heard, it is an indication of trouble.

Feed for the Horse.—One of the most sensible articles on the treatment of a horse is that which is given from a physiological standpoint by Colvin.

It is the opinion of this authority that the horse's stomach has a compacity of only about 16 quarts, while that of the ox has 250. In the intestines this proportion is reversed, the horse having a capacity of 190 quarts against 100 of the ox. The ox, and most other animals, have a gall bladder for the retention of a part of the bile secreted during digestion; the horse has none, and the bile flows directly into the intestines as fast as secreted. This construction of the digestive apparatus indicates that the horse was formed to eat slowly and digest continually bulky and innutritious food. When fed on hay it passes very rapidly through the stomach into the intestines. The horse can eat but about five pounds of hay in an hour, which is charged, during mastication, with four times its weight of saliva. Now, the stomach, to digest well, will contain but about ten quarts, and when the animal eats one-third of his daily ration, or seven pounds, in one and one-half hours, he has swallowed at least two stomachfuls of hay and saliva, one of these having passed to the intestines. Observation has shown that the food is passed to the intestines by the stomach in the order in which it is received. If we feed a horse six quarts of oats it will just fill his stomach, and if, as soon as he finishes this, we feed him the above ration of seven pounds of hay, he will eat sufficient in three-quarters of an hour to have forced the oats entirely out of his stomach into the intestines. As it is the office of the stomach to digest the nitrogenous parts of the feed, and as a stomachful of oats contains four or five times as much of these as the same amount of hay, it is certain that either the stomach must secrete the gastric juice five times as fast, which is hardly possible, or it must retain this food five times as long. By feeding the oats first, it can only be retained long enough for the proper digestion of hay, consequently it seems logical, when feeding a concentrated food like oats, with a bulky one like hay, to feed the latter first, giving the grain the whole time between the repasts to be digested.

Feeding Horses.—Another authority writes as follows: The horse has the smallest stomach, in proportion to his size, of any animal. This space is completely filled by four quarts of oats and the saliva that goes into the stomach with it. Horses are generally overfed and not fed often enough. For a horse with moderate work six or eight quarts of bruised oats and ten pounds of fine hay are sufficient. This should be fed in three meals, and is better if fed in four. A horse's digestion is very rapid, and therefore he gets hungry sooner than a man. When he is hungry he is ineffective, and wears out very rapidly. Water fills the stomach, lowers the temperature, and dilutes the gastric juice; therefore a horse should not drink immediately before eating. Neither should he be watered immediately after eating, because he will drink too much and force some of the contents of the stomach into the large intestine, which will cause scouring. Scouring is also caused by too rapid eating, which can be prevented by putting half a dozen pebbles half the size of the fist into the manger with the oats. Give only a moderate drink of water to a horse. A large drink of water before being driven will have a very quieting effect on a nervous horse. A race horse always runs on an empty stomach. Digestion progresses moderately during exercise, if the exercise is not so violent as to exhaust the power of the horse. I consider bruised oats worth twenty per cent. more than whole. They are more perfectly digested. I prefer oats to any other grain for horses. Cracked corn is good under some circumstances, but I would not use meal or shorts. The disease called big head is caused by feeding corn. When a horse comes in hot I would give a moderate feed immediately. If the horse is too tired to eat I would take the feed away. A heated horse is a reason against watering and for feeding, for the system is just then in a condition to begin digestion. A horse will not founder if fed immediately when hot. I prefer dry feed, unless the horse has some disease of the throat and lungs. I do not consider it worth while to cut hay. I always feed hay from the floor, then the horses do not get particles in their eyes.

Raising a Colt.—A colt is regarded as an incumbrance because he is useless until he arrives at a suitable age for work, but it really costs very little, compared with his value, to raise a colt. When the period arrives at which the colt can do service, the balance sheet will show in its favor, for young horses always command good prices if they are sound and well broken. One of the difficulties in the way is the incumbrance placed on the dam, which interferes with her usefulness on the farm, especially if the colt is foaled during the early part of the spring. Some farmers have their colts foaled in the fall, but this is open to two objections. In the first place, spring is the natural time, for then the grass is beginning to grow, and nature seems to have provided that most animals should bring forth their young in a season beyond the reach of severe cold, and with sufficient time to grow and be prepared for the following winter.

Again, when a colt is foaled in the fall he must pass through a period of several months' confinement in the stable, without exercise, or else be more or less chilled with cold from time to time. Should this happen, the effect of any bad treatment will be afterward manifested, and no amount of attention can again elevate the colt to that degree of hardiness and soundness of body that naturally belongs to a spring colt. Besides, a colt foaled in the spring will outgrow one foaled in the fall. An objection to spring colts may be partially overcome by plowing in the fall, or keeping the brood mares for very light work, with the colts at liberty to accompany them always. A colt needs but very little feeding if the pasture is good and there is water running through it. He needs then only a small feed of oats at night—no corn —and if he is given hay it is not necessary to give him a full ration. What he will consume from the barn will not be one-third his value when he is three years old, and if he is well bred the gain is greater.

When a farmer raises his horses he knows their disposition, constitution and capacity. It is the proper way to get good, sound, serviceable horses on the farm. It should not be overlooked that a colt must be tenderly treated from birth, and must be fondled and handled as much as possible. He should never hear a harsh word, but should be taught to have confidence in everybody he sees or knows. This is an easy matter if his training begins from the time he is a day old. He can be thus gradually broken without difficulty, and will never be troublesome. No such thing as a whip should be allowed in a stable that contains a colt. Colts should not be worked until three years old, and then lightly at first, as they do not fully mature until they are six years old, and with some breeds of horses even later. Mares with foals at their side should be fed on the most nourishing food.

To Bit a Colt.—The true way to bit a colt is not to bit him at all; that is, let him bit himself. When my colts are one year old, I begin to teach them to hold the bit in their mouth. The bit is of pine, some half-inch in diameter, and five inches in length. This piece of soft pine is held in the mouth by a cord tied to either end, and fastened on the head, back of the ears. The colt loves to have the bit in his mouth, because it enables him to bring forward the saliva process. He will bit, and work it over in his mouth, and enjoys it hugely. He will welcome it, and will actually reach out and open his mouth for it, as a trained horse will for a bit. After a few days, you can tie strings making miniature reins to this bit, and teach the colt the proper use of it. When this is done, he is ready for the regular steel bit. Put your bridle on with a leather bit, large and pliant; throw your checkline, if your bridle has one attached, into the pigsty; get into your wagon and drive off. This is all the "bitting" a colt needs. Treated in this way, he will have a lively, yielding, sensitive mouth. He will take the bit bravely when working up to his speed, but yield readily to the driver's will. A horse, bitted in this sensible way, can be driven a forty-clip with the lines held in one hand, or be lifted over a five-barred gate with the strength of a single wrist. If you do not believe it, try it and see.

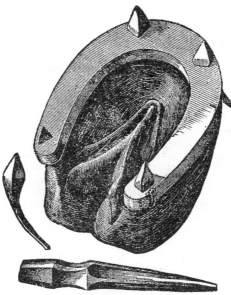

HORSESHOE.—FIG. **1.**

A Convenient Horseshoe.—Among the numerous horseshoes lately devised in this and other countries, that invention in England, by Mr. Joseph Offord, seems worthy of special notice. Its object is to fit the hoof with a movable but firm covering, which can be readily adjusted to fit every kind of work and road, so that, like its master, the horse may own several sets of shoes for different occasions. The device consists in having one or more perfectly wedge-shaped holes in the side and close to the edge of each shoe (Fig. 1), in which triangular cogs, or wedges, are inserted. These are fastened by the fangs being brought, without touching the hoof, to the outside of the shoe, over which they are clenched with a small hammer. The cogs do not penetrate the hoof, and there is no risk of hurting the horse. The holes being wedge-shaped, cannot fill up with stones or dirt, and the fangs being malleable, the wedges are easily removed or inserted at pleasure. It is necessary, however, to get the holes punched in the shoes before the horse is shod, and for the coachman to be provided with a supply of these patent cogs to insure safety on any road in frost or on wood.

As many are accustomed to use a cog which screws into the shoe, Mr. Offord has prepared a steel wedge-shaped one (Fig. 2) for this purpose. The screw cogs are, of course, more expensive. In using them the shoe has to be drilled and tapped with

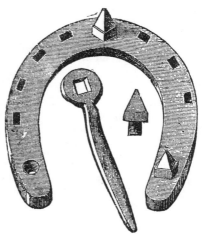

HORSESHOE.—FIG. 2.

one or more holes before the horse is shod. The cogs are inserted into these holes when needed, or removed at pleasure by means of a wrench provided for this purpose. We give two illustrations, reproduced from the *Agricultural Gazette*, showing both these methods, with the punch, wrench, and cogs, both of which have stood the test of many years' experience, and have given great satisfaction.

To Break Horses from Pulling at the Halter.—Two methods of breaking a horse of this habit are here illustrated, as follows:

TO BREAK HORSES FROM PULLING AT THE HALTER.—FIG. **1.**

Fig. 1.—Get a strong half-inch cord twenty-two feet in length; put the center under the tail like a crupper; twist them a few times as you bring them forward over the back; pass forward on each side of the body, the pass them forward through the halter below the jaw. Tie firmly to a tree, post, or stall, and excite the animal by any means that will cause him to pull, until the habit is overcome. You may even whip across the nose keenly until there is perfect submission, which will not require long. Hitch in this way for a few days, or so long as there is is any predisposition to pull on the halter.

Fig. 2.—This contrivance consists of an ordinary ring halter, with the two side rings connected by a strong, flexible cord. Whenever the horse pulls, the inner part of the cord is drawn forcibly against his jaw, and the effect is a severer punishment than he is willing to endure.

TO BREAK A HORSE FROM PULLING AT A HALTER.—FIG. 2.

Warts on Horses.—A correspondent of an English agricultural journal writes: "Inquiries are made for a cure for warts on horses, mules, and cattle. Many remedies are prescribed

—many barbarous and cruel to the animal. I will give you a remedy often tried, and never known to fail. Anoint the wart three times with clean, fresh hog's lard, about two days between times. I have had warts on my horses—bleeding warts, of large size, rattling warts and seed warts, to the number of more than one hundred on one horse's head. I have never been able to find the warts for the third application of the lard. All disappear after the second application. I have sent this prescription to several agricultural papers, hoping it would be of some use to farmers. But they all seem slow to believe, perhaps, because the remedy is at hand and costs nothing. I own I was slow to believe myself; but, having a fine young mare with large bleeding warts, that covered parts of the bridle and girths with blood whenever used, I thought there would be no harm in trying lard on them. When the mare was got up for the third application, there were no warts, and the scars are there now, after more than fifteen years, with very little change. I may say that for cuts, bruises, galls, etc., the application of fresh lard—either for man or beast—is worth more than any patent liniment in use. It will remove pain instantly, and does not irritate raw flesh, as all liniments do.

Stumbling Horses.—The Pittsburg *Stockman* says: " Some good horses are addicted to stumbling while walking or moving in a slow trot. A well-versed veterinarian states that there are two causes that would tend to produce this faulty action; one a general weakness in the muscular system, such as would be noticed in a tired horse; the other a weakness of the exterior muscles of the leg, brought about by carrying too much weight on the toe. To effect a cure, he adds, lighten the weight of each front shoe about four ounces; have the toe of the shoe made of steel instead of iron, it will wear longer, have it rounded off about the same as it would be when one-third worn out, in order to prevent tripping, allow one week's rest; have the legs showered for a few minutes at a time with cold water through a hose, in order to create a spray; then rub dry briskly, from the chest down to the foot. Give walking exercise daily this week, for about an hour, twice a day. When you commence driving again omit the slow jog—either walk or send him along at a sharp trot for a mile or two, then walk away, but do not speed for at least several weeks. By this means the habit of stumbling from either of the above causes will be pretty well overcome.

Cure for Balky Horse.—Hermann Koon, my German neighbor, writes a correspondent of the *Prairie Farmer*, is as patient a man as belongs to that patient race. Coming along the road a month or so ago, I saw Hermann lying in a fence corner, under the shade of an elm, quietly smoking his pipe. A quarter of a mile or so beyond I saw Hermann's horse and buggy by the roadside, the horse evidently tied to a post. This was a queer condition of affairs, for my neighbor is one of the most industrious men I know. My curiosity was aroused, and I stopped for an explanation. In broken English he told me his horse, a recent purchase, had proved balky, had stopped near where he now stood and no amount of coaxing could induce him to go on. Hermann did not curse the animal, he did not lash it with his whip, beat it with a club, build a fire under its belly, nor resort to any other of the brutal means some men use in such cases. He quietly got out of the buggy, tied the horse to the post, and walked off. Hermann had been taking it easy under the tree for three long hours. He thought the horse would be glad to go now if requested to do so. It had once before stopped with him, and after a patient waiting alone, for an hour, it went on all right. He expected about four hours, this time, would effect a permanent cure of the bad habit. I went on about my business, leaving the stolid German to his pipe and his thoughts. To-day I met him again. He said the horse was eager to start when he went back to the buggy, and though he has used it every day since, no disposition to balk has been manifested. He believes there will be no repetition of the offense. Most men think they cannot afford to waste time in this way, perhaps, but if the horse is cured he is a valuable one, whereas, if it had become a chronic balker, through cruel management, it would be worthless. Hermann thought he could not make money faster than by saving the reputation of his horse. It is a new system, but Hermann says it will work well every time, if the horse is not naturally vicious. It looks reasonable to me, and if my nag ever tries the stop game with me, and I can command patience sufficient, I will try his plan.

Kicking Horses.—We present herewith a method that will be found available in all cases of kicking by horses. The beast should have a good

pair of bits in his mouth, to which should be attached a strap or rope sufficiently long to reach back between and behind the fore legs about eight inches, and should pass through the girt or surcingle. A loop should be made in this, the back end of the rope or strap, about two inches or more in length. Now take a rope about seven or eight feet long. (The length of the rope will depend upon the size of the horse; the rope should be long enough to allow of a free use of the horse's hind legs in traveling.) Pass one

HOW TO PREVENT HORSES FROM KICKING.

end of the rope round the leg, upon the inside, so the fastening shall come upon the outside, to prevent interfering, and bring it round upon the outside of the leg, and pass the end over and around the middle of the rope and wind it round the rope upon the outside of the leg, as illustrated. Draw the noose up round the pastern—i. e., between the fetlock and hoof—and pass the unfastened end of the rope through the loop in the rope or strap which passes through the surcingle, and fasten the end round the other leg, as was done the first time in fastening. This mode of fastening is simple, is easily done and undone, and will not work off, provided the noose is drawn up tightly around the pastern. If you have a horse that is addicted to the unpleasant habit of kicking, try this experiment, and you will find that it works admirably.

Training Vicious Horses.—A new and very simple method of training vicious horses was exhibited in West Philadelphia, and the manner in which some of the wildest horses were subdued was astonishing. The first trial was that of a kicking or "bucking" mare, which her owner said had allowed no rider on her back for a period of at least five years. She became tame in about as many minutes, and allowed herself to be ridden about without a sign of her former wildness. The means by which the result was accomplished was a piece of light rope which was passed around the front jaw of the mare just above the upper teeth, crossed in her mouth, and thence secured back of her neck. It was claimed that no horse will kick or jump when thus secured, and that a horse, after receiving the treatment a few minutes, will abandon his vicious ways forever. A very simple method was also shown by which a kicking horse could be shod. It consisted in connecting the animal's head and tail by means of a rope fastened to the tail and then to the bit, and then drawn tightly enough to incline the animal's head to one side. This, it is claimed, makes it absolutely impossible for the horse to kick on the side of the rope. At the same exhibition a horse which for many years had to be bound on the ground to be shod suffered the blacksmith to operate on him without attempting to kick while secured in the manner described.

Galls and Sores on Horses.—If the owner of the horses, the farmer

ONE CAUSE OF HIDE-BOUND.

himself, could always be among his work animals, they would receive more attention and better treatment; but as he has so much to think about and look after, he cannot give this department his careful supervision, and many errors creep into the management which could not otherwise be found there. There are some horses which chafe more readily than others, while some do not have the collars and harness fit them, which will invariably cause galls or sores; and even when the harness does fit properly, the warm weather, or giving the horse a hard, warm day's work, may cause shoulder or saddle galls to appear, which will soon become larger and bad sores, if not promptly attended to. Bathing the shoulders, with spring or well water hardens them, and decreases the tendency toward galling. When galls appear, wash the affected parts with good white castile soap (only use the best castile and none other), and warm water to cleanse them. After the parts have been dried with a soft cloth or rag or sponge, anoint the parts with a mixture of pure glycerine in which a little carbolic acid has been mixed. Do this at night after work. In the morn cleanse well again, as above, and put on some pulverized alum if you work the horse regularly. Continue this course until the sores are perfectly healed up.

Working Mares in Foal.—It is quite common to see or hear inquiries as to how near the time of foaling, a mare may be worked without injury to her or the colt, on the supposition that it is necessary for her to go idle for a month or two before.

This is not the case; and in the hands of a careful man she may be kept at such work as plowing, harrowing, or cultivating without the least danger, until she is ready to foal. Of course, fast driving or working to a heavy wagon tongue, on rough or muddy roads, or where heavy backing is to be done, should not be allowed. The writer has always worked mares moderately on the farm, when necessary, until it was evident they were likely to foal within a few hours, and has known of their foaling in harness, en route from the plow to the barn, but never with any bad results. While we think it more humane to let a mare have a few days' liberty before this trying event, there seems to be little necessity for losing the work of a strong mare for any great length of time before foaling, and we would prefer to allow the extra holidays afterward. Ordinarily, she will do first-rate work with a ten days' vacation, provided that she is not put immediately to work that is too severe, and fed partly with something else than corn.

Kicking in the Stall.—The habit of kicking in the stable arises from idleness. Regular day work is the best remedy, but when that is not sufficient, a branch or two of some prickly shrub, nailed to the posts, will often stop the habit, care being taken to arrange it so as not to prevent the animal from lying down and obtaining needed rest. Mares are supposed to be much more subject to this vice than geldings or stallions; but so far as our personal experience goes, there is little difference. A broad leather strap, to which is tied a small wooden log, are commonly applied to one or both legs, but they are not always sufficient. A heavier weight than two pounds should not be used, for if a horse is frightened by it, he may kick worse and do himself injury. When, however, he is well used to a wooden log, and has got over his first alarm, a heavier one may be put on if required. The strap, which should be broad, is buckled around the leg above the fetlock, and the weight suspended from it, which should not reach farther down than an inch and a half above the coronet, as the coronet would inflame to a mischievous extent if bruised. Sometimes a weight is required for each leg, if the animal kicks at both stall posts. Occasionally, when all other remedies fail, the practice will cease when the animal be turned loose in a roomy box stall.

Reining Horses.—The habit of reining in horses very tightly finds less favor with many persons than it did. It is not easy to see in what way the habit originated. If a man has a load of anything to pull, he wishes to get his head as far forward as possible to pull with ease. But the horse is denied this. His head is reined back tightly, thereby making it much harder for him to pull the load. To our view, a horse looks better, and we know he feels better, when pursuing a natural, leisurely, swinging gait. It is as necessary for his head to oscillate in response to the motions of his body, as it is for a man's hands to do the same thing. A horse allowed his head will work easier and last longer than one on which a check is used. Blinds are another popular absurdity in the use of horses. They collect dust, pound the eye, and are in every way a nuisance. A horse that cannot be driven with safety without them should be sold to a railroad grader. No colt should be broken to them. Animals fear noises they cannot see the cause of much more than those they can. We would dispense with tight reining and with blinds.

Colic in Horses.—This disease is caused by indigestion, over-feeding, or by giving cold water in large quantities, or by eating sour grain. If colic occurs from eating sour grain, one of the best remedies is a few lumps of charcoal. Pulverize it fine and pour on it about a quart of boiling water. When cool, strain off and give. If the above does not give relief, stimulants should be given, with a view to arouse the stomach and get relief from the fermented food which it contains. Purges are of no sort of use for the purpose of relieving an overloaded stomach, and therefore if inflammation is present, their use is positively injurious. The use of saleratus and turpentine, which is so popular an agent with horsemen, are not always the proper remedies. To make use of the former, being an anti-acid it is supposed to combine with the free acid in the digestive organs, and thus neutralize it, but if its use is persisted in, it will injure the mucous membrane of the stomach. Turpentine is a powerful irritant, and it should never be made use of except by those who understand its action, and neutralize it by mixing it with linseed oil. The following has been used with good results, and can be recommended as safe and efficacious: Sulphuric ether, 1 1-2 ounces; oil of pepperment, 2 ounces; water, 16 ounces. Mix and shake well before giving. If not relieved, give again in half an hour, and an injection composed of soap suds to be thrown into the rectum.

Dr. N. Rowe, of Chicago, gives the following as the best simple remedy for colic in a horse: If it is ordinary colic, or gripes without flatulence, give him a dose of whisky, say from two to four ounces, that being generally handy; or a strong dose of peppermint or spearmint tea, hot; but if a drug store is near, give from one to two ounces each of laudanum and spirits of nitre; repeat the dose in half an hour if necessary. If it is flatulent colic, the horse bloated with gas, give a teaspoonful of saleratus in half a pint of warm water, repeat it in ten minutes; if this does no good, give an ounce of turpentine in half a pint of linseed oil; or you may give half an ounce of chloral hydrate in half a pint of cold water. In addition to the above directions, in all cases give warm water injections, and let the horse remain quiet, allowing him to roll if he wants, to give friction to the belly, and give soft feed and rest afterward for a day or two.

The *Massachusetts Ploughman* recommends salt, and as this is known among housekeeepers as useful in colic, we give what the writer says: "Spread a teacupful of salt upon the back of the animal over the kidneys and loins, and keep it saturated from twenty to thirty minutes, or longer if necessary. If the attack is severe, drench with salt water. I have a valuable bull, weighing nineteen or twenty hundred pounds, which had a severe attack of colic a year ago last summer. I applied salt to his back as above, and it being difficult to drench, we put a wooden bit into his mouth, keeping it open about two inches, and spread salt upon his tongue, which, together with the salt upon his back, relieved him at once, and within a very short time equilibrium appeared fully restored. I have for several years past successfully applied this treatment to other animals in my herd."

An officer who commanded artillery during the late war used the following simple remedy for colic in horses, which he has tried with perfect success in hundreds of cases: Rub the horse well between the fore legs and around the girth with spirits of turpentine. Immediately relief follows.

Another remedy is the following: Take some good home-made soap, and make about half a gallon of warm soap suds; then take a quart bottle, fill it, and drench the horse. Sometimes as much as a half-gallon may be needed.

Bots.—The bot larvæ are liable to be found domiciled in the horse at any and at all times. It only does noticeable damage when the number accumulates in the passages, or when there is some disturbance in the digestion of the horse, when, it is said, it cuts through the membrane of the stomach, causing death to ensue. The bot-fly lays its eggs in the hair of the horse, about the flanks and front legs, where they get to the tongue, and from thence are swallowed and hatch in the stomach. They live a certain period of time and are discharged, to become flies again. Several doses are recommended to be given to dislodge the grub, but when it is doing no perceptible harm many horsemen prefer to let it alone rather than medicate the horse. But some remove them by giving powdered aloes, asafœtida, each one-fourth ounce; mix in hot water, and when cold add oil of turpentine, sulphuric ether, each one ounce. Give in linseed tea as a drench.

Another authority says: Bots in horses may be known by the animals occasionally nipping at their sides, and also by red pimples rising on the inner surface of the upper lip, which may be plainly seen by turning the lip up. The cure is effected by taking two quarts new milk, one quart of molasses, and giving the horse the whole amount. In fifteen minutes afterward give two quarts warm sage tea; thirty minutes after give one pint of currier's oil, or enough to operate as physic. The cure will be complete, as the milk and molasses cause the bots to let go, the tea puckers them up, and the oil carries them entirely away.

Another remedy is as follows: Give the animal one quart of sage tea, in which a large teaspoonful of soda or saleratus is dissolved. If not relieved in one hour, repeat the dose, and repeat hourly until relief is obtained.

Founder.—Founder consists of inflammation of the laminæ, or leaves of the hoof—the most sensitive portions of the foot, which serve to connect the interior part to the outer protecting covering of horn. It may be very severe and acute, or a simple stiffness of the limbs and muscles. In this case two drams of lobelia may be given, and the limbs bathed with hot water and rubbed with liniment or kerosene oil. This may be continued for three or four days. Warm blanketing, with hot fomentations, will be useful. When the horse suffers very much, and the feet are hot and painful, a pound of salts should be given, followed by twenty-drop doses of tincture of aconite; the feet enveloped in large poultices of bran, or even sawdust, steeped in hot water, and the legs bathed in hot water and wrapped up. A deep, soft bed should be given, and the horse induced to lie down. After the worst symptoms are over the hoof and sole should be rasped down and the feet kept in a puddle of clay and water. The shoes should be removed.

The following remedy, says an experienced farmer, of Texas, is a sure cure for founder, viz: "A large tablespoonful of pulverized alum and a tablespoonful of pulverized saltpetre mixed. Moisten the dose and administer it by pulling out the tongue and placing the spoon as far back in the mouth as possible."

Heaves.—If you want to have no trouble with heaves in your horses be sure that they are fed no dusty and dirty hay, which is the prolific source of this annoyance. Ordinary clean hay can always be fed with safety if properly cut up, moistened, and mixed with ground grain; but to feed the musty or dirty sorts is very injurious. Clover, owing to its liability to crumble, often gets dirty, even after storage, and should never be fed without being previously moistened.

Very bad cases of heaves have been cured by simply feeding the animal upon cut and moistened feed, of very good quality and in small quantities, three times a day. For instance, four pounds of timothy hay and three quarts of feed made of equal quantities of oats, corn, and wheat bran ground together. With this was mixed a small quantity of salt, and twice a week one dram of sulphate of iron and half an ounce of ground gentian root were given in the feed. A liberal bran mash every evening will also be very useful. A horse that cannot be cured by this treatment is of no value, and may be considered past cure.

The following is recommended by an agricultural authority: One dram of tincture of aromatic sulphuric acid in a pint of water night and morning, allowing the animal to drink from a bucket. The horse should also receive in his food, night and morning, equal parts of powdered ginger, gentian, sulphur, cream of tartar, charcoal, licorice, elecampane, caraway seed and balm of Gilead buds (chopped fine), the dose to be an ounce. Be careful and not overfeed the animal.

Still another remedy is the following: Asafœtida, pulverized, one ounce; camphor gum, pulverized, one-half ounce; mix and divide into four powders; feed one every other night for a week.

Epizootic in Horses.—The disease known as " the epizootic " is a common one, but is rarely so general as to be justly entitled to that distinction. It is simply a catarrhal affection of the bronchial tubes, the lining of the air-passages of the lungs, and the nasal sinuses, in fact, what may be called a very bad cold, with some fever. It is treated by a saline purgative, as 8 to 12 oz. of Epsom salts, and afterwards half an ounce of saltpetre daily, with warm drinks, general good nursing, and frequent rubbing of the limbs and body to excite the circulation.

Shying Horses.—A horseman whose horse is given to shying, ought never to permit himself to evince symptoms of nervousness nor punish the animal for exhibitions of timidity. Whenever a horse directs the points of his ears in a certain direction, as though distrustful or afraid, the reins should be pulled in another direction, thus diverting the attention of the animal from the object causing the perturbation. If, on the other hand, force or harsh means are used to compel an acquaintance with the object feared the horse will be doubly excited, if not unmanageable. We have found, in cases of shying or halting at real or fancied objects of disquiet, that stopping the horse and using soothing language, answers a very good purpose. If the object is stationary, the horse, after a short time, will most usually advance in the direction of it, approaching cautiously till satisfied no danger is to be apprehended, when he will resume his way in a quiet mood. But if chastised for shying, he will have two objects of fear instead of one, and become more confirmed in the habit of distrustfulness.

Best Material for Stable Floors.—A Western writer says: " I have used plank, macadam, cinders and coal-tar mixed, and clay pounded hard for stable floor, but the best material for the purpose, and which gives me the most satisfaction, especially on the score of cleanliness, is good, hard brick, laid edgeways, with an inclination of about one-quarter of an inch to the foot; the more level the floor is, the easier it is for the horse. Many a horse has been ruined by standing on a stable floor with too much inclination. Persons making stable floors should study the comfort of their animals. Another great advantage of brick is, that it is always moist, which is an object to be taken into account, as the hoof never becomes dry, consequently there is no danger of contraction, providing the shoer leaves the frog alone, which should not be cut, not even the ragged edges of it. I have used the brick floor for the last three or four years, and am well satisfied that there is nothing better.

Scratches on Horses.—A veterinary authority says he has never known a failure of carrot poultice for scratches on horses, and he gives the following directions, probably valuable, as carrot has an excellent effect on many unhealthy sores: Wash the sores thoroughly with warm, soft water and castile soap, then rinse them off with clear water, after which rub dry with a cloth. Now grate some carrots (about a pint after grated) and bind them on the sores. The best way to bind it on is to take a cloth and wrap it around the sores, letting the lower edge come close down to the hoof; then tie a cord around this lower end, after which put the grated carrot into the opening at the top of the cloth, press it down around the sores, then tie another cord around the top of the cloth, a little above the fetlock. This should be repeated every day for four or five days, when the scratches will be cured.

Ringbones on Colts.—For ringbones on colts, first pay attention to shoeing. If he walks on the toe, have a high heel to the shoes; but if he strikes the heel first, let it be thin and the toe high. If there is inflammation, reduce it by rest and water bandages. Then blister with the following: Powdered cantharides, Venice turpentine, and rosin, each two ounces; lard, two pounds. Melt the last three together, and when not too hot stir in the cantharides. When the pustules appear, omit for a few days. Then apply again and alternate for three or four times. Remember that in all diseases or troubles of this kind there will be more or less fever, and attention should be given to the general health of the animal, even when no particular symptoms of illness are seen

Cure for Spavin and Ringbone.—Venice turpentine and Spanish flies, of each, two ounces; euphorbium and aqua ammonia, of each, one ounce; red precipitate, one half ounce; lard, one and a half pounds. Pulverize all, and put into the lard; simmer slowly over coals, not scorching or burning, and pour off, free of sediment. For ringbones, cut off the hair, and rub the ointment well into the lumps once in forty-eight hours. For spavins, once in twenty-four hours for three mornings. Wash well previous to each application with suds, rubbing over the place with a smooth stick, to squeeze out a thick, yellow matter. This has removed very large ringbones.

Treatment of Sick Horses.—The practice of forcing a horse to stand on his legs, or walk about, while laboring under an attack of colic, is most inhuman. The same remark is also applicable to the plan of exercising a horse during the time he is under the purgative action of a dose of physic. He should be moved gently about before the medicine commences to operate, but never after. Do those barbarians who knock the animal about while enduring the pains of colic or when suffering the purgative action of medicine, ever think of what they are doing? If they were treated themselves on the same plan under similar circumstances, they would soon come to their senses regarding the management of the unfortunate animal which is placed under their charge.

A Muzzle for Biting Horses.—This dangerous habit is taught the horses by thoughtless owners or drivers by playing with them when colts, or teasing them when full grown. A sharp cut with a whip across the horse's nose when he bites may serve to break him from the habit; but when the case is worse and incurable, a muzzle for this purpose may be made of strips of light hoop iron or of leather. A band may be made to encircle the muzzle to which strips of leather or iron are fastened. At the bottom of the muzzle a round piece of leather should be fastened by rivets to keep the strips in their place.

How to Save Oats in Feeding.—A saving may be effected in the consumption of oats for horses by simply soaking them in tepid water. Practical experiments which have been made show that by this method the ration for each animal may be reduced by a third. Horses whose teeth have seen their best days masticate the grain in its ordinary condition insufficiently, and younger animals often eat so greedily that the greater proportion of it is swallowed whole. This waste may be obviated by the simple method recommended, which so far softens the grain that it is more completely masticated and digested, and consequently yields more nutriment. Three hours is a sufficient length of time to soak the grain, provided the water is not too cold.

How Blindness is Produced.—It is said that dark stables tend to produce blindness in animals. A veterinary surgeon says: "Darkness produces blindness, because nature is outraged in the fact that the sight of the eyes is destroyed by want of light to present objects properly to the vision, and thus, by continued inactivity, producing blindness. Even so is blindness, or imperfect vision, produced by an over-action of light upon the retina of the eye, as is always the case when light is admitted by a window directly in front of the horse. Nothing is worse than this light, so admitted. Nature is outraged, and as a penalty we have nervous, fretful horses, shyers, cribbers, balkers, runaways, and anything but a reliable and pleasant horse."

Care of Horses' Legs.—Few men who handle horses give proper attention to the feet and legs. Especially is this the case with the farmer. Much time is often spent in rubbing, brushing and smoothing the hair on the sides and hips, but the feet are not properly cared for. The feet of a horse require ten times as much, for in one respect they are almost the entire horse. All the grooming that can be done won't avail anything if the horse is forced to stand where his feet are filthy, for his feet will become disordered and then the legs will get badly out of fix, and with bad legs and feet there is not much hope for anything. In short, to those owning horses we would say attend to the feet and legs.

How to Tell a Horse's Age.—The editor of the *Southern Planter* says: The other day we met a gentleman from Alabama, who have us a piece of information as to ascertaining the age of a horse after it has passed the ninth year, which was quite new to us, and will be, we are sure, to most of our readers. It is this: After the horse is nine years old, a wrinkle comes in the eyelid, at the upper corner of the lower lid, and every year thereafter he has one well-defined wrinkle for each year of his age over nine. If, for instance, a horse has three wrinkles, he is twelve; if four, thirteen. Add the number of wrinkles to nine, and you will always get at it. So says the gentleman; and he is confident it will never fail.

Sawdust for Stables.—Nothing makes so soft and easy a bed for our " dumb animals " as sawdust, more particularly the horse, as it is natural, before lying down, either by pawing or stepping back and forward, to brush all their bedding, if straw is used, under their hind feet, but would be less liable to move the sawdust. As regards injury to horses' feet or lungs on account of inhaling the dry dust, we know of a stable where horses are let, and I was informed by the owner that he had used sawdust for twelve years and never had been able to discover any bad effects from the use of it, and pointed out several horses that had been thus bedded for ten or twelve years; and had sold the manure at the usual rates, and never had heard of any objections on account of the sawdust.

The Watering of Horses.—M. P. Cartledge, member of the Royal College of Veterinary Surgeons, urges the great necessity of allowing an unlimited supply of water to horses; and he alludes to the very mistaken notion among grooms and others having the control of horses that water *ad libitum* is injurious. While grooms and others drink without stint themselves, they profess to know when a horse has drank sufficient, and so take away the pail before his natural wants are half satisfied. Horses will not drink to excess if watered frequently, and in their case drinking does no harm.

Cribbing.—Cribbing is a vice which springs from habit more than any other cause. It begins frequently from a desire to ease the teeth from inconvenience or perhaps pain, at that period when the dentition is perfecting, and then becomes fixed upon the horse as a vice. It is not injurious except when accompanied with " wind sucking," which is a series of deep inspirations by which flatulence and belly-ache are caused. When the habit is fixed' on a horse it is difficult to break it, and the only effective method is to use a muzzle which prevents him from thus using his teeth.

Linseed Oil for Horses.—Linseed oil is not only a valuable restorative for sick horses, but is exceedingly useful in cases of inflammation of the membranes, peculiar to the organs of respiration and digestion; it shields and lubricates the same, tranquilizes the irritable state of the parts, and favors healthy action. Put a couple of handfuls of seed into a bucket and pour a gallon and a half of boiling water upon it; cover it up a short time, then add a couple of quarts of cold water, when it will be fit for use. In case of an irritating cough add some honey.

Windgalls or Puffs.—Windgalls are puffy swellings occurring along the tendons of the legs of horses, below the knee. They are the results of sprains or strains of the tendons, and are generally filled with synovial fluid, or lymph, or serum. A padded bandage, with astringent lotions applied two hours a day at first, adding two hours every day after, until it is kept on continually, is the usual remedy. Rest from work is helpful to a cure.

Brittle Feet.—Some horses have such brittle feet that it is difficult to keep their shoes on. This is often caused by a sudden change from excessive and long-continued wetness to extreme dryness. The best treatment is to rub the soles and shells of the feet with a mixture composed of the following: Tar, two parts; beef suet, two parts; whale oil, four parts; beeswax and honey, one part each; melt over a slow fire, and mix well.

Ignorance in Shoeing.—Some blacksmiths who shoe horses do not know that the frog of the foot should be allowed to come to the ground; that it should not be pared down, as is frequently done, nor should it be touched when healthy. It is meant to pound upon the ground, and it is the pounding that it gets that is the life of the foot, and those horse-shoers who have not yet learned this very important fact ought to learn it or quit business. Most of the diseases and defects of horses' feet come from cutting away the frog or by raising it by high shoes clear away from the ground.

Avoiding Indigestion in Horses.—It is best to give a horse water before giving oats. The water stays in the stomach a very short time, but is quickly absorbed or passed into the bowels, where it is absorbed and goes into the blood. The horse secretes a very large quantity—more than four quarts—of saliva while eating a meal, which is sufficient to reduce the food to a pulp suitable for its digestion. So that to give water soon after eating, except in very small quantity, would be apt to cause indigestion and waste of the food by excessive dilution.

Flies and Horses.—A physician writing to the London *Daily News* recommends, to prevent the torment inflicted by the flies on horses, application to the latter, before harnessing, of a mixture of one part crude carbolic acid with six or more parts of olive oil. This should be rubbed lightly all over the animal with a rag, and applied more thickly to the interior of the ears and other parts most likely to be attacked.

To Cool Horses When Hot.—There is danger of congestion when cold water is thrown on the body of a horse when very hot and tired; and yet, how many do it? The better way is to throw water freely on the fore legs of the animal. This corresponds to the well-known custom of persons, when overheated, bathing the wrists for some time before drinking much.

To Recruit a Hide-Bound Horse.—To recruit a hide bound horse, give nitrate potassa (or saltpetre), four ounces; crude antimony, one ounce; sulphur, three ounces. Nitrate of potassa and antimony should be finely pulverized, then add the sulphur, and mix the whole well together. Dose a tablespoonful of the mixture in a bran mash daily.

Sprains and Bruises in Horses.—Dissolve an ounce of camphor in eight ounces of spirits of wine; then add one ounce of spirits of turpentine, one ounce of spirits of sal ammonia, half an ounce of oil of origanum and a tablespoonful of laudanum. Rub in a quarter of an hour with the hand, four times a day.

Flies in Horse Stables.—It is said that kerosene oil slightly sprinkled on the floor of the horse stables will serve to abate the nuisance of flies. It may be shaken out of a bottle through a hole in the cork. A pint will last a week for the purpose.

Hemlock Cribs.—A horse will not bite a crib made of hemlock lumber, nor will rats, mice, or other vermin gnaw through it.

Worms in Horses.—Worms in horses are caused by hard work, poor food, and general neglect. For ordinary cases of worms, common salt, nutritious food, and pure water will prove satisfactory. Salt should always be kept in the stalls of horses.

Over-Reaching.—An over-reaching horse, one whose hind feet is frequently hitting the forward shoes, should wear heavy shoes forward and light ones behind. The theory is that the heavier hoof will be thrown a little farther ahead than the lighter one.

Worms in the Rectum.—When a horse is affected with worms in the rectum there should be injected in the rectum, once daily for a week, a mixture of one pint of linseed oil and two drams of oil of turpentine. Feed at the same time bran mashes and oil meal.

Sensitive Jaws.—Some horses are more sensitive than others in the upper jaw, and will not go up on the steel bar or snaffle upper-jaw bit. In such cases have a bit made of plain round leather, the usual size of the upper-jaw bit.

Best Method of Cleaning Horses.—The best thing to clean a horse with is a corn-cob scrubbing-brush. It never can scratch his legs, as the curry-comb of tin does, while it does more work in the same time than curry-comb and brush put together.

Hints to Breeders of Shorthorns.—To learn a trade, is to do things precisely upon the same principles, and up to the same general standard that experts in the same trade attain to. The principles are simple, though the parts are complicated. So of Shorthorn cattle. They are merely machines for converting crude grain or grass into bone, muscle, adipose matter, and hair; and the whole secret of excellence—the superiority of one beast over another—consists in their ability to convert the most crude food in a given time into the finest quality of the tissues named, so distributing these as to give us a roomy frame of bone in the parts where we want room for the vital organs and for the choicest cuts, and thick, fleshy, well-marbled roasts, and broad, well-marbled steaks, in the parts where best fiber is produced. Such a conformation should be secured as will answer these ends so effectively as the engine is expected to generate steam through the consumption of fuel in the furnace. The conformation of the trunk of the cow is a subject worthy of very careful study. The bony frame is of secondary importance, the vital organs within being of the first importance, and the size and vigor of these, if accompanied by a liberal distribution of cellular tissue throughout the system, ensures a rapid conversion of food into nutritive particles and the disposition of these in the various tissues. Large lungs, and large heart, stomach and liver give size and rotundity to the trunk and width to the bosom. A large stomach is of the utmost importance, because furnishing a large surface. From this the gastric juice issues, and when we consider the inner surface of the stomach, and the air cells of the lungs, we must prize an extended surface in those organs as highly as we do a large surface in a steam boiler if we expect great results. Two of the worse faults in the construction of a Shorthorn are the following, viz.: the ribs starting from the spine in a downward direction, giving a wedge shape to the upper third of the chest; the other is a long rib deficient at the lower end, causing a curve upward in the lower line immediately back of the fore leg. We doubt if any other two defects are so hard to breed out as these. A drooping rump or low carriage forward may be brought up in one or two crosses, so that with after care they may not reappear; but the defects in the chest pointed out above depend upon deficient vital organs within. The re-organization and enlargement of the heart, lungs, stomach, and liver require many discreet crosses to accomplish. Passing from the chest backwards, we would call attention to the importance of the short ribs being long, and standing out horizontally from the spine, forming a level plane forward of the hips. This broad, level loin generally keeps company with a round, deep chest and is a point of excellence that should always be sought. The hind quarter that holds its width well back, carries a large amount of meat not represented in the quarter that narrows in rapidly from the hip back. A perfect symmetrically-organized frame, with the fleshy part so well distributed and packed as to make it difficult to tell where one portion of the carcass ceases and the next begins This is the goal to be aimed at. The third and last subject, "quality," we will treat very briefly. No intelligent breeder while striving to increase the depth and breadth of the carcass, loses sight of the equally important point, the texture of those parts of the animal that are to be consumed as human food. This idea of texture is never lost sight of by the fruit grower, and the excellencies which fix the value of the apple, viz., fair size, smooth surface, and tender, juicy meat, are the three things upon which we base our estimate of a Shorthorn. Now, the common notion is that all animals that handle mellow have high flavored, tender flesh. This is an erroneous idea, proved every day upon the butcher's block. We couple two animals together, expecting to secure well-fattened, ready feeders in the progeny they will generally transmit it. But if both the parents have dark, unsavory flesh, they and all their get, and all the progeny after for all time, will have the same, unless modified and improved by new crosses having light-colored, savory flesh.

Selecting Breeding Males.—The first object which any breeder of cattle or sheep must keep in view is that his stock must be healthy. In the selection of a male animal, therefore, the first things to be considered are the indications by which it may be possible to form a judgment as to his constitution. There can be no doubt that this is one of the important points of form or shape to which it is material for a breeder to look into in the selection of either a bull or ram. It is not enough to observe that they have wide breasts or bosoms, but the width which is noticed in looking at them from the front, should be continued along the brisket, which should show great fullness in the part under the elbows; it is also important that they should be thick through the region of the heart.

Another point to be carefully considered is the muscular system. Great muscular power is not only indicative of a good constitution and good health, but it has a merit in itself. Large muscles are the usual accompaniment of strength of constitution, and it also shows that when ready for the shambles there will be a good proportionate mixture of muscle and fat in the meat. In both bulls and rams a thick neck is proof of large muscles, and there can hardly be a greater fault in either animal than to have this wanting. Other indications of muscle will be more difficult to observe in sheep than in cattle. In a good bull there should be a full muscle on each side of the backbone, just behind the top of the shoulder blades. He should also have the muscles at the outside of the thigh full and extending nearly to the hough. A bull having these indications will seldom be found deficient in muscle.

Ringing a Bull.—We give an illustration of a plan for putting a ring through the nose of a bull worthy of the attention of stock-breeders. A ring is undoubtedly the safest mode of controlling the bull. Clamp rings having two knobs, which press into the nostrils, may be useful for occasional use, but a good stout copper ring should be put through the cartilage of the nose of every thoroughbred bull before he is four years old. This will last him for his lifetime, and whether tied up in the stable or out for exercise, it will effectually control him. The old-fashioned plan of inserting the rings was

by burning a hole through the cartilage with a hot iron, but this was a cruel and difficult process. The plan suggested is to use a weapon styled a trochar, similar to the surgical instrument employed for "tapping" in case of dropsy, and for "hoove" in cows. It is a sharp-pointed, round dagger (the point three-sided), carrying a silver-plated shield reaching from the upper part of the point to the handle. The above illustration will further explain.

The sheath being on the dagger when the operation is performed, the whole is easily pushed through the nose, the sharp point of the dagger piercing the nostril with so little pain that one man can easily hold the head still. The dagger is then withdrawn, leaving the sheath in the hole. The ring is then inserted into the end of the sheath, which is slowly withdrawn, leaving the ring in place. This is then closed and fastened with a screw.

These rings should be so well made that both the hinge and the screw should be perfectly smooth, and so fitting as to take a practiced eye to notice the joining.

The manner in which the operation is performed will be seen at a glance at the accompanying engraving.

The ring should turn freely round in the incision, which, having been made with a three-cornered cut, will be more sensitive against a pull than the smooth-burned hole. Indeed, it is sometimes necessary with the latter cruel operation to take the ring out after a time and resort again to burning, in order to make the cartilage sufficiently sensitive for the ring to be effective in managing the animal.

An Inexpensive Relish for Stock.—Stock men of large experience appreciate the need of salt for stock, and usually make such provision that animals under their care are daily provided with this relish. There are, however, many farmers who look upon salt as a luxury enjoyed by their stock when placed within reach, but not necessary to their thrift or comfort. Observation and experience have proven to those who have given most attention to the subject that cattle require for best results the salt they crave.

The French Government at one time commissioned a number of practical and scientific men to investigate the subject of salt as a relish for stock, and ascertain the quantity required for different animals. While only approximate figures could be arrived at in the numerous experiments made to settle this matter, a scale was fixed upon by this commission as the minimum daily allowances for the different animals in ordinary condition. In this a working ox or a milch cow is allowed two ounces of salt per diem. Repeated trials appeared to prove that the amount specified produced in milch cows the greatest flow of milk. Oxen fed the same amount presented sleek coats, while others receiving no salt were rough, mangy, and ill conditioned. The scale in question allowed for fattening stall-fed oxen, two and a half to four ounces of salt per day, and for fattening pigs, from one to two ounces. For sheep, from one-half ounce to two-thirds of an ounce was allowed. One ounce was set down as the daily portion for horses and mules.

The figures given above possess a practical value to feeders of stock, in that they represent the respective amounts best calculated to produce desirable results in the different animals named, and give an idea of the amount required by each kind. On small farms with few animals salt can be dealt out in small quantities each day, but where herds and flocks are numerous, salt boxes and troughs become a necessity, and are in any case a convenient and economical arrangement. These troughs or boxes ought, of course, to be in sheltered places and at points where animals can have daily access to them. Some should be placed at elevations to suit horses and cows, and others set within reach of sheep.

A plan in favor in the far West, and which recommends itself on the ground of economy, is mixing salt and hardwood ashes in equal proportions, combined with a sufficient amount of water to make a solid lump or mass. These lumps are distributed in the trough, where, with diligent licking, each animal gets a small quantity, the belief being that they will take in this form no more than they really require. In addition to the fact that salt is necessary to the thrift of animals, a strong argument in its favor in localities where cattle and sheep are allowed extended runs during the day, is that it proves a strong attraction, bringing them home at night without other incentive.

Cattle in Cornstalks.—A Kansas farmer writes: If cattle are allowed to run in stalk fields for an indefinite time they are apt to die from eating too much food of an indigestible character. Cornstalks when left standing in the field become woody and indigestible. Cattle when allowed to run, fill themselves so full that the stomach becomes clogged, the food heats, does not pass off, and the animal dies. For three winters I have fed my cows on shocked cornstalks, feeding no hay or straw, and in all cases they have done better than when fed on hay. In the winter of 1880 and 1881, I wintered 3,500 head of working oxen. I bought all the stalk fields that were accessible, allowed the cattle to run in them three hours each day, when I had them driven out. My reasons for so doing was not on account of smut, but because the stalks had become hard, woody and indigestible. I lost no cattle from this management, and returned them in the spring with a loss of only two to the hundred. Feeders have fed beef cattle for years on shock corn; they consider it the best and safest kind of feed.

Relieving Choked Cattle.—The accompanying engraving represents the instruments employed for relieving choked cattle, as recommended by Prof. Simonds, of the Royal Veterinary College of England.

In cases of choking," says Prof. S., " the amount of danger may mostly be calculated by the abdominal distension, for death results from the lungs being unable to expand in conse-quence of the pressure of the ru-men against the diaphragm."

He says: " In many c a s e s prior to unchoking the patient, the gaseous compounds which are disengaged from the ingesta and distend the rumen, must be given an exit to, by puncturing the rumen, to prevent suffoca-tion."

The instrument for unchoking, as shown in the sketch, c o n - sists of a probang and a gag; the latter is to be placed in the mouth as shown. Two assistants are re-quired. One of these should be placed on either side of the ani-mal, holding the handle of the gag, which protrudes from the side of the mouth, with one hand, and the opposite horn with the other. They must also keep the head elevated so as to bring it as near as possible in a straight line with the neck. We give Prof. Simonds's instructions in opera-ting as follows:

RELIEVING CHOKED CATTLE.

" The probang being held as represented, is to be p a s s e d through the opening in the gag and carried carefully over the dorsum of the tongue into the pharynx, and from thence pushed inwards until it reaches the ob-struction. Sufficient and well-regulated pressure is now to be made until the obstruction yields, when it is to be driven by the in-strument into the rumen. Care should always be taken to *propel the root into the first stomach*, and we should never rely on the power of the esophagus to do this after we have succeeded in removing it from its origi-nal situation. Want of attention to this simple rule has often protracted suf-fering to the animal, and not unfrequently death. The probangs in ordinary use are seldom of sufficient length, nor are the bulbs with which they are tipped of a proper shape. The instrument should not be less than six and a half feet long, and the bulbs should be large and slightly cup-shaped."

Bone Disease in Milch Cows.—For more than half a century there have been occasional outbreaks of a peculiar disease in New England, mostly affecting milch cows, and commonly known as bone-ail or stifle joint lameness. Heretofore the trouble has been chiefly confined to hilly sections, but seems now to be approaching the valleys.

This disease, technically called *Cachexhia ossifraga*, is not confined to the stifle joint, frequently affecting the hip and other joints also. In one case, where the hip joint was affected, examination showed that the articular surface of the head of the tibia or shank bone had been worn through by its friction with the femur, or thigh bone, by the absorption of the floating cartilage between the ends of the bones. Similar conditions were noticed in other instances. As it is believed this cartilage cannot be regenerated, it was at first a question whether the disease was curable. Before investigation, its cause was attributed to the phosphatic materials in the feed, and this idea has been fully established. Where such materials were supplied in the form of bran, the disease was thought to be occasioned by the excessive use of such feed, as it was known that such excess changes the bone into a sort of phosphate, while the healthy bone is an insoluble phosphate.

In former outbreaks, bone meal was found to be an effective remedy, and in recent instances it has been used with good results. A Suffield, Conn., man, of considerable experience, says that two ounces of the meal in a pint of bran, three times a week during the early summer and fall feeding, will generally cure, if accompanied with plenty of salt. In aggravated cases, however, the free use of this material is recommended. Still, care must be exercised lest it should be supplied too freely, as an excess is sometimes liable to injure the butter, because the putrid, oily matter of the bone is excreted by the udder as a sort of oleomargarine. But if the meal has been thoroughly clarified, this trouble is less apt to occur, and it may be avoided altogether by the use of cotton-seed meal, which is rich in phosphates without containing the obnoxious matter liable to be in bone meal. Bran is also largely made up of phosphates, but it is well to add corn meal.

The necessary mineral element can probably be furnished in hay that has been manured with superphosphates, which furnish lime and phosphoric acid that are greedily taken in by the plant. Indeed, the recent outbreak is accounted for by the fact that where it occurs, little, if any, mineral fertilizers are used. They are now being applied more extensively, and the gradual disappearance of the disease will doubtless follow.

Marks of a Good Cow.—Those who keep but one or two cows naturally want them for general purposes, do not want a mere butter cow nor yet a mere milk animal, but one which combines both in as great a degree as can be found. Such cows are not plentiful, we admit, or at least are not often for sale at a moderate price, so that when they are offered, it behooves would-be purchasers to be able to tell them.

We do not believe in very small cows, nor yet in large, heavy animals, as neither, as a rule, are capable of filling the bill, the former too often falling short in the quantity, while the large ones are apt to run too much to flesh to make them profitable dairy animals. The medium-sized ones invariably produce the best results, and a heavy milker and a large butter maker is seldom fat, as the majority of the food she consumes is converted into milk and butter. The head should be fine but bony, with small horns, large, mealy nose and shapely ears. The base of the horns and the inside of the ears should be of a bright golden color. We have never yet seen an animal with horns and ears well colored (golden yellow) which failed to make a fine quality of butter and highly colored. It is an unmistakable sign. The body should be of good size, and the width and depth rapidly increase as it runs to the rear or hind quarters. The milk veins should be large and prominent, and the udder need not necessarily be large, so it is not meaty, but is small when milked out. The teats should be of good size, and only have a single hole in each; we have seen quite a number with teats having two holes. The hair should be fine and soft, while the skin should be pliable, and almost as soft to touch as velvet or kid. In color it should be tinged deeply with yellow, especially on the shoulders and flank and along the back. Color of the hair is rather a secondary matter, though the best cows are generally yellow, tawn, gray or white, with dark marks edged with yellow. Black cows but seldom prove to be good general-purpose ones, though of course there are exceptions frequently met with.

Cattle Rack.—We give the following illustrated design for a rack to feed cattle from in the yard. We think it far superior in point of economy and convenience to anything of the kind we have seen. It can easily be made by anyone possessing ordinary skill in using tools:

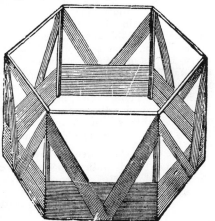

CATTLE RACK.

The shape, as will be seen, is six sided, or in the form of a hexagon. It consists of six upright posts five feet long (3 by 4 scantling will answer, or round poles 3 or 4 inches through will do very well), and twelve boards, each one foot in width and five feet long. These latter nailed to the posts horizontally will form the box. To strengthen the whole and keep the cattle from stepping over the sides, nail strips of thick boards or plank flatwise across the upper end of the posts. Then nail two boards diagonally upon each side, extending from the top of the posts to the bottom of the box, leaving a space of about a foot and a half in the center on a line with the upper edge of the box. These slanting boards serve as braces, and give strength and firmness to the whole structure, and make six feeding places for the cattle. If scantling is used for posts, it would be well to hew off the corner from each, so as to make the boards fit well.

Mode of Construction.—Nail the boards to two sets of posts to form two opposite sides. Cut two strips of boards about ten feet four inches long; stand the side upright and nail these strips across the top and bottom— across the diameter—then bring the other ends within five feet, and nail on the boards across the end; you will then have three sides formed. Nail on the other two opposite sides and end. Put on the braces and it is done. It can be moved to different parts of the yard, and with care will last for years.

Economy in Feeding Cattle.—There is more waste in feeding than in anything else on the farm. Wheat straw, corn-stalks, and even chaff may be fed, if properly prepared. With a fodder cutter that not only cuts but crushes, corn fodder can be made as palatable as clover hay, and wheat straw, when cut into short lengths and mixed with hay, answers excellently when grain is fed with it. Cows will always eat chaff if it is mixed with cut food. If all such feeding material as corn fodder and wheat straw is cut up fine, and well moistened, salted, and mixed with bran, shorts and meal, with a pound of linseed or cotton-seed meal additional, a mess will thus be prepared that is not only nourishing and healthy, but superior to hay alone. It is not intended here to recommend straw in the place of better food, but we claim that if a saving can be effected by feeding straw in connection with concentrated food, there will be a saving, not only of the hay in the loft by reason of the substitution, but also of much that annually goes to waste.

How wasteful it is to throw fodder and straw over the fence into the farm-yard to be picked over and trampled in the dirt without being consumed. Every pound of fodder and straw is valuable and can be put to useful service, which is very important when the winter's supply of hay seems unlikely to last, and when the cold season is unusually long. Nor is it proper to allow fodder to remain all the year stacked in the fields, for it is almost every time that the winds blow it down, where it remains until fed, but it is not then in as proper condition as if well cured and placed under cover. As to using straw for bedding, this, also, is wastefully done, as if it possessed no value; and if chaff is not preferred for feeding, let it be used as an absorbent in the stables, for which purpose nothing is superior to it. A crop of turnips, or what may be better, beets, parsnips, and carrots, should be grown for stock, not only for their value for feeding purposes, in proportion to their cost, but also because they afford a succulent diet in winter when every other kind of food is dry, and at times not relished.

How Good Cows are Ruined.—Milking is an art, and the farm hand who knows how to milk properly is more valuable to the careful dairyman than any other help. Of course, anybody can milk, and some can milk a dozen cows before breakfast. The careful manager, however, is not so anxious for fast help as he is to employ those who are careful. The operation should never be hurried, but the milk should be drawn steadily, and, as it flows, naturally. Some cows have very tender teats, and the rapid milkman forgets this fact in his endeavor to make speed. The cow that is naturally impatient and fretful does not like to submit to rough handling, and her disposition is soon ruined by such treatment. With the constant irritation she will fail in quantity, and be less productive, just as any human being would fail to perform faithful service when laboring under mental affliction or trouble. As the udder becomes distended and filled with milk, the desire on the part of the cow is to be relieved of its contents, and she willingly submits to it for the relief it occasions. The constant practice of being milked at stated intervals impresses itself strongly upon her, and she will seldom offer resistance without cause. When a cow, therefore, that has been a patient deliverer of milk becomes fractious, the fault can always be traced to the milkman. The careless dairyman is the one who complains of the failure of his cows to keep up the flow, and bloody milk, garget and other evils are the results of his own bad management. There is another point in the treatment of cows that demands attention, and that is allowing them to stand a long time waiting to be milked. With cows that give large yield it is very painful, and when the udders have been filled to their utmost, and the milkman is not on hand to relieve them, they become exceedingly nervous and restless. This will do more to cause a cow to go dry before her period than anything else, and many a good cow has been sent to the shambles through diminution of quantity, simply because nature has revolted at her sufferings, and allowed her to dry up because her storehouse was not emptied of its contents at the proper times. She should also be milked to the last drop, if possible, and as the last portion of milk is claimed to be the richest, the udder should be left with nothing in it. With regularity in feeding and milking, and kind treatment at all times, the cow will not only become gentle, and remain so, but will milk on several weeks longer than otherwise. An experienced dairyman needs help that are skillful, and he knows how to judge the milkman's work by the behavior of his cows. When a stable of cows begin to give trouble in milking, it is only necessary to observe the manner in which

they are milked in order to cure the evil. The udder of a cow is a very delicate structure, and she quickly rebels at rough usage or improper periods of milking.

To Prevent Cattle from Hooking Fences.—The mode herewith illustrated will be found a sure cure for cattle that hook or put their heads through fences. Take a one-eighth inch annealed wire ten inches long; make a ring in one end (one inch and a half); grind the other end sharp, to punch through the gristle in the nose. The animal's head has to be fastened securely in the stanchions, in order to bore the holes through the horns, which should be

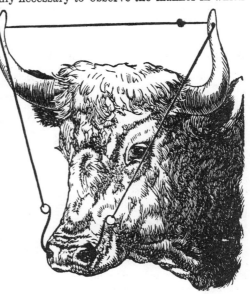

TO PREVENT CATTLE FROM HOOKING FENCES.

done with a three-eighth inch bit; then punch the wire through, and make the same sized ring in the sharp end; now take a cord that will run easily through the holes in the horns, and tie one end to the ring on one side and pass the cord through the holes in the horns to the other ring; the wire should be bent up above the nostrils to prevent the breath from rotting the cord; the cord should not be very tight when put on, for the rains will tighten it enough.

To keep a bull from jumping and hooking fence, put on the above and a poke with the sword or arm running through a wire ring in the nose, long enough to keep the arm from bearing on the wire, and the animal is at home all the time.

Currying Milch Cows.—To the farmer the idea of currying a cow, milch or otherwise, is an absurdity; but to dairymen who have highly-bred cows, who take a pride in their business and get the top price of the market for their produce, it is a matter of moment, in that it is known to increase the milk flow and the butter produce by ten to twenty per cent.

There are many points in the conduct of a dairy, unknown, indeed, unthought of by farmers, that will presently have a prominent place in their management, very much to the benefit of themselves and those who receive and make use of their produce.

Among those are: Succulent food, protection from inclement weather, kind handling, thorough and careful milking, full and regular feeding, clean stabling (when stabled), and an absence of foul odors, good ventilation, plenty of light and that thorough cleansing of the skin without which no milch cow can perform her duty thoroughly and well. With all these we must, to have a " tip top " article of butter, have the washing of the udder and teats before milking, and with this an entire absence of the filth accumulated in feeding and lounging between milkings.

Of all these, one of the most important is that of periodical currying, in that it cleanses the hide of superfluous hair, keeps it active and healthful and void of that peculiar odor so commonly found in milk and sometimes in butter. It promotes the secretion and disposition of the putrid particles of the animal system which would otherwise be absorbed by the secretery glands and be carried off in the milk, and leaves the latter not only purer but of a much better quality, and gives promise to the butter maker of a higher color and a purer flavor to the butter from the churn, hence a higher price in the market.

TO PREVENT COWS KICKING.

Herein may seem lots of trouble over details, but when reduced to a system they occupy little of time, labor or expense.

To Prevent Cows Kicking.—We give an illustration of a patented device for preventing a cow from kicking, which is said by those who have used it to be effectual. It consists of a light iron semi-circle intended to go over the back of the animal, with a joint and ratchet at the side, and a wooden block at each end, which fits to the flank of the cow, and prevents her from moving her foot forward. The inventor claims that it can be affixed in three or four seconds and that its operation is neither cruel nor harsh. On the contrary the habit has been entirely cured after it is used for a short time. It will doubtless suggest a modification that will be useful to farmers without infringing upon the patent.

Black Tongue in Cattle.—The symptoms are inflammation of the mouth, swelling of the head and face, discharge of bloody saliva, and high fever marks the first stages. Ulcers soon appear under and on the sides of the tongue. Then the throat and neck swell, and if the disease is not checked gangrene ensues and the animal dies. The disease is said to yield readily to early and proper treatment. The following has proved very successful: The animal should be bled from the neck vein. Give him castor oil, one pint, to be repeated in ten hours if it should not operate. Then use the following: Powdered burnt alum, four ounces; chloride of lime, two ounces; corn meal, two quarts. Mix, and with this powder swab the mouth frequently.

Lice on Cattle.—A correspondent of the *Country Gentleman* says on this subject: The more common remedies recommended for relieving cattle and stock from lice are more or less dangerous to life or health, and must be used with extreme care. An unfailing remedy which may be used by any one without danger to life or limb would be a boon to many farmers. Such a remedy we have in the bee-larkspur of our flower-gardens. A strong tea made from the seeds or foliage of the plant can be used as a wash with perfect safety. Any part of the plant may be used in making the wash, either green or dried. The plant should be gathered before it is frosted, and cured and preserved as other herbs are. In the use of kerosene, mercurial ointment, tobacco, etc., great care must be used or injury results from absorption; it enters the limbs or other parts of the animal and is often a permanent injury. No such danger need be apprehended in the use of larkspur. All the parts where the vermin lodge should be well scrubbed with the wash, and if thoroughly well done in a pleasant, mild day, one application is sufficient. In former days, when school children were troubled, I have heard old people tell their experience in using this remedy to their complete satisfaction. Another equally harmless remedy is aloes in fine powder, which may be used dry by filling a common pepper box with the powder and sprinkling it freely into the hair on the neck, back, sides and rump of the infested animal. Rub it thoroughly through the hair and on the skin with the ends of the fingers. Leave the animal undisturbed for a week, then card thoroughly and apply as before. Continue this at intervals of a week, till not a living parasite is left. Usually two applications, if thoroughly made, will suffice.

Another writer says that to destroy lice on live stock he has found nothing better than strong carbolic soapsuds. The soap usually sold under that name is not strong enough for the purpose. It may be easily prepared and at any degree of strength that may be required. Get a pound of carbolic acid crystals, which may be had at any wholesale druggist's. I get them in Boston at a cost of sixty cents per pound. Take ten pounds of common bar soap, put in a pan with a little water and heat until dissolved. Take out the cork from the bottle containing the acid, and set it in hot water, which will cause the acid to become fluid; add this to the soap and stir well. Set away to cool and you will have a soap at a small cost that will be strong enough to kill any vermin which infest domestic animals, and which will cure barn itch or any cutaneous diseases to which they are liable. It is good to cleanse and heal sores, and a wash of it will be found good where animals are hide-bound and the skin out of condition; it will be found good to wash the inside of poultry houses to render them sweet and kill and prevent vermin. It is a cheap, safe and sure remedy, and should find a place in all well regulated premises.

A stock-grower, writing to the New York club, gives his mode of destroying lice on cattle. He says: "I destroy them with brine—any kind of salt water will do it. I find two kinds of lice; the blue lice, and I think the other is hen lice. I tried red precipitate one year; it killed the lice, two yearlings, and a two-year old. But washing the cattle with brine is easier, and they get into the habit of licking one another, and are more gentle toward each other.

Another writer recommends grease. He says: "Insects breathe by means of small pores on their sides. Grease or oil that comes in contact with the insects closes the pores and stops the breathing. Mercurial ointment kills as much by the lard in it as by the mercury—that is, so far as the vermin are concerned, but not as to the animals that lick it off from their bodies, so that almost any oily or greasy application will be destructive to insect vermin that infest animals if it is applied where it will do the most good."

Still another authority says: " A good remedy for lice on cattle is water in which potatoes were boiled. For every one of your cattle take two quarts of water and eight middle-sized potatoes cut in half. If you have ten cattle, you must take eighty potatoes and twenty quarts of water. When the potatoes are soft take them out. Get a large sponge and wash the cattle freely, choosing a warm day. Comb them with a currycomb, and you will be astonished to see the effects of the potato water."

Cheap Shelter for Stock.—Shelter for stock is one of the great needs of farmers. It is costly to build a barn and shed, but for simple purposes of shelter farmers might make greater use of their abundance of straw. In some localities it is customary to burn this as the readiest means to get it out of the way. A much better use might be made of it in constructing shelter for all kinds of stock, both against rain and cold. A very good plan is to make a frame of poles (as the engraving represents), and stack straw over them. This work should be done at threshing time, but if it has been

neglected it may be done at any later time. It pays richly in health, thrift, and in the saving of food, to provide shelter.

The Soiling System with Cows.—It is a question of economy as to whether it is wise in us to allow the herd the full occupancy of a pasture, in order to reap the products in the shape of butter and milk. A large herd re-

CHEAP SHELTER FOR STOCK.

quires a large pasture, and before any estimate can be made in the way of profit and loss, the value of the pasture itself, and the probability of what it may yield if cultivated, should be considered.

The soiling system, which demands that the cattle shall be fed at the barn instead of pasturing in the field, has many advocates, and the reasons in its favor are that fewer fences are required, more manure is saved, larger yields of milk and butter are procured, and less space is required. Those who oppose the method say that it requires extra labor, and that the health of the stock is improved by their having the liberty of the pasture.

Every consideration should be made, however, regarding the conditions. If the stock is kept on farms that are too large for cultivation, and where space is no object, with an unlimited supply of grass that cannot be utilized except by being pastured, then the soiling system is not economical, for no necessity arises for its practice; but on small dairy farms, where land is valuable and the products within easy reach of the best markets, the system of stall feeding of cattle is one that should be carried to an extreme, for the result will be very profitable, any other method being suicidal in the extreme. The extra labor required is equalized by the saving in fences, and the care and management is balanced by the savings of the liquid and solid manure. Both systems, therefore, are profitable under certain circumstances, the whole matter being regulated by soil, climate, capacity for production, and distance from market.

Raising Calves.—A stock grower writes: As a general rule, I let the calf suck the cow for three days, then I take it away; and after it has been twelve hours without food, I give it some new milk—about ten pounds, if I can get him to eat it. If, while the calf is running with the cow, you can handle it a little, so as to make it tame, it will learn to eat much easier. I am a large, stout man, and can easily hold a calf. If the calf is tame, so that it will come up to you and suck your hand, you can get it to eat the first time without much trouble; but if it is not tame, I get a-straddle of the calf, back him up in a corner, hold the pail between my knees, put one finger in the calf's mouth, and with the other hand hold the calf's head in the pail, and keep doing so until the calf commences to suck. Sometimes he will begin right off, and others will refuse for maybe ten minutes; but I never had one but what would suck after a while. By the third time I feed him I commence to take my finger out of his mouth, and do so more and more until he drinks without having a finger to suck. I feed entirely on new milk for ten days, then give about half new and half twelve-hours-old skimmed milk (using the cream I take off the milk on the table); then, after another ten days, I drop the new milk, having done so by degrees, and feed half twelve-hours-old skimmed milk and half skimmed milk. I work it so for a little while; but soon give him all skimmed milk, giving about eleven or twelve pounds at a feeding, and feed twice a day, without any meal or bran. I give in winter all the hay they want, keeping some before them all the time. After a calf is three months old you can give it some meal or shorts, if you wish; but I do not think it is best if it can have plenty of milk. I feed calves until about five months old, and then commence to wean them by degrees. If calves scour while they are being fed milk, I give them about two teaspoonfuls of salt. In the summer I feed them their milk cold, and it is generally thick, sour milk. In the winter I warm it a little, about milk-warm or blood-heat. It is well to handle your calves some while they are eating, so as to make them tame, and that is one advantage of raising them by hand, for they are generally tame.

Charcoal for Sick Animals.—In nine cases out of ten, when an animal is sick the digestion is wrong. Charcoal is the most efficient and rapid corrective. The hired man came in with the intelligence that one of the finest cows was very sick, and a kind neighbor proposed the usual drugs and poisons. The owner being ill and unable to examine the cow, concluded that the trouble came from over-eating, and ordered a teaspoonful of pulverized charcoal to be given in water. It was mixed, placed in a junk bottle, the head turned downward. In five minutes improvement was visible, and in a few hours the animal was in the pasture quietly grazing. Another instance of equal success occurred with a young heifer which had become badly bloated by eating green apples after a hard wind. The bloat was so severe that the sides were as hard as a barrel. The old remedy, saleratus, was tried for correcting the acidity. But the attempts at putting it down always raised coughing, and it did little good. Half a teaspoonful of fresh powdered charcoal was given. In six hours all the appearance of the bloat had gone, and the heifer was well.

How to Break a Heifer or a Vicious Cow to Milk.—A vicious cow becomes so only by education, or, as it is sometimes said, by being spoiled. The case is much worse than that of a heifer, and when the cow is apparently cured of a bad habit, it is liable upon slight provocation to return. The principle involved in the treatment of all brutes is to employ kindness together with the means of proper restraint. In the case of the young or the vicious cow, place her in stanchions or fasten her securely. Pass a girth—either a strap or a rope—around the body, just in front of the bag, letting it pass in the rear of the right hip and in front of the left. Draw the girth somewhat tightly—more or less so, to correspond with the severity of the case. Take pail and stool, and sit down to the milking. The case must be a very obstinate one which will give any lasting trouble. The philosophy of the treatment is that the strap so restrains the actions of the muscles of the hind legs that the animal cannot kick to harm, or get its foot into the pail, while the restraint is steady and sure and the punishment not severe. A woman or boy can manage an ordinary case. Heifers broken in this way, we think, become more thoroughly gentle and submissive. Of course an even temper and kind treatment must be strictly observed.

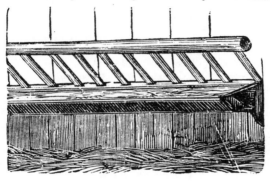

FEED RACK FOR STOCK.

Feed Rack for Stock.—The rack represented in this engraving is designed to be placed against a building or wall, under cover. It may be adapted to any kind of stock by placing it at the proper height. The cut plainly explains its construction. The trough below the slats may be used for feeding grain or roots. This style of rack is very popular in Europe.

Science Applied to Stock-Feeding.—It is often necessary to mix different kinds of food to secure the best combination of flesh and fat-producing elements. Experiments have been made in Germany to ascertain what is the proper combination of these principles. Ordinary food contains two leading elements, one of which supplies the flesh and muscle of the animal frame, and the other the fat and heat. These two elements should bear a certain relation to each other. In the combination producing the best results, the ratio is one of the muscle-producing to three or four of the fat-producing. Our common crop contains these elements in very different ratios. In corn-fodder it is 1 to 10, which is too small proportion of the muscle-producing element in proportion to the fat-producing. In wheat straw, they are 1 to 15; in oat straw, they are 1 to 16; in German millet, they are 1 to 3, so that this, when cut in the dough state, possesses the proper combination. In corn (grain) they are 1 to 7 or 8, too much of the fat for the muscle-producing elements. This corresponds to our experience. Corn is too heating for work stock in our climate in summer. It is, however, excellent for fattening animals. In oats (grain) these elements are 1 to 5, nearer correct than in corn. In wheat bran, 2 to 8 1–2; in rye, 1 to 6. European field bean has 1 to 1.8 (one and eight-tenths), showing too much muscle-producing for the fat-producing elements. The proper medium may be attained by mixing two kinds of food. Thus corn and peas mixed make the ratio about correct. Clover hay is 1 to 3; lucerne, 1 to 2; vetch, 1 to a little more than 2.

How Practical Farmers Manage their Cattle.—A well-known firm of practical farmers give the following information of the method pursued by them: "Unless the weather is stormy, we turn our breeding bulls out for exercise half of every day, often with the cows in the pasture, when none of them are in heat. After breeding our cows we keep them in a stable, where they cannot be with the other cows for from ten to fifteen hours. We have a few stalls that are specially designed for cows that are due to calve during cold weather, and, of course, these are made as warm as we can get them. We turn the cows out with their calves three times each day, until the calves are six to eight weeks old, then only twice a day. We rarely allow calves to run with dam in pasture, though we put the calves out to grass as soon as they have learned to eat it. Feed young calves well on shelled corn, oats and meal. Have separate pastures for bulls and heifer calves and do not allow them to pasture together after the bulls are three or four months old. Our dry cows we winter principally on hay, feeding very little grain, except to young stock and those that have calves at their sides, or those designed for the show-ring. We breed our heifers when about twenty months old."

CALF WEANER.

Calf Weaner.—This invention relates to the class of calf weaners adapted to be attached to the central cartilage of the calf's nose, like a bull ring, the parts of the weaner being provided with sharp points that come against the cow's bag when the calf attempts to suck. The parts or sections of the device are attached together by a pivot forming a part of one of the points. They are held closed by means of a small screw. This device is very effective, simple and cheap.

Training Horns.—If it is desirable to straighten a horn, you may frequently scrape with a piece of glass, or a knife, the hollow side, which will cause it to grow faster on that side; but in that case it must not be scraped deeply, for then it becomes weaker on that side, and will be turned toward the weaker side. Some scrape the side toward which they wish to turn the horn quite thin, and then scrape the opposite side just enough to make it grow faster, and that will turn it toward the thinly scraped side. If you wish to turn a horn up, scrape on the under side just enough to make it grow faster on that side. A very barbarous way to turn a horn is sometimes practiced, by searing with a hot iron on that side toward which the horn is to be turned. This prevents the growth of horn on that side, and the growth upon the other side turns the horn. The horns may be polished by rubbing them with fine sand paper, and then with pumice-stone, and then oiling them. But this artificial manipulation of horns is seldom necessary. The horns of well-fed cattle will generally grow in comely shape if let alone.

The hair is sometimes oiled to give it a glossy appearance, but the best gloss is put upon the hair by rich and appropriate feeding. Nature, under proper conditions, does this work best.

Hollow Horn.—The first symptoms of the disease are readily seen. The animal affected refuses to eat, and shows an indisposition to move about. It not properly treated at once, the disease soon becomes so severe as to prevent the animal from feeding at all, and death is generally the result. The old plan of boring the horns and pouring in turpentine should never be resorted to, as it does no good, and gives the animal unnecessary pain. The horns are not effected, and consequently need no doctoring. The tongue is the member wherein lies the trouble. By securing the animal's head, so as to prevent injury to yourself from its horns, and then pulling out the tongue and pressing it downward, over the under lip, hundreds of little black heads of so-called flesh-worms will rise above the surface. Take a dull table knife and scrape off these black heads carefully and gently; then throw on the tongue a little salt or pepper, or both mixed together, which will bring up the saliva and set the animal's tongue to working. In a few hours at most the animal will begin to eat, and the trouble will be ended. We have never known this remedy to fail, no matter how severe the case.

Taste of Turnips in Milk.—There are several remedies, says the *American Agriculturist,* to prevent the taste of turnips in milk, but we believe no one of them can be strictly relied upon as effectual; we will, however, give them in order:

1. The objectionable taste comes from the crown of the turnip. If this is cut off and thrown away entire, the remainder will not affect the milk. 2. Dissolve a teaspoonful of carbonate of soda in a teacupful of warm water, and add this to six gallons of milk when first set in the pans. For a single gallon, of course one-sixth of the above would be sufficient, and for two or three gallons in due proportion. The turnips ought to be given to the cow immediately after milking. 3. Pulp or crush the turnips so fine as to make them quickly and easily digested after eating, and when fed mix with cut hay or straw. 4. Scald the milk as soon as drawn from the cows. The best way to do this is to insert the milk can into a large pan or kettle about three-quarters full of boiling water, and stir the milk until it reaches 80 to 90 degrees of heat, and then set it away to gradually cool off. The cream then rises thick, comes off in a lump, and is churned quickly. All the above remedies are so simple as to be easily tried, and if they do no good, cannot effect harm.

Leaves for Bedding.—An economical farmer writes: "In the scarcity of rye straw, and the absence of saw-dust and other material for bedding cattle, we have been forced to use forest leaves to keep the horse and cow in cleanly condition, and on the whole are much pleased with them. The gathering was from the roadside, and along the walls, where brush and leaves had accumulated for years. A few basketfuls were put under the animals every morning, and kept there until they were well saturated with the urine, and then thrown out into the manure heap. With a plenty of this material, kept dry under a shed, and used abundantly, there is very little loss of liquid manure. As an absorbent, it is much more effective than we expected to find it. Leaves have a high reputation as a material for the hot-bed and the compost heap, and are worth the labor of gathering, in most cases for their fertilizing properties. Cords of them are going to decay in the sight of almost every rural home, and it is the rare exception that they are utilized. Meanwhile the fields and garden are famished for want of manure, or supplied with concentrated fertilizers at forty dollars a ton.

The First Milk.—The custom of weaning the calf from the cow when it is only three days old is a barbarous one. We are familiar with the fact that cows are sometimes injured by such a course, also, especially if she is naturally of a nervous, anxious disposition, she soon learning the habit of holding up her milk, and when a cow holds up her milk she has become addicted to the most incurable vice known. There is another thing connected with the weaning of the calf at so early an age, which is the plain statement that we make in claiming that the milk is unfit for use, although the calf is usually taken away in order that the milk may be sold. Those who have had experience in the dairy know that milk from cows that have recently come in is ropy, and possesses a distinct characteristic in appearance from that of cows that have been in service for a longer time. Thus, it is not only unnatural to deprive the cow of her calf so early, but to use the milk. It also pays to keep the calf on the milk until it is old enough to be sold at a fair price.

Obstructed Teats.—The more the udder is stimulated to extra secretion of milk, so much the more is it liable to congestion and inflammation. The pressure, too, of a great quantity of milk in the udder upon the circular muscle (sphincter), which closes the end of the teat, tends to set up more or less irritation there, and this will sometimes result in excessive thickening of the walls and hard milking, or even complete closure of the orifice. The simplest and best treatment is to slightly dilate the opening of the teat, once or twice a day, with a perfectly smooth probe. A silver milking tube, about a twelfth of an inch in diameter, will answer; or, when this is not available, a probe of the same size made of gutta percha. A small size will be necessary at first, and, after a day or two, when that passes easily, a larger one, until finally the orifice is easily dilatable and the milking sufficiently free. In every case the probe should be well oiled, and introduced with caution, so as to avoid injury to the internal parts. A silver tube should be warmed before it is introduced.

To Test the Health of a Horse or Cow.—In horses the pulse at rest beats forty times, in an ox from fifty to fifty-five, and in sheep and pigs about seventy to eighty beats per minute. It may be felt wherever a big artery crosses a bone. For instance, it is generally examined in the horse on the cord which crosses over the bone of the lower jaw in front of its curved position, or in the bony ridge above the eye, and in cattle over the middle of the first rib, and in sheep by placing the hand on the left side, where the beating of the heart may be felt. Any material variations of the pulse from the figures given above may be considered as a sign of disease. If rapid, hard and full, it is an indication of high fever or inflammation; if rapid, small and weak, low fever, loss of blood or weakness. If slow, the possibilities point to brain disease, and if irregular, to heart troubles. This is one of the principal and sure tests of the health of an animal.

Black Leg.—Black leg in young cattle generally attacks calves in the fall when they get the rank growth of feed and are subject to sudden changes of weather from rains and frosts. It sometimes attacks thrifty calves in the winter when they are in the house and eating dry feed. We believe the herdsman can trace the disease back to the cause, and we believe the cause is the same in winter as in fall and spring; that is, rapid growth from generous feed and liability to sudden chills from being kept in too warm houses and exposures to cold while out during the day. Stables should not be too warm, nor should calves be deprived of exercise. Saltpetre in salt is used by experienced herdsmen as a preventive; bleeding will prevent the disease spreading among calves; for, although it is not contagious, the cause that produces it in one is apt to produce it in others.

Treatment of Horn Brittleness.—In treating cows for horn brittleness, a stock raiser in Austria found no good resulting from feeding bone meal when the water used from a spring was perfectly soft—that is, without mineral matter. But upon changing them to the water of another spring containing carbonate, sulphate and phosphate of lime, and chlorate of magnesia in small quantities, the effects were as follows: 1. The animals drank half as much again as before. 2. The cows gave more and better milk than before. 3. The worst diseased cows at once began to get better, and this was the first case in which any of them recovered without removal. 4. The oxen showed far better condition than could be previously attained on the best of food and with the most careful attention. No fresh cases occurred as soon as the change of water was introduced.

Sores on Cattle.—There are many sores on cattle, which if kept constantly washed clean with cold water and kept free from dirt, would heal of themselves. A very careful herdsman says his practice of curing hoof-rot is to thoroughly cleanse the affected parts with warm water and soap; and then apply warm tar between the hoofs. In very bad cases there will be a large core to come out; remove it carefully with the thumb and finger, cleanse the cavity as above with soap and water, and then fill it with warm tar. Keep the parts thoroughly covered with tar, even if it is necessary to use a bandage. Keep the animal in a clean, dry pasture. It is no more liable to affect the whole system than any other ulcer. When once cured there is no danger of its appearing again unless from the same cause.

How to Milk a Cow.—The most economical way to milk a cow, all things considered, is to milk the two fore teats clean, leaving off with a pretty full stream, and then milk the hind ones down to a short stream, and, returning to the fore ones, milk them to the same condition, not touching the hind ones again. This will leave the teats empty, and the bag, too. It is a false notion that tugging away at the teats stimulates a cow to give more milk; but, on the contrary, emptying the bag as soon as possible yields more; then the cow can have the extra time to eat, which is a better stimulus than either. A slow milker is never tolerated in the dairy districts, and a " stripper " is an injury anywhere. The sooner a cow is milked, and all the organs connected with feeding, digestion, and secretion are left in their natural condition, the better it is for the cow.

Caked Udder.—When a cow's milk suddenly dries up and becomes clotted in the udder, it is probably due to garget or inflammation of the udder from some one of many causes. The udder is then hard or lumpy, and hot. A remedy is to give the cow at once eight or twelve ounces of Epsom salts, with half an ounce of saltpetre, repeating the latter in six hours. If the milk is difficult to draw, a solution of one ounce of carbonate of soda in a pint of water should be injected in the teats with a syringe, and then milked out. This will bring away the curded milk which, if left in, will make matters very much worse. If the cow is feverish, the saltpetre may be repeated for a day or two. To bathe the udder in cold water, rubbing and squeezing it gently for a considerable time, is useful.

Another remedy is to wash and rub thoroughly with water as hot as you can bear your hand. Then rub with a dry cloth. Then apply hog's lard, or what is better, grate good yellow carrot fine and simmer it in the lard to an ointment and apply and rub as above.

Cows Winter Themselves.—Many farmers are accustomed to dry off their cows early, milking them only about eight months. We think it improves the milking qualities of the cows to milk them ten months, but they should be well fed. We have a neighbor, who, ten years ago, found himself short of hay in the fall, and lamented that he should have to pay out nearly all of the product of his cows through the summer to purchase hay at high prices to winter them. He had a moderate amount of straw, and we suggested that the product of his cows from the first day of December, if well fed, would pay for all the corn and meal, middlings, etc., necessary to winter his cows in fine condition. He tried this, keeping account of purchases of feed and sales of butter, and found that the butter came out ten dollars ahead in the spring.

Cornstalks for Cattle.—A Maine farmer says: Farmers justly set a high value on well cured corn stalks, but some find a difficulty in getting their stock to eat them as cleanly as they wish. I have overcome this difficulty this winter by sprinkling them with hot brine. I withheld dry salt from the stock a while, also husks, and made a brine by putting salt into a watering pot and pouring on hot water; gave the husks a bountiful sprinkling and fed them the last thing at night, instead of feeding them in the morning, as formerly. I think if I had tried this plan years ago I should have saved a great amount of fodder that was thrown out and trodden under foot.

Foul Foot in a Cow.—Cows and horses are subject to a disease of the feet similar to scratches in horses. Diseased granulations, similar in appearance to the heart of a cauliflower, break out and excrete a thin acrid matter. The treatment should be, to dress the diseased part with caustics, such as powdered sulphate of copper (blue vitriol) or sulphate of zinc (white vitriol), rubbed up smoothly, with clean, sweet lard, and give the animal repeated doses of one ounce hyposulphite of soda, as an alterative. The soda should be given every other day for a week or ten days.

Kicking Cows.—A writer says he once had a very valuable heifer which was an exceedingly vicious kicker. To cure her of the habit, he put a common garden hoe end in front of her off hind leg, and behind and above the gambrel joint of the nigh hind leg. Then sitting down on the right to milk, he put the handle of the hoe well up under his arm and began milking. The heifer could not stir either hind leg, and after one week she could be milked safely without fettering, and proved to be a valuable and gentle animal.

Warm Water for Cows.—Warm water is an excellent thing for cows giving milk; it is as good as two or three quarts of meal a day; but if you mix meal and shorts with it cows must be allowanced, as they will drink too much—enough to diminish the flow of milk. The quantity will vary with the character of feed and the cow. A little good judgment is a nice thing here, as everywhere else.

Roots for Stock.—The value of roots for stock is not appreciated to the extent that it should be. In the rotation of crops in England turnips rank high, and it is not uncommon for a farmer to devote from twenty to fifty acres to this crop. Cattle are kept there in fine condition in winter on raw turnips, and the latter also make excellent food for sheep. On rich land the crop produces very largely, and a comparatively small space is sufficient for ordinary wants.

Jumping Cattle.—To stop a cow or steer from jumping over fences nail a horseshoe on one forward foot. This prevents the hoof from spreading, and consequently renders the animal unable to spring. This is calculated to be very effectual.

Mixing Hay for Stock.—A mixture of one-third clover hay with timothy and redtop is recommended for any kind of stock. This mixture, it is said, will produce more milk, more growth, and more fat in stock than clear timothy and redtop.

Proportions of Food.—A milch cow, on the average, requires daily three per cent. of her weight in hay to keep her in health, an ox two per cent., or two and a half per cent. if working moderately. An ox fatting, five per cent. at first, and four and a half per cent. when half fat; sheep three and a half per cent. to keep in store order. If other food is substituted for hay, or a part of it, its comparative value as a nutriment must be ascertained. Thus, eight pounds of potatoes are equal to four pounds of good hay, while eight pounds of turnips are only equal to one and three-fifths pounds of hay.

Carrots for Stock.—It is asserted, by those who have tested the matter, that for stock-feeding an acre of carrots is worth about two hundred per cent. more than the same ground will do in grass. This will pay for increased expense of cultivation, and leave a fair margin of extra profit. Cattle take readily to carrots as a portion of their daily food, and the large yield per acre should make them a greater favorite with farmers than they generally are. The thinning and weeding appear to be a great drawback to their more general cultivation. But with this expense the crop pays well.

Celery Tops for Cows.—A writer in an Australian paper states that in many instances the leaves of celery are highly esteemed as food for milch cows, and are often preferred to red clover. The cows are said to eat them greedily, and to yield on this food a far richer milk than on any other. Sometimes leaves are cut up small, scalded with hot water, and given as a mash mixed with bran, and sometimes they are fed whole in their natural state along with the other ordinary food

The Best Feed for Cattle.—We have seen pumpkins fed quite freely with excellent result in quantity and quality of milk; but it is not fit or economical to feed too largely of any one food. Potatoes fed in moderation are excellent for milk; but given in too great a quantity they will reduce the yield. Turnips or beets must not be given too liberally; corn fodder, given as a sole ration, is unprofitable; but fed with half pasture will keep up the yield of milk and add largely to the profit of the season.

Phosphates for Cattle.—A natural instinct leads cattle to eat bones when their pastures are deficient in lime or phosphates of lime. If these bones are brought home and reduced to a fine powder, mixed with salt, and placed in a box or boxes fixed in the barn-yard, the cows will lick them and derive very great benefit from them. This will save their teeth, and prevent them from choking themselves, as they might readily do with a piece of bone. Those who have no old bones should purchase a few, and treat them in the way indicated.

Straw and Bran.—Professor Henry, of the *Wisconsin Experimental Farm*, holds that it is wise economy on the part of the farmer who has a great straw stack, and small herd of cattle, and some hay, and who will not enlarge his herd, to sell the hay at $7 or $8 per ton, and spend the money in buying bran at $11 and $12, and feed it with the straw, together with some oil-meal. Good bright straw is made equal to hay by the addition of the protein in the bran and meal, and the whole is thus made into a far better quality of manure than usually comes from the usual way of feeding the hay, and half washing the straw.

Feeding Bran with Meal.—For winter feeding, where cattle are kept in stalls and heavily fed, there is no better divisor for corn meal than wheat bran. It is also cheap, and furnishes what the corn meal lacks. When cattle are fed on corn meal as the principal food for fattening, it is apt to clog if fed in too large quantities; hence, our best feeders are in the habit of using bran as the cheapest and best means for rendering the meal fed more digestible.

Rings on Cows' Horns.—The first ring appears when the bovine is two years of age, and sometimes before. The ring gradually increases during the third year, and is fully formed at three years; the second ring appears during the fourth year, and is complete at the end of the fifth year; after that one additional ring is formed each year. A cow with three rings is six years old; with four, seven years old. After nine or ten years the rings are no indication of the age.

Care of Oxen.—Oxen that work on frozen roads, although there is no ice, should be shod. The rough, hard surface wears down the hoofs very fast, and causes inflammation of the interior; the trouble may not become apparent until later, when the mischief is difficult to repair. If the feet are tender and hot, and a slight lameness is perceived, examine the hoofs between the claws, cleanse the feet, and apply the needful remedies without delay, and so save trouble in the future.

To Exterminate Rats and Mice.—An English agricultural paper says: "Several correspondents write to announce the complete extirpation of rats and mice from their cow-stalls and piggeries since the adoption of this simple plan: A mixture of two parts of well-bruised common squills and three parts of finely chopped bacon is made into a stiff mass, with as much meal as may be required, and then baked into small cakes, which are put down for the rats to eat."

Garget in Cows.—It is said that eight drops of tincture of aconite dropped on a piece of bread and mixed with the food at night, and next morning four drops more given in the same manner, will generally complete the cure of garget in cows.

Scours in Calves.—For scours in calves, a raw egg broken into their milk is the most effectual remedy. A piece of rennet soaked in milk is also good, but we prefer the raw egg.

A Winter Piggery.—The object sought in the erection of this piggery is to secure a neat, clean, cheap and comfortable shelter for young pigs. The structure is thirty feet long, six feet wide, five and a half feet high in front, and four feet high at the rear. The roof slopes only one way, and projects fifteen inches, to throw water away from the pens. First make the spot on which it is to be built a foot higher than the natural surface, with stiff, good clay soil. Gravel must be put on this several inches deep. Set round white oak posts a few inches in the ground at every corner of each pen or division. Nail on, with double-ten nails, scantling, two by four inches. Board up with vertical boarding, one by twelve inches. Cover the roof of building with the same material, and make slatted divisions for the pens inside. Our illustration shows the trough into which slops and water are poured from the outside. These have a one-inch hole at one end, with peg to let off surplus water in cleaning. A piggery of this size will hold from ten to thirty, according to size and age. It should be built facing the south, so as to allow as much sunshine as possible to enter the doors. Whitewash the inner apartments for health; also the outside, which gives the structure a pleasant appearance. The ornamental verge board is sawed out of one-inch plank a foot wide, and a one-inch auger hole put through the center of the figure, as shown in the cut. The rafters project a foot over the front, which proves a solid basis upon which to nail the verge board. A little venetian red in some lime is good to color the verge board, the corners and doors. The doors are made of open slat-work, and are furnished with small chains for fastening, and strap hinges. This piggery can be built for about $35.

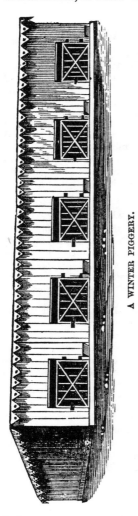

A WINTER PIGGERY.

Will it Pay to Steam Fodder?—Taking the word fodder in its broadest sense, says the *American Agriculturist*, as any kind of food for granivorous animals, we may say that it will always pay to steam or cook feed for swine, and often for cows, in stables containing twenty-five head or more, while for sheep and horses it will be of doubtful expediency, and usually not advisable under any circumstances. The cooking of feed for fattening swine is so important as a matter of economy, that it will pay, even though done with little regard to the saving of labor and fuel. On the other hand, to cook the feed for neat cattle with profit, not only should there be animals enough to make it pay, but the rations should be so carefully planned, that by mingling of palatable, with less relished and coarse fodder, a saving may be effected in that way. Besides the object for which the cattle are kept, is an important factor to be considered in the feeding.

The flow of milk is increased by steaming the fodder—the color of the butter is, however, injured. The same ration will prove more fattening, while, at the same time, there will be little or no waste, if the steam is well managed. It is best to have the steamed ration composed of a variety of feed, such as corn-fodder roots, hay or oat straw, with bran and corn meal, or cotton-seed, or linseed-cake, or meal. The substitution of one kind of fodder or meal for another, gives variety and relish. The coarse fodder is cooked soft, and the flavor of the roots and of the meal pervades the mass. It is not likely that any of the small agricultural steamers can be made to economically cook the food for as many as twenty-five or thirty head of cattle. When a boiler of several horse-power is employed to do other work, as pumping, thrashing, sawing wood, grinding, cutting hay and corn fodder, etc., steam may be economically used for cooking fodder. Of this there can be little doubt. The steam box in which the fodder is placed for cooking, if it is big enough, need not be filled oftener than twice a week, and if, as already intimated, every pains is taken in the operation to save in the items of labor and fuel, steaming fodder for cattle will be found profitable.

Convenient Trough.— This trough is designed more especially for an outdoor or field trough for summer and fall use. It is very desirable with many to feed their swine outside of pens in those seasons, and every farmer is aware that it is almost a necessity to have the trough arranged to keep the swine away, both from the person who feeds them and from the receptacle into which their food is placed while the latter is being prepared. The trough

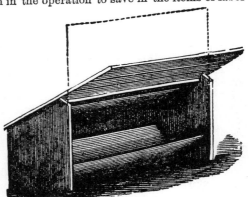

CONVENIENT TROUGH.

which we illustrate is adapted very perfectly to this purpose. It may form part of the fence, so that the swine cannot come to the rear, from which side the food is placed in it, and the additional advantage is the shelter of both trough and animals from storms.

The cut requires little explanation. The cover is hung on pins and fastened by a hook and staple on the rear side to keep it down. When food is to be placed in the trough the hook is unfastened and the cover lifted up in the position shown by the dotted lines. By this movement the swine are completely shut away, and it is very convenient to place and mix their food. A slight effort brings the cover back to its place, and they can then " go in." Perhaps sheep feeders might take a useful hint from this plan.

Pig Raising.—We will suppose that the farmer has a litter of good, healthy pigs of good stock, one day old. He congratulates himself that, having escaped the dangers which are so thick at the critical period of farrowing, he will have no further trouble. The pigs are lively, and well developed; the mother shows no disposition to eat them, and is careful not to overlie them. There are still two dangers right before the pig raiser into which he may ignorantly run—but which may be easily avoided—which have caused the death of pigs by the million. The first is overfeeding the sow with rich, heat-producing feed. I think there is no one cause that has occasioned so much loss as this. Make it an invariable rule to feed sparingly of corn for the first week. A failure to pay close attention to the matter of diet at this time will often result in fever, which dries up the milk, the insufficiency of which actually starves the pigs to death. When the result is not so bad as this, the sow loses appetite, runs down rapidly in flesh, and although the pigs live they do not thrive, and before weaning the mother is a skeleton. For the first week feed house slops and bran, with but one ear of corn at a feed, and then increase gradually, and by the end of the second week you can feed as heavily as you please. The second danger to young pigs is that they become diseased for want of exercise. It the sow is kept in a close pen and proves to be a good suckler, it is often the case that in two or three weeks the pigs get so fat as to die. Many a farmer, with a valuable litter of pigs shut up in a close pen, has seen them die one after the other until the litter disappeared, and yet he had no idea what was the matter. Lay it down, then, as a second rule in pig raising, that young pigs must have exercise.

Still another important thing is a clean bed. If allowed to sleep in dust they are likely to die of thumps, and if in a wet place or a manure pile, they become mangy, or contract colds and die. But we will suppose that the farmer is wise enough to guard against the dangers I have spoken of, and has brought the litter safely to the age of four weeks, with the mother in good condition, and having a good appetite. It is now time to begin to prepare the pigs for weaning. Make a pen near where you feed the sow, and arrange it so that the pigs can go in and out at pleasure, but let it not be accessible to the sow, and begin feeding with milk and soaked corn. The quantity must be very small at first, and only what they will eat clean. Increase gradually, and by the time they are eight weeks old they will be eating enough so that they can be weaned without checking their growth. If, as is often the case, there are in the litter two or three pigs that are not quite up to the average, it will be good, both for them and the sows, to let them run with the mother a week or two longer than the remainder of the litter. For four months after weaning feed liberally. No matter whether your pigs are to be kept for breeders, fattened the first fall, or wintered over to be pastured the next summer and fed the second autumn, the treatment should be the same. Do not aim to make them fat, but get all the development of bone and muscle you can. The food should not be corn exclusively, for we want more of the flesh-formers, and they should have the run of pasture, and be fed on bran slop with the corn. Exercise, a varied diet, with part bulky food and not too much corn, will give a profitable hog.

Overfeeding Stock.—Overfeeding an animal is worse in its effects than a spare diet. A great many more young animals are checked in their growth, and otherwise injured, by overfeeding than by a deficiency of food. In illustration of this statement, a correspondent tells the following story of his own experience:

A rather opinionated and willful hired man, who requires the closest watching in feeding the stock, in defiance of strict orders, gave some Berkshire pigs some cotton seed meal in their feed, in the expectation that it would help them to grow. Their feed had been skimmed milk, with a quart of wheat middlings to the pailful. Considerable more cotton seed meal was added to the feed during my absence from home for a day and night, and on my return the next day two of the young pigs were taken with convulsions and severe spasms. They died the next day, when two more were taken, and soon after two more. The whole six died in the same way. First they slowly turned around and around, then stood with the head in a corner and pressed against the wall or yard fence; the jaws were chopped together, and they foamed at the mouth. After a few hours they lay upon their sides and struggled violently with the legs until they died. A dose of lard oil allayed the symptoms for a time, and had it been given at first, would probably have saved them. On opening them the lungs were found congested and very red in patches, and the brain, also, was much congested, the blood vessels being dark blue. The stomach and intestines were filled with cotton seed meal, the milk having been digested. So short a case of indigestion, or stomach staggers, as it is popularly called, is rare; but the pigs were but two months old, and had probably been misfed previously.

A Convenient Feeding Trough.—We give an illustration of a convenient trough for feeding hogs or sheep. It is especially well designed for feeding hogs, and may be placed in the pen, the swing door above the trough forming one side. If desirable to use it out of doors, it may form part of a fence. The construction is simple. Two upright board standards, about four feet high, are nailed to the ends of the trough to support a swing door or partition, which is adjusted so that the lower edge plays back and forth just over the top of the trough. The view given is of the rear side of the

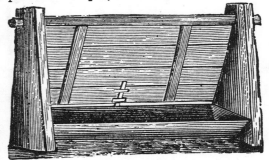

A CONVENIENT FEEDING TROUGH.

trough, and the partition is swung forward to shut the animals away while their food is being prepared. When ready, the slide is withdrawn, the partition swings over the rear side, and the hogs can "go in." Slats of wood should be placed across the trough to keep the animals from standing in it. By swinging the partition high enough, the hogs may pass under.

Sanitary Management of Swine.—One great fault in the management is to keep too many hogs together in one shed or inclosure. From want of proper protection in the way of housing, hogs are very apt to crowd together in bunches during cold weather; and, coming into the sheds wet and dirty, and being obliged to lie either on old and filthy straw bedding or on a wet and damp floor, their sweating and steaming soon produces a foul atmosphere, and the bedding, not being removed at proper intervals, gets rotten, and adds to contamination of the air. Being thus packed together in the building, the hogs, in a warm and perspiring condition, are next exposed to the influence of cold winds and wet, by being turned out in the morning hours to run in the field among grass wet with cold dew or from rain or hoar-frost, or to be fed from troughs in the yard. Among the common consequences are congestion, cold or catarrh, and, if the so-called hog cholera happens to be prevailing, they are almost certain to be affected with that disease, as their systems, under such management, are rendered predisposed or susceptible thereto. In many places the hogs are kept in miserable sheds, no provision being made for proper drainage, the ground sloping toward the sheds, which frequently being unpaved, or without proper flooring, are constantly damp and wet, while pools of urine and filth abound, and with wind and sleet approaching from all quarters. In proportion as the standard of breeding has become higher, so has the vital force, energy, and hardiness become lessened; and the effects of improper quantity and quality of food, filthy or stagnant water, faulty construction of houses, and undue exposure to atmospheric influences, have become proportionately more baneful.

A Good Pig Sty.—We furnish herewith a plan for a good pig sty, with a detailed description showing the best manner of constructing the same. Our illustration represents the ground floor, 25 feet wide by 32 feet long. A is an entry five feet wide, running the whole length of the building, with a door at each end; it is used for feeding, as the troughs in boxes b, b, b, b, run along one side of it. The roof extends only over the entry (a) and the boxes

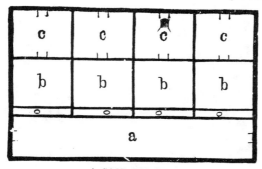

A GOOD PIG STY.

b, b, b, b. The boxes c, c, c, c, are not under the roof. The whole building is floored with plank, with a slight depression in grade toward the front of about half an inch to the foot, for the purpose of drainage. The inside partitions need not be more than about four feet high. The small door between b and c is hung by hinges from the top, so as to open either way, made to work easy, not reaching quite to the floor. The pig soon learns to push it open and pass through, and the door closes after it. When pigs are put into the boxes, one corner of the box floor (c) should be made *wet*, and the pigs will be careful not to wet anywhere else. O, o, o, o, are feeding troughs. The height of the building should be seven or eight feet. No bedding is required. Keep the floor clean.

Hog Cholera.—The Lewistown *Gazette*, published in Fulton County, Ill., says: "Every paper in the United States ought occasionally to keep the fact before its readers that burnt corn is a certain and speedy cure for hog cholera. The best way is to make a pile of corn on the cobs, effectually scorch it, and then give the affected hogs free access to it. This remedy was discovered by E. E. Lock at the time his distillery in this county was burned, together with a large lot of store corn, which was so much injured as to be unfit for use, and was hauled out and greedily eaten by the hogs, several of which were dying daily. After the second day not a single hog was lost, and the disease was entirely conquered. The remedy has been tried in a number of cases since, and never failed."

The Washington (Iowa) *Gazette* says Mr. Donahey, of that place, furnishes the following recipe for the cure of hog cholera: To prevent hogs from having cholera, quinsy, or pneumonia, use one gallon of soft soap, four ounces of saltpetre, and half a pound of copperas. Mix well in swill, and feed to about forty hogs in one day. In four or five days give the following: Carbolic acid, eight drams, black antimony, two ounces, half pound of sulphur. Mix well in swill, and feed to about forty hogs in two days. Repeat the above once a month, and it will prevent any of the above diseases. I have used it for ten years without a single case of any disease among my hogs.

A simple cure for hog cholera, says the *Kentucky Live Stock Record,* is an infusion of peach-tree leaves and small twigs in boiling water, given in their slop. Peach leaves are laxative, and they probably exert, to a moderate extent, a sedative influence over the nervous system. They have been used as a worm destroyer with reported success. They have also been recommended as an infusion for irritability of the bladder, in sick stomach and whooping cough. The cases of fatal poisoning from their use in children are on record, as peach leaves contain prussic or hydrocyanic acid, but as it is almost impossible to poison a hog, their use would not be objectionable. The specific is worth a trial.

The report of the Georgia Agricultural Department has a statement to the effect that forty cases of hog cholera were averted, if not cured, by turning the animals on to a quarter of an acre of clover, to graze for one week. It has long been held that this disease springs mainly from malnutrition, and too much feeding on corn or other carbonaceous food. The fact that clover —a nitrogenous fodder—in this case averted the threatened disease is of great interest. The culture and use of clover in the South may through this knowledge be greatly extended.

Nancy Agree, of Missouri, some years since claimed the $10,000 premium offered by the legislature of that State for a cure for hog cholera. Her specific is as follows: "Take inside bark of the wild cherry tree and boil it down with water so as to make a strong solution, and give it to the hogs to drink, excluding them from water. It has proven a perfect cure, even in the last stages of the disease. I also recommend an admixture of the root of the bull nettle."

A correspondent of the *Journal of Agriculture* recommends a half tea-spoonful of carbolic acid in a gill of milk. This remedy, he states, has been successful in every case and not only cures but stops the spread of the disease. It is administered from the mouth of a long-necked bottle.

The Pig as a Plowman.—Farmers everywhere, says the *American Agriculturist,* are influenced by the construction of railroads and other means of quick transportation, but none of them more so than those who grow meat as a branch of their farm operations. The pork-raisers in the older States come in competition with the swine products of the prairie States, where the pig is a condenser of the corn crop, and among the most economical methods of sending that cereal to market—yet even with cheap freights, it will not do for Eastern farmers to abandon the sty, and look to the West for their salt pork and hams. There are economies to be practiced in swine raising that will make the Eastern farmer successful in his competition with the West. He has the protection of freights over long distances which can never be very much reduced. The home market will always be remunerative, so long as pork products are in demand. His lands need manure, and that which is made in the sty and under cover, is among the best of the home made fertilizers. Herding swine upon pasture, or old meadow, that needs breaking up, is not very much practiced, but is one of the best methods of raising pigs. They are as easily confined within a movable fence as sheep, utilize the grass and coarse feed quite as well, and perform a work in stirring the soil that sheep cannot do. The nose of the pig is made for rooting, and we follow Nature's hint in giving him a chance to stir the soil. A movable yard, large enough to keep two pigs, can be made of stout inch boards, about fourteen feet long, and six inches wide. For the corner posts use two by four inch joists. Nail the boards to the posts six inches apart, making four lengths or panels four feet high. Fasten the corners with stout hooks and staples, and you have a pen or yard fourteen feet square, which is easily moved by two men. If you place two fifty-pound pigs into this yard they will consume nearly all the grass and other vegetation in it in three or four days, and thoroughly disturb the soil several inches in depth. When they have done their work satisfactorily, the pen can be moved to the adjoining plat, and so onward through the season. The advantages of this method are, that it utilizes the grass and other vegetation, destroys weeds and insects, mixes and fertilizes the surface of the soil about as well as the ordinary implements of tillage. In the movable yard there is thorough work. Even ferns and small brush are effectually destroyed. Worms and bugs are available food for the pig. And it is not the least of the benefits that the small stones, if they are in the soil, are brought to the surface, where they can be seen and removed. The pig's snout is the primitive plow and crowbar, ordained of old. No longer jewel this instrument, but put it where it will do the most good, in breaking up old sod ground, and help make cheap pork.

Charcoal for Hogs.— We have but little doubt that charcoal is one of the best known remedies for the disordered state into which hogs drill, usually having disordered bowels, all the time giving off the worst kind of evacuations. Probably the best form in which charcoal can be given is in the form of burnt corn—perhaps, because when given in other forms the hogs do not get enough. A distillery was burned in Illinois, about which a large number of hogs were kept. Cholera prevailed among these hogs somewhat extensively. In the burning of buildings a large amount of corn was consumed. To this burned and partially burned corn, the hogs had access at will, and the sick commenced recovering at once and a large portion of them got well. Many farmers have practiced feeding scorched corn, putting it into the stove or building a fire upon the ground, placing the ears of corn upon it, leaving them till pretty well charred. Hogs fed on still slops are liable to be attacked by irritation of the stomach and bowels, coming from too free generation of acid, from fermentation of food after eaten. Charcoal, whether it be produced by burning corn or wood, will neutralize the acid, in this way removing the irritating cause. The charcoal will be relished to the extent of getting rid of the acid, and beyond that it may not be. Hence it is well to let the wants of the hog be settled by the hog himself.

Iron Hog Troughs.— Upon the subject of the best material for hog troughs, a writer says: "I make them out of iron, not out of iron-wood, but cast iron. I grappled with this problem a half dozen years ago and mastered it. I became an inventor. I had an invention put into the form of a model and got the proprietor of an iron foundry to cast eight troughs after the model. They were put into the different pens and they are there now, bright, clean, smooth, sound, and all right, and I expect to leave them just in this shape to my heirs. The model cost $18, and the troughs 6 cents a pound, and they weighed an average of at least 100 pounds. The spout is cast with the trough in one solid piece, and there are also feet cast and attached, by which it is fastened to the floor. The corners are made rounding and so is the bottom, so that freezing does not crack them, as the ice does not press against the corners or sides, but around the whole. They are easily cleaned out, as the sloping sides allow the dirt to slide out before a broom, are always in place, and will never wear out. The wear and waste and annoyance of modern troughs became unbearable. Now I contemplate this part of farm experience with a feeling akin to perfect satisfaction. The trough is not patented."

Phosphates Essential to Pigs.—Experiments made by Lehman upon young animals showed that food containing an insufficient amount of phosphates not only affects the formation of the skeleton, but has an essential influence upon its separate parts. A young pig was fed one hundred and twenty-six days upon potatoes alone; a result of this insufficient food, *rachitis* (rickets, or softening of the bone). Other pigs, from the same litter, fed upon potatoes, leach-out-meat, and additional phosphates, for the same length of time, had a normal skeleton; yet even in these animals there was a difference according to the kind of phosphate added. Two that were fed on phosphate of potash had porous bones, specifically lighter than the others, which were fed upon phosphate and carbonate of lime.

Pig Scraping Table.—This table can easily be made by a handy man. It is formed by bars of wood fixed into a frame. By using a table of this description when scraping pigs, the water and hair fall to the ground, and the latter is effectually disposed of. It is a simple arrangement, and its construction and use will materially aid in neatness and despatch.

PIG SCRAPING TABLE.

Preparing Food for Swine.—A writer gives the following opinion: " The present practice with the greater number, I believe, is to prepare food for pigs either by steeping, steaming, or boiling, under the belief that cooking in any shape is better than giving in the raw state. I am not at present prepared to say definitely what other kinds of food may do, raw or cooked, with pigs or other domesticated animals, or how the other animals would thrive with peas or corn, raw or boiled; but I now assert on the strongest possible grounds—by evidence indisputable, again and again proved by actual trials in various temperatures, with a variety of the same animals, variously conducted—that for fast and cheap production of pork, raw peas are fifty per cent. better than cooked peas or Indian corn in any shape."

Hogs as Producers of Manure.—One hog, kept to the age of one year, if furnished with suitable material, will convert a cartload per month into a fertilizer which will produce a good crop of corn. Twelve loads per year multiplied by the number of hogs usually kept by our farmers would make sufficient fertilizing substance to grow the corn used by them; or, in other words, the hog would pay in manure its keeping. In this way we can afford to make pork at low prices, but in no other way can it be done without loss to the farmer

Swine Raising.—The *American Agriculturist* contains the following sensible advice regarding the raising of swine: Pure air helps to make pure blood, which, in the course of nature, builds up healthful bodies. Out-of-door pigs would not show so well at the fairs, and would probably be passed over by judges and people who have been taught to admire only the fat and helpless things which get the prizes. Such pigs are well adapted to fill lard kegs, whereas the standard of perfection should be a pig which will make the most ham with the least waste of fat, the longest and deepest sides, with the most lean meat; it should have bone enough to allow it to stand up and help itself to food, and carry with it the evidence of healthy and natural development in all its parts. Pigs which run in a range or pasture have good appetites—the fresh air and exercise give them this—hence they will eat a great variety of food and much coarser than when confined in pens. Nothing need go to waste on the farm for lack of a market. They will consume all the refuse fruits, roots, pumpkins, and all kinds of vegetables, which will make them grow. By extending the root patch and planting the fodder corn thinner, so that nubbins will form on it, and by putting in a sweet variety, the number of pigs may be increased in proportion. A few bushels of corn at the end of the season will be ready the next year for any crop, and ten times the advantage accrue to the farm than if as the pigs are usually managed.

Bone Meal for Strengthening Hogs.—Most farmers have noticed that in fattening swine, especially when they are crowded rapidly, they always appear weak in their hind legs, and sometimes lose the use of them entirely. An intelligent farmer says that he and his neighbors have made a practice of feeding bone meal in such cases, and find that a small quantity mixed with the daily feed will prevent any weakness, and strengthen the animals so as to admit of the most rapid forcing. As bone meal is known to be a preventive of cripple ail and weakness in cows, it looks reasonable that it should also be a benefit to hogs, which are often confined to a diet containing but little bone-making material.

Keeping Hogs Clean.—The floor of a hog pen should be of plank. The pen and hogs can then be kept clean. If the animals are permitted to root up the floor of the pen and burrow in the earth, they will always be in an uncleanly and unwholesome condition, and much food will be wasted. It is quite unnecessary for either the comfort or health of the hogs to let them exercise their natural propensity to root in the ground. The exercise is really a waste of food and takes so much from their growth. Hogs will fatten most quickly when they eat and sleep and remain perfectly quiet, as they will do in a dry, warm pen, with a clean plank floor, and bedding of clean straw and plenty to eat.

How to Give a Pig Medicine.—At a recent meeting of an English Farmers' Club, Professor McBride spoke of the difficulty of administering medicine to a pig. He said: "To dose a pig, which you are sure to choke if you attempt to make him drink while squealing, halter him as you would for execution, and tie the rope end to a stake. He will pull back until the rope is tightly strained. When he has ceased his uproar, and begins to reflect, approach him, and between the back part of his jaws insert an old shoe, from which you have cut the toe leather. This he will at once begin to suck and chew. Through it pour your medicine and he will swallow any quantity you please."

Hay for Hogs.—Very few are aware of the fact that hay is very beneficial to hogs; but it is true, nevertheless. Hogs need rough food as well as horses, cattle or the human race. To prepare it you should have a cutting-box (or hay cutter), and the greener the hay the better. Cut the hay short and mix with bran, shorts or middlings, and feed as other food. Hogs soon learn to like it, and if soaked in swill or other slop food, it is highly relished by them. In winter use for hogs the same hay you feed to your horses, and you will find that, while it saves bran, shorts or other food, it puts on flesh as rapidly as anything that can be given them.

Paralysis in Pigs.—Pigs are frequently subject to a partial paralysis of the nerves of the lumbar region, by which motion of the hind quarters is rendered difficult or impossible. It sometimes results from inflammation of the covering membrane of the spinal cord, caused by exposure to cold. The remedy is to rub turpentine or mustard paste upon the loins, and to give a teaspoonful of saltpetre in the food once a day. Dry pens and protection from rains in the hot season are the best preventives.

Poisonous Swill.—A correspondent of the *Prairie Farmer*, having complained of a disease among his hogs, is told by another correspondent that the symptoms are similar to those of hogs of his own, which he is satisfied died from eating swill that had become poisoned by standing too long. He says: " Chemists say that when swill stands a certain length of time after it has soured, it becomes poisonous. I don't *know* that this is so, but I *do* know that I shall not feed any more old swill."

Roots for Hogs.—Parsnips, carrots, Swedish turnips, and especially mangel-wurtzels, will all fatten pigs. The roots ought not to be given in a raw state, but always cooked and mixed with beans, peas, Indian corn, oats, or barley, all of which must be ground into meal. When pigs are fed on such cooked food as we have stated, the pork acquires a peculiarly rich flavor, and is much esteemed, especially for family use.

Economy in Hog Raising.—One man who let his hogs run on grass and artichokes all summer, was sure that his hogs paid him from fifty to sixty cents per bushel for the corn they consumed (not counting anything for the grass). Another man, who kept his hogs in a pen all summer without anything but corn and water, did not realize more than ten or fifteen cents per bushel for the corn consumed.

Water for Hogs.—Hogs require free access to water in the summer time. If they can have a place to bathe or wallow in, it is beneficial to them, as it cools and cleanses the skin. Mud is not filth—it is a good disinfectant and healthful. Sometimes mud baths have been found useful as medicinal treatment for sick people.

Scurvy Pigs.—It is said by a farmer who has tried the experiment so often as to be sure of his ground, that buttermilk poured over the back of a scurvy pig will entirely and speedily remove the scurf. The remedy is simple.

Squash for Fattening Hogs.—A New York farmer declares that an acre of Hubbard squash will fatten ten more hogs than the corn that can be raised on the same ground. He has gathered from six to eight tons from an acre.

Hurdling Sheep.—The accompanying illustration shows how an English man fed his sheep on an irrigated pasture, by the use of hurdles of

AN ENGLISH METHOD OF HURDLING SHEEP.

a peculiar description. The hurdles are twelve feet long and are made with a stout pole bored with two series of holes twelves inches apart; stakes six feet long are put into these holes so that they project from them three feet on each side of the pole. One series of holes is bored in a direction at right angles to that of the other, and when the stakes are all properly placed they form a hurdle, the end of which looks like the letter X. The engraving shows how these hurdles are made and the method of using them. A row of these hurdles is placed across the field. The field in which they are used consists of six acres. A strip of ten feet wide is thus set off, upon which four hundred sheep feed. They eat up all the grass upon this strip and that which they can reach by putting their heads through the hurdles. The hurdles are then turned over, exposing another strip of rather more than four feet wide at each turn. When this is fed off, the hurdles are again turned over. The sharp points presented by the hurdles prevents any trespassing upon the other side of them, and by using two rows of hurdles the sheep are kept in the narrow strip between them. Their droppings are very evenly spread over the field, and it is richly fertilized by them. At night the sheep are taken off and the grass is watered. The growth is one inch per day under this treatment, and when the field has been fed over, the sheep are brought back again to the starting point and commence once more eating their way along.

Raising Feed for Sheep.—The corn raised especially for sheep should be planted in drills, three and one-half feet apart, and about six inches in the drill. It will ear sufficiently, and should be shocked when the ear is just passing out of the milk, in large, well-built shocks. And the most profitable use that can be made of this for winter feeding is, to run it through a cutter, directly from the shock, reducing to fine chaff, stalks, ears, and all. If cut one-fourth of an inch long, the sheep will eat it all clean; this we know from practical experience. With a large cutter, a ton can be cut in twenty to thirty minutes. This cut corn, fed in properly constructed troughs, will furnish both grain and coarse fodder. The only improvement you can make on this ration, without cooking, is to feed with it some more nitrogenous food, such as bran, linseed meal, or cotton seed meal. Wool is a nitrogenous product, and corn is too fattening a ration when fed alone.

To Tell the Age of Sheep.—The books on sheep have seriously misled flock-masters on this subject. Almost any sheep owner will tell you that after a year the sheep gets a pair of broad teeth yearly; and if you show that his own three-year-olds have four pairs of broad teeth, he can only claim that they are exceptions, and protest that they do not exceed three years of age. Now these cases are no exception, for all well-bred sheep have a full mouth of front teeth at three years old. Some old, unimproved flocks may still be found in which the mouth is not full until nearly four years old, but fortunately these are now the exceptions, and should not be made the standard, as they so constantly are. In Cotswolds, Leicesters, Lincolns, South-Downs, Oxford-Downs, Hampshire-Downs, and even in the advanced Merinos, and in the grades of all of these dentition is completed from half a year to a year earlier. The milk or lamb teeth are easily distinguished from the permanent or broad teeth by their smaller size and by the thickness of the jaw bone around their fangs where the permanent teeth are still inclosed. As the lamb approaches a year old, the broad exposed part of the tooth becomes worn away, and narrow fangs projecting above the gums stand apart from each other, leaving wide intervals. This is even more marked after the first pair of permanent teeth have come up, overlapping each other at their edges, and from this time onward the number of small milk teeth and of broad permanent teeth can usually be made out with ease. Another distinguishing feature is the yellow or dark coloration of the fangs of the milk teeth, while the exposed portions of the permanent teeth are white, clear, and pearly. The successive pairs of permanent teeth make their appearance through the gums in advanced breeds at about the following dates: The first pair at one year; the second pair at one year and a half; the third pair at two years and three months; the fourth and last pair at three years. It will be observed that between the appearance of the first two pairs there is an interval of six months, while after this each pair come up nine months after its predecessors. For backward grades, and the unimproved breeds, the eruption is about six months later for each pair of teeth, but even with them the mouth is full at three years and six months.

Sheep Ticks—How to Get Rid of Them.—Sheep ticks are much more numerous and more annoying than many suppose. Men of experience with large flocks generally know and apply the necessary remedies, but there are hundreds of farmers whose time and attention are principally directed to grain growing, etc., and who keep but a few sheep, whose flocks are sorely troubled by this parasite, and they never discover the cause of the evil. The accompanying engraving of the insect in its different stages, is from the Cyclopædia of Agriculture.

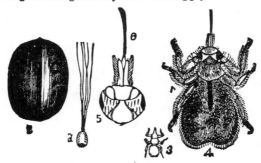

FIG. 1.—SHEEP TICKS, MAGNIFIED.

The sheep tick or louse lives amongst the wool, and is exceedingly annoying to lambs. Their oval, shining bodies, like the pips of small apples, and similar in color, may be found attached by the pointed end to the wool. (See engraving Fig. 1; Fig. 2, the same magnified.) These are not the eggs, but the pupæ, which are laid by the female, and are at first soft and white. From these issue the ticks (Fig. 3; Fig. 4, the same magnified), which are horny, bristly, and dull ochre; the head is orbicular, with two dark eyes (Fig. 5), and a rostrum in front, enclosing three fine curved tubes (Fig. 6), for piercing the skin and sucking the blood. The body is large, leathery, purse-shaped and whitish when alive, and notched at the apex. The six legs are stout, very bristly, and the feet are furnished with strong double claws. The English remedies are a wash of arsenic, soft soap and potash, decoction of tobacco, train oil with spirits of turpentine, and mercurial ointment.

Ticks, when very numerous, greatly annoy and enfeeble sheep, and should be kept out of the flock if possible. After shearing, the heat and cold, the rubbing and biting of the sheep, soon drive off the tick and it takes refuge in the long wool of the lamb. Wait a fortnight after shearing to allow all to make this transfer of residence; then boil refuse tobacco leaves until the decoction is strong enough to kill ticks beyond a peradventure. This may be readily tested by experiment. Five or six pounds of cheap plug tobacco may be made to answer for one hundred lambs. The decoction is poured into a deep, narrow dipping tank kept for this purpose, and which has an inclined shelf on one side covered with a wooden grate, as shown in our illustration below (Fig. 2). One man holds the lamb by the hind legs, another clasps the fore legs in one hand, and shuts the other about the nostrils to prevent the liquid entering them, and then the lamb is entirely immersed. It is immediately lifted out, laid on one side on the grate, and the water squeezed out of its wool. It is then turned over and squeezed on the other side. The grate conducts the fluid back into the box. If the lambs are annually dipped, ticks will never trouble a flock.

Early Lambs.—In many localities an early lamb will sell for more money than will the ewe and her fleece; therefore, where there is a market for early lambs the breeding of these is a very profitable business, if the person who attempts it is provided with ample shelter and understands the management of both ewes and lambs.

Lambs for early market are bred so as to be dropped in February and March. February is a hard month to bring them through, and without judicious treatment and warm shelter many lambs will be lost. The chief aim is to get the lambs ready for market as soon as possible, as it is the earliest arrivals that gain the highest prices. It is necessary to keep the dams in good condition with sufficient food to make plenty of nourishing milk. Experi-

FIG. 2.—TANK FOR DIPPING SHEEP.

ence and judgment are required in feeding the lambs; they must have food enough to promote rapid, healthy growth, and yet of a character that will not produce scouring. While the lambs are still with the ewes, it is well to supply them additional food. They can soon be taught to drink milk which is fresh and warm from the cow. Later on, oats, rye and wheat bran finely ground together make an excellent feed. As a gentle laxative a few ounces of linseed oil-cake will be found beneficial and at the same time nourishing.

As the lambs approach the period for weaning extra food should be increased; indeed, the weaning must be very gradually accomplished. The sudden removal of the lambs from their dams is injurious to both. A plan generally followed to avoid the evil effects of a sudden change, is that of removing the lambs to a good pasture of short, tender grass, and at night returning them to the fold with the ewes. The ewes must not be neglected. Their feed should be gradually diminished so as to diminish the yield of milk.

How to Make Sheep Pay.—Any farmer in the Eastern or Middle States having a farm of one hundred acres in good fence can keep a flock of fifty sheep and receive larger profits than from any other investment of the same amount, providing they will care for them in the following manner, viz.: Have your sheep in good condition when you take them from pasture to winter. Have a sheltered pen, with plenty of room, to protect them from the cold and storms; have an out-yard where they can be allowed to go in on nice sunshiny days, in which throw cornstalks, oat or wheat straw, if you have plenty of it, for what the sheep do not eat will make manure, so there will be nothing lost. Also keep the sheltered pen dry, by throwing in straw, as fast as it is cut up in manure. Feed them on clover hay. If you do not grow any buy it, for one ton of clover hay is equal to two tons of any other for sheep, in my experience. Try and have your lambs dropped in January or February. Build a small pen alongside of your sheep pen, cut a small hole, so the lambs can get in, but not large enough to admit the sheep. Put troughs in the lambs' pen, and feed them on ground feed. They will soon find the hole and learn to eat, and if you have never tried it before, you will be surprised how much faster they will grow, and you will also find that the butcher will buy your lambs earlier, and pay a larger price for them than he will for your neighbor's, who does not observe the above advice.

Feed Rack for Sheep.—Feed racks for stocks are indispensable articles of furniture in the sheds and yards of the farm. We give an engraving of one of these, designed especially for sheep. Its dimensions are thirty inches high, twenty-eight wide, bottom formed by nailing together four boards, eight or nine inches wide, in the shape of two troughs, or the letter W, resting on the

FEED RACK FOR SHEEP.

cross piece B. The novel feature, perhaps, is the cant boards A A, which are hinged and then fastened by movable braces. These boards serve as particular shelter to sheep, both from storm and chaff from fodder; and by moving the braces they assume a vertical position, and thus keep out the sheep while one is filling in the grain.

Why Sheep are Profitable.—Sheep are profitable for several reasons, among them being the small expense of maintaining a flock. By that we do not mean the plan pursued by many of turning them into the woods and fields to be called up occasionally to be " salted," but they cost but little when cared for, because they are not choice in the matter of feeding. They greedily devour much that would be unserviceable, and for that reason are a necessary adjunct on a farm as a measure of economy. Where they become serviceable mostly is on those pastures that are deficient in long grass, and which are not used for making hay. It is on this short grass, even if scattering, that the sheep pick up good feeding and thrive well. In fact, long grass is not acceptable to sheep, as they graze close to the ground. A flock of sheep would almost starve in a field of tall clover, and will quickly leave such for the privilege of feeding on the short herbage that grows in the fence corners, in the abandoned meadows, and among the wheat stubble. The crab grass, which becomes a weed on light soils, is highly relished by sheep when just beginning to spread out, and even the purslane is kept down by them. Fields from which the corn has been harvested afford them much valuable pasturage, and they are always able to derive something for food on places that would support no other animal. In saying this it is not inferred that they require no care at the barn. They surely do, but require less than may be supposed.

They are also great renovators of the soil, scattering manure evenly and pressing it in, thus improving the ground on which they feed. They multiply rapidly, a small flock soon becoming a large one, and they produce profit in three directions—wool, mutton and lambs.

Tar the Noses of Sheep.—The months of July and August are the ones when sheep in many localities are subject to a most aggravating annoyance from a fly (*oestrus bovis*), which seems bound to deposit its larvæ in the nostrils. It infects wooded districts and shady places where the sheep resort for shelter, and by its ceaseless attempts to enter the nose makes the poor creature almost frantic. If but one fly is in a flock they all become agitated and alarmed. They will assemble in groups, holding their heads close together and their noses to the ground. As they hear the buzzing of the little pest going from one to another, they will crowd their muzzles into the loose dirt, made by their stamping, to protect themselves, and as the pest succeeds in entering the nose of a victim, it will start on a run, followed by the whole flock, to find a retreat from its enemy, throwing its head from side to side, as if in the greatest agony, while the oestrus, having gained his lodging place, assiduously deposits its larvæ in the inner margin of the nose. Here, aided by warmth and moisture, the eggs quickly hatch into a small maggot, which carrying out its instincts, begins to crawl up into the nose through a crooked opening in the bone. The annoyance is fearful and maddening, as it works its way up into the head and cavities.

The best known remedy is tar, in which is mixed a small amount of crude carbolic acid. If the scent of the acid does not keep the fly away he gets entangled in the tar, which is kept soft by the heat of the animal. Any kind of tar or turpentine is useful for this purpose, and greatly promotes the comfort of the sheep, and prevents the ravages of the bot in the head.

Increasing the Growth of Wool.—The use of chloride of potassium is recommended in Germany as a means of increasing the growth of wool on sheep. Some German chemists have made experiments with the article, proving that the growth of wool is promoted by its use. It is administered in the proportion of one part of chloride to nine parts of salt. It not only increases the production of wool, but improves the quality, and promotes the general health of the animal, we are told; but the proper quantities to administer are not stated.

To Cure Poisoned Sheep.—Take rue leaves, as many as you can grasp between thumb and forefinger. Bruise them; squeeze the juice into a half teacup of water, and drench the sheep with it. If the sheep are poisoned very bad, drench the second time, which will never fail to cure.

Crossing Merino on Common Sheep.—A Merino ram crossed on a flock of common sheep will double the yield of wool through the first cross alone, thus paying for himself the first season.

THE POULTRY YARD--Update

Even if one were not interested in their flesh to eat, eggs would be a great inducement to raising chickens. Even if one didn't like eggs, it might be worthwhile to raise chickens for the manure they furnish.

Like the apple industry, the poultry industry has gone through large changes since 1888. In the same way that mechanical and marketing processes have led to a decrease in the varieties of apples available, so have breeds of chickens diminished. In 1888 a farmer might raise Brahmas, Dorkings, Barred Rocks, Rhode Island Reds, Wyandottes, Polish, Hamburgs, Sussex, Sultans, Sumatras, Cochins, Dominiques, Minorcas, Andalusians, Spanish or Hollands. But an egg industry grew up around the turn of the century which used hybridized Leghorns exclusively. This industry has fluctuated between boom and bust a number of times in the last fifty years.

Readers of this book won't have to know much about the poultry industry. A small number of farmers with huge operations supply the chicken egg and meat market. There's little place in the market for small-timers. But the *Cyclopaedia's* advice for small-time poultrymen is excellent, and the practices will supply a family and friends with eggs. The *Cyclopaedia* recommends fresh air, exercise and a frequent change of location for chickens. The modern egg industry raises chickens in cages in which they can barely move.

The plans given here for chicken coops are sound--these buildings will keep the chickens from severe weather, are economical and easily cleaned, and will protect the flock from predators. The incubators shown will work if fitted with a small heat coil or light bulb. The diet outlined will serve well--whole grains at night and soft food in the morning. Chickens are excellent for disposing of garbage; they'll eat anything.

Eggs can be preserved uncooked in the ways described or sunk in water. My favorite way of preserving them, though, is the pickled hard-boiled egg, done with a standard cucumber pickle solution with perhaps a touch of cayenne.

There are a number of chicken-raising handbooks about. For technical considerations, I like the booklet in the "Have-More" Series called *Starting Right with Chickens*, ed. Ed Robinson, (Charlotte, Vt.: Garden Way Publishing Co., 1971). A more poetical treatment of the history, folklore and uses of chickens is Page Smith & Charles Daniel's *The Chicken Book*, (Boston: Little, Brown & Co., 1975). It is a good, readable book for background but it isn't practical. A lucky person may find an old, useful handbook at a flea market or yard sale. *Poultry Culture: A Text Book on Poultry* would be a good one to run across.

For the farmer interested in turkeys, the "Have-More" Series offers *Starting Right with Turkeys* by G.T. Klein (Charlotte, Vt.: Garden Way Publishing Co., 1972).

THE POULTRY YARD.

A Poultry House for Chickens.—The poultry house we have illustrated is designed for young chicks. It can be attached to a coop, and is made of laths. It is the length of a lath and half a lath in height.

Such an arrangement allows the mother some room to move about, and enables the young chicks to reach air and sun. Almost any bright boy can nail the laths together, and it will materially increase the chickens' chances of life. Remember that the first few days are the most critical and require extra attention.

More fowls are destroyed in infancy, like humans, by injudicious feeding than at any other time. The first four weeks' management of the young chicks is everything, for no after cares can compensate for neglect during the critical period. For the first twenty-four hours no food should be given the chicks of any kind. At first there may be given hard-boiled egg, chopped fine. This need only be given for two or three days when the food should be changed to one consisting of oatmeal cooked in milk, to which an egg has been

A POULTRY HOUSE FOR CHICKS.

added. The second week the milk and oatmeal gruel, stiffly made, should be continued, and good wheat screenings allowed also. After the second week the food may be varied so as to consist of anything they will eat, but do not confine them to a single article of diet, as disease of the bowels may occur. Green grass, cooked vegetables and milk may be given freely. The chicks should not be allowed to roam outside with the hen, if possible, until the sun is well up, as dampness is more injurious to them than cold. When very young feed every two hours, as feathers, bone and meat are forming fast, requiring plenty of nourishment. When cleanliness is observed but few diseases appear. Never let a surplus of food remain after the feeding is over, but see that they are sufficiently supplied before taking the excess away. Young chicks are not troublesome to raise if a little system and care are practiced.

A Model Hennery.—The breeding of new and choice varieties of poultry has grown to be quite an extensive industry in this country during the past few years, and it is not entirely confined to those who make it a business, either, as many of our farmers have learned, at last, that it pays to devote more time and attention to the raising and care of poultry than they formerly were willing to give to it. The model hennery herewith illustrated and described combines all the essential requisites for convenience, cleanliness, the health of the fowls, and the separation of the different varieties, together with all the modern improvements, from which many good hints may be obtained, if not wishing to adopt the plan just as it stands.

This building is nearly 75 feet long, 13 feet high, and 12 feet wide. It is built of wood, the roof shingled. To the highest pitch of the roof it is 13

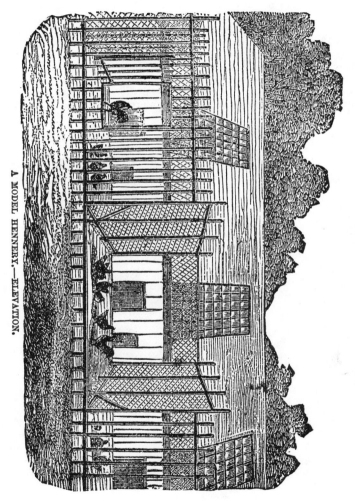

A MODEL HENNERY.—ELEVATION.

feet. The elevation or height from the ground or foundation in front is 4 feet, which cuts a twelve-foot board into three pieces; the length or pitch of the roof in front is 12 feet—just the length of a board, saving a few inches of a ragged end; the pitch of the rear roof is 6 feet, and the height of the building from the ground to the base of the roof is just 6 feet, which cuts a twelve-foot board into two pieces. The ground plan and frame work are planned on the same principles of economy of timber. By this plan no timber is wasted, as it all cuts out clean; there is also a great saving of labor. The foundation of the building rests on cedar posts set four feet into the ground.

This house contains eight pens, each one of which will accommodate from twenty-five to thirty fowls; each pen is nine feet long and eight feet wide. All the pens are divided off by wire partitions of one inch mesh. Each pen has a glass window on the southern front of the house, extending from the gutter to within one foot of the apex of the roof, fixed in permanently with French glass lapping over each other, after the fashion of hot-bed sashes; they are about eleven by three feet. Each pen is entered by a wire door six feet high, from the hallway, which is three feet wide; and these doors are carefully fastened with a brass padlock.

The house is put together with matched boards, and the grooves of the boards are filled in with white lead and then driven together, so as to make the joints impervious to cold or wet. On the rear side of the house there are

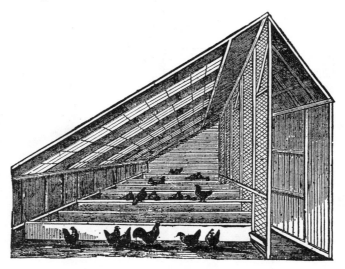

A MODEL HENNERY.—END VIEW OF INTERIOR.

four scuttles or ventilators, two by two feet, placed equidistant from each other, and to these are attached iron rods which fit into a slide with a screw, so that they can be raised to any height. These are raised, according to the weather, every morning, to let off the foul air. Each pen has a ventilator besides the trap door at the bottom, same size, which communicates with the pens and runs. These lower ventilators are used only in very hot weather, to allow a free circulation through the building, and in summer each pen is shaded from the extreme rays of the sun by thick shades fastened upon the inside, so that the inside of the house is cooler than the outside.

The dropping boards extend the whole width of the pen, and are about two feet wide and sixteen inches from the floor; the roosts are about seven inches above and over this board. They are three inches wide and crescent-shaped on top, so that the fowls can rest a considerable portion of their bodies on the perches. Under these dropping boards are the nest boxes, where the fowls lay, and are shaded and secluded. The feeding and drink-

'ng troughs are made of galvanized iron, and hung with hooks on eyes, so that they can be easily removed when they require cleaning.

One can stand at one end of this long house and see all the chickens on their roosts. By seeing each other in this way the fowls are made companionable and are saved many a ferocious fight; at the same time each kind is kept separate from the other. Each pen has a run 33 by 12 and 15 feet; these runs are separated by wire fences 12 feet high, with meshes of 2 inches.

The house is surrounded with a drain which carries off all the moisture and water, and prevents dampness. Inside the house is cemented all through, and these cemented floors are covered with gravel two inches deep. The house is heated in the cold weather just enough to keep water from freezing. The plan of this hennery is remarkable for its simplicity and hygienic arrangement. The cost of the labor and material is under $500.

Movable Poultry House.—Those who have tried movable poultry houses regard them as exceedingly profitable arrangements, and very desirable. We give an illustration of one in use in England, which is mounted on wheels, with a floor raised high enough above ground to form a dry run. It has a set of movable laying nests at back, outside flap-door with lock, large door with lock, for attendant, small sliding door and ladder for fowls, two shifting perches,

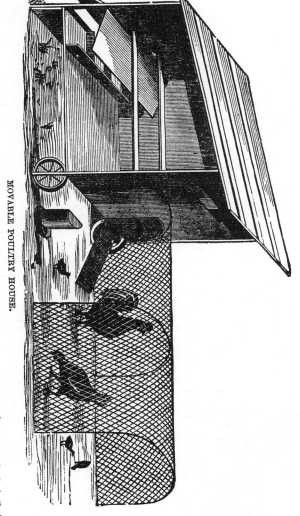

MOVABLE POULTRY HOUSE.

and sliding window. The benefit birds of all description derive from change of place, not only arises from the pleasure every animal as well as man derives from changes of scene, but by being preserved from the exhalations emitted by excrementitious matter and decaying food.

Model Poultry House.—We give a plan of poultry house and yards,

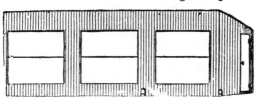

combining many g o o d points and conveniences. The building is enclosed with worked spruce or pine boards, put on vertically, and the height so arranged that each bo..rd will cut to avoid waste. All the pieces are cut off of the full lengths in front, making just half a rear length. The rafters

ELEVATION.—LENGTH, 24 FEET; WIDTH, 11 FEET; HEIGHT, IN FRONT, 9 1-2 FEET; HEIGHT, IN REAR, 6 1-2 FEET.

of thirteen feet joist, with either battened or shingle roof as preferred. The building is supposed to face the south. The entrance door, E, opening into the passage, P, three and a half feet wide, which runs the length of the building; smaller doors, D, each two feet wide, opening into the roosting room, R. The nests are raised about a foot from the floor, and also open into the room R, with a hinged board in the passage, so that the eggs can be removed without entering the roosting rooms. The perches, A, are movable, perfectly

level, and raised two feet from the floor. The partition walls are tight, two boards high, above which is lath; the passage wall above the nest, and also the doors, D, being of lath also.

The roosting-rooms are seven and a half by eight feet, large e n o u g h f o r twenty-five fowls each. Windows are six feet square, raised one foot from the floor. We prefer the glass to be six by eight or seven by nine inches—as these small sizes need no protection strips to prevent the fowls from breaking them. The holes, H, for egress and

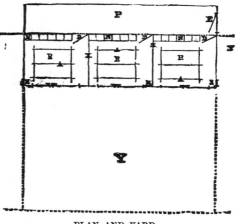

PLAN AND YARD.

ingress of the fowls, are closed by a *drop* door worked by a cord and pulley from the passage way. Another door can be placed in the other end of the passage way if desirable. This arrangement of the yards, Y, of course would not suit every one; some would prefer smaller yards, making each yard the width of the room and adding to its height. The house above is designed for only three varieties; but by simply adding to the length, any number of breeds may be accommodated. The simplest and most economical foundation is to set locust or oak posts about four feet deep, every eight feet, and spike the sills on them. There is then no heaving from frost; and all the underpinning necessary is a board nailed to the sill and extending into the ground a couple of inches. A setting room can be added by making the building four feet longer. The room should be in the end next the door, so as to be always within notice.

Such a house built of seasoned lumber and well battened, will shelter any fowls — excepting, perhaps, the Spanish, Leghorns, and a few of the more tender varieties—from all ordinarily cold weather; and we believe it to be the cheapest and most convenient house for general use.

Chicken and Duck Inclosure.—We present herewith a plan for chicken or duck coops, with inclosures, which will be found very convenient fixtures in any poultry-yard. These coops are made so that they are movable, and can be constructed by almost any one conversant with the use of a hammer and nails. Any refuse boards and odd pieces are all that are necessary to build them. The coops can be set in any desired position, then fenced in with boards twelve to sixteen inches wide, as shown in our engraving, with stakes driven in the ground on each side of the boards at intervals, to keep them from falling over. Put up in this manner the stakes can be withdrawn at will and the inclosure moved as often as desirable. For partitions our engraving has shown a light wire mesh, which is easy to handle and

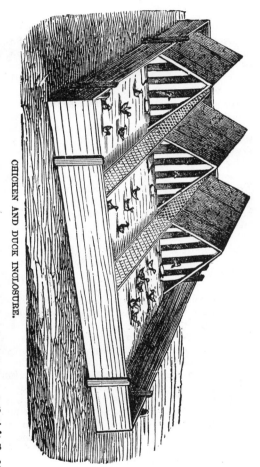

CHICKEN AND DUCK INCLOSURE.

can be procured at a very small cost. This is fastened into position by pinning down with wooden pins, which, in this way, is made also movable.

Caponizing.—Caponizing is not a very difficult operation, and any one who is blessed with the average amount of brains and common sense can soon learn to caponize as quickly and as successfully as an "expert." We know that some one will probably tell you that the instruments used are "very delicate," and the operation can only be safely performed by an expert; but don't believe it. We once wrote out the directions for caponizing, and sent them to a lady who was anxious to know how to perform the operation. With the written directions before her, she first operated on some half-dozen of cockerels that had been killed for table use, and then tried her hand on the living birds, with excellent success. In three days, besides doing her usual housework, she caponized 162 cockerels, and only three of them died from the effects of the operation.

If you live near any one who understands caponizing, and is willing to teach others, go and learn how, but if you cannot do that, go and get a set of instruments and teach yourself. A set of caponizing instruments consists of a pointed hook, a steel splint with a broad, flat hook at each end, a pair of tweezers, and a pair of crooked concave forceps. In the first place, kill a young cockerel and examine it carefully, so that you will be able to tell the exact position of the organs to be removed. You will find them within the cavity of the abdomen, attached to the back, one on each side of the spine. They are light colored, and the size varies with the age and breed.

After you have "located" the parts to be removed, practice the operation on chickens that have been killed, until you are sure that you can operate quickly and safely; then you may try your hand on the living birds. Place the bird on its left side in a rack that will hold it firmly in position without injuring it, or else draw the wings back and fasten them with a broad strip of cloth; draw the legs back and tie them with another strip; then let the attendant hold the fowl firmly on the table, one hand on the wings and head, the other on the legs, while you perform the operation. Remove the feathers from a spot a little larger than a silver dollar, at the point near the hip, upon the line between the thigh and shoulder. Draw the skin backward, hold it firm while you make a clean cut an inch and a half long between the last two ribs, and lastly through the thin membrane that lines the abdominal cavity. In making the last cut, take care and not injure the intestines. Now take the splint and separate the ribs by attaching one of the hooks to each rib, and then allowing the splint to spread; push the intestines away with a teaspoon handle, find the testicles; take hold of the membrane that covers them and hold it with the tweezers; tear it open with the hook; grasp the spermatic cord with the tweezers, and then twist off the testicle with the forceps. Remove the other in the same way. The left testicle is usually a little farther back than that on the right, and should be removed first. During the operation take care not to injure the intestines, or rupture the large blood vessels attached to the organs removed. The operation completed, take out the splint, allow the skin to resume its place, stick on some of the feathers that were removed, which will absorb the blood and cover the wound; give plenty of drink, but feed sparingly on soft cooked food for a few days, or until they begin to move around pretty lively.

To prepare cockerels for caponizing, shut them up without food or drink for twenty-four hours previous to the operation, for if the intestines are full the operation will be more difficult and dangerous. Cockerels that are intended for capons should be operated upon between three and four months of age. Cockerels of any breed may be caponized, but of course the larger breeds are the best. A cross between the Light Brahmas and Partridge Cochins will produce extra large cockerels for capons, but only the first cross is desirable. Capons grow fully one-third larger than the ordinary male fowl of the same age and breed. Their flesh is more delicate and juicy, and they command prices, from thirty to fifty per cent. higher than common poultry, but outside the largest cities there is no market for them.

Good and Cheap Incubators.—For the benefit of those who desire to experience some of the pleasures and profits of artificial incubation, we here give a model of a very simple and reliable incubator, with directions for making the same.

Have a pine case made somewhat like a common washstand (see Fig. 2) without the inside divisions.

About a foot from the floor of this case, place brackets like those in Fig. 1, and on a level with these screw a strong cleat across the back of the case inside. These are to support the tank.

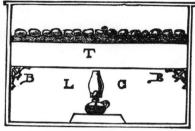

The tank should be made of galvanized iron, three inches deep and otherwise proportioned to fit exactly within the case and rest upon the brackets and cleat. The tank should have a top or cover soldered on when it is made. At the top of this tank in the center should be a hole an inch in

FIG. 1.—INSIDE OF INCUBATOR. FRONT SECTION—T, TANK; L C, LAMP CLOSET, B B, BRACKETS.

diameter with a rim two inches high, and at the bottom, toward one end, a faucet for drawing off the water. When the tank is set in the case fill up all the chinks and cracks between the edges of the tank and the case with plaster Paris to keep all fumes of the lamp from the eggs.

Fill the tank at least two inches deep with boiling water.

To find when the right depth is required, gauge the water with a small stick. Over the top of the tank spread fine gravel a quarter of an inch thick; over this lay a coarse cotton cloth. Place the eggs on the cloth, and set a kerosene safety-lamp under the center of the tank.

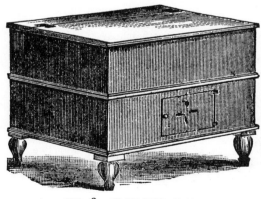

The door of the lamp-closet must have four holes for ventilation, otherwise the lamp will not burn. The lamp-closet is the space within the incubator under the tank. Turn the eggs carefully every morning and evening, and after turning sprinkle them with quite warm water. Two thermometers should be kept in the incubator, one

FIG. 2.—INCUBATOR CLOSED.

half way between the center and each end; the average heat should be 105 degrees.

If the eggs do not warm up well, lay a piece of coarse carpet over them. If they are too warm, take out the lamp and open the cover for a few minutes, but do not let the eggs get chilled. If they should happen to get down to 98 degrees, and up to a 108 degrees, you need not think the eggs are spoiled. They will stand such a variation once in a while; but of course a uniform temperature of 105 degrees will secure more chickens, and they will

be stronger and more lively. In just such an incubator as the one described, the writer hatched over two hundred chickens two years ago.

For those who are ambitious to try top heat, the same sort of a tank is

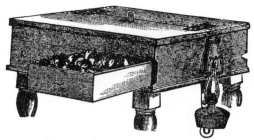

required, but a boiler must
be attached at the side with
an upper and lower pipe for
circulation. Any plumber
can attach the boiler, and
the faucet must be at the
bottom of the boiler on one
side.

The drawers containing
the eggs should slide be-
neath the tank. A stand
for the lamp should be
screwed to one end of the

FIG. 3.—TOP HEAT INCUBATOR, ON TABLE.

case in such a position as to bring the lamp under the boiler (see illustration
above). This incubator can be cooled by raising the lid, turning down the
lamp and pulling the drawers part way out.

In both incubators while the eggs are hatching sprinkle them two or three
times with quite warm water. After the chicks are hatched they need a

warm cover, a good run, plenty
of clean gravel, fresh water, fine
cracked corn, and green food
every day.

**How to Raise Artificially-
Hatched Chickens.**—The fol-

FIG. 4.—FORM OF TANK.

lowing article is from the pen of a gentleman who has given the matter of
the artificial hatching of chickens much careful study, and he tells how to
successfully raise the young chicks after being so hatched:

"It is evident to the most casual observer that chickens hatched without
a mother must be raised without a mother. Born orphans, they must remain orphans. When my incubator produced the first chick, what a com-

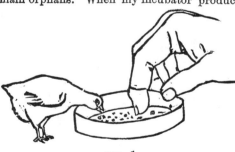

FIG. 1.

motion there was in the house.
The birth of a baby wouldn't
have been a circumstance to
it; and while the women-folks
would have known what to do
with a new baby, we all
looked at one another with
blank bewilderment when the
question was asked what we
should do with the new chick.
The thermometer outside was
down nearly to the freezing
point, while in the incubator

the temperature was 105 degrees. The little chick's hair stood on end, and
he was panting for dear life. He must come out of there, and as his brothers
and sisters were following him out of the shells, we began to prepare all
sorts of receptacles for them. We rigged up a mother on the heater, and
put in it several chicks that lived a few hours and then died. We decided it was too cold, so we put others in a box and put them back in the

Incubator, where some of them were smothered with the heat. It was evident something must be done, or we would soon have no chicks to experiment with. I determined in my own mind that a temperature of about ninety degrees would be correct, so I rigged up the brooder and started the lamp, put in the thermometer, and when the proper degree of heat was reached, put what was left of the chicks into the brooder, and they began to brighten up. The problem was solved, though its solution cost me the lives of many fine chicks.

"With further experience, I find the following treatment a complete success: After the chick breaks the shell, let him scramble around and dry himself in the incubator, which will generally take a few hours, though some are much stronger than others. After too much exercise they begin to pant, and should, of course, be removed. I have a box twelve inches square and six inches high. To the lid of this tack strips of woolen cloth an inch wide and two inches apart. These rags should hang within two inches

FIG. 2.

of the bottom. Put a half inch of dry sand in the box. The brooder is kept at a temperature between eighty and ninety degrees. The young chicks, when perfectly dry, are taken from the oven and put in the box, and the box put in the brooder where the other chicks are. Air holes should be cut in the *lid* of the box, for if cut in the side the other chicks peck out the feathers of the little ones through these holes. This box keeps the chicks warm, and they soon brighten up, and at the end of twelve hours are ready to take the first lesson in eating. Take a hard boiled egg and chop the white and yelk up together as fine as grains of wheat; with it cover the bottom of a little pan —the top of a blacking box will do. Place this in the box with the chicks,

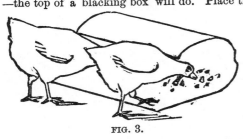

FIG. 3.

and, while tapping with the finger in the feed, repeat 'tuck, tuck,' like the clucking of a hen (Fig. 1). A little patience, and one chick will see something and peck at it, when the others will follow suit, and in a few minutes the first lesson is learned. After a few meals, with this process repeated, it will be only necessary to rap on the box, and the little fellows will be ready for their meal, and also be spry enough to be put out of the box and run with the others in the brooder.

" The next lot of chicks I feed as follows: Stale wheat bread is soaked in water. A cupful of oatmeal or rice has boiling water poured over it, and is stirred until it takes up all the water. I mix two handfuls of soaked bread, with the water squeezed out, with one handful of this oatmeal, and dry it all with unbolted cornmeal until it crumbles freely. A little salt is mixed up with it. This, with a little meat once a day, is their sole feed, and it is given about every three hours until the chicks are a week old, or until the wings are large enough to cover their backs, when they are put in a pen. This lot is fed the above mixture five or six times, with meat or worms once a day, and a head of cabbage is hung in the pen for them to peck at. The bottom of this pen is covered with dry sand and ashes, with a pile of old mortar and broken oyster shells to be picked over.

"For a water fountain I use a small tin pan, covering with a stone all the top except just enough to allow the chicks to drink, as shown at Fig. 2. Turn the open part next to the wall, so the little things cannot scratch dirt into it. Chicks are very fond of scratching the feed out of the pan. To prevent this I take a sheet of tin (Fig. 3), bend it over, and put the feed under the bent part. This prevents their treading on or scratching out the feed, and caters to their natural taste for hunting under things for food. It is also cleaned more readily than a pan.

"The body of the brooder (Fig. 4) is made of zinc, with an air-chamber over and under the back end. The lamp setting under it sends the heat up through the heater and out through the top, where a nursery for young or sick chicks is placed to utilize the waste heat. This form of brooder, with a warm chamber and the chicks feeding in the open air, I believe to be better than those where the chicks are never subjected to a cool atmosphere. The short stay while they feed in the open air tends to harden and invigorate them. All brooders, boxes, or pens, used to keep large numbers of chicks in, should have the bottom lined with zinc, as wood or earth is sure in time to become saturated with excrement, no matter how clean you try to keep it, and

BROODER.—FIG. 4.

it is the ammonia arising from these tainted floors that causes such pens in time to prove fatal to the chicks. I promised to tell the truth about my experience in hatching the eggs, and here it is: The last eggs that hatched out were bought October 10th. Up to that time I had purchased one hundred and five eggs at thirty cents a dozen. About one-third of these proved unfertile, and were cooked and eaten, or hard-boiled and fed to the young chicks, leaving about seventy-five eggs for the incubator to work on. Out of these I now have twenty-seven as fine chicks as I ever saw. By my own awkwardness and want of experience, I have killed or lost fully one dozen. My machine was an old one, and the battery was worn out. The gauge never was worth a cent. All the defective parts have been renewed except the gauge, and I have learned to doctor that. Owing to the above faults, the temperature in the oven has run too low for days at a time, and for hours it has been at 82 degrees, while it has taken short trips as high as 110 degrees. The only wonder is that I got a chicken out of any of the eggs. It is astonishing how much an egg will stand.

"From my experience with hens I am satisfied I will be able to get more chicks from a given number of eggs with the incubator than I ever could with hens. It would be a poor hand who could not raise from a fourth to a third more chicks with brooders than with the best hens."

Packing Eggs for Market.—We present herewith three different styles or methods of packing eggs for shipment or for storage, any one of which will be found simple, inexpensive and practical.

Our illustration, Fig. 1, represents a substantial carrying case, with nine drawers, the frames of which are of wood covered with canvas or sacking,

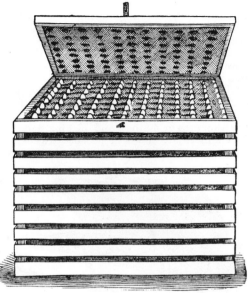

FIG. 1.—CANVAS COVERED CASE.

with cords or strings underneath, for the purpose of keeping the eggs in their places. The sacks, at the top and bottom, have depressions, as shown in the cover of the engraving, so that the eggs fit snugly and are not liable to be displaced by handling or transporting. Each alternating layer, coming between these depressions in each box or drawer, fills up the interstices perfectly. With proper care these cases will last for years, are always ready for packing and can be filled as the eggs are laid, thus avoiding repeated handling. The eggs can also be kept in them perfectly secure when the owner desires to hold his stock for better market. There are nine layers or drawers of eggs in this box,

FIG. 2.—COMMON TRANSPORTING CASE.

each layer containing eight dozen, or a total of seventy-two dozen of eggs.

Fig. 2. shows a cheaper case in every respect. It is a common packing box, made with paste or binders' board partitions, and each layer of eggs covered with the same material. One point connected with packing in these boxes the shipper should know and guard against; that is, it is sometimes the case that the pasteboard cover, on which the eggs are placed, is composed of two pieces, and during transporting or handling these pieces become displaced, or pass each other; then the eggs above drop down on the lower ones and break them. This difficulty, however, can easily be avoided by passing a piece of stiff paper over the joints, which will prevent them passing each other. Any sized box desired can be used for this style of case, and, with a little care on the part of the packer of the eggs, can be carried as safely as with any of the patent boxes now in vague.

Fig. 3 consists of an outside case or crate, in which are fitted a number of trays with cord laced through the sides and ends, dividing the spaces into small squares or meshes, and making a delicate spring, which responds to the slightest jar. Rows of pockets are suspended from the cord work, giving to each a separate apartment, and so arranged that no jar nor jolt the carrier may receive can cause one egg to strike another, and being thus separated, a free circulation of air is obtained, which prevents heating by any possibility. Each tray is provided with a protector, which keeps the eggs in the pocket even though the carrier be overturned. As each tray contains a certain number, no errors in count can ever occur, and the purchaser can determine at a glance both the number and quality of the eggs. By using this carrier a child can pack as well as a man.

FIG. 3.—SUSPENSION EGG CARRIER.

One of these carriers, the size shown, will hold sixty dozen of eggs.

Milk for Hens.—Fanny Field thus expresses herself as to the food value of milk for hens: "I quite agree with the correspondent of the *American Poultry Yard*, who declares there is no feed on earth so good for fowls and chicks as milk in some form. For very young chicks we make the clabbered milk into Dutch cheese, and use the whey to mix feed for other fowls and chickens. From the time they are a week old till sent to market for broilers, our early chicks have all the milk, sweet or sour, or buttermilk, that they can drink. If the home supply of milk falls short of the demand, we buy skim milk at two cents a quart, and consider it cheap at that. For laying hens in winter there is nothing better than a liberal supply of milk. A pan of warm milk, with a dash of pepper in it, every morning, will do more toward inducing hens to lay in cold weather than all the egg-food in creation. For fattening fowls, we find that boiled vegetables mixed with milk and barley or cornmeal will put on flesh at an astonishing rate. Don't be afraid to give milk to fowls or chicks; from the time when the chicks are given the first feed up to within the last day of the old fowl's life, milk may be safely and profitably given."

Poultry Keeping for Profit.—During the year 1884, Mr. Henry Stewart contributed to the *New York Times* a series of articles containing many valuable suggestions for those who wish to make poultry-keeping a business. His plan is briefly as follows: Each yard is to consist of a plot of ground about 100x400 feet, containing nearly one acre, with a suitable fence. The house is placed in the center of the yard and a cross-fence on a line with the house divides it into two parts. These two parts are alternately sown thickly with some crop that will afford forage for the fowls. In September they are placed on one side sown thickly with turnips. The other is immediately plowed up and sown with rye. The fowls will do very well for the winter in one side, with an occasional day in the green rye. In November wheat is sown, after the turnips are eaten off. In April we may sow oats, in May corn, in June rape or mustard seed and in July begin the rotation again with rutabagas.

As a rule a house twenty-five feet long, ten feet wide, eight feet high in the front and five feet in the rear, will be quite large enough for the one hundred fowls to be kept in each yard. This should be cleaned at least once a week, the oftener the better. The inside walls are quite smooth, having no fixtures except the roosting poles, which are on a level one foot from the ground. This leaves no harbor for vermin. The nests are loose boxes. Mr. Stewart also suggests that where a series of yards are kept, the inside fences may be movable, so that while the fowls are all confined to one side, the fences may be removed from the other, thus facilitating the plowing and planting.

"It is evident," he adds, "that this system will greatly enrich the soil, and this may be turned to good account by raising fruit trees in the poultry yards. No other fruit crop pays so well as plums, but none is so hard to grow on account of the pestiferous curculio. But when plums are grown in a poultry yard this insect has no chance. The sharp eyes of the fowls let no rogue escape, and one can raise plums with success and profit. As 200 of these trees can be planted on one acre, there is a possibility of $400 per acre from the fruit as well as $200 from the fowls; for every hen well cared for should make a clear profit of two dollars in the year. The yards may be planted with dwarf pear trees, with equal profit or more, because 300 of them may be placed on one acre. The shade of these trees is invaluable." It is also recommended that a row or small grove of Norway Spruce, Arbor-vitæ or Austrian pine be planted each side of the house to serve as a wind break for the fowls in winter.

Raising Chickens by Artificial Mothers.—Mr. E. S. Renwick writes from a large experience upon the above subject, in the *American Agriculturist*. He says:

When a fancier raises forty or fifty chickens a year, as amusement, the amount of care which he gives them is never taken into account; but if the number of chickens be increased to several hundreds, some means must be provided by which so large a number can be taken care of without too much labor. For supplying warmth and protection to young chickens, various "artificial mothers," or "brooders," have been devised. Those in the market are well enough adapted to the raising of a small number of chickens of nearly the same age, but it becomes a difficult matter when from two hundred and fifty to five hundred are to be raised, and of all ages, from those just hatched to those large enough for broilers. Young chickens must have plenty of air, exercise and wholesome green food; and means of protection against injury must be provided. Where young chickens of different ages are together, the elder tyrannize over the younger, the newly-hatched chickens being frequently trampled to death, or are driven away from their food by the stronger. Young chickens are very often lost in the grass when at liberty, and are frequently wet and chilled. Hence, to successfully raise a large number of chickens by hand, various means must be provided by which those of different ages can be separated, and by which the chickens can be protected and at the same time have sufficient liberty for exercise and development in the open air.

A Rustic Poultry House.—The rustic poultry house here illustrated is not only convenient, but designed to beautify the poultry yard of any amateur or breeder. For the rustic work, join four pieces of sapling in an oblong shape for sills; confine them to the ground; erect at the middle of each of the two ends a forked post, of suitable height, in order to make the sides quite steep; join these with a ridge pole; put on any rough or old boards from the apex down to the ground; then cover it with bark, cut in rough pieces, from half to a foot square, laid on and confined in the same manner as ordinary shingles; fix the back end in the same way; and the front can be latticed with little poles, with the bark on, arranged diamond fashion, as shown in the engraving. The door can be made in any style of rustic form. The roosts, laying and setting boxes can be placed inside of the house, in almost any position, either lengthwise or in the rear.

A RUSTIC POULTRY HOUSE.

From the directions here given one can easily build a house of any desired size, and in any location in the poultry yard he wishes; but to make the rusticity of the house show off to the best advantage it should be placed amid shrubbery.

The Hatching Period.—Setting hens should have a daily run. Do not remove them forcibly from their nests, but let the door be open every day at a given hour for a certain time while the attendant is about. Perhaps for the first day or two you may have to take them gently off their nests, and deposit them on the ground outside the door. They will soon, however, learn the habit and come out when the door is open, eat, drink, have a dust-bath and return to their nests.

While hens are off their nests some people dampen the eggs with luke-warm water. It is claimed that moisture is necessary, and that the chicks gain strength by the process. This may be correct, and in very dry weather, perhaps, necessary. It is generally, however, a mistake to meddle too much with nest or eggs; the hen is only made restless and dissatisfied by so doing. While the eggs are hatching out it is best not to touch the nests. It is very foolish to fuss the old bird and make her angry, as she may tread on the eggs in her fury, and crush the chicks when they are in the most delicate stage of hatching.

Picking off the shell to help the imprisoned chick is always a more or less hazardous proceeding, and should never be had recourse to unless the egg has been what is termed " billed " for a long time, in which case the chick is probably a weakly one and may need a little help, which must be given with the greatest caution, in order that the tender membranes of the skin shall not be lacerated. A little help should be given at a time, every two or three hours; but if any blood is perceived stop at once, as it is a proof that the chick is not quite ready to be liberated. If, on the contrary, the minute blood vessels which are spread all over the interior of the shell are bloodless, then you may be sure the chick is in some way stuck to the shell by its feathers, or is too weakly to get out of its prison-house.

The old egg shells should be removed from under the hen, but do not take away her chicks from her one by one as they hatch out, as is very often advised, for it only makes her very uneasy, and the natural warmth of her body is far better for them at that early stage than artificial heat. Should only a few chicks have been hatched out of the sitting, and the other remaining eggs show no signs of life when examined, no sounds of the little birds inside, then the water test should be tried. Get a basin of warm water, not really hot, and put those eggs about which you do not feel certain into it. If they contain chicks they will float on the top, if they move or dance the chicks are alive, but if they float without movement the inmates will most likely be dead. If they (the eggs) are rotten they will sink to the bottom. Put the floating ones back under the hen, and if, on carefully breaking the others, you find the test is correct (one puncture will be sufficient to tell you this), bury them at once.

Chickens should never be set free from their shells in a hurry, because it is necessary for their well-being that they should have taken in all the yelk, for that serves them as food for twenty-four hours after they see the light, so no apprehension need be felt if they do not eat during that period, if they seem quite strong, gain their feet, and their little downy plumage spreads out and dries properly. Their best place is under the hen for the time named.

When all are hatched, cleanse the nest completely, and well dredge the hen's body with sulphur powder; give her the chicks, and place chopped egg and bread-crumbs within reach. The less they are disturbed during the first two or three days the better. Warmth is essential, and a constantly brooding hen is a better mother than one which fusses the infant chicks about and keeps calling them to feed. Pen the hen in a coop and let the chicks have free egress. The best place to stand the coops is under sheltered runs, guarded from cold winds, the ground dry, and deep in sand and mortar siftings. Further warmth is unnecessary if the mothers are good; and if the roof is of glass, so as to secure every ray of sun, so much the better. Cleanliness of coops, beds, flooring, water vessels and flood tins must be absolute. The oftener the chicks are fed the better, but food must never be left; water must be made safe, or death from drowning and chills may be expected. The moment weather permits, free range on grass for several hours daily is desirable, but shelter should always be at hand.

Packing Poultry or Market.—All poultry should be thoroughly cooled and dried before packing, preparatory for shipment to market. For packing the fowl provide boxes, as they are greatly preferable to barrels. Commence your packing by placing a layer of rye straw, that has been thoroughly cleaned from dust, on the bottom of the box. Bend the head of the first fowl under it, as shown in our illustration (Fig. 1), and then lay it in the left hand corner, with the head against the end of the box, with the back up. Continue to fill this row in the same manner until completed; then begin the second row the same way, letting the head of the bird pass up between the rump of the two adjoining ones, which will make it complete and

solid (see illustration, Fig. 2). In packing the last row, reverse the o r d e r, placing the head against the end of the box, letting the feet pass under each other. Lastly, fill tight with straw, so that the poultry cannot move. This gives a firmness

PACKING POULTRY.—FIG. 1.

in packing that will prevent moving during transportation. Care should be taken to have the box filled full.

Poultry Raising as a Business.—Mr. P. H. Jacobs, a practical poultry man, writes as follows in the *American Agriculturist:* A flock of ten hens can be comfortably kept in a yard twenty feet wide by fifty deep. An acre of ground will contain forty such yards, or four hundred hens. No cocks are necessary unless the eggs are desired for incubation. To estimate $1.50 as a clear profit for each hen, is not the maximum limit, but the profit accrues according to the management given. Poultry thrives best when running at large, but this applies only to small flocks. Hens kept by the hundred become too crowded while at large, no matter how wide the range, and sickness and loss occur. Large flocks must be divided, and the size of the yard required for a flock is of but little importance compared with that of the management. There is much profit to be derived from the sale of young chicks—and, where one pays attention to the business—they receive the greatest care. Each brood, like the adult, is kept separate from the others in a

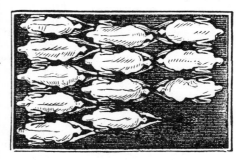

PACKING POULTRY.—FIG. 2.

little coop, which prevents quarreling among the hens, and enables the manager to count and know all about the chicks. This is very important, as there are many farmers who hatch scores of broods and yet cannot tell what became of two-thirds of them. Hawks, crows, cats, rats, and other depredators take their choice, and the owners are no wiser. Each setting hen should be in a coop by herself, and each coop should have a lath run. The critical period is the forming of the feathers, which calls for frequent feeding, and when they have passed that stage, the chicks become hardy. The houses need not be more than eight feet square for each family, and can be doubled. If possible, it is best to have changeable yards, but, if used, a less number can be kept to an acre. If the yards are kept clean by an occasional spading, however, green stuff may be grown elsewhere and thrown over to them. This may consist of cabbage, grass, turnip tops, kale, mustard, lettuce, etc. Watering must not be neglected, or the meals given irregularly. Care must be observed not to feed too much, as over-fat fowls will lay few eggs, and such eggs will not hatch. A good poultry manager is always among his fowls, and observes everything. The breeds have special characteristics also. The large fowls must be hatched in March, if early pullets are desired for winter laying. This applies to Brahmas, Cochins and Plymouth Rocks. If the manager finds this impossible, he should at once substitute cocks of the Leghorn breed, which crossed with large hens, make good marketable chicks, and produce pullets that mature early. A knowledge of the characteristics of the several breeds is indispensable to success. Crossing pure-bred cocks with common hens is excellent, but " fancy poultry " is not profitable to any but those who understand thoroughly the mating and selection of the several breeds.

Poultry on a Large Scale.—People thinking of raising chickens on a large scale will do well to note the following sound advice by the *Poultry Monthly:*

" There are many persons of moderate means who have had perhaps some little experience with breeding poultry, and who get to wondering if it will pay to breed poultry on a large scale; whether it will pay to embark in the breeding of poultry for market purposes as a business, and if it is good policy to give up a fair paying clerkship or small business to engage in it. Such questions are very difficult to determine to the satisfaction of all persons concerned, for much more really depends on the person than on the business in nearly every department of human industry, and where one person may make a success of any undertaking another one may fail, though having started with equally as good chances of success. Poultry, to be successful on a large scale, must be kept in small colonies of about fifty birds each, for many more than that number in a single house is apt to cause sickness or disease, ere long, among them. Small flocks like that can be given better attention than larger ones, and the first approach of disorder can be seen readily and promptly checked, while there is less danger of great loss when thus kept in small flocks, as the trouble can usually be confined to the flock in which it started by proper and prompt sanitary measures. When the breeder is not too far away from large retail markets, and especially where the breeder can market them himself, thus saving commission, freight, and loss, it pays best to breed and keep poultry for the eggs they produce, as eggs known to be strictly fresh are always in good demand at quite an increase in price over that received for the ordinary " store " eggs. Such breeds as the white and the brown Leghorns, and birds bred from them, either pure breed or cross breed or grade, as a basis, are first-class egg producers, while a game cock is also valuable to breed to good common hens, producing, as a rule, vigorous, active pullets, which are invariably good layers. Those who wish to raise poultry principally for the flesh should raise the light Brahmas, Plymouth Rocks, dark Brahmas, or some of the Cochin breeds, the first two named, however, being general favorites in this respect, and also combining with it good laying qualities under favorable circumstances. Those who cannot or will not give the poultry regular or constant attention, shelter them properly, supply proper food in liberal quantities and at frequent and regular intervals, and pay a strict attention to cleanliness and thoroughness in all the details of the management, need not expect even to succeed, not to even consider the question of loss or profits, for success and profit here means work, work, work."

Feeding Hoppers for Fowls.—We give herewith designs for two styles of feeding hoppers for fowls, deeming anything that has a tendency toward economy will be beneficial to the farmer as well as to the amateur breeder of fowls.

FIG. 1.—FEEDING HOPPER.

The illustration, Fig. 1, represents a very good and easily constructed hopper, that can be made to contain any quantity of corn required, and none wasted. When once filled it requires no more trouble, as the grain falls into the receiver below as the fowls pick it away, and the covers on that which are opened by the perches, and the cover on the top, protect the grain from rain, so that the fowls always get it quite dry; and as nothing less than the weight of a fowl on the perch can lift the cover on the lower receiver, rats and mice are excluded.

Our illustration, Fig. 2, represents "a perfect feeding hopper," which, from the description here given, can be easily constructed by any person. A is an end view, eight inches wide, two feet six inches high, and three feet long; B, the roof projecting over the perch on which the fowls stand while feeding; C, the lid of the receiving manger raised, exhibiting the grain; E, E, cords attached to the perch and lid of the manger or feeding trough; I, end bar of the perch, with a weight attached to the end to balance the lid, otherwise it would not close when the fowls leave the perch; H, pully; G, fulcrum. The hinges on the top show that it is to be raised when

FIG. 2.—A PERFECT FEEDING HOPPER.

the hopper is to be replenished. When a fowl desires food it hops upon the bars of the perch, the weight of which raises the lid of the feed box, exposing the grain to view, and after satisfying its hunger jumps off, and the lid closes. Of course the dimensions of either of these feeding hoppers may be increased to any size desired.

Winter Egg-Production.—The following is from the *Country Gentle-man:* To obtain a breed of fowls that are perpetual layers is the object that many aim at. This is an impossibility, for nature will exhaust itself and must have a period of rest. In order that we have a perpetual production of fresh eggs, the business must be arranged beforehand. There is a difference in breeds, some laying better than others at any time of the year, and others, again, giving their eggs in winter. There is little difficulty in obtaining eggs in summer, but the winter eggs must be worked for, and the fowls managed beforehand. Hens that have laid well during the summer cannot be depended on for late fall or early winter, even if well fed, but will generally commence in January, and keep it up throughout February and March, giving a good supply of eggs if not too old. But it is better not to allow such birds to go into the winter. They are generally fat, after having finished the annual moult, and should be killed for the table. After the second annual moult hens are apt to become egg-bound, especially if well fed and fat. The excess of fat that accumulates about the lower intestines and ovaries weakens these organs and renders them incapable of performing their offices. Hence the fowl suffers and becomes profitless. When left too long the bird becomes feverish and the flesh is unfit for food. The better way is to avoid this trouble, since there is no cure, by not allowing the birds to go into the second winter. Trouble of this kind seldom occurs with pullets or young hens.

To obtain a supply of winter eggs, we must have the chicks out in March or April. Leghorns and some of the smaller breeds will do in May or the first of June, but the Brahmas and Cochins must come off early, that they may have the full season for growth. The Asiatics are generally good layers in winter, and need less artificial heat, as nature has not furnished them with any ornamental appendages which suffer by exposure to frost. For them it is not necessary to spend large sums in warm buildings. What they can dispense with in this respect they demand in feed, which must be given regularly. The feed must be kept up and varied with animal and vegetable diet. The supply of water must never fail. We must feed and feed a long time before the eggs will come. Any breed of hens will consume an enormous quantity of feed before commencing to lay, but after having once begun they will not require, or even take so much grain. When laying, their great craving is for vegetable and animal substances, and crushed clam or oyster shells.

Fowls that are regularly trained have certain portions of the day for their different feeds. My birds require their shells at night, as well as their greens, and their grain in the morning, and always fresh water. When one has the time and convenience, and enjoys the petting of fowls, making warm stews on very cold days is an admirable plan, and the birds relish them marvelously. Take beef or pork scraps, and put into an old kettle, having them previously chopped fine, and fill it half full of water. While stewing, throw in a dozen chopped onions, two dozen cayenne peppers, and the day's coffee and tea-grounds. Thicken the mixture with cornmeal, and serve it around among the hens hot. They relish it amazingly when once taught to eat it, and will look for the ration daily at the certain time. On cold winter days give this feed between two and three o'clock in the afternoon, and the chicks get their crops warmed up for the coming cold at night. If scraps are not handy, boil unpeeled potatoes, and serve in the same manner, adding a little grease or cold gravies left over from yesterday's dinner.

The combed varieties require warmer quarters and sunnier exposure than the Asiatics, and are good winter layers after December and early January. They will lay in the fall if early hatched, but the change of fall to winter, and the getting into winter quarters affects them, and they seldom commence again before the days begin to lengthen, at which time Brahmas will cease egg-production and become broody. Where one has the convenience it is well to keep both kinds, in order to insure a supply of eggs. It is useless to expect many eggs from old fowls of any variety. Have the buildings ready early, and the fowls of the right age and in condition to insure success. The business of our domestic hen is to produce eggs, and we must feed her for it.

CHICKEN COOP.—FIG. 1.

A Chicken Coop.—Nail short pieces of matched boards together as indicated in the cut; then board up the rear end tightly, and nail narrow strips of boards or lath in front; put a floor of boards in the back part of the coop, large enough for the hen to brood her young upon, and lay a wide board in front to feed upon, as long as the width of the coop. The coop should be at least two feet high, and from two to three feet deep. The board in front may be turned up at night to prevent the young against rats, cats, etc., and should remain in the morning until the dew is off from the grass. The coop should be moved every two or three days to a clean place. The second engraving shows a coop of another construction, the tight apartment at the end with a slide door to let down every evening, keeps the little inmates secure from all enemies. A few auger holes must be made for ventilation. The front is a simple frame, with lath attached at sufficient distances to allow the chickens to pass through. The top should be made separate, and attached to the side by leather hinges.

Feeding and Laying. —The best of feed sometimes fails to induce the hens to lay. This is not because the fowls do not get enough,

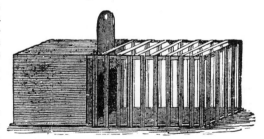

CHICKEN COOP.—FIG. 2.

but because it is not the kind they desire. It may be feed consisting of everything that serves to satisfy the demand for egg material, and yet no eggs will be the result. There are several causes for these complaints, one of the principal being the fact that a plentiful supply of pure fresh water is not always within reach, and unless water is plentiful the fowls will not lay. Water being the principal substance in an egg, it cannot be limited. Unless the water can be procured for the egg the fowl cannot lay. And in cold weather it must be so situated as to be either protected from freezing or else have a little warm water added to it occasionally. Now this is a troublesome job in winter, but water will freeze on cold days, and consequently if useless to the fowls when in a frozen condition. The feed, however, even when of the best quality, may not give satisfaction. In that case, when no eggs are being derived, change it entirely for three or four days. Give something entirely different in the morning from that previously given, even if inferior, but still give whole grains at night in cold weather, for then the fowls go on the roost early in the evening, and have to remain in the coops until daylight, which is nearly thirteen hours, and so long a period demands the solid food in order to keep them warm during the long cold nights. Whole corn and wheat is best for them then, but in the morning any kind of mixed soft food makes a good meal for a change. The changes can be made by using good clover hay, steeped in warm water, after being chopped fine, slightly sprinkled with meal, and fed warm, which will be very acceptable. A few onions chopped fine will also be highly relished. Parched ground oats or parched cracked corn is a splendid change of food for a few days from the ordinary routine of every day. It stimulates them if fed warm, and is a good corrective of bowel complaints, especially if some of the grains are parched till burned. The matter of feeding is to give variety, and if the food is of good quality also, a good supply of eggs may be expected at all times, but with good quarters and plenty of water the prospects will be better.

Successful Poultry Raising.—Mr. Charles Lyman, a successful raiser of poultry, writes as follows: In raising poultry or stock of any kind, it should be the aim of every one to keep it healthy and improve it. You can do it very easily by adopting some systematic rules. These may be summed up in brief, as follows:

1. Construct your house good and warm, so as to avoid damp floors, and afford a flood of sunlight. Sunshine is better than medicine.

2. Provide a dusting and scratching place where you can bury wheat and corn and thus induce the fowls to take the needful exercise.

3. Provide yourself with some good, healthy chickens, none to be over three or four years old, giving one cock to every twelve hens.

4. Give plenty of fresh air at all times, especially in summer.

5. Give plenty of fresh water daily, and never allow the fowls to go thirsty.

6. Feed them systematically two or three times a day; scatter the food so they can't eat too fast, or without proper exercise. Do not feed more than they will eat up clean, or they will get tired of that kind of feed.

7. Give them a variety of both dry and cooked feed; a mixture of cooked meat and vegetables is an excellent thing for their morning meal.

8. Give soft feed in the morning, and the whole grain at night, except a little wheat or cracked corn placed in the scratching places to give them exercise during the day.

9. Above all things keep the hen house clean and well ventilated.

10. Do not crowd too many in one house. If you do, look out for disease.

11. Use carbolic powder occasionally in the dusting bins to destroy lice.

12. Wash your roosts and bottom of laying nests, and whitewash once a week in summer, and once a month in winter.

13. Let the old and young have as large a range as possible—the larger the better.

14. Don't breed too many kinds of fowls at the same time, unless you are going into the business. Three or four will give you your hands full.

15. Introduce new blood into your stock every year or so, by either buying a cockerel or settings of eggs from some reliable breeder.

16. In buying birds or eggs, go to some reliable breeder who has his reputation at stake. You may have to pay a little more for birds, but you can depend on what you get. Culls are not cheap at any price.

17. Save the best birds for next year's breeding, and send the others to market. In shipping fancy poultry to market send it dressed.

Fish for Poultry.—In preparing fish for fowls, we prefer to chop them up raw, add a very little salt and' pepper, and feed in small quantities in conjunction with grain and vegetables; but for young chicks it is advisable to boil before feeding, and simply open the fish down the line of the back bone, leaving to the chicks the rest of the task. This food shall be given to layers sparingly, or we may perceive a fishy smell about the eggs, especially if the fish is fed raw. All who can will do well to try this diet for their flocks, and note its effect on egg production. We have always marked a decided increase in the rate of laying following an allowance of fish fed in moderate quantities.

There are hundreds of our readers who live near or on rivers or lakes, or the sea shore, where they can get considerable offal fish, such as are either too small to market, or are cast out as unfit to be sold. Hundreds of bushels of these fish are annually used for manure, either composted or plowed in direct. In this connection they are very good, though many a basketful could be put to better account by feeding them to your fowls; and they are very fond of this diet, though care must be taken not to feed it exclusively, for it may cause extreme laxity.

To Cure Pip.—This is a troublesome and somewhat fatal complaint to which all domestic poultry are liable; it is also a very common one. Some writers say it is the result of cold; others, that is promoted by the use of bad water. But, whatever the cause, the disease is easily detected. There is a thickening of the membrane of the tongue, particularly at the tip; also a difficulty in breathing; the beak is frequently held open, the tongue dry, the feathers of the head ruffled and the bird falls off in food; and if neglected, dies. The mode of cure which, if put in practice in time, is generally successful, is to remove the thickened membrane from the tongue with the nails of the forefinger and thumb. The process is not difficult, for the membrane is not adhesive. Then take a lump of butter, mix into it some strong Scotch snuff, and put two or three large pills of this down the fowl's throat. Keep it from cold and damp, and it will soon recover. It may, perhaps, be necessary to repeat the snuff balls. Some writers recommend a mixture of butter, pepper, garlic, and scraped horseradish; but we believe the Scotch snuff to be the safest, as it is the most simple.

Eggs and Pullets.—Unless you want a large proportion of cockerels do not sell all the largest eggs you can pick out. There are no means known by which the sex of eggs can with certainty be determined. Although many thought some sign indicated the sex, yet after repeated fair trials, all these indications have entirely failed with me, except the one which follows: With regard to the eggs of most of the feathered kingdom, if you pick the largest out of the nest, they are the ones that generally produce males, especially if they happen to be the first laid. Even in a canary's nest it is noticeable that the first egg laid is very often the largest, the young from it is the first out, keeps ahead of its comrades, is the first to quit the nest and the first to sing.

How to Produce Layers.—Mr. L. Wright says: In every lot of hens some will be better layers than others. Let us suppose we start with six Houdans—a cock and five hens. Probably out of this five two may lay thirty eggs per annum more than either of the others; their eggs should be noticed and only these set. By following this for a few years a very great increase in egg production may be attained. My attention was drawn to this subject by a friend having a Brahma pullet which laid nearly three hundred eggs in one twelve-month, though valueless as a fancy bird, and the quality descended to several of her progeny; and I have since found other instances which prove conclusively that a vast improvement might easily be effected in nearly all our breeds were that careful selection of brood stocks made for this purpose which the fancier bestows on other objects. It is to be regretted more is not done in this way, and having more room than I had, I hope myself to make some experiments in this direction shortly. I will say now that I am perfectly certain the number of two hundred eggs per annum might be attained in a few years with perfect ease were the object systematically sought; and I trust these few remarks may arouse a general attention to it among those who keep poultry for eggs only, and who can easily do all that is necessary without any knowledge whatever of fancy points, or any attempt to breed exhibition birds.

A Grain Chest for Fowls.—We illustrate an excellent grain chest for fowls. The trough (1), two inches high. The front of the chest extends downward no further than the top of the trough, thus leaving a free passage for grain from the chest into

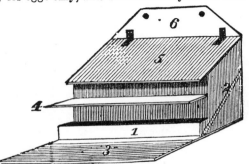

GRAIN CHEST FOR FOWLS.

the trough. The dotted line (2) shows the position of a board in the chest, placed there to conduct the grain into the trough as fast as it is eaten out by the fowls. The platform (3) is for the fowls to stand upon while eating. It should not be wide enough to induce them to form a habit of sitting upon it. A board (4) is fastened to the front of the chest and extends over the trough to prevent filth from falling into it. The cover of the chest (5) should extend a little over the front, that it may be handily raised, and should rest inclined to prevent fowls from roosting on it. An extension of the back of the chest (6), with two holes in it, is provided so that it may be hung on corresponding wooden pins. If it is hung up in that way it will be necessary to put some kind of a key through each of the pins, to prevent its being jarred off from them. It should be hung so that the platform will be at least two feet from the floor. It may be made any length. A square chest, for a post in the yard, can be made on the same principle.

How to Fatten Turkeys.—Nothing pays better to be sent to market in prime condition than the turkey crop. Many farmers do not understand this. Their turkeys grow on a limited range, getting little or no food at home through the summer, and if fed at all with regularity it is only for two or three weeks before killing. I see these lean, bony carcasses in the local markets every winter, and feel sorry for the owner's loss. They have received a small price for their birds and a still poorer price for the food fed out. The average life of a turkey is only seven months, and the true economy of feeding is to give the chicks all they can digest from the shell to the slaughter. If they get all they can eat on the range, that is well. Usually this should be supplemented by regular rations when they come from the roost in the morning and two or three hours before they go to roost at night. The food may be slack in the morning, so that they will go to the range with good appetites, and fuller at night. They should be put upon a regular course of fattening food as early as the middle of October, when you propose to kill the best birds at Thanksgiving. The younger and lighter birds should be reserved for the Christmas and New Year's markets. They continue growing quite rapidly until midwinter, and you will be paid for the longer feeding. There is nothing better for fattening than old corn, fed partly in the kernel and partly in cooked meal mashed up with boiled potatoes. Feed three times a day, giving the warm meal in the morning, and feeding in troughs with plenty of room, so that all the flock may have a chance. Northern corn has more oil in it than Southern, and is worth more for turkey food. Use milk in fattening if you keep a dairy farm. Feed only so much as they will eat up clean. Cultivate the acquaintance of your turkeys as you feed them. No more charming sight greets your vision in the whole circle of a year than a large flock of bronze turkeys coming at call from their roosts on a frosty November morning. New corn is apt to make the bowels loose, and this should be guarded against. There is usually green food enough in the fields to meet their wants in the fall, and cabbage and turnips need not be added until winter sets in. If the bowels get loose give them scalded milk, which will generally correct the evil. Well-fattened and well-dressed turkeys will bring two or three cents a pound more than smaller birds. It will not only be better for the purse, but for your manhood, to send nothing but finished products to the market.

Preserving Eggs.—Several Practiced Methods.—Several ways of preserving eggs are practiced. The object is to prevent evaporation from the egg. Cutting off the air from the contents of the egg preserves them longer than with any other treatment. An egg which has lain in bran even for a few days will smell and taste musty. Packed in lime eggs will be stained. Covered with a coat of spirit varnish eggs have kept so perfectly that after the lapse of two years chickens were hatched from them. A good egg will sink in a body of water; if stale, a body of air inside the shell will frequently cause it to float. When boiled, a fresh egg will adhere to the shell, which will have a rough exterior; if stale, the outside will be smooth and glassy.

Looking through a paper tube directed toward the light, an egg held to the end of the tube will appear translucent if fresh; but if stale it will be dark—almost opaque.

Spirit varnish for preserving eggs is made by dissolving gum shellac in enough alcohol to make a thin varnish. Coat each egg with this and pack, little end down, so that they cannot move, in bran, sawdust, or sand; the sand is best. Whatever is used for packing should be clean and dry. For preserving in lime, a pickle is made of the best stone lime, fine, clean salt and water enough to make a strong brine, usually sixty or sixty-five gallons of water, six or eight quarts of salt, and a bushel of lime are used. The lime should be slacked with a portion of the water, the salt and the remainder of the water is added. Stir at intervals, and when the pickle is cold and the sediment has settled, dip or draw the liquid off into the cask in which the eggs are to be preserved. When only a few eggs are to be pickled a stone jar will answer.

At the Birmingham Poultry Show, England, prizes were offered for the best dozen preserved eggs that had been kept two months. The eggs were tested by breaking one of each set competing for the prize into a clean saucer, also by boiling one of each lot.

The eggs that had been preserved in lime-water, it was found on breaking them, presented cloudy whites. Eggs preserved by rubbing over with bees-wax and oil showed thin, watery whites.

Eggs that stood best the test of boiling and which gained the first prize had been simply packed in common salt. These had lost little, if any, by evaporation, had good, consistent albumen, and were pleasant to the taste. The exhibit which took the second prize was served as follows: Melt one part of white wax to two parts of spermaceti, boil and mix thoroughly; or two parts clarified suet to one of wax and two of spermaceti. Take new-laid eggs, rub with antiseptic salt and fine rice starch. Wrap each egg in fine tissue paper, putting the broad end downward; screw the paper tightly at the top, leaving an inch to hold it by. Dip each egg rapidly into the fat heated to 100 degrees. Withdraw and leave to cool. Pack broad end downward in dry, white sand or sawdust. The judges were inclined to believe that had the trial been for a longer period than two months, this latter method would perhaps have proven the better of the two. The eggs were excellent, and on stripping off the waxed paper the shells presented the clean, fresh appearance of newly laid eggs.

The following is a recipe for packing in salt: Cover the bottom of a keg, cask, jar, hogshead, or whatever you choose to pack in, with a layer of fine salt two inches deep; upon this place the eggs, small end down, and far enough apart so that they will not touch each other or the sides of the receptacle; then put on another two inch layer of salt, then another layer of eggs, and so on until the package is full. This is the method that we used, and is on the whole the best method for housekeepers and for those who have only a small number to pack for market. The salt can be used over and over again.

The following recipe is also given for keeping eggs: Put them in an open-work basket or colander and immerse them for a moment in boiling water; let them stay just long enough to form a film on the inside of the shell; this excludes the air. Then place them in some convenient vessel, small end down, and set them in the coolest part of the cellar, where they will keep till wanted for use.

Cheap Poultry Houses.—The following directions for building cheap poultry houses are clipped from W. H. Todd's descriptive catalogue:

We find the best and most successful plan to manage and make fowls pay is to scatter them over a large range in fields and orchards. For this purpose cheap, convenient, and comfortable houses are best. My plan is to build 16 feet long and 8 feet wide, 7 1-2 front (facing south), and 4 1-2 back, boarded upright and battened, with a shed roof, shingled. Sills are 2x4 inch-plank halved together. Plates, same size. Rafters, 2x2. Lay the sills on sleepers, and on these lay a tight floor, which cover with dry earth 4 to 6 inches deep, removing and renewing twice a year. This keeps fowls dry, warm and healthy. Place an entrance door near one end, on the front, and at least two windows of six 8x10 lights. Partition across the middle, with a door. Fix ventilators at the highest point in each end, sheathed to exclude storm and wind. Erect roosts 20 inches high, for twenty fowls, with a movable nest or two, and a box, partly filled with dust and ashes, and you are ready for " business." Forty large fowls can be accommodated and thrive well. Since the house is double we are in shape for running two breeding yards. Fence can be built cheaply with lath nailed upright to two 1-inch-thick pieces, the lower one 8 or 10 inches wide, and the upper about 2, 30 inches apart; the lath may be 3 inches apart, and a short piece 16 inches long, tacked to the bottom board, and to a light strip running lengthwise the panel. It is best to make this fence in panels about 12 feet long. Set a post where they come together, and pass a wire around panels and post, fasten, and you have light, cheap, strong fences. The house can be made warmer if necessary by lining with tar-board sheathing.

An Inexpensive Chicken Coop.—A correspondent writes as follows: " Having made a good discovery, I am desirous of giving it to the people. Being engaged in raising chickens for profit, it was necessary to make cheap coops to keep them in for a few weeks. I take an old barrel and tack every

AN INEXPENSIVE CHICKEN COOP.

hoop on each side of a seam between the staves with an inch wrought nail; after clinching the nail, I saw the hoops off on the seam. Then I spread the barrel open, as shown in the illustration, by cutting a board about twenty inches long for the back of the coop, and two small pieces to tack laths on for the front part. I have the upper section of the back fastened with leather hinges, so that I can open it at pleasure. Everybody has old barrels which are almost valueless, and the trouble and expense of making a coop of this description is so small that it is not worth mentioning, while to buy the material and make a coop of the same size, it would cost about one dollar."

Chicken Cholera.—A New Jersey correspondent gives this remedy: Take of pulverized copperas, sulphur, alum, cayenne pepper and rosin, of each equal parts, and mix one teaspoonful in four quarts of meal. Give three days in succession, then once a week as a preventive. I have seen it used successfully. It will not cure those which have it, but will prevent spreading of the disease. For a disinfectant, use crude carbolic acid—one tablespoonful in one gallon of water. Sprinkle the hen house often, say about twice a week.

Another correspondent says: I used a strong tea made of white oak bark, which I used in the drinking water as a preventive. When a fowl was taken sick I used it pure, giving several teaspoonfuls at a time, four or five times a day. I have taken fowls so far gone that they were past eating or drinking, and cured them in a few days with this simple remedy. As a disinfectant I use crude carbolic acid, pouring it on a board in the chicken house and on the perches, coops, etc., or anywhere that the fowls frequent. If you will try this plan for awhile, removing all infected fowls from the flock, and keep the surroundings clean, I think you will soon get rid of the disease.

The following prescription we find in the *Southern Cultivator*, and it is said to be very efficacious in chicken cholera: Glycerine and water, each a half ounce; carbolic acid, ten drops. When the first symptoms of the disease are apparent, give five drops, and repeat at intervals of twelve hours. Usually the second dose effects a cure. A neighbor informed me that cholera was very destructive among his poultry, and at my suggestion he tried the foregoing recipe. He reports that the progress of the disease was promptly arrested, and in almost every case a cure was accomplished.

Infertile Eggs.—There are many reasons why eggs hatch so poorly, when from pure bred stock, one of the greatest being want of *stamina* in the flock from which the eggs came, caused by being kept too closely confined. As a rule it is best to procure eggs for hatching from fowls which have free range, which is a great promoter of healthfulness, though there is no reason why eggs should not hatch well when from fowls in confinement, *if* those fowls are given good care, plenty of food, and have good sized yards to run in. Want of fertility may be due to running too many hens to a cock; about ten hens of the Asiatics (Brahmas and Cochins), and from ten to fifteen of the laying breeds (Leghorns, Hamburgs, etc.) to a cock being about the right number to secure good results, other things being equal.

A Cheap Chicken Fountain.—Take an emptied tomato can, bend in the ragged edges where it has been opened, make a hole in the side one quarter of an inch from the edge, fill it with water, put a saucer on it, and quickly invert both. The water will then stand in the saucer constantly at the height of the hole. Chickens can drink, but cannot get in the water, which remains clean.

A CHEAP CHICKEN FOUNTAIN.

Chicken Lice.—The first signs of lice are with the early setting hens. From their nests soon a whole house will be overrun with the pest. Chicks show the presence of lice very quickly, and lice are certain death to them if they are not protected. Have all nests movable, and change the contents frequently. With sitting hen's nests be sure to have the nest clean and the box and surroundings whitewashed before she is placed. Whitewash and the dust box are the surest preventives of lice. Put two or three coats of whitewash on every interior spot in the building; the lice harbor in the crevices of the rough sidings, and on the under side of the perches. Let the fowl house have a dust box. Mix hot ashes with the dust occasionally to dry it. Do all this early in the year, before spring laying and sitting. Kerosene and lard when applied is a sure cure, but they are too often dangerous in their effects. A little castor oil on the head and under the wings of sitting hens is very effective. Don't keep a brood hen in a little coop without a dust wallow. If you want your fowls to be free from lice you must keep their habitation clean. The best way to do that is by occasional change of the nest contents and a thorough whitewashing of the apartment.

Raising Turkeys.—The difficulty of raising turkeys is a serious draw-back to the profits of the business, but the exercise of care will obviate the difficulty. At first, and for about six weeks, turkey chicks are very delicate, so much so that even a warm shower will finish them. If they can be kept alive for about two months they begin to assume a more robust character, and will soon become the very hardiest of poultry. The chicks, therefore, should be provided with shelter, and the shed which furnishes this would be all the better if it had a wooden floor. The best feed for the first week is hard boiled eggs, mixed with minced dandelion. It is thought the dandelion serves to keep the bowels in order. At all events the young birds prefer dandelion to all other green food. At the end of the first week add gradually to the boiled eggs bread crumbs and barley meal, constantly lessening the amount of egg until at the end of three weeks it may be entirely discontinued. Now give boiled potatoes as a part of the food, and a small portion of some small grain may be added, in fact making the food very much like that of other poultry. If fed in this way and kept dry, they will come along all right.

How to Raise Ducks.—A writer who thinks unlimited water a bad thing for young ducks, recommends the following treatment for them: "Ducks are easily hatched, and, if properly managed, they are easily raised—much more so than chickens or turkeys. Probably the worst thing for ducklings is the first thing they usually receive, and that is unlimited range and water to swim in. The little things are, in a measure, nude, and should be kept in pens with dry soil floors or stone pavements that can be washed down daily. No kind of poultry will succeed on bare boards. All the water they need is best furnished by burying an old pot in the ground and laying a round piece of board on top of the water with room for the ducks to stick their heads in and fish out the corn that is put in the water. This amuses them and does no harm, while, if allowed to go off to ponds or streams, they are very liable to fall a prey to vermin in some shape, or to get their bodies wet and chilled from remaining too long in the water. Their pens must be kept clean if they are expected to thrive.

Gapes in Fowls.—The parasite that causes gapes in fowls is of a red color and about three-quarters of an inch long. The remedies are numerous, but chiefly consist in removing the worms. One way is to moisten a feather from which all but the tip of the web has been stripped, with oil, salt water, or a weak solution of carbolic acid, introduce it into the windpipe, twist it around once or twice, and then withdraw it. A teaspoonful of sulphur mixed with a quart of corn meal and water, and fed to the fowls morning and evening, is also a good remedy.

The *Poultry World* says: As soon as we discover any symptoms of gapes among our chickens, we know that there are worms—very small red worms —in their windpipes, and we give them camphor in their drinking vessels strong enough to make quite a taste of the camphor. Then, if any get the disease quite badly before we discover it, we force a pill of gum camphor down the throat, about the size of a small pea, and the fumes of that dose will kill the worms. No kind of worms can live in camphor; hence, camphor must be a powerful vermifuge.

A Connecticut poultry raiser writes: "Perhaps some who raise fowls will be interested in my experiment tried last season on a chicken with the gapes. I gave it about a quarter of a teaspoonful of kerosene, and as it seemed better for a day or two, I repeated the dose, giving nearly one half a teaspoonful for the second time. The chicken was about the size of a robin at the time, but is now full-grown, weighing several pounds. I cured chickens affected with a disease we thought cholera, by giving powdered alum dissolved in water."

Eggs.—How Increased.—If an increase of eggs be desired in the poultry yard, before large sums are expended in the purchase of everlasting layers, we would recommend the system of keeping no hens after the first, or at most, after the second year. Early pullets give the increase, and the only wonder is that people persist, as they do, in keeping up a stock of old hens, which lay one day and stop the next. In some parts of Europe it is the invariable rule to keep the pullets only one year. Feeding will do a great deal—a surprising work indeed—in the production of eggs, but not when old hens are concerned; they may put on fat, but they cannot put down eggs. Their tale is told, their work is done; nothing remains to be done with them but to give them a smell of the kitchen fire, and the sooner they get that the better.

Late Chickens.—Late chicks may be more profitable than early ones. Chickens from eggs set in August and September may be kept warm in a tight, glazed house, and fed so that they will grow continually through the winter, and if they come later all the better, if they are well kept and fed. The early broods will be salable at good prices, when the market is bare of chickens, and the later ones will furnish spring chickens long before the usual supply comes to hand. Spring chickens hatched in fall, or even in winter, are rare, but not entirely unknown to a few persons who made the discovery that with good feed, warm quarters, a warm mess at least once a day, warm drink and cleanliness, there is no difficulty at all about raising them, and at a good profit.

Cure for Scaly Legs in Fowl.—A sure cure of scaly legs in fowl is effected thus: Insert a feather in the spout of a coal oil can so that too large a stream will not run out; get some one to hold the fowl by the wings; take hold of a toe of one foot at a time, and pour a fine stream from the hock joint to the end of each toe, taking care that all parts of the foot are wet with it. One application a year is enough, if done at all, and at the time when they need it, say during January or February. The scaly appearance is caused by an insect, which the oil most effectually kills, and leaves the legs clear and bright looking. This will answer even when the legs are twice their natural size, which is frequently the case when neglected.

Roup.—Fowls exposed to dampness in severe weather are apt to take cold, which often culminates in roup. The writer has cured this disease by injecting kerosene into the nostrils by the means of a bulb syringe, and then using it to gargle the throat. The latter is effected by holding the throat close enough to prevent swallowing, and, after the gargling, pouring the liquid out on to the ground. Repeat this once the next day; then feed with boiled rice and scalded milk, keeping water away for a few days.

To Get Rid of Skunks.—To rid your poultry yard of skunks, purchase a few grains of strychnine, roll it up in a ball of lard, and then throw it at night outside the yard, where the animals' tracks are seen. As they are very fond of lard, they will swallow it quickly, and in the morning you will find your enemy dead. But you must be careful to shut up the dogs and cats, as they are equally fond of lard. It is the easiest way to kill any vermin, as they die very soon. Skunks will kill and eat full-grown ducks and hens, and suck their eggs, whenever they can gain entrance into the poultry-house.

Road-dust for the Hennery.—Collect a few barrels of dry earth, road-dust, fine dry dirt in the cornfield or potato patch, or anywhere that is most convenient. This is a handy thing to have in the fall and winter for sprinkling under the roosts and on the floor of the poultry-house. It absorbs ammonia, keeps down smells, and keeps things ship-shape. It will pay to attend to this when it can be so easily done. It costs but little, and is a real advantage.

The Langshans.—There is a prominent feature of the Langshans not possessed by the Black Cochins, which is activity. They come in as an extra desirable breed, between the leghorns and the sitters, for they commence to lay early, and when about to enter upon incubation are easily broken. They are large in size, fine-boned, hardy, and grow rapidly. They are the strongest rivals for public favor that the Plymouth Rocks have, and are just as certain to go to the front as if they had been known for centuries. Their qualities as a farmer's fowl are good, and they will entirely supersede many other breeds in time.

Poultry Manure.—Collect the droppings as often as possible, and compost them with dry dirt. If dry dirt is inconvenient on account of the earth being frozen, use good ground land plaster instead. The mixture of ground plaster and poultry droppings is better than either alone, and the ammonia is thereby saved. A good dusting of plaster over and under the roosts, and plentifully scattered all over the floor of the poultry house, conduces to the health of fowls and destroys foul odors.

How Nests Should be Made.—Eggs hatch much better if the nests are made by placing a cut turf, and shovel of mold, sand or ashes in the box or basket, and on this a little short straw, than if straw only is used. In this way a convenient hollow is obtained that prevents the eggs rolling out from under the setting hen. In cool weather the eggs are thus kept of a much more equable temperature than in nests made simply of loose straw.

To Fatten Geese.—To fatten geese, an experienced practitioner says: Put up two or three in a darkened room and give each bird one pound of oats daily, thrown on a pan of water. In fourteen days they will be found almost too fat. Never shut up a single bird, as geese are sociable and will pine away if left alone.

Nests of Sawdust.—To prevent hens from scratching their nests make the nests of sawdust. Do not have the boxes too large—only long enough for two nests, with a partition. Place a little hay on the sawdust until the hens get accustomed to it; also sulphur, to prevent vermin.

Hens Eating Eggs.—If hens get into the habit of eating eggs, take enough bran and corn meal of equal parts for one feeding, and enough vinegar warmed to make the meal wet enough for the hens to eat. Mix together and feed it to the hens.

THE DAIRY--Update

A friend who keeps a small number of milk cows and raises some veal calves looked at the drawings in this chapter and wondered aloud, "How did they ever keep it clean?" Indeed, dairying has changed considerably since 1888, and the greatest progress has been made in cleanliness. Modern dairy farmers couldn't conceive of using the implements shown here. Their equipment is made of glass and stainless steel. Their milk is stored in bulk tanks for pick-up. Such equipment is very expensive but it's absolutely necessary to pass state health requirements for marketing milk. The cost of milking and milk storage equipment is, however, a minor expense compared to the vast outlays necessary for beginning a large-scale dairy. Dairy farmers may have half a million dollars tied up in their land, stock and barns.

The milk industry is dominated by large-scale producers who combine to supply urban areas. Small dairymen get less per gallon of milk.

Luckily we don't have to compare the family cow with such vast industries. Reasonable health precautions and a modest investment can supply a family with milk and milk products. My friend the small dairyman suggests if a person wants to make money from a small farm that now would be a good time to be raising milk-fed veal. Prices on veal are high, and a single cow can feed three calves. Mortality rates are significantly lower for calves left with their mothers than for calves raised on formulas.

Once you have milk, it must be used or kept. It can be kept simply as whole milk but for long-term storage, the farmer might consider making the milk into butter, cheese, or yogurt. The churns shown here have worked and will work well. Churning cream to butter has always utilized the excess energy of children, though churns may be run by waterwheel, treadmill or windmill.

Don't buy a cow in a poke. Different breeds have different strengths and weaknesses. Holstein-Friesians are most popular with the dairy industry as they give very large quantities of moderately rich milk on economical feed. Guernseys are known for their gentleness, adaptation to climate, and rich milk. Ayrshires are rugged and produce good quality milk for many years. Jerseys graze well, are tolerant to hot climates and their milk is the richest in butterfat. The Brown Swiss is known as docile, rugged, and gives rich milk; veal calves are often Brown Swiss. Milking Shorthorns are considered 'dual-purpose' because they produce profitable milk and are good for meat.

Many dairy farmers respond to complaints about the manure smell of their operations with "It smells like money to me." Careful manure handling will greatly benefit the land and the health of the cows.

There are many handbooks for dairy-farming but I like the older ones best. They are better adapted to what the small dairyman will need to know. An excellent but hard-to-get book is J.H. Frandsen's *Dairy Handbook and Dictionary* (Amherst, Ma.: J.H. Frandsen, 1958). Check your local library. This book contains sections on care and management of the herd, milk treatment, marketing, buttermaking, cheesemaking, equipment, breeds, and a reference section. Its eight hundred pages contain most of what a beginner would need to know. *The Cow Economy* by Joanne & Merrill Grohman (Coburn Press, 117 Main St., Bridgton, Maine, 04009) is recommended by a dairyman friend as a good guide to a small operation.

THE DAIRY.

Apparatus for Milking.—Absolute cleanliness in milk is as much to be desired as in any other article of food. We fear that farmers and dairymen, as a rule, do not give as much attention to this matter as it really requires. We present herewith an illustrated article on this subject from the pen of a practical dairyman, which we consider worthy of attention, and trust that many will profit by its suggestion:

"Every reasonable person desires to have his or her food perfectly clean. Milk and dairy products are not always clean, to put it very mildly, and the filth that finds its way into milk is of a very disagreeable, if not unwholesome, kind. As a large portion of the milk of a family cow—and much of that sold —is used by children, owners of cows should be excessively

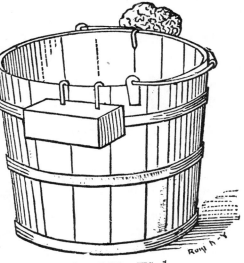

DAIRY PAIL.—FIG. 1.

careful to have the milk perfectly clean and pure. This is easy to be done if it is desired. It requires only the determination to do it, and a very little attention. The cow is not a cleanly animal, by any means, and some cows seem to delight in making themselves filthy. One of my best cows will take pains to lie down directly in her droppings, so that the udder is always besmeared, and other cows are very careless about it, at the best, so that it is necessary that a part of every milking apparatus should consist of a pail of water, a sponge and towel. Before the cow is milked the udder should be washed and wiped dry. For this purpose I have used a pail arranged as shown in the engraving (Fig. 1), which is taken to the barn at every milking. Previously the stable-man has brushed and carded the cows, and has cleaned and sanded or littered the

MILKING PAIL.—FIG. 2.

floor, so that there is no coarse filth to remove, and only the remaining smears. But if these are left on the teats, the filth will get into the pail in spite of all efforts. The pail has a hook on one side upon which the sponge is carried, and a box on the other, in which an old towel or pieces of cloth are kept. With these the udder and teats are washed and dried before the cow is milked. The time used—not lost—is well spent.

"The milking pail should be provided with a strainer, and I have found none made for sale free from some objection, either as regards the difficulty of cleaning or durability. I have my pails made to order with the strainer upon the half cover of the pail at the edge, and with a lip at the edge to cause the milk to flow easily. (See Fig. 2.) There is no difficulty in washing this pail, the wire gauze cannot be broken in the washing, and it is perfectly cleaned with ease. Hairs *cannot* be kept out of milk at some seasons, and a fine hair carried lengthwise *will* pass through the finest wire cloth. It is therefore necessary to use precautions in straining. A hair will not pass through a cotton cloth, and in straining milk into a deep pail I use the strainer shown at Fig. 3, which has a piece of washed, somewhat coarse and thin, white muslin, fastened around the bottom hoop. This causes the milk to pass through three strainers at one time, which is sufficient. Where the milk of several cows is strained, the strainer should be rinsed after each use, otherwise the after milk passes over all the impurities gathered in the strainer. For shallow pans the double strainer, Fig. 4, is excellent. The middle strainer fits closely into the bottom of the basin over the fixed strainer, and

STRAINER.—FIG. 3.

the basin rests in the perforated hoop which stands in the milk pan. A cloth may be tied over the top of the basin if thought proper. With all these precautions the most complete cleanliness is within easy reach, and if the cow is healthy and well fed, the most fastidious person may drink the milk without any apprehension. While it is so easy to be clean the conscientious dairyman need have no excuse for violating propriety, and excuse himself by the idea that it can't be helped.

"Every dairy utensil should be of tin. No wooden vessel should be used in milking, as the wood absorbs the milk, which sours in the pores and there curdles, and every particle of curdled milk, whether effected by rennet or by acidity, like the leaven of yeast, is an active agent for souring other milk. As

DOUBLE STRAINER.—FIG. 4.

curd of milk is hardened by heat and made insoluble, dairy utensils should first be washed with cold water and soap, and when thoroughly well cleaned they may then be scalded. Curd is dissolved by alkali, and the free alkali of the soap not only removes the grease of the milk, but also any particles of milk which by an accident may have been retained in a crevice or corner, and there soured or curdled. To make the cleaning of dairy vessels more easy, it is well to have no sharp corners, but to have all the joints made round, and this may be done easily if one has the milk pails made to order."

Milk Cooler.—There are quite a number of devices for this purpose, and some of them are too complicated, which must always be a serious objection. Our engraving represents an English milk cooler, which is heartily commended. In this apparatus a very small quantity of cold water, passing upward in a very thin stream between two corrugated sheets of metal, rapidly abstracts the heat from two shallow streams of milk descending outside the metal sheets (Fig. 1). D is the inlet and F the outlet of the water, which, being supplied from a higher level, flows through the refrigerator (B) by the force of gravity. A tap of the milk receiver (A) regulates the flow of milk into a small trough at the top of the refrigerator, punctured with holes, through which the milk runs, and is spread into so fine a sheet that, instead of

MILK COOLER.—FIG. **1.**

falling rapidly from step to step, it follows the corrugations of the surface. In the enlarged section (Fig. 2) of a part of the refrigerator the descending arrows indicate the current of milk gradually cooling as it descends. The current of water passing upward is warmed, so that when it passes out of the spout at F it is very nearly of the same temperature as the milk in the receiver. This device appears to be quite simple.

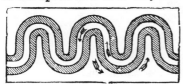

MILK COOLER.—FIG. **2.**

How to Make Good Butter.—Be sure the pasture is of the best, and that it contains a variety of the sweetest grasses. Do not change from winter feed to spring pasture too suddenly, and, particularly, do not turn out your cows too early to shift for themselves. Let the milking be done by quiet persons, whether male or female, at regular times morning or evening, knowing always that the milking is conducted as cleanly as it is quietly.

Know that the utensils for holding the milk are of the best description and always scrupulously clean.

See that the milk is perfectly cooled to free it of animal odor. A thermometer is an absolute necessity in all well regulated dairies.

Be sure the room for setting milk is cool, and so it may be darkened at will. Thorough ventilation is one of the golden rules in dairying. The temperature of the dairy room should never be more than sixty degrees, nor less than forty degrees.

Skim the milk as soon as the first indications of getting thick from lopper

POWER FOR CHURNING.—FIG. 1.

are shown. Turn the cream slowly into the jar, and stir thoroughly when more cream is added. Keep the receptacle for the cream cool, from fifty to sixty degrees, and cover with some fabric that will keep out minute insects, and at the same time allow access of air.

Churn when the cream is ripe, that is, when the cream is sour, every day in spring, and every day in summer. Do not allow the cream in the churn to rise much above sixty degrees. Do not churn too fast. There is nothing gained by seeking to bring the butter in a few minutes. From twenty to thirty minutes is about right.

Good grass will make nice colored butter. At such seasons, when the color of butter is pale, use coloring carefully. It is better that butter be rather light than a dark yellow.

When the butter comes in granules, stop churning. Wash with cold water or cold brine; work only enough to bring it to a firm uniform mass. Do not salt heavily; from three-quarters to one ounce of salt to a pound of butter is enough. Pack in tight, clean, sweet packages; fill to within a half inch of the top, cover with a clean cloth, and add brine to fill until sold. Keep it in the coolest place you have, and there is no reason why you should not get the top prices for your butter.

POWER FOR CHURNING.—FIG. 2.

Power for Churning.—
We present four illustrations, with brief descriptions, showing practical methods for labor saving in the usually tiresome and monotonous business of churning, from which may be gleamed some valuable hints.

Fig. 1, although not a power churn, is, nevertheless, a labor-saving arrangement. It is simply a hickory sapling about twelve or fourteen feet long, fastened firmly at the butt end, while at the other end is fixed a seat in which a child can sit and perform the work with more ease than a grown person in the ordinary way. The dash of the churn may be fastened at any point to accommodate the spring of the pole. Fig. 2 is a vertical wheel with a rim about two feet in width, on the inside of which the animal treads. It is necessary to have this wheel as much as eight or ten feet in diameter. The engraving gives ample insight into its mechanical construction.

Fig. 3 is a water-power churn, showing the water wheel fitting easily into the box or flume, at the outlet of the dam, or it may be simply placed in a swift-running brook, as it does not require much power or speed. The wheel should be about three feet in diameter. The power can be transmitted any distance by means of two wires fastened upon poles with swing trees that receive a backward and forward motion from the crank of the water-wheel.

Fig. 4 represents a cheap churn power, which is both simple and practical. A is a log, squared and set in the ground far enough to be solid.

POWER FOR CHURNING.—FIG. **3.**

B is the sweep—a four-inch scantling sixteen feet long, with a two-inch hole in one end and an axle on the other, and holes in the center for the standard, according to the length of the dash. C is the drive-wheel, eighteen inches in diameter, three inches thick. D, the churn, which stands still on a small one-legged table, with the leg running through the sweep (B) and into the stationary block. This arrangement gives the dasher (E) two motions, and causes the butter to "come" in shorter time. F, beam guide; G, beam; H, standard; I, hitching stick; J, whiffletree; K, pitman. It is very easy to operate.

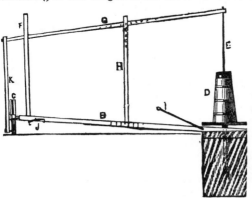

POWER FOR CHURNING.—FIG. **4.**

Hard Churning and Blue Cream.—It is a very common thing for a person with one cow to complain that her cream will not churn, or that it churns with great difficulty. The reason is the cream is kept so long to get a churning that it becomes too sour. Putting in either bicarbonate of soda or sal soda will reduce the acid and help the butter to come, but the butter thus made is always inferior. The remedy is to churn oftener, say every other day, or if the weather is a little cool, twice a week, and to put in milk to make sufficient bulk for churning. The skimming, too, should be done early—as soon as the cream is all up, or pretty near all up. It is better to take in the top of the milk in which the last rising of the cream lingers, than wait for the milk to get stale before removing the cream. The practice which many people follow of letting the whey start on the milk before skimming or on the cream before churning, is to a high degree detrimental both to the churning and to the quantity and quality of butter. If easy churning is desired, the cream must be churned while it has a fresh and new taste—not later than the first stage of sourness.

The " blue or moldy-looking cream " is not peculiar to any breed, and it occurs in the milk of all cows if they and their milk are improperly cared for. The cream of any milk may take on a dark or moldy appearance if too long exposed to light and to a damp atmosphere. It is more easily induced in the milk of cows which, from any cause, have had their blood heated, or by exposure to hot sun, by too fast or too much driving or from feverishness by excessive feeding, etc. Milk inclined to have flecks in its cream is very easily made to assume a moldy condition, for the dark color is derived from an actual fungus which develops in the milk and cream. An unusually ready development of it is evidence that the cow is in some way sick—from over feeding or other causes. There is always in milk a variable quantity of albuminous matter which turns dark-colored upon exposure to air and light, but it is heavier than cream and heavier also than the serum of milk, and is inclined to settle to the bottom. This has probably no connection with dark-colored cream; it is more likely the result of unfavorable health and dampness of cellar.

To Keep Butter.—It is said that a compound of one part sugar, one part nitre, and two parts of the best Spanish salt, beaten together into a fine powder and mixed thoroughly with the butter in the proportion of one ounce to the pound, would keep the butter in every respect sweet and sound during two years. It is also said to impart a rich marrowy flavor that no other butter ever acquires, and tastes very little of the salt.

Cream and Cold.—It has been discovered by a French scientist that the rising of cream is quicker, and its volume greater, the nearer the temperature is to that of freezing water; further, that the yield of butter is greater, and the skim milk, butter and cheese are all of the better quality under like conditions. These facts should be worth the attention of dairy keepers.

Waterproof Butter Wrappers.—At the Pennsylvania State Fair in 1882 waterproof butter wrappers attracted considerable attention from dairymen. Advocates of the waterproof paper claim for it that, being airtight, it preserves the freshness and flavor of the butter, and is about one-sixth as expensive as cloth.

To Restore Rancid Butter.—Rancid butter can be restored by first washing it thoroughly in cold water, then to every one hundred pounds add two pounds pulverized sugar, two ounces powdered saltpetre, and salt to suit.

An Improved Butter-Worker.—This butter-worker consists of a table of maple (Fig. 1), or other hard sweet timber, in the form shown in the engraving, with three feet sides and six feet on curve, without side pieces. At each edge is a deep groove to conduct the brine. At the front end is a rim, projecting one-half inch above the plank. At the lower end is a deeper cross-groove, with outlet at one side of the projecting bed-piece. In this bed-piece is loosely set a post with a round tenon fastened by a pin beneath. In this post is set the lever, so loosely as to admit of lifting the handle of the lever a foot or more. This lever is held in the mortise by a pin, and sets one-eighth of an inch above the table at the post; is of maple, four inches wide and three inches thick; lower side square cornered plain, upper side rounded or cornered. The handle is wrought at the upper side,

IMPROVED BUTTER-WORKER.—FIG. 1.

leaving a shoulder below, which sets just within the rim of the table.

Fig. 2 shows the frame-work of the table, into which the legs are formed. The entire cost of this butter-worker will not exceed $3. The operation, which differs from that of other workers in use, consists of pressing the butter with a direct vertical pressure—no grinding strokes allowable. Then strike the left side of the butter with a right upward motion of the lever a few strokes, and it lies in a roll parallel to the lever. Now turn the roll at right angles to the lever, and continue the three operations of pressing, rolling, and turning, until it is sufficiently worked.

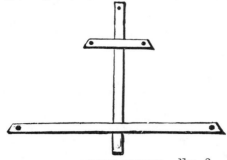

IMPROVED BUTTER-WORKER.—FIG. 2.

French Butter Making. —In the French system the butter is made from very sour cream, is washed in the churn, not salted, but sold for present use in Paris and England, and the keeping quality is not much studied. Notwithstanding the extreme sourness of the cream when churned, the butter has almost the same appearance as that made from sweet cream—this is the result of the washing. The finest French butter is shipped at once to the consumers, and generally consumed before the end of three days; so its keeping qualities are not material. No salt is used for the home market. It is put up in large balls of 28 lbs. to 40 lbs., each ball being covered by a piece of fine flannel and placed in a willow basket. Second and third-class butter is made up in one pound rolls and packed in grape leaves. For the English market, butter is put up in one pound rolls and covered with jaconet and lace paper, and packed in small boxes 14x9x6 inches, twelve rolls in each box.　M. Lepelletier is the largest exporter of this kind of butter, and is said to ship 1,200 boxes per week, his trade amounting to 12,000,-000 francs per year.　It is sent in refrigerating cars.　In Paris all butter is sold by auction at ten markets.　Women are mostly the buyers.　Three or four hundred lots are sold every hour.　Sworn officials weigh and register the butter, and make up the accounts of sale.　The different kinds of butter are named from the places where they are made, and classified according to quality.　The best butter is sold at 50 and 75 cents per pound.

Preparing Butter for Market.—After the milk has been kept in the spring or cooling house about forty-eight hours, it is then taken out and skimmed, and after the butter is made it is put up in half-pound prints for market.　It is shipped in boxes, having an ice chamber in the center.　The boxes are 31 by 16 1-2 inches and 15 inches deep.　The ice chest is of tin, placed in the center of the box, and is 16 1-2 by 5 inches, 15 inches deep.　At the bottom there is a hole, which extends also through the box, for the escape of water from the ice as it melts.　Movable shelves with cleats on the edges, are fitted in each side of the ice chest, one above the other, for holding the prints.　The box holds 10 shelves, 5 on each side of the ice chamber,

and the shelves, when in place, leave a space between each of 2 1-2 inches.　We give a rough draft of the movable shelf in our illustration.　Each shelf holds 20 prints, or 10 pounds of butter.　In packing the butter a plain board is used to receive the prints at the bottom of the box; then the shelf, as illustrated, is placed on top, and thus con-

MOVABLE SHELF FOR HOLDING BUTTER PRINTS.

tinued until the whole number of prints are in.　A movable shelf just coming to the top of the box is placed over the top prints, so that when the lid of the box is brought down it presses tightly on it and thus keeps the shelves from shaking and prevents any injury to the prints.

Keeping Butter for Winter Use.—Good butter put up after the following directions will keep in sound condition one year: Use for a package a tub somewhat tapering, with heavy staves and heads provided at both ends, so as to make a package that will not leak.　In packing the tub is turned on the small end, and a sack of cotton cloth is made to fit the tub, and into this the butter is packed until it reaches to within an inch of the groove for holding the upper head.　A cloth is next laid upon the top of the butter and the edges of the sack brought over this and neatly pressed down; then the head is put in its place and the hoops driven home.　The package is now turned upon the large end and the sack of butter drops down, leaving a space on the sides and top.　Strong brine is then poured into a hole in the small end and until it will float the butter.　The hole is tightly corked and the butter is pretty effectually excluded from the air.　Where only a small quantity of butter is to be preserved, pack it in self-sealing fruit jars.　By this plan a little brine is put into the jar, which is then packed not quite full of granulated butter.　Some bleached muslin is laid over the butter, then the little place above filled with salt, and finally enough strong brine, made from butter salt, poured in to fill the can. When packing roll butter in jars the brine should be made strong enough to bear an egg. To three gallons of this brine add a quarter of a pound of white sugar and one tablespoonful of saltpetre. Boil the brine, and when it is cool strain carefully. Make the butter into rolls and wrap each roll separately in white muslin cloth. Pack the jar full, weight the butter down, and submerge in brine.

Suggestions in Milk-Setting.—Professor L. B. Arnold says:

First—To make the finest flavored and longest-keeping butter the cream must undergo a ripening process by exposure to the oxygen of the air while it is sweet. This is best done while it is rising. The ripening is very tardy when the temperature is low.

Second—After cream becomes sour, the more ripening the more it depreciates. The sooner it is then skimmed and churned the better, but it should not be churned while too new. The best time for skimming and churning is just before acidity becomes apparent.

Third—Cream makes better butter to rise in cold air than to rise in cold water, but it will rise sooner in cold water, and the milk will keep sweet longer.

Fourth—The deeper milk is set the less airing the cream gets while rising.

Fifth—The depth of setting should vary with the temperature; the lower it is the deeper milk may be set; the higher, the shallower it should be. Milk should never be set shallow in a low temperature nor deep in a high one. Setting deep in cold water economizes time, labor and space.

Sixth—While milk is standing for cream to rise the purity of the cream, and consequently the fine flavor and keeping of the butter, will be injured if the surface of the cream is exposed freely to air much warmer than the cream.

Seventh—When cream is colder than the surrounding air, it takes up moisture and impurities from the air. When the air is colder than the cream, it takes up moisture and whatever escapes from the cream. In the former case the cream purifies the surrounding air; in the latter, the air helps to purify the cream. The selection of a creamer should hinge on what is most desired—highest quality, or greatest convenience and economy in time, space and labor.

First Principles in Butter Making.—Butter is *finished* in the dairy, but *not made there*. The stamp of the dairywoman puts the gold in market form; but the work must be commenced in the field ◆ in the feeding stables; and this leads at once to the consideration of feeding for butter. During the early, sunny summer month, when nature is profuse of favors, there is little to be done beyond accepting her bounty. The tender grasses are full of the needed nutrition, and they afford the constant supply of moisture without which the secretion of milk is greatly lessened. Yet, at this season, as well as all others, a pure supply of water is absolutely necessary. It does not meet the requirement if cattle have a wet hole full of surface drainage in the pasture, or a frog pond. While it is not probable that the tadpoles and wrigglers sometimes found in city milk have been drunk by thirsty cows, many infusions do exist in such pools that are hardly eliminated or rendered entirely harmless by the wonderful milk secretions of the animal. The cattle should drink from spring-fed boxes; and as often as these, under the hot sun, are seen to produce green growth or floating scum a pail of coarse salt may be put in, and the current checked until the fresh-water growths are killed; the salt water is then drawn off, and for a long time the trough will remain pure and the water bright.

Bitter Milk.—Bitter milk is a matter of frequent occurrence every fall and winter, or soon after the cows are off from grazing. It is caused, first, by bitter herbs in the hay—such as May weed, rag weed, John's wort, etc.—and also by the use of too much over-ripe food, such as straw, corn stover, or late-cut hay. It never occurs when cows are f'd on good food, and are thriving, or even holding their own, and are kept comfortably warm. It can be avoided, first, by correcting the error in feeding and exposure; and, secondly, by scalding the milk when it is first drawn, by setting it in pans over a kettle of boiling water till the skin which forms on its top is well wrinkled, and then setting it away to cool for the cream to rise. This treatment will drive out the cause of the bitter flavor, and improve the butter and make it easy to churn.

Borax for Salting Butter.—The Italian minister of agriculture addressed a communication to the chamber of commerce of Milan relative to experiments in salting butter with borax which have been carried out at the agricultural station at Florence. From the account which appears in the *Giornale di Agricoltura*, borax would appear to have a most marvelous effect in insuring its absolute preservation. Samples of fresh butter made at the Florence station, and purposely not carefully freed of their buttermilk, were found, on the addition of about eight per cent. of borax, to maintain their natural fine flavor, without the least change whatever, for upward of three months. To attain this satisfactory result, it is necessary that the borax should be perfectly dry, and in a very fine powder, and care must be taken to its thorough mixture with the whole mass of the butter operated on. Among the further advantages of this plan, it is noted that borax imparts no flavor of any kind to the butter, while it is entirely harmless in its nature, and also reasonably cheap. Still later experiments have shown that a very much smaller proportion of borax suffices to produce the desired effect, and also that simple solutions of the salt act quite as well as the dried powder.

Don't Flavor Your Butter too Much.—It is too true that unless we adopt the improvements of the day and look carefully after our interests, we shall be left in the background as to quality and profit. But why is it that western creamery butter brings a better price? We are told it is because of its uniformity of quality. The butter is made from day to day, from week to week under the same conditions, and always free from anything that would impart unpleasant flavors. Milk set in a farmer's kitchen or in any place where it will absorb unpleasant odors from cooking vegetables, from tobacco smoke or from clothing fully charged with the odor of the stables, cannot make butter free from unpleasant flavor. We complain of low prices received when we ourselves are to blame. The flavor of the butter is affected by the feed of the cows. We lay the blame at the door of the dairy woman, when he who feeds the cows is responsible.

To Color Butter.—As a rule, it is absolutely essential in the winter to color butter in order to make it marketable, or at all attractive as an article of table use at home. There may be a possible exception to this rule, in cases where cows are fed largely upon yellow corn, pumpkins, carrots, etc., but this does not lessen the importance of the rule. Of the various substances used in coloring butter, we think that carrots (of the deep yellow variety) give the most natural color and most agreeable flavor. Annatto, however, is principally used, with most satisfactory results. If carrots are used, take two large-sized ones, clean them thoroughly, and then with a knife scrape off the yellow exterior, leaving the white pith; soak the yellow part in boiling milk ten or fifteen minutes. Strain boiling hot into the cream; this gives the cream the desired temperature, colors it nicely, and adds to the sweetness of the butter.

How to Detect Oleomargarine.—A Frenchman points out in a note to the Belgian Academy a simple way of distinguishing between natural and artificial butter, based upon the different behavior of the two substances when exposed to a temperature of from 150 degrees to 160 degrees in a capsule or test tube. At this temperature artificial butter produces very little froth, but the mass undergoes a sort of irregular boiling, accompanied by violent jerks, which tend to project some of the butter out of the vessel. The mass grows brown, but this is by reason of the caseous matter separating into clots on the walls. The fatty portion of the sample sensibly retains its natural color. Natural butter, on the other hand, at the same temperature, produces abundant froth, the jerks are much less pronounced, and the mass grows brown, but in a different way. A good part of the brown coloring matter remains in suspension in the butter, so that the whole mass has a characteristic brown look. All natural butter behaves in the same way.

Firm Butter Without Ice.—In families where the dairy is small, a good plan to have the butter cool and firm without ice is by the process of evaporation, as practiced in India and other warm countries. A cheap plan is to get a very large-sized, porous, earthen flower-pot, with a large saucer. Half fill the saucer with water, set it in a trivet or light stand—such as is used for holding hot irons will do; upon this set your butter; over the whole invert the flower-pot, letting the top rim of it rest in and be covered by the water; then close the hole in the bottom of the flower-pot with a cork; then dash water over the flower-pot, and repeat the process several times a day, or whenever it looks dry. If set in a cool place, or where the wind can blow on it, it will readily evaporate the water from the pot, and the butter will be as firm and cool as if from an ice-house.

THE APIARY--Update

The keeping of bees today is governed by law in many states. Therefore, although the basic advice in this chapter is valid, the amateur beekeeper will have to seek help (and a free brochure) from a County Agent on the state requirements for a permit and inspection of hives.

Besides the standard channels like a county agent, don't forget to seek advice from small local beekeepers. They usually love to tell you what works for them. Buy some honey and talk. Many folks will go even further and help you get started.

Here is a calendar of beekeeping activities supplied by a friend up the road:

> *March--Feed the weakest hives sugar syrup or honey and pollen.*
> *April--Pack and get the bees ready to be sent out to blooming orchards.*
> *Mid-May--Divide up the strongest hives, or they will divide themselves by swarming elsewhere.*
> *Late July--Collect off the first honey and extract it from the combs in the centrifuge.*
> *August--Add more supers (tiers) to hives for the fall wildflower splurge.*
> *September--Take off more combs and extract the honey.*
> *Early October--Feed heavily with sugar syrup or honey to help the bees get ready for winter.*
> *November--Wrap hives, tar paper over insulation, for wintering.*
> *January--Check hives on a nice day to see if supplies of food are adequate.*

If you are thinking of planting specially for your bees, consider buckwheat and clover. Buckwheat may be sown in wet lands where other crops will not grow. It also furnishes excellent flour (for pancakes particularly). A field of clover will supply your bees with food and will also yield a good cutting of hay.

Equipment for beekeeping may be purchased from many sources but two of the best mail-order firms are Dadant & Sons of Hamilton, Ohio, 62341 and Walter Kelly of Clarkson, Kentucky, 42726.

The beginning beekeeper might find it useful to buy several books such as *The Hive and the Honeybee,* ed. Dadant & Sons (Hamilton, Ohio: Dadant & Sons, 1973) and *Let's Build a Bee Hive* by Wilbert Miller (available from the author, 2028 Sherman St., Phoenix, Ariz., 85009) and a subscription to the *American Bee Journal* (Hamilton, Ohio, 62341) or to *Gleanings-in Bee Culture* (A.I. Root Co., Box 706, Medina, Ohio, 44256). If you plan to build your own hives, *Let's Build a Bee Hive* will be very useful as the bees are very fussy about the dimensions of their accomodations. Not only living and storage space but ventilation and temperature control are important to them. Other inexpensive, useful books are John F. Adams' *Beekeeping: The Gentle Craft* (Garden City, NY: Doubleday & Co., 1974) and *The Complete Book of Beekeeping* by Herbert Mace (NY: Van Nostrand Reinhold Co., 1976).

THE APIARY.

Wintering Bees.—For the benefit of those who are interested in the subject of bee-keeping, we present herewith an illustrated article upon wintering bees, the suggestions in which we think will be found both valuable and timely.

FIG. 1.—PLATFORM.

Prepare, of any sound matched flooring, a platform nailed to 2x4 or 3x3 joists. When ready, set it upon blocks or stones, and it will appear as shown in Fig. 1. On this you are to put the bee hives, eight in number, and arranged as stated further on; also a north-end board, two side boards, a south-end board and a movable cover or roof. The arrangement of your hives should be as shown in Fig. 2, where a is the north-end board, made square, but with cleats, as in the next figure; and bb are two hives with their entrances facing the south; ccc are three hives with their entrances to the east; ddd are three hives with their entrances to the west. The object of this arrangement is to vary as far as possible the entrances, that the bees be less confused when they fly out in winter.

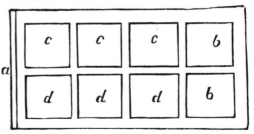

FIG. 2.—ARRANGEMENT OF HIVES.

Experience shows that most of them find out their own hives by this arrangement.

Fig. 3 shows the inside of the north-end piece of the boxing about the hives, the outside of which is perfectly plain, and aa are two cleats that hold the boards together, with the square wall cleat at the bottom and the longer cleat close by the first cleat, the three cleats making an inch space, marked dark, which dark places allow the side pieces

FIG. 3.—INSIDE OF END PIECE.

to rest in and be held to the north piece. Fig. 4 shows first the outside of the south-end piece, and that it has two cleats, but that the boards do not go down to the bottom of them. The construction of this south piece is further seen in the end view, at the right hand of the larger view.

Fig. 5 is a view of the west side boxing piece. It has two cleats at the ends, *a a.* The one at the left hand is a little in from the end, as that end fits the dark place in the left end of Fig. 3. Two cleats, shaped as in the small figure of Fig. 4, are on the middle parts of the view. They serve the same purpose as in the large figure in Fig. 4. You need not be told that a corresponding east piece is to be made.

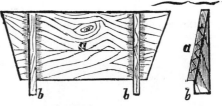

FIG. 4.—OUTSIDE OF END PIECE.

FIG. 5.—VIEW OF SIDE PIECE.

Now arrange hooks, or other contrivances, and put this boxing together about your hives, arranged as shown in Fig. 2, and you have it ready to pack the bees. The best packing is dry saw-dust, or cut straw; cut it not over an inch long. Pack all about the hives, and at least six inches thick over the top of the hives. Now make a roofing; the form, as shown by Fig. 6, which is made of triangular boards, with boards nailed on the top of them. When done, the whole will appear as in Fig. 7, which shows the two hives, the south-end having three small entrances, too small for a mouse or rat to get in at, and an inch round hole just over the three entrances, which hole is covered with wire cloth; these are all the holes for ventilation necessary. The dotted lines show the form of an ordinary box hive, a foot square and a foot high. Of course, in making your platform and boxing, you will make them to fit the hive you use, which will alter lengths and breadths a little, but not the general shape of what we have described. The side view would be so similar to Fig. 7 that we do not give it. Observe this in putting your bees in winter quarters: If November 1st to 16th passes so cold that bees fly little, this is a good time to pack them in this boxing. If it is so warm that they fly a good deal till December 1st or 16th, then that time is the best.

FIG. 6.—DESIGN OF ROOF.

FIG. 7.—APPEARANCE WHEN COMPLETE.

Let them have a few coolish days without protection, and be shut up a week or so before you change them from their summer stands to this winter packing. Leave the bottom boards of your hives on, and put a little sawdust under them. A bee-house is useful if it has a large window in the floor, for all operations that require to let the bees out in a room; then they fly to the window and get in bunches at its bottom near the floor, and when you are through with the changes to be made, they go easily into the hive. Make a tin reeling machine; reel out your honey; put it in neat glass packages; make holes on the side of your old-fashioned box hives, and g e t boxes everywhere—that is the secret of non-swarming; and make winter packing sheds as we have told you.

THE MAIN BEE HOUSE, SHOWING TIERS OF HIVES.

Bee Farming in Australia.

—We present herewith a very interesting article on the subject of bee farming, as practiced in New South Wales, Australia, where, as will be seen, the industry is carried on on a very extensive scale. The article is carefully illustrated and the methods employed plainly described, and we trust that all who take an interest in the subject of bee keeping may gain some valuable hints and suggestions from a perusal of the same.

The operations in bee culture going on in Paramatta are well deserving of being ranked as bee farming. They are carried on after the most approved system of the German apiarians, which differs only in the form of hive used and a few minor details from the approved system followed in Britain and America. But to get at the history of the company whose operations we illustrate: It appears that, in December, 1881, a skilled bee master, Wilhelm Abram, arrived in Sydney from Germany, where bee culture is a recognized industry and subsidized by the State, and is under the care of scientific entomologists, for the purpose of teaching the art of bee culture to those desirous of making it their study, and at such an institution Mr. Abram was trained. Before leaving Germany he purchased some of the prize swarms at an exhibition of Italian bees in Germany, and the Italian Bee Company commenced operations with these at Parramatta, in January, 1882. An importation of prize queens from America was made, and the operation of queen rearing

THE SWARMING BAG, A GREAT IMPROVEMENT.

was entered on. In the meantime a number of colonies of the common black or English bee had been secured and transferred to frame hives, and as Italian queens were reared, the black queens were removed and replaced by Italians, the progeny of which replaced the black bees, as the latter died out. Not much attention was paid to producing honey until the race of Italian bees could be firmly established, and the result was that in the spring of last year there were about eighty colonies of gold-banded Italians actively at work.

The bee master is an adept at his profession. With a pipe in his mouth,

THE QUEEN BREEDING HIVES.

he opens hive after hive, blowing a whiff of smoke upon them, to give the bees something else to think about when they seem any way refractory, a projection from the stem of the pipe allowing this to be done conveniently. The hives used are of the German bar-frame kind. They open from the back, and each hive is two stories high, so that ample space can be given to the bees when they are storing honey rapidly. The main house is about 150 feet in length, 10 feet high, 10 feet wide, and two tiers of hives are arranged on each side, as shown in the sketch.

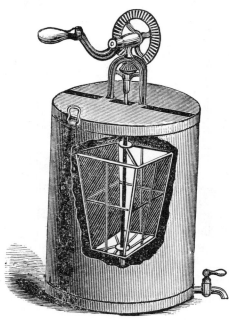

CENTRIFUGAL MACHINE, SHOWING INSIDE.

The swarming bag is one of the best things we have seen in bee culture. It is about six feet in length and one foot in diameter, and formed of alternate lengths of calico and mosquito netting, each length having a ring of cane inside to hold out the bag, as shown in the sketch. When the bees are about to swarm, the bag is fastened on to the front of the hive, and the other end fastened to a stake. When the queen emerges she bounds up into the upper end of the bag, and is quickly surrounded by her followers. Thus the swarm is captured with ease, the alternate breadths of mosquito netting and calico making the interior light and enticing for the bees to enter and cluster. They are then shaken into a bar-frame hive.

The queen breeding hives are much smaller than the others, and are arranged at distances of about twenty feet apart alongside the fences. Two or three frames of brood comb are put into each hive, with a queen cell coming to maturity. When the queen bee hatches out of the cell she makes a flight

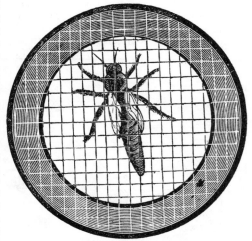

THE QUEEN CAGE.

(the only flight of her life) in order to meet a drone or male bee. She is then fertilized, and becomes the mother and queen of a family, laying eggs at the rate of 2,000 daily when the season is good and stores abundant. The centrifugal machine is used for extracting honey without destroying the comb. The caps with which the bees seal up each cell of honey are sliced off with a very thin-bladed knife of simple form, and the frames are set in the metal basket of the inside of the machine. Then, by turning the handle, the honey is thrown out and runs down the sides of the machine, from which it is drawn by a tap, leaving the comb undamaged and ready to be returned to the hives for the bees to fill over and over again with nectar. In this way absolutely pure honey is got without any other substance whatever, and without injuring the bees or annoying them. The queen cage, as shown in illustration, is drawn to scale, as is the queen or mother bee seen inside.

The Culture of Buckwheat for Bees.—Prof. Cook gives the following on this subject:

Buckwheat is valuable as a honey plant, as it can be made to bloom when there would otherwise be a dearth of flowers. We have found in our experimental beds that the Silver Hull variety has more flowers in the panicles, and yields more to the acre. The honey is dark, but is preferred to all other kinds by some people. It blooms from four to six weeks after sowing.

It will do fairly well on any soil, but thrives best on a rich soil. It should be sown broadcast, three pecks to the acre. It is usually sown here late in July, but for bees it had better be sown early in June. Then it will bloom about the middle of July, when bloom is usually absent, and will, I think, yield just as well; though I judge simply from observing small plots. The cultivation before sowing should be deep and thorough.

When ripe it is cut and allowed to lie on the ground to dry. When dry it is bound and drawn to the barn, where it may be threshed at once, if it is desirable to do so. In fact, the cultivation, soil and harvesting of buckwheat are much the same as that given to oats.

It is safe in estimating that each acre of buckwheat sown within one and one-half miles of an apiary is worth $100.

Buckwheat, like other plants, is capricious. Some seasons it yields but little honey. It is not a favorite of bees; at least I have known bees to leave it for other plants. Perhaps it contained no nectar at the time.

Will Bee Keeping Pay?—Of course it will. There is nothing that either men or women can engage in that will pay anywhere as well as bee culture; and there is nothing so well adapted for the farmers' sons and daughters as bee keeping, and if they would take hold of four or five colonies of Italian bees they never would want for a few dimes to go to a strawberry festival, or perhaps they might want to go to that world-renowned exposition that always visits every village about the July days, and if they have been good, industrious boys and girls, and will have looked after bees, they will have the satisfaction of having their own money, and will not have to ask father for the money when he is so pushed with his crops and so short of money to pay his hands. But to make the keeping of bees a success, you must go into it understandingly, and if you have not already the bees on hand, you will have to purchase a few colonies, and be sure to get Italians. If they are not in a movable comb they will have to be transferred. You will then have them in a hive that you have complete control over, even to examine every comb and seeing every bee or queen in the hive.

Clipping the Queen's Wing.—The clipping of the queen's wing having become a matter of acknowledged good policy, as we knew it would, the question naturally arises, What is the best method for clipping it? We have tried all plans, and find the quickest, easiest and the least risk attending the following: Lift from the hive the comb on which you find the queen, slant it toward the hive with the lower end resting on the ground and the upper end against the hive, make no rapid motions to alarm the queen, but deliberately wait till she is in a position that you can grasp the end of one wing between the thumb and forefinger of the left hand, then with a sharp pocket knife and an up and backward motion cut off about one-third of the wing. If deliberate in your movements, the queen will not become nervous, nor will she be aware she had been meddled with, no scent of the fingers will be left on either her wings or body, and no commotion created in the hive.

BEE HIVE.—FIG. 1.

An Unpatented Bee Hive.—Apiarians know full well the importance of providing the honey bee with a properly constructed and well arranged hive, in which these little workers may safely store the nectar carefully gathered from the blossoming sweets of earth. Many good and valuable hives for this purpose have been constructed, and are the subject of letters patent, for the manufacture and use of which a royalty is required by the owners thereof.

The hive shown in connection with this article is, beyond question, the simplest, cheapest, and best arranged unpatented hive extant. Fig. 1 is a perspective view of the hive as it appears upon the sand. In appearance it has a neat, unpretending look of self-recommendation.

The advantages gained by having a passage for the bees at the bottom, and six inches upward therefrom, at one side of the hive, are: *First.* During winter snow and ice accumulate in sufficient quantities to entirely fill and cover the lower series of holes, while the upper ones remain open, admitting fresh air, the importance of which all apiarians are familiar with. *Second.* Bees alighting at the upper series of holes, upon returning from a long and fatiguing flight, have but a short distance to traverse to reach the place where the accumulated sweets are to be deposited.

The hive proper is 12x12x15—2,160 cubic inches, inside measurement. When filled with honey it weighs eighty pounds—a sufficient quantity to feed a large colony of bees during the season not fruitful of flowers.

For supporting the comb in the desired position, small round sticks are used in the same manner as in the old box hive. The cover to this portion has its upper surface beveled near the edges, to receive and retain in position a small or upper hive, seven inches high and twelve inches square, inside dimensions. It is shown in proper place in Fig. 1, and raised in Fig. 2, disclosing the surplus honey boxes, which are two in number, 11 1-2 x 6 x 5 1-2 inches, outside measurement, made from quarter-inch pine lumber, with glass ends or sides, either plain or ornamental, as the contents may be designed for home consumption or exhibition at the sale-room, or to compete for premiums at fairs. Each of said boxes connects with the lower hive by four one-inch holes, which are made in hive and boxes at the time of their construction. They afford a sufficient passage-way to and from said boxes. The top of the hive is delineated in Fig. 3. One series of holes is shown, while the

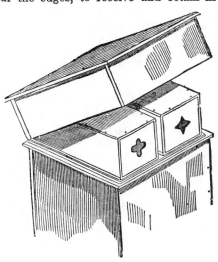

BEE HIVE.—FIG. 2.

other is covered (in use both should be) by securing a thin strip in the proper position by screws. They remain thus until the hive is thought to be filled, or a sufficient quantity accumulated to successfully winter the bees. At this juncture carefully remove the screws, slightly raise the strip, place one of the surplus boxes at the end of the strip, and gradually, or by a dextrous movement, get it in place, as shown in Fig. 2. When both are in position, place over them the cover, and, unless you are careless, not one bee is injured by the operation. Should the surplus boxes be provided with glass ends you may at any time during the season view the stores therein accumulated by raising the cover. At or soon after the appearance of autumnal frosts, remove the surplus boxes, cover the series of holes as above stated. At the approach

BEE HIVE.—FIG. 3.

of winter again remove them; thereby all vapor arising from the breathing of so great a number of insects passes into the empty space above, thus in a great measure, preventing death by the congealing of this vapor. Other points of merit could be noticed, but will suggest themselves.

Advice to Young Bee Keepers.—Beginners in bee keeping should not, when going into the business, build costly bee houses, provide high-priced, untested, patented hives, purchase a large number of colonies, or buy "three-banded" Italian queens at a time when, as yet, they can hardly tell a drone from a worker. Begin moderately and hasten slowly. The needful experience in practical bee culture is much more easily and far more efficiently acquired by careful attention to a few choice stocks, than by a hurried supervision of a large number, even with the aid of manuals and text-books. Plain, simple, movable frame-hives, too, will be found better suited for the requisite manipulations than fanciful and complicated contrivances devised by persons really ignorant themselves of the habits and wants of bees. And colonies placed in an open situation, with their hives readily accessible from all sides, and somewhat sheltered or shaded by trees or vines, will be much more conveniently managed than when placed in ordinary sheds or out-door bee houses. Study first to know what is required for success, and then extend your operations when you are sure that you can have the business "well in hand."

How to Catch Swarms.—For the past ten or twelve years, says a correspondent of the *American Bee Journal*, I have not cut my fruit trees to catch swarms. I get an ordinary sized basket, and nail a three-eighth-inch board on the bottom, with some suitable springs under it; then bore a hole in the center, and put an iron down through, with a loop on the top and a nut on the inside, and screw it fast; buckle a strap, six or eight inches long with a snap on it, in the loop. Have a pole cut from the edge of a two-inch plank, dressed any length, from eight to ten feet, with a ferule on each end and one-quarter inch iron rod sixteen inches in length; take a small ring, and bend an eye on the end of the rod, with the ring in it; taper the other end, and make it secure in the end of the pole; then curve it so as to project it six or eight inches, in which snap the basket catcher.

To use it, push it among the branches of the tree which the bees are making for, and if they do not light upon it, when they begin to cluster, put the catcher up against them, and when you get part of them on your basket, move it a little away and toward the branch that they are on, and they will all settle on the basket in five minutes.

To complete the pole, get a one-half inch rod of iron, twelve inches long, tapered at each end, and secure it in the lower end of the pole; and when the bees begin to settle on the basket, stick the spear in the ground and let it stand, while you are preparing the hive, etc. Then take down the pole and unhook the basket with bees, which may be carried any distance you wish. Shake off the bees on an open sheet in front of the hive, showing them the way, and they will go in faster than a flock of sheep into a yard after the gate is open.

Mice in the Apiary.—During the winter mice are sometimes troublesome guests in the apiary, especially if the hives are surrounded by straw in which they can harbor. The best preventive is to have hives so tight that they can gain no admittance. For the sake of ventilation it is not well, however, to have the entrance closed air-tight; therefore, fasten a piece of wire gauze over the entrance of the hives that may be in the cellar, or that may be buried in the ground; this will exclude mice and admit air; and over the entrance of hives that are covered with boxes, fasten a piece of tin about a quarter of an inch above the bottom board, so that the bees can just pass under the edge of it, while the mice are excluded.

FARM IMPLEMENTS--Update

Though the author of the *Farm & Housekeeper's Cyclopaedia* discusses horses in the Livestock chapter, I'll discuss the team of horses' modern equivalent, the tractor, here. Perhaps the largest single investment a farmer of 1888 would have to make, beyond land and house, would be the team of horses. He might pay as much as $200 for a good pair. Now, the tractor is one of a number of large investments a beginning farmer must make. I recommend visiting farm auctions and used equipment dealers. The question always is: can it be made to work? An old, well-cared-for, medium-sized tractor will give good service and is certainly more practical for the beginner with limited capital. New machines cost phenomenal amounts.

All sorts of other equipment may be dragged or powered by the tractor's driveshaft. Couplings vary. The size and power of the tractor will determine how many bottoms the plow may have and whether a disc harrow can be attached directly behind the plow. Land can be prepared too much, as repeated passes over it may lead to compaction below the plow level. The designs furnished in this chapter for simple rollers and riding clod-crushers will work but would give a shattering ride.

Once the land is fitted for seed, the farmer will have to decide on planting procedures. Simple, old-fashioned seed drills are often sold for a song, but once again the buyer must ask: can it be adjusted to work properly?

Simple cultivators may be built according to the directions in the *Cyclopaedia* or purchased second-hand. Some crops will repay hand-weeding; others are best cultivated by machine.

The designs for various forms of hoes indicate that much of the cultivation was still being done by hand in 1888.

In 1888 a sizable amount of the small grains were still being harvested by a man with a scythe and cradle. The grain was stacked in sheaves in the field to cure, and then moved to the threshing floor of the barn where it was threshed with flails. By 1888, however, machines for harvesting and threshing the grain were being perfected. Threshers were not uncommon, and the invention of the twine binding harvester, coinciding with Dakota wheatlands boom, greatly speeded the harvest.

The treadmill shown on page 245 was used to power a thresher or loader, removing grains from straw and conveying them to storage. Larger models were used to power sawmills and smaller ones for churns.

Now huge, costly combines cut the grain, thresh it, store the kernels and redistribute the chaff and straw on the field. These machines are most profitable when they can be run in long, straight lines, without interference from hedgerows, fences, streams or hills. Old-fashioned harvesters, threshers and loaders may be found second-hand which will better suit the small operation's needs and pocketbook.

Though a correspondent small farmer in Gasport, NY writes that a decent second-hand tractor may run more than $1500, the tractor is the key to successful farming, large or small. Hand work may do to keep the crop cultivated and to harvest and prepare it for storage, but nothing can beat the tractor for preparing land for use. If tractors produced manure, we would be completely pleased.

A good primer on farm equipment is Harrison Pearson Smith's *Farm Machinery and Equipment* (NY: McGraw-Hill Book Co., 1948). Since it was first printed in 1929 and last updated in 1948, it's a good guide to what might be found second-hand.

FARM IMPLEMENTS.

Combined Roller and Vibrating Harrow.—The thorough pulverization of the soil is, and will be, an important item in the tillage of the earth. The most effective method, therefore, of attaining this result, is one of interest to every individual. Our engraving on this page is intended to represent an arrangement of a combined roller and vibrating harrow, the successful working of which we have had the opportunity of witnessing. The invention consists of the frame, A, roller, B, which may be constructed of either iron or wood, the axle of which terminates at each end in a strong crank, C, C, of from six to nine inches in diameter. These cranks are keyed upon the axle in opposite positions. Connected to the wrist pins of each crank are the connecting rods, D, D, which extend backwards, and are attached to opposite corners of the harrow, E. The attachment of the connecting rods to the cranks is made with universal joints, so as to allow of a free and easy working of all the parts, and to permit the roller and harrow separately to accommodate themselves to the inequalities of the ground. The manner in which the harrow is vibrated through the medium of the crank in rotating with the roller, it is not necessary further to explain. If the machine is used as shown in the drawing, the last operation performed will be that of harrowing, but if it is desired to leave the ground in a rolled condition, all that is necessary to do is to turn over the tongue, F, of the roller, until it rests upon the cross pieces, G, and attach the team by a chain, to what will then be the front corner of the harrow. Or should it be desired to use

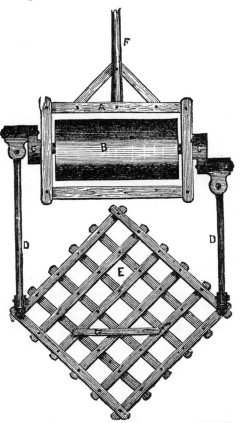

COMBINED ROLLER AND VIBRATING HARROW.

the roller or harrow separately, they may be readily disconnected by driving out two of the bolts in the universal joints. This invention is public property for the benefit of the world at large.

Hay Elevating Apparatus.—We present herewith a sketch and description of a new hay elevator, in the form of a suspended track and hay-fork traveler, which we think will not only prove a timely suggestion, but a positive boon to many farmers. This track can be suspended in any barn, high or low, without any additional timbers. The hay can be run up, and over beams, without any scattering or dragging. Another great advantage in this plan is having the rope double from the fork to the traveler. This gives the

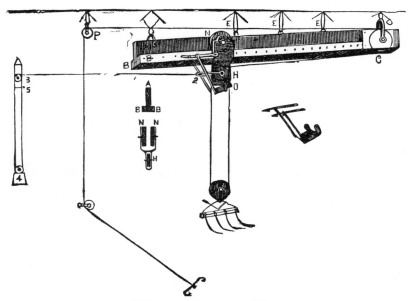

HAY ELEVATING APPARATUS.

horse great power on the fork just where it is needed, that is, when the forkful of hay is separating from the load.

It consists in part of a track made of hard wood, in the form shown. The center piece A is six inches wide and one and a half inches thick, put together with dowel-pins, until as long as wanted. The slats B B are two inches wide and one inch thick. They are nailed on the lower edge of A, breaking joints as they are put on. They are put on each side of A as shown in sketch. There is a pulley C, six inches in diameter by one and a half inches thick, put in the back end of the track. The box for this pulley is made by bolting a short piece, six inches wide and one inch thick, on each side of A. A, clevis; D goes over the track and is fastened on with the bolt that goes through the pulley. C, a rope is put through the clevis and this end of the track is drawn up close to the rafters. The front end is suspended by a clevis and two ropes; it is hung a foot or so lower than the back end. Screw into A the hooks that come with the fork, about eight feet apart, and into each put a strong link six inches long by one and a half inches in the opening, as shown at E, E, E; these are for the rope to pass through, and also to suspend it by.

The traveler consists of a pulley and pulley box, H, with sides four inches apart, extending up some seven or eight inches, which carry two rollers, N N, four inches in diameter and one inch thick, which roll on each side of A, and directly on B B. There is an eye, O, on the traveler, in which one end of the haul rope is tied; it then passes around a pulley on the fork, then through the pulley in box H, around pulley C, through the links E E E, around pulley P, and around a pulley at the floor, then to horse.

There is a latch, as shown at the right of the drawing, to hold the traveler over the load until the fork is elevated; when the pulley on the fork strikes the bottom of the latch and raises the catches up, then the fork moves back; when the fork returns, the catches slide over the pin.

There is a small rope (1) fastened to the traveler by a clevis, 2; said rope passes over a pulley, 3, down to weight, 4, around the pulley fastened to the weight, up to the eye, 5, where it is tied.

By this arrangement a long track can be used in a low barn. The weight will bring the fork back without pulling on the trip cord.

In using this plan, the horse, after he has drawn up a forkful, is turned to the left; around to the side of the rope, and walked back to the starting place; he is then turned around to the right, on the same side of the rope that he came back on; by so doing, there is no stepping over the rope, which generally twists or untwists it, and renders it very liable to loop around a horse's legs as the fork comes back. The weight must be only just heavy enough to bring the fork back slowly, then the rope will not pull on the horse when he is coming back.

HOME-MADE TOOL.—FIG. 1.

Home-Made Tools.—Frequently the farm and garden tools and contrivances that are home-made are quite as effective as expensive boughten ones, and farmers that are blessed with a little ingenuity are continually "fixing" up some kind of a labor-saving machine to work with. Our illustrations represent two very handy and useful implements, of which a farmer writes as follows: "While using to-day a tool which just suits me for killing weeds, it struck me that it might just suit others, even if it is home-made and not patented. To make it, take an old twelve or fourteen-inch half round file; grind off the teeth, bend it as shown in Fig. 1, and put it in an ordinary handle. Now, if you want to loosen the soil, or pull out sods or large weeds, you have a light pick to do it. If you want to kill ordinary weeds turn the hoe flat on the ground and scrape away. Now, as the file or hoe has two sharp edges, you can use either side; as it is long it will work very rapidly; as it is narrow it will work easily, and not draw the dirt over the weeds and re-plant them, but will tumble them on top for old Sol to deal with.

" Another home-made tool now in season, and which has saved me much labor between rows of mangel wurtzel, carrots, etc., is made by taking a piece of old, thin, sharp tire, reversing the bend so as to bring the flat side down, bending it to fit between the rows and with the two ends brought together so as to bolt to an old plow beam, as shown in Fig. 2. Make one, hitch old Tom before it, and go to work, and if it don't work to a T, tell."

Care of Farm Implements.—

Any implement that with good usage and protection will last eight years, will become weak and defective and generally useless, if exposed during four years to dews, rain and sun. It cannot be otherwise. Dew is very destructive to all wood, and sun cracks admit rain and moisture to the interior fibres, to work injury there. To leave implements thus exposed is a direct loss of fifty per cent., a heavy tax. But to state it mildly: An implement which, left unprotected would last five years, will undoubtedly last six years if always kept dry and in the shade when not in actual use. This will save one-fifth of its efficiency, or twenty per cent. A few boards or a straw cover, and attention to having implements always put under, is far more profitable than to " work out " the twenty per cent. to buy new ones.

HOME-MADE TOOL.—FIG. 2.

Woodwork that must be left exposed, will be greatly benefitted by a frequent application of paint, or simply a coat of painting oil and by filling up all sun cracks, as soon as formed with such oil. The use of crude petroleum tends to the preservation of wood, and may be applied to all unpainted woodwork of implements.

Improved Tread Power.—

In the tread-mill power we have here illustrated, the endless traveler consists of cast-iron chain links joined together and carrying lags which are connected to the links by a tenon on each end fitting in a corresponding mortise in the link. Carrying rollers are fitted to run in boxes attached to the frame, so that the chain links run along on them from one to another, and in order that the rollers may be of larger than ordinary size and placed farther apart, the chain links have abutting shoulders above the pivot joints, which hold the lags up level for the horse to walk on. Each lag has a rib or cleat nailed on the upper surface just back of the front edge. The rollers that sustain the weight of the horse may be larger, stronger, and easier running than where the rollers are attached to the chains. For a brake to regulate the speed of the machine, a couple of centrifugal levers are pivoted to a couple of the arms of the flywheel, and having a brakeshoe on the short arm to act on a friction rim attached to the frame, the long arms of the levers being connected to the rocker bar by rods, and to the rocker one of the levers is connected by a coiled spring and adjusting screw, which tend to keep the brakes off the rim when the speed is not too high; but

IMPROVED TREAD POWER.

when excess of speed throws out the centrifugal levers the shoes will be pressed on the rim till the speed slows to the proper limit. The machine is provided with a simple stop device and is improved in other details.

A Good Corn-Marker.—The worst difficulty with ordinary three or four tooth corn-markers results from the inflexibility of the long bar to which the teeth or marker are attached. In passing over uneven ground some of the teeth will not touch the earth, and consequently the planter must guess the position in which the seed should be planted. The marker we herewith illustrate is constructed to surmount this difficulty—t w o joints being made in the bar which allow each tooth to

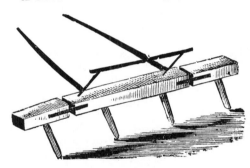

A GOOD CORN-MARKER.

make its proper furrow on a very uneven surface. The joints are made by sawing the bar apart at the places indicated in the engraving, then connecting the sections by bolting on two stout iron straps, the bolts passing entirely through the bar of wood. Four straps of light wagon tire iron, each six inches long, and four six inch bolts will make the two joints. A space of one inch left between the sections of the bar will give sufficient flexibility to it for the purpose required.

A Good Clod Crusher.— Take two pieces of board 2x6 or 8, and round the end of each with an ax. Nail boards 6 feet long on the bottom. They should be

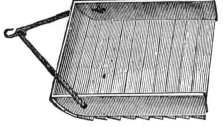

A GOOD CLOD CRUSHER.

about 1 1-2 or 2 inches thick, beveled and lapped, as shown in our engraving. Bore 2 holes (in place where indicated) with a half-inch bit; take 8 feet same sized rope, and tie loop in middle; put ends through holes and tie knot in each to keep it there. Hitch your team to it, jump on yourself, and drive ahead. Once going over will be sufficient. Your land will be finer than you could harrow it in a week. It is better than a roller, for it levels the land, does not pack it, and draws easier than either harrow or roller, and can be made by a boy ten years old in half an hour's time.

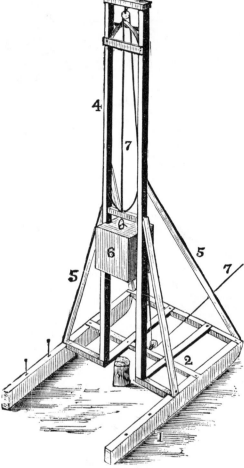

SPILE OR POST DRIVER.

Spile or Post Driver. —Every farmer has often seen the time, we believe, when he could have saved himself or his men a great deal of hard labor, if he could only have had the use of a spile or post driver to sink a few spiles here on this marshy land, to build a dam, or to drive down a few posts there to erect a small building upon or to drive down a line of fence posts; but, not being the possessor of one himself, and not knowing where he could borrow one conveniently from a neighbor, the work has been done without it, and much unnecessary labor wasted thereupon. We consider a post driver one of the most useful implements, for general use, to be found upon a farm. We present an illustration of a good and substantial post driver, with simple directions how it can be made, and would offer the suggestion that the dull months of the winter season will afford a good opportunity for those who wish to provide themselves with one of these useful implements, to do so, and thus have it in readiness for use when next season's work begins.

The machine we have illustrated is of quite simple construction, and with the exception of a little iron work, the pulleys and rope, may be made by any farmer who is handy with tools. The pair of runners (1) are 9 feet long, made of oak 7 inches wide and 4 inches thick. The cross pieces (2) are of 4 by 4-inch scantling. The distance from the rear cross piece to the next one is 10 inches, and from that to the front one is 2 1-2 feet. The rear one is left open in the middle, as represented, for the post. Two pieces of 2 by 4-inch scantling **are** bolted across the top of the cross pieces near the middle, as seen in the cut. The two upright pieces (4) are 20 feet long, of 2 by 6-inch scantling **stiffened** by a 2 by 4-inch piece spiked on the outside edgewise. They would be better made of 4 by 6-inch stuff, or even 6-inch square, as they are required to be stiff. The braces (5) are 2 by 4 inches, the front ones a foot the longest. The weight, or block (6), may be round or square, 20 inches in diameter, and 2 or 2 1-2 feet long, of solid, heavy oak, and grooved on the sides next to the uprights. In the top of this is a strong staple, to which the shears, which are fastened in the sliding block above, catch. The grooves in the weight are 6 inches wide, to take in the whole width of the uprights (four pins on each side would answer the purpose of the grooves). Two 2-inch auger holes are bored through the rear portion of each runner, in order to drive in stakes or a crowbar to keep the machine from being drawn forward while driving the post. The working will be readily understood. A chain is fastened to the front cross-piece at the points where the top pieces are joined, to which the whiffletrees are hooked. It is then drawn forward by the team (a span of horses or mules) until the weight is over the mark for the post. The post being placed, the whiffletrees are then unhooked from the chain and hooked to the rope which pulls up the weight. One to three blows will drive the post in to the required depth. It is then drawn forward to the next post. Two men and a span of mules will drive three-fourths of a mile of posts in a day, and one man will mark for the posts and face them ready for the boards in the same time. The posts are slightly pointed, and thus driven, set very firm. The cost of such an implement is about $25, and it will pay for itself in a few days.

A Convenient Tool.—A cheap tool that will prove very handy and can be made very cheaply and quickly, and used for setting out plants such as sweet potatoes, cabbage, tomatoes, etc. Take a round piece of wood one and a half inches in diameter and about a foot long; sharpen one end neatly; at the other end cut down to one inch in diameter, one inch below the end; this will give a small shoulder all around.

Take another round piece of wood the same size, or if a little larger it will answer as well. Cut it four inches long, in the center bore a hole with an inch auger, and fasten this on the top of the other piece; this will serve as a handle, and the stick can be pushed down into the soil easily and pulled out, and can also be used to press the dirt firmly around the roots of the plants that you are setting out. Ten minutes' work will make one, and you will find it very convenient for use, so as not to have to hunt around for a sharp stick every time you want to set out a few plants.

Implement for Small-Crop Hoeing.—A Massachusetts farmer writes: "I beg to introduce a small hoe which has not been used among the agriculturists yet. It can be made of old discarded scythe-blades, cut sloping at the corners, so that the face next the ground is nine inches wide and the back six inches wide. At the corners, a quarter or half inch can be turned up at an angle to make a hook like a blacksmith's knife used to finish off horses' feet. Then a shank of three-eighths inch wrought iron can be welded on to the center, and the other end into a good handle. Any person skilled in hoeing trying this hoe to single out carrots, parsnips, etc., will wonder why he did not think of it before. I get an old table knife and heat it, turning about two inches of the end to a hook shape, to thin out my cabbage seed and onion beds, cutting the ground clean and quickly between the plants."

Coulter Cleaning Plow Attachment.—Our engraving represents a simple attachment to a plow, intended to keep the coulter free from obstructions when plowing in stubble or turning under long manure. It consists of a rod of iron, one end of which is attached to the wheel of the plow in such a manner that its turning will give the rod a backward and forward motion. The rod passes along under the beam and is bent around its base, or the shank of the plow in wooden beamed ones, just above the mold board, and forms a loop against the coulter. This loop, working backward and forward, works off all obstructions from the coulter.

COULTER CLEANING PLOUGH ATTACHMENT.

A Farm Tool House.—One of the most useful and money-saving buildings that a farmer can place on his premises is a spacious and convenient tool house. It is generally the case that there is room enough in the various outbuildings to house the farm implements if it is economized; but it is a corner here and a few feet of barn or shed floor there; sometimes in a cellar and sometimes in a loft, possibly easy of access, but probably difficult, and in all such instances it is space originally intended and needed for some other purpose. The main reason why so many farmers neglect protecting their implements from the weather when not in use, is the lack of convenient and roomy storage. We lay great stress on its being spacious and handy; for if it is thus, James will always drive the lumber wagon inside to take the hay rack off, and he will draw in the stone boat with the plow and harrow and cultivator on it, and they will escape the next rain or dew and the consequent coat of rust. A farmer needs a tool house as much as a horse-barn or a woodshed. Our illustration is suggestive. It is adapted to a locality abounding with stone. The walls of the building are made of that material, laid without mortar. The foundation is placed below the frost, and the earth is banked on the outside to further protect them and to throw off water. The top of the wall is leveled with mortar, and a two-inch plank laid on, to which the rafters are spiked. The latter are braced on the inside by nailing on cross strips. The roof may be made of the cheapest material, which varies with localities. There is one window in the end opposite the door. The doorway should be twelve feet wide to admit a reaper, and if the location is not too much exposed there is little need of doors. The ground is the floor. The walls are but six feet high, and the structure should be twenty wide by thirty or forty long. Such a building will cost but little where stones are in the way. The farmer can

build it, and will save many dollars in twenty years, and many steps each year otherwise taken after mislaid implements.

A Home-Made Corn-Sheller.—This is simply the use of a bar of iron laid across a box. The box is made of a convenient height to sit upon, say twelve or fourteen inches, and is eighteen by thirty inches square. This size will hold over two

FARM TOOL HOUSE.

bushels. The bar of iron (or, better, of steel) should be 3-4 by 1-4 of an inch in size, and a little longer than the box. Put a staple sufficiently large to admit the bar into the middle of the upper edge of one end of the box, and cut a notch the size of the bar in the other end. Put in the bar, put a piece of board across the notched end for a seat and go ahead with your shelling. Both hands are used in the operation, the left clasped tightly around the bar between the legs of the operator, while the ear is drawn upward by the right hand, the fingers of the left holding it firmly against the bar, and slightly pushing it upward. Shell two thirds of the small end first, then turn and shell the butt. Two bushels of our small corn can be easily shelled in an hour, after getting a little accustomed to the manipulation. I

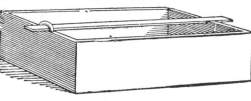

CORN-SHELLER.

have tried many other ways, but none have proved at once so easy and so rapid as this. We present a sketch of the box and bar.

A Good Weeding Implement.—We give a sketch of an excellent weeding implement which is valued very highly by those who have used it. It saves at least the wages of three men. By actual experiment one man will do more weeding with it in the same time, and do it better, than four men with hoes. The implement costs about three dollars—not more, certainly—and will save fifty dollars worth of labor during one season. The frame is eighteen inches long and twelve inches wide. It is light, made of two or two and a half inch material. The wheel is ten inches in diameter, of inch and a half or two inch plank, with a tire of sheet iron. The knife in the rear is a bar of steel two inches wide and a quarter of an inch thick, bent so as to lift the frame about five inches from the ground as it **sits** upon the surface. Each edge is sharp in order that it may cut both ways—the operator pushing it before him by means of the handles, cutting off the weeds, then drawing it back the same distance and lifting the knife at the same time, in order to insure a displacement of the weeds. The knife may be made of a width to suit any space between rows of vegetables. The form of the knife is such as that it may be run as close to the rows as is desired, without endangering the roots of plants—for it cannot cut under. Weeders of this character are sometimes made with the knife before the wheel. Anybody can make the woodwork of this weeder who has the tools. Ordinary plow handles that can be purchased for twenty-five cents will answer. The knife, the braces to the handles, and the tire of the wheel, is all the iron about it. We have devoted this much space to its description and commendation because there are many farmers who are turning their attention to root culture and to the culture of small fruits, and there are many others who would devote more acres to these crops were labor available. Those who grow carrots, onions, turnips, parsnips, the sugar beet, or even strawberries, will find, for money invested in one of these implements, a sure return. There is no patent on it that we know of, and any man with gumption can make one.

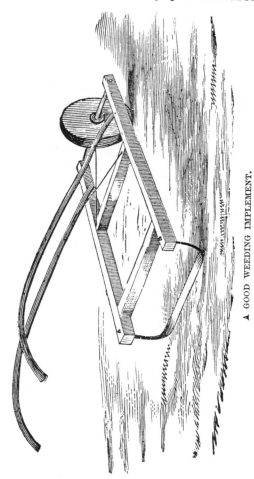

A GOOD WEEDING IMPLEMENT.

Thomas' No-Patent Scraper. — Our illustration represents a practical and very useful implement for use on public or private roads, and as there is no patent upon it, it can be easily made by any one as follows:

Take a hard wood plank, say three by fourteen inches, seven feet long. Bevel the back side, rivet on an old mill saw for the edge. Put in a mortise wide enough to receive the tenon of the pole on an angle—a common ash wagon pole with a tenon say two by four inches, and five feet of medium size cable chain fastened on each side of the pole two and a half feet from the tenon. Fasten to the plank, on a line below the mortise, one grub hook two and a half feet from the mortise, on each side of said mortise, to hitch to the chains on the pole. Unhook the chains, and your scraper is in two pieces, handy to pack away under cover. Estimated cost:

Pole, 25c.; plank, 25c.; old saw, $1.00; making woodwork, 50c.; chains and iron work, $1.50. Total, $3.50.

Set your scraper at the right angle to carry the gravel or earth toward the center of the road, and drive on at a good brisk walk, the driver to ride or place on weights when necessary. If the road is very rutty or uneven, it is better to change the angle and drive back on same side, as the scraper would cross its own angle going back, and still carry the earth toward the center of the road.

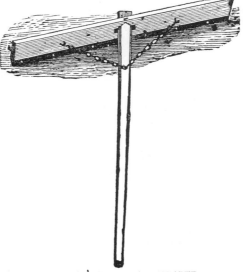

THOMAS' NO-PATENT SCRAPER.

A Clod Crusher.—We illustrate a very cheap, simple, but efficient implement —first made and used, we believe, in E n g l a n d—for breaking lumps of earth on plowed fields and leaving the surface smooth and finely pulverized. It is a very good substitute for the roller to smooth the surface of the field and cover grass seed sown after spring rains. It is made in this wise: Lay two oak scantlings, 3x3 inches square and three and one half feet long, parallel on the shop floor, three feet apart. Then spike a strip 2x2 and five feet long across two ends of the scantling; then four two-inch planks eight inches wide and five feet long, spiking

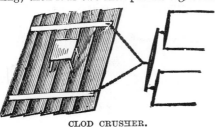

CLOD CRUSHER.

them on like clap-boarding, and finish with a plank fourteen inches wide for the front. Turn your crusher over, affix a stool for the driver and the chains to the crosspieces for the team to draw by, and the implement is completed.

Improvement of Roads.—A **Good Scraper.**—We would like to call the attention of all lovers of good roads, and especially of those who are overseers, to the importance of some system in constructing and repairing public highways.

In the first place, all roads should be made and kept rounding. The ditches at the side should be deep, and of such a grade that the water may quickly run off. A road constructed in this manner may be kept rounding for a number of years by the frequent use of the large A scraper, drawn by four horses abreast. Perhaps this important road implement in some districts is an unheard-of contrivance. Judging from the looks of many roads, we think it must be so, and for the benefit of overseers in such districts, we give a drawing on this page of the best large scraper we have ever seen. The scraper here represented is constructed of oak plank 11 feet long, 14 inches wide, and 2 1-2 inches thick, set up edgeways, in shape of the letter

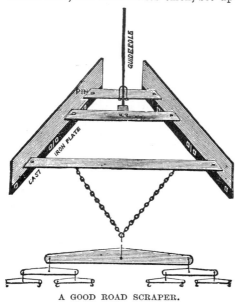

A, with the top cut off. The rear cross-piece is near the end, and also near the top edge of the plank. The next is distant from the other 1 1-2 feet, and 2 inches lower, for the purpose of allowing the guide-pole to pass over the rear one, and the end under the other, giving the other end the right length to take hold of. The front cross-piece is also near the end, and is the center of the plank. The rear end should be one foot throat; the front any desired width. To the inside of the plank, at the lower edge, are bolted plates of cast iron 5 inches wide and 1 1-2 inches thick, the holes through the same being slots longest up and down, that the iron may be lowered as it wears away. The cut of the scraper may be altered by moving the draw-clevis in

A GOOD ROAD SCRAPER.

the chain to one side of the center, causing one side to do the whole work, as is many times necessary. The great advantage of this scraper over others is that it continually draws the dirt toward the center, and leaves the road perfectly smooth and rounding.

A Snow Plow.—The snow plow here illustrated is built so as to be fixed upon the forward part of a double sled. The frame is made of 4x4 oak scantling, and is similar in form to a double mold-board plow. One runner is fixed to the forward part, at such a distance below the edge of the plow as to raise it to clear obstacles such as stones or frozen mud which may be in its way. Four inches would

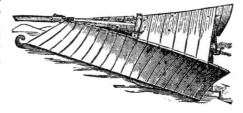

SNOW PLOW

probably in general be a safe distance. The hinder part of the plow rests upon the sled as shown in the engraving, and is bolted to it. A long tongue is fixed into the place of the ordinary one, and is fastened to the front of the plow by an iron strap, which is bolted to the frame. The hinder portion of the plow may be covered over with boards, and a seat fixed firmly upon it. When it is used, it is best to load it as much as possible. The sides of the plow are made of half-inch oak or basswood strips, steamed and bent into shape. The outer surface of these strips should be dressed smoothly, which will make the draft easier.

Bag Holders.—Farmers who raise crops of cereals for market are well aware of the trouble and labor involved in the one operation of bag filling. It oftentimes happens that one person is required to hold open and fill the bag at the same time; this, however, is a slow and tedious process, and to expedite this important operation, at the same time render it less laborious, the bag holders shown in our illustration were invented. A proper size of the one delineated in Fig. 1 is platform K, 24x14x2 inches, either pine or oak; standard B, 4x3x36 inches; hopper P, 16x16 inches at the top, beveled to admit of the hooking thereon of the bag D, as shown. It is obvious that, by having the upper portion of the hopper of

FIG. 2.   FIG 1.

BAG HOLDERS.

larger dimensions than the top or mouth of the bag, the operation of filling can be performed much quicker, and with less liability to spill the grain; the bag holder also dispenses with one hand.

Fig. 2 illustrates a simple arrangement for the purpose. The hopper is of the size of that in Fig. 1. It is supported by three short straps or chains, R R R, attached to as many of its several sides, which in turn are attached at the

HAND PLOW.

point M. This bag holder is cheap, simple, portable, and durable. It can be attached to the granary wall, or any portion of the barn above the floor. By providing the main chain M with a hook, it can be raised or lowered to accommodate bags of various lengths.

Hand Plow.—Most vegetables are greatly benefitted by having the ground stirred frequently around them. Hoeing is a tedious operation both for time and patience.

We give a drawing of a small shovel plow with a wheel set in the tram, which can be pushed like a wheelbarrow. When loosening the soil is the object, it is a very expeditious machine. The tram is made by screwing together pieces of hard wood boards. The wheel should have a "broad tread" to prevent cutting in. A large cultivator tooth does tolerably well for a shovel. It works well for boy-power, by tying a drag rope to the end of the tram. With this a garden can be gone over in less than a fourth of the time required to hoe it, the same time may be given on different days with so much greater result, as the plowing is nearly as good as hoeing each time.

Keep the Farm Tools Sharp.—Too often these things are not thought of until the articles are wanted, when much valuable time is lost in putting in order what might as well have been done during the dull winter days. It has been computed that the same man can do as much in two days with a sharp scythe as in three days with one comparatively dull, and the same expenditure in force. And it is just the same in regard to all other tools or implements, whether operated by hand, steam, or horse power. The engineer continually oils the machinery, and a good saw or file is oil to hand implements. We know one who has a great deal of hand hoeing to do by hired labor, and he believes the continued use of the file on the hoes makes a difference of nearly one-half in the labor. His calculation is that every ten-cent file he buys saves him ten dollars in his laborers' bills. Look after the spades, scythes, hoes, chisels, saws, etc. A good grindstone and a set of files are among the best of farm investments. The best of all forehandedness is that which prepares in advance a full set of good and well-repaired tools to work with.

AROUND THE FARM--Update

This chapter aims at catching up loose ends from other more specific chapters on farm and home management. I find a great deal of interesting and worthwhile material here, but I'll have to jump about as the author jumped.

Dairying in the U.S. was radically changed by the ensilage systems mentioned here as being under experimentation. Dairy farmers now raise different kinds of crops, harvest them differently and store the chopped mash in silos. Cribs for corn storage and barns for hay storage decreased in importance once the farmers began building silos.

Smoking and curing are excellent ways to keep meat. For a small outlay of money and a good deal of strenuous labor, even the amateur could construct a smokehouse like one of those described in this chapter. An excellent handbook for the person who wants to butcher and preserve meat is Frank G. Ashbrook's *Butchering, Processing and Preservation of Meat* (NY: Van Nostrand Reinhold, 1955).

Fish ponds serve and protect the farm in a number of ways. A well-situated, well-cared-for pond, one whose banks have been kept clear of brush and trees, is a pleasure to the eye. The pond also serves as fire protection, furnishing an easily available and adequate supply of water for the fire pumper. Properly fenced, the pond will provide water for livestock without being turned into a mudhole. The pond may be stocked with fish to supplement the farmer's diet. I would not suggest carp but bass will multiply and afford good eating. Often the County Soil & Water District runs an inexpensive fish stocking program.

The whitewash and paint recipes are quite good. We are given two recipes for paint, oil-based and caseine, the caseine paint will stick well to wood but not plaster. Wherever there is a possibility of paint being gnawed off and eaten by humans or animals, the caseine based paint would be advisable. Paints with oil and lead stick best but constitute a health hazard. Whitewash was widely used in 1888. Lime serves as a mild disinfectant and whitewashed objects show the dirt more, indicating when they need cleaning and a new coat. The rice paste whitewash is a cheap and efficient way to improve the looks of a barn or shed.

Draining land is a subject dear to my heart, since I have worked several years as a technician with the Ontario County Soil & Water Conservation District. Almost all of our work has involved using tile or open drains to improve wet croplands. Government policy now states that draining practices should be used to increase the yields of wet land, rather than bringing new land into production. Therefore, land which has been farmed in any manner for two out of the last five years is eligible for drainage assistance under federal cost-sharing programs. Technicians from the local Soil & Water District or from the Soil Conservation Service will aid you in planning a drainage system to improve your wet croplands. The reasons outlined in this chapter for drainage continue to be useful. I have never seen land drained by drilling through an impervious layer of clay to sand beneath, but I have seen thousands of acres brought into fuller and earlier production with the use of ditches and tile.

AROUND THE FARM.

Making and Keeping Ice.—The method of making and keeping ice we here illustrate and describe will be of practical use only to those who are fortunate enough to have a spring or stream of running water upon their place; but the same result might be obtained by pumping in the water, though it would involve much more labor and trouble.

The icehouse should be built firmly of rough boards, as shown in our illustration. Put high up on the outside of the house a penstock, with which connect, by means of a hollow plug, a tin pipe about two inches in diameter, on the inside, making a hole through the siding for the purpose. This tin pipe may pass through the center of the icehouse, or it may be fastened to the side walls, passing partly or entirely around. If passing through the center, conical tubes similar to the muzzle of an oil can, about an inch in altitude, should be soldered on either side of the tin pipe so as to discharge jets at an angle of about 30 degrees to a perpendicular.

MAKING AND KEEPING ICE.

If passing around the sides, cones should be so soldered on that the jets shall be thrown inward. The aperture through the apex of these cones should be very fine, about the size of a small pin. At the discharge end of this pipe, passing through or around the icehouse, should be fastened a rubber pipe of from four to six feet in length. By raising the movable end of this rubber pipe we give whatever head we desire to the jets; in severe cold weather the greater head, and as the weather moderates less. Should it be thawing or too mild to freeze, then lower the rubber pipe so that the water will flow through the pipe without being discharged from the cones. For this purpose the pipe should have a gradual descent toward the discharge end. Should this not effectually prevent any water flowing on the ice, then bore a hole in the penstock below the pipe passing through the icehouse, and let the water discharge from this hole during mild weather. The jets may be within two feet of each other. Better results attend a large number of fine jets than a less number discharging the same amount of water. In starting, the bottom of the icehouse should be covered with sawdust. The ice will form very slowly at first, but after the bottom is covered it will congeal more rapidly. After a sufficient quantity of ice has been formed, the sawdust may be put on, covering thickly around the edges, so that as the ice melts the dust will fall down and protect it. Ice formed in this way will keep better than if sawed and packed in the usual way. We consider this mode of saving ice worth a practical test by all who have running water and sufficient fall.

Whitewash for Buildings and Fences.—If people knew how easily whitewash is made, and how valuable it is when properly applied, it would be in more general requisition. It not only prevents the decay of wood, but conduces greatly to the healthfulness of all buildings, whether of wood or stone. Out-buildings and fences when not painted, should be supplied once

SMOKE HOUSE.—FIG. **1.**

or twice a year with a good coat of whitewash, which should be prepared in the following way: Take a clean, water-tight barrel, or other suitable cask, and put into it a half-bushel of lime. Slake it by pouring water over it boiling hot, and in sufficient quantity to cover it five inches deep, and stir it briskly till thoroughly slaked. When the slaking has been thoroughly effected, dissolve it in water and add two pounds of sulphate of zinc and one of common salt; these will cause the wash to harden and prevent its cracking, which gives an unseemly appearance to the work. If desirable, a beautiful cream color may be communicated to the above wash by adding three pounds of yellow ochre; or a good pearl of lead color by the addition of lamp, vine, or ivory black. For fawn color, add four pounds of umber, Turkish or American—the latter is the cheaper—one pound of Indian red, one pound of common lamp-black. For common stone color, add four pounds of raw umber and two pounds of lamp-black.

Smoke Houses.—Our first illustration, Fig. 1, represents a smoke house built of brick, 6x7 feet square, and suitable for a large farm. The bottom is excavated the size of the building, two feet deep, filled in with small stones, and on this a brick floor, well cemented, is laid. This insures dryness. The walls are of brick, eight inches thick and seven feet high, with a small door on one side, lined on the inside with sheet-iron or zinc. Hooks should be firmly attached to the joists, on which to hang the hams and shoulders. This style of smoke house is not very expensive, is safe from fire, and when not in use for smoking meat, is an excellent receptacle for ashes, which ought never to be kept in contact with wood, on account of the danger from spontaneous combustion.

Our next illustration, Fig. 2, represents one of the best arranged smoke houses that we have ever seen. It was large and built of brick, with an iron door which is generally kept locked. In the gable end there is a fire-place with a door. "A" shows the fireplace with door, for making the smoke, a chimney leading up on the inside of the wall letting the smoke into the room. The advantage of this arrangement is that the fire for smoking is built without entering the building, and simply by opening the door of the fireplace. The smoke passing up the chimney on the interior side of the

SMOKE HOUSE.—FIG. 2.

wall is cooled, and thus the meat does not come in contact with heat from fire. In the ordinary smoke-house, as is well known, the pieces of meat often break loose from their fastenings and fall into the fire or ashes underneath, and are injured or destroyed. In this plan the ash room may be partitioned off and the meat kept in a room by itself, and the door being always kept locked, except at such times as the meat is desired for the table, there is no chance of loss from thieves or flies. One can keep meat in this house in perfect condition from one end of the year to the other, and no losses can accrue from any source.

For those who want a cheap, easily made smoke house, our illustration, Fig. 3, will meet the requirement. It is made in a slight rise of ground, by an archway of brick, at the lower end of which the

SMOKE HOUSE.—FIG. 3.

fire is made, while at the upper end is placed a barrel or box containing the hams and other meat to be cured. The lower end is closed after the fire is well started, to prevent a too rapid burning of the corn cobs or other material used in smoking the meat, and also to direct the smoke to the upper orifice for escape.

Ensilage.—This word, which is only a few years old, grows out of the discovery made by a Frenchman, Auguste Goffart, that green crops, when stored in water-tight pits called silos, under a heavy pressure, do not rot, but are preserved fresh and sweet, and retain all their nutritive juices for a year or more; and that, when offered to cattle in this condition, in the winter, are preferred to any dry food. It is not surprising that the discovery made a sensation among farmers and cattle feeders in this country, and that there is exhibited a keen desire to know all about it; for, not only can a great deal more in weight, of green food than dry, be raised on an acre, but ensilage possesses the advantage of supplying cattle with succulent summer feed in the winter—an advantage of great value to milch cattle. Any green crop that stock are fond of when in a growing state is good material for ensilage—grass, clover, rye, young corn, sorghum and vegetables; but corn, clover and the grasses are most generally used, because when growing they are full of juice, which is lost in curing into hay or fodder, but preserved in the silo. Several kinds of green crops may be packed in the same silo, and the ensilage is said to be improved by the variety. Corn, either drilled or cultivated or sown broadcast, and cut in its most juicy condition, is the basis of most ensilage experiments in this country; it may be packed in the same silo with clover or grass of any kind cut green, and successive crops of corn may be planted for mixture with different kinds of grasses in their season. As it is estimated that ten to twenty tons weight of green crops may be cut from an acre of good soil—five to ten times as much as the weight of a dry crop of grain or hay—it is easy to see how much more profitable it is to save green crops in the form of ensilage than to allow them to mature and dry. Col. J. W. Wolcott, of Boston, who owns a farm near that city, raised 460 tons of ensilage on thirty-four acres—being fourteen tons to the acre—one year. By raising two crops on the same soil he has gathered as much as twenty-one tons per acre. On one piece of ground he gathered thirty-one tons per acre, but "that corn was fourteen feet high," he says. He adds: "I am satisfied that an acre of ground will keep a cow twenty-four months." When the silo is opened in winter the contents are found in a sort of cheesy condition, and require to be sliced off with a sharp axe. They have undergone a slow and slight fermentation which does not impair their merits as feed and is not offensive to cattle. Indeed, the first smell of ensilage is said to "set cattle wild for it," and they prefer it to any other kind of feed.

Silos are variously constructed. The usual plan is to dig pits ten feet wide, fifteen feet deep, and as long as may be desired, on sloping ground, and make them water-tight with cement. Mr. C. W. Mills, of Pompton, New Jersey, prefers to build a strong frame, boarded up tight and close with thick lumber, entirely above the ground, something in the fashion of an ice house. The green crops may be packed into them, either whole or cut up with a cutter; each plan has its advocates, though the weight of opinion is in favor of cutting, as it allows of closer packing. As the crops are thrown in they are tread down as closely near the edges as possible, and when the silo is full it is covered and weighted with heavy rocks or earth, and then shedded over to protect it from the weather. In a few weeks the ensilage is

" ripe " and ready for use. One end of the silo, if built along the ground, may be opened and the ensilage cut out and fed as it is wanted. Its quality will depend on the crops of which it is made and the care with which they are packed away. Nearly all animals will eat it; cattle like it and thrive on it, and for milch cows it is particularly valuable, as it increases their flow of milk and keeps them in cheerful, healthy condition.

What Goes with a Farm.—When a farm is bought or sold, questions often arise as to what goes with it, and disputes may often be avoided if farmers know just what their farm deeds include. In brief, says Mr. Haigh, of the Detroit bar, in the *American Agriculturist*, where no reservations are made in the deed, the conveyance includes the land, the buildings upon it, and all such chattels or articles as have become so attached or fixed to the soil or to the buildings, as to become what is known in law as "fixtures." What constitutes a fixture depends largely on the intention of the owner in putting it there, and also upon the manner in which it is affixed. Anything so affixed to the roll or the buildings that it cannot be removed without injury nearly always goes with the farm, and anything of a permanent nature, fitted for permanent use, and annexed thereto by the owner with that intention, generally goes with the land, though it might be severed without any injury, as the following examples will illustrate: All fences on the farm go without, but not fencing materials, as rails, etc.; if bought elsewhere and piled upon the farm, and not yet built into a fence, they have never yet been " annexed." But rails built from timber standing on the farm and piled up for future use go with it; their original annexation is not severed by being changed from standing trees to rails. If, however, they were cut with the intention of using them elsewhere than on the farm, they would then be personal property and would not pass. The bare intention in the mind of the owner in this instance makes the difference between real estate and personal property. Hop poles, if they have once been used upon the farm, are regarded as a part of it, though at the time of sale they are stored away for future use. Loose scaffold poles, however, laid across the beams of a barn, have been held not to be a part of the realty. Standing trees, of course, are a part of the farm; so are trees cut or blown down, if left where they fall, but not if corded up for sale; the wood has then become personal property.

To Tan Hides.—We think that many farmers would tan sheep and other skins, with the hair and wool on, if they were told how. They are very convenient for sleighs, wagons, house rugs, and many other purposes. We give the following from a reliable source, remarking that it is essentially the same that we found in use by the trappers and hunters in the wilderness: All fatty and fleshy matter should first be removed from the skin, and with sheep skins the wool should be washed clean with soft soap and water, and the suds be thoroughly rinsed out. For each skin take four ounces of salt, four ounces of alum, and half an ounce of borax; dissolve these in one quart of hot water, and when cool enough for the hand to bear, stir in sufficient rye meal to make a thick paste. This paste is to be spread thoroughly over every part of the flesh side of the skin, which is then to be folded together lengthwise, and left for two weeks in an airy place. Then remove the paste, wash and dry the skin. When nearly dry, it must be worked and pulled, and scraped with a blunt knife made for the purpose, shaped like a chopping knife, or with a piece of hard wood worked to a sharp edge. The more the skin is worked and scraped as it dries, the more pliable it will be. Other furs can be tanned with the fur on.

Weasel, Rat, and Vermin Traps.—The common steel rat-trap is frequently used with good success in destroying these vermin, but we give herewith an engraving of a trap in this connection (Fig. 1), which we think will be found more effectual, and it is so simple in its construction that any one can make it. The trap consists of an oblong box, the end of which draws out, and is provided with a looking-glass in the internal side, which attracts the vermin on looking in. The entrance of the trap is formed of two spring doors made of wire, which allow the vermin to enter with least pressure.

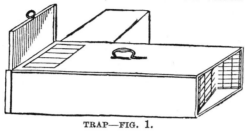

TRAP—FIG. 1.

These doors have s h a r p p o i n t s where they meet, which, although not felt by the vermin when entering, will prevent it from withdrawing after having once introduced its head. Near to the looking glass a bait is suspended, and a cage is also fixed with a chicken to serve as a decoy. These traps are self-setting, simple, inexpensive, fit for all sizes of vermin, and safe for the house, farm-yard, or game preserve.

We also give an illustration of another trap (Fig. 2), which can be easily made by any person conversant with the use of a saw, hammer and nails. The top and bottom of the trap are made of oak board one inch thick and twenty inches square. It is divided into two parts, making really two distinct traps. The corners are of wire about one-quarter of an inch in diameter, and the sides and partitions of No. 7 wire. Holes are bored both top and bottom, and the wires inserted. The corner wires are riveted, holding the trap firmly together; the doors are of oak, three quarters of an inch thick, and are kept in place by a cross wire on the top board of the trap, and by two small staples near the bottom edge of the door, which slide on the upright wires on each side. The treadle X is also oak, working on the upright pin O, as a fulcrum, and being held in place by the wire hook V working on a pivot at P, and on the lower end of which the bait is placed. One side of the trap is represented as set, the other as sprung.

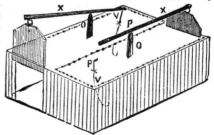

TRAP—FIG. 2.

Trapping the Mink, Skunk, Etc.—Next to the weasel, the mink is most dreaded among poultry. In localities near salt marshes, swamps, ponds, and sluggish streams they most abound. The ravages of the mink are easily told from those of the weasel or any other animal. He almost always carries off a portion of his prey and tries to secrete it. If you find a half-grown chicken or old fowl dead and dragged wholly or partly into a stone wall or under some building, you may be certain it is the work of a mink; and if you go to work *right*, you will be just as certain to trap him.

One peculiarity of the animal makes his capture easy—he *always* returns to a spot where he has hidden his quarry, or where he has made a raid; and if he misses it, will go searching around for it. A knowledge of this fact led to the invention some years since of the trap we now illustrate. It is unpatented and our readers our free to make and use it.

The trap should be three feet long, one foot wide, and one foot high, outside measurement, and may be made of ordinary faced pine boards.

N is the only *solid* part of the *top*, to which is hinged the lids L and D, and also in which the standard S is mortised. The lid L is held up by the rod A, in which are one or more notches to elevate it the desired height, catching or hooking over the pin B, and projecting a few inches beyond. Under A, and hinged into the standard by the pin P, is the lever T, also projecting an inch or more beyond. C is a treadle board, hinged at Y to the bottom of the trap, and connecting by the wire W to the lever T, elevating it about two inches when set. H is the *bait* box, separated from the main trap by a wire screen, X X. O is a window, of which there should be one on each side about three or four inches square, also covered with wire or wire cloth, and D is the lid of the bait box, fastened down by the pin E.

If you have a chicken or fowl that has been killed by the mink a night or two preceding put *that* into the bait box and close the lid, placing the trap as near the spot where the dead fowl was found as you can. If a live fowl is put in, no harm can be done to it, the screen effectually protecting it. The

mink enters the trap, and as soon as his weight gets well up on the treadle it pulls down the lever T, the projecting end of which dislodges the rod A, and drops the lid L. It is best to have a *weight* upon L, or else a catch to hold it down when sprung, as we have known an old mink to pry up the lid and get out.

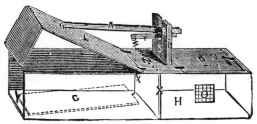

A MINK TRAP.

We have never known this trap to *miss* when set immediately succeeding the depredations of one of those *varmints.*

Next to the mink, the skunk is the most destructive to poultry. The best way to trap him is with eggs, of which they are passionately fond. They are not particular about the *quality*, as they seem to favor a rotten one, or one with a dead chicken in it. Tie the egg in a piece of netting, and fasten it to the treadle of a steel trap, or to a common box trap. Find their burrow, and set your trap near the mouth. It is nearly useless to set a trap where a theft has been committed. The animal may not go back there for months. He might possibly be caught in a night or two. But the chances are against it.

Crows and hawks are to be classed among the enemies of poultry. The former prey only on young chickens and eggs. Catch one and hang it in your poultry yard; no other crow will come near it. The quickest and surest trap for crows is to place a steel trap in the shallow water of a pond, so that the jaws when open, are just under water. On the treadle place a small tuft of grass or moss, making a miniature island. Then cut a small stick with three branches, forking in such a manner as to support an egg on them; stick this about six or eight inches from the trap; lay a little moss, grass, or leaves over it, and place the egg on the forks, so it will appear as if floating on the water; cover the remainder of the trap lightly with grass, so as to hide it from sight, for Mr. Crow is very observant. To obtain the egg the crow will light on the "island," and find too late he is caught. When hawks are troublesome the only remedy is to shoot them. You will soon notice that he visits your yard about a certain time every day, and by watching for him you can soon rid yourself of the troublesome visitor—of course provided you are a good shot.

Trapping Ground Moles.—We give an illustration upon this page of a very good and simple trap that may be successfully used in catching that troublesome little pest, the ground mole. It is made of two ash boards, a full inch in thickness, seven inches in width, and two feet six inches long, attached to one end by a broad butt hinge. The form given to the bottom board is shown in the cut, the central slit being made to admit the free play of the trigger, which is represented by itself in the right-hand corner of the sketch. It is of iron, ten inches long; the lower part shaped like a paddle, five inches long, one and one-eighth inches wide, and the left-hand end, notched as shown, and three-quarters of an inch wide perpendicularly. The post, sixteen inches high, is curved to the circular sweep of the top board on its hinge. The teeth, six in number, on each side, are riveted seven-eighths

of an inch apart, in a plate five and one-fourth inches long and one inch wide, containing four screw holes, placed zigzag, and this is found much firmer and more secure than if the teeth were inserted directly in the upper plank. The trap is set, as shown in the cut, across a mole track, first digging a hole eight inches square and six inches deep,

A GOOD MOLE TRAP.

and returning the soil, taking care to exclude all stones and large pebbles. Press the earth down pretty firmly, and set the trap so that the trigger touches the surface of the ground exactly over the line of the track. When the mole goes along his accustomed road, and finds it obstructed, his movements in reopening the track inevitably heaves up the surface, so as to set off the trigger, and the teeth on one side or the other will catch him. Weight the trap with a heavy flat stone.

Ridding the Land of Stumps.—We have frequently noticed persons when clearing land make a brush pile over a green stump, with the expectation, apparently, that they were pursuing the right course to effectually rid the land of its presence immediately, while in fact no better means could be resorted to in order to insure its indefinite preservation. It has been the experience of the writer that a stump should never be fired until it has become sufficiently "seasoned" to insure its entire consumption, else the charred remnant becomes impervious to the action of the elements, and it will remain a troublesome customer to deal with for long years after.

These thoughts are suggested from a quite recent experience in dealing with some very "old settlers," which the hands on the farm wished to fire several years **back,** and were only prevented from doing so by a positive command to the contrary. By a little patient waiting we are gratified with seeing "the places which once knew them, know them no more forever." This is one plan of treatment.

Martin Boxes.—The box-house does very well if made of any small box about fifteen inches square (which can be had of any grocer), with a division put in it so that two families can inhabit it. A square hole should be sawed out at the bottom edge opposite each division, and the bottom nailed on. Place the box on a pole from twelve to fifteen feet high, or on the gable end of a roof, or even in a tree, and your house is finished. It can be painted or not, or even made in fancy designs, which are quite attractive to the eye. The illustration given on this page will convey the idea. A hop, or other rapid-growing climber, if planted at the bottom of the pole, will climb up it and cause it too look quite ornamental and picturesque. We have seen them built two stories high, made like a diminutive gothic cottage, which is quite pretty. The house should be made before the martins come, as they are generally in a hurry to locate and go to "housekeeping." By all means give them some kind of a home.

MARTIN BOX.

Cisterns.—Many who have cisterns and depend upon them for their supply of water for family use, hardly realize the importance of keeping them sweet and clean. Rain water as it comes down from the clouds is probably as pure as any water can be, but after it has washed over a roof and down the conductors into the cistern, carrying with it dust, leaves, and other rubbish that may have gathered on the roof or in the gutters, it is not strange that the cistern should need to be cleaned out every year or two. If the cistern is not much used the water is quite likely to become bad. It may look all right, and not taste very bad either, and yet not be healthful. Of course all cistern water should be filtered, and a soft brick filter is perhaps the best; but even then it will become necessary to clean the cistern as often as every two years, and better every year.

To Purify Cisterns.—Throw in two ounces powdered alum and two ounces borax to a twenty barrel cistern of rain water that is blackened or oily, and in a few hours the sediment will settle, and the water will be clarified and fit for washing

Silos and Ensilage.—The new system of preserving and feeding ensilage, says an intelligent writer, is one of such simplicity that doubting minds
are incredulous as to possible results.   If the building of a silo and the subsequent process of filling with ensilage were some wonderful secret, or perhaps a new discovery protected by a series of patents—if the use of the system were permitted only under the payment of heavy royalties—there is a
class of skeptical minds who fatten on uncertain qualities, and who have but
little faith in any practice which is within the reach of persons of ordinary
intelligence and common sense.   It is difficult for many minds to realize the
facts claimed for ensilage or to explain to themselves why such results
should be secured by processes so simple and by apportions so economical.
Yet proof, absolute demonstration, is within the reach of every inquiring
mind, or of every enterprising farmer who is willing to spend fifty dollars
for commencing experiments upon his own farm.

It is a most singular fact that the doubting minds are those who have
had no practical experience on the subject, but whose conservatism is on
the parade.   It is equally surprising that no intelligent, practical attempt at
silo building or ensilage feeding has resulted in failure, although men of all
classes and attainments have experimented with the new system.   It would
be reasonable to expect many failures among so many beginners of varying
capacities, were there anything intricate or uncertain in the process and its
auxiliaries.   No authority in this country is competent to pronounce positively upon the future success or failure of this new system; it is for the interest of no one to urge or induce the adoption of the system by any unwill-
ing farmer, and no one is to be enriched by the multiplication of silos,
except, perhaps, the individual owners.   Many a conservative farmer will
await the report of his more enterprising neighbor, who has built a silo, yet
it is certain that before many years every one will have an opportunity to
judge the merits and drawbacks of the system of ensilage.

New Way with a Silo.—A Massachusetts farmer records his experience as follows: We had always raised more or less Indian corn, using the
stalks for wintering our limited number of cattle.   After increasing our herd
we planted fodder corn to help out our stock of corn stalks.   However, the
hard labor attending the cutting, binding, shocking, and curing the fodder
made us willing investigators of the new and highly recommended system
of ensilage feeding.   From all who had constructed silos and tested ensilage
we heard uniformly favorable reports.   We could not learn of a failure,
hence we determined to test ensilage for ourselves, only hesitating on account of the probable labor and expense attending the erection and weighting of a stone silo.

Learning that wooden silos found favor with some farmers who pronounced them equally as good, so long as they lasted, as the more costly
stone affairs, we determined upon constructing our silo of wood.   Our barn
is a two-story building, measuring 40x80 feet.   It contains several large
bays, the dimensions of which are 20x24 feet.   We sealed up one of these
bays with 1 1-4 inch matched spruce boards covered with tarred paper.   We
cemented the bottom of the silo, also the walls under the sills of the barn.
We coated the inside of the silo with coal oil to prevent the effects of moisture upon the boards.

We stored about 125 tons of corn fodder in the silo, treading it down by
men, instead of horses, by reason of the small size of the silo.   We were
about three weeks storing the whole of our fodder on account of the lack of

help. **For** covering the silo we used hemlock boards and tarred paper, no other weighting being applied until some three or four weeks later, when we stored a quantity of dry corn stalks upon the top of the silo. Upon opening the silo we found the fodder in a perfect state of preservation, the ensilage showing no mold, except a little on top, just under the cover. In preparing the fodder, we employed a two-horse power to run our cutter, the latter being provided with a carrier for delivering the fodder in the silo.

Rustic Seats for the Lawn.—The garden and lawn are incompletely furnished if they are not supplied with some kind of seats whereon one may recline at ease. Fortunately these seats need not be costly; it would, indeed, show bad taste to have them so. Something easy, graceful, fantastic, rustic—

RUSTIC SEAT.—FIG. **1.**

something that the sunshine or the wind will not harm, or have its beauty destroyed by the rain. The materials for such seats are nearly always at hand—at least on every farmer's premises. All that is required is a little skill and patience to construct them. The branches of the trees may be bent and shaped into tasteful chairs, and any desired form given to them. The branches of the red cedar tree and wild grape vine furnish the best of material for this style of rustic seat. Our illustration, Fig. 1, shows a very pretty chair made in this manner. A few pine boards cut out and nailed together, as

RUSTIC SEAT.—FIG. **2.**

represented in the engraving, Fig. 2, will form a cheap and convenient rustic seat, which will be admired for its very simplicity and quaintness.

A favorite shade tree on the lawn may be surrounded with seats so attached that one in sitting may lean against the trunk Our illustration, Fig. 3, will give a good idea of how seats of this kind may be constructed.

Of materials there are plenty around almost every homestead—tasteful labor only is wanting to make appropriate rustic seats. The position of such seats is worthy of consideration. As they are mainly intended for use in warm weather, they should be amply shaded. A

RUSTIC SEAT.—FIG. **3.**

position should be chosen that commands a good prospect—if not a distant landscape, then of the beauties of the lawn and the flower garden. Some, at least, should be screened from observation by shrubbery—fragrant if possible—where one may read or work. It is during the warmer months that the garden and lawn offer their greatest attractions, and everything that tends to make them more enjoyable should be provided.

How to Preserve Cider.—A pure, sweet cider is only obtainable from clean, sound fruit, and the fruit should, therefore, be carefully examined and wiped before grinding.

In the press use hair cloth or gunny in place of straw. As the cider runs from the press let it pass through a hair sieve into a large open vessel, that will hold as much juice as can be expressed in one day. In one day, or sometimes less, the pomace will rise to the top, and in a short time grow very thick. When little white bubbles break through it draw off the liquid through a very small spigot placed about three inches from the bottom, so that the lees may be left behind. The cider must be drawn off into very clean, sweet casks, preferably fresh liquor casks, and closely watched. The moment the white bubbles before mentioned are perceived rising at the bunghole, rack it again. It is usually necessary to repeat this three times. Then fill up the cask with cider in every respect like that originally contained in it, add a tumbler of warm sweet oil and bung up tight. For very fine cider it is customary to add at this stage of this process about half a pound of glucose (starch sugar), or a smaller portion of white sugar. The cask should then be allowed to remain in a cool place until the cider has acquired the desired flavor.

In the meantime, clean barrels for its reception should be prepared, as follows: Some clean strips of rags are dipped in melted sulphur, lighted and burned in the bunghole and the bung laid loosely on the end of the rag so as to retain the sulphur vapor within the barrel. Then tie up half a pound of mustard seed in a coarse muslin bag and put it in the barrel, fill the barrel with cider, and add about a quarter of a pound of isinglass or fine gelatine dissolved in hot water. This is the old fashioned way, and will keep cider in the same condition as when it went into the barrel, if kept in a cool place, for a year.

Professional cider makers are now using calcium sulphite (sulphite of lime) instead of mustard and sulphur vapor. It is much more convenient and effectual. To use it, it is simply requisite to add one-eighth to one-quarter of an ounce of the sulphite to each gallon of cider in the cask, first mixing the powder in about a quart of the cider, and giving the latter a thorough shaking or rolling. After standing bunged several days to allow the sulphite to exert its full action it may be bottled off. The sulphite of lime (which should not be mistaken for the sulphate of lime) is a commercial article, costing about forty cents a pound by the barrel. It will preserve the sweetness of the cider perfectly; but unless care is taken not to add too much of it, it will impart a slight sulphurous taste to the cider. The bottles and corks used should be perfectly clean, and the corks wired down.

A little cinnamon, wintergreen or sassafras, etc., is often added to sweet cider in the bottle, together with a dram or so of bi-carbonate of soda at the moment of driving the stopper. This helps to neutralize free acids, and renders the liquid effervescent when unstopped; but if used to excess, it may prejudicially affect the taste.

What Birds Accomplish.—The swallow, swift, and hawk are the guardians of the atmosphere. They check the increase of insects that otherwise would overload it. Woodpeckers, creepers, and chickadees are the guardians of the trunks of trees. Warblers and flycatchers protect the foliage. Blackbirds, crows, thrushes, and larks protect the surface of the soil. Snipe and woodcock protect the soil under the surface. Each tribe has its respective duties to perform in the economy of nature, and it is an undoubted fact that if the birds were all swept off the face of the earth man could not live upon it, vegetation would wither and die; insects would become so numerous that no living being could withstand their attacks. The wholesale destruction occasioned by grasshoppers which have devastated the West is to a great extent, perhaps, caused by the thinning out of the birds, such as grouse, prairie hens, etc., which feed upon them. The great and inestimable service done to the farmer, gardener, and florist by the birds is only becoming known by sad experience. Spare the birds and save the fruit; the little corn and fruit taken by them is more than compensated by the quantities of noxious insects they destroy. The long-persecuted crow has been found by actual experience to do more good by the vast quantities of grubs and insects he devours than the harm he does in the grains of corn he pulls up. He is, after all, rather a friend than an enemy to the farmer.

Recipe for Curing Meat.—To one gallon of water take one and one-half pounds of salt, one-half pound sugar, one-half ounce saltpetre, one-half ounce potash. In this ratio the pickle can be increased to any quantity desired. Let these be boiled together until all the dirt from the sugar rises to the top and is skimmed off. Then throw it into a tub to cool, and when cold pour it over your beef or pork. The meat must be well covered with pickle, and should not be put down for at least two days after killing, during which time it should be slightly sprinkled with powdered saltpetre, which removes all the surface blood, etc., leaving the meat fresh and clean. Some omit boiling the pickle, and find it to answer well, though the operation of boiling purified the pickle by throwing off the dirt always to be found in salt and sugar. If this recipe is strictly followed, it will require only a single trial to prove its superiority over the common way, or most ways of putting down meat, and will not soon be abandoned for any other. The meat is unsurpassed for sweetness, delicacy, and freshness of color.

Value of Drainage.—As a matter of fact there is very little land in our country that would not be improved by drainage. Many light soils are springy, and the crops are injured in them by stagnant water. Heavy land can never do its best until drained. Vast areas of low-lying but rich land are practically valueless for want of drains to carry off the redundant moisture which forbids the growth of any but aquatic plants. Many who admit the importance of this improvement are puzzled about the ways and means of effecting it. The *Drainage Journal* mentions the following plan, which is well worthy of serious consideration: " Some enterprising tile manufacturers select careful farmers who own flat lands, and make them something like the following proposition: That the farmer make a careful estimate of his average crops, and the tile manufacturer proposes to furnish the tile necessary to drain thoroughly the lands designated in the agreement, the farmer to furnish the labor of putting in the drains at a stipulated price, to be paid out of the excess of crops grown on the land over and above the average yield before agreed upon, and the tile manufacturer agreeing to take the balance of the increase in four or five crops (as agreed) to cover the cost of the tile. On level lands, where the average crop runs low and the land by nature is rich, it is a safe proposition for the tile manufacturer, if the farmer honestly performs his part of the contract. On rich level lands that need drainage, and need it badly, it will pay twenty-five per cent. annually on the investment, and in some instances more."

Rustic Garden House.—No accessories to the garden add more to its beauty and comfort than pleasant, comfortable seats and resting places. They may be composed of a few sticks, forming a simple seat under the shade of some tree, or may be made in the form of rustic houses. Simplicity, however, must not be lost sight of, and no foolish attempt should be made to eclipse the simple beauty of nature by any expensive display of art. In our travels on the Hudson we once stopped at the beautiful garden of A. J. Downing, and after admiring the fine specimen trees it contained, and surveying the finely-kept lawn, we found ourselves reclining in a pretty rustic house, a view of which is given in the engraving on this page, and we now present it as a model for this kind of work. A little patience and taste and a very few tools will enable one with ordinary mechanical skill to erect such a house at leisure times, almost without cost.

RUSTIC GARDEN HOUSE.

How to Make Sorgo Vinegar.—A correspondent writing from Loutre Island, Mo., in the *Rural World*, tells how he made 1,000 gallons of No. 1 vinegar mostly from sorgo skimmings. He says: "Of course the first skimmings are not used. I had two 160-gallon tubs. Into these I put about 70 gallons of apple pomace (cider and all), 25 to 30 gallons of skimmings, according to thickness, then filled up with rain water. I let it remain for two or three days, then drew it off and put in a large 1,000-gallon cask, which I finished filling by the latter part of October. Next spring I drew it off in 40-gallon barrels, put them in a warm place where the sun shone on them part of the day, and I soon had the very best of vinegar. The above casks were in an out-house where it was as cold as out of doors. Of course it had no time to sour that fall, as winter set in early in November; consequently freezing did not hurt it, though it should not freeze after once becoming sour. Pressed or dry pomace is just as good, only add skimmings and water for the cider taken. Vinegar made this way is better, I think, than when made of sorgo alone. It can hardly be detected from pure cider vinegar, and is just as good. Bear in mind that only enough water should be added to reduce the strength of the skimmings to about that of cider. You need saccharine to make good vinegar. You can't make vinegar from a few apple peelings and a barrel of rain water."

Blasting Stumps.—The following is the *modus operandi* of blasting stumps with dynamite: Make a hole an inch in diameter near the stump, inclining at an angle of about forty-five degrees, so as to reach underneath the body of the stump. This hole may be made with a crowbar through the soil, but if there be a large deep tap-root it will be necessary to continue the hole into the body of the tap-root by means of a long auger. A cartridge containing three or four ounces of dynamite is then inserted to the bottom of the hole, and a slow match having a peculiar percussion cap on the end is inserted in the cartridge. The hole is then tampered with earth, and when all is ready the outer end of the match is lighted, and the operator retires to a safe distance. The explosion usually not only extracts the stump from the ground, but tears it into pieces small enough to handle easily. The dynamite costs about forty cents per pound, so that a three or four ounce charge, with its fuse, would cost about ten cents—making the cost of blowing up a stump about ten cents, besides the labor.

How to Thatch Roofs.—Rye straw threshed with a flail and kept straight, with the short or broken straws raked out, is the best material. The roof is made ready for thatching by nailing strips of boards, say one by two inches, across the rafters, putting them a foot apart. The pitch should be steep, to insure a waterproof and durable roof. The straw should be cut to a uniform length, and care taken to have it straight and all right. The sketch shows how the

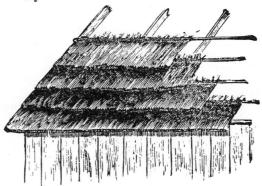

HOW TO THATCH ROOFS.

roof is prepared for the straw, and the manner the courses are laid. Tie the straw in bundles that will average six inches in thickness. The band should be close to the upper end, the one which is fastened to the cross strip. The courses should overlap, so as to make the roof the thickness of three bundles.

Fish Culture for the Farm.—No farm should be without a fish pond, well stocked, any more than it should be without poultry. This may be a startling announcement to farmers who have to go one hundred feet to water, but it is none the less practical, as much as to keep stock on such a farm. Water must be produced in either instance. On most farms the drainage is favorable to ponds by throwing a dam across some sag or ravine and retaining the water that would naturally run off. The pond would serve the purpose of both stock and fish. Where this plan is not practicable, a pump worked by a wind-mill will answer as well if kept running; the surplus water drained into an artificial pond would supply the water. The pond should be at least eight feet deep in the center. This would give the fish an opportunity to place themselves beyond the reach of ice. A pond of fifty feet in diameter would accommodate a reasonable supply of fish for an ordinary family if the fish are properly fed. Perhaps there is no fish so well calculated for this character of farming as the carp. It feeds on vegetables, and in its habits has about the relation to an ordinary game fish that the farm yard fowl has to the game fowl.

A Suggestion for Drainage.—A Missouri farmer relates an experience which offers suggestions, which, while they may not be exactly new, may have for many, great practical value. There were upon his farm several depressions which in wet seasons held ponds of water. To drain these by ordinary means would have been very expensive, because no gravel could be got near the farm, and there was no tile factory in that vicinity. Open ditches were out of the question.

The services of an expert well-borer were secured. He sank several test shafts in various parts of the farm, and found that the underlying ground was a tenacious blue clay, fourteen to sixteen feet thick, and almost perfectly impervious. Beneath this was found a strata of white sand. The well-borer and his machine were placed in a wagon, which by means of a long rope was hauled to the deepest parts of a pond about an acre in extent. Here he bored a well down to the sand, completing the operation before sunset of the day when the work began. In thirty-six hours the water had disappeared and the pond was dry. To make this short perpendicular drain permanent he had it cleared of sediment, sunk the shaft about two feet into the bed of sand, and filled to the top with clean, coarse gravel from a creek bed. The gravel was heaped about a foot high above the shaft to strain the water properly that the shaft might not become choked.

They are thousands of places in the West where, year after year, farmers have plowed around such wet spots, giving them up to the possession of rushes and frogs. Yet they could be drained easily by a few hours' work. In Western Michigan a large swamp lay for years on the southern edge of a village, a noisome barrier to progress and a bone of contention in village and township politics. To drain it a large ditch a mile or two long would have been required; but some one, fortunately, discovered that a thin sheet of clay was all that kept the water from going down into a deep strata of gravel, boulders and sand. The wells were sunk and the swamp thoroughly drained at an almost nominal cost, leaving rich black soil, which is the most productive and valuable in all that district. There may be thousands of similar swamps, where two or three days spent in sinking test shafts would show a ready means for converting sloughs or swamps into fields of wonderful fertility.

Important Use of Coal Oil.—A Southern farmer says: "I once read an article enumerating some of the practical uses to which coal oil can be successfully put, in which the writer suggested that it would be an effective remedy against the apparently indestructible bott or grub in horses. I had a horse which had always been so hopelessly infected with both grubs and the small intestinal worm, that he could never be kept in a better condition than that of a skeleton, and with a ravenous appetite, and the best of treatment with the use of all known remedies, appeared to be nothing more or less than an improved type of a successful worm manufactory. Out of patience and disgusted with my patient, and not knowing how much kerosene a horse could take without injury, yet determined to "kill or cure"—not caring much which—I commenced to drench with a gill of oil, intending to double the dose every day till a "cure" or a "kill" was effected. On the first day I gave a gill, on the next a half a pint, and on the third a pint, and it was very soon apparent that that was enough both for the worms and the horse. Large quantities of both kinds passed, and the horse appeared to be on the point of passing too, but he didn't; and soon after all the usual symptoms of worms had disappeared, and the horse commenced to improve rapidly in flesh and general condition, and is now in better condition than I have ever seen him, and still improving.

" I also experimented with kerosene on cut nails to make them take the place of wrought nails in a cart body I was building. I brought the nails to a red heat, dropped them into the oil and let them stand until cool, when they could be clinched, bent and twisted into any desirable shape almost with as much ease and safety as a piece of wire, of the same size. My cart body required 100 nails, for which any blacksmith would have charged me one dollar. Two pounds of ten penny nails cost ten cents, leaving a balance of ninety cents in favor of the kerosene. This is a small item, but the farmer can save many such during the year, and it is the little things that pay."

Draining Wet Land.—The objects of draining are:

1. To carry off surface water, by open drains.

2. To lower the water line.

3. To prevent waste of the surface-applied manure, by washing off the soluble elements before they become incorporated in the soil.

4. To put the soil in a condition to be benefitted by the use of lime, ashes and alkaline substances. There is no use in manuring or liming land that lies under water half the year.

5. To make the land a better absorbent of ammoniacal, nitrogenous and carbonic acid gases—so necessary for the growth of all crops.

6. To make the soil more porous, so that rains and melted snow shall descend through the soil, leaving their fertilizing elements in the earth that has acted as a filter, instead of flooding the surface and carrying all their rich freights off of the land.

The infinitely wise Father has provided a vast reservoir of the richest agricultural elements which He pours upon the earth, in the rain and snow, for us to utilize. The science of agriculture is teaching the wise how to secure and utilize these elements. One way to do it is, to render the soil porous and friable, ready to receive and hold the nitrogen and carbonic acid gas that is precipitated upon it in showers and snow. The nitrogen thus precipitated by rains goes down to the alkaline elements constantly being liberated in the soil and unites with the potash, soda and lime, forming the nitrates of lime and soda and potash, thus making the soil one vast laboratory, on nature's grand scale, for the production of a fertilizer that will never deplete but constantly enrich the lands of the intelligent agriculturist.

7. To enable the farmer to start his plow from ten days to three weeks earlier in the spring, and to keep it going when lands undrained are unfit to work. The time lost on undrained lands in the spring and fall and after heavy rains, which can be improved on well drained lands, will be sufficient in from one to three years to satisfactorily drain most farms.

8. To make the land earlier and later. Well drained land is much warmer and advances the growth of plants faster than land saturated with water. As we can start our plows from ten days to three weeks earlier on drained fields than on undrained, there is more than a corresponding difference in maturing of the crops in consequence of a warmer and quicker soil. And as the plow can run later in the season when the fall rains are made to

percolate through the soil into drains, so the season is not only earlier in the spring but correspondingly prolonged in the fall, enabling one team to accomplish during the season much more work. Every farmer knows what a rush and hurry there is, when ground is undrained, to push things when soil is tempered just right for work. Well drained land is always tempered right. Steady work, which accomplishes the most, and not hurry, becomes the order of the day, while there is always time to do everything well.

9. Another object of draining is to deepen the soil. Where the water line has been six inches from the surface, that is the depth of the man's farm for all practical purposes. Neither cereals nor root crops will go down below the water line. Trees do badly. Apples, pears and quinces blight when the top roots go below the water line. Lowering the water line twelve inches gives the tiller of the soil a new farm more valuable than the first. The potash, soda, phosphoric acid and lime of the first six inches has sunk down into the strata below. As these substances, so necessary to the growth of plants, sink down into the earth when wet, so they rise in the form of nitrate when the ground is dry. So that underdraining gives the farmer control by clovering and root cropping, of more valuable elements and greater quantities of them, than he can afford to buy.

10. The last object of draining we will mention is, to render the farm and neighborhood more healthy. This is no unimportant consideration. We know of districts of country many miles square which twelve years ago were greatly subject to chills and fevers, but which, by only partially draining and liming, have become almost entirely free from these maladies. It is just what any thinking person would suppose. Where the land is low and the water lies either on the surface or within an inch or two of it, the surface vegetation is decomposed by the action of the moisture as soon as the warm rays of the sun fall upon it. Malarial marsh gas is eliminated; bilious and intermittent fever, stomach and bowel afflictions, that carry off numbers of children, follow as a natural and necessary consequence. Where there is only a small pond hole, that dries up in summer, near the house, doctors are sure to be in demand. We hardly know where to stop writing on this important subject. Many other reasons for draining will readily suggest themselves, and farmers should study the various methods of draining wet land.

How to Cure Hams.—This receipt is fifty years old, and it is the best. To each twenty pounds of fresh meat make a mixture of one-fourth of a pound of brown sugar and a dessertspoonful of ground saltpetre; rub this well by hand into the meat; then with coarse salt cover the bottom of a barrel, say to half an inch; put in hams, and cover with half an inch of salt, and so on until the barrel is full; hams should remain in a cool place four weeks; when salted, wipe and dry them, and get some whole black pepper, which you must grind yourself, and pepper thoroughly, especially about the hock and bone; let the ham lie for two days; then smoke for eight weeks.

Axle-Grease.—A first-rate axle-grease is made as follows: Dissolve half a pound of common soda in one gallon of water; add three pounds of tallow and six pounds of palm oil, or ten pounds of palm oil only. Heat them together to 200 or 210 degrees Fahr.; mix, and keep the mixture constantly stirred until the composition is cooled down to 60 or 70 degrees. A thinner composition is made with half a pound of soda, one gallon of water, one gallon of rape oil, and a quarter of a pound of tallow, or palm oil,

Driving Nails Into Hard Wood.—The editor of an agricultural periodical witnessed an experiment of driving nails into hard seasoned timber, fairly dried. He says that the first two nails, after passing through a pine board, entered about one inch, and then doubled down under the hammer; but on dipping the points of the other six or eight nails into lard, every one was driven home without the least difficulty. Carpenters who are engaged in repairing old buildings sometimes carry a small lump of lard or tallow for this purpose on one of their boots or shoes.

Good Well Curbing.—The best timber for curbing a well is hemlock, which is very durable when under water, and gives no flavor to the water. Of the woods some mention, all would rot very quickly except pine and tamarack, but pine is objectionable on account of its strong flavor. If hemlock cannot be procured, tamarack would be the best. The timber should be cut in two or three inch planks, and put together by halving the timbers at the end, and holding the halved parts dovetailed or cornered together, so that the sides cannot be forced in by the pressure of the earth, the upper half of one piece fitting upon the lower half of the other piece.

To Repair Leaky Roofs.—One of the very best preparations for repairing roofs that leak is to procure coal tar at the gas-works, and mix finely-sifted coal ashes or road dust with it till about as thick as mortar. Plaster with this carefully around leaky-roofed valleys or gutters, or about chimney flushings. It will soon set as hard as stone, and apparently as indestructible. This preparation is very cheap, and would probably answer equally well spread all over a roof previously laid with felt or roofing paper. Once put on properly, it would seem to be there for all time.

A Cheap Rain Gauge.—To make a rain gauge for farmers' use, just as good as if it cost three dollars, take a quart fruit can free from dents, hold the top in the fire until the solder is melted, then knock it off; place the can on a post, with brackets nailed around to keep it in place. Make a rule six inches long, divided into tenths of inches—one made out of a strip of slate is best. Measure the rain every morning after falling. An inch of rain is a good rainfall, if it comes gently. This in weight will be 226,875 pounds, or 113 tons 875 pounds to the acre.

Burning Stumps.—Tree stumps are said to be easily removed by boring a two-inch hole eighteen inches deep into the stump. Do this in the fall, and fill with a concentrated solution of saltpetre, and plug up to keep out water. By spring it will have permeated every part. Then fill the hole with kerosene, set on fire, and the whole stump, it is said, will be consumed, even to the roots. It would seem to be feasible, and it is certainly an easy way to get rid of stumps. The ashes will remain to fertilize the soil.

How to Get Rid of Rats.—The *English Standard* says: "Several correspondents write to announce the complete extirpation of rats and mice from their cow-stalls and piggeries since the adoption of this simple plan: A mixture of two parts well-bruised common squills and three parts finely-chopped bacon is made into a stiff mass, with as much meal as may be required, and then baked into small cakes, which are put down for the rats to eat."

Whitewash That Will Stick.—To make whitewash that will not wash off by the rain, one peck of lime should be slaked in five gallons of water, in which one pound of rice has been boiled until it is all dissolved. The rice water should be used hot, and the mixture covered up closely until the lime is slaked. Then add a pound of salt, and the wash heated to boiling when used. It is not an expensive preparation. It can be prepared by any person wishing to use a good wash, and is highly satisfactory. Brother farmers, try it.

Signs of a Prosperous Farmer.—When lights are seen burning in his house before the break of day, in winter especially, it shows that the day will never break on the breaking in of the winter of adversity.

When you see him drive his work instead of his work driving him, it shows that he will never be driven from good resolutions, and that he will certainly work his way to prosperity.

When he has a house separate from the main building purposely for ashes, and an iron or tin vessel to transport them, it shows that he never built his dwelling for a funeral pyre for his family, and perhaps himself.

When his hog-pen is boarded outside and in, it shows that he is " going the whole hog or none," in keeping plenty inside his house and poverty out.

When his sled is safely housed in summer, and his farming implements covered both winter and summer, it plainly shows that he will have a good house over his head in the summer of early life and the winter of old age.

When his cattle are properly shielded and fed in winter it evinces that he is acting according to Scripture, which says that " a merciful man is merciful to his beast."

When he is seen subscribing for a newspaper and paying for it in advance, it shows that he is speaking like a book respecting the latest movements in agriculture, and that he will never get his walking papers to the land of poverty.

To Clean an Old Roof.—Those wishing to know the best means of removing moss and earth accumulations from an old shingle roof, are advised to sprinkle lime freely along the comb of the roof, and let the rains dissolve and carry it over the shingles. Every particle of dirt and moss will be removed by it. If kept clean, shingles will last much longer. This method is as good and cheaper than any direct application to the shingles.

Paint for Farmers.—Farmers will find the following profitable for house or fence paint: Skim milk, two quarts; fresh slaked lime, eight ounces; linseed oil, six ounces; white burgundy pitch, two ounces; Spanish white, three pounds. The lime is to be slaked in water, exposed to the air and then mixed with about one-fourth of the milk; the oil in which the pitch is dissolved to be added a little at a time, then the rest of the milk, and afterward the Spanish white. This is sufficient for twenty-seven yards, two coats. This is for white paint. If desirable, any other color may be produced; thus, if cream color is desired, in place of the part of Spanish white use the other alone.

To Prevent a Carriage from Spotting.—A newly-varnished carriage is liable to spot. To prevent this some wash the carriage two or three times in clean cold water applied with a sponge instead of using a hose; this will help harden the surface, and prevent it to some extent from being injured by the mud or water getting splashed on the job. Never let mud dry on the surface, and then wash off expecting to see no spots on the varnish. You will certainly be disappointed, and the only way to remedy this evil will be to have it revarnished. Soft water is better than hard water for the washing of carriages, as the lime which is in the hard water is very liable to injure the varnish.

Removing Carbonic Acid Gas or Foul Air from Wells.—A correspondent gives an account of an extemporized apparatus for removing carbonic acid gas from wells. It was simply an opened out umbrella let down and rapidly hauled up a number of times in succession. The effect was to remove the gas in a few minutes from a well so foul as to instantly extinguish a candle previous to the use of the umbrella. Whenever there is an escape of gas in an apartment, the adoption of this plan will be found useful.

To Render Wood Uninflammable.—Professor Kedzie, of the Agricultural College of Michigan, an expert chemist, says that a paint or wash made of skim milk, thoroughly skimmed, and water brine, will render wood uninflammable, and he proved it by experiment. He said this paint, or whitewash, is durable, very cheap, impervious to water, of agreeable color, and, as it will prevent wood from taking fire, urged its use, particularly on roofs, outbuildings, barns, etc.

Remedy for Burdocks.—It is said that a certain and speedy remedy for burdocks has been found in kerosene oil. A small quantity poured into the heart of a plant, directly after cutting, leaves no trace of their existence save a small hole in the earth where they stood. Refined or crude oil will accomplish the purpose just as well.

Paint for One Cent a Pound.—To one gallon of soft, hot water, add four pounds sulphate of zinc (crude). Let it dissolve perfectly, and a sediment will settle at the bottom. Turn the clear solution into another vessel. To one gallon of paint (lead and oil), mix one gallon of the compound. Stir it into the paint slowly for ten or fifteen minutes, and the compound and paint will perfectly combine. If too thick thin it with turpentine.

A Good Word for Toads.—Toads, according to Prof. Miles, live almost entirely upon slugs, caterpillars, beetles and other insects, making their rounds at night, when the farmer is asleep—and the birds, too—and the insects are supposed to be having their own way. French farmers understand these facts so well that they purchase toads, at so much a dozen, and turn them loose.

Protect the Swallow.—Among insectivorous birds the swallow is worthy of great encouragement. An examination of the stomachs of eighteen swallows killed at different seasons of the year showed that they contained an average of 406 undigested insects each, and not a single grain of corn (of any kind), or the least particle of fruit or a trace of any vegetable.

Plan for Keeping Hams.—A very good way of keeping hams is to wrap them in strong brown paper so that the ashes cannot come in contact with them. Then pack them in clean, hard wood ashes, in dry boxes or barrels. This will keep well cured hams quite sweet, as the ashes serve as a protection against insects. The boxes should be set in a cool, dry place.

Improving Lawns.—For ridding lawns of unsightly weeds, such as plantain and dandelions, the following plan is recommended by an experienced gardener: To the end of a light wooden rod attach a small sponge, or better, wind a few thicknesses of cloth around it, dip the sponge in oil of vitriol, and with it touch the heart of the weed.   The oil of vitrol may be carried in a wide-mouthed bottle at the end of another rod.

Mold in Cellars.—To get rid of mold in cellars, put some roll brimstone into a pan and set fire to it; close the doors, making the cellar as nearly air-tight as possible, when the fungi will be destroyed and the mold dried up. Repeat this simple and inexpensive operation every two or three months for two or three hours at a time.

Thawing Frozen Apples.—It is stated by those who have had the advantage of experience, that if apples which have been frozen are thawed in the dark they are uninjured; but if in the light, they very soon become unfit for use.   We should suppose the same result would most likely appear if the experiment were tried with potatoes.

Washing Harness.—It is bad policy to wash harness with soap, as the potash injures the leather.   If the harness becomes rusty rub off the dirt as well as possible with a soft brush, and apply a dressing of grain black, followed with oil or tallow, which will fasten the color and make the leather soft and pliable.

A Good Suggestion About Harness.—Add a little glycerine to the grease applied to harness, and it will be kept in a soft and pliable state, in spite of the ammoniacal exhalations of the stable, which tend to make it brittle.

Gas Tar for Wagon Wheels.—A farmer who has tried it speaks in the highest praise of gas tar for painting wagon wheels, stating that it tightens tires and spokes better than anything that can be tried.

Mice in the Grain Chest.—If you are troubled about the grain chest with mice, watch for their holes and scatter a little copperas in them.   A few grains will drive them away.

Rats and Mice.—Rats and mice will go into a trap much more readily if a piece of looking-glass is put in any part of the trap where they can see themselves.   They are social little creatures, and where they can see any of their tribe, there they will go.

COOKING RECIPES--Update

The feeling for food, its taste and texture, is extraordinary in these recipes. It must be that food was not easy to come by in 1888, that people sweated for whatever they put on the table. Food must have been a precious substance to be treated with utmost tenderness. That feeling comes through in these recipes.

However, valuable though these recipes are, they may be difficult for a novice to follow. There is a certain level of expertise assumed of the reader. For instance, in the bread section it is assumed that the reader knows what a bread sponge is. Since this knowledge is valuable, I will go through the preparation of a bread sponge.

In a big bowl, put a cup of bread flour, either white or whole wheat and add a sufficient quantity of water to make a paste, stirring all the while with a wooden spoon. Add an envelope of dry yeast dissolved in a bit of water or a small package of fresh yeast, crumbled into a little water and dissolved. Stir. Add a tablespoon of honey or molasses or white sugar and stir again. Cover with a plate. This is a bread sponge. If you let it rise an hour at 70°, it will get full of bubbles, and breadmaking can proceed. If you use less yeast and the room temperature is 10° to 20° cooler, you can let this sponge rise overnight and proceed with bread making in the morning.

The point of bread sponge is that it activates the yeast before the major part of bread making has begun. Yeast treated this way is more powerful than yeast added with all the rest of the ingredients. It can rise many more loaves of bread. And more important, the yeast itself is more effective.

Actually, most of the recipes can be followed if the reader has a reading knowledge of cookbooks. If there is a point where the reader is stymied, I would suggest checking out a later cookbook for fuller directions on the same recipe. I have used a 1906 cookbook to good advantage.

You can see from this chapter what was readily available in 1888 and what was scarce. Fresh fruits and vegetables were obviously available only at short intervals in the year. The rest of the time, it was potatoes and cabbage. The quantity of potato recipes here, the quantity of cabbage recipes–I would trust these implicitly. I would be more cautious, say, with the asparagus recipes. I myself cook asparagus in as little water as possible. Victorians tended to overcook vegetables.

Individual recipes that strike me as I read through this chapter: the recipe for boiling potatoes (really, great skill involved here), green corn pudding, Something Nice (green tomatoes, spiced), Airy Nothings (flat sugar cookies), Watermelon Cake, Hard Times Pudding, Sand Hearts, Brown Bread and so on. They really knew what they were doing in those days.

THE HOUSEHOLD.

COOKING RECIPES.

Breakfast Dishes.

To Make Good Coffee.—French cooks are famous for the excellence of their coffee, which they make so strong that one part of the liquor requires the addition of two parts to reduce it to the proper strength. This addition is made with hot milk. The large proportion of hot milk, in the place of so much warm water, gives the coffee a richness like that made by the addition of cream in the ordinary way. By this means any housekeeper desirous of making good coffee, can have it without cream.

Hominy Muffins.—Take two cups of very fine hominy, boiled and cold; beat it smooth and stir in three cups of sour milk, half a cup of melted butter, two tablespoonfuls of salt and two tablespoonfuls of white sugar; then add three eggs well beaten, one tablespoonful of soda dissolved in hot water, and one large cup of flour; bake quickly.

Corn Muffins.—One pint of corn meal, one pint of sour milk, two tablespoonfuls of soda, two eggs, two tablespoonfuls of sugar, three tablespoonfuls of melted butter, a little salt. Stir soda into the milk and mix with the meal; add the eggs, melted butter, sugar and salt. Beat briskly, and bake in cups in a hot oven. Very nice breakfast cakes.

Breakfast Muffins.—Set a rising as for bread over night. In the morning, early, warm a pint of milk and beat into the dough sufficient to make it as for ordinary muffin batter; beat well for five or ten minutes and set to rise for breakfast. Bake in rings on a very hot griddle, and turn frequently to prevent burning.

Buttermilk Muffins.—One quart of sour milk, two eggs, one teaspoonful of soda dissolved in warm water, a teaspoonful of salt, and flour sufficient to make a good batter. Beat the eggs well, stir them into the milk, then add the flour and salt, and lastly the soda. Bake in a quick oven.

Bread Griddle Cakes.—To a pint of bread crumbs add one pint of boiling milk; cover closely and let it stand over night. In the morning mash to a smooth paste and beat in the yelks of two eggs; then slowly add one-half pint of cold milk, beating all the time; and one-half pint of flour with which a measure of baking powder has been sifted; lastly add the whites of the eggs, beaten to a stiff froth; fry like griddle cakes.

Buckwheat Cakes.—The best buckwheat cakes are made with an addition of corn meal flour and oat meal flour to the buckwheat, in this proportion: Six cups of buckwheat, three cups of oatmeal flour, or if this cannot be obtained, substitute graham flour in its place, and one cup of corn meal flour; to this add a dessertspoon evenly filled with salt, two tablespoonfuls of molasses, and lukewarm water sufficient to form a batter; stir through the flour well four teaspoonfuls of baking powder before wetting; but these cakes are much better raised over night with yeast.

French Pancakes.—To make French pancakes, take two eggs, two ounces of butter, two ounces of sifted sugar, two ounces of flour, half a pint of new milk. Beat the eggs thoroughly and put them into a basin with the butter, which should be beaten to a cream; stir in the sugar and flour, and when these ingredients are well mixed, stir in the milk, keep stirring and beating the mixture for a few minutes. Serve with a cut lemon and sugar, and pile the pancakes on a dish, with a layer of preserves or marmalade between each.

Egg Pancakes.—Beat six eggs light, add some salt, and one pint of flour, and stir in gradually enough milk to make a thin, smooth batter. Take a hot griddle or skillet, butter the bottom, and put in enough batter to run over it as thin as a dollar piece. When brown turn it. When done take it out on a dish; put a little butter, sugar and cinnamon over it. Fry another and treat likewise, and so on until a plate is piled. Send hot to table for dessert or breakfast or tea.

Cream Pancakes.—Take half a pint of thick cream, two ounces of sugar, and a teaspoonful of finely-powdered spice; beat the yelks of three eggs, add them to the cream; mix well together; simply rub your pan with a bit of *friture*, make it hot, put in a small quantity of the batter, so as to have the pancakes as thin as possible. Serve them sprinkled over with grated lemon peel and pounded loaf sugar.

Corn Griddle Cakes.—Two cups of coarse corn meal, two cups sour milk, or buttermilk, one egg, one tablespoonful graham flour, one teaspoonful soda dissolved in boiling water; make a batter of the meal, milk, eggs, and flour; if it is too thick add a little milk; then stir in the dissolved soda, beat well, and bake immediately on a hot griddle; do not scorch the cakes.

Wheat Griddle Cakes.—One quart of sour milk, two even teaspoonfuls of soda and one even teaspoonful of salt, flour enough to make a good batter; stir until the lumps are broken; fry at once.

To Make Batter Pancakes.—Well beat three eggs with a pound of flour, put to it a pint of milk and a little salt, fry them in lard or butter, grate sugar over them, cut them in quarters, and serve them up.

Breakfast Corn Cakes.—Two eggs, one cup sweet milk, two tablespoonfuls sweet cream, one-half cup sugar, three-fourths cup flour, two cups Indian meal, three teaspoonfuls baking powder.

Lemon Flapjacks.—One pint of milk, four eggs, juice of one lemon, a pinch of soda, and flour enough to make a light batter. Fry in hot lard. Serve with sugar and nutmeg.

Delicious Waffles.—One and one-half pint sweet milk; one teacup butter and lard, or one cup of either melted and put in the milk, then stir in the flour; next beat the yelks of four eggs, and add with two tablespoonfuls of yeast and beat very hard. Beat the whites last, and stir them in gently. The consistency of the batter should be about like griddle cakes, or so it will run easily in the irons.

Hominy Fritters.—Cook the hominy well; let it boil down pretty thick before using; add to one quart of boiled hominy about half a cup of sweet milk, one egg, a little salt, and flour enough to fry and turn without running; only enough lard required in frying to prevent burning; too much milk and flour toughens them.

Omelet.—Comparatively few of our housekeepers dare attempt an omelet, but there is nothing difficult about it. The chief cause of failure lies in not having the spider hot enough, or in making an omelet too large for the pan. For a spider eight inches in diameter, not more than four eggs should be used. For an omelet of this size, use four eggs, one teaspoonful of salt, and two tablespoonfuls of cream, or in place of that, use milk. Beat the yelks alone to a smooth batter, add the milk, salt and pepper, and lastly, the well-beaten whites. Have the frying-pan very hot. Put in a tablespoonful of butter, which should instantly hiss. Follow it quickly with the well-beaten mixture, and do not stir this after it goes in. Cook over a hot fire, and as the egg sets, loosen it from the pan without breaking, to prevent burning. It should cook in about ten minutes. When the middle is set, it is a good plan to place the pan on the high grate in the oven to brown the top. This is not needed if you turn half of the omelet over upon itself before turning the whole from the pan upon a hot dish. Eat while hot.

Scrambled Eggs.—Many use only eggs with butter and salt for this dish—for four eggs, one tablespoonful of butter. Melt the butter and turn in the beaten eggs, and stir quickly one or two minutes over a hot fire. A common practice is to increase the quantity without impairing the quality by adding milk—a small cup to six eggs, and a tablespoonful of butter with salt and pepper as preferred. Stir these ingredients over a hot fire, putting in the butter first, until the whole thickens. It should be soft and creamy when done. It is very fine served on toast.

Eggs a la Creme.—Hard boil twelve eggs, and slice them in thin rings. In the bottom of a deep baking dish spread bits of butter, then a layer of bread crumbs, and then a layer of boiled eggs. Cover with bits of butter, and sprinkle with pepper and salt. Continue thus to blend these ingredients until the dish is full or nearly so. Crumbs over which bits of butter are spread, must cover all of these bits of eggs, and over the whole mixture a pint of sweet cream or sweet milk must be poured, before it is baked in a moderately heated oven.

Eggs Newport Style.—Take one pint of bread crumbs and soak in one pint of milk. Beat eight eggs very light, and stir with the soaked crumbs, beating five minutes. Have ready a saucepan in which are two tablespoonfuls of butter, thoroughly hot, but not scorching; pour in the mixture, season with pepper and salt, as the mass is opened and stirred with the "scrambling," which should be done quickly with the point of the knife, for three minutes, or until thoroughly hot. Serve on a hot platter, with squares of buttered toast.

Stuffed Eggs.—Six hard boiled eggs cut in two, take out the yelks and mash fine; then add two teaspoonfuls of butter, one of cream, two or three drops of onion juice, salt and pepper to taste. Mix all thoroughly, and fill the eggs with the mixture; put them together. Then there will be a little of the filling left, to which add one well-beaten egg. Cover the eggs with this mixture, and then roll in cracker crumbs. Fry a light brown in boiling fat.

Cupped Eggs.—Put a spoonful of high-seasoned brown gravy into each cup; set the cups in a saucepan of boiling water, and, when the gravy heats, drop a fresh egg into each cup; take off the saucepan, and cover it close till the eggs are nicely and tenderly cooked; dredge them with nutmeg and salt. Serve them in a plate covered with a napkin.

Eggs a la Mode.—Remove the skin from a dozen tomatoes, medium size, cut them up in a saucepan, add a little butter, pepper and salt; when sufficiently boiled beat up five or six eggs, and just before you serve, turn them into the saucepan with the tomato, and stir one way for two minutes, allowing them time to be well done.

A Nice Dish for Breakfast.—Take some slices of bread cutting, off the crust; make a batter of three eggs and a pint of milk; soak the bread in it; put some butter in the frying pan; fry the slices of bread till brown.

A Good Way to Cook Eggs.—Heat and grease the muffin irons; take a dozen eggs, break an egg in each muffin ring; put pepper, salt and a lump of butter on each; then put in the oven; as soon as it is slightly browned remove with a fork; dish and send to the table hot.

Breakfast Dish.—A nice dish for breakfast is made by taking bits of ham that have been left from previous meals, cutting in small pieces, and heating them with two or three eggs stirred in. Pieces of beef may also be used, and enjoyed if properly cooked. Chop them fine, season with butter, pepper and salt, and serve hot. The excellence of these dishes depends upon the way in which you cook and season them. Anything which is warmed over, in order to be palatable, must be nicely prepared.

Potato Cakes for Breakfast.—Save from dinner a soup-plate of mashed potatoes, add to it half a saltspoonful of pepper, the same of nutmeg, a little salt and the yelk of an egg; form into small cakes, put in a buttered baking-pan, brush the top with the white of an egg, and brown in a quick oven.

A Cheap Breakfast Dish.—Stale bread may be made into a palatable dish for breakfast by dipping it in batter and then frying in lard or butter. Make the batter with eggs—a teaspoonful of corn starch mixed in a table-spoonful of milk to each egg. A little salt should be added.

Soups.

Asparagus Soup.—Three pounds of knuckle of veal will make a good strong stock. Put the veal to boil with one and a half bunches of asparagus, a gallon of water, and let it boil rapidly for three hours. Strain and return to the pot, adding another bunch of asparagus, chopped fine, and boil twenty minutes. Take a cup of milk, add a tablespoonful of flour; let it all just come to a boil and serve. Season well with pepper and salt.

Potato Soup.—Mash to a smooth paste one pound of good mealy potatoes, which have been steamed or boiled very dry; mix them by degrees in two quarts of boiling water, in which two ounces of the extract of meat have been previously dissolved, pass the soup through a strainer, set it again on the fire, add pepper and salt; let it boil for five minutes, and be served with fried or toasted bread. Where the flavor is approved, two ounces of onions, minced and fried a light brown, may be added to the soup, and stewed in it for ten minutes before it is sent to table.

Green Pea Soup.—Put two quarts green peas into four quarts of water, boil for two hours, keeping the steam waste supplied by fresh boiling water —then strain them from the liquor, return that to the pot, rub the peas through a sieve, chop an onion fine, and a small sprig of mint, let it boil ten minutes, then stir a tablespoonful of flour into two of butter, and pepper and salt to taste; stir it smoothly into the boiling soup. Serve with well-buttered sippets of toasted bread.

Cream-of-Rice Soup.—Two quarts of chicken stock (the water in which the fowl has been boiled will answer), one teacup of rice, a quart of cream or milk, a small onion, a stalk of celery, and salt and pepper to taste. Wash the rice carefully, and add to the chicken stock, onion and celery. Cook slowly two hours (it should hardly bubble). Put through a sieve; add seasoning and the milk or cream, which has been allowed to come just to a boil. If milk, use also a tablespoonful of butter.

Chicken Cream Soup.—Boil an old fowl with an onion in four quarts of cold water until there remains but two quarts. Take it out and let it get cold. Cut off the whole of the breast and chop very fine. Mix with the pounded yelks of two hard boiled eggs, and rub through a colander. Cool, skim, and strain the soup into a soup pot. Season; add the chicken and egg mixture, simmer ten minutes and pour into the tureen. Then add a small cup of boiling milk.

Saturday Soup.—Collect all the bones which you have on hand, beef, veal, mutton or fowl, and boil together one day. The next morning remove the fat and put the soup on to heat. If you have a little cold hash or a few croquettes, put them in, and add a saucer full of canned corn, salt and pepper to taste, a few slices of onion, half a teaspoonful of celery salt, one cup of stewed tomato. Boil all together, and just before serving put in a few drops of caramel to make it a good brown.

Cauliflower Soup.—Cauliflower and butter. Peel the cauliflowers, and put them in boiling water. When they are perfectly soft, strain the water off, and put them in the saucepan again with some butter. Moisten them with water or beef broth, and finish cooking them. Put some slices of fried bread in the soup, and let the whole boil gently until it is thick; then serve it.

Minute Soup.—Excellent for supper where something warm is desired, or for the little folks when they return from school "almost starved to death." Light bread or crackers crumbed in a bowl or deep dish, add a lump of butter, half a cup of sweet cream, plenty of pepper and salt; if fond of onions, cut a few slices thin and lay over the top and pour over plenty of boiling water, and you will be surprised to see how good it is. If not fond of onions, add an egg well beaten, after the water is poured over, and stir well.

Veal Cream Soup.—Boil the remnants of a roast of veal until the meat falls from the bones; strain and cool. The next day put on to boil, with a slice of onion and one-third of a cup of raw rice. Let it simmer slowly for an hour. Add salt and pepper to taste. Just before serving add one cup of rich milk, or cream if you have it, heated first in a separate dish. Serve with grated Parmesan cheese.

Macaroni Soup.—Put into a stewpan of boiling water four ounces of macaroni, one ounce of butter, and an onion stuck with five cloves. When the macaroni has become quite tender, drain it very dry, and pour on it two quarts of clear gravy soup. Let it simmer for ten minutes, taking care that the macaroni does not burst or become a pulp; it will then be ready to serve up. It should then be sent to the table with grated Parmesan cheese.

Beef Soup.—Three pounds beef, three onions, three quarts water, one-half pint pearl barley. Boil beef slowly about an hour and a half, then add onions, sliced, and pearl barley (previously well washed and soaked half an hour); then boil about an hour longer. More water may be added, sufficient to have two quarts of soup when done. Season to taste with pepper.

One Day Soup.—Half a can of tomatoes, five or six cold boiled or baked potatoes, half an onion, one stalk of celery or a few celery tops. Boil all together until the vegetables are very soft. Put through a colander, add pepper and salt, and a pinch of sugar. Just before serving pour in one cup of hot milk with a pinch of soda dissolved in it. Sift over the top a few very dry bread crumbs.

Mutton Soup.—Take the water that remains in the steamer after the mutton is cooked; there should be about three quarts; add one-half cup English split peas, nicely washed, one small onion, and cook gently three hours, adding a little more water if it cooks away much. Before taking from the fire add salt and pepper to taste.

Poultry Soup.—Take the carcass and bones of any poultry, turkey particularly, and put in a kettle with plenty of water, and boil all the forenoon, filling up with hot water if necessary, and at dinner time you will find to your surprise a most savory soup; season with salt and pepper.

Bean Soup.—Put one quart of beans to soak over night in lukewarm water. Put over the fire next morning with one gallon cold water and about two pounds salt pork. Boil slowly about three hours, add a little pepper. It is better to shred into it a head of celery. Strain through a colander and serve with slices of lemon to each guest.

Julienne Soup.—Put a piece of butter the size of an egg into a soup kettle; stir it until melted; fry three onions and then put in three quarts of good stock, salt, pepper, mace and celery seed, two chopped carrots, two chopped turnips, a pint of dried peas that have been soaked in water over night. Boil two hours.

Codfish Soup.—Boil a teacup of codfish in three pints of water for twenty minutes; add three tablespoonfuls of flour and a little hot water; boil up once; add two pints of milk, let it boil; add three eggs. When served in a tureen, add one poached egg for each person.

Vegetable Soup.—Take one turnip, one potato and one onion; let them be sliced, and boiled in one quart of water for an hour; add as much salt and parsley as is agreeable, and pour the whole on a slice of toasted bread.

Tomato Soup.—Pour a quart of boiling water over a pint of canned tomatoes. Let them boil for an hour, or until they become soft. Strain and return to the fire. Stir in a teaspoonful of soda; this will make it effervesce, and while it is still foaming add a pint of boiling milk, a large piece of butter, pepper and salt. Thicken slightly with cracker-dust and serve immediately.

Summer Soup.—Eight potatoes boiled soft, piece of butter size of two eggs; boil one quart of milk and one quart of water together, and pour boiling hot on the soft potatoes; strain, and then boil half an hour in the milk and water.

Plain Soup.—Boil fresh beef or mutton bones three hours, salt; to one gallon liquid add one teacup washed rice, two or three cloves, boil one-half hour, and it is done.

Okra Soup.—To five quarts of water and a shin of beef add four dozen okras, sliced thin, and a few tomatoes; boil from six to seven hours, and add salt and red pepper to taste.

Meats and Poultry.

Potted Beef.—Choose lean beef; rub it over with saltpetre, and let it lie twelve hours; salt it well with a mixture of bay salt and common salt. Put it into a jar of the requisite size, immerse it in water, and let it remain four or five days. Then take it out, wipe it dry, and rub it with ground black pepper; lay it in a pan, cover it with a crust, and bake seven hours. Take it out when done and let it cool; then pick out the skins and strings, and beat it in a strong mortar, adding seasoning of mace, cloves, and nutmeg, in powder, and a little melted butter and flour. Press it closely into pots, and pour over it clarified butter.

French Beefsteak.—Cut the steak two-thirds of an inch thick from a fillet of beef; dip into melted fresh butter, lay them on a heated gridiron and broil over hot coals. When nearly done sprinkle pepper and salt. Have ready some parsley, chopped fine and mixed with softened butter. Beat them together to a cream, and pour into the middle of the dish. Dip each steak into the butter, turning them over, and lay them round on the platter. If you desire, squeeze a few drops of lemon over, and serve very hot.

An Excellent Dish.—A dish equal to the best steak and cheap enough for any man, is prepared from a shank of beef with some meat on it. Have the bone well broken; wash carefully to remove bits of bone; cover with cold water; watch when the boiling begins and take off the scum that rises. Stew five or six hours till the muscles are dissolved; break the meat small with a fork—far better than chopping—put it in a bread pan, boil down the gravy till in cooling it will turn to a stiff jelly. Where this is done, gelatine is quite superfluous. Add salt, and, if liked, other seasoning, and pour it hot upon the meat; stir together and set aside over night, when it will cut into handsome mottled slices for breakfast or supper.

Chicken Viennese Style.—Procure two very young spring chickens, pluck and draw them carefully, without injuring the skin. Take a very sharp knife and cut each exactly in two; sprinkle with a little pepper and salt, rub a little fresh salad-oil over each piece, and thoroughly egg and breadcrumb them. Rub a little suet on a clean gridiron, place it over a very clear fire, with the four pieces of chicken, broil them very carefully until of a nice brown color; then having ready a hot dish, with four pieces of toasted bread on it, lay half a chicken on each piece of toast, and pour over all a good white sauce, which must be made with a little raw cream.

Chicken Patties.—Chicken patties are made by picking the meat from a cold chicken and cutting it in small pieces. Put it in a saucepan with a little water or milk, butter, pepper and salt. Thicken with a little flour and with the yelk of one egg. Line some patty-pans with crust, not rich and yet not tough, rub them over with the white of the egg, and bake. When done, fill with the chicken, and send to the table hot. Cut out round cakes of the crust for the tops of the little pies, and bake on a common baking tin. It is very little trouble to do this, and the pleasure afforded each child by having a little chicken pie of his own amply pays the right-minded cook.

Smothered Chickens.—Cut the chickens in the back, lay them flat in a dripping-pan, with one cup of water; let them stew in the oven until they begin to get tender; take them out and season with salt and pepper; rub together one and one-half tablespoonfuls of flour, one tablespoonful of butter; spread all over the chickens; put back in the oven, baste well, and when tender and nicely browned take out of the dripping-pan; mix with the gravy in the pan one cup of thickened milk with a little flour; put on the stove and let it scald up well and pour over the chickens; parsley, chopped fine, is a nice addition to the gravy.

Virginia Fried Chicken.—Dice and fry one half pound of salt pork until it is well rendered. Cut up a young chicken, soak for half an hour in salt and water, wipe dry, season with pepper, roll in flour, and try in hot fat until each piece is of a rich brown color. Take up and set aside in a warming closet. Pour into the gravy one cup of milk—half cream is better; thicken with a spoonful of flour, and add a spoonful of butter and chopped parsley; boil up and pour over the hot chicken, or, if preferred, serve without the cream gravy, with bunches of fried parsley. Plain boiled rice should accompany this.

Beef Rolls.—The remains of cold roast or boiled beef, seasoning to taste of salt, pepper, and minced herbs; puff paste. Mince the beef tolerably fine, with a small amount of its own fat; add a seasoning of pepper and salt, and chopped herbs; put the whole into a roll of puff paste and bake for half an hour, or rather longer, should the roll be very large. Beef patties may be made of cold meat by mincing and seasoning beef as directed above, and baking in a rich puff paste in patty tins.

Veal Cutlets.—The cutlets should be cut as handsomely as possible, and about three-quarters of an inch in thickness; they should, before cooking, be well beaten with the blade of a chopper, if a proper beater be not at hand; they should then be fried a light brown and sent up to table, garnished with parsley, and rolls of thin-sliced, nicely-fried bacon; they are with advantage coated previously to cooking with the yelk of an egg, and dredged with bread crumbs.

A la Mode Chicken.—Pick and draw a fine young chicken, wash and wipe dry and season with salt and pepper. Make a nice pastry, roll out an inch thick; wrap the chicken in it, tie in a cloth, and boil an hour or two, according to the tenderness of the fowl. Make a dressing of one tablespoonful of flour, one of butter, and sufficient boiling water to make a smooth paste. Place the chicken on a dish, and pour the dressing over it, garnish with parsley or celery leaves and a hard-boiled egg cut in slices.

Curry.—Take cold chicken, turkey, or cold lamb, cut it in small pieces, and put in a frying-pan with about a pint or more boiling water; let it stew a few moments, then take the meat out, thicken the gravy with a little flour, add a teaspoonful of curry powder, pepper and salt to taste, and let it boil up once; have some rice boiled whole and dry; put it around the outside of the platter, and in the center put the meat; throw the gravy over the meat, not the rice, and serve.

Tripe a la Lyonaise with Tomatoes.—This economical dish, which is in the reach of every family, is very fine. Take two pounds of dressed and boiled tripe, cut into small strips two inches long and put into a saucepan. Parboil and drain off the first water; chop a small onion fine and let all stew twenty minutes; add half a teacup of thickening and then stir in half a can of tomatoes. Season with salt and pepper. This dish has become very popular in all the hotels throughout the country.

Boiled Corn Beef.—This is much improved if cooked in plenty of water, and when thoroughly done, left until cold in the same water that it was boiled in. Lift the pot off the fire, and let pot, water, and meat grow cold together. This will make it much more moist and juicy, besides tender and sweet, than if taken out hot and all the moisture in it dried out by standing and steaming until it grows cold. Hams, tongues, etc., should be cooked in the same way.

To Cook a Rabbit.—When nicely dressed lay it in a pan and cover with cold water, and add half a teacup salt and soak over night; in the morning drain off water and cover the rabbit inside and out with dry corn meal, and let stand till time to cook for dinner; then rinse, cut up and parboil in slightly salted water until tender; take out, roll in corn meal and fry a nice brown; an onion sliced and laid over it while parboiling is an improvement for those who like the flavor.

Baked Ham.—Make a thick paste of flour (not boiled) and cover the ham with it, bone and all; put in a pan on a spider or two muffin rings, or anything that will keep it an inch from the bottom, and bake in a hot oven. If a small ham, fifteen minutes for each pound; if large, twenty minutes. The oven should be hot when put in. The paste forms a hard crust around the ham and the skin comes off with it. Try this, and you will never cook a ham in any other way.

Sauce Piquante.—Put a bit of butter, with two sliced onions, into a stewpan, with a carrot, a parsnip, a little thyme, laurel, basil, two cloves, two shallots, a clove of garlic, and some parsley; turn the whole over the fire until it be well colored; then shake in some flour, and moisten it with some broth and a spoonful of vinegar. Let it boil over a slow fire; skim, and strain it through a sieve. Season it with salt and pepper, and serve it with any dish required to be heightened.

Minced Veal and Eggs.—Take some remnants of roast or braised veal, trim off all browned parts, and mince it very finely; fry a shallot, or onion, chopped small, in plenty of butter; when it is a light straw-color add a large pinch of flour and a little stock, then the minced meat, with chopped parsley, pepper, salt, and nutmeg to taste; mix well, add more stock if necessary, and let the mince gradually get hot by the side of the fire; lastly, add a few drops of lemon-juice. Serve with sippets of bread fried in butter round, and the poached eggs on top.

Boned Chicken.—This is nice for picnics. First take out the breast-bone; then remove the back with a sharp knife, and next the leg bones; keep the skin unbroken, and push within it the meat of the legs. Fill the body with alternate layers of parboiled tongue, veal force-meat, the liver of the fowl, thin slices of bacon, or aught else of good flavor which will give a marbled appearance to the fowl when served; then sew up and truss as usual.

Pigeon Pie.—Border a dish with fine puff paste, lay a veal cutlet (or tender rump steak) cut in thin slices at the bottom of the dish; season with salt, cayenne, nutmeg, or pounded mace. Put as many young pigeons as the dish will contain, with seasoning as above, and in the interstices the yelks of some hard-boiled eggs; put some butter over them, fill up with good gravy, cover with paste, glaze with the yelk of an egg, and bake.

Mutton Cutlets in the Portuguese Way.—Cut the chops, and half fry them with sliced shallot or onion, chopped parsley, and two bay leaves; season with pepper and salt; then lay a force-meat on a piece of white paper, put the chops on it, and twist the paper up, leaving a hole for the end of the bones to go through. Broil on a gentle fire. Serve with sauce Robert; or, as the seasoning makes the cutlets high, a little gravy.

A Brown Sauce.—For one quart. Stir gently in a stewpan over a slow fire, till of a light golden color, two ounces of butter and two ounces of flour, then add two pints of stock; stir till perfectly smooth; add four teaspoonfuls (one and one-third ounce) of the extract of meat and a sprig of marjoram, one of thyme, and two of parsley; boil a quarter of an hour slowly; strain, season, and it is fit for use.

Fried Meat Cakes.—Chop lean raw meat, as you would for sausage, season with salt, pepper, and onion; shape into flat cakes, dip the cakes in egg and breadcrumbs, and fry in dripping. Any meat may be used for this dish, but it is particularly nice of beef, and the finest portions need not be put to this use. Drain on a strainer; have ready a dish of nicely mashed potatoes, on which put your beef-cakes, and serve.

Veal Scollop.—Put a layer of cold chopped veal in a buttered dish; season with salt, pepper and butter; then strew over it a layer of finely powdered cracker, and pour over a little milk to moisten it; add another layer of veal and so on. When the dish is full wet well with gravy and warm water, cover with a tin plate and bake. Remove the cover ten minutes before it is done to let it brown.

Thick Gravy.—Melt in a stewpan a piece of butter the size of a walnut; add two tablespoonfuls of flour; mix well; then add one pint of hot water, half a teaspoonful of the extract, and sauce to taste. This will be found suitable for poultry, or wherever thick gravy is required. The above may be made richer by using a larger proportion of extract.

Hashed Fowl.—Take the meat from a cold fowl and cut it in small pieces. Put half a pint of well-flavored stock into a stewpan, add a little salt, pepper and nutmeg, and thicken with some flour and butter; let it boil, then put in the pieces of fowl to warm; after stewing sufficiently, serve with some poached eggs laid on the hash, with a sprig of parsley in the center, and garnish round the plate with pieces of fried bread.

Chicken Fried.—Cut some cold chicken into pieces and rub each with yelks of eggs; mix together some bread crumbs, pepper, salt, nutmeg, grated lemon-peel and parsley; cover the pieces of chicken with this and fry them. Thicken some good gravy by adding flour, and put into it cayenne pepper, mushroom powder or ketchup, and a little lemon juice, and serve this with the chicken as sauce.

To Remove Fishy Taste from Game.—Pare a fresh lemon very carefully without breaking the thin white inside skin, put inside a wild duck and keep it there forty-eight hours, and all the fishy taste so disagreeable in wild fowl will be removed. Every twelve hours remove the lemon and replace with a fresh one. A lemon thus prepared will absorb unpleasant flavors from all meats and game.

Chicken Fritters.—Cut into neat pieces some tender cold chicken and let them stand awhile in a mixture of lemon juice, salt and pepper. Make a batter of milk, egg, flour and salt, stir the chicken into it, and then fry in boiling lard, putting one bit of chicken in each spoonful of batter. Serve very hot, taking care to drain the fat off well. Garnish with parsley.

Chicken Croquette.—Two sweet breads boiled; one teacup of boiled chicken, hashed; one boiled onion, one teacup of boiled bread and milk, quarter pound butter, salt and pepper. Chop chicken and sweet breads very fine, mix in well the other ingredients, shape into rolls, then dip in the yelk of an egg, then in cracker dust; drop into boiling lard and fry brown.

New Way of Cooking Chickens.—A new way of cooking chickens is to parboil them and then drop them into hot lard, *a la* doughnuts, and fry a few minutes. This will serve to make variety in the bill of fare, but will not wholly take the place of the favorite method of browning in butter. Nice gravy may be made by adding milk and flour to the butter in which chickens have been fried.

French Chicken Pie.—A tender chicken cut in joints, half pound salt pork cut in small pieces, boil the two together till nearly tender in a little water; line a deep dish with pie-paste, put in the meat, season with salt, pepper and chopped parsley, put in a little water and cover over with the pie-paste, which should be rich; bake forty minutes.

Pickled Tongue.—The remains of pickled tongues are very nice intermixed and placed in a pan and pressed, when they will turn out resembling collared meat. A little thick jelly may be poured into the pan with them. Slices of cold tongue may be warmed into any kind of savory sauce and laid in a pile in the center of a dish, the sauce being poured over them.

A Delicious Beefsteak.—Have your frying pan very hot, wipe the steak dry, place in it and cover tightly; turn frequently and keep covered. When done, add to the gravy one tablespoonful hot coffee, a good size lump of butter; salt and pepper to taste. Pour over the steak and serve hot.

A Veal Omelet.—A veal omelet is prepared by chopping a little cold veal and adding to it the beaten egg. Cold boiled ham may be chopped and added in the same way; also veal and ham together, which is very nice. Three or four tablespoonfuls of meat are enough. A little chopped parsley is sometimes added, but herbs are not now so much used in cooking as formerly, though they are an addition to the flavor.

How to Pickle Tongues.—A good-sized tongue requires to boil at least three hours. It is a good plan to soak it over night in cold water. To cook it, put it on in cold water and let it come slowly to the boil. Some cooks change the water when it is half done; if this course is taken, be sure that the fresh water is boiling before the tongue is placed in it.

Roast Partridge.—Lard them well with fat pork; tie the legs down to the rump, leaving the feet on; while cooking, baste them well with butter. They require twenty-five or thirty minutes to cook. To make a gravy, put the drippings into a saucepan with a piece of butter about the size of an egg, and a little flour and hot water. Let it boil up once.

To Dress Cold Fowl.—Take the remains of a cold fowl, remove the skin, then the bones, leaving the flesh in as large pieces as possible; dredge with flour, and fry a light brown in butter; toss it up in a good gravy well seasoned and thickened with butter rolled in flour; serve hot with bits of toasted bread.

Bread Sauce for Partridges.—Cut up an onion, and boil it in milk until it is quite soft; then strain the milk into a cup of stale breadcrumbs, and let it stand one hour. Then put it into a saucepan, with about two ounces of butter, a little pepper, salt, mace and the boiled onion. Boil it all up together, and serve it in a sauce-tureen.

Stewed Liver.—Cut up into slices half a pound of calf's liver and the same quantity of fat bacon; put first, a layer of bacon at the bottom of a pie-dish, then one of liver; sprinkle with pepper and salt, add one medium-sized onion and one apple, both cut up; cover down and let it stew gently in the oven for about one hour and a quarter. No water is required.

How to Make Meat Tender.—Cut the steaks the day before into slices about two inches thick, rub them over with a small quantity of soda; wash off next morning, cut into suitable thickness, and cook as you choose. The same process will answer for fowls, legs of mutton, etc. Try, all who love delicious, tender dishes of meat.

A Nice Supper Dish.—Grate or mince lean ham very fine; mix with it the yelk of an egg and some cream; season with a very little nutmeg. Have ready some small slices of bread half an inch thick; toast them a delicate brown; then, while hot, spread the meat over it; break the yelk of an egg over the top and brown slightly in the oven, and send to table hot.

Spiced Veal.—One pound of veal, chopped very fine; season with two well-beaten eggs, a tablespoonful of butter, teaspoonful of salt and sage each. Put it into a cake-pan, and bake about an hour. Slice when cold.

Mint Sauce for Lamb.—Two full tablespoons of very finely-chopped young mint, one of pounded and sifted loaf-sugar, and six of the best vinegar. Stir all these ingredients together until the sugar is dissolved.

Delicious Flavor to Lamb.—To give a delicious flavor to lamb which is to be eaten cold, put in the water in which it is boiled whole cloves and long sticks of cinnamon. To one leg of lamb allow one small handful of cloves, two or three sticks of cinnamon. If the lamb is to be roasted, boil the cloves and cinnamon in water, and baste the lamb with it.

Fillet of Veal Boiled.—Bind it round with tape, put it in a floured cloth, and in cold water; boil very gently two hours and a half, or if simmered, which is, perhaps, the better way, four hours will be taken; it may be sent to table in bechamel or with oyster-sauce. Care should be taken to keep it as white as possible.

Cold Tongue on Toast.—Take cold smoked tongue or ham; mince or grate fine, mix it with the beaten yelks of eggs and cream or milk, with a dash of cayenne pepper; prepare thin, small, square pieces of buttered toast; place on a heated platter, putting a spoonful of the meat on each piece; cover with dish cover, and send to table hot; for breakfast or lunch.

Veal Sausages.—Take fat bacon and lean veal in equal quantities, with a handful of sage, a little salt, pepper, and, if at hand, an anchovy. Let all be chopped and beaten well together, floured, rolled, and fried. Veal sausages are better suited for persons whose digestion is not very strong than those made of pork.

Excellent Tea Dish.—A delicious dish for tea or lunch is made thus: On a very fine wire gridiron (or one made of wire net used for screens), place some slices of salt pork, cut as thin as possible; on each slice lay a good sized oyster, or two small ones; broil and serve hot. This, with coffee, crisp toast, with chopped cabbage, makes an almost ideal lunch.

A Good Breakfast Dish.—A good dish for breakfast is made by chopping pieces of cold boiled or fried ham just as fine as it is possible to chop them; mix them with cold mashed potatoes, an egg or two, a little butter or cream, or both, form into balls, flour them, melt a little butter in a frying pan, and brown the balls. Serve hot.

Mutton Pie.—Take the mutton chops from the forequarter, season highly with pepper and salt and put into a baking dish with alternate layers of apples, pared and sliced, and a little sprinkling of chopped onion. Put a crust of not very rich pastry over the top, and bake for twenty or thirty minutes in a hot oven.

To Cook a Duck.—To cook a duck satisfactorily, boil it first until tender; this can be determined by trying the wing, as that is always a tough part of a fowl. When tender, take it out, rinse it in clean water, stuff and put in the oven for about three-quarters of an hour, basting it often.

Pressed Chicken.—Boil two chickens tender, take out the bones and chop the meat fine, add a small handful of bread crumbs, season to taste, with butter, pepper, salt, and a little sage; pour in enough of the liquor to make it moist; mold in any shape you choose, and, when cold, cut in slices.

Scrambled Mutton.—Three cups of cold boiled mutton chopped fine, three tablespoonfuls of hot water, one-fourth of a cup of butter; put on the stove, and when hot break in four eggs and stir constantly until thick. Season with pepper and salt.

The Right Way to Cook Steak.—Broil steak without salting. Salt draws the juice in cooking. It is desirable to keep this in if possible. Cook over a hot fire, turning frequently, searing on both sides. Place on a platter. Salt and pepper to taste.

Boiled Tongue.—If the tongue is not hard, soak it not more than three hours. Put it into a stewpan with plenty of cold water and a bunch of herbs; let it come to a boil, skim and simmer gently until tender, peel off the skin and garnish it with parsley and lemon.

Frizzled Beef.—Chip the beef as thin as paper with a very sharp knife. Melt in a frying-pan butter the size of an egg, stir the beef about in it for two or three minutes, dust in a little flour, add half a teacup of rich cream, boil and serve in a covered dish.

Roasted Tongue.—Soak for two hours; sprinkle salt over it, and drain in a colander; this should be done with fresh tongues before using; boil it slowly for two hours; take off the skin, roast, and baste with butter. Serve with brown gravy and currant jelly sauce.

Spiced Beef.—Five pounds of the shank, boiled five hours, with celery seed. Drain off the gelatine, and then chop the meat very fine, add pepper and salt to taste, and put it into a cloth on a platter. Cover with the cloth and press it.

Broiled Ham.—Cut into thin slices, pour boiling water over them, letting it remain ten minutes. Wipe the ham a little and place it on the gridiron; this takes out the salt. Ham that has been boiled broils nicer than the uncooked meat.

Liver Fried as Cutlets.—One egg to one pound of liver; have the liver cut thin; scald; wipe dry with a towel; beat up the egg; dip the liver in the egg, then into powdered cracker; fry brown. This is very nice; serve with tomatoes, if preferred.

A Good Way to Cook Liver.—A good way to cook liver is to fry it in butter, with an onion cut in small pieces scattered over it. Cook slowly; when done, add a lump of butter and a little flour; stir well, and turn over the liver. Serve with Saratoga potatoes.

Fish.

Oyster Omelet.—Twelve oysters, if large, double the number if small; six eggs, one cup of milk, one tablespoonful of butter, chopped parsley, salt and pepper; chop the oysters very fine; beat the yelks and whites of the eggs separately, as for nice cake, the whites until they stand in a heap. Put three tablespoonfuls of butter in a frying-pan, and heat while you are mixing the omelet. Stir the milk in a deep dish, with the yelks and seasoning. Next add the chopped oysters, heating them well as you add gradually. When thoroughly mixed pour in melted butter, and finally whip in the whites as lightly as possible. Have the butter in the pan very hot, and pour in the mixture. Do not stir it, but when it begins to stiffen, slip a broad-bladed knife around the sides and cautiously under the omelet, that the butter may reach every part. As soon as the center is fairly set, and the bottom brown, turn out into a hot dish. Lay the dish bottom upward over the frying-pan, which must be turned upside down dexterously. This brings the brown side of the omelet uppermost. This is a delicious breakfast or supper omelet.

Fish Chowder.—Take a cod or haddock weighing about four pounds; skin it, cut in small pieces and wash in cold water; take one-fourth pound (scant) of salt pork, cut in pieces and fry brown in the kettle in which the chowder is to be made; pare and slice five medium-sized potatoes and one small onion; place a layer of potato and onion in the kettle; then a layer of fish, dredge in salt, pepper and flour; put in alternate layers until all is used; add hot water enough to cover, and boil gently thirty minutes; add one pint of milk, six crackers split and dipped in cold water; then cook ten minutes longer.

Spiced Oysters.—For 200 oysters, take one pint vinegar, one grated nutmeg, eight blades of whole mace, three dozen whole cloves, one teaspoonful salt, two teaspoonfuls whole allspice, and as much red pepper as will lie on the point of a knife; put the oysters, with their liquor, into a large earthen vessel; add vinegar and all other ingredients; stir well together and set over a slow fire; keep covered; stir them several times to the bottom; as soon as they are well scalded they are done; put into jars; if a larger quantity is made it can be kept for a long time; of course these are eaten cold.

Fried Oysters.—Use for frying the largest and best oysters you can get. Take them from the liquor, lay them in rows upon a clean cloth and press another lightly upon them to absorb the moisture; have ready some beaten eggs and some cracker dust. Heat enough butter in the pan to cover the oysters. Dip each one in the egg first, then into the cracker, rolling it over, that it may be completely covered. Drop them into the frying-pan and fry quickly to a light brown. Do not let them remain in the pan an instant after they are done. Serve dry, on a hot dish.

Broiled Oysters.—Choose large, fat oysters; wipe them very dry; sprinkle them with salt and pepper, and broil upon one of the gridirons with close bars, sold for the purpose; you can dredge the oysters with flour if you wish to have them brown, and many persons fancy the juices are better preserved in that way; butter the gridiron well, and let your fire be hot and clear; broil quickly and dish hot, putting a bit of butter upon each oyster as it is taken from the gridiron.

Codfish with Cream.—Pick out carefully in flakes all the flesh from the remnants of some boiled codfish; melt a piece of butter in a saucepan, and add to it a large pinch of flour and a gill of milk or cream, with pepper, salt, and grated nutmeg to taste, also the least bit of cayenne; stir well; put in the fish, and gently shake it in this sauce until quite warm. If the composition be too dry, add a little milk or cream; then add, off the fire, the yelks of two eggs, beaten up with a little milk, and serve.

Broiled Salmon.—The middle slice of salmon is the best. Sew up neatly in a mosquito-net bag, and boil a quarter of an hour to the pound in hot, salted water. When done, unwrap with care, and lay upon a hot dish, taking care not to break it. Have ready a large cup of drawn butter, very rich, in which has been stirred a tablespoonful of minced parsley and the juice of a lemon. Pour half upon the salmon, and serve the rest in a boat. Garnish with parsley and sliced eggs.

Oyster Patty.—Scald the oysters in their own liquor, beard them, drain them perfectly dry, and flour and fry them lightly in butter. Take each oyster separately with a fork and put them into a stewpan, strain the liquor in which you have scalded the oysters into the butter and flour that remains in the frying pan, stir well together, and season with a little pepper, salt and a little juice of lemon; pour the whole on the oysters, and let them stew. When nearly done thicken with a small quantity of butter rolled in flour, and fill your patties.

Salmon Croquettes.—Mix the fish thoroughly with an equal quantity of boiled rice, adding a little melted butter, and salt and pepper to taste. Mold into small sausage-shaped forms, and roll them first in finely-powdered crackers, then in beaten egg yelk, and again in the cracker crumbs. Fry in hot fat like doughnuts. A palatable, nutritious food, easily prepared, and as the egg prevents the entrance of much fat they are readily digestible.

Clams with Cream.—Chop fifty small clams, not too fine, and season with pepper and salt. Put into a stewpan butter the size of an egg, and when it bubbles sprinkle in a teaspoonful of flour, which cook a few minutes; stir gradually into it the clam liquor, then the clams, which stew about two or three minutes; then add a cup of boiling cream, and serve immediately.

Baked Bluefish.—Chop up an onion and fry it in butter; then add half a pound of soft, fine bread crumbs, a tablespoonful of fresh butter, a little chopped parsley, pepper, salt, and a few drops of lemon. After cooking a very little, take it up and add a well-beaten egg. Stuff your bluefish with this. Serve the fish with a drawn butter sauce having a little finely-chopped pickled asparagus in it.

Deviled Crabs.—Boil your hard crabs, and take out the meat and mince it. Grate two ounces of bread crumbs and mix with them two hard-boiled eggs chopped fine, some cayenne, salt, and lemon juice. Add all this to six ounces of the crab meat, make moist and rich with cream, clean the shells, fill them with the mixture, and put some bread crumbs over the top, and brown in a hot oven.

Crab Sauce.—Mix about two or three ounces of butter with a little flour, and melt it in about a pint of milk. Stir it over the fire for a few minutes. Pick the meat from a fine boiled crab, chop it into small pieces, season it with a little cayenne, powdered mace and salt, and stir it into the melted butter and milk. Then warm it gradually and simmer for a minute or two, but do not let it boil.

Panned Clams.—Allow one patty-pan with nearly upright sides to each person. Cut stale bread in rounds to fit the bottom of each pan, butter it, and wet with clam liquor. Fill each pan nearly full of clams, pepper and salt them, and lay a bit of butter on each. Put them in a dripping-pan, cover with another, and bake till the edges curl—about ten minutes. Serve in the pans.

Codfish Balls.—Boil and pick the codfish. Boil potatoes, mash well, mix with them a piece of butter, season with pepper and salt, and add cream enough to moisten them. Mix codfish and potatoes together in like proportion, and add three or four chopped hard-boiled eggs, and a little finely-minced onion. Make into cakes and fry in boiling lard,

Oyster Toast.—Toast white bread nicely, then place oysters with their juice on the fire; as soon as boiling remove, take out the oysters, set the juice back again and stir in a large tablespoonful of butter rubbed with a little flour, let this boil five minutes, remove, then add the yelks of two eggs, pepper, salt, a little chopped parsley, and the oysters, which have been pounded fine; use the mixture to spread over toast; set in the oven to heat thoroughly.

How to Cook Clams.—Take one dozen clams—open, saving juice and meat—chop the meat fine. Take six eggs, mixing the whites and the yelks; then mix the clams (juice and meat) with the eggs, and cook over a *slow fire*, stirring constantly till the mixture has the consistency of stiff cream. Take off and serve—a dish fit for a king.

Fish Croquettes.—Take one pint of any cold white fish, flake it very fine, remove all bones and pieces of skin; season it highly with salt, pepper, cayenne and onion juice. Let the taste decide, but remember that fish needs more than meat. Moisten the fish with one cup thick cream sauce.

Clam Cakes.—Make a batter of one egg, beaten light, with one cup of milk, two and one-half cups of flour, and a little salt; beat well together and then stir in lightly three dozen clams that have been washed and drained, and drop in hot fat with a tablespoonful of batter, and one or two clams in each spoonful, fry brown and drain in a colander. Serve immediately.

Cornish Fish Pie.—In Cornwall almost every kind of fish is put into a pie, well floured over, with a little chopped parsley and onions, a little pepper and salt, some broth or water, and a nice short crust over it; there is a hole left in the crust at the top, and through this hole some cream is poured in just before serving.

Pickled Oysters.—Open the oysters, and take each one away from its liquor; boil some vinegar, equal quantities, with the liquor of the oysters; put in some whole mace; drop the oysters into the boiling liquor, and lift them speedily from the fire; then bottle them. This method keeps the oysters from shriveling.

To Broil Smoked Halibut.—Select halibut of a dark-brown color, the thinnest and hardest; soak twenty-four hours in cold water, with the flesh side down; only cover with water; broil over hot coals; serve with a little butter, or poach eggs and dish them with the halibut as if for ham.

Clam Soup.—Twenty-five clams, opened raw and chopped fine; add three quarts of water; boil them one-half hour, then add a pint of milk, one onion chopped fine, thicken with butter and flour, beat three eggs in the tureen, and pour your broth over them boiling hot.

Broiled Mackerel.—Split down the back and clean; be careful to scrape all the thin black skin from the inside. Wipe dry and lay on a greased gridiron; broil on one side brown, and then on the other side. The side that has the skin on should be turned to the fire last.

Oyster Macaroni.—Boil macaroni in a cloth, to keep it straight. Put a layer in a dish seasoned with butter, salt, and pepper, then a layer of oysters, alternate, until the dish is full. Mix some grated bread with a beaten egg. Spread over the top and bake.

Oyster Loaf.—Cut a round piece five inches across from the top of a nicely-baked round loaf of bread; remove the crumbs, leaving the crust half an inch thick; make a rich oyster stew and put it in the loaf in layers, sprinkled with bread crumbs; place the cover over the top, cover the loaf with the beaten yelk of an egg and put it in the oven to glaze; serve very hot.

Sauce Piquante for Fish.—Make a brown sauce by frying a chopped onion in a little butter, adding a large teaspoonful of flour and a tumbler of stock. Simmer a little, strain, and put in a teaspoonful of vinegar, one of chopped cucumber pickle, and one of capers.

Fish Sauce. Take half a pint of milk and cream together, two eggs, well beaten, salt, a little pepper, and the juice of half a lemon; put it over the fire, and stir it constantly until it begins to thicken.

Vegetables.

Boiling Potatoes.—To boil a potato well requires more attention than is usually given. They should be well washed and left standing in cold water an hour or two, to remove the black liquor with which they are impregnated, and a brackish taste they would otherwise have. They should not be pared before boiling; they lose much of the starch by so doing, and are made insipid. Put them into a kettle of clear cold water, with a little salt, cover closely, and boil rapidly, using no more water than will just cover them, as they produce a considerable quantity of fluid themselves while boiling, and too much water will make them heavy. As soon as *just* done instantly pour off the water, set them back on the range, and leave the cover off the saucepan till the steam has evaporated. They will then, if a good kind, be dry and mealy. This is an Irish receipt, and a good one.

Snap Beans and Potatoes.—Snap some beans and parboil them; then pour into a colander and let the water drain off. Take several potatoes, peel, and cut into small pieces; put into a saucepan a spoonful of lard and an onion cut up small, the potatoes, and last, the snap beans. If you have any beef broth, pour just enough into the skillet to cover the beans; if not, use boiling water; season with salt and pepper; let it boil till the potatoes are done. Should there be any broth, pour it off; add a piece of butter the size of a walnut and dredge a little flour over the beans; mix thoroughly by stirring, and let it simmer a few minutes longer, then remove from the fire.

To Cook Asparagus.—Scrape the stalks till they are clean; throw them into a pan of cold water, tie them up in bundles of about a quarter of a hundred each; cut off the stalks at the bottom all of a length, leaving enough to serve as a handle for the green part; put them into a stew pan of boiling water, with a handful of salt in it. Let it boil and skim it. When they are tender at the stalk, which will be in from twenty to thirty minutes, they are done enough. Watch the exact time of their becoming tender; take them up that instant. While the asparagus is boiling, toast a slice of bread about half an inch thick; brown it delicately on both sides; dip it lightly in the liquor the asparagus was boiled in, and lay it in the middle of a dish; melt some butter, but do not put it over them. Serve with butter.

Asparagus with Eggs.—This dainty luncheon-dish is made of whatever asparagus may be left over from the previous day. Supposing there are a dozen heads of asparagus, cut the green part into pieces the size of peas, melt an ounce of butter in a saucepan, add a tablespoonful of cream or milk, a tablespoonful of gravy, a little pepper and salt, and three well-beaten eggs. Throw in the asparagus, stir the eggs quickly over the fire for half a minute till they are set, and pour the mixture neatly upon slices of bread which have been dipped in boiling water and buttered.

Stewed Cucumbers.—Cut the cucumbers fully half an inch thick right through; put them in a saucepan, just covering them with hot water, and let them boil slowly for a quarter of an hour, or until tender, but not so as to break them, then drain them; you want now a pint of good cream, and put your cream with a teaspoonful of butter, in a saucepan, and when it is warm pop in the cucumbers, season with a little salt and white pepper, cook five minutes, shaking the saucepan all the time, and serve hot. It is just as delicate as asparagus, and a very nice dish, indeed.

Stuffed Turnips.—Peel and boil in boiling water well salted a quart of medium-sized turnips; as soon as they are tender drain them, cut a slice from the top of each, scoop out half the middle with a teaspoon, mash the part taken out, with a little salt, pepper, butter and the yelk of an egg, and fill the turnips with the mixture; put on each one the slice cut from the top, brush them over with the beaten white of an egg, set them in a baking dish and brown them in a hot oven. Serve them hot.

Macaroni.—People who like macaroni will find pleasure in eating it when prepared in this way: Boil it until it is tender, taking care to preserve the shape so far as possible. When it is done drain off all the water and pour over it a little sweet milk, with a lump of butter and plenty of pepper and salt. While the macaroni is boiling, cook in a separate saucepan enough tomatoes to make a pint when stewed. When the macaroni is ready for the table, pour the tomatoes over it; serve hot.

Stuffed Egg Plant.—Cut them in half lengthwise, and parboil them in salted water; scoop out most of the inside and pound this to a paste in the mortar with a little fat bacon and some mushrooms previously chopped up, a little onion also chopped, pepper and salt to taste, and a little crumb of bread soaked in stock. Fill each half with this mixture, lay them in a well buttered tin and bake for about a quarter of an hour.

Stuffed Squash.—Pare a small squash and cut off a slice from the top; extract the seeds and lay one hour in salt water; then fill with a good stuffing of crumbs, chopped salt pork, parsley, etc., wet with gravy; put on the top slice; set the squash in a pudding dish; put in a few spoonfuls of melted butter and twice as much hot water in the bottom; cover the dish very closely and set in the oven two hours, or until tender; lay within a deep dish and pour the gravy over it.

Saratoga Potatoes.—Cut raw potatoes in slices as thin as wafers with a thin sharp knife; lay them in cold water over night, a bit of alum will make them more crisp; next morning rinse in cold water and dry with a towel. Have ready a kettle of lard, hotter than for fried cakes, and drop in the potatoes a few at a time. They will brown quickly, skim out in a colander and sprinkle with salt, or lay them on a double brown paper in the oven till dry. If any are left over from the meal, they can be warmed in the oven, and will be just as good for another time.

Baked Onions.—Peel ten large onions without breaking the layers; boil them for half an hour in well-salted boiling water, and drain them; when cool enough to handle cut a half-inch slice from the top of each, and take out a teaspoonful of the middle part; chop these pieces fine, mix them with half a cup of stale bread crumbs, a saltspoonful of salt, quarter of that quantity of pepper and the yelk of a raw egg; use this force meat to stuff the onions, lay them on a baking dish, brush them with the white of the egg beaten a little, dust them with fine bread crumbs and bake them slowly for forty minutes. Serve them hot.

Potato Dumplings.—Peel some potatoes and grate them into a basin of water; let the pulp remain in the water for a couple of hours, drain it off, and mix with it half its weight of flour; season with pepper, salt and chopped onions. If not moist enough add a little water. Roll into dumplings the size of a large apple, sprinkle them well with flour, and throw them into boiling water. When you observe them rising to the top of the saucepan, they will be boiled enough.

An Appetizing Entree.—Take cold boiled cabbage, chop it fine; for a medium-sized pudding dish full add two well-beaten eggs, a tablespoonful of butter, three tablespoonfuls of cream, with pepper and salt *ad libitum.* Butter the pudding dish, put the cabbage in and bake until brown. This may be eaten cold, but it is much better if served hot. It is especially good with roast pork or pork chops.

Fried Cauliflower.—Pick out all the green leaves from a cauliflower and cut off the stalk close. Put it, head downward, into a saucepan full of boiling, salted water. Do not over boil it. Drain it on a sieve, pick it out into small sprigs, and place them in a deep dish with plenty of vinegar, pepper and salt. When they have laid about an hour in this, drain them, dip them in batter, and fry in hot lard to a golden color.

Irish Stew.—This is the stew that is mostly made in Ireland. Put some slices of boiled corned beef (never fresh) into a stewpan with a good deal of water, or thin stock, two large onions sliced, and some cold boiled potatoes (whole) and a little pepper. Stew gently until the potatoes are quite soft and have taken up nearly all the gravy; some will break; but they should be as whole as possible. Turn all out on a flat dish and serve.

To Cook Spinach.—Boil spinach in the ordinary way; drain it and get off all the water; chop it just as finely as possible—it cannot be divided too much. Take a small onion, slice it very fine and brown it in butter; chop this fine and mix it with the spinach; have a teacup of milk, a tablespoonful of flour, a dessertspoonful of butter, some salt and pepper; stir in the spinach and cook about ten minutes.

Tomato Pie.—Peel and slice enough green tomatoes to fill one pie; to this allow four tablespoonfuls of vinegar, one of butter, and three and a half of sugar, flavor with nutmeg, bake with two crusts very slowly. If you choose you may stew the tomatoes first, and then there is no danger of the pie being too juicy.

Excellent Way to Cook Tomatoes.—A delicious dish (especially suitable with cutlets, steaks, broiled ham, or anything served without gravy) may be made by cutting tomatoes into thin slices, and grilling them over a sharp fire for ten minutes, or thereabouts; they should then be coated with a mixture of bread crumbs, fresh bu''er, mustard, salt, pepper and sugar (proportions according to taste), and returned to the gridiron, or put into a hot oven to crisp.

Baked Beets.—One of the most satisfactory ways to cook beets is to bake them; when boiled, even if their jackets are left on, a great deal of the best part of the beet is dissolved and so lost. It will, of course, take a little longer to bake than to boil them, but this is no objection; allow from fifteen to twenty minutes more for baking; slice them and eat as you would if they were boiled. One nice way to serve them is to chop them fine. After they are cooked season with pepper, salt and butter.

Lille Cabbage.—Wash a large cabbage, cut it in inch pieces, rejecting the stalk, and drain it in a colander. Meantime peel and chop an onion, fry it for one minute in two tablespoonfuls of drippings of butter, add the cabbage, with a teaspoonful of salt, and a quarter of a saltspoonful each of pepper and grated nutmeg, cover it, and simmer it for twenty minutes, stirring it frequently to prevent burning. Serve it hot.

Vegetable Hash.—Chop, not very fine, the vegetables left from a boiled dinner, and season them with salt and pepper. To each quart of the chopped vegetables add half a cup of stock and one tablespoonful of butter. Heat slowly in the frying-pan. Turn into a hot dish when done, and serve immediately. If vinegar is liked, two or more tablespoonfuls of it can be stirred into the hash while it is heating.

Baked Cabbage.—Boil a firm head for fifteen minutes, then change the water for more boiling water; boil till tender, drain and set aside to cool. Mince some boiled ham; mix with bread crumbs; add pepper, one tablespoonful of butter, and two eggs well beaten, and three tablespoonfuls of milk; chop cabbage very fine; mix all together, and bake in a pudding-dish till brown. Serve hot.

Succotash.—Cut the corn from eight or ten cobs; mix this with one-third the quantity of Lima beans, and cook one hour in just enough water to cover them. Drain off most of the water; add a cup of milk, with a pinch of soda stirred in. When this boils, stir in a great spoonful of butter rolled in flour, season with pepper and salt, and simmer ten minutes longer.

Potatoes a la Duchesse.—Take some cold, boiled potatoes, cut them into rounds, cutting with a cake cutter wet with cold water. Grease the bottom of a baking-pan and set the rounds in it in rows, but not touching one another, and bake quickly, first brushing them all over—except, of course, on the bottom—with beaten egg. When they commence to brown, lay a napkin, folded, upon a hot dish and range them regularly upon it.

Macaroni Cheese.—Boil two ounces of macaroni, then drain it well. Put into a saucepan one ounce of butter; mix it well with one tablespoonful of flour; moisten with four tablespoonfuls of veal stock and a gill of cream; add two ounces of grated cheese, some mustard, salt and cayenne to taste, put in the macaroni and serve as soon as it is well mixed with the sauce and quite hot.

Stewed Mushrooms.—Slice the mushrooms into halves. Stew ten minutes in a little butter seasoned with pepper and salt and a very little water.

Drain, put the mushrooms into a pie dish; break enough eggs to cover them over the top; pepper, salt and scatter bits of butter over them; stew with bread crumbs and bake until the eggs are set. Serve in the dish.

Stewed Carrots. —Boil the carrots until they are half done, then scrape and cut into thick slices; put them into a stewpan with as much milk as will hardly cover them; a very little salt and pepper, and a small quantity of chopped parsley; simmer them until they are perfectly tender, but not broken. When nearly done add a piece of butter rolled in flour. Serve hot.

Potato Croquettes.—Take six boiled potatoes, pass them through a sieve; add to them three tablespoonfuls of ham, grated or minced finely, a little grated nutmeg, pepper and salt to taste, and some chopped parsley; work into this mixture the yelks of three or four eggs, then fashion it into the shape of balls, roll them in bread crumbs, and fry in hot lard, and serve with fried parsley.

Imitation Duck.—Boil two onions until nearly soft; then chop them fine, and mix with pieces of stale bread crusts that have been soaked awhile in cold water or milk. Add a little powdered sage, some pepper and some salt. Grease a baking tin, put the mixture in, and strew over the top some grated bread and bits of butter. Bake it for half an hour and serve for breakfast, or a side dish at dinner.

Potatoes Fried Whole.—When nearly boiled enough, put small potatoes into a stewpan with butter, or beef dripping; shake them about to prevent burning, till they are brown and crisp; drain them from the fat. It will be an improvement if they are floured and dipped in the yelk of an egg, and then rolled in finely-sifted bread crumbs. This is the ordinary French method.

Scalloped Squash.—Boil and mash the squash in the customary way and let it cool; beat the yelks of two eggs, and when the squash is nearly cold, whip these into it, with three tablespoonfuls of milk, one of butter rolled in flour and melted into the milk; pepper and salt to taste; pour into a buttered bake-dish, cover with fine crumbs, and bake to a light brown in a quick oven. To be eaten hot.

Potato Pie.—Peel and grate one large white potato into a dish, add the juice and rind of one lemon, the beaten white of one egg, one teacup of white sugar, one cup cold water; pour this into a nice under crust and bake; when done have ready the beaten whites of three eggs, half cup powdered sugar, flavor with lemon, spread on the pie and return to the oven to harden.

A Delicious Dish.—Take a large fresh cabbage and cut out the heart. Fill the place with stuffing, or veal chopped very fine, and highly seasoned, rolled into balls with yelk of egg. Then tie the cabbage firmly together and boil in a kettle for two hours. It makes a very delicious dish, and it is often useful for using small pieces of meat.

Haricot Beans.—Soak half a pint of the small white beans over night in just enough cold water to cover them; the next day boil two hours, strain and put in a pie-dish with one-half ounce of butter, a teaspoonful of finely-chopped parsley, previously fried; cover with slices of raw bacon, and bake a quarter of an hour.

Potatoes Fried with Butter.—Nicely wash and pare some floury potatoes; cut each into any form you fancy, such as a large lozenge, etc.; then thinly slice them, so that the pieces may be of a uniform shape; dip them into either a sweet or savory batter, fry them in plenty of butter, and serve them quite hot, with either salt or pounded loaf-sugar strewn upon them.

Scalloped Tomatoes.—Pare and slice; scatter fine crumbs in the bottom of a bake-dish; cover with slices of tomatoes, seasoned with sugar, pepper, salt and butter; cover with crumbs and then with tomatoes; fill the dish in this order, covering all with crumbs, with bits of butter sprinkled upon them. Bake, covered, half an hour, and brown.

Celery Sauce.—Pick and wash two heads of celery, cut them into pieces an inch long, and stew them in a pint of water and a teaspoonful of salt until the celery is tender. Rub a large tablespoonful of butter and a spoonful of flour well together; stir this into a pint of cream, put in the celery, and let it boil up once. Serve hot with boiled poultry.

Fried Potatoes.—The French method of cooking potatoes affords a most agreeable dish. The potatoes are peeled, wiped, and cut into thin slices, and thrown into a frying-pan containing an abundance of hot lard. As soon as they become brown and crispy, they are thrown in a colander to drain them; then sprinkle with salt, and serve hot.

Onions and Tomatoes.—A side dish, which will be new to many cooks, is made by slicing very thin some onions and green tomatoes, in about equal proportions, and frying them together just as you fry onions alone. Salt them well, and, if there is any danger of their being greasy, drain before serving.

Sauce Robert.—Put two medium-sized onions, chopped very fine, with a large lump of butter, in a stew-pan; let them brown well, constantly stirring; add a teaspoonful of flour mixed with half a pint of good stock; salt and pepper; cook about five minutes; add a teaspoonful of mixed mustard and one of vinegar.

Tomato and Onion Omelet.—Take equal parts of sliced onions and tomatoes, peeled and freed from pips, chop them both coarsely. Fry the onions in butter. When cooked, without being colored, add the tomatoes, with pepper and salt, and stir the mixture on the fire. Make a plain omelet in the usual way, and insert this in the fold on dishing it.

Scalloped Onions.—Boil, till tender, six large onions. Take them up, drain and separate them; put a layer of bread or biscuit-crumbs in a pudding-dish, then a layer of onions alternately, until the dish is full. Season with pepper and salt, add a little butter, moisten with milk, and brown half an hour in the oven.

Baked Cauliflower.—Put cauliflower to soak in salted water for an hour or more; look over carefully; remove the hard stalks and leaves; scald for five minutes; cut into pieces and put into a pie-dish; add a little milk, and season with pepper, salt and butter; cover the whole with dry grated cheese and bake.

Green Corn-Cakes.—Cut the corn from the cob and stir it into a graham batter made with sweet milk; fry, and serve hot with melted butter.

Scalloped Potatoes.—Pare the potatoes, cover the bottom of a baking-dish with bread crumbs, then add a layer of sliced potatoes, then bits of butter, salt and pepper, fill the dish with the alternate layers, wet the whole with milk, and bake the whole for an hour and a half.

Lima Beans with Cream.—Put a pint of the shelled beans into just enough boiling salted water to cover them, and boil them tender; then drain off the water; add a cup of boiling milk (or better, cream), a little piece of butter, pepper and salt. Let the beans simmer a minute in the milk before serving.

Corn with Tomatoes.—Cut the corn from the cob and put it with an equal quantity of tomatoes that have been sliced and peeled; stew these together for half an hour; then season to taste with salt and pepper and a little sugar; stir in a liberal piece of butter and simmer a few minutes longer.

Browned Potatoes.—Steam or boil small-sized potatoes, peel and place them in a stewpan with some melted butter, shake occasionally, and when all are well browned serve upon thin slices of toast which have been dipped in Chili sauce that has been thinned with a little weak vinegar.

Tomato Sauce.—Pare, slice and stew the tomatoes for twenty minutes. Strain and rub through a colander, leaving the hard and tough parts behind. Put into a sauce-pan with a little minced onion, parsley, pepper, salt and sugar. Bring to a boil; stir in a good spoonful of butter rolled in flour. Boil up and serve.

Baked Tomatoes for Breakfast.—Take a quart of cold stewed tomatoes, beat into it two eggs, two tablespoonfuls of bread crumbs, a tablespoonful of chopped parsley, a little more salt and pepper, and bake for twenty minutes in a quick oven.

Potato Snow.—Take large white potatoes and boil them in their skins until tender, drain and dry them near the fire, and peel; put a hot dish before the fire and rub the potatoes through a coarse sieve into it; do not touch afterwards or the flakes will fall; serve immediately.

Potato Puffs.—Take any outside slices of cold meat, chop and season with pepper, salt and cut pickles. Mash potatoes, making them into paste with an egg; roll cut with a dust of flour; cut round with a saucer. Put the seasoned meat on one-half and fold like a puff. Fry a light brown.

Potato Fritters.—Grate six cold boiled potatoes, add to them one pint of cream or new milk, and flour enough to make as stiff a batter as for other fritters, the yelk of three eggs, then the beaten whites, salt, and fry in sweet butter.

Fried Egg Plant.—Peel and parboil five minutes, cut slices crosswise, season with pepper and salt, roll the slices in the beaten egg, then in fine bread crumbs (or they may be dipped in batter); fry a light brown in hot lard.

Horseradish Sauce.—Grate the horseradish, boil an egg hard, pound the yelk, and add to the above a little raw cream, mustard and vinegar added the last thing. It must all be mixed cold and then heated.

Potato Balls.—Mash boiled potatoes; add butter, size of an egg, two spoonfuls of milk, a little salt; stir it well; roll with your hands into balls; roll them in egg and crumbs; fry them in hot fat, or brown in the oven.

To Prepare Potatoes for Breakfast.—A nice way to prepare potatoes for breakfast is to cut cold boiled ones in square pieces, and dip them in beaten egg, and put them on a buttered pie-plate in the oven; when they are hot and brown send them to the table.

Green Corn Pudding.—Take twelve ears of sweet corn, grated, one and one-half pints of milk, four well-beaten eggs, and one and-half teacups of sugar. Mix the above. Bake it for two hours in a buttered dish.

Cauliflower Omelet.—Take the white part of a boiled cauliflower; after it is cold chop it very small and mix with it a sufficient quantity of well-beaten egg to make a very thick batter.

Tomato Toast.—Prepare the tomatoes as for sauce, and while they are cooking toast some slices of bread very brown, but not burned; butter them on both sides, and pour the tomato sauce over them.

Tomatoes Fried.—Do not pare them, cut in slices; dip in pounded crackers sifted. Fry in butter.

Salads and Relishes.

Fine Cucumber Pickles.—Make a brine that will bear an egg, and drop in the cucumbers; cover them with grape leaves; weight them down, and let them stand ten or more days. Then take them out, drain well, and soak a day or two in plenty of clear water, frequently changed. Afterward put them in a kettle with grape and cabbage leaves and a lump of alum. Cover with weak vinegar, and let them stand until they turn green. Then take out, drain, and put into stone jars. For each three gallons of pickles use one gallon of cider vinegar, and place into it one ounce each of mace and celery seed, two ounces of ginger, three ounces each of cloves and stick cinnamon, four ounces each of mustard seed (black and white mixed), choice black pepper and allspice, two tablespoonfuls of ground mustard, a handful of chopped horseradish, two pods of red pepper, four onions, and two pounds of sugar. Boil, and pour it hot over the pickles. More sugar can be added to suit the taste. Cover the jar very closely, and expose to the sun every day during hot weather.

Egg Pickle.—Obtain a moderate-sized, wide-mouthed earthen jar, sufficient to hold one dozen eggs; let the latter be boiled quite hard; when fully done, place the same, after taking them up, into a pan of cold water. Remove the shells from them, and deposit them carefully in the jar. Have on the fire a quart (or more, if necessary) of good white wine vinegar, into which introduce one ounce of raw ginger, two or three blades of sweet mace, one ounce of allspice, half an ounce of whole black pepper and salt, and half an ounce of mustard seed, with four cloves of garlic. When it has simmered for half an hour, take it up and pour the contents into the jar, taking care to observe that the eggs are wholly covered. When quite cold, stopper it down for use. It will be ready after a month. When cut into quarters they serve as a garnish, and afford a nice relish to cold meat of any kind.

Delicious Beet Salad.—Boil some Bermuda beets and set them on ice to get thoroughly cold. If they are large they will take many hours of boiling, and must be cooked neither too long nor too quickly—in either case they will be tough and hard. Cut them up in small, not too thick, slices, add some nicely-sliced cold potatoes, and a shred or two of onion—just enough to flavor the salad. Now dress it with plain French dressing of much oil, a little vinegar, salt and pepper. Arrange it in your salad dish, and having chopped finely a hard-boiled egg, arrange it over the salad, leaving a rim of almost an inch and a half uncovered. On this rim arrange sprigs of the small watercress. With the deep red of the beets showing through the delicate green of the cress and the white and yellow of the egg, the salad looks beautifully, and it tastes so deliciously that it can never go begging. The Bermuda beets must be used, as they are the sweetest and richest. Some people add a little raw sliced apple—the fruit must be tart and soft.

Celery Salad.—Take three bunches of celery, chop fine in a chopping bowl, sprinkle over it salt and a little pepper, then beat up one egg in a saucepan, add half teacup of vinegar, two tablespoonfuls of sugar, and four tablespoonfuls of salad dressing; stir it altogether and when it comes to a boil put in the celery and let it all boil for about five minutes, stirring constantly, then put it into a dish and have an egg boiled hard, which cut in slices and lay over the top; garnish around the edge with the tops of the celery. It is best when cold. I make chicken salad the same way, by taking as much chicken as celery, and a little more vinegar and salad.

Potato Salad.—To one pint mashed potatoes (those left over from dinner are just right), add the smoothly-rubbed yelks of three hard-boiled eggs, reserving the whites cut in transverse slices to garnish the dish; slice one cucumber pickle, one teaspoonful ground mustard, pepper and salt to taste; heat one teacup good vinegar, dissolving in it a lump of butter the size of a walnut; pour the vinegar over the pickle and seasoning, and add the mashed potatoes by degrees, rubbing and incorporating thoroughly. We think you will find it an agreeable addition to the table.

Chicken Salad.—Cut the meat from two chickens, or one if you want a small dish. Add an equal quantity of shred lettuce, after you have cut the chickens into narrow shreds two inches long. Mix in a bowl. Prepare a dressing thus: Beat the yelks of two eggs, salt lightly and beat in, a few drops at a time, four tablespoonfuls of oil; then, as gradually, three teaspoonfuls of hot vinegar and half a teaspoonful of best celery essence. The mixture should be thick as cream; pour over the chicken, mix well and lightly, put into a salad dish and lay sections of two hard-boiled eggs on top, with a chain of sliced whites around the edge.

Pickled Cauliflower.—Take half a dozen small heads of cauliflower and break them into sprigs; then boil them in enough salt and water to cover them; let them scald until a sprig from the broom can be run through them, or a fork will pierce them easily; then skim out into jars and make a pickle of one gallon of vinegar, half a pound of brown sugar, one ounce of unground pepper, half an ounce of cloves, one ounce of white mustard seed, one ounce of celery seed and one ounce of turmeric; boil all together for twenty minutes, and pour while very hot over the cauliflower; cover closely and it will keep all winter.

Tomato Catsup.—Cut one peck of ripe tomatoes in halves, boil them in a lined saucepan until the pulp is all dissolved, then strain them well through a hair sieve and set the liquor on to boil, adding one ounce of salt, one ounce of mace, one tablespoonful of black pepper, one teaspoonful of red pepper, one tablespoonful of ground cloves, five of ground mustard; let them all boil together for five or six hours, and stir them most of the time. Let the mixture stand eight or ten hours in a cool place, and add one pint of vinegar, and then bottle it; seal the corks and keep in a cool, dark place.

How to Dress Salad.—Take one-half a lemon and rub the inside of the salad bowl. Rub the yelks of two hard-boiled eggs, mashing them with a wooden spoon smooth; mix with them a tablespoonful of water and two tablespoonfuls of sweet oil. Add by slow degrees a saltspoonful of salt, a teaspoonful of mustard and a teaspoonful of powdered sugar. When these are all blended evenly pour in three tablespoonfuls of vinegar. Have your lettuce quite fresh and crisp, and picked over nicely; place in the salad bowl; do not stir it around, as that would cause it to wilt. Decorate the top of it with boiled red beet, cut in different forms, and the hard boiled whites of your eggs.

Asparagus Pickled.—Cut and wash the green heads of the largest asparagus; let them lie two or three hours in cold water; scald them very carefully in salt and water, then lay them on a cloth to cool; make a pickle according to the quantity of your asparagus, of white wine vinegar and salt, and boil it. To a gallon of pickle put two nutmegs, a quarter of an ounce of mace, the same of whole white pepper, and pour the pickle hot over them; cover the jar with a thick cloth, and let it stand a week, then boil the pickle; when it has stood another week, boil it a third time, and when cold cover the jar close.

Lobster Salad.—Eight eggs, one pint vinegar, four tablespoonfuls melted butter or sweet oil, one tablespoonful mixed mustard, one tablespoonful salt, one teaspoonful black pepper; mix altogether, put it over the fire to cook. Do not let it boil, it will thicken when done; stir constantly. Chop the lobster not fine, and lettuce the same, mix, but not till about time for eating. Add as much of the dressing as seems necessary to make the salad creamy, and then spread a little over the whole. The dressing will keep bottled a long time. It is nice with any meats.

Cauliflower Salad.—Boil a cauliflower in salted water till tender, but not overdone; when cool, cut it up neatly in small sprigs. Beat up together three tablespoonfuls of oil, and one tablespoonful of Tarragon vinegar, with pepper and salt to taste; rub the dish very slightly with garlic, arrange the pieces of cauliflower in it, strew over them some capers, a little Tarragon, chervil, and parsley all finely minced, and the least bit of dried thyme and marjoram powdered. Pour the oil and vinegar over, and serve.

Tomato Salad.—Tomato salad is an agreeable entree, and goes well with almost any dinner, but particularly well with fried or roast meats. To half a dozen medium-sized tomatoes, with the skins removed and the tomatoes sliced, add the yelks of two hard-boiled eggs, also one raw egg, well beaten and mixed with a tablespoonful of melted butter, a teaspoonful of sugar, with cayenne pepper and salt to suit the taste. When all these are mixed thoroughly, add half a small cup of vinegar,

Herring Salad.—Soak two herrings over night; boil two quarts of potatoes with the skins on; when cold, peel and cut in dice; bone and skin the herrings and cut in dice; chop a large onion fine; mix all together with pepper and vinegar, enough to moisten. To be eaten with cream poured over. Serve on a large, flat dish, and garnish with hard-boiled eggs and beets cut in slices. (This is the Swedish way.)

Cabbage Salad.—One pint of good vinegar, four well-beaten eggs, half a cup of butter; put them on the fire, and stir constantly until the mixture begins to thicken; then add a tablespoonful of made mustard, two of salt, and one of black pepper; chop one head of cabbage very fine, with one bunch of celery, and soak in salt and water for two hours; drain and pour the dressing over it, and mix it. It will keep all winter in a cool place, if kept well covered. By mixing lobster or chicken with it, you will have a nice salad.

Something Nice.—Take the seeds out of green tomatoes, and cut the tomatoes in fine strips with scissors until you have six pounds of them. Add four or five good-sized bell peppers, green, after taking out the seeds and cutting fine. Add also two and a half pounds of white sugar and one quart of cider vinegar, a half ounce of cloves, and a small quantity of mace. Cook all about an hour, and you will have nice spiced tomatoes.

Sweet Cucumber Pickles.—Take ripe cucumbers, cut out the inside, pare, and slice in squares an inch or two long and one wide, as you fancy. Take seven pounds of this, boil in salt water until tender, then drain. In a porcelain kettle put one quart of vinegar, three pounds of sugar, one ounce cassia buds, one of cloves, one-half allspice. Boil together, then add the cucumber, and simmer all two hours.

German Salad.—Take six medium-sized cold potatoes, and slice thin, three good-sized sweet apples, also cut in small slices, four silver skinned onions chopped fine, and a little parsley cut in bits; dress these with two tablespoonfuls of oil, salt, pepper, sugar, and a little mustard and vinegar to blend the whole; beat it very light, and stir through the salad; garnish with hard-boiled eggs cut in rings.

Carrot Salad.—Wash and scrape tender, rich-colored carrots; throw them into fast-boiling water, and boil until soft; cut them into very thin slices; put them into a glass bowl, and sprinkle with sifted loaf sugar; add the juice of a large lemon, and a wineglassful of olive oil; garnish the dish with very thin slices of lemon, and any kind of green salad leaves.

Pickled Onions.—Peel small silver butter onions and throw them into a stew pan of boiling water; as soon as they look clear take them out with a strainer-ladle, place them on a folded cloth covered with another, and when quite dry put them into a jar and cover them with hot spiced vinegar. When quite cold pack them down and cover with a tight cover.

Winter Salad.—Chop very fine some nice cabbage with a little onion and celery; salt and pepper to taste; take the yelk of an egg and stir with a fork, and drop one drop at a time into some salad oil until the egg is quite thick; add four tablespoonfuls strong vinegar, one tablespoonful mustard. You must stir the egg very quickly while putting the oil and vinegar in. This is very nice when made right.

Ham Salad.—Take your fragment of cold boiled ham left after slicing, remove all dark and dry portions, also all the fat; mince evenly and fine; take enough rich, sweet cream to set the mince, a saltspoonful of strong, ground mustard, the same of fine sugar, and a good pinch of cayenne pepper; mix thoroughly with the ham; garnish with sprigs of parsley, and you have a nice dish for tea.

French Mustard.—Slice up an onion in a bowl; cover with good vinegar; leave two or three days; pour off vinegar into a basin; put into it one teaspoonful pepper, one of salt, one tablespoonful brown sugar, and mustard enough to thicken; smooth the mustard for vinegar as you would flour for gravy; mix all together; set on the stove and stir until it boils, when remove, and use it cold.

Spiced Apples.—Eight pounds of apples, pared and quartered; four pounds of sugar; one quart of vinegar, one ounce of thick cinnamon, one-half ounce cloves; boil the vinegar, sugar, and spice together; put in the apples while boiling, and let them remain until tender (about twenty minutes); then put the apples in a jar; boil down the syrup until thick, and pour over them.

To Pickle Red Cabbages.—Slice them into a sieve, and sprinkle each layer with salt. Let the whole drain three days; then add some sliced beet-root, and place the whole in a jar, over which pour boiling vinegar. The purple-red cabbage is the finest. Mace, bruised ginger, whole pepper, and cloves may be boiled with the vinegar, and will make a great improvement.

Cucumber Catsup.—Grate three dozen large cucumbers and twelve white onions; put three handfuls of salt over them. They must be prepared the day beforehand, and in the morning lay them to drain; soak a cup and a half of mustard seed, drain it and add to the cucumbers, with two spoonfuls of whole pepper; put them in a jar, cover with vinegar, and cork tight; keep in a dry place.

Salad Dessert.—Boil and mash a white potato, add the yelks of two hard-boiled eggs. While the potato is warm, beat all smoothly together, add melted butter or oil-prepared mustard, salt and vinegar to taste. The potato increases the quantity of dressing, and cannot be distinguished from eggs.

Pickled Oysters.—Select the largest oysters, drain off their liquor, and wash them in clear water; put them in a stew-pan with water proportioned to the number of oysters, some salt, blades of mace, and whole black pepper. Stew them a few minutes, then put them in a pot, and when cold, add as much pale vinegar as will give the liquor an agreeable acid.

Clover Vinegar.—Put a large bowl of molasses in a crock and pour over it nine bowls of boiling rainwater; let it stand until milk warm, put in two quarts of clover blossoms, and two cups of bakers' yeast; let it stand two weeks, and strain through a towel. Nothing will mold in it.

Salad Dressing.—Six tablespoonfuls of melted butter, six tablespoonfuls of cream, one teaspoonful of salt, half teaspoonful of pepper, one teaspoonful of ground mustard, one cup of vinegar; then add three eggs beaten to a foam, remove from the fire and stir.

Fruit Salad.—A new dish with which epicures tempt fate and give an impetus to stomach anodynes is composed of sliced oranges, sliced pine-apples, sliced bananas, sliced hard-boiled eggs, sliced cucumbers, vinegar and sugar. It is called a fruit salad.

Sweet Pickles.—Take eight pounds of green tomatoes and chop fine; add four pounds of brown sugar, and boil down three hours; add one quart of vinegar, a teaspoonful each of mace, cinnamon, and cloves, and boil about fifteen minutes. Let it cool, and put into jars or other vessel.

Chili Sauce.—Twelve ripe tomatoes, pared, two large peppers chopped fine, one large onion chopped fine, two teacups of vinegar, one tablespoon-ful salt, one cup brown sugar, one teaspoonful each of allspice, nutmeg, cloves, and ginger. Boil all together.

Currant Catsup.—To five pints of strained currants add three pounds of sugar, one pint of vinegar, and a tablespoonful of cinnamon, one of pep-per, one of cloves, one of allspice, one-half of salt; scald them well three-quarters of an hour; then put it in bottles and cork tight.

Grape Catsup.—Five pounds of grapes; boil and press through colan-der; two and a half pounds of sugar, one pint of vinegar, one tablespoonful each of cinnamon, cloves, allspice, and cayenne pepper, and half a table-spoonful of salt. Boil until the catsup is rather thick.

Preserved Tomatoes.—A pound of sugar to a pound of tomatoes. Take six pounds of each, the peel and juice of four lemons, and a quarter of a pound of ginger tied up in a bag. Boil very slowly for three hours.

Spiced Currants.—Three pounds of sugar to seven pounds of currants, one teaspoonful of cinnamon, one of cloves, one of allspice, pepper if desired. Boil half an hour, stirring enough to prevent burning. Spiced currants are especially good with meat.

Tomato Butter.—Sixteen pounds nice tomatoes, one quart vinegar, eight pounds sugar. Boil all together until thick. When half done add two large spoonfuls of cinnamon, one of ground mace, and a teaspoonful of cloves or allspice.

Hot Slaw.—Shave the cabbage fine; put it on with just water enough to cook it; when it is done put a little milk in, salt and pepper; then rub a little flour in some butter and stir in. An egg may be stirred in in place of the flour.

Cucumber Salad.—Peel and slice cucumbers, mix them with salt, and let them stand half an hour; mix two tablespoonfuls salad oil and the same quantity of vinegar, and a tablespoonful of sugar and one of pepper for the dressing.

Bread and Rolls.

Eight Points in Bread-making.—1. Good wheat flour. Some va-rieties of wheat, such as are deficient in gluten, will not make good flour.

2. A good miller to grind the wheat. The bread-maker should be sure to find the good miller.

3. The wheat should not be ground when very dry. Choose a "wet spell" for the grinding.

4. The flour should be sifted before using, to separate the particles.

5. Good yeast. This made from new hops. Stale hops will not, with certainty, make lively yeast.

6. Thorough kneading. After it has had enough, knead it a while longer.

7. Do not let the dough rise too much. Nine out of every ten bread-makers in this country let their bread "rise" until its sweetness has been destroyed.

8. The oven can be too hot as well as too cool. The "happy medium" must be determined and selected.

There are three kinds of bread, viz.: Sweet Bread, Bread and Sour Bread. Some housewives make sour bread, a great many make bread, but few make sweet bread. "Sweetness" in bread is a positive quality that not many bread-makers have yet discovered.

To Make Graham Bread.—Set the sponge to rise over night, using milk instead of water, and adding for every three quarts of flour a cup of molasses. In the morning, add a little salt and enough of flour to make a dough just thick enough not to be molded. Put in baking-tins to rise, and when light bake in a moderate oven. Do not mold at all. Rye bread and graham bread should be made soft; molding spoils the bread, making it hard, dry, and chippy.

To Keep Bread Moist.—Have the dough stiff when it is set for the last rising. The larger the proportion of flour to that of moisture in the dough the longer it will keep moist. After the bread is baked and cold, put it in a tin box or an earthen jar with close cover, and keep it covered tightly. Bread thus made, and kept cool, and always from the air, will last and be moist for a week.

Home-Made Crackers.—Beat two eggs very lightly, whites and yelks together; sift into them a quart of flour, a teaspoonful of salt; add a table-spoonful each of butter and lard, and nearly a tumblerful of milk; work all thoroughly together; take a fourth of the dough at a time and roll out half as thick as a milk cracker, cut in small rounds, and bake quickly to a light brown.

Rice Bread.—Rice bread makes a pleasing variety at the breakfast table. Take one pint of well-cooked rice, half a pint of flour, the yelks of four eggs, two tablespoonfuls of butter melted, one pint of milk and half a teaspoonful of salt; beat these all together, then, lastly, add the whites of the four eggs, which you have beaten to a stiff froth. Bake in shallow pans or in gem tins. Serve warm.

Southern Batter-Bread or Egg-Bread.—Two cups white Indian meal, one cup cold boiled rice, three eggs well beaten, one tablespoonful melted butter, two and a half cups milk, or enough for soft batter, one tea-spoonful salt, a pinch of soda. Stir the beaten eggs into the milk, the meal, salt, butter, last of all the rice. Beat well three minutes, and bake quickly in a shallow pan.

Indian Bread.—One pint of sweet milk, two tablespoonfuls of molasses, a little salt, one yeast cake, and for every cup of wheat flour put in two of Indian meal until as thick as pound cake. Turn into well-buttered tins and set in a warm place to rise over night. Then set in a slow oven to bake about three-fourths of an hour.

Squash Biscuit.—One pint of strained squash, one half cup of yeast, one small cup of sugar, and a piece of butter the size of an egg; beat the squash, butter and sugar thoroughly, add yeast and beat again, add flour till quite stiff to stir with a spoon, let it stand over night, in the morning put in gem pans, or make into biscuit, let rise and bake; these should be eaten while hot.

Brown Bread.—One pint cornmeal, pour over it one pint boiling water, teacup molasses, shorts or graham flour enough to make a stiff batter, two eggs, one teaspoonful of soda dissolved in a little boiling water; steam three hours by putting in a pan in a steamer over a pot of hot water; keep the water boiling all the time.

Bread Cheesecakes.—Slice a penny loaf as thin as possible, pour on it a pint of boiling cream. When well soaked, beat it very fine, add eight eggs, half a pound of butter, a grated nutmeg, half a pound of currants, a spoonful of brandy or white wine. Beat them up well together, and bake in raised crusts or patty pans.

Graham Gems.—Take cold water and make a batter of graham flour, a trifle thicker than for griddle cakes; salt a little if you like; bake in iron gem pans; the pans should be well heated before the batter is put in; bake in a very hot oven about twenty minutes. It will improve them to use part sweet milk, though they are good without.

Oatmeal Crackers.—One teacup of oatmeal, and water enough to make a dough; mix well and quick; if it will bear to be rolled out with the rolling pin, roll it; keep at it in the same way until it is one-quarter of an inch thick; do it very quickly or it will dry; make only dough enough at one time for one cracker; do not brown in baking.

Rosettes.—Beat the yelks of three eggs very light until they thicken. Add one quart of milk and one tablespoonful of melted butter and a teaspoonful of salt. Mix three teaspoonfuls of baking powder with three cups of flour, and add to the milk and eggs. When all the lumps are beaten out add the whites of the eggs whipped to a stiff froth. Bake immediately in muffin pans in a quick oven.

French Rolls.—One pint milk, small cup yeast, and flour enough to make a stiff batter; let them rise well, add one egg, one tablespoonful batter, and flour enough to make it stiff enough to roll; knead well and let it rise; then knead again, roll out, cut with round tin, put in a pan and let them rise until very light; bake quickly and you will have delicious rolls. Mix in the morning and have them for tea.

Tea Rolls.—One pint of milk, one quart of flour, two tablespoonfuls of butter or butter and lard, one-half Vienna yeast cake. This makes the sponge. Let it raise, salt it, dissolve a very small quantity of soda, and put into the sponge. Mix it with a quart of flour and let it raise again, then cut out and put in pans, to raise very light before putting into the oven.

Scotch Shortbread.—Rub together into a stiff short paste two pounds of flour, one pound of butter, and six ounces of loaf sugar. Make it into square cakes about a half-inch thick, pinch them all along the edge at the top, dock over the whole surface of the cake, put them on tins so as to touch each other by their edges, and bake in a moderate oven.

French Toast.—Beat four eggs very light, and stir with them one pint of milk; slice some nice white bread, dip the pieces into the egg and milk, then lay them into a pan of hot butter and fry brown. Sprinkle a little powdered sugar and cinnamon or nutmeg on each piece, and serve hot.

German Cream Biscuits.—Take four ounces of butter, six ounces of powdered loaf sugar, seven ounces of flour, one tablespoonful of fresh cream, and one egg. Make the above into a dough, beating it well; then roll it out very thin, cutting it into square pieces two inches long and one broad. Bake in a quick oven, and when done they should be a light yellow brown.

Graham Biscuits.—Three cups graham flour, one cup white do., three cups of milk, two tablespoonfuls of lard or butter, one heaping large spoonful of white sugar, one saltspoonful of salt, one teaspoonful of soda, two teaspoonfuls cream of tartar; mix and bake as ordinary soda biscuit. They are good cold.

Oatmeal Gems.—One beaten egg, one cup of sweet milk, one cup of cold oatmeal pudding, beat all together, add half a teaspoonful of soda, and one and one-half cups of flour. This quantity will fill the gem pan. Does not hurt some dyspeptics.

Breakfast Rolls Without Soda.—Two eggs, one and a half cups of milk, a teaspoonful of salt, and flour enough to make a thick batter. These must be baked in an iron gem pan, or they will be a complete failure. A quick oven is desirable.

Dyspepsia Bread.—One pint bowl of graham flour; dissolve one-half a teaspoonful of soda in two-thirds of a cup of yeast and add to the mixture one teacup of molasses; pour in sufficient warm water to make it somewhat thinner than flour bread.

Oatmeal Wafers.—Oatmeal wafers are relished by babies and older children, too. Take a pint of oatmeal and a pint of water, with almost a teaspoonful of salt; mix and spread on buttered pans; make it just as thin as it is possible and yet have the bottom of the pan covered; bake slowly.

Oatmeal Biscuit.—Take half a pound medium oatmeal, quarter of a pound flour, one dessertspoonful of baking powder; mix with two ounces butter and half a gill of milk, made hot in a saucepan. Roll out quickly, and bake in very thin cakes.

Light Rolls.—Boil four potatoes; mash them and put into a pint of boiled milk, two tablespoonfuls of butter melted in the milk; flour enough to make a stiff batter; half a pint of yeast, one teaspoonful of salt.

Graham Wafers.—Put a pinch of salt into one-half pound of graham flour; wet it with one-half pint of sweet cream; mix quickly and thoroughly; roll out as thin as possible, and cut in strips; prick and bake in a quick oven.

Good Brown Bread.—Four cups of cornmeal, three of rye, one of molasses, one large teaspoonful of soda dissolved in warm water. Mix very thin, steam three hours, and bake half an hour. Try it.

Railroad Yeast.—One tablespoonful of ginger, one teaspoonful of soda, one pint of boiling water; thicken with coarse flour or middlings; let it rise, and set in a cool place. Use a teaspoonful to a baking of salt-rising bread.

Rice Biscuits.—Take half a pound of sugar, half a pound of the best ground rice, half a pound of butter, and half a pound of flour, and mix the whole into a paste with eggs (two are sufficient for this quantity).

Indian Meal Puffs.—In one quart of boiling milk stir eight tablespoonfuls of meal, four spoonfuls of sugar; boil five minutes, stirring all the time; when cool add six beaten eggs; pour in buttered cups; bake half an hour.

Steamed Brown Bread.—One quart of Indian meal, one pint of rye flour; stir these together and add one quart of sweet milk, one cup of molasses, two teaspoonfuls of soda, and a little salt. Steam for four hours.

Tea Puffs.—Two and one-quarter cups flour, three cups milk, three eggs —whites and yelks beaten separately; three teaspoonfuls of melted butter, a little salt. Bake in muffin tins in a hot oven.

Block Biscuits.—Half a pound of butter beaten up to a cream, half a pound of ground rice, three-quarters of a pound of flour, half a pound of loaf sugar, four eggs, and a little sal volatile.

Old Maid Bread.—One quart of flour, two eggs, two tablespoonfuls of lard, one teaspoonful of salt, one teacup of yeast, one cup of milk; make up in a soft dough; reserve one-third of the flour for second rising.

Rice Biscuits.—Sift seven ounces of sugar; then add to it half a pound of the best ground rice, seven ounces of butter, seven ounces of flour, and mix it into a paste with eggs—two are sufficient for this quantity.

Ginger Biscuits.—One pound of flour, half a pound of fresh butter, half a pound of powdered lump sugar, three-quarters of an ounce of ground ginger, two eggs. Bake five minutes in a quick oven.

Indian Bread.—Two cups of Indian meal, one-half cup each of rye meal and wheat flour, two thirds of a cup of molasses, one pint of sour or buttermilk, one teaspoonful of saleratus or cooking-soda, one teaspoonful of salt.

Egg Sandwiches.—Boil fresh eggs five minutes; put them in cold water, and when quite cold peel them; then, after taking a little white off each end of the eggs, cut the remainder in four slices. Lay them between bread and butter.

Corn Gems.—Two cups cornmeal, two cups flour, two cups sweet milk, two eggs, three heaping teaspoonfuls of baking-powder, one-half cup butter, one-half cup sugar; bake in gem pans.

Improving Bread.—If, when bread is taken from the oven, the loaves are turned topside down in the hot tins, and are allowed to stand a few minutes the crust will be tender and will cut easily.

Tea Rusks.—Three cups of flour, one cup of milk, three-fourths of a cup of sugar, two heaping tablespoonfuls of butter, melted, two eggs, three teaspoonfuls of baking-powder.

Johnny Cake.—Take one pint of milk, one pint of meal, three tablespoonfuls of flour, two tablespoonfuls sugar, one tablespoonful butter and one egg.

Tea Biscuits.—Two pounds of flour, two ounces of butter, one cup of milk, one or two eggs, half a cup of sugar, one cup of yeast, set at night, bake in the morning.

Cottage Bread.—One quart of flour, one large spoonful of sugar, one of butter, one egg, one teacup of yeast; put to rise, and bake as biscuits.

Jellies and Preserves.

To Preserve Pine-Apples in Slices.—This can be made with the West Indian pines. Choose ripe but sound ones, and cut them into slices about one inch thick, and cut off the rind. Weigh the slices, and to every two pounds of fruit put one pound and three-quarters of white sifted sugar. Boil them together in a preserving pan for half an hour, and, if the slices are then tender, take them out carefully with a wooden spoon and place them upon a deep dish, boil the syrup for a short time longer, and then pour it over the slices of pine-apple. This process must be repeated for three successive days, after which the preserves may be put into jars and covered.

Russian Jelly for Invalids.—Instead of throwing away the peel and core of apples from making a pie or pudding, put them in a jar and pour over them a pint of hot water; put the jar by the fire or in the oven until the water tastes strongly of the apples; strain the apple-water off, and throw away the peel; then add to the apple-water one tablespoonful of large sago; set it to the fire until the sago has absorbed all the water; then put it in a mold, and it will be ready for use; to be eaten either hot or cold. A little lemon juice added improves the flavor. The proportion of peel and water must be according to the quality of the apples, as some are so much sharper than others. No decay should be allowed to be in the peel. Rhubarb may be used in the same way. The jelly should taste strongly of fruit. This jelly is most refreshing in sickness.

Grape Preserves.—Grapes partly ripe are delicious preserved in the following manner: Pick out those that are knotty or wormy; take the rest, a few at a time, in a coarse sieve, working them around with the hand until the seeds are loosened, when they will drop through, leaving the skins and pulp in the sieve. Drain the juice off the seeds, and to every pound of pulp, skin, and juice, allow half a pound of white sugar. Put all into the preserving kettle and cook slowly about three-quarters of an hour. Put hot into jars, a brandy paper on top, and seal up.

Frosted Currants.—Currants, white of egg, cold water, pulverized sugar. Pick fine, even bunches, and dip them one at a time into a mixture of frothed white of egg and a very little cold water; drain them until nearly dry, and dip them in pulverized sugar; repeat the dip in sugar once or twice, and lay them upon white paper to dry. They will make a beautiful garnish for jellies and charlottes, and look well heaped in a dish by themselves or with other fruit. Plums and grapes are very nice frosted in the same manner. Currants mixed with a sufficient quantity or raspberries, put in a glass bowl and eaten with powdered sugar and plain cream, make a very nice dish.

Chicken Jelly.— Cut half of an uncooked chicken into small pieces and break the bones; pour over it a quart of cold water, and boil slowly until it is reduced to less than half; season with salt and a little pepper, if the latter is allowed the invalid. Strain through a colander, then through a jelly-bag into a mold or bowl. If the chicken is quite tender, boil carefully the breast of the other half of it; cut it into dice and put it into the mold or bowl, and cover it with the liquid. When the jelly has hardened, scrape off the layer of fat at the top of the mold before turning the jelly on a platter.

Mock Champagne Jelly.—Take one quart of fine cider, mix this with one pound of loaf sugar or sugar to taste, the juice of four lemons, the grated rind of one, and some pieces of stick cinnamon, the whites of two eggs well beaten, one box of gelatine; soak the gelatine in a pint of cold water one hour, then add a pint of boiling water, the cider and other ingredients; stir the mixture until the gelatine is well dissolved; then put it on the fire and boil five minutes, strain through a jelly-bag into molds, set in a cool place or on ice to harden.

Preserved Cherries.—To ten pounds of cherries allow five pounds of sugar; stone the fruit and put in a porcelain kettle in layers with the sugar; let it heat slowly until the juice is drawn out, or it may stand in a cool place, even over night; when stewed until tender, take the cherries from the syrup in a little strainer, and put them in cans placed on a board in boiling water. Boil the syrup until thick, then fill the cans and fasten the covers.

Hints About Making Preserves.—It is not generally known that boiling fruit a long time, and skimming it well, without the sugar and without a cover to the preserving pan, is a very economical and excellent way—economical, because the bulk of the scum rises from the fruit, and not from the sugar, if the latter is good; and boiling it without a cover allows the evaporation of all the watery particles therefrom; the preserves keep firm and are well flavored. The proportions are, three-quarters of a pound of sugar to a pound of fruit. Jam made in this way, of currants, strawberries, raspberries, or gooseberries, is excellent.

Lemon Syrup.—Take a dozen lemons; slice them thin; take ten pounds best white sugar; place a layer of sugar and one of lemons in an earthen jar; let them remain over night, then pour as much water over them as will make a syrup; place the jar in a kettle of water, and let them simmer but not boil; strain and bottle, and you will have a delicious flavoring when lemons are expensive. Lemonade can be made from it by using a few spoonfuls in water. The lemons can be placed on a plate after they are strained from the syrup and used in preserves for flavoring.

Apple Jelly.—Make a syrup of a pound of sugar, putting in sufficient water to dissolve it; when boiled enough, lay it in the peeled and cored halves of some large sour apples, let them simmer till tender, then lay them carefully in a dish so that they will remain unbroken and in good shape; add another pound of sugar to the syrup, let it boil, skim it, and when partly cool pour it over the apples; when the dish gets cold each dainty piece of apple will be surrounded by a delicious jelly; eat them with cream.

Orange Jelly.—One-half box of gelatine soaked in one-half pint of cold water for half an hour; then add the juice of five oranges and two lemons and one and one-half cups white sugar; turn on one pint of boiling water and set the pail containing the ingredients in a kettle of boiling water to heat, but do not let it quite boil; then strain into an earthen vessel to cool.

Before bringing to the table cut in squares and place in a glass sauce dish. This is much liked, and is very nice for the sick.

Citron or Watermelon Preserves.—Peel and cut eight pounds of rinds, soak twenty-four hours in salt water (three tablespoonfuls in water enough to cover), soak again in alum water, three tablespoonfuls of alum as above; then soak in fresh water twenty-four hours. Take one ounce white ginger root to one and a half gallons water, boil till tender enough to pierce with a straw; then to eight pounds of fruit make a syrup of seven pounds of sugar, boil till transparent and season with cinnamon; delicious.

Orange Marmalade.—Take equal weights of sour oranges and sugar. Grate the yellow rind from a fourth of the oranges. Cut all the fruit in halves at what might be called the "equator." Pick out the pulp, and free it of seeds. Drain off as much juice as you conveniently can, and put it on to boil with the sugar. Let it come to a boil. Skim and simmer for about fifteen minutes, then put in the pulp and grated rind, and boil fifteen minutes longer.

Uncooked Currant Jelly.—To one pint of currant juice add one pound of granulated sugar, stir the juice very slowly into the sugar until the sugar is dissolved, then let it stand twenty-four hours and it will be stiff jelly. Tie it with paper dipped in brandy, and set it in the sun. Half a bushel of currants makes twenty-two one-half pint glasses of jelly.

Calf's Foot Jelly.—Take two calves' feet; add to them one gallon of water; boil them down to one quart; strain, and when cold remove all fat; then add the whites of six or eight eggs (well beaten), half a pound of sugar and the juices of four lemons; mix well. Boil for a minute, constantly stirring; then strain through a flannel bag.

Raspberry Jam.—To every quart of ripe raspberries, allow a pound of the best loaf sugar. Put sugar and berries into a pan, and let them stand two or three hours. Then boil them in a porcelain kettle, taking off the scum carefully. When no more scum rises, mash them and boil them to smooth marmalade. When cold, put them in glass tumblers.

Peach Butter.—Pare ripe peaches and put them in a preserving kettle, with sufficient water to boil them soft; then sift through a colander, removing the stones. To each quart of peach put one and one-half pounds sugar, and boil very slowly one hour. Stir often, and do not let them burn. Put in stone or glass jars and keep in a cool place.

Coffee Jelly.—Take one package of Cox's gelatine and dissolve it in a pint of cold water. Let it stand until well dissolved, and then put two teacups of strong hot coffee in a quart cup, fill the measure up with boiling water and stir gelatine, coffee and water together with a pint of sugar; after stirring let it settle, and pour the mixture through a strainer into molds. To be eaten cold with cream and sugar.

White Currant Jam.—Boil together quickly for seven minutes equal quantities of fine white currants carefully picked from their stalks, and of the best pounded white sugar passed through a sieve. Stir the preserve gently the whole time, and be careful to skim it thoroughly. Just before it is taken from the fire, throw in the strained juice of one good lemon to four pounds of the fruit.

Preserved Citron.—Cut the citron in thin slices, pare off the outside rind and take out all the seeds, put in the preserve kettle with water enough to cover it; boil till it can be pierced easily with a fork, skim it out and strain the water, placing it back in the kettle; allow three-quarters of a pound of sugar to a pound of citron; dissolve the sugar in the liquor; cut three or four lemons into it and let it boil till it is as thick as required, then put in the citron and boil; when it is transparent, then it is done; if boiled too long the citron will be tough.

Plum Marmalade.—Rub the plums, after draining, through a sieve or colander to take out the stones and skins. Add half a pound of sugar for each pint of pulp, boil slowly, stirring well to prevent burning, until it is a smooth thick paste. Excellent marmalade is made by mixing the sifted pulp of wild plums and crab apples.

Gooseberry Jelly.—Boil six pounds of green unripe gooseberries in six pints of water (they must be well boiled, but not burst too much); pour them into a basin and let them stand covered with a cloth twenty-four hours; then strain through a jelly bag, and to every pint of juice add one pound of sugar; boil for an hour, then skim it and boil for one-half hour longer.

Spiced Peaches.—Pare, stone, and halve the fruit; allow nine pounds of peaches to four of sugar, and nearly one pint of vinegar; boil the fruit in water until tender; then pour off, and add the sugar and vinegar, with a few whole cloves, cinnamon and a little mace. Boil half an hour.

Quince Marmalade.—Pare, core and quarter the quinces; boil them gently, uncovered, in water until they begin to soften; then strain them through a hair sieve, and beat in a mortar or wooden bowl to a pulp; add to each pound of fruit three-quarters of a pound of sugar; boil it till it becomes stiff, and pour into small molds.

Blackberry Jelly.—This preparation of the blackberry is more agreeable than the jam, as the seeds, though very wholesome, are not agreeable to all. It is made in the same way as currant jelly; but the fruit is so sweet that it only requires half the weight of the juice in sugar.

Jellies Without Fruit.—To one pint of water put one-fourth of an ounce of alum; boil a minute or two; then add four pounds of white sugar; continue the boiling a little; strain while hot; and, when cold, put in half a twenty-five cent bottle of extract of vanilla, strawberry, lemon, or any other flavor you desire for jelly.

Crab Apple Jelly.—Cut out the eyes and stalks of the apples; halve them and put in a preserving kettle with enough water to prevent burning. Cook until soft; then strain through a sieve, and afterward through a muslin bag; to every pound of juice allow one and one-quarter pounds of sugar. Boil gently for twenty minutes.

Lemon Jelly.—Isinglass, two ounces; water, one quart, boil; add sugar, one pound, clarify, and, when nearly cold, add the juice of five lemons, and the grated yellow rinds of two oranges and two lemons; mix well, strain off the peel, and put it into glasses or bottles.

Blackberry Jam.—To each pound of fruit add three-fourths of a pound of sugar; then put together and boil from one-half to three-fourths of an hour.

Currant Jelly.—Fill a jar with currants and place it in a kettle of boiling water. Boil till the fruit is well softened, stirring frequently, then strain through a cloth, and to every pint add a pound of white sugar. Boil ten minutes, skimming until quite clear. Black currant or grape jelly can be made in the same way.

Apple Jam.—Core and pare the apples; chop them well; allow equal quantity in weight of apples and sugar; make a syrup of the sugar by adding a little water, boiling and skimming well, then throw in a little grated lemon peel and a little white ginger. Boil until the fruit looks clear.

Plum Preserves.—Weigh your plums, scald them, put on a dish or waiter; be sure to strain; weigh as much sugar as fruit, and to every pound add a gill of water; let sugar boil, skim, add scalded fruit, cook two hours and a half; put in air-tight jars.

Pickled Peaches and Plums.—To seven pounds fruit, three pounds sugar, one quart vinegar, one ounce cloves, one ounce cinnamon. Scald vinegar and sugar three mornings in succession, and pour on the fruit. The third morning scald altogether.

Tapioca Jelly.—Wash eight ounces of tapioca well; then soak in one gallon fresh water, five or six hours; add the peels of eight lemons, and set all on to heat; simmer till clear; add the juice of the eight lemons with wine and sugar to taste; then bottle.

Isinglass Jelly.—Put four ounces isinglass and two ounces cloves into one gallon water, boil it down to half a gallon; strain it upon four pounds of loaf sugar; add, while cooling, a little wine; then bottle.

Gooseberry Jelly.—Sugar, four pounds; water, two pounds; boil together; it will be nearly solid when cold; to this syrup, add an equal weight of gooseberry juice; give it a short boil, cool, then pot it.

Cranberry Jelly.—Make a very strong isinglass jelly. When cold, mix it with a double quantity of cranberry juice. Sweeten and boil it up; then strain it into a shape. The sugar must be good loaf, or the jelly will not be clear.

Peach Marmalade.—Peaches too ripe for preserving answer for marmalade. Pare and quarter them, allowing three-quarters of a pound of sugar to each pound of fruit, and half a pint of water to each pound of sugar. Boil one hour and a half, stirring constantly.

Gooseberry Jam.—Take what quantity you please of red, rough, ripe gooseberries, take half the quantity of lump sugar, break them well and boil them together for half an hour or more, if necessary. Put into pots and cover with paper.

Pickled Apples.—Apple pickles are delicious. Pare and halve the apples, removing the cores carefully, to keep them in good shape. Steam till soft. Put spiced vinegar over them.

Puddings, Pies, Etc.

Apple Fritters.—First pare the apples, and then with an apple-corer cut out the core from the center of each; then cut them across in slices about one-third of an inch thick, having a round opening in the center. Next make a fritter batter by the following recipe: Beat three eggs well; add a part of one pint of milk and a little salt; then the remainder of the pint of milk and one pint of flour alternately, beating it all quickly. The slices of apples must now be immediately dipped in this batter and fried in boiling lard; sprinkle over with sugar and serve in a circle, one overlapping the other, with or without sweet sauce in the center.

Amber Pudding.—Four eggs, their weight in sugar, butter and flour, peel of one lemon, and grated rinds of two; beat the butter with your hand to a cream, then add the flour, sugar and beaten eggs by degrees, then the peel and juice of the lemons; butter a mold, and when all is well mixed fill it quite full; put a buttered white paper over the top and tie well over with a cloth, put in a pan of boiling water and boil for about four hours.

Apple Charlotte.—Take a loaf of stale bread, and butter the slices; pare and slice a dozen apples; take a lemon, grate the skin, and save the juice; place at the bottom of a stoneware baking dish a layer of apples; scatter brown sugar on it, some of the lemon gratings, and a little juice; then put in a layer of the buttered bread; keep on until your dish is full, having the crust on top; bake in a moderately hot oven. Do not make it too sweet.

Apple Pudding.—Peel and quarter enough apples to cover the bottom of a deep tin plate; then make a batter of sour milk, soda and flour, with a tablespoonful of lard to enough flour to make a batter that will cover the apples. This should not be thicker than for pancakes. Pour it over the apples and bake till brown. Then, when done, turn it on a large plate with the crust down. Over the apples scatter sugar and cinnamon.

Apple Souffle.—One pint of steamed apples, one tablespoonful of melted butter, half a cup of sugar, the white of six eggs and the yelks of three, and a slight grating of nutmeg. Stir into the hot apples, the butter, sugar, and nutmeg, and the yelks of the eggs well beaten. When this is cold, beat the whites of the eggs to a stiff froth, and stir into the mixture. Butter a three-pint dish, and turn the souffle into it. Bake thirty minutes in a hot oven. Serve immediately with any kind of sauce.

All the Year Round Pudding.—Line a pie-dish with paste, spread on three ounces of any kind of jam (raspberry is the best); then beat well in a basin the following: Three ounces of bread crumbs, the same of sugar and butter, the rind and juice of half a large lemon; add this to the pastry and jam, and bake half an hour.

An Excellent Pudding.—One-half pound suet, shred fine; one half pound grated bread crumbs; one-quarter pound of loaf sugar, the yelks of four eggs and whites of two well beaten; two tablespoonfuls of orange marmalade or sliced citron, if preferred. To be put into a butter mold and boiled for two hours. To be served with wine poured over it, or sauce.

Pudding a l'Elegante.—Cut thin slices of light white bread, and line a pudding-shape with them, putting in alternate layers of the bread and orange marmalade, or any other preserve, till the mold is nearly full. Pour over all a pint of warm milk, in which four well-beaten eggs have been mixed. Cover the mold with a cloth, and boil for an hour and a half. Serve with wine sauce.

Delicious Apple Sauce.—Pare and slice thin as many apples as you wish. Put them into a tin basin or pudding dish, with enough sugar to make them sweet and a little water. Bake slowly until soft. They will turn a rich red, and have a flavor far exceeding stewed apples.

Apple Dumplings.—Make them the usual way, place them in a deep pudding dish; make a liquor of water, sugar, butter, and a little nutmeg; the liquor should very nearly cover the dumplings; bake on one side, turn them on the other; bake about three-fourths of an hour.

Albany Puffs.—Beat the yelks of six eggs until they are very light; stir in a pint of sweet milk, a large pinch of salt, the whites of the eggs beaten to a froth, and flour enough to make a batter about as thick as boiled custard. Bake in gem pans in a quick oven.

Apple Custard.—Take a half cup of melted butter, two cups sugar, three cups stewed apples, four eggs, whites and yelks separately beaten. Bake in pie plates in bottom crust.

Brown Betty.—Take one cup bread crumbs, two cups chopped sour apples, one half cup sugar, one teaspoonful cinnamon, two tablespoonfuls butter cut into small bits. Butter a deep dish and put a layer of chopped apple at the bottom, sprinkle with sugar, a few bits of butter and cinnamon, cover with bread crumbs, then more apple. Proceed in this way until the dish is full, having a layer of crumbs on top. Cover closely and steam three quarters of an hour in a moderate oven, then uncover and brown quickly. Eat warm with sugar and cream, or sweet sauce. This is a cheap but good pudding, better than many a richer one.

Bread Pudding.—Soak two or three French rolls cut into slices in a pint of cream or good milk; add the yelks of six eggs, beaten, some sugar, orange-flower water, three pounded macaroons, and a glass of white wine; tie it up in a basin, or buttered cloth; put the pudding in boiling water, and let it boil for half an hour. Serve with wine sauce.

Baked Lemon Pudding.—Mix the following ingredients together in the order in which they are placed: Moist sugar, one-quarter pound; bread crumbs, six ounces; eggs, well beaten, three; lemon peel grated and juice, two; bake one and a half hours in a moderate oven.

Bird's Nest Pudding.—Pare and core as many apples as will stand in a dish, and fill the holes with sugar. Make a custard of a quart of milk, eight eggs, and a quarter of a pound of sugar. Pour it over the apples, grate a nutmeg over the top, and bake one hour.

Fried Bananas.—Peel and slice the bananas, sprinkle with salt, dip in thin batter, and fry in butter. Serve immediately.

Cup Plum Pudding.—Take one cup each of raisins, currants, flour, bread crumbs, suet, and sugar; stone and cut the raisins, wash and dry the currants, chop the suet, and mix all the above ingredients well together; then add two ounces of candied peel and citron, a little mixed spice, salt, and ginger, say half a teaspoonful of each; stir in four well-beaten eggs and milk enough to make the mixture so that the spoon will stand upright in it; tie it loosely in a cloth, or put it in a mold; plunge it then into boiling water, and boil for three and a half hours.

Cranberry Sauce.—Wash and pick over the cranberries; put on to cook in a tin or porcelain vessel, allowing a teacup of water to each quart. Stew slowly, stirring often until they are thick as marmalade. Take from the fire in little over an hour, if they have cooked steadily; sweeten plentifully with white sugar and strain through a coarse net into a mold wet with cold water. Do this the day before using, and at dinner time turn from the mold into a glass dish.

Chocolate Pudding.—One quart of milk, fourteen even tablespoonfuls of grated bread crumbs, twelve tablespoonfuls of grated chocolate, six eggs, one tablespoonful vanilla; sugar to make very sweet. Separate the yelks and whites of four eggs; beat up the four yelks and two whole eggs together very light with the sugar. Put the milk on the range, and when it comes to a perfect boil pour it over the bread and chocolate; add the beaten eggs and sugar, and vanilla; be sure it is sweet enough; pour into a buttered dish; bake one hour in a moderate oven. When cold, and just before it is served, have the four whites beaten with a little powdered sugar, and flavor with vanilla, and use as a meringue.

Chocolate Cream Custards.—Set to boil a quart of milk; mix with half a cup of cold milk two ounces of grated sweet chocolate, pour some of the boiling milk into it, and then pour all back into the pan of boiling milk, stirring it all the time; when quite heated and about coming to the boiling point, add the yelks of six eggs which have been beaten with a cup of powdered sugar; when these are nicely blended add three whites, beaten with a little vanilla, keeping the three other whites for frosting; put in cups, and a tablespoonful of the frosting on the top of each cup.

Cranberry Pudding.—Cranberry pudding is made by pouring boiling water on a pint of dried bread crumbs; melt a tablespoonful of butter and stir in. When the bread is softened add two eggs, and beat thoroughly with the bread. Then put in a pint of the stewed fruit and sweeten to your taste. Bake in a hot oven for half an hour. Fresh fruit may be used in place of the cranberries. Slices of peaches put in layers make a delicious variation.

Coffee Custard.—Mix one egg with a cup of freshly-ground coffee, pour on it a pint of boiling water; boil five minutes. Pour it off clear into a saucepan, add a pint of cream and boil. Beat from five to eight eggs with one and one half cups of sugar, and pour the boiling mixture over this, stirring it well. Set the whole in boiling water, and stir until it thickens.

Cranberry Roll.—Stew a quart of cranberries in just water enough to keep them from burning. Make very sweet, strain and cool. Make a paste, and when the cranberry is cold spread it on the paste about an inch thick. Roll it, tie it close in a flannel cloth, boil two hours, and serve with sweet sauce. Stewed apples or other fruit may be used in the same way.

Delicious Fritters.—Put three tablespoonfuls of flour into a bowl, and pour over it sufficient hot water to make it into a stiff paste, taking care to stir it well to prevent its getting lumpy. Leave it a little time to cool, and then break into it, without beating them first, the yelks of four eggs, the whites of two, and stir and beat all together. Have your fat or lard hot, and drop a dessertspoonful of batter in at a time, and fry a light brown. Serve on a hot dish with a spoonful of jam or marmalade dropped in between each fritter.

Crow's Nest.—Fill a deep pudding tin or dish with apples cut in thin slices; sugar and cinnamon, or lemon, to sweeten and flavor to taste, and a little water; cover with a thick crust; bake until apples are tender; serve hot with hard sauce, or with cream and sugar; be sure to cut air holes in the crust to let the steam escape.

Cream Fritters.—Beat three eggs to a froth, add half a pint of cream, the same of milk, a teaspoonful of salt, one pint flour, two teaspoonfuls baking powder; stir to a smooth batter; fry in hot lard the same as doughnuts. These are good hot or cold. Serve with sweetened cream or maple molasses.

Cake Pudding.—Take odd bits of cake (if two or three kinds all the better), break in small pieces, put them in a pudding dish which has been previously buttered, make a rich custard; pour over the cake; bake or steam. It is made still nicer by adding cocoanut frosting, and setting in the oven till of a light brown.

Cocoanut Pudding.—One-half pound of butter, one-half pound of sugar, whites of eight eggs whipped to a froth. The white portion of one cocoanut grated into minute particles. Grease pan with butter, and bake. For this pudding desiccated cocoanut answers as well as fresh cocoanut.

Custard Pudding.—Take a pint of cream, six eggs well beaten, two spoonfuls of flour; half a nutmeg grated, and salt and sugar to taste; mix them together; butter a cloth and pour in the batter; tie it up, put it into a saucepan of boiling water, and boil it an hour and a half. Serve with melted butter.

Cream Batter Pudding.—Half pint sour cream, half pint sweet milk, half pint flour, three eggs, half teaspoonful soda, a little salt. Beat eggs separately, adding the yelks last. Bake in a slow oven, and you will find this the queen of puddings.

Egg Pudding.—Take any number of eggs, their weight in flour, brown sugar and butter, and a few currants or chopped raisins, as preferred. Mix well together by means of the eggs. Bake in buttered molds; serve hot, with wine sauce.

Cracker Pudding.—Pour one quart boiling water over six soft crackers, let stand until very soft; add three or four eggs, one cup raisins, one-fourth spoonful salt, sweeten, flavor or spice, bake. Very nice.

Citron Pudding.—Mix one quart of cream with three spoonfuls of sugar, one-half pound of flour, one-half pound of citron peel, yelks of six eggs and a little nutmeg. Bake in teacups in a quick oven.

Cottage Pudding.—One cup of sugar, one cup of sweet milk, one pint of flour, two tablespoonfuls of melted butter, one teaspoonful of soda, two teaspoonfuls of cream tartar, one egg.

Cracked Wheat Pudding.—Cracked wheat mixed with milk in the proportion of half a cup to a quart, and flavored with cinnamon and a raisin or two, makes a very good pudding.

Cream Custard.—Eight eggs, beat and put into two quarts of cream; sweeten to taste; add nutmeg and cinnamon.

Date or Prune Pudding.—Take a quart of milk, beat six eggs, half the whites in half a pint of milk, and four spoonfuls of flour with a little salt, and two of beaten ginger; then by degrees mix in all the milk and a pound of dates, tie it in a cloth, and boil it an hour; melt butter and pour over it. Damsons are very nice instead of the dates or prunes.

A Delicious Pudding.—Sift two tablespoonfuls of flour, and mix with the beaten yelks of six eggs, add gradually one pint of sweet cream, a quarter of a pound of citron cut in very thin slices, and two tablespoonfuls of sugar; mix thoroughly, pour into a buttered tin, and bake twenty-five minutes. Serve with vanilla sauce.

Dandy Pudding.—One and one-half pints of milk, four eggs, sugar to taste. Boil the milk and yelks and one teaspoonful of corn starch. Beat the whites to a stiff froth, after the cream is cooked, put it in a dish to cool. Then drop the whites, after sweetening, on the cream. Brown the top a few minutes.

English Plum Pudding.—One-half pound currants, one pound raisins, one-half pound of beef suet, butter the size of an egg, three eggs, one nutmeg, two teaspoonfuls of lemon, three-fourths of a pint of milk, a little salt, flour sufficient to stiffen, mix well together; put into a bowl and bake four hours; cover bowl with a cloth. *Sauce.*—Three tablespoonfuls corn starch, one-half pint milk, one-half cup of sugar, one tablespoonful of butter; boil five minutes.

Economical Family Pudding.—Bruise with a wooden spoon, through a colander, six large or twelve middle-sized potatoes, beat four eggs, mix with a pint of good milk, stir in the potatoes, six ounces sugar and flavoring, butter a dish, bake half an hour. This receipt is simple and economical, as cold potatoes, which may have been kept two or three days, till a sufficient quantity is collected, will answer quite well.

Egg Sauce.—Boil half a dozen eggs hard, when cold remove the shell, cut each egg in half crosswise, and each half into four quarters. Put them into one pint of melted butter.

Floating Island Custard.—One-half gallon sweet milk, eight eggs beaten to a froth, yelks and whites beaten separately, add one tablespoonful of flour and a little milk. Set the milk on the stove in a tin basin or a porcelain kettle, bring it to a boiling heat, add the mixture of yelks of eggs and flour, let it boil up thick, stirring constantly. Flavor with lemon unless some other flavoring is preferred (lemon is best), beat the whites of the eggs to a stiff froth, sweeten the custard to your taste, place the white of eggs on top, let it remain over the stove a minute, then take it off and serve. This makes a very nice dessert if made properly, and is good either hot or cold. This receipt is enough for eight or ten persons.

Orange Fritters.—One pound of flour, one pint of milk with a teaspoonful of salt in it, and one-quarter of a pound of melted butter, and three eggs beaten very light. Prepare four oranges by removing the yellow rind and every particle of white pith; divide into small pieces without breaking the skin. In each spoonful of batter put a piece of orange, and fry a golden brown; sift powdered sugar over as soon as taken from the pan.

Fruit Roll.—Make a crust as usual, which roll out in a long sheet. Cut a quantity of fruit, peaches, apples, or plums, or small fruit mashed, or jam, which spread thickly over and sprinkle with sugar; roll up and fold the ends over; then wrap in a strong cloth and tie closely, and place in a steamer. Serve with sauce or sweetened cream.

Fig Pudding.—Take a quarter of a pound of figs, pound them in a mortar, and mix gradually half a pound of bread crumbs, and four ounces of beef suet, minced very small, add four ounces of pounded sugar, and mix the whole together, with two eggs beaten up, and a good teacup of new milk. When all these ingredients are well mixed, fill a mold and boil for four hours.

Farmers' Pudding.—Heat one quart of milk to boiling, then stir in, slowly, one teacup of maizena. Mix with this about six good apples, pared and sliced, and add two tablespoonfuls of sugar, one of butter, and a little allspice and nutmeg. Pour the whole into a deep dish, and bake until done, which will be in about forty minutes.

Fruit Pudding.—One egg well beaten, one cup sweet milk, one and one-half cups of berries, half cup of sugar, one spoonful of butter, one cup bread crumbs. Bake in a shallow dish.

Ginger Pudding.—Five eggs, two cups of sugar, two cups of butter, four cups of flour, one cup of molasses, one cup of sour milk, one teaspoonful of soda, ginger and allspice to taste. Bake in a pan or steam in a mold or pan.

Sauce for Ginger Pudding.—One-half pint of molasses, one pint of sugar, one-half pint of butter, ginger to suit the taste, and a little water. Boil all together until the sauce becomes somewhat thick.

Golden Pudding.—Half a pound of bread crumbs, quarter of a pound of suet, quarter of a pound of marmalade, quarter of a pound of sugar, four eggs; mix the suet and bread crumbs in a basin, finely minced, stir all the ingredients well together, beat the eggs to a froth; when well mixed put into a mold or buttered basin, tie down with a floured cloth, and boil two hours. Serve with powdered sugar over it.

Graham Pudding.—One cup of graham flour, half a cup of sweet milk, a little salt, a teaspoonful of baking powder. Turn over a pudding-dish full of sliced apples sweetened with either sugar or molasses. Bake till thoroughly done. This is a good dish for those who cannot eat rich pie-crust, and may be varied by using different kinds of fruit.

Hard Times Pudding.—Half a pint of molasses, half a pint of water, two teaspoonfuls of soda, one teaspoonful of salt. Thicken with flour enough to make a batter about like that for a cup cake. Put this in a pudding-bag; allow room to rise. It would be safe to have the pudding-bag about half full of the batter. Let this boil steadily for three hours. Sauce to serve with it is made thus: Mix two teaspoonfuls of either white or brown sugar with a lump of butter the size of a butternut; a little salt and one large spoonful of flour should be mixed with the butter and sugar. When free from lumps pour boiling water slowly over it, stirring all the time. Let it boil up once or twice to make it of the desired thickness.

Hard Sauce for Puddings.—Stir to cream one cup of butter with three cups powdered sugar; when light, beat in juice of a lemon, two teaspoonfuls nutmeg.

Home Pudding.—One pint of milk, yelks of two eggs, three crackers rolled fine, and bake. Use three-fourths of a cup of sugar, and the whites of the eggs for frosting; spread over the pudding and return to the oven for a few minutes.

Indian Pudding.—Boil two quarts of milk, and while boiling stir in cornmeal enough to make it of the consistency of mush; take one cup of suet, one cup of molasses, one tablespoonful each of cinnamon and ginger and stir into the pudding; scald all together well, and then set away to get cool; add three well-beaten eggs, butter, size of egg, one cup each of currants and raisins, salt and sugar enough to serve without sauce if you wish; then bake three hours slowly. Brandy sauce makes it equal to English plum pudding.

Indian Apple Pudding.—Pour three pints of scalded milk over one pint of sifted Indian meal, stir in two large spoonfuls of molasses, two teaspoonfuls of cinnamon or ginger, and one teaspoonful of salt, add a dozen apples, pared and sliced very thin. Bake in a yellow nappy for three hours. Serve with a sweet sauce.

Kiss Pudding.—One quart milk, three tablespoonfuls cornstarch, the yelks of four eggs, one-half cup sugar and a little salt. Place part of it, with salt and sugar, on the stove and boil. Dissolve the cornstarch in the rest of the milk and stir into the boiling milk; also, add the yelks of the eggs and flour. *Frosting.*—The beaten whites of the four eggs, with one-half cup of sugar flavored with lemon. Cover the pudding and nicely brown. Save a little frosting to moisten the top, then put grated cocoanut over top to give it the appearance of snowflake.

Kent Pudding.—One quart of milk, six ounces of ground rice, three eggs, currants, sugar, and spice to taste. The milk and rice should be boiled overnight, and the other ingredients mixed in the next morning. Stir the mixture well before putting it into the oven.

Lemon Meringue Pudding.—One quart milk, two cups bread crumbs, four eggs, one-half cup butter, one cup white sugar, one large lemon, juice and half the rind grated; soak the bread in the milk; add the beaten yelks with the butter and sugar rubbed to a cream, also the lemon. Bake in a buttered dish until firm and slightly brown; draw to the door of the oven and cover with a meringue of the whites whipped to a froth, with three tablespoonfuls of powdered sugar and a little lemon juice. Brown very slightly; sift powdered sugar over it and eat cold. You may make an orange pudding in the same way.

Lemon Custard. One cup of sugar, one of sweet milk, one tablespoonful of butter, three eggs, one lemon—mix lemon juice with yelks and sugar, add milk next, then the butter and flour. When the custards are cool spread on the whites, well sweetened, and set back in the stove to brown.

Magic Pastry.—Two tablespoonfuls of pounded sugar, four ounces of fine flour, two eggs. Mix all together very smoothly, and fry in lard,

Lemon Fritters.—Among the nicest of fruit fritters are those made of lemon. To one cup of milk and one egg allow the juice and pulp of one lemon. These may be served with sauce; with the grated peel of half the lemon added to flavor the sauce.

Lemon Pudding.—One pound of sifted sugar, one pint of cream, one-half pound of butter, six eggs, and one lemon. Beat the butter and sugar to a cream, add the well beaten eggs, the grated lemon both pulp and peel, and the cream. Stir well, and bake.

Lemon Flap-Jacks.—One pint of milk, four eggs, juice of one lemon, flour to make a light batter, pinch of soda. Fry in hot lard. Serve with sugar and nutmeg.

Molasses Sauce.—One cup of molasses, half a cup of water, one tablespoonful of butter, a little cinnamon or nutmeg (about a half teaspoonful), one-fourth of a teaspoonful of salt, three tablespoonfuls of vinegar. Boil all together for twenty minutes. Lemon juice may be used in place of vinegar if desired. This is very nice for an apple or rice pudding.

Maple Sugar Sauce.—Break half a pound of maple sugar in small bits, put it into a thick saucepan over the fire and melt the sugar until it forms a clear syrup; then remove it from the fire and stir in two heaping tablespoonfuls of butter cut in small bits. Serve the sauce hot with any fruit pudding.

Mountain Dew Pudding.—Three crackers, rolled, one pint of milk, yelks of two eggs, and a small piece of butter. Bake one-half hour, then take the whites of the eggs, beat to a stiff froth, add one cup of sugar, and put it on the top and bake fifteen minutes.

Orange Pudding.—Peel and cut in bits five oranges, rejecting the seeds. Sprinkle a cup of sugar over it. Boil a pint of milk, to which add the yelks of three eggs, well beaten, with one tablespoonful of cornstarch. When it thickens pour it over the fruit. Beat the whites of eggs with a tablespoonful of white sugar. Frost the pudding and brown it in the oven. Substitute strawberries or peaches if you like.

Peach Pudding.—Beat the yelks of six eggs and one cup of sugar light; moisten one tablespoonful of cornstarch with milk and stir in the yelks of the eggs; flavor to taste. Stir this mixture in one quart of boiling milk. Let it boil up once. Line bottom of a pudding dish with peaches, peeled, cut in half, and sugared. Pour over them a layer of the custard; then peaches, and so on until the dish is full, leaving the last layer of custard; cover the tops with the whites of the eggs whipped to a froth; put in the oven and brown. Serve hot or cold.

To Ice Pastry.—To ice pastry, which is the usual method adopted for fruit tarts and sweet dishes of pastry, put the white of an egg on a plate and beat it to a stiff froth. When the pastry is nearly baked, brush it over with this, and sift over some powdered sugar. Put it back into the oven to set the glaze, and in a few minutes it will be done. Great care should be taken that the paste does not catch or burn in the oven, which it is very liable to do after the icing is laid on.

Orange Roly Poly.—Make a short, light dough, the same as is used for any dumplings, roll into an oblong shape and cover the paste thickly with sweet oranges, peeled, stirred thin and seeded; sprinkle with sugar, roll up closely, folding and pinching down the edge to keep in the syrup. Steam an hour and a half. Serve with cream and sugar or hard sauce.

Pan Pudding.—This is a New England dish, and is nice where appetites are expansive. Take three cups of fine rye meal, three cups of Indian meal, one egg and three tablespoonfuls of molasses; add a little salt and allspice, and enough rich sweet milk to make a batter stiff enough to drop from a spoon. Fry to a good brown in hot lard.

Pineapple Fritters.—One pint of flour, half pint of milk, three eggs, half teaspoonful soda, three-fourths teaspoonful cream tartar, one tablespoonful sugar, salt to taste. Peel and slice one juicy pineapple, and cover with sugar; let it stand over night; stir in the batter when ready to fry. To be eaten while hot, with sugar.

Pineapple Pudding.—Peel the pineapple, taking care to get all the specks out, and grate it; take its weight in sugar, and half of its weight in butter; rub these to a cream and stir them into the apple; then add five eggs and a cup of cream. It may be baked with or without the paste crust, as you may prefer.

Peach Potpie.—Put a plain pie crust round the edge of a pan; cut up some peaches, and put a layer of them into your pan, then a layer of sugar and nutmeg; cover with a crust, and bake slowly for two or three hours.

Plum Pudding.—One pound raisins, one pound currants, one-half pound citron, one-half pound candied fruit, one pound suet, one pound sugar, one pound mixed flour and bread crumbs, eight eggs, spices to taste; boil four hours.

Pop-Overs.—One pint milk, one pint flour, butter size of a walnut, three eggs, beaten light, pinch of salt, add eggs last. Bake in cups, filling them half full.

Puff Pudding.—One and a half cups of flour, one of milk, two eggs, and a little salt; bake in a hot oven twenty minutes in pattypans. Serve with sauce.

Queen of Puddings.—One pint of bread crumbs, one quart of sweet milk, yelks of four eggs, piece of butter size of an egg. Flavor and bake. Beat the white of an egg to a froth with a cup of pulverized sugar. Spread over the pudding a layer of jelly, pour the eggs over and brown slightly. Serve with cold sauce.

Quick Pudding.—Boil some rice; when done soft, break in three eggs, half a cup of cream or milk, and flavor to suit the taste. Give it one boil, and send it to the table with bits of butter on the top.

Sweet Potato Pudding.—Beat to a cream one pound of sugar and one pound of butter, and two pounds of potatoes, mashed fine, five eggs, one wineglass of wine, and half a pint of milk. Bake in a crust.

Steamed Pudding.—One coffeecup of buttermilk, one-third of a cup of sugar, one egg, a little salt, a heaping teaspoonful of soda, about three and one-half teacups of flour, and one small cup of raisins. Steam two hours.

New Rice Pudding.—Mix four large teaspoonfuls of rice flour with half a pint of cold milk, and stir it into a quart of boiling milk until it boils again; then remove, stir in butter the size of an egg and add a little salt; let it cool, and add four eggs, well beaten, two-thirds of a cup of sugar, grated nutmeg, half wineglassful of brandy or other flavoring; bake in a buttered dish twenty minutes. To be eaten hot with sauce.

Rice and Apples.—Core as many nice apples as will fill a dish; boil them in light syrup. Prepare one-quarter of a pound of rice in milk with sugar and salt, put some of the rice in the dish, and put in the apples; then fill up the intervals with rice, and bake it in the oven until it is a fine color.

Raspberry Fritters.—Make a batter of a pint of milk, one egg, a little salt, and enough flour to make a mixture that will drop from a spoon. Add a cup of fine raspberries, with a tablespoonful of granulated sugar mixed with them. Fry in hot lard and dash with powdered sugar.

Raisin Pudding.—One quart of sweet milk, six eggs, one-half teacup of butter, one-half teacup sugar, one teacup raisins with seeds removed, flour sufficient to make thick batter. Pour into a mold and steam until cooked. Butter and sugar flavored for sauce.

Rice Fritters.—Take one cup of cold boiled rice, one pint of flour, one teaspoonful of salt, two eggs beaten lightly, and milk enough to make this a thick batter; beat all together well and bake on a griddle.

Raspberry Custard.—Take three gills of rasberry juice and dissolve in it a pound of white sugar, mix it with a pint of boiling cream, stir until quite thick, and serve in custard glasses.

Strawberry Short-Cake.—To make a nice strawberry short-cake, make a nice, rich biscuit crust, bake in a round tin, and when baked cut in two parts with a sharp knife; put a thick layer of berries, sweetened to taste, on one half, then lay on the other half and fix in the same manner. Some think a cup of sweet cream poured over the top layer a great addition. The berries should be mashed before placing them on the cake.

Swiss Pudding.—Put layers of crumbs of bread and sliced apples with sugar between, till the dish is quite full; let the crumbs be the uppermost layer; then pour melted butter over and bake it. Or butter a dish, strew bread crumbs thickly over it, add apples, raspberries, or any fruit sweetened, alternately with bread crumbs, until the dish is full; then pour melted butter, or rather small lumps of butter, over the top and bake.

Steamed Apples.—Select nice, sweet apples; wash and place them in a pan; turn a little water in the pan and stew; one-half cup sugar over as many apples as will cover the bottom of the pan; then cover with another pan and cook till done. If preferred, you can stew the juice down and turn it over the apples. They are much nicer than when baked.

Suet Pudding.—Chop fine one cup of raisins and one-half cup of suet (one cup, if wanted very rich), add two cups of sweet milk, one cup of sugar, four cups of flour, one teaspoonful of cream of tartar, two teaspoonfuls of soda, and a little salt. Cover tight and steam or boil two hours. Leave room to swell. Pork chopped very fine, or a little less in measure of pork fat, may be used. Eat with liquid sauce.

Simple Dessert.—Put eight crackers in a deep dish, pour enough warm water or milk over them to just cover them, and when soaked, which will not take longer than ten minutes, sprinkle with sugar, cover with cream, garnish with preserved peaches, pears, or quinces, and serve. Try it.

Snow-Ball Pudding.—Take two teacups of rice, wash, and boil until tender; pare and core twelve large sour apples (leaving the apples whole); fill the apples with rice, and put it around outside; tie each one in a separate cloth and drop in boiling water; serve while hot with cream and sugar, or any sauce desired.

Pudding Sauce.—One cup of sugar, an even tablespoonful of flour, and the same of butter. Mix to a cream. Put boiling water to them, mix thoroughly and put on the stove to boil fifteen minutes, stirring occasionally. Flavor with grated nutmeg.

Pudding Sauce.—Take the superfluous juice from a can of peaches, and heat it to boiling. Mix flour, butter and sugar in about equal quantities, add a little vanilla, and cook the mixture in the hot peach juice. This is delicious for almost any kind of steamed or fruit pudding.

A Fine Pudding Sauce.—When a sponge pudding is to be eaten hot an excellent sauce is made of sugar and butter whipped to a cream, strawberries or other fruit crushed into it, and a little good wine. If properly made no better sauce can be used for a sponge pudding.

Stewed Apples.—Pare your apples and place them in a steamer, with a clove in each; then put the steamer over a pot of boiling water, until soft; then take them up in the fruit dish and shake powdered sugar over them.

Sweet Apple Custard.—Pare and core sweet apples; stew them in water till tender; strain them through a colander, add sugar and spice to taste, and make them like pumpkin pies.

Sallie Lunn.—One quart of flour, four eggs, one pint of milk, one tablespoonful of lard, same of butter, two spoonfuls of sugar, one gill of yeast.

Tapioca Custard.—After soaking a cup of tapioca until perfectly soft, drain off any surplus water and add a quart of new milk; set the dish in one of boiling water to prevent sticking or burning; sweeten to suit the taste; when it begins to grow a little thick, add the yelks of four eggs, beaten, with one tablespoonful of sugar; remove from the fire as soon as it becomes the consistency of cream, or it will be too hard when cold; flavor to taste after it is done, and spread the whites of eggs over the top; brown a delicate color in the oven.

Tiptop Pudding.—One pint of bread crumbs, one quart of milk, one cup of sugar, the grated peel of a lemon, yelks of four eggs, a piece of butter size of an egg, then bake. When done spread fresh strawberries over the top, or if not in season for strawberries, use a cup of preserved raspberries; pour over that a meringue made with the white of the egg, a cup of sugar, and the juice of the lemon. Return to the oven to color; let it partly cool, and serve with milk or cream.

Tapioca Pudding.—Soak four tablespoonfuls tapioca in a little water over night; boil one quart of milk and pour over it while hot; when cool add one-half cup sugar, one egg, and the yelk of one egg, well beaten; bake slowly one hour, spread with the whites of two eggs, beaten, return to oven, brown slightly; flavor with orange.

Wine Sauce for Pudding.——Half a pint of sherry or Madeira wine, and half a gill of water; boil together, and add four tablespoonfuls of sugar, the juice of one lemon, and the rind cut into small pieces. To be poured over the pudding just before the latter is to be eaten.

Waffles.—One pint of sour cream, one pint of flour, three eggs, half a teaspoonful soda, beat up, and bake on hot waffle irons, well buttered, and butter well as soon as removed from the iron.

Yorkshire Pudding.—Make a batter with five tablespoonfuls of flour, one egg, and about a pint of milk. Put some of the fat out of the dripping-pan into the Yorkshire pudding tin, and when it is boiling hot pour in the batter. Bake it in the oven for half an hour, and set it for a few minutes in front of the fire under the meat.

Apple Meringue Pie.—Stew and sweeten juicy apples when you have pared and sliced them; mash smooth, and season with nutmeg, or stew some lemon peel with them and remove when cold; fill your pans and bake till done; spread over the apples a thick meringue, made by whipping to a stiff froth the whites of three eggs for each pie, sweetening with a tablespoonful of powdered sugar for each egg; flavor this with rose or vanilla; beat until it will stand alone and cover the pie three-quarters of an inch thick. Set back in the oven until the meringue is well set. Should it color too darkly sift powdered sugar over it when cool; eat cold. Peaches are even more delicious when used in the same manner.

Cherry Pie.—Stone the cherries; make a paste as for any pie, put in the fruit, add sugar, and about three tablespoonfuls water; sprinkle a tablespoonful flour over fruit; take a piece of butter the size of a walnut, and cut it in small bits over the top; make a paste of one teaspoonful of flour to two of cold water, and wet the edges of the crust before putting on the cover; if properly done it will prevent the juice from running out; or, roll the edges together; while hot, see if it is sweet enough; if not, raise the cover and put in more sugar. Eat while slightly warm.

Spring Mince Pies.—A cup and a half of chopped raisins, one cup of sugar, one cup of molasses, one cup of warm water, half a cup of vinegar or good boiled cider, two well-beaten eggs, five crackers, pounded fine; stir all together and season with spices as other mince pies; bake with rich crust. For the top crust, roll thin, cut in narrow strips, and twist and lay across.

Cream Pie.—One pint milk, two large spoonfuls sugar, one tablespoonful flour, yelks of two eggs and white of one. Beats eggs, sugar, and flour together, let the milk get boiling hot, pour in the beaten parts and stir until thick, make the crust and bake it; fill with the custard. Beat the remaining white of egg till stiff, spread evenly over the top, return to the oven to brown slightly. Flavor with lemon or vanilla.

Custard Pie.—One quart milk, three eggs, one tablespoonful corn starch, one dessertspoonful extract vanilla, one cupful sugar, a very small pinch salt; beat the sugar and eggs together, mix the corn starch in a little of the milk, and stir all well together. This is far superior to the ordinary custard pie made with four eggs. Less sugar may be used if preferred.

Mock Lemon Pie.—One cup of sugar, one heaping tablespoonful of flour, the yelks of two eggs (save the whites for the top of the pie), one teaspoonful of extract of lemon, two-thirds of a cup of boiling water, two-thirds of a cup of stewed pie plant; mix the sugar, flour, eggs and extract together; then pour on the water, then the pie plant; bake with one crust; when done, beat the whites to a stiff froth and spread it over the pie, setting it back in the oven for four minutes.

Pie-Crust Without Lard.— Take good, rich buttermilk, soda, and a little salt, and mix just as soft as can be mixed and hold together; have plenty of flour on the molding-board and rolling-pin; then make and bake as other pies, or rather in a slow oven, and when the pie is taken from the oven do not cover it up. In this way a dyspeptic can indulge in the luxury of a pie.

Oatmeal Pie Crust.—Scald two parts of fine oatmeal with one part of hot water; mix well and roll thin. As this bakes very quickly fruit which requires much cooking must be cooked first before making the pies. This crust is very tender, possessing all the desirable qualities of shortened pie crusts without their injurious effects.

Beverly Pie.—Pare and grate some sweet mellow apples—about a dozen; to a pint of the grated pulp put a pint of milk, two eggs, two tablespoonfuls of melted butter, the grated peel of a lemon, and half a wineglass of brandy; sweeten to your taste; to be baked in a deep plate, with only a lower crust.

Corn-Starch Custard Pie.—Very nice pies are made with two eggs, and two large tablespoonfuls of corn starch to a quart of milk; sweeten and spice to taste; the corn starch should be mixed smooth with milk and eggs beaten up in it, then thin out with more milk; sweeten, season, pour into pans lined with paste, and grate a little nutmeg over the top.

Lemon Pie.—The juice and grated rind of one lemon, one cup of water, one tablespoonful of corn starch, one cup of sugar, one egg, and a piece of butter the size of a small egg. Boil the water, wet the corn starch with a little cold water, and stir it in; when it boils up, pour on it the sugar and butter; after it cools, add the egg and lemon; bake with under and upper crust.

Lemon Pie.—Four lemons, one cup sugar, one cup molasses, three and one-half cups water, half cup flour. Grate the rind of two lemons and use with the inside of the four (but do not use the white skin, as it is bitter), cook these ingredients a few minutes before putting it between the crust.

Lemon Meringue Pie.—Beat the yelks of four eggs, ten tablespoonfuls of sugar, three of melted butter, and the juice of one lemon and a half, add three tablespoonfuls of milk or water; bake in an undercrust, then beat the whites, pour over the top and put back in the oven to brown.

Apple Custard Pie.—Two well-beaten eggs, one cup grated sweet apple, one pint sweet milk, two large spoonfuls of sugar, a little salt and flavor.

Rhubarb Cream Pie.—One pint stewed rhubarb, four ounces sugar, one pint cream, two ounces powdered cracker, three eggs. Rub the stewed rhubarb through a sieve, beat the other ingredients well together, and just as the pie is ready for the oven stir in the rhubarb; pour the whole into a plate lined with pastry. Cover with strips and bake.

Orange Pie.—Take the juice and grated rind of one orange, one small cup of sugar, yelks of three eggs, one tablespoonful of corn starch, make smooth with milk, piece of butter as large as a chestnut, and one cup of milk. Beat the whites of the three eggs with sugar, and place on the top after the pie is baked—leaving in the oven till browned.

Buttermilk Pie.—Beat together a heaping cup of sugar and four eggs, add half a cup of butter; beat thoroughly, and add one and a half pints of fresh country buttermilk. Line the pie tins with crust; slice an apple thin and lay in each pie; fill the crust with the mixture, and bake with no upper crust.

Buttermilk Pies.—One cup sugar, two cups buttermilk, two eggs, two tablespoonfuls flour, two tablespoonfuls butter; flavor with lemon. This makes two pies.

Rice Pie.—To a pint of boiled rice add a pint of rich cream, two eggs, salt, and a little mace. Let these ingredients be well mixed, spread half the quantity in a deep baking dish, lay pieces of chicken upon it and cover them with the remainder of the rice, and bake in a hot oven.

Pumpkin Pie.—Stew the pumpkin as dry as possible without burning; rub it through a colander. To one pint of the pumpkin add three eggs, one quart of milk, one teacup sugar, half teaspoonful salt, and nutmeg or ginger to taste. The above quantity will make two large pies.

Marlborough Pie.—Grate six apples, one cup of sugar, three tablespoonfuls melted butter, four eggs, juice and grated rind of a lemon, two tablespoonfuls brandy or wine, if you choose; if not, omit it. Bake in an under, but without top crust.

Washington Pie.—Three eggs, one cup sugar, a scant half cup milk, half teaspoonful soda, a teaspoonful cream tartar, cup flour, a piece butter size of a hen's egg, spice to taste; this makes three layers; spread with jelly.

Cocoanut Pie.—Grate one cocoanut, add one pint of milk, three eggs, one cup of sugar and a little salt; add the cocoanut milk. Enough for two pies.

Peach Pie.—Line the pie pans with rich pastry, fill with ripe, juicy peaches, peeled and cut in quarters, sprinkle well with sugar, cover with a thin crust, bake half an hour. Serve cold.

Prune Pie.—Stew the prunes as for sauce, stone and sweeten, and with nice pie crust I think you will call them good. Be sure and not have them too dry.

Fancy Dishes.

Pineapple Bavarian Cream.—One pint of fresh or canned pineapple, one small teacup of sugar, one pint of cream, half a package of gelatine, half a cup of cold water. Soak gelatine two hours in the water. Chop pineapple fine, put it on with the sugar to simmer twenty minutes. Add gelatine and strain immediately through a cloth or sieve into a tin basin. Rub the pineapple through as much as possible. Beat until it begins to thicken, then add cream which has been whipped to a froth. When well mixed, pour into a wet mold, and set away to harden. Serve with whipped cream.

Lemon Float.—Boil one quart of sweet milk and three tablespoonfuls of sugar, and mix it with one tablespoonful of corn starch, stirred smoothly, and the grated peel of one lemon. When it has boiled ten minutes, add the yelks of three eggs, well beaten, and stir constantly for five minutes. Put the pail it was cooked in directly into a pail of cold water, and stir it some time, then strain it into a pudding dish. Beat the whites of the eggs to a very stiff froth, add the juice of the lemon and two tablespoonfuls of sugar. Put them over the pudding and serve ice cold. Desiccated or fresh cocoanut grated finely can be added to the whites of the eggs, and will improve the dish very much.

Peaches with Rice.—Take some peaches and cut them in halves; simmer them in a syrup for half an hour, then drain, and when cold arrange them on a dish round a shape of rice made as follows: Boil three tablespoonfuls of rice, picked and washed clean, in a pint of milk, with sugar to taste, and a piece of vanilla; when quite done put it into a basin to get cold. Make a custard with a gill of milk and the yelks of four eggs; when cold mix it with the rice. Beat up to a froth a gill of cream, with some sugar and a pinch of isinglass dissolved in a little water; mix this very lightly with the rice and custard; fill a mold with the mixture and set it on ice. When moderately iced turn it out on a dish and serve.

Coffee Cream.—This is a delicate and agreeable dish for an evening entertainment. Dissolve one ounce and a quarter of isinglass in half a pint of water. Boil for two hours a teacup of whole coffee in about half a pint of water (ground coffee is not so good for the purpose); add a teacupful to the melted isinglass. Put them into a saucepan with half a pint of milk, and let the whole boil up; sweeten with loaf sugar, and let it stand ten minutes to cool, then add a pint of good cream; stir it well up and pour it into a mold and put it in a cool place to fix; turn it out on a glass dish before serving up.

Charlotte Russe.—Take one-fifth of a package of gelatine and one-half a cup cold milk; place in a farina boiler and stir gently over the fire until the gelatine is dissolved, pour into a dish and place in a cool room; take one pint of rich cream and whisk it with a tin egg-beater until it is thick; flavor the cream with either vanilla or wine, and sweeten to taste; when the gelatine is cool strain carefully into the prepared cream; line a mold with lady fingers; then pour the cream in carefully until it is filled; cover with lady fingers and ice the top if you desire it.

Snow Eggs.—Snow eggs are formed by putting over the fire a quart of rich milk, sweetening it and flavoring it with orange flower water. Separate the whites and yelks of six fresh eggs, and beat up the whites to a stiff froth. Drop a spoonful at a time into the boiling milk, turning them as quickly as possible, and lifting them out of the milk with a skimmer, place them on a sieve. Beat up the yelks and stir them into the milk; let them have one boil and put in a glass dish. Arrange the whites around the edges and serve either hot or cold; the last is preferable.

Airy Nothings.—To three eggs put half an egg-shell full of sweet milk, and butter the size of a walnut; work in flour until you can roll the dough into as thin a sheet as possible. Cut into cakes with a saucer and stick as you do biscuits; bake them quickly but not brown; heap them up on a dish and strew them thickly with powdered sugar. *Note.*—Allow one pint of flour to the other ingredients named above, although every bit may not be required; always reserve a little for the rolling out of cakes on a board.

Snow Custard.—Boil eight eggs, leaving out the whites of four; add to them one quart of milk and five ounces of sugar; have a shallow pan of hot water in the oven; set the dish into it, and bake till the custard is thick; then set away to cool; beat the remaining whites very light; add half a pound of sugar and a teaspoonful of lemon juice; when the custard is cold lay the whites over the top in heaps, but do not let them touch.

Cream Pie and Orange Dessert.—Cut the oranges in thin slices and sprinkle sugar over them; let them stand two or three hours; serve on ordinary fruit plates. The pie is made with a bottom-crust only, and that not thick, but light and flaky. Take one coffeecup of thick, sweet cream, half a cup of pulverized sugar, a tablespoonful of flour, one egg; flavor with lemon extract; bake until you are sure the crust is brown and hard, so that it will not absorb the custard.

Whipped Cream.—Take one pint of very thick cream, sweeten it with very fine sugar and orange flower water; boil it. Beat the whites of ten eggs with a little cold cream, strain it, and when the cream is upon the boil, pour in the eggs, stirring it well till it comes to a thick curd; and then take it up and strain it again through a hair sieve. Beat it well with a spoon till it is cold, then place it in a dish in which you wish to serve it.

Watermelon Tea Dish.—Take a fully ripe watermelon, put on ice until thoroughly cold, slice, remove seeds and cut any shape you prefer, squares, diamonds, stars, size sufficient for mouthful, put layer into glass dish, sprinkle with granulated sugar, another layer with sugar, until you fill your dish, sprinkle sugar over top, return to ice-box until wanted for tea. Dish and eat the same as any kind of fruit. You will be delighted.

Compote of Oranges.—Put a handful of loaf sugar to boil with a gill of water in a saucepan; when it boils, add the rind of three oranges minced finely or cut into very narrow strips. Let the whole boil five minutes, add a liquor glass of brandy, and pour the syrup (hot) over half a dozen whole oranges, peeled and cored, or cut up in any form you like. Leave the oranges in a basin with the syrup till quite cold; then pile them up on a dish and serve.

Gooseberry Trifle.—Scald the fruit, press it through a sieve, and add sugar to taste. Make a thick layer of this at the bottom of the dish. Mix a pint of milk, a pint of cream, and the yelks of two eggs; scald it over the fire, stirring it well; add a small quantity of sugar and let it get cold. Then lay it over the gooseberries with a spoon, and put on the whole a whip made the day before.

Hen's Nest.—Take four eggs, make a hole with a pin in one end, take out all the yelk and white, fill this with a liquid blanc mange, stand each shell in an egg cup and put it away to cool; put some orange marmalade on a dish; when the blanc mange is hardened, break off the shells, and stand the whole eggs in the center of the orange marmalade. This looks like a nest of eggs, and has a pretty effect for a supper table.

Dessert.—Make a batter as if for waffles; to one pint of milk allow two eggs and enough flour to thicken; one teaspoonful of baking-powder should be stirred into the flour. Fill a sufficient number of teacups with this and fruit in layers. Then set the cups in the steamer, and let the water boil underneath it for a full hour. Serve while hot with sugar and cream. Any jam is nice for this, or raw apples chopped fine.

Orange Butter.—Pare eight large oranges, cut into thin slices, pour over them one and one-half cups of powdered sugar; boil one pint of milk; and, while boiling, add the yelks of three eggs, one tablespoonful of corn starch made smooth with cold milk; stir constantly, and when thick pour over the fruit; beat the whites of the eggs to a froth, sweeten, pour over the custard and brown in the oven. Serve cold.

Cocoanut Cones.—One pound powdered sugar, one-half ditto of grated cocoanut, and the whites of five eggs; whip the eggs as for icing, adding the sugar as you go on, until it will stand alone, then beat in the cocoanut; mold the mixture with your hands into small cones, and set these far enough apart not to touch each other upon buttered paper in a baking pan; bake in a very moderate oven.

Dorcas American Cream.—Four eggs, half box gelatine, one quart milk. Put the milk and gelatine on the stove, and when nearly boiling, mix in the yelks well beaten. Beat the whites very stiff; then add sixteen table-spoonfuls of sugar. After they are well beaten, add to the other ingredients just as they come off the stove. Flavor with vanilla or anything you may fancy.

Velvet Cream.—One ounce isinglass, a teacup of wine, the juice of a large lemon, one pint of rich cream. Dissolve the isinglass in wine; rub large lumps of sugar over the lemon to extract the oil; squeeze out the juice, and sweeten to taste. Boil this mixture and strain it; when quite cool add the cream, and put it into molds

Spirals.—Two eggs beaten quite light, sufficient flour stirred in to make the mixture very stiff; add a pinch of salt and stir again; then roll out quite thin, cut strips about two inches wide and four long, and roll round the fingers as if curling hair. Fry in butter till of a delicate golden shade, and sprinkle powdered sugar just before serving.

Ambrosia.—One pineapple chopped quite fine, one-half box of straw-berries, six bananas sliced and the slices quartered, six oranges sliced and the slices quartered, one lemon cut fine. Sweeten to taste; add one wine-glassful of sherry or Madeira, and set away until very cold.

Corn Starch Blanc Mange.—Dissolve three tablespoonfuls of corn starch in new milk; heat a pint of new milk nearly boiling hot, pour in the starch, stir briskly, and boil for three minutes; flavor with lemon or vanilla.

Apple Charlotte.—This is a seasonable dish. Take two pounds of apples, pare and core them, slice them into a pan, and add one pound of loaf sugar, the juice of three lemons, and the grated rind of one. Let these boil until they become a thick mass, which will take about two hours. Turn it into a mold, and serve it cold with either thick custard or cream.

Snowflake.—Dissolve in one quart of boiling water a box of gelatine; when thoroughly dissolved add four cups of white sugar and the juice of two lemons; when nearly cold strain; beat to a stiff froth the whites of six eggs; mix the whole together, pour into molds and set on ice, or in a very cool place. This served with a boiled custard makes a very pretty dish.

Lemon Conserve.—One pound powdered white sugar, quarter pound fresh butter, six eggs, leaving out the whites of two, adding the juice and grated rind of three fine lemons. Put all into a saucepan, stir the whole gently over a slow fire until it gets thick as honey. A delicious spread for bread, biscuits or rolls.

Orange Tart.—Grate the yellow of one orange, squeeze out the juice, being careful to avoid the seeds, the juice and yellow of half a lemon, fourth of a pound of sugar, two ounces butter, carefully melted, two eggs, leaving out the white of one, beat well, stir all together, line a tart tin, or pattypans with thin paste, fill and bake fifteen or twenty minutes.

Snow Balls.—Two cups of sugar, one cup of butter, one cup of sweet milk, three cups of flour, three teaspoonfuls of baking powder, whites of five eggs. Bake in deep square tins. The day following, cut in two-inch squares, taking the ouside off so as to leave it all white; take each piece on a fork and frost upon all sides, and roll in freshly grated cocoanut.

Spanish Puffs.—Put into a saucepan a teacup of water, a tablespoonful of powdered sugar, half a teaspoonful of salt, and two ounces of butter; while it is boiling add sufficient flour for it to leave the saucepan, stir in, one by one, the yelks of four eggs, drop a teaspoonful at a time into boiling lard, fry them a light brown; pour white wine and melted butter over them.

Peach Butter.—Pare ripe peaches and put them in a preserving kettle, with sufficient water to boil them soft; then sift through a colander, removing the stones. To each quart of peach put one and one-half pound sugar, and boil very slowly one hour. Stir often, and do not let them burn. Put in stone or glass jars and keep in a cool place.

German Trifle.—Put one quart of strawberries, or any other fresh fruit, in the bottom of a glass dish; sugar the fruit, cover it with a layer of macaroons, pour over it a custard made with one quart of milk and the yelks of seven eggs, well beaten; sweeten to your taste; when cold, place on the top of the eggs, beaten to a stiff froth, with a little sugar.

Havana Butter.—One and a half cups white sugar, whites of three eggs, yelk of one, grated rind and juice of a lemon and a half, or two small ones. Cook over a slow fire twenty minutes, stirring all the while. Very nice for tarts or to be eaten as preserves.

Blanc Mange.—One ounce isinglass to one quart of milk, add sugar, cinnamon and mace to your taste; put it by the fire until the isinglass is dissolved; strain it, and put it in molds to cool.

Banana Pie.—One who retains the " sweet tooth " of his childhood will find this to his liking: Make a banana pie with a lower crust only; bake the crust first, then fill it with sliced bananas and powdered sugar; the fruit will soften sufficiently in a few moments. Cover the top with whipped cream and eat at once.

Orange Salad.—Peel one dozen oranges, and cut in slices; put in layers, in a glass dish, sprinkling each layer plentifully with sugar. Squeeze over this the juice of six oranges, and pour over all a glass of wine or brandy. Sweet oranges are best for this dish with very little sugar, but Messinas are very good, well sweetened.

Apple Snow.—Put twelve apples in cold water and set them over a slow fire; when soft, drain them, take off the peelings, core them, and put them in a deep dish; beat the whites of twelve eggs to a stiff froth, put half a pound of sugar in the apples, beat them light, then beat in the whites. Elegant.

Apple Cream.—Peel and core five large apples; boil them in a little water till soft enough to press through a sieve, sweeten, and beat with them the whites of five eggs. Serve with cream poured around them.

Chocolate Cream.—Put over the fire one quart of milk; when it comes to a boil add three tablespoonfuls of chocolate. Thicken with corn starch and sweeten to taste. Flavor with vanilla. Serve cold with cream.

Caledonian Cream.—Two teaspoonfuls of white sugar, one teaspoonful of raspberry jam, two whites of eggs, juice of one lemon. Beat for half an hour. Serve up sprinkled with fancy biscuits.

Quince Snow.—One-third pound of quince marmalade to whites of two eggs and quarter pound of sugar; pile in a pyramid in a dish and bake a pale yellow.

Cakes.

Weights and Measures.—Two cups flour weigh one pound; one pint flour, one pound; one pint white sugar, one pound; two tablespoonfuls liquid, one ounce; eight teaspoonfuls liquid, one ounce; one gill liquid, four ounces.

Bon-ton Wedding Cake.—Beat to a cream six cups butter and four of white sugar, add sixteen eggs beaten, then roll six cups currants washed and dried, three cups seeded raisins, two cups minced citron, two cups almonds blanched and cut fine, half cup lemon peel minced fine, and one tablespoonful cinnamon, nutmeg, cloves and allspice, in three pints sifted flour, till they are well dredged with the flour, then add them all at once to the butter, sugar and eggs, add half pint brandy; mix very thoroughly and smooth, put in a large cake pan well buttered and lined with paper, and bake in a very *even* oven for eight hours, watch it carefully, and your cake will be elegant; ice it the next day with " transparent icing."

Snow Jelly Cake.—Beat two eggs in a teacup and fill with rich, sour cream; one teacup of white sugar, one cup of flour, a little soda; not quite half a teaspoonful unless the cream is very sour. Bake in four round tins and brown as little as possible. Have a jelly prepared by soaking four tablespoonfuls of tapioca in warm water until transparent, then add more water and place your dish in boiling water on the stove and cook until a transparent jelly; flavor strong with lemon, almond, or wintergreen. Gelatine is just as nice as tapioca. This cake is not expensive and is very nice, and can be eaten by dyspeptics.

Rich Coffee Cake.—Two cups of butter, three of sugar, one of molasses, one of very strong coffee, one of cream or rich milk, the yelks of eight eggs, one pound each of raisins and currants, one-half pound of citron, the same of figs, and five cups of brown flour after it is stirred. Put the flour in the oven until a rich brown, being careful not to burn it. When cold sift with it three teaspoonfuls of good baking powder and a little salt. Cut the figs in long strips, dredge all the fruit with flour, beat the cake well up, and bake in moderate oven from four to five hours.

Marble Cake.—*Light Part.*—Whites of three eggs, one-half cup of butter, one-half cup of sugar, one-half cup of milk, two cups of flour, one-half teaspoonful of soda, one teaspoonful of cream of tartar.

Dark Part.—Yelks of three eggs, one cup of molasses, one-half cup of butter, two cups of flour, one teaspoonful soda, one-third cup of milk, and flavor with mixed spices, cloves, cinnamon, nutmeg. Butter the tin and put in the pan alternate layers of light and dark parts, having the light part on top.

Lemon Cake.—One cup of sugar, four eggs, three tablespoonfuls of sweet milk, three tablespoonfuls of melted butter, three teaspoonfuls of baking powder and one cup of flour.

Sauce.—One lemon (juice and grated rind), one cup of cold water, one cup of sugar, one egg, and tablespoonful of cornstarch. Beat lemon rind and egg together; stir in sugar and lemon juice; dissolve cornstarch in cold water. Cook in a tin over hot water till it jellies.

Good Plain Cookies.—Two cups of white sugar, two eggs, one cup of butter (melted), one teaspoonful of soda, six tablespoonfuls of cold water; roll thin. You may scatter cocoanut over the top before baking. Another good recipe for cookies: Two cups of molasses, one cup of sugar, one cup of butter, one cup boiling water, two teaspoonfuls of soda, two tablespoonfuls of ginger, one tablespoonful of cinnamon; roll as soft as possible. If you like the flavor of coffee, you can use half cold coffee and half water.

Sand Hearts.—Two pounds of flour, two pounds of sugar, one pound of butter, three eggs. Make up into a dough, and work till the ingredients are well incorporated. After rolling out and cutting into heart-shape, place the cakes on a pan and beat up one egg, spread some of it over them with a feather, and then sprinkle with granulated sugar. If a little coarse-grained all the better, mixing with it a little finely-powdered cinnamon.

Watermelon Cake.—White part, two cups of white sugar, two-thirds cup of butter, two-thirds cup of milk, three cups of flour, whites of five eggs, one teaspoonful of soda, and two teaspoonfuls of cream of tartar. Red part, one cup of red sugar, one half cup of butter, one-half cup of milk, two cups of flour, one cup of raisins, whites of five eggs, one teaspoonful of soda, and two teaspoonfuls of cream of tartar. Stone and roll the raisins in powdered sugar, stir into the cake, and turn into the middle of the pan, and pour the white part over and around it.

Frosting for Cake.—Allow sixteen tablespoonfuls pulverized sugar for each egg. Take part of the sugar at first and sprinkle over the egg; beat them for half an hour, gradually stirring in the rest of the sugar; then flavor. A little lemon juice whitens icing. Strawberry juice or cranberry syrup gives a pretty pink shade. It may be colored yellow by using some of the yelk of the egg or by putting the grated peel of a lemon or orange in a thin muslin bag and squeezing it hard into the egg and sugar.

Currant Cookies.—One pound flour, one-half pound of butter, three-quarters of a pound of sugar, four eggs, one half pound of currants well washed and dredged, one half teaspoonful of soda dissolved in hot water, one-half lemon, grated rind and juice, one teaspoonful of cinnamon. Drop from a spoon upon a baking tin lined with well-buttered paper and bake quickly.

Cocoanut Cake.—Three eggs (the whites of two of them to be used for frosting), two-thirds of a cup of sugar, two-thirds of a cup of sweet milk, one and two-thirds cups of flour, one teaspoonful of cream of tartar, and a half teaspoonful of soda. Bake in thin round tins; make a frosting of the whites of the two eggs, well beaten, with four dessertspoonfuls of white sugar; spread on the top of the cakes and sprinkle the grated cocoanut with the frosting.

Apple Cake.—A pleasant variation on the jelly and cream filling used for double cakes may be made of apples. Beat one egg light in a bowl, and into it a cup of sugar. Add to this the strained juice and grated rind of a lemon. Peel and grate three firm pippins or other ripe, tart apples directly into this mixture, stirring each well in before adding another. When all are in, put into a farina kettle and stir over the fire until the apple custard is boiling hot and quite thick. Cool and spread between the cakes.

Angel Cake.—Sift together four times, one and one-half cups of sugar, one cup flour, one teaspoonful cream of tartar; stir in this very lightly whites of eleven eggs thoroughly beaten. Flavor with one-half teaspoonful of rose extract. Bake fifty minutes in a slow oven, not opening the oven for thirty minutes. Turn pan over on a rack and let cake remain in pan one hour. This is the simplest rule for angel cake that we have ever seen, and is excellent.

A Useful Cake.—One-third cup of butter, two cups light brown sugar, two eggs, beat all together. One cup of new sweet milk, three cups of sifted flour, three teaspoonfuls baking powder. Stir all together, and bake in seven layers. For jelly cake take jelly, for orange cake juice and grated rind of one orange, whites of two eggs, make stiff with sugar. For lemon cake white of one egg, juice of one lemon, and teaspoonful extract of lemon. For cocoanut, whites of two eggs, thickened with sugar and grated cocoanut.

Dolly Varden Cake.—Two cups of sugar, two-thirds of a cup of butter, one cup of sweet milk, three cups of flour, three eggs, one-half teaspoonful of soda, one teaspoonful of cream tartar. Flavor with lemon. Bake one-half of this in two pans. To the remainder add one tablespoonful of molasses, one cup of chopped raisins, one-half cup of currants, piece of citron chopped fine, one teaspoonful of cinnamon, cloves and nutmeg. Bake in two pans and put in sheets alternately with a little jelly or white of an egg beaten to a froth.

Almond Cake.—The following recipe for almond cake is a good one. It makes a very nice cake for the basket. Take one cup of butter, one cup and a half of sugar, three eggs, half of a cup of milk, two teaspoonfuls of baking powder, about two cups of flour; flavor with a little almond extract; blanch one pound of almonds; lay aside enough to cover the top of the cake when they are cut in halves; chop the rest and put into the cake. After the cake is in the tin, lay the split ones over the top of the cake; they will rise and brown as the cake bakes. This is delicious; try it.

Raised Raisin Cake.—Dissolve half a square of compressed yeast in one large cup of milk and stir in one pound of flour, let rise; when light beat together eight ounces each of butter and sugar, yelks of four eggs, cup of stoned raisins, some fine cut citron, and grated peel of a lemon; stir now into the dough, beating it very light (it is best to use the hand), let it rise again in a round cake pan and bake in an even but moderate oven.

Strawberry or Red Cake.—Whites of five eggs; butter, one cup; sugar, one cup; red sugar sand, one cup; or if wanted very dark, two cups of red sugar, leaving out the white; sweet milk, one cup; corn starch, one cup; flour, two cups; baking powder, three teaspoonfuls; then make a white cake and bake same as marble cake, or, if desired, bake in layers and put together with frosting.

Farmer's Fruit Cake.—Soak three cups of dried apples over night in warm water. Chop slightly in the morning, and simmer two hours in two cups of molasses. Add two well-beaten eggs, one cup of sugar, one cup of butter, one dessertspoonful of soda, flour enough to make rather a stiff batter. Flavor with nutmeg and cinnamon to the taste. Bake in a quick oven.

Ice Cream Cake.—Take the whites of five eggs, one and a half cups of sugar, one-half cup of butter, one cup of milk, one-half teaspoonful of soda, one teaspoonful cream tartar, three cups of flour. Separate this mixture and color half with strawberry coloring. Flavor this with vanilla, the white with lemon. Put in the white, then the pink. Bake slowly.

Rice Cake.—Take half a pound of clarified butter, eight eggs well beaten, leaving out the whites of two, three-quarters of a pound of pounded sugar, and the grated peel of a lemon; mix these well together; then add grounded rice and dried flour, half a pound of each; currants and candied peel may be added, when approved.

Pineapple Cake.—Three cups sugar, one cup butter, five eggs, three and one-half cups of flour, one-half cup cold water, two teaspoonfuls baking powder. Bake in layers; spread each layer with a thick icing, then cover with grated pineapple. Place on next layer and treat as before.

Gelatine Frosting.—One tablespoonful gelatine, two tablespoonfuls of cold water; when the gelatine is soft, one tablespoonful of hot water. When entirely dissolved add one cup of powdered sugar, and beat while it is yet warm until white and light; lemon to taste. Give good measure to all the ingredients. This frosts one sheet of cake

Molasses Cookies.—Two cups and one-half hot molasses, one cup of shortening (half butter and half lard), one teaspoonful of ginger and one of cinnamon; dissolve two teaspoonfuls of saleratus in a cup of lukewarm water and throw in as quickly as possible; add some flour and stir a few minutes as you would soft cake, then add more flour; mix as soft as you can conveniently and roll out.

Banana Cake.—One cup of butter, two cups sugar, one cup of water or of sweet milk, three eggs, four cups of flour, three small teaspoonfuls of baking powder; mix lightly and bake in layers. Make an icing of the whites of two eggs, and one cup and a half of powdered sugar. Spread this on the layers, and then cover thickly and entirely with bananas, sliced thin. This cake may be flavored with vanilla. The top should be simply frosted.

Buttermilk Cakes.—We advise those ladies who live in the country, where buttermilk can be easily procured, to try the following receipt, which makes a very good light cake: Into two pounds of flour rub one pound of butter, add three-quarters of a pound of currants, two ounces of candied peel, one pint of buttermilk, and one ounce of carbonate of soda. Mix and beat them well together, and bake in a tin.

Bachelors' Buttons.—These delicious little cakes are prepared by rubbing two ounces of butter into five ounces of flour; add five ounces of white sugar, beat an egg with half the sugar and put it to the other ingredients. Add almond flavoring according to taste, roll them in the hand about the size of a large nut, sprinkle them with lump sugar, and place them on tins, with buttered paper. They should be lightly baked.

Bread Cake.—Two cups of very light bread sponge, take one cup butter and lard mixed, one cup sugar, one cup molasses, one tablespoonful cinnamon, half teaspoonful cloves, one teaspoonful soda, one tablespoonful rich milk, two eggs; mix these ingredients well and add to the risen sponge, with flour to make as stiff as cup cake, and one cup of raisins; let rise until light and bake slowly.

Coffee Cakes.—Three cups of bread sponge, one-half cup of butter, two tablespoonfuls of sugar, two eggs. Roll thin, cut out as for biscuit; sprinkle with sugar, cinnamon, and bits of butter. Bake slowly.

Black Cake.—One and three-quarter pounds of flour, one and one-quarter pounds of brown sugar, one pound of butter, one and one-half pounds of raisins, one and one-half pounds of currants, one-half pound of lard, four eggs, one pint of milk, one nutmeg, and mace, one teaspoonful of baking powder. Wine and brandy.

Filling for Layer Cake.—A delicious filling for a layer cake is made of one cup of stoned raisins and one lemon peeled, chopped together; mix with this half a cup of cold water and one cup of sugar. Beat this well together; if the cake is well baked, so that there is a crust on the top, put the filling in while the cake is still warm. Be sure to remove the seeds from the lemons.

Old-Fashioned " Muster Gingerbread."—One cup molasses, two large spoonfuls butter, one teaspoonful soda dissolved in three tablespoonfuls boiling water, one teaspoonful ginger; knead well but not hard; roll into sheets, mark with a fork and bake quickly; this will make three common sized sheets; after it is baked and while hot, mix one teaspoonful sweet milk and one of molasses and wet the top.

Chocolate Jumbles.—One and a half teacups of white sugar, one-half a teacup of sweet cream, one-half a teacup of butter, one teacup of chocolate, half a teaspoonful of soda dissolved in cream, one teaspoonful cream of tartar, one egg. Work very stiff with flour, mix the chocolate and cream of tartar in the flour, roll thin, cut with a cutter.

Honey Cakes.—Three and one-half pounds of flour, one and one-half pounds of honey, one-half pound of butter, one-half pound of sugar, half a nutmeg, one tablespoonful of ginger, one teaspoonful of soda; roll thin and cut in small cakes; bake in a quick oven, cover tight and let stand till moist. They will keep a long time. This recipe has been used in one family for twenty-five years.

Huckleberry Cake.—One cup butter, two cups sugar, three cups flour, five eggs, one cup sweet milk, one teaspoonful soda dissolved in hot water, one teaspoonful each of nutmeg and cinnamon. One quart of ripe berries dredged well with flour. Stir them in carefully so as not to burn them. Bake in loaf or card.

Boston Cake.—One pound of flour, one pound of sugar, half a pound of butter, cup of sour cream, five eggs, teaspoonful of soda, spice. Beat butter and sugar to a cream, then yelks of eggs beaten very light, dissolve soda in cream, and add then flour alternately with whites of eggs beaten to a froth; spice to taste; fruit can be added; bake in a moderately hot oven, especially if fruit is added.

Queen's Cake.—One pound flour, one pound of sugar, half pound of butter, five eggs, flavoring essence to taste, cup of milk, one pound of currants, spice and citron. Beat butter and sugar to a cream, add eggs well beaten, then milk, flour, spice and fruit. Chopped raisins can be used in place of currants, if preferred. Bake two hours in a pretty hot oven.

Cream Cake.—One-half cup of butter, two cups sugar, three eggs beaten in one cup of milk, three cups of flour, two teaspoonfuls of cream of tartar, one teaspoonful of soda. Cream for middle, one pint of milk, let it come to a boil, one-half cup of flour, one cup of sugar, two eggs, flavor with vanilla and a lump of butter. This is worth trying.

Cream Tea Cakes.—Two pounds of flour, a teacup of butter, half pint of sour cream, half a teaspoonful of saleratus, and a little salt. Mix well. If necessary, add more cream. Make into small round cakes, and bake fifteen or twenty minutes. When done, open one side, and insert a piece of butter, or serve otherwise, hot.

Mrs. Crabtree's Cake.—One cup sugar, one-half cup butter, three eggs, leaving out whites of two for frosting; one-half cup of sweet milk, one-half teaspoonful soda, one teaspoonful cream of tartar, two cups, not quite full, flour. *Frosting.*—Whites of two eggs, beat to a froth, one and half cups sugar; one cup raisins chopped fine, one cup English walnuts, chopped fine.

Lady Fingers.—Take two eggs, one cup of sugar, half a cup of butter, half a cup of sweet milk, two teaspoonfuls of baking powder; add enough flour to form a soft dough. Take a small piece of dough, flour it and roll with your hands as large as your finger; cut off in four-inch lengths and put closely in buttered pars. Bake quickly.

Loaf Seed Cake.—Take one loaf of dough, one cup of brown sugar, half cup of butter or drippings, half ounce of caraway seeds, or a quarter pound of currants, a little spice, two eggs; mix thoroughly with the hands, and set to rise. Do not bake until real light; bake in a deep tin.

Kisses.—Beat the whites of three fresh eggs to a stiff froth; mix with five spoonfuls powdered sugar and flavor with lemon. Butter a pan and lay in it white paper. Drop the mixture upon it in teaspoonful cakes, at least an inch apart. Sift sugar over; bake half an hour in a slow oven.

Adelaide Cake.—One pound of flour, one pound of sugar, one-half pound of butter, six eggs, one cup of milk; rub the butter and sugar together, then add the yelks of the eggs, then the milk, with soda and cream tartar in it; flavor with lemon; mix the flour and whites of eggs in alternately.

Fruit Cream Cake.—One cup of brown sugar, one egg, butter the size of an egg, one cup of cream, one teaspoonful of soda, one teaspoonful of cinnamon, one small nutmeg, two cups of flour, one cup and a half of seeded raisins. This will make one good-sized loaf.

Hickorynut Macaroons.—Make frosting as for cake; stir in enough pounded hickorynut-meats, with mixed ground spice to taste, to make convenient to handle. Flour the hands and form the mixture into little balls. Place on buttered tins, allowing room to spread, and bake in a quick oven.

Tea Cake. –Beat two eggs in a teacup, fill the cup with sweet milk, add one cup sugar, ten even teaspoonfuls melted butter, one and three-fourths cups flour, two teaspoonfuls baking powder. This is the most reliable, easily made, and accommodating of cakes. Delicious baked in layers, and spread with jelly, chocolate icing, or cream. May be baked in a loaf or small patty pans, and served warm with tea.

Boston Tea Cakes.—One well beaten egg, two tablespoonfuls sugar, one cup of sweet milk, one teaspoonful of soda dissolved in the milk, two teaspoonfuls of cream of tartar sifted into the dry flour, two heaping cups of sifted flour, one tablespoonful of butter, melted. Bake in small tins.

Soft Cookies.—One heaping cup of butter, one and a half of sugar, two eggs, three tablespoonfuls of sour milk, a small teaspoonful of soda, and as little flour as will roll them out. Do not roll them thin. Sprinkle over before cutting out, and press it in slightly with the rolling pin.

Ginger Snaps.—One cup molasses, one cup brown sugar, half cup lard and butter melted together, three tablespoonfuls ginger, one teaspoonful cinnamon, half teaspoonful cloves, one teaspoonful soda dissolved in half a cup of boiling water; thicken with flour; roll and bake.

Christmas Cake.—Butter, blanched almonds, sugar, grocers' currants, and candied peel, half a pound of each; half a pint of cream, a measured half pint of eggs out of their shells, and enough French brandy and Madeira wine in equal parts to make the whole sufficiently moist; the eggs are to be whisked, the cream whipped, and the butter beaten as for a pound cake; bake it for two hours in a hoop or tin.

Molasses Sponge Cake.—One cup molasses, one and a half of flour, three eggs, one teaspoonful soda; bake in a quick oven.

Corn Cake.— Three eggs whipped light, yelks and whites separately, two cups sour or buttermilk, three tablespoonfuls melted butter, one teaspoonful soda dissolved in boiling water, one tablespoonful white sugar, one small teaspoonful salt. Corn meal enough to make a rather thin batter. Bake in a shallow pan, or in small tins, thirty minutes in a hot oven.

Fruit Cake.— Three pounds of flour, three pounds of sugar, three pounds of butter, thirty eggs, one ounce of cinnamon, four or five nutmegs, cloves to your judgment, half a pint of wine and brandy each, six pounds of currants, five pounds of stoned raisins, one citron and a half.

Jelly Cake—to Roll.— Three eggs beaten well with one cup of sugar; when light add one cup of flour, teaspoonful of cream of tartar, one-half teaspoonful of soda dissolved in water. Baking powder can be used instead of cream of tartar and soda.

Sponge Drops.— Beat to a froth three eggs and add one teacup of sugar: beat five minutes; stir into this one and a half cups of flour, in which one teaspoonful of cream of tartar and one half teaspoonful of soda are thoroughly mixed; flavor with lemon; butter tin sheets, and drop in spoonfuls about three inches apart.

Mother's Tea Cake.— Break an egg in a teacup, filled with sugar, beat thoroughly together, add one cup thick, sour cream, one teaspoonful soda, a little salt, half a nutmeg, and flour to make a stiff batter; bake twenty minutes in a moderate oven.

Choice Fig Cake.— A large cup of butter, two and a half cups of sugar, one of sweet milk, three pints of flour with three teaspoonfuls of baking powder, the whites of sixteen eggs, a pound and a quarter of figs (the choicest), well floured and cut in strips like citron; no flavoring.

Fried Cakes Without Eggs.— Take one and one-half cups of sugar, one cup of thick cream, two cups of buttermilk, one teaspoonful of cinnamon, about two and one-half teaspoonfuls of soda, and flour to mix. Roll, cut into rings, and fry in very hot lard.

Coffee Snaps.— Half cup molasses, half cup sugar, half cup lard and butter, mixed, a little salt, half teaspoonful soda, dissolve in quarter cup of strong coffee. Beat well; add flour enough to roll. Bake in a quick oven.

Currant Cake.— One-half cup of butter, one cup of sugar, two eggs, one-half cup of milk, one and one-half cups of flour, two teaspoonfuls of baking powder, one cup of washed currants dredged with flour.

Layer Cake.— The layer cake, so popular now, made of two layers of white cake with one of fruit cake in the middle, may be varied deliciously by making the middle layer of walnut cake. For this, if the cake is a large one, take two-thirds of a cup of sugar, one-third of a cup of butter, one cup flour, one egg, one teaspoonful baking powder, and nearly one cup of hickory-nut meats.

Hickorynut Cake.— One cup broken hickory meats, one and one-half cups sugar, one-half cup butter, two cups flour, three-fourths cup sweet milk, two teaspoonfuls baking powder, and the whites of four eggs, well beaten. Add the meats last.

Chocolate Icing.—Put into a saucepan half a pound of powdered loaf-sugar, two ounces of grated chocolate, and about a gill of water; stir on the fire until the mixture assumes the consistence of a thick, smooth cream.

Hickorynut Cookies.—Take two cups of sugar, two eggs, half a cup of melted butter, six tablespoonfuls of milk or a little more than a third of a cup, one teaspoonful of cream of tartar, half a teaspoonful of soda, and one cup of chopped kernels stirred into the dough.

Cookies.—Two eggs, half a cup of butter, or half lard with the butter, one cup of white sugar, flavor with lemon extract and nutmeg, three teaspoonfuls of baking powder sifted with flour enough to make the consistency to roll.

Molasses Cake.—Two cups of New Orleans molasses, four cups of flour, one cup of water, one cup of butter, one egg, two teaspoonfuls of soda, one orange; grate the peel, put that in, and also the juice and pulp.

Sponge Cake.—Beat four eggs, two cups sugar, two cups of flour with two heaping teaspoonfuls baking powder sifted in, all together thoroughly; then add a little lemon and two-thirds cup of boiling water. Beat well and bake, and you will have as fine a cake as was ever eaten.

Clove Cake.—Two cups flour, half cup molasses, one-half cup butter, one-half cup milk, two eggs, two cups raisins, one teaspoonful of soda, half teaspoonful each of cloves, cinnamon, and allspice, half a nutmeg.

Macaroons.—The whites of three eggs, beaten to a stiff froth; half a pound of cocoanut, half a pound of rolled and sifted crackers, and an even tablespoonful of extract of bitter almond. Drop them upon a greased paper, in a dripping-pan, and bake a light brown.

Feather Cake.—One cup of milk, one cup of flour, one egg, half a cup of sweetened milk, one tablespoonful of melted butter, one teaspoonful of baking powder, one teaspoonful of lemon juice. Bake to a dark brown.

Ginger Cookies.—One cup of sugar, one of butter, one of molasses, one tablespoonful of ginger, one of cinnamon, and two teaspoonfuls of saleratus, dissolved in three tablespoonfuls of hot water. Bake quickly.

Snowden Cake.—Beat to a cream half a pound of butter, three-quarters of a pound of granulated sugar, the whites of six eggs, half a teacup of cream, and one pound of Bermuda arrow-root. Add the beaten yelks of two of the eggs, and a little salt. Bake in a mold one hour.

New Way to Prepare Chocolate Cake.—Lovers of chocolate cake will rejoice at a new way of preparing it. Use the usual recipe for the cake, omitting one-third of a cup of flour. Grate the chocolate as for layer cake, add to the dough, mix thoroughly, and bake in a loaf.

Fruit Cake.—One cup of butter, one cup of sugar, one cup of molasses, three cups of flour, one half cup of milk, one cup of chopped raisins, one teaspoonful of cloves, cinnamon and allspice, two eggs, and two teaspoonfuls of baking powder or one teaspoonful of soda.

Doughnuts.—One egg, one cup sugar, one teaspoonful of butter, one cup of sweet milk, one teaspoonful of soda, two teaspoonfuls of cream tartar.

Cocoanut Cookies.—Two cups of white sugar, one cup of butter, two cups of grated cocoanut, two eggs, one teaspoonful of baking powder, and mix with enough flour to roll easy. Roll very thin, bake in a quick oven, but not brown.

To Flavor Cake.—An economical and really delicious way to flavor cake which is to have icing over the top, is to grate part of the peel of an orange or lemon over the cake before putting the icing on.

White Mountain Cake.—One tablespoonful of butter, four tablespoonfuls of milk, one cup of flour, one cup of sugar, two teaspoonfuls of yeast-powder, and two eggs; cream, whites of two eggs, six ounces of pulverized sugar.

Railroad Sponge Cake.—One and a half cups of sugar, two even cups of flour, four eggs, one teaspoonful of baking powder. Mix and add one-third of a cup of hot water.

Plum Cake.—One pound flour, one pound sugar, one pound butter, five pounds currants, ten ounces citron, three-quarters of an ounce of cloves, three-quarters of an ounce nutmegs, ten eggs, one wineglass brandy.

Crullers.—Two coffee cups sugar, one coffee cup milk, four eggs, six spoonfuls lard, two teaspoonfuls cream tartar, one teaspoonful soda, flour to make stiff enough to roll; fry in boiling lard; spice to suit the taste.

Virginia Snow Cake.—The whites of nine eggs, two cups sugar, four cups flour, one cup sweet milk, one cup butter, two teaspoonfuls baking powder.

Water Pound Cake.—One cup of butter, three cups of sugar, one cup of water or milk, four cups of flour, six eggs, one teaspoonful of soda, two teaspoonfuls of cream of tartar.

No Egg Cake.—Two and a half cups of flour, half a cup each of butter and milk, one and a half cups of brown sugar, and one teaspoonful of soda. Flavor with nutmeg.

Cup Cake.—Two cups of sugar, one cup of milk, one-half cup of butter, two teaspoonfuls of baking powder, four eggs, two and one-half cups of flour.

Gold Cake.—Yelks of five eggs, one and three-fourths cups butter, one-half cup milk, one and one-quarter cups flour, one cup sugar, two spoonfuls baking powder.

Ice Cream and Summer Drinks.

French Vanilla Ice Cream.—One quart rich sweet cream, half a pound of granulated sugar, and the yelks of six eggs. Place the cream and sugar in a porcelain kettle on the fire, and allow them to come to a boil; strain through a hair sieve, and having the eggs well beaten add slowly to the cream and sugar while hot, at the same time stirring rapidly. Place on the fire again, and stir for a few minutes; then pour into the freezer, and flavor with one tablespoonful of vanilla.

Crushed Strawberry Ice Cream.—Three pints best cream, twelve ounces pulverized white sugar, two whole eggs, and two tablespoonfuls of extract of vanilla. Mix in a porcelain basin, place over the fire, and stir constantly until it reaches a boiling point. Strain through a hair sieve into the freezer, select, hull and crush to a pulp one quart ripe strawberries, with six ounces pulverized sugar. Add this pulp to the frozen cream, mix well, and give the freezer a few additional turns to harden.

Coffee Ice Cream.—One quart best cream, half a pint strong coffee, fourteen ounces white pulverized sugar, yelks of eight eggs. Mix in a porcelain-lined basin, place on the fire to thicken, and strain through a hair sieve. Put into a freezer and freeze.

Lemon Ice Cream.—One quart best cream, eight ounces of pulverized sugar, three whole eggs, and a tablespoonful of extract of lemon. Place on the fire, stirring continually until it reaches the boiling point, then remove and strain into the freezer.

Italian Orange Ice Cream.—One pint of best cream, twelve ounces of pulverized sugar, the juice of six oranges, two teaspoonfuls of orange extract, the yelks of eight eggs, and a pinch of salt.

Biscuit Glaze.—One pint and a half of cream, the yelks of eight eggs, and one tablespoonful of vanilla; take six ounces of crisp macaroons and pound to a dust; then stir into it another tablespoonful of vanilla; mix the cream, sugar and vanilla; place on the fire and stir until it begins to thicken; strain into freezer, and when nearly frozen add the macaroon dust and finish. Eggs can be left out of all ice cream recipes if desirable.

Orange Ice.—Squeeze the juice from six large oranges and two lemons; pour about five gills of boiling water over the broken peel and pulp and let it stand until cool; then strain and add the water to the orange and lemon juice. Sweeten to taste with loaf sugar, and freeze.

Lemon Water Ice.—Rub on sugar the clear rinds of lemons; squeeze the juice of twelve lemons, strain them, boil the sugar into a strong, thick syrup; add to the juice half a pint of water, or good barley water, sweeten it with your syrup, and add the white of an egg and jelly.

Oranges Cold.—Frozen oranges, for dessert at any season of the year, are delicious. Remove the peel and slice the oranges; to each pound of oranges add three-quarters of a pound of sugar and one-half pint of water, and freeze.

Red Currant Fruit Ice.—Put three pints of ripe currants, one pint of red raspberries, half a pint of water in a basin. Place on the fire and simmer for a few minutes, then strain. Add twelve ounces of sugar and half a pint of water.

Raspberry Water Ice.—Press sufficient raspberries through a hair sieve to give three pints of juice, and add one pound of pulverized sugar and the juice of one lemon.

Egg-Nogg.—To make a quart take three eggs, nearly a pint of good fresh milk, sugar and spice to suit the taste. Put these in a pitcher; add hot water to make a quart; then stir, or change from one vessel to another until completely mixed; then add a wineglass or more of the best whiskey. Wine may be used instead of whiskey. The eggs and sugar must be thoroughly beaten before being put with the hot water.

Ginger Beer.—White sugar, twenty pounds; lemon juice, eighteen ounces; honey, one pound; bruised ginger, seventeen ounces; water, eighteen gallons; boil the ginger in three gallons of the water for half an hour; then add the sugar, the juice and the honey, with the remainder of the water, and strain through a cloth; when cold, add the white of an egg and half an ounce of the essence of lemon; after standing four days, bottle. This beverage will keep for many months.

White Spruce Beer.—Mix together three pounds of loaf sugar, five gallons of water, a cup of good yeast, adding a small piece of lemon peel, and enough of the essence of spruce to give it flavor. When fermented, preserve in close bottles. Molasses or common brown sugar can be used, if necessary, instead of loaf, and the lemon peel left out. Sometimes, when unable to obtain the essence of spruce, we have boiled down the twigs. This will be found a delightful home drink.

Sham Champagne.— A good temperance drink is made as follows: Tartaric acid, one ounce; one good-sized lemon; ginger root, half ounce; white sugar, one and a half pounds; water, two and a half gallons; brewer's yeast, four ounces. Slice the lemon, bruise the ginger, and mix all except the yeast. Boil the water and pour it upon them; let it stand until cooled down to blood heat, then add the yeast and let it stand in the sun all day, and at night bottle. In two days it will be fit for use.

Berry Sherbet.—Crush one pound of berries, add them to one quart of water, one lemon sliced, and one teaspoonful of orange flavor, if you have it. Let these ingredients stand in an earthen bowl for three hours; then strain, squeezing all the juice out of the fruit. Dissolve one pound of powdered sugar in it, strain again, and put on the ice until ready to serve.

Cherry Effervescing Drink.—Take a pint of the juice of bruised cherries, filter until clear, and make into a syrup with half a pound of sugar; then add one ounce of tartaric acid, bottle and cork well. To a tumbler three parts full of water, add two tablespoonfuls of the syrup and a scruple of carbonate of soda; stir well, and drink while effervescing.

Orangeade or Lemonade.—Squeeze the juice, pour boiling water on a little of the peel, and cover close; boil water and sugar to a thin syrup and skim it. When all are cold, mix the juice, the infusion, and the syrup with as much more water as will make a rich sherbet; then strain. Or, squeeze the juice and strain it, then add to it water and capillaire.

Ginger Lemonade.—Take half cup of vinegar, one cup of sugar, two teaspoonfuls of ginger, stir well together; put in a quart pitcher and fill with ice water. If one wants it sweeter or sourer than these quantities make it, more of the needed ingredients may be put in. It is a cooling drink, and almost as good as lemonade, some preferring it.

Iceland Moss Chocolate.—Dissolve one ounce of Iceland moss in one pint of boiling milk; boil one ounce of chocolate for five minutes in one pint of boiling water; thoroughly mix the two, and give it to the invalid night and morning. This is a highly nutritive drink for invalids.

Staffordshire Syllabub.—Put a pint of cider and a glass of brandy, sugar and nutmeg, into a bowl, and pour milk on the top of it; or pour warm milk from a large teapot some height into it.

Effervescing Lemonade.—Boil two pounds of white sugar with one pint of lemon juice; bottle and cork. Put a tablespoonful of the syrup into a tumbler about three parts full of cold water, add twenty grains of carbonate of soda, and drink quickly.

Cool Summer Drink.—Take one pound finely powdered loaf sugar, one ounce of tartaric or citric acid, and twenty drops of essence of lemon. Mix immediately, and keep very dry. Two or three spoonfuls of this, stirred briskly in a tumbler of water, will make a very pleasant glass of lemonade.

Table Beer.—A cheap and agreeable table beer is made as follows: Take fifteen gallons of water, and boil one-half, putting the other into a barrel; add the boiling water to the cold, with one gallon of molasses and a little yeast. Keep the bung hole open till the fermentation is completed.

Root Beer.—To make Ottawa root beer, take one ounce each of sassafras, allspice, yellow dock, and wintergreen, half an ounce each of wild cherry bark and coriander, a quarter of an ounce of hops, and three quarts of molasses. Pour boiling water on the ingredients, and let them stand twenty-four hours. Filter the liquor, and add half a pint of yeast, and it will be ready for use in twenty-four hours.

Milk Lemonade.—Dissolve three-quarters of a pound of loaf sugar in one pint of boiling water, and mix with them one gill of lemon juice and one gill of sherry; then add three gills of cold milk. Stir the whole well together and strain it.

Nice Lemon Beer.—Slice two good-sized lemons, put with them one pound of sugar; over these pour one gallon of boiling water, and when about milk warm add one-third cup of yeast. Let it stand over night, and it is ready for use.

Confectionery.

To Make Tomato Figs.—Pour boiling water over the tomatoes, in order to remove the skin; then weigh them and place them in a stone jar; with as much sugar as you have tomatoes, and let them stand two days; then pour off the syrup, and boil and skim until no scum rises. Then pour it over the tomatoes, and let them stand two days, as before; then boil and skim again. After the third time they are fit to dry, if the weather is good; if not, let them stand in the syrup until drying weather; then place on large earthen plates or dishes, and put them in the sun to dry, which will take them about a week; after which, pack them down in small wooden boxes, with fine white sugar between every layer.

Walnut Creams.—One cup granulated sugar, one-half cup hot water; boil like mad two or three minutes or until it jellies in water; cool it (almost), beat it very fast until it creams; spread on a platter, halve and put on walnuts. This cream is same as chocolate cream. Chocolate for cream as follows: One ounce or one square Baker's chocolate in a bowl over the teakettle and melt; add one teaspoonful pulverized sugar, a piece of butter size of a walnut with the salt washed out; dip the balls of cream into this and dry on sheets of paper. The above directions make forty drops, or cream for one pound walnuts.

Peppermint Drops.—The best peppermint drops are made by sifting finely powdered loaf sugar in lemon juice, sufficient to make it of a proper consistence; then, gently drying it over the fire a few minutes, and stirring in about fifteen drops of oil of peppermint for each ounce of sugar, dropping them from the point of a knife. Some persons, instead of using lemon juice, merely mix up the sugar and oil of peppermint with the whites of eggs; beating the whole well together, dropping it on white paper, and drying the drops gradually before the fire, at a distance.

Pop-Corn Balls.—Take a three-gallon pan and fill it nearly level full of popped corn, and then take a cup of molasses and a little piece of butter and boil until it will set, or try it in cold water; just a drop will do in water, and if it sets, then pour the molasses all around on the corn. Then take a large iron spoon and stir well; when well mixed, butter your hands well and take corn in both hands, as much as you can press well together, and you will have a large and splendid ball. You can use sugar in the place of molasses if you wish it.

To Sugar or Crystallize Pop Corn.—Put into an iron kettle one tablespoonful of water, and one teacup of white sugar; boil until ready to candy, then throw in three quarts of corn nicely popped; stir briskly until the candy is evenly distributed over the corn; set the kettle from the fire, and stir until it is cooled a little and you have each grain separate and crystallized with the sugar; care should be taken not to have too hot a fire lest you scorch the corn when crystallizing. Nuts of any kind prepared this way are delicious.

Walnut Candy.—The meats of hickory nuts, English walnuts, or black walnuts may be used according to preference in that regard. After removal from the shells in as large pieces as practicable, they are to be placed on bottom of tins, previously greased, to the depth of about a half inch. Next boil two pounds of brown sugar, a half pint of water and one gill of good molasses until a portion of the mass hardens when cooled. Pour the hot candy on the meats and allow it to remain until hard.

Almond Candy.—Take one pound of sugar and about half a pint of water; put in part of the white of an egg to clarify the sugar; let this boil a few minutes, and remove any scum that rises. When the sugar begins to candy drop in the dry almonds; first, however, you should blanch the nuts by pouring hot water over them, and letting them stand in it a few minutes; then the skin will slip off readily. Spread the candy on buttered plates to cool.

Sugar Taffy.—One pound sugar put in a pan with half tumbler cold water, add one teaspoonful cream tartar, lump of butter size of hickory nut, one teaspoonful vinegar (do not stir at all), boil slowly twenty-five minutes, and drop a little into cold water, and if crispy it is done; turn on to plates and pour on flavoring—lemon and vanilla, half each—pull till very white.

Butter Scotch.—Take two cups of sugar, two tablespoonfuls of water, piece of butter the size of an egg. Boil without stirring until it hardens on a spoon. Pour out on buttered plates to cool.

Chocolate Candy.—One cup brown sugar, one cup white, one cup molasses, one cup milk, one cup chocolate, butter the size of a walnut.

Lemon Drops.—Squeeze the juice of six lemons into a basin; pound some lump sugar, and sift it through a fine sieve, mix it with the lemon juice, and make it so thick that you can hardly stir it. Put it into a stew pan, and stir it over the fire for five minutes, then drop out of a teaspoon on writing paper, and let it stand till cold.

Candied Lemon Peel.—Peel some fine lemons, with all the inner pulp, in halves or quarters; have ready a very strong syrup of white sugar and water; put the peels into it, and keep them boiling till the syrup is nearly reduced. Take them out and set them to dry with the outer peel downward.

Cocoanut Candy.—Grate the meat of a cocoanut, and, having ready two pounds of finely sifted sugar (white) and the beaten whites of two eggs, also the milk of the nut, mix together and make into little cakes. In a short time the candy will be dry enough to eat.

Candied Orange Peel.—Make a very strong syrup of white sugar and water; take off the peels from several oranges in halves or quarters, and boil them in the syrup till it is nearly reduced. After this take them out and set them to dry with the outer skin downward.

Vanilla Candy.—Three teacups of white or coffee sugar, one and a half teacups unskimmed sweet milk to dissolve it; boil till done, and flavor with vanilla; after it cools a little, stir until hard and eat when you please.

LADIES' FANCY WORK--Update

Ever wander through an antique store and see the collectibles of the Victorian era and wonder how they were made? This chapter tells you how they did it.

Some of the fancy work is functional--the instructions for lining a quilt, or making knitted dressing slippers or star mats.

I was struck by the instructions for making floral transparencies. Leaves, ferns or flowers are arranged between panes of glass, thus preserving "their beautiful appearance throughout the winter."

LADIES' FANCY WORK.

Work Table Cover.—This cover if of fawn-colored cloth, ornamented elaborately on the ends in application embroidery. The design figures, which look dark in the illustration, are applied in broken cloth; on the middle of each leaf of the large middle application figure apply a piece of dark-brown velvet. Edge all the applied figures with fawn-colored soutache, and ornament the pieces of velvet besides in point Russe embroidery with fawn colored saddlers' silk. For the lines of the design sew on brown soutache in two shades. The cover is bordered with light brown open silk fringe an inch and a quarter wide. Brown percale lining.

WORK TABLE COVER.

Imitation Coral Hanging Baskets.— Take old hoops with the covering on; bend and tie in any shape desired; tie with wrapping-twine, with ends of the twine left one-fourth of an inch long; cover the basket when formed with knots or ties about one inch apart all over the basket. Then take one half pound of beeswax, melt it in a shallow pan, stir in enough Japanese vermilion to get the color you wish, then roll the basket in the melted wax until it is covered completely. We have one made in this way, that has hung exposed to the weather for two years, and is still as good as new.

A Pretty Tidy.—The requisites are a ball of number fourteen tidy cotton, and a wooden frame about twenty inches square, with an inch sprig

FIG. 1.—BLACKBERRY.

driven half down in the center of each corner, and similar ones along the sides in line with these, and an inch apart.

Fasten your cotton to the second side sprig, and weave from this sprig to the one directly opposite, passing round each sprig three or four times; then draw the thread to the next sprig and weave in the same manner. Continue this until you reach the second sprig from the side you are working toward. Now cross these threads in the same way from the other two sides, then cross with the same number of threads diagonally in both directions. You will then have in your frame four warps, each in different directions. With a needle and tidy cotton securely fasten as they are every place where four sets of threads intersect, drawing the cotton from one to another. Cut the cotton at every sprig, and it is finished, except trimming the fringe a little. Made in this way they are serviceable, and less work than you would think.

Embroidery Designs.—We give a design from natural forms (Fig. 1) to which the artist has added an imaginative edge, although that has the outlines of some leaf forms. For fine delicate needlework in pure white this forms a most graceful design. But, where embroidered in the colors natural to the leaves and fruits, on a boy's or girl's jacket, stand cloth or ottoman cover, on cloth of scarlet or gray, is pretty enough for the most fastidious. Moreover, this leads you to observe and study

FIG. 2—INITIAL LETTER.

these things, which from your life-long intimacy with them may have failed to specially interest you.

For an initial letter for the corner of a handkerchief, we give two designs (Figs. 2 and 3), which serve the treble purpose of use, ornament, and memory of delicious fruits. For a gentleman's handkerchief, nothing can be in better taste than his initials wrought in such becoming drapery. And so through the whole alphabet you can weave something synonymous from nature about each letter. Such work flavors of botany, which is a science everybody should study. Aside from its being a most delightful study in itself, it is the key to a marvelous world of infinite and ever-varying delights; it keeps you from going through life with your eyes blinded; it tends to make you gentle, large-hearted and thankful. These forms will, or ought to, stimulate your pencil for drawing. Drawing cultivates your eye as nothing else will. It educates your hand; it civilizes you generally. Make a sketch of anything, and it will ever after possess a new interest. You tread

on a thousand forms of vegetation every day. Can you make a drawing of one? The fine drawing we give would be a nice design for a center of a pillow sham.

Persian Rugs Made at Home.—It is easy enough after you once know how, and, for that matter, so is everything you undertake. To make a rug you will need plenty of perseverance, for it is a large contract to make one of ordinary size; but it is very pretty work, and can be done with ease by even those ladies whose failing eyesight compels them to give up the various fascinating forms of fancy work, which are too apt to prove a tax to the best of eyes.

Purchase from come carpet dealer a supply of scraps of tapestry Brussels carpeting; pieces that are too small to be worked up into hassocks are

FIG. 3.—INITIAL LETTER.

quite large enough for the purpose. Cut these into strips of any length their size allows; but let them be of uniform width, say three inches. Ravel these all out, rejecting the linen, and collecting in a box the little crimped worsted threads. Then provide yourself with a pair of the largest-sized steel knitting-needles, and a ball of the coarsest crochet cotton, either white or colored. Set on ten stitches, and after knitting a row or two to make a firm beginning, go on as if you were making a garter, but with every other stitch lay a thread of the crimped wool across the needles. After knitting the stitch, take the end of wool which shows upon the wrong side, and turn it toward the right side, knitting a stitch above to secure it. Then put in another thread of wool and repeat the process. The back of the strips should have something the appearance of that of a body Brussels carpet, while the front should be like a sort of thick, long napped plush. The colors may be used without selection, making a sort of *chene* effect; or carpets may be chosen for raveling which show only shades of scarlet or blue; **or brown** carpets may be used for the center of the rug, and a border of scarlet or blue sewed on all around. After doing a little of this work, many ideas as to arrangement of colors will suggest themselves, and a little practice will enable the knitter to produce some very pleasing results.

When the strips are all finished they must be sewed together at the back. It is only for convenience that they are knitted in strips—the rug, as a whole, would be very cumbersome and unwieldy to handle. Some ladies edge a Brussels or velvet carpet hearth-rug with a strip of this knitting, thus giving a very pretty finish. Small mats for placing in front of bureaus are also very pretty made upon the same plan.

Work Basket.—The basket is of fine wicker-work, the sides are lined with gathered satin, and the bottom with embroidered plush; both are fin-

WORK BASKET.

ished with silk cord. The outside is ornamented with fringe of crewels of various colors. Handles of cord.

Crochet Macrame Tidy.—Use seine cord No. 8.

Crochet 57 chain stitches.

1st row.—Put thread over hook and crochet in first loop, and so on until you have made 9 single shell stitches. Crochet 7 chain, shell 9, chain 7, shell 9, chain 7, shell 9.

2d row.—Turn, chain 3, shell 9 on top of the last made in the first row, chain 9, shell 9, chain 9, shell 9, chain 9, shell 9.

3d row.—Turn, chain 3, then same as last row only making 7 chain instead of 9.

4th row.—Turn, chain 3, shell 9, chain 5, place the hook in the fifth stitch of the chain in the 2d row; secure the chain of 7 in with it, chain 4, shell 9, and so on to the end of the row.

Begin again at the beginning and crochet the desired length. Finish all around with scallop, with fringe across the lower edge. Run satin ribbon through the openings to match your room.

A Home-Made Hassock.—Hassocks, or footstools, are convenient for many purposes. Well, let me tell you how easily you can make one out of articles that one considers only lumber, and are often at a loss to know what to do with. Take seven tin fruit cans, put one in the middle, and the other six around it; draw around this a band of unbleached muslin and fasten it so as to keep them firmly in place; set them on a piece of paper and cut a pattern of the bottom, which then cut in heavy pasteboard. Cover this with gray paper muslin for the bottom, as it slips better than anything else. Cut out of cretonne a similar-shaped piece for the top, also a band to fit the

PILLOW SHAM.

sides; cord the top piece around the edge, and sew on the band. Stuff the cans with hay or excelsior, and let it be good and thick on top of the cans, also, as it will pack in a little while. Draw your cretonne over it, and sew firmly to the bottom, and you have your hassock to use on the porch in summer, or as a footstool before the fire. It is strong as well as very light, and can be moved easily with the foot.

Pillow Sham.—Made of linen. The edges cut out like design, turned in and basted, then the lace overhanded on, making sure to have it full enough on the points; cut a long buttonhole in the end of each point, and run colored ribbons through. It is easily made and the effect is very pretty.

Clothes Brush Holder.—The basket is of very fine wicker, in the form of a cone; it is ornamented with an embroidered drape, which may either be finished with a narrow furniture gimp or tufts of crewel; the bottom is covered with silk, which is drawn to a point at the end and finished by a tassel; the top is ornamented with two woolen tassels and a rosette.

Table Covers, Etc.—A rich and handsome cover may be made of aida canvas, either square or in scarf style, with a wine-colored plush square in the center, fastened on with feather stitching in yellow floss. The edge of canvas should be raveled out and knotted into fringe, about three inches from which feather-stitch a band of plush, and above this may be a design worked in crewels if it is a scarf, or, if square, in each corner.

"Crazy silk patchwork" bands are much used for decorating table covers, curtains and chair covers. The pieces must be small and of elegant silk, satin and velvet.

A simple and pretty table cover for a bedroom lamp-stand may be made of pale blue canton flannel trimmed with antique lace or with black velvet ribbon, feather-stitched on with yellow floss, and the edge finished with a fringe of blue worsted tied in. One similar to this made of cardinal all-wool canvas or basket flannel is pretty for the sitting-room.

NO. 1.—CLOTHES BRUSH HOLDER.

Neat and pretty bureau or wash-stand covers are made of scrim or dotted muslin in scarf shape, trimmed with deep lace and lined with pink or blue silesia.

Serviceable and pretty covers for the sofa pillow and chair cushions in the sitting-room are made of the striped or plaid turkish towels, which are so inexpensive and yet pleasing to the eye. The prettiest pillow shams used are those made of four

NO. 2.—BACK OF NO. 1.

small hem-stitched handkerchiefs, joined with lace insertion, finished with a frill of lace, and lined to match the other appointments of the room. They need not be made of expensive handkerchiefs; the thinner the better. Fortunate are those who possess one of those large wicker or rattan chairs, as they may be decorated so handsomely with colored satin ribbon, run in and tied in bows, or a handsome scarf about twelve inches wide, and long enough to hang over the back and go down the back and seat, and hang over the seat a little. It may be made of a strip of plush in the center, and a strip of embroidery in crewel work on felt, satin, momie cloth or canvas of some contrasting color, or worsted work. Line and join the seams with fancy stitches in silk, and finish the ends with fringe. Another handsome decoration of a rocker would be a cushion covered with plush or embroidered canvas. Put a puff of satin around the edge, and cover the seam with small chenille cord. A pillow roll for the head-rest at the back should be made to match, and tied on with ribbons. Double-faced canton flannel in wine color and olive green is much used for lambrequins, table covers, curtains for archways and double-doorways, and also for windows, but it may fade when brought in such close contact with the sun and light. The trimming is usually a band of old gold, feather-stitched on, and the edge is finished with fringe or a hem.

HANGING BASKET.

Hanging Basket.—

The basket is wicker-work, and the band at the top is of light blue cloth four inches deep, with a scalloped piece a darker shade over it. The long stitches on the dark cloth are of the lightest shade of blue silk, with a silver thread running with it. Through the wickers run satin ribbon. Combine the two shades of blue in the tassels, with the silver wound round the tops of them. Heavy cord and tassels to hang it up by. The same design of trimming will answer for any shaped basket.

Ornamental Scrap Bag or Basket.—This basket, to hang against the wall, is composed of cardboard, covered with gray linen, embroidered with brown wool, and fastened in a cane stand. Cut out first a piece of cardboard for the back and the bottom, and five pieces for the front. Bind them with a crossway strip of gray linen, cover them with gray linen, and work on the outside with brown wool the design in point russe, the stitches being taken through the cardboard. Then line the pieces with linen and sew them

ORNAMENTAL SCRAP BAG.

together. Next prepare five pieces of thin cane, four and one-half inches long, for the edges of the back, and five four and one-half inches long, five four inches long, and six five inches long, for the front of the basket. At one-half inch from the ends cut a little hollow in the canes, and then fit them to each other and tie them together, first with strong thread and then with brown ribbon, according to illustration, and secure the basket into the stand. For the cover, cut a piece of cardboard according to the shape of the upper part of the back, doubled. Cut it in half through along the center, cover the side on which you made the incision with linen, and work on one-half of the design seen in illustration to the back of the basket, double the cover, sew the edge of the linen together, and sew on a cord,

leaving a loop in the middle. Two brass rings sewn at the back serve
to hang up the
basket.

Toilet Pin-cushion. -- The
foundation is a
square of lining
about seven
inches, stuffed
with sawdust; it is
covered with plain
satin; satin rib-
bon of a contrast-
ing color is folded
into points, and
disposed accord-

TOILET PINCUSHION.

ing to design; tassels ornament the corners; a square of fine Irish linen, six
inches when hemmed (the hem
one inch deep), is placed corner-
wise over the cushion; this square
is ornamented with drawn
threads and cross-stitch embroidery in silk the color of the
satin.

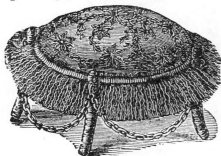

NEEDLE CUSHION.

Needle Cushion.—We give a
design for a needle cushion, the
frame of which can be made of
rustic work. The feet can be
connected by a chain, as the
sketch indicates. The cushion
can be filled with emery and or-
namented with any kind of needle-work that may suit the fancy. The edge
may be ornamented with fringe,
gimp, or other convenient and
suitable material.

Pen Wiper.—Twelve disks of
cloth of various colors are edged
with crystal beads. The rounds
may be of any size wished, according as the pen wiper is required,
large or small. They are then
folded in four, and fastened together in the center with a few
stitches of strong silk.

Wheat Ear Edging.—Cast
on five stitches. 1. Two plain
stitches; thread over, one plain,
thread over twice and purl two
together. 2. Thread over twice,
purl two together, four plain.

PEN WIPER.

3. Knit three plain, thread over one, plain,

thread over twice, purl two together. 4. Over twice, purl two together, five plain. 5. Knit four plain, over, one plain, over twice, purl two together. 6. Over twice, purl two together, six plain. 7. Knit six plain, thread over twice, purl two together. 8. Over twice, purl five together, three plain; then commence again at first row.

Music Portfolio and Stand.—This stand, as we illustrate it, is made of turned wood, with a portfolio made of pasteboard, covered with a design of needle-work. Music stands of this sort are very convenient, as every musical family knows; but such a stand can be made as well, look as appro-

MUSIC PORTFOLIO AND STAND.

priate and perhaps more ornamental, if made of rustic work. The woods, and often even the wood-pile, will afford abundant material for its manufacture, and when made by ingenious and loving hands, renders it, though o' homely and inexpensive materials, nearly priceless in value.

Basket for Fruit.—Pretty baskets for serving large fruit for luncheon are easily made. Take four pieces of cardboard and cover with any material preferred, and on each piece work or paint the flower of the fruit which the basket will contain. Fasten the pieces together by a knotted cord. **Over** the fruit throw a square of delicate macrame lace.

A Lesson in Decorating.—Choose a plain, smooth, red-clay flower-pot. If it is rather stupid-looking all the better. With your box of water-color paints, lay broad bands of dull blue around top and bottom. If you prefer, you can paint the intervening strip black, instead of leaving it red, and the bands may be divided by a narrow line of yellow. Now you are ready for the pictures. If you possess some sheets of little scrap-chromos, you will soon be rid of your task. Select some very odd, grotesque ones, that will surprise each other as much as possible—a huge butterfly, tiny Madonna, reptiles, sprays, zebras, and the like. Paste them on in the most disorderly order you can imagine, and your work is complete. Another method is to cut from picture papers a quantity of small designs, being careful to trim them very neatly. Paint these all black, and lay on a dull red or blue ground. Whichever plan you choose, be careful and not decorate too profusely, as that would be quite unlike the Japanese, while it would hint most strikingly of a merry, mischievous little girl.

Fancy Card Basket.—The foundation of this basket is of wire, and it is lined with quilted satin. The drapes are of cloth pinked at the edges and embroidered with silk.

FANCY CARD BASKET.

Antique Lace.—Cast on fifteen stitches.

1. Knit three, over, narrow, knit three, over, knit one, over, knit six.
2. Knit six, over, knit three, over, narrow, knit three, over, narrow, knit one.
3. Knit three, over, narrow, narrow again, over, knit five, over, knit six.
4. Cast off four, knit one, over, narrow, knit three, narrow, over, narrow, knit one, over, narrow, knit one.
5. Knit three, over, narrow, knit one, over, narrow, knit one, narrow, over, knit three.
6. Knit three, over, knit one, over, slip two, knit one, pass the slipped stitches over the knitted one, over, knit four, over, narrow, knit one, begin again from the first row.

How to Make a Screen.—The accompanying illustration is that of a beautiful but expensive screen, which, however, may serve as a guide in the making of a much cheaper one. The frame-work of this is of carved wood, the screen itself of embroidered silk, covered with sheer white muslin, with a plaited edge, which is put over the silk for protection. The height and width of a screen may vary, of course, according to the size of the heater or grate, and may consist of one piece as in the illustration, or of two, three, or half a dozen, joined by by hinges and resembling the construction of cloth bars. Black walnut is a handsome wood of which to make the frame, which may be fashioned plainly or ornamented to one's taste; but if that be to expensive, a cheaper wood may be employed, and stained to imitate something better. Cherry is again growing into great favor, and nothing could be prettier than a frame made of that.

SCREEN.

For the shade or screen proper a great variety of materials may be used. For convenience, make a light frame (like those over which mosquito netting is drawn for windows), which will neatly fit inside the other; over this stretch smoothly and nail a piece of strong muslin or canvas, as the ground work for the ornamentation; in lieu of this tin might be used; wood is too much warped by the action of the heat. The canvas may be covered with gay-colored chintz, at twelve and a half cents per yard, or handsome cretonne at sixty cents, or brocaded silk, painted satin, or a large fine print or engraving or embroidered cardboard or canvas—almost anything one's fancy may devise.

A very showy screen recently seen on exhibition had a black background on which was pasted all sorts, sizes, colors, and kinds of cheap prints, carefully cut out and applied without any regularity of design, and then the whole heavily varnished. The effect was very gay and sparkling. Pressed ferns and autumn leaves, artistically arranged on a white or light background, or even black look finely; the back of the leaves should be well touched with mucilage, so as to adhere firmly. For a black background, velveteen, or plain black paper, to be had where wall paper is sold, are good.

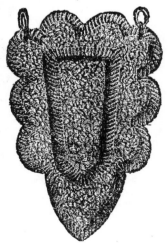

SLIPPER CASE.

Slipper Case.—Cut two pieces of cardboard the size desired; cover them with momie cloth. Then cut of cardboard a smaller piece for the pocket; cover it on one side with the cloth, and fasten it in the center of one of the large pieces; then finish where it is joined with a worsted cord. Overhand the two large pieces together, and sew the cord all around the edge. To hang it, sew on two large brass rings at the back of the two top-side scallops.

A Handsome Lace Spread.—With forethought and some money one can easily make a beautiful set of pillow shams and spreads without any great expense. From time to time buy, as you see those which please you and are cheap, squares of antique lace; they come in all kinds of pretty designs. Choose those of uniform size and of the same quality. When you have enough set them together with a stripe of satin. Remnants of satin can be purchased sometimes at very low figures. For a border, catch the squares together diagonally and fit it in half squares of the satin. Put the edge of the lace squares over the satin, having first taken the precaution to overcast very delicately the edges of the satin. The spread may be lined or not, as you please. The pillow covers should be made to match. With proper care a set of this kind will last a long time, and when one considers the comfort of always having a handsome covering for the bed at hand to dress it up for great occasions, the outlay of time and money does not appear to have been wasted.

Hanging Card-Receiver and Watch Case.—Take two pieces of card, ten inches long and three and one-half inches wide, and cut the ends pointed as the design shows. Cover both pieces with velvet or silk, and embroider a vine of flowers on one end, or if preferred paint in water colors. Overhand the two pieces together and finish the edge with gilt cord. Make a ring of twisted cord at the top. Bend the card up at three inches to form the rack, and fasten at the sides with cord and tassels. Twist a large hook with gilt wire and sew an inch below the ring at the top, for the watch.

CARD-RECEIVER AND WATCH CASE.

To Prepare Skeleton Leaves.—A ready method of preparing skeleton leaves is the following: Make a solution of concentrated lye in hot water, in the proportion of about two ounces of lye to a quart of water; or, if this is not convenient, prepare the lye by dissolving four ounces of common washing soda in a quart of water, adding about two ounces of fresh quick lime, boiling for about a quarter of an hour, and when cool decanting the liquid from the sediment. Place the leaves in this solution, and allow it to boil for about an hour, or until by trial the pulpy part of one of the leaves allows itself to be readily removed. When this is the case, the leaves are carefully removed, one by one, floated on a sheet of glass, and the pulp is removed by gently tapping or beating with a painter's stiff brush, or the like, taking care not to apply a rubbing motion, which would destroy the fibres as well. From time to time the disintegrated pulp should be washed away by allowing a stream of water to flow on the glass. When this operation has been properly performed, nothing of the leaf remains behind but the network of fibres, or the skeleton.

The next step is to bleach the skeleton leaves, which is easily done by placing them in a shallow dish of water, to which a small quantity of chloride of lime has been added (say about a teaspoonful to a quart). In a day or two, at most, the fibres will be found bleached to a pure white, when they should be removed to a vessel of fresh water for final cleansing, in which they should remain for another day. From this they should be removed, placed between

TOILET BOTTLE CASE.—FIG. 1.

the folds of a soft linen cloth, and allowed to dry; they are then ready to be pressed, curled, or arranged into ornamental designs, according to fancy.

Another method of disintegrating the pulp of the leaves, which is sometimes followed, is to place them in a dish of water, keeping them beneath the water by the use of a sheet of glass, and exposing them to the sunlight. The disintegration takes place slowly, requiring two weeks or thereabouts to complete it. The subsequent operations are the same as those above described.

Toilet Bottle Case.—The case is made on a circular foundation of cardboard, four inches wide, lined with black silk and covered with black cloth vandykes round the edge. The latter is embroidered in satin overcast and feather stitch (see Fig. 2). The flowers are worked alternately in white and blue, the rosebuds with pink, and the wheat ears with maize silk. The branches and sprays are worked with several shades of olive and fawn-colored silk. On this foundation is sewn a cylindrical case of cardboard, two and a half inches high, and lined within and without with black satin. Two box-plaited ruchings of satin are arranged round it, and above these is a vandyke strip of black cloth embroidered in the same designs and colors as above described.

TOILET BOTTLE CASE.—FIG. 2.

Parlor Ornament.—Purchase a plain Indian straw basket, one of neat manufacture and pretty shape; paint it black; this gives an effective background for the fruit designs painted on the sides and ends; line the basket with brightly tinted velvet, cover the handle with silver or gold cord; the same should run along the edges of the opening. This dainty piece of home art forms a lovely card basket. A common straw hat, a size to fit a boy of six years, can be made into an artistic novelty. Face the brim with satin nicely pleated; fill the crown with artificial flowers; secure them from tumbling out by long loops of threads; suspend the hat from the top of a cabinet or music stand; the effect is very bright and pleasing. Industrious fingers willing to devote time to the manipulation of home decoration may shape out many lovely things from bits of silk, satin, velvet, and scraps of all wool goods. The top of a table covered with work of this kind is very handsome, and a like decoration for a carved bracket is remarkably showy.

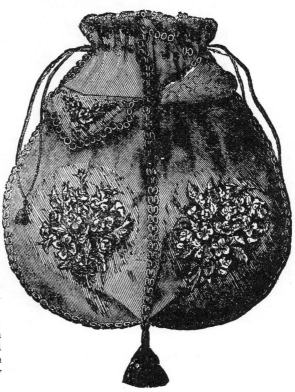

CATCH ALL.

Catch-All.—The frame-work of this article is made of pieces of cardboard sewed together The materials required for the outside are drab Holland cretonne, flowers, fancy braid, and worsteds to match flowers in color. A cord is drawn through eyelet holes at the top of the bag, and a large tassel of worsted finishes the bottom.

A Rosette.—Rosettes are often useful in tidies, borders and the like. To make the above, begin with a chain of four stitches, and unite in a ring. In this loop work twenty trebles.

Second round.—Work one chain and one treble over each treble of the last round. Third round.—* On the treble and next chain make a leaf thus: The cotton twice round the needle, take up the stitch, work through two, cotton on the needle, draw through two; cotton on the needle, take up the stitch again, work through two, cotton on the needle, work through two: cotton on the needle, take up the next stitch, and work all off the needle, two loops at a time; then four chain. Repeat from *. Fourth round.—One DC on the middle of the four chain, * five chain, one DC on the middle of the next four chain; repeat from *. Fasten off neatly at the end of the round.

Ottoman.—*Materials:* Wine and canary-colored cloth, heavy cord and tassels. Make a cushion of ticking a foot square, fill it tightly with curled hair, then make a case of

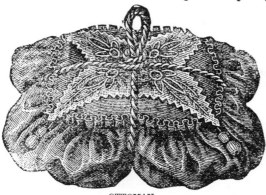

the wine-colored cloth, and in the seam round the edge of the case full in one edge of the piece to form the puff, then turn it up, and turn in the upper edge and box-plait it, and sew firmly on the top of the case, leaving a space in the center nine inches square. Cut of the light cloth a piece for the center like the design, and braid it with gilt, red, blue, and b l a c k braids, having the edge

OTTOMAN.

of the star pinked. Fasten it to the cushion in each point with a large bead, and finish each corner with a tassel. Draw the cord round the ottoman firmly, and tie in a knot, leaving a loop in the center to lift it by.

Toilet or Work Basket.—Use black, polished, round wooden or bamboo rods, an inch in circumference, two thin plates of wood four inches long and two and three-fifths inches wide, white satin, green velours, shaded green, pink, purple, and brown twist silk, fine gold cord, green silk ribbon one-fifth of an inch wide, four white Venetian beads, four bronze rings, stout cardboard, small steel tacks, white sewing silk.

The frame of our model is constructed of four pillar-like rods, each eight inches long, and h o l d i n g between them two boxes, each consisting of eight wooden or bamboo rods, and a thin wood bottom four inches long, and two and three-fifths inches wide. The lower box, which is one and four-fifths inches high, requires four rods five and three-fifths inches long, and four rods four and one-fifth inches long. The upper box, which is two and one-fifth inches high, is of

TOILET OR WORK BASKET.

exactly the same size at the bottom, while for the top, which curves outward, the two long rods must be each six inches long, while the cross rods require a length of five and one-fifth inches. Small steel tacks connect the various parts, those which are arranged into squares being notched where they intersect. Each of these squares encloses a pasteboard box covered with green velours on the inside, and on the outside with white satin, decorated by an embroidery of colored silks. The box is fastened at the top to rods by means of overhand stitches of gold cord, making the rod appear as if twisted with the gold cord. The bows decorating the upper corners of the boxes are made of green ribbon, ten inches long, sewed to the rods in the middle and then tied. The handle, which is fastened to the upper box by means of steel tacks, and is decorated with two ribbon bows, measures fifteen inches in length, and is to be wound about with gold cord. The four pillars are decorated at their tips by Venetian beads resting on bronze rings.

Sofa Pillow.—Knitting or crochet. An exceedingly comfortable pillow to hang on a chair-back or to use when traveling is well illustrated in the cut herewith presented. Knit or crocheted in squares of different colors,

CROCHET SOFA PILLOW OR BOLSTER.

almost any stitch may be used, according to the fancy of the workers, and when stuffed and finished, with cord and tassels for the ends, and hung on the back of the "old rocking chair," it forms no mean addition to the comfort and ornamentation of a room. The predominant colors of the room will suggest the appropriate ones to be used, but should there be no decided color prevailing, a pillow made of alternate dark red and olive squares will be found both handsome and durable, as far as showing dust or soil from the head.

Plush Mosaic.—The designs for this new and beautiful work can be purchased all ready prepared for use; but as many would like to try it who may find it difficult to procure them, they can, by following the given directions, cut and arrange their own. One best suited to it is a border of autumn leaves, as the rich, variegated colors can be very effectively rendered in gold, crimson, brown and green. Maple leaves are prettiest, both in form and color, and the size should be varied, some large, others small, arranging them as a border. If possible, select several of the natural leaves, and cut the exact pattern in paper. The plush may be purchased in small quantities, an eighth of a yard of each color sufficing for a number of leaves. Lay the paper patterns on the plush and cut with a pair of sharp scissors leaves from the different colors. The groundwork is of plush; for instance, a scarf for the top of an upright piano may be of olive plush with a lining of cardinal satin, and a border of autumn leaves. These should be prettily arranged across the ends of the scarf, and each leaf basted to keep it in place. The edges are fastened down with tinsel or gold thread, and as it sinks into the soft plush, shows only a slight, glistening outline. The stems should be worked with silk matching the different shades of the leaves. The veining of the leaves is also worked with the same color of silk, and as it makes only a slight depression or crease in the plush, gives a very pretty natural effect. The leaves can be shaded by using different shades of plush. For instance, one-half of a leaf may be light crimson, the other a shade or two darker; or the point of a leaf may be turned over, showing light green against dark. Arranging them in this way gives variety, also less stiffness of design.

HANDKERCHIEF BOX.

These same plush designs may be used on sateen or cloth, although in this case the term "mosaic" would not be applied. The design described would, however, be very pretty arranged on a ground-work of either of these materials. This work is very beautiful for table covers, lambrequins, portieres or any large article that may require a decorative border.

Handkerchief Box.—Take a fancy letter-paper box that is square, and opens in the center; make a tufted cushion of satin on the top, and put an insertion of white lace around it with the same color underneath. If careful, with a very little glue, the sides can be covered with satin, finishing the edges with a silver or gilt cord. Complete the box by placing a little perfume sachet inside. This makes a pretty present and is not expensive, as often small pieces of silk will answer the purpose of covering.

Knitted Insertions.—No. 1, Twist pattern—Cast on six stitches for each pattern. First six rows: Plain. Seventh row: Slip three loops on a spare needle, leave them and knit the next three; then knit those on the spare needle. Repeat these seven rows. No. 2, Feather Pattern—Cast on twenty-five stitches for each pattern.   First row: Knit two together four times; then over and one plain eight times; then knit two together four times, and purl the last stitch.   Second, third, and fourth rows: Plain.   Repeat from first row.

Wall Pocket.—We give herewith an illustration of a wall-pocket, which is ornamental and useful.   It may be used for visiting cards, letters, papers, sewing-materials, slippers, and various odds and ends.   Almost any kind of

WALL POCKET.

material may be used, but something bright has more attractiveness.   The one the drawing was made from was of silk, of blue silk, lined with corn color, with cord of blue and gold, and with raised embroidery in silk.   The framework is cut from stiff paper.   When designed with especial reference to slippers, the pocket is cut quite in the shape of a slipper, with a loop at the heel, from which it is hung.   For Christmas gifts they form pretty objects for devoted fingers to manufacture.

Floral Transparency.—The pretty transparency represented on next page is made by arranging pressed ferns, grasses, and autumn leaves on a pane of window-glass, which should be obscured, laying another transparent pane of the same size over it, and binding the edges with ribbon, leaving the group imprisoned between (use gum tragacanth in putting on the binding). It is well to secure a narrow strip of paper under the ribbon. The binding should be gummed all around the edge of the first pane, and dried before the leaves, ferns, etc., are arranged; then it can be neatly folded over the second pane without difficulty. To form the loop for hanging the transparency, paste a binding of galloon along the upper edge, leaving a two-inch loop free in the center, afterward to be pulled through a little slit in the final binding. These transparencies may either be hung before a window, or, if preferred, secured against a pane in the sash. In country halls a beautiful effect is produced by placing them against the side-lights of the hall door. Where the side-lights are each of only a single pane, it is well worth while to place a single transparency against each, filling up the entire space, thus affording ample scope for a free arrangement of the ferns, grasses, and leaves, while the effect of the light is very fine. Leaves so arranged will preserve their beautiful appearance throughout the entire winter.

FLORAL TRANSPARENCY.

Flower Patterns for Embroidery.— Great taste can be displayed in selecting appropriate flower patterns for an embroidered design. The double and single hyacinths, combined with a tulip, give a lovely effect. The fine dark blue of the former and the scarlet-margined yellow of the latter show to splendid advantage on black velvet or deep brown satin. White and purple lilacs mixed with the gold and yellow crocus give a striking design for floss and bead needlework, on a dark brown of some rich goods. The light blue crocus, with its pretty tippings of snow white, combines richly with the double red anemone, a design well suited for a center-piece on a table or a piano cover. The border would look handsome worked in some sort of creeping plant, with the corners finished off in star anemones clustered with autumn leaves. The Belle Laura tulip is of a lovely violet hue enhanced in beauty by the mixture of white; this flower is very effective in large pieces of embroidery with a touch of brilliant green foliage. A cluster of oxalis, with their brilliant hues and dark green leaves, give a charming effect. Combined with pansies, this design is a lovely pattern for the center of a sofa pillow; the border should be worked in buds and smilax. A bunch of heliotrope wrought in silk and worsted on black velvet gives a handsome design for applique work on satin to be used for various decorative effects in upholstery. The best and most correct designs in flowers are made from the natural plants. The tints are easily matched in silk and worsted, and even in beads the various colors are given.

Lamp Shade.—*Materials:* Three sheets of tissue paper, each one a shade darker than the other; six fancy colored pictures, one-eighth yard of white tarlatan, and one sheet of gilt paper. Cut six pieces of cardboard the shape of pattern, cover them with the tarlatan, then glue the gilt paper on

LAMP SHADE.

one side of each, just turning it over the edges. Then cut of the tissue paper square pieces the size of pattern; fold them across from corner to corner; then fold again, and run the four edges together and draw up tightly, forming the leaves. Sew them on as seen in the design, putting in the different shades. Fasten each section of the shade together by just tying at the top and bottom with coarse, waxed thread. Glue a fancy picture in the center of each section.

Quilt Lining.—A handsome lining for a fancy silk quilt is made of plain surah silk, or, if that is too expensive, plain soft cashmere of a pretty color serves very nicely. It is often a question how the lining shall be tacked to the outside without marring its beauty. A very pretty way is to first baste the outside carefully on the lining—then divide the lining into squares, marking the corners of each square with a thread. A pretty star may then be embroidered at every point, catching the two sides together, but taking care that the stitches do not show on the right side. A cardinal lining with stars embroidered in yellow silk is quite showy. A darker or lighter shade of the same color as the lining used for the stars makes a tasteful combination.

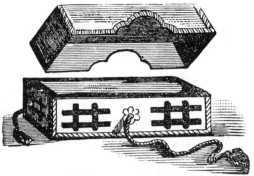

GLOVE BOX AND COVER.

Glove Box and Cover.

—A glove box of the kind we illustrate may be cut and made from a large paper box. After the edges are neatly sewed, paste neatly over the outside a cover of white muslin, to make the box strong. Line and cover both box and cover with silk, finishing the edges with large silk cord or chenille. The outside may be ornamented in a variety of ways. Additional ornamentation may be secured by cutting curves in the sides of the cover. Both admit of much ingenuity and display of taste in arrangement and trimming. Attached covers are convenient for careless users, and much more easily trimmed, being simply fastened at the back, and lifted and closed like a trunk cover. Instead of using silk as a covering, perforated paper (never get that in white, as it soon soils) lain against a smooth paper or cloth of a different color, and the silver and gold paper, perforated with large, square meshes, with initials or other ornament wrought in chenille, silk, or worsted, may be used to advantage.

Sachet.—The sachet is of old-gold plush, embroidered with rosebuds and leaves, and trimmed with lace and bows of ribbon.

Handkerchief Cases.—If for a gentleman, the size of the case would be eleven inches by eighteen inches, doubling down the center; for a lady, fourteen inches square; it should be lined with silk, and lightly wadded, the wadding being scented. Cut a piece of satin, twenty-six inches long, and eleven inches broad, and line it with fine flannel, and a piece of satin quilted beforehand over it. Turn in the edges all round, and sew over neatly; fold the two ends in toward each other, until they meet to within about an inch. Sew over the double edges at the sides, and fold up the case. The handkerchiefs slip in on either side, into the two

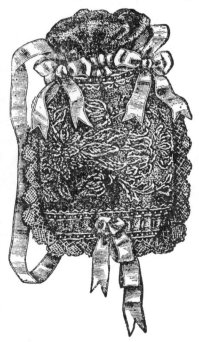

SACHET.

pockets thus formed, the plain ones being arranged on one side and the fancy ones on the other. These cases are convenient if they are scented, which is done by sprinkling sachet on to the flannel before the satin lining is added, and with a thin layer of cotton wool above. We may add that the satin should be quilted on to a thin piece of lining. We have given the dimensions to allow for turning in. There is another shape made like a large envelope. The size and shape must be similar to the other, only the upper part which forms the flap to the envelope is brought to a point in the center, with each side turned in. A silk cord is sometimes added all round the sachet, and finished off at the point with a loop, which forms the button-hole, while the button is placed on the lower side of the case.

Ladies' Fancy Bag Purse.

—The lower part of the purse bag is formed of black silk, in spider-web lace, lined with crimson silk, as also the upper part of the bag. Cords of crimson silk draw the purse together near the top, and tassels are placed at each division and one at the bottom.

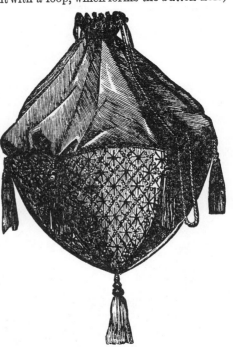

Crocheted Shawl.—*Material:* Six ounces of Shetland wool.

Make a chain the length of the longest edge of the shawl, which is three-cornered. The chain should be a multiple of six. After making the chain * throw the thread over the needle and catch into the third stitch from the needle, draw the thread through, thread over, draw through two, thread over, through two. This is the treble crochet stitch. Make eight more of these stitches in the same

LADIES' FANCY BAG PURSE.

chain stitch. Put the needle through the third stitch from the shell and draw the thread through this stitch and the one on the needle. This is single crochet stitch. Repeat from * to the end of the chain and break the thread.

2. Catch the thread in the middle stitch of the first shell of the preceding row. * Make three chain stitches, thread over the needle, put the needle through the next stitch to the one in which the thread is fastened, draw thread through, thread over, through two; keeping this loop and the former one on the needle, put thread over and make the same kind of stitch in the next stitch of the shell. Continue in this manner until there are ten stitches on the needle, then throw the thread over and draw through all the stitches, four chain and single crochet into the middle stitch of the next shell. Repeat from *

3. Catch the thread in the same stitch as the preceding row and * make nine trebles in the middle of the first shell of the second row, single crochet into the single crochet at the end of the first shell in second row. Repeat from *.

4. Like second row.

5. Like third row.

Scissor Case and Needle Cushion.—This is a neat little case intended to hang upon the wall near the sewing machine or work table. Our pattern is made up of brown silk, and finished with three rows of cords. The cords are also stitched on as finish for the pockets, which are sewn on the case itself. Cut from the illustration a pattern in pasteboard and a similar one in silk, allowing a margin to turn in. To make it more substantial line the silk with thin muslin. The back can be covered with cambric to match the color of the silk. The needle cushion measures three inches across, lined with muslin, and drawn in at the edge with a small cord to give it the proper curve; fill with emery, fine sand, or wool, if preferred.

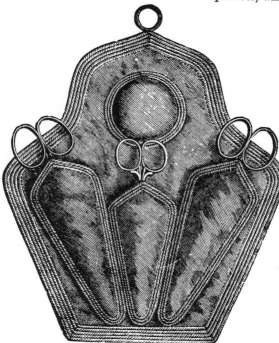

SCISSOR CASE AND NEEDLE CUSHION.

Table Mats.—Make a chain of twenty-five stitches.

DC. all around to the beginning and turn the work. There is one stitch upon the hook; put the hook back through the last loop through which the cotton was drawn, put the cotton over the hook and draw it through that loop alone; then put the cotton over the hook and draw through the two loops upon the hook—DC. the row of loops on the back side of the mat to the end.

Crochet twice in each of the three adjoining loops at the end—DC. to the other end. Crochet twice in each of the two adjoining loops at that end, bringing the ends of the first row around the mat together.

Bring the cotton in front of the hook which has upon it one loop, put the hook through a loop at the end of this row where it commenced, and draw the cotton through the two loops upon the hook joining the row.

Turn the work over, put the hook back through the last loop that the cotton was drawn through, put the cotton over the hook, draw through that loop alone, put the cotton over the hook and draw through the two loops. Crochet twice in the first loop of each of the two loops that had two stitches put in them.

Proceed down the side to the other end—crochet twice in the first of each of the three loops that had two stitches put in them, then go on to the beginning of the row, join and turn over the mat as before.

Continue until the mat is of sufficient size.

For the border pass one loop and make in the second five TC. stitches. Pass one loop and fasten down by DC. in the next and so on around the mat.

The length of the chain in the middle of course determines the size of the mat. For coffee and tea pots make a chain of six, and fasten together. Crochet twice in every stitch to start the six points for widening.

The cotton suitable is Dexter's No. 6 four threads. A hook small enough to make it very compact should be used. The stitches to be crocheted all the time are upon the back of the mat.

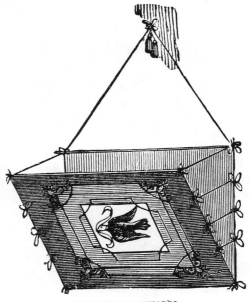

The mat is worked in ribbed (DC.) crochet, the hook being placed in the outside half of each loop, and the work turned at the end of each round. The increasings are, of course, to turn the corners, and the rounds are completed by an SC. before turning back.

Hanging Portfolio.— This is made of pasteboard, covered with gilt or white satin paper. It can be of any size you wish. It may be left plain or a picture pasted on

HANGING PORTFOLIO.

in front. Lace the sides together with a cord or ribbon. Hang with a cord and tassel. This is ornamental and useful for holding small articles.

Plush Thermometer Frame.—Remove from the tin frame an ordinary thermometer, and cut a piece of stiff pasteboard to fit it like a picture frame. It should be about two inches wide. Cut a piece of light blue plush to fit the frame exactly, and gum it on the back. Draw this smoothly over the frame and turn the raw edges of the plush over to the under side of the frame. Paint on the plush a pretty design of golden-rod. Cut a piece of pasteboard, exactly the size of the frame, and cover with light-blue silk or paper muslin. Overhand the edges of this and the plush together with blue sewing silk. Sew across the back a loop by which to hang it, or if it is preferred standing, fasten securely at the back a long wire, shaped like a hairpin. This makes a very good stand.

Visiting Card Stand.—The frame is made of black varnished rattan, but may be made of wood in the form of rustic work. There are two flat plates which may be ornamented to suit by painting. The edges of these are hung by bead ornaments. Take a small strip of oil-cloth which fits around the edges of the respective plates, measure equal distances, sew black jet buttons on and string bronze beads, thus constructing the first row. Then take gold or amber-colored beads and make a second row; the third row of white beads. Stick these around the jet buttons to the oil-cloth. The four double twisted rows may be made of different colored beads. The ends of these can be sewed on to the oil-cloth, and, after they are securely fastened, cut the oil-cloth which shows from under the ornaments, and then fasten it to the edges of the plates.

VISITING CARD STAND.

Bag for Knitting-Work.—In these days of knitting and crocheting, a small pocket or bag is convenient to hold the balls of wool, silk or cotton, and the needles or crochet hooks. This knitting-work pocket is worn attached to the belt, and is made of ecru linen and lined with red satin, or any other material that one may fancy. Cut from each of these materials five pieces of the following dimensions: Two inches wide at the top, not allowing for seams, one-half inch wide at the bottom and six inches long. These pieces are cut so as to bulge out at the sides, and are each four inches in width at the widest part. Embroider the linen in any design that you may fancy, but it seems desirable that this should be in outline stitch, and done with red silk. Join the linen pieces so that the seams are on the right side; notch them so that they will lie flat, and cover them with red silk braid, cross-stitched with some contrasting tone or color. Join the lining and place inside this, and bind the top with the same braid and fasten down in the same manner. Work a red silk eyelet hole in one of the side pieces to allow the end of the wool you are working with to come through. Close the bottom of the bag with a bunch of loops of red satin ribbon, and sew an end of the same ribbon at the top of each of the seams, joining them together with a bow of the ribbon, in which is sewed quite a large shield pin to fasten it to the dress belt.

Pin-Cushion.—A pretty little pin-cushion in the shape of a bellows can be made as follows: First cut four pieces of cardboard (visiting or invitation cards are **the** best), to the size required, and the shape of a small bellows; cover these four pieces singly with pretty silk or satin, by turning over the edges and lacing them from side to side with a needle and thread to make them fit. Then join two pieces together, and sew over the edges neatly;

FIG. 1.—WORK BASKET (OPEN).

sew a little piece of fine flannel or merino filled with needles to one joined side piece at the point; then put the two sides together and sew them well together at the point, leaving space enough for a gilt bodkin to pass through and make the real point. Put pins in all around the edge, add a narrow ribbon band fastened by a pin at the handle end, to keep the sides together. The inside of the bellows looks best with satin or plain silk, and the outside with brocade. If a small design is embroidered or painted on the outside, it has a very beautiful effect. A common length of the bellows is three inches from the handle to the point.

Work Basket.—An octagon-shaped box or basket is used for the foundation; it is lined with quilted blue satin, ornamented with a small silk button at the corner of each diamond. The outside of the basket is covered with old-gold satin, put on in four large puffs; each puff is divided by a band of blue velvet embroidered with a cross-stitch design; it is edged with lace and a fine gold cord. The lid is covered with velvet, also ornamented with lace, and a handle of wire covered with gold cord. In Fig. 1 the basket is shown open, and in Fig. 2 closed. Fig. 2 shows plain velvet bands, and in this figured silk is used instead of the old-gold satin.

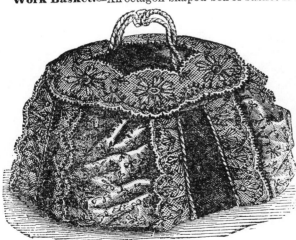

FIG. 2.—WORK BASKET (CLOSED).

Knitted Dressing Slipper.—*Materials required:* Four ounce blue and four ounce white Berlin wool; four pins No. 12 (Walker's gauge), and a pair of cork soles.

Commence the slipper at the toe with blue w o o l, cast on ten stitches, increase by putting the wool over the pin at beginning of

FIG. 1.—KNITTED DRESSING SLIPPER.

each row to make a stitch. Fig. 2 shows the outside of work, and Fig. 3 the inside with loops of white wool. When knitting with the white wool take it from two balls so as to have two lengths.

1st Row: Knit plain.

2d Row: Make one, knit one, * take the double white wool, turn it twice over the pin to form a loop of about three-quarters of an inch (see design), with the left-hand pin pass the last knitted loop over the four loops of white, knit two, repeat from * to the end of the row.

3d Row: Make one at the beginning of the row, slip the loops of white wool, knit the blue; in knitting the blue stitch pass the blue wool with which you are knitting round the double white wool; in knitting the

FIG. 2.—DETAIL OF FIG. 1.

FIG. 3.—DETAIL OF FIG. 1.

next stitch this will draw up the white wool close to the work, and so carry it to the other side to be ready for working the next row of loops.

4th Row: Make one, knit the blue stitches plain, knit the four white loops at the back as one stitch.

5th Row: Make one, knit to the end of the row. Repeat from second row, increasing at the beginning of each row until the work is wide enough across the instep.

Now divide the stitches for the sides, casting off ten in the center; with the third pin continue to work on the side stitches as before, without increase or decrease, until you have the length from the instep to the back of the heel, then cast off and work the other side in the same way; sew the two sides together at the back with a needle and wool.

Now pick up the stitches round the top of slipper, on three pins, and with a fourth pin and blue wool knit ten rows, cast off, turn this plain piece over, and hem it down to the top of inside of slipper to form a roll round the edge. Sew the bottom of slipper neatly and firmly to a strong cork sole lined with wool.

Stand for Cigar Ashes.—Our engraving represents a stand for cigar ashes. It consists of a bowl with a piece of wire running around it, by which it is mounted on three sticks, which are joined together in the middle. The upper ends are fastened to the bowl, and the fastening and bowl covered by lace or pressed leather, or any other material. The stand may be made by any young man or woman, of rustic work, using for the bowl piece the half of a cocoanut-shell, scraped, finished, and varnished. It will make a neat, unique, and useful ornament.

STAND FOR CIGAR ASHSS.

The Hungarian Bow.—This is a novelty in home decoration, and is used instead of a scarf upon chairs and sofas. It is formed of a long scarf with embroidered and fringed ends, but plain in the middle, and is arranged in a knot or bow. This is fastened to the back of the chair or sofa, and the ends prettily draped over it. Bronze and gold colors are the most used, embroidered in tulip design, with shaded red silk and gold thread. The fringe may be of gold, or red silk and gold. Handsome Roman scarfs that were bright for personal wear, but are now a little " off-style," may be utilized in this way, and are as handsome as anything bought at the decorative or art stores.

Star Mats.—Have four knitting needles; cast on three stitches, on each of three needles, then tie like the beginning of a stocking; then knit two plain rounds, then widen every stitch all around, then knit one plain round, then widen every two stitches all around, then one plain round, then widen every three stitches all around, then a plain round. Continue so till you get thirteen stitches between. Knit a plain round every time after widening, then widen and narrow, and widen again, then knit two plain rounds, then widen and narrow, widen and narrow again, then widen, then knit two plain rounds. Continue so till the star is complete, adding one more widened stitch every two rounds. Then bind off.

A Table Scarf.—A useful table scarf, and one that is particularly pleasing to the eye, because it does not suggest almost endless labor, is made by taking a strip of all wool Java canvas of the proper length for the table on which it is to be used. Line it with some stiff cloth and then with silesia. At about three inches from the outer edge sew on two strips of black velvet ribbon two inches wide. Through the center work a handsome scroll pattern, using bright yellow silk; the velvet stripes may be put on perfectly plain, or may be worked in old-fashioned cross-stitch, or in some modification of feather stitch. Finish the bottom of the scarf with yellow silk balls. This is suitable for the common sitting-room; it is so bright that the dust can be shaken from it with ease.

Baby Basket.—Procure a large brown basket and a small camp-stool.

BABY BASKET.

Measure the size round the top of the basket; get that quantity of material; measure the depth of the basket, and allow for the scallops to fall over the edge. Bind the scallops; fasten it to the edge of the basket; draw it down lightly to the bottom in plaits. Cut a round piece of material the shape of the bottom of the basket; fasten it round the edge, and finish with a box-plaiting of ribbons. Make the cushions and pockets to please the fancy. A box-plaiting round the top of basket; also round the scallops. Between each scallop put a bow or cord and tassels of worsted; fasten this on the camp-stool, around which put a ruffle of the same material the basket is lined with.

Neat Mats can be made by cutting a stiff piece of woolen goods into the shape desired, and crocheting an edge or border of fancy-colored yarn

Star Stitch.—Crochet a chain of twenty stitches. Without putting the wool over first, put the needle into the second chain, thread over and draw through, leaving the two loops on the needle; do the same in the next three chain successively, drawing the wool up longer and having five loops on the needle, put wool over and draw through all, and make one chain to hold it *. Put needle into the stitch where the five loops are, draw thread through, put the needle into the back part of last loop of the star before, draw through, put the needle into the next two chain just the same, drawing them up longer and thread over, draw through all five loops and make one chain *; repeat between the stars.

Embroidered Chair Cover.—Embroidered slips are much used now instead of chintz covers for chairs. They can be made of thin woolen material, or of linen. When of wool they are embroidered with crewels.

The better way to have the covers fit nicely, is to lay the material on the chair, pin it in place to hold it firmly, and lay the plaits and seams just where they should be, and cut the material then. There are no two chairs exactly alike in shape, and it will be found far more easy to fit them in this way. The seams and edges are bound with braid and the corners are laced down with cords. The caps for the arms are fastened with buttons and button-holes.

EMBROIDERED CHAIR COVER.

Feather Edged Braid Trimming.—Fasten the thread to a loop in the braid —chain seven stitches, put the needle in the second loop from where you commence, draw the thread through the loop and the stitch on the needle, chain four more and fasten in the next second loop, then take up three more loops by putting the needle through each one, and drawing the thread through the loop, and the stitch on the needle, chain four stitches and fasten as before, chain four more and fasten, take up eight loops as the three were taken, chain two and fasten around the last four chain stitches, chain two more and fasten in the second loop from the eight taken up stitches, chain two, and fasten around the next four chain stitches, chain two, and fasten in second loop, then take up three loops, chain two, fasten around the four chain stitches, chain two, fasten in second loop, chain two, fasten around the seven stitches, chain four, fasten in second loop, double the braid together from this loop, and on the right side of the work take up a loop of each piece of the braid, draw the thread through these loops, leave the stitch on the needle, and so continue until all have been taken up, as far as the loop above the eight taken up stitches, on the opposite side of the braid, then draw the thread through two stitches at a time until only one stitch remains on the needle, then commence the second scallop same as before. Crochet across the top of the completed edging, to sew on by. And I think it washes and wears better to crochet a chain of three between each loop on the lower edge, except those close between the scallops, simply drawing the thread through these. The needle must be fine and straight.

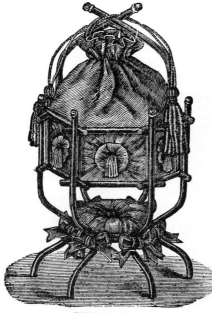

WORK-STAND.

Ladies' Work-Stand.—The skeleton of the work-stand we have illustrated is made of rattan. The squares between the rods should be covered with green, plaited silk, which is drawn together and either fastened with a button or a small rosette and a flat tassel. The bag, for the reception of embroidery or other fancy work, is made of green silk, drawn together by a green cord, at the end of which is a tassel of the same color. To hide the joints of the rods, a scarf of green ribbon is put at each juncture. In the lower part of the stand is a pincushion, which is made in the same style as the filling-in of the squares above, and also drawn and held together with a button.

Mosaic Embroidery.—Mosaic embroidery is very effective for mantel drapes, piano covers, and screens, and is quite easily made. Take whatever material is chosen for the ground work and sew on to it with some fancy stitch odd patterns cut from various colored plushes

FLORICULTURE--Update

There are more plants now available for home gardening than there were in 1888. Sprengeri ferns, various bromeliads, palms, rubber plants and other semi-tropical plants have been transported north for the benefit of house gardeners. These plants often require special treatment such as misting and fertilization but will respond well to the general practices contained in this chapter. For instance, I have used tobacco sprays to good advantage with my plants.

Light, water, soil, and pot size are basic considerations for healthy house plants. Most problems can be traced to one or more of these factors. Some plants will tolerate the limited light they receive from north and west windows; others will not. In areas with chlorinated water, the plant water should be let stand for a few hours to allow the harmful chlorine to pass off. The benefits of good drainage cannot be overstated. Potting soils often contain vermiculite or pearlite for lighter soil and better drainage. Many plants need a period of dryness for healthy root growth. They should never be allowed to stand in water. Top watering is best; bottom watering promotes excess root growth. Soil acidity and alkalinity are important to many plants, so lime water or egg shells will benefit the growth of some plants but not others. Plants put into too large pots will devote too much energy to filling the soil with roots. Begonias, for example, seem to enjoy being root-bound. If a plant is root-bound, it should be moved to the next larger size pot, not a pot twice the size. Glass and plastic pots should be strenuously avoided as they afford neither the 'breathing' nor the drainage of clay pots.

The Wardian case mentioned in this chapter is nothing but a terrarium with Victorian doo-dads. Slow-growing plants should be chosen for terraria, and the gardener should take care to add charcoal and ample drainage material to keep the atmosphere and soil free of mold. A properly balanced terrarium takes little care.

Many greenhouses sell plants ill-equipped to survive in the home. Greenhouse plants are used to much sunlight, much water vapor in the air, and have perhaps been heavily fertilized. This is particularly true of flowering plants. The home gardener should try to cushion the shock of moving plants to a non-greenhouse environment by misting the plants, finding them a space with good light and by being aware of their fertilizer needs. Too much fertilizer is as dangerous as too little; too much leads to excess, rapid leaf growth. I've found fish emulsion a mild and effective fertilizer.

The home gardener may be interested in duplicating greenhouse conditions in the home. Kits now on the market can convert a spare room or window into a miniature greenhouse.

Setting plants out in the summer, whether in or out of the pot can lead to considerable growth. Care must be taken when bringing the plants in in the fall that they are not infested and that they accustom themselves again to indoor life. Roots and stems should be pruned at the same time and about the same amount.

With the renewed interest in house plants in the last five years, there is no lack of books on the subject. Though the *Cyclopaedia's* advice is apt, it can be supplemented by one of the numerous house plant books. The best I've encountered is *Simon & Schuster's Complete Guide to Plants and Flowers* (NY: Simon & Schuster Fireside, 1974).

FLORICULTURE.

Ivy for Picture Frames.—Ivy is one of the best plants to have in the house, as it bears a large amount of neglect and abuse, and gratefully repays good treatment. It is not rare to see a pot of ivy placed where it can be trained around picture frames or mirrors, and thus border them with living green. A good plan is to dispense with the pot, or rather, have a substitute for it, which is kept out of sight. Our illustration shows a picture frame wreathed with ivy after this method. Only a good-sized picture or mirror can be treated in this way, and as such are usually hung so that the top of the frame leans forward, the space between the frame and the wall is available for the receptacle for the plant. A pot or pan of zinc, of a wedge shape, and size to suit the space between the frame and the wall, can be readily made by any tinsmith. This is to be hung against the wall so as to be quite concealed by the picture, and the ivy tastefully trained over the frame. A rustic frame is better suited to this purpose, as it not only affords better facilities for attaching the stems to the frame, but its style seems better adapted to this kind of decoration than more pretentious

IVY FOR PICTURE FRAMES.

ones. Still, a gilt frame may be made beautiful in the same way. There is only one precaution to be used, viz.: not to hang such a frame over the fireplace, for the combined heat and dust would soon destroy the plant. Let it hang so that it may face a north or east window. Don't forget the water; the pan holding the plant is out of sight, and, therefore, should be kept in mind.

Diseases of Room Plants.—The leaves of plants when in a normally healthy state are generally of a deep green color, but when diseased they become yellowish or white In the majority of cases such a diseased appearance is produced by an excess of light or a lack of it, too much or too little water, unsuitable, overrich, or impoverished soil, or lack of drainage. When the discoloration first shows itself—and this is generally on the younger shoots —the condition of the roots should be ascertained by turning the plant out of the pot. If the roots are healthy and fill the ball, or appear overcrowded, the discoloration indicates lack of nutriment, or too little or too much light. In the first case it can be remedied by shifting the plant into a larger pot, or watering the plant with liquid manure. If excess or lack of light is the cause, reference must be had to the character of the plant. Ferns, selaginellas, and plants of similar character that naturally grow in shady places, become pale or yellowish when grown in bright light, while those whose habitat is in open, exposed situations, become discolored when not having a sufficiency of light. In either case, when grown in pots, plants are more liable to become diseased through this cause than when grown in the open air. The remedy, of course, is only to shift the position of the plant and place it where the light will better suit its nature.

If the ball is not filled with roots, and they do not appear to be fresh and healthy, the discoloration, in all probability, proceeds from excess of moisture or unsuitable soil. To remedy the first, see that the drainage outlet is kept free and unchoked; if after a week or two this does not affect a change, then it is probable that the diseased appearance arises from unsuitable soil. Some plants, such as azaleas, camelias, and rhododendrons, in such case will not throw out a single rootlet from the old ball into the new soil, but gradually die back or make but weakly, spindling shoots. If the discoloration has been produced by bad drainage, excessive watering, or unsuitable soil, and is of such long standing as to cause the roots to decay, or the soil has become sour, the proper remedy is to shake off all the earth from them and wash them by shaking them thoroughly in clean water, cutting off the decayed parts with a sharp knife, and replanting into light fresh earth, and seeing that the drainage is kept free. Rich soil or large pots should not be used, the latter should be but little larger than the diameter of the roots. When the roots are well developed the plant may be shifted into a larger pot and richer soil. The leaves of plants from warm countries—oranges, for instance—will sometimes become yellow when exposed to a low temperature, especially when accompanied with much moisture; the remedy in this case either to raise the temperature or decrease the amount of water given.

Sometimes the discoloration is caused by insufficiency of water, which causes the roots to shrivel up. It may also proceed from giving too much water at one time, and then letting the ball become dry, or by only giving enough of water to moisten the surface of the soil for an inch or two, while below it may be as dry as powder. Carefulness and watchfulness are the only modes of preventing injury to the plants from such causes. When the leaves of deciduous plants fall off as their season of rest approaches, they should be placed in a lower temperature, and not have as liberal a supply of water as when growing. If evergreen plants, such as we generally grow in greenhouses, shed their leaves profusely and suddenly, it indicates that they have not light enough, or that the temperature of the room is too high, or the atmosphere is too dry; the proper mode of treatment in such cases is self-apparent.

Occasionally plants will die off suddenly near the surface of the soil, although the roots, leaves and shoots look quite healthy. This is often caused by the collar of the plant—the part where the roots are joined to the stem—being set too deep into the soil. Watering with very cold water when the soil in the pots has been exposed to the sun will also cause them to die off suddenly. Plants in pots should never have the pots exposed to the full blaze of sunshine, especially in the middle of the day. The crowns of herbaceous plants that have been kept dry, or comparatively so, during their season of rest, will rot away if the balls of roots are too liberally supplied with water. They should be kept in the shade, and but sparingly supplied with water, and that rather tepid, until they develop a leaf or two.

Some plants, especially roses, when kept in rooms, are very apt to become mildewed, to the certain destruction of the leaves and flower buds. As soon as it shows itself the leaves should be washed with soap and water, rinsed off and flowers of sulphur dusted on with a dredging-box or a pepper-box, washing it off after it has been on for two or three days.

The whole art of keeping plants in rooms is to provide an equable, moist temperature, light according to the nature of the plants, regular moderate watering, good drainage, suitable soil, cleanliness, and an avoidance of all sudden checks or shocks to the plant either in temperature or humidity. These are always injurious, as they produce disease and render the plant liable to the attacks of insects and fungoid growths.

Cheap and Pretty Hanging Baskets.—The sweet potato, which is basket and contents in one, has, when successful, a very ornamental effect. Truth compels us to state that it is not always successful, and a yellow, scraggy appearance of foliage will sometimes reward the best-intentioned endeavors; but given ordinarily favorable surroundings, which include heat and sunshine, this curious hanging basket thrives and covers a large space with bright-hued verdure. A large, sound root should be selected, and the top for some distance down is then removed. Next comes the disagreeable process of removing the inside—leaving a wall all around, and a thicker one at the bottom. Three holes are then bored at equal distances, about half an inch from the top; and into these the suspending cords, which unite at the upper ends, are fastened. When filled with water up to the holes, the sweet potato basket is completed; and if placed in a sunny window, it should be covered with shoots and leaves in a few weeks' time. Some of the sprays can be trained upward, and others allowed to droop. The red-skinned sweet potato has a pretty streak of silver in the foliage, and the two varieties on either side of a window make an agreeable contrast. If preferred, the hollow root can be filled with earth or sand instead of water—if with the latter, there should be two or three small pieces of charcoal at the bottom. A carrot treated in the same way sends forth a mass of feathery foliage whose vivid green brings a sort of sunshine into the dreariest day; and even a large sponge suspended by cords, thoroughly moistened and planted with flax, rape-seed, or any low growing verdure, is not to be despised. A very pretty basket can be manufactured by taking an ordinary one of wire and fastening to it raisin-stems, or bits of thin wire properly bent, and then dipping the whole into melted sealing-wax of a vermilion color until it is thoroughly coated. Brushing it over with the mixture would take less material. The effect of theses coralized sprays, glowing through delicate green vines, is really beautiful. Every one cannot succeed with a basket of growing plants. but almost any one can succeed with ivy; and a very ornamental hanging basket that requires little care can be made in the following way: Almost any kind of basket will answer, and there should be a good collection of autumn leaves varnished and prepared in sprays. Six or eight two ounce bottles should be filled with water, and have one or two well-grown sprays of ivy in each, placed in wads of cotton to keep them upright, the leaves arranged in between and around the edge of the basket. The ivy will grow, and can be trained to run up the cords, as well as to hang over the sides; the only care required is to fill up the bottles as the water evaporates, and to keep the leaves free from dust.

Window Gardening.—What adds more to the cheerfulness of the home during the lonely, dreary days of winter, than flowers? All can have

FIG. 1.—DOUBLE WINDOW WITH PLANT SHELF.

them, the poor as well as the rich, if a little care and forethought is used in growing and arranging them.

The preparatory work consists in transplanting and fairly starting in small pots, in August or September, the Madeira vine, creeping Charlie, cypress vine, balloon vine, the common English, the German, or the Kenilworth ivy, or morning glory, flowering bean, or sweet-scented pea, or, if you are disposed to be more aristocratic, smilax, lophiospermum, or, if the window is large and the foliage is not deemed too rank, the clematis or the passion vine. Nearly all of these, if thus started, will grow finely and festoon your windows in a few weeks; some of them have fine blossoms, which will add to the beauty of their foliage. Next, for the plants to make a display in your windows. What these shall be, and how they shall be arranged, depends very much upon the size, shape and character of your windows. If you have a bay or oriel window, either large or small, you can make it the most attractive feature of your room at a very small expense. First place your pots with climb-vines at the sides on low brackets, and the vines to make a beautiful frame for your windows. If the window is a deep bay, other and more delicate vines may be placed between the side windows and the main one—such as smilax, the Kenilworth ivy, or the cypress vine—and trained over the ceiling of the bay. At the base of the windows have a shelf six or eight inches wide (eight is best), supported by the ordinary

FIG. 2.—PRETTY ARRANGEMENT FOR SITTING-ROOM WINDOWS.

metal brackets, and in front tack the expanding framework (such as is shown in Fig. 1), which is now to be found for sale by the yard very cheap at all the flower stores—the black walnut is the prettiest, though the holly wood is very neat; stretch it to its full extent before tacking it on. Then selecting your hardiest and most freely-blooming plants—geraniums, pelargoniums, rose geraniums, all from slips potted in July or August, periwinkles, fuchsias, heliotropes, bouvardias, cuphias, and newly-potted slips of verbena, with such other beautiful small plants as you may find desirable—place each pot in one about three sizes larger, which is partially filled with fine earth, and the space between loosely packed with moss. Set these on your shelf, arranging them with reference to complementary colors; put in the center where the main partition between the two divisions of the central window is, a good and shapely ardisia, which, if it has been plunged during the summer, will, by this time, be loaded with its beautiful berries, **which** are in November just beginning to turn to a beautiful scarlet. These berries will hang on till June; and, while the plant is of very moderate price, **it** has no superior as an ornamental shrub. In the corners put callas, which should have been heeled or turned over to rest, as early as July or August 1st. Their position should be partially shaded, and where they will not have too much heat; when they begin to bud, they should have a plenty of warm, almost hot, water furnished them daily. They, too, should be placed in a

FIG. 3.—BAY WINDOW WITH PLANT PLATFORM.

pot surrounded by a large pot, and the interstices filled in with moss. Across the center of the windows place other shelves with pots of smaller flowers, and, among the rest, creeping plants, such as verbenas, sweet alyssum, nemaphila lobelia, mesembryanthemum, etc., etc. On a table in the center, if you can have a neat box, zinc-lined, you can set in pots, hyacinths, amaryllis, cyclamens, iris, and the finest sorts of crocus, and, packing moss around them, keep them moist. From the ceiling of the bay may be suspended hanging baskets, taking the precaution to keep them moist. The outlay **for** all this is very little, and if you are ingenious you can do it all yourself.

But everybody has not bay windows, or even double windows. For these unfortunates, among whom we are sorry to be obliged to reckon ourselves, the simpler arrangement indicated in Fig. 2 is almost as effective. A shelf at the foot of each window supported on brackets, and, if preferred, protected by the expanding framework, will give room for four or six pots at each window, while the vines can be trained around the windows, as in the other case. A swinging bracket large enough for two pots can be attached to the outer side of the framework of each window, midway of its height, and a rustic basket attached to a hook projecting from the top of the window frame, if desired. On a table or slab between the windows a small jardiniere, containing an ardisia, or Tahiti orange, can be placed. In the selection of climbers for trimming the windows, avoid the climbing fern, which is offered so abundantly at all the flower stores. It cannot be made to live in parlors,

FIG. 4.—DEEP BAY WINDOW WITH BRACKETS.

and in spite of all the care which may be taken with it will soon become dry and unsightly. The ivies, Madeira vine and cypress vine are the best, though several other climbers are pretty. The blossoms of the Madeira vine, which will come out if it is well cared for in February or March, are very fragrant, and will fill the parlors with their delicate perfume.

The wall pockets so plenty in these days of scroll sawing, can be very easily adapted to the purpose of plant cultivation, and add greatly to the beauty of these simple decorations.

How to Kill Insects on Plants.—Slugs are occasionally seen eating large holes or notches in the leaves of all succulents and begonias. They usually feed at night. Cut potatoes, turnips, or some other fleshy vegetable in halves, and place conveniently near the plants. The slugs will gather upon the vegetable, and are easily destroyed. The white worm which infests, occasionally, all soils where plants are kept in pots, may be removed as follows: Sprinkle lime water over the soil, or sprinkle a little slacked lime on the earth, and in the saucer of the pot. Lime water may be easily made by slacking a large piece of lime in a pail of cold water, letting this settle, and then bottle the clear water for use. Give each pot a tablespoonful twice a week.

To destroy the little bugs on the oleander, take a piece of lime the size of a hen's egg, and dissolve it in about two quarts of water. Wash the stock and branches with this water.

To destroy plant lice, take three and a half ounces of quassia chips, add five drachms Stavesacre seed in powder, place in seven pints of water, and boil down to five pints. When cold, the strained liquid is ready for use, either by means of a watering-pot or a syringe.

Hot alum water will destroy red and black ants, cockroaches, spiders and chintzbugs. Take two pounds of alum and dissolve it in three or four quarts of boiling water. Let it stand on the fire until the alum is all melted, then apply it with a brush (while nearly boiling hot) to the places frequented by these insects.

Any choice plants may be preserved from the ravages of slugs by placing a few pieces of garlic near them. No slugs will approach the smell of garlic.

Greenhouse slugs often become a nuisance in the greenhouse. A certain remedy is to sprinkle salt freely along the edges of the bench or table, the crossing of which is sure death to the slug.

Another way of destroying insects on flowers is to water the plants with a decoction of tobacco, which quickly destroys. Independently of the removal of the insects, tobacco-water is considered by many persons to improve the verdure of the plant. Prepare it as follows: Take one pound of roll tobacco and pour over it three pints of water, nearly boiling. Let it stand for some hours before it is used.

Kerosene oil may be used for destroying insects on plants by taking a tablespoonful of oil and mixing it with half a cup of milk, and then diluting the mixture with two gallons of water. Apply the liquid with a syringe, and afterward rinse with clear water. This substance is death to plant insects, and we have never heard of its injuring the most delicate plants when used as here directed.

The following is recommended as a means of destroying the rose slug: Add a teaspoonful of powdered white hellebore to two gallons of boiling water. Apply when cold, in a fine spray, bending the tops over so as to reach the under surface of the leaves. One application is usually sufficient. This is a good way to treat the currant worm.

The red spider may be banished from plants by the simple process of cutting off the infected leaf. A leaf once attacked soon decays and falls off; but then the animals remove to another. By carefully pursuing this amputation plants will become remarkably healthy.

A new method for the getting rid of worms which destroy the house plants is a number of sulphur matches placed in the flower pots with their heads down. The experiment has been tried with success.

Ammonia for Plants.—If the house plants become pale and sickly, a dose of ammonia, a few drops in the water you water them with, will revive them like magic. It is the concentrated essence of fertilizers, and acts upon plant life as tonics and sea air upon human invalids,

Ornamental Wardian Case.—The sides of the box are of mahogany, 1 1-4 inch in thickness, and the bottom of deal, 1 1-2 inch thick, well framed and dovetailed together, and strengthened with brass bands, and with two cross-bars beneath. The upper edge of the box is furnished with a groove for the reception of the glass roof, and this groove is lined with brass, to

ORNAMENTAL WARDIAN CASE.

prevent the wood from rotting. The roof is composed of brass, and glazed with the very best flattened crown glass. The brass astragals are grooved for the reception of the glass, and not rebated, as in ordinary glazing. Eyed studs are cast on the inner side of the ridge astragal, about half an inch in length, for the purpose of suspending small orchids or ferns from the roof. The inside of the box is lined with zinc, and at one of the corners an aperture is formed into which a copper tube, two inches long, is inserted, and furnished with a cock for withdrawing any superfluous water that may at any time accumulate within the box. One of the panes is made to take out—this provision is necessary for the occasional arrangement and airing of the plants, but the general arrangement is made by lifting the top off entirely.

Rose Culture.—*Situation.*—A place apart from other flowers should be assigned to them, if possible, sheltered from high winds, but open and not surrounded by trees, as closeness is very apt to generate mildew; where they cannot have a place to themselves, any part of the garden best fulfilling these conditions will answer.

Soil.—A most important item in their successful culture. That in which they especially delight is a rich, unctious loam, that feels greasy when pressed between the fingers. Where this is not to be had the soil must be improved; if light, by the addition of loam, or even clay, well worked in; where heavy, good drainage and the addition of coal ashes in small quantities will help it, but in such places draining is more important.

Planting.—Mix some loam and well-rotted manure together, open a good sized hole, and fill it with fresh soil; plant firmly. Shorten any very long shoots, and, if exposed to winds, secure the plant by short stakes.

Manuring.—Roses are strong feeders, and will take almost any amount of manure; pig manure is the best, except in hot soils, when cow manure is preferable; stable manure is generally available and good. Exhibitors generally apply a top-dressing in spring, but it does not improve the appearance of the beds; a good top-dressing may be laid on the beds in autumn, and be dug in in the spring.

Watering.—When coming into bloom, if the weather be dry, give a good drenching twice or three times a week; continue after blooming to prevent mildew. If greater size be required, liquid manure may be used. Syringe daily for green fly.

Pruning.—This may be done any time after the beginning of March, according to the season. Cut out all wood over two years old and all weakly shoots. Weak-growing kinds should be pruned hard—that is, down to three or four eyes; stronger growing kinds may be left longer. Cut to an eye that points outward, so as to keep the inside of the plant open. Teas and noisettes require less cutting back; the tops should be shortened and the weak shoots cut out, and they should not be pruned until May. Use a sharp knife.

Rustic Hanging Basket.—The accompanying drawing represent a rustic hanging basket that any person can make with the common house tools, axe, saw, knife, hammer and a few brads. First, procure from the woods two or three sticks of iron wood, or such as may suit the fancy. They should be selected, small trees, about three inches in diameter. After selecting the tree, cut it up into pieces fourteen or fifteen inches in length; then, taking one of these round sticks, split off the four sides; this, if it splits well, will give eight pieces from two sticks, the number required to make the basket. The sticks, or pieces, should be narrower and thinner at one end than the other, as shown in the cut, and rounded at each end. Then procure a block or piece of inch board, and cut out a circular piece about three inches in diameter, slanting it a little so that the pieces will have the taper towards the bottom when tacked to the block. This gives the basket a little flare. They should fit close together at the point where the block is, and may be a little open, nearer the top, in order to fill between with moss.

Now, the pieces being nailed to the block with brads, begin to ornament it with grape-vines and roots. Roots are tacked to the under side of the block, to fill it all up, and at the lower points of the pieces where they match, always keeping in view one thing—to preserve the tapering form and matching the roots in every way that will bring them all towards the center with uni-

formity. Next put vines on the sides, as per engraving, bringing two together over the places where the sticks match; also, weave in around the top two vines, in and out alternately, and, fastening with brads, tack roots on the pieces between the ornamental work.

Next put on a handle of grape-vine, giving it a single knot; tie at the top to form a loop, interweaving it with a smaller vine; then give the basket a coat of varnish and put in suitable plants. Keep the basket partially in the shade, and occasionally dip it in a barrel of rain water.

To Prepare Plants for Winter.—It is a great mistake to delay the work of preparation for winter until it is suggested by cool nights or a warning given by blighting frosts. When a plant has been taken from a pot and planted in open ground it usually outgrows its former place, and is too large for any vessel of convenient size. The root should be cut away to a considerable extent and likewise the top or foliage must be correspondingly reduced. Novices often fail at this point, for they dislike to part with any of the new growth, and set the plant in a pot unpruned, and expect what is not possible, that it will flourish.

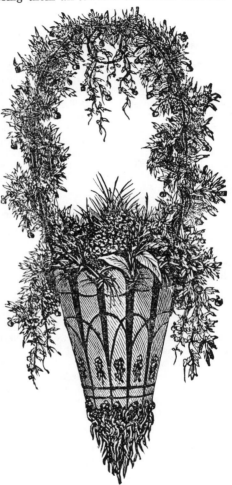

RUSTIC HANGING BASKET.

Cut back root system and branch system equally is the rule. Plants when thus transplanted need to be favored by being kept in the shade and sheltered from the drying winds until they have made a good start in the pots. Many of the house plants are kept in their pots during the summer and will need repotting, or the pot washed and the surface soil replaced by fresh, rich earth. A larger pot is needed by those plants whose roots have formed a mat along the inner surface. The ball of earth can be examined quickly by spreading the left hand on the vessel—the stem passing between the fingers, and with the other hand on the bottom invert the pot and give the edge a downward tap against some object. If this does not succeed, pour some water around the edge, and after a short time repeat the operation. All old pots should be clean, and if the new ones are used soak them in water until the pores are filled. A piece of broken vessel is placed over the bottom hole before filling in the potting earth. All the necessary pots, soil, etc., should be abandoned now, that they may be at hand when needed at any time during the winter.

Selection of House Plants.—Select fresh, healthy plants for winter culture, for they will repay all the labor you bestow upon them by bright flowers. The old geraniums, heliotropes, fuchsias, etc., which have flowered all summer, will be of no value for window gardening, while young plants will soon be covered with buds and flowers. Small plants in small pots are far more desirable for house culture than large plants in such cumbrous pots that it requires a man's strength to move them.

There are several winter-flowering fuchsias which will continue to bloom from October until May, in beautiful luxuriance, if you will only give them a spoonful of "*Soluble Pacific Guano*" once in two or three weeks, or give it in a liquid form by dissolving a tablespoonful of it in three quarts of hot water. It will also destroy the white worms which are so apt to infest the soil of plants that have not been repotted frequently. At least it proved an antidote with me last season. But if it does not exterminate them, take a piece of unslacked lime as large as a man's fist, and slack it in hot water in an old pail, and when the lime has sunk to the bottom, water the plants with it, and it will make their foliage luxuriant and destroy worms of all kinds. The lime can be used over several times.

Tea roses, if well treated, make lovely plants for winter. Purchase well-rooted plants of *Bon Silene, Safrano, Bella,* and other varieties, and put them close to the glass and stimulate weekly with weak liquid fertilizers; or a *Jacqueminot* rose which bloomed in the summer may be taken up and potted in an eight-inch pot, with the richest compost made friable with sand or sharp grits, cut back all the old wood and pull off every leaf and place it in a frost-proof window, but where the sun shines in well, and you can force as handsome rose-buds as the florists.

For a small amount of money a collection of winter-flowering plants can be procured; and though they will neither feed nor clothe the body, yet they will minister to the needs of the soul, which sometimes hungers, thirsts, and shivers, while the body is luxuriously fed, and clothed in fine raiment.

Soil for Plants.—Knowing that nearly every lady in the city finds it hard to get manure of the right quality for her plants, I thought this suggestion might be of some use to them. Gather up the fallen leaves and put them in an old box, or in some obscure corner where they will not have to be removed. After getting all you want, pile them in as close quarters as possible, then throw on them all of your dish-water, wash-water, or any water that will help to make them rot. Every week or two take a stick and turn the leaves over, and keep on doing this until they are all rotten, which they will be in a short time, and you will have as good a manure as any florist could want. If you could get the droppings from a cow and put them in an old dish and pour water on them; let it stand for a day or two; then take the liquid and pour it around the roots of the plant; it will give it a dark green color and make it grow very fast; but in putting the last named on the roots do not let any get on the leaves. As nearly every lady has some plant which they cannot pot, from its large size, they would be very glad to know of some way in which they can enrich the soil without going to the trouble of taking the plant out of the pot. By putting the liquid on every month it will make the soil nearly as rich and do the plant as much good as if they had put it in rich soil. Fine charcoal is excellent to mix with the soil when potting plants, or to sprinkle on the surface of the soil of those already potted. It stimulates the growth of the plants and deepens the colors. Iron filings from a blacksmith or machine shop worked into the soil for plants, will add greatly also to the rich and bright color of the flowers.

Smilax for a Curtain.—Last season, writes a lady, I slipped some smilax out of a small pot into a box which I set on a shelf that was on the outside of a south window. This shelf was eight inches below the top of the window-sill. The box was six inches deep, and so was a little lower than the sill. With a red-hot poker I burned a row of holes around the sides of the box, and filled it with a light, rich soil. When the plant was fully established and had sent up nice thrifty sprouts, I drove nine small nails along the top of the window-pane, and slipped on to them the looped-up ends of a fine cord; the other ends of the cord were tied each to a nail which was stuck in the box by the sprout it was intended to support. The vines grew rapidly, and in a few weeks' time had reached the top of the window; a week or two more, and the ends were drooping down from the top, thus forming a graceful valance to my beautiful curtains—a curtain far more beautiful than any made by mortal hand could ever be. In October, when the nights were growing frosty, I slipped the looped ends of the cords that supported the vines off the nails, and placed the box with the vine on a stand on the inside of the window and slipped the loops over nails, and so, without any trouble at all, had my window adorned with this lovely vine until Christmas. This vine so airily light, and so graceful, is peculiarly appropriate for the adornment of thin evening dresses, and as lovely for the hair.

Hot-Water Cure for Sickly Plants.—M. Willermoz some time since stated that plants in pots may be restored to health by means of hot water; ill-health he maintains, ensues from acid substances in the soil, which, being absorbed by the roots, act as poison. The small roots wither and cease to act, and the upper and younger shoots consequently turn yellow, or become spotted, indicative of their morbid state. In such cases the usual remedy is to transplant into fresh soil, in clean pots with good drainage, and this often with the best results. But his experience of several years has proved the unfailing efficacy of the simpler treatment, which consists in watering abundantly with hot water at a temperature of 145 degrees Fahr., having previously stirred the soil of the pots so far as may be done without injury to the roots. Water is then given until it runs freely from the pots. In his experiments, the water at first came out clear; afterwards it was sensibly tinged with brown, and gave an appreciable acid reaction. After this thorough washing, the pots were kept warm, and the plants very soon made new roots, immediately followed by vigorous growth.

Golden-Leaved Horseshoe Geranium.—If those who have the golden-leaved horseshoe geraniums will put them in the brightest sunlight, the colors will be brought out so that the plant will be as beautiful as if it were covered with blossoms.

The Mud System of Slipping Plants.—The following interesting article we find in the *Babyhood Magazine:* A child of five years can cut off a slip from a geranium, verbena, heliotrope, carnation, fuchsia, or even a rosebush, taking care that the slip is made from the young or green shoot; and in a plate or saucer filled with wet sand it will root just as quickly and as well as if put in by the hands of a gardener—provided care is taken that the sand in the saucer is kept wet by adding a little water to it each day until the slips show the small roots. The slip should be cut in the way shown in the drawing, taking it off either between or below the joints. The saucer holding the slips should be placed in some sunny window where it is warm enough for a little child. Nearly all kinds of slips can be rooted at any time of the year; but some, such as the coleus, salvias, and various plants called " warm-blooded," had better not be slipped until the warm weather comes in May.

The slips will begin to show the little roots in from two to three weeks after being put in the saucers. They should then be potted in little pots about two inches deep, which the gardeners call thumb-pots. The slips should be potted in rich, soft mold, which can be procured from any florist. Good garden earth will also do, only it must not be wet and sticky. If it can only be got in a very wet condition, dry stove-ashes may be mixed with it.

When the slips are to be potted, first fill the little flower-pot full of earth, then with the fore-finger make a hole in the center big enough to put the roots in. Gently press the earth all around the roots, making it level and smooth on the top; then with a watering-pot sprinkle slightly the slips, now plants. Every other day they will require watering until they begin to put little white roots to the edge of the pot, which can be seen by giving the pot a tap on the table, and turning the contents out just like jelly from a glass. After

the soil in the little pots gets filled with roots, which will be in four or five weeks from the time the slips were placed in them, it will be well to transplant into pots three or four inches deep. By May the slips that were put in the saucers to root in February or March will have made plants large enough to set out in the open garden, and by midsummer will be fine bushes covered with blossoms.

Fuchsias.—Fuchsias, after being exhausted with blooming, should have the terminal shoots all clipped off, and be repotted in a soil composed of leaf mold. In a few weeks new shoots full of flower buds will start all over, growing rapidly.

Rustic Flower Stand.—A very simple and graceful arrangement for flowers requiring no more space than the tiny violet or crocus, or some

RUSTIC FLOWER STAND.

bright blossoming dwarf plant. A box frame, with four "posts" to support the roof, is all the foundation required. The rest is made of neatly cut pieces of straw, braided with three rows of red-stained willow or cane. The pretty flower pavilion is ornamented with wheat sheafs and grasses. Bright colored autumn leaves, pressed and varnished, would look charming mingled with grasses. They can be fastened about the frame with wire

The Verbena.—The verbena is one of our most popular bedding plants, and is also used by many persons as a window plant, though for this purpose it is not generally recommended, as it does not do well in an atmosphere warmer than 50 degrees or 55 degrees, and must have plenty of sunlight, two requisites which but few persons can command. In the conservatory they should be given a top shelf, kept moderately dry and never watered in the morning, or when the sun would be likely to shine upon them before the foliage is dry, as it causes mildew; give fresh air whenever it is practicable to do so, and keep the plants stout and bushy by pinching back stray branches. A soil composed of two parts loam, two parts well-rotted manure and one part sand suits them best. Keep the surface soil loose and porous, to allow air to reach the roots, and provide good drainage. If green fly appears fumigate with tobacco. To perpetuate the verbena use small cuttings taken from fresh growth instead of layers or old roots. The best way is to start the plants from seeds in the spring. By this means the plants do not bloom quite so early, but they are more hardy and vigorous, and flower more profusely than those grown from cuttings. Seedling plants are always the most satisfactory for bedding, and the only fault that can be found with them is, that the colors do not always come true from seeds.

Preserving Autumn Leaves.—Autumn leaves are used in various methods, the most popular being, perhaps, to dry them flatly and carefully, and take great care to preserve their stalks. When thoroughly dry they are varnished, which gives them a pretty gloss and also acts as a preservative to them from all insects and moths. After this they are carefully laid aside for the decoration of the winter dinner table, and may be most safely preserved in a tin box with a well fitting cover. Grasses added to them are very effective, and when dry they may be dyed. They may be also frosted when dry, by dipping each stalk into a solution of alum and leaving them to dry upright. With the grasses and leaves may be used the dried everlasting flowers and the prepared moss, but I must warn my readers that no little taste is needed in their arrangement to avoid the least heaviness of effect. I have found that glass vases and stands are the most effective for their arrangement, as the transparency of these increases the wished-for likeness and grace. Another way of using the dried leaves is for the ornamentation of tables, blotting books, or boxes. Old cigar boxes, when painted black, are very favorite articles for decoration, but now we know the value of varnished unpainted wood, I fancy that many people will prefer the effect of the cigar boxes unpainted, with the unvarnished leaves gummed on, and the box and leaves varnished afterward. If, however, a black ground be especially desired, use " Brunswick black " to stain the wood, or " Brunswick black " and turpentine mixed to make a rich looking brown grounding. Then gum on the leaves in a central group, being careful to cut away all the under parts of the leaves, which will be hidden by others above, as too many thicknesses of leaf will make an uneven surface, and give an ugly appearance to the work when finished.

The Tuberose.—Because many farmers' wives cherish the belief that some wonderful skill attends the cultivation of this plant, they deny themselves the pleasure of its possession. The bulbs must be lifted before there is any danger from frost, and spread in a warm, sunny place to thoroughly dry. If they become chilled in any way, either before being lifted or during the winter, their value is destroyed. But if kept in a warm closet, they will repay for all the trouble by their spikes of beautifully pure and fragrant blossoms.

Tuberoses are reproduced very rapidly. Therefore, after a start has once been made with a collection of bulbs of one, two and three years' growth, the owner can continue to set the same, and there will be no trouble in having all that are desired.

There is no difficulty about the planting and cultivation. They will do well on any soil that will produce a good crop of corn. The soil should be made mellow, so as to be easily worked, and the bulbs set at such distance apart as the extent of surface will allow, and covered with the soil. All the cultivation that is necessary is to keep the soil mellow and free from weeds.

If desired for early blooming the bulbs may be set in boxes the latter part of the winter, and kept watered, and in a warm room. They will then come to flowering earlier than if not set in the ground until all danger from frost is past.

Let every farmer's wife and daughter cultivate a few of these plants that so beautify and adorn the home.

A Miniature Green House.—This is a convenient and ornamental apparatus for growing flowering house plants, or for starting cuttings or seeds early in the season that are afterwards to be transplanted to open ground. B B is a large earthen vessel or pot, in the center of which, at the bottom, the small pot, A, is inverted. The space G G around this is filled with drainage material. On the top of this pot a smaller one, C, of porous earthen, and having straight sides, is set, and the space around this, D D and E E, is filled

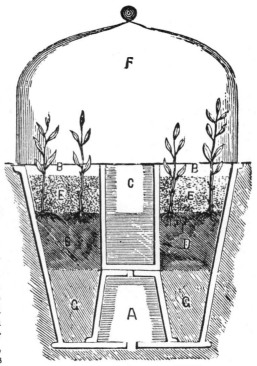

A MINIATURE GREEN HOUSE.

with mold and sand in which two circles of plants may be set. The pot, C, is filled with water, which percolates through the porous sides and keeps the mold moist enough for purposes of vegetation. Over all the bell glass, F, is placed. If the bell glass and large pot cannot be obtained conveniently, the same principles can be nearly carried out by constructing a square box of wood and framing panes of glass for the cover.

Novel Method of Enriching Plants.—A French writer recommends a novel mode of enriching and promoting the growth, especially of geraniums. Namely: Watering the plants with a solution of 150 grains of glue in about two gallons of water.

A Beautiful Basket Plant.—The finest hanging baskets we have ever seen, have been of single plants of the ivy-leaved geranium. The richness and elegance of the foliage, and the drooping or trailing habit of this plant are qualifications it possesses, rendering it eminently serviceable for baskets and vases. One plant is enough for a basket, but except in rare cases, it will require more time than is afforded the first season to show in its best condition. The plant is easily kept over winter, and the second season, if attention is given by the use of manure-water to sustain it, the growth will be exuberant. There are now so many varieties of this plant, that one has the opportunity to indulge his taste in selection. There are golden yellow-leaved ones, bronze, green with white margin, and one, L'Elegante, that has its green leaves margined with white that is tinged and streaked with pink. The colors of the flowers are different with each variety; there are scarlet, and crimson, and rose, and pink and white; again, there are single and double flowers. One of the best varieties for a hanging basket, on account of its fine foliage and free growth, is the double-flowered sort, Kœnig Albert, having mauve or purplish lilac-colored flowers. The double flowers last much longer than the single ones, and this adds much to the value of the plant. For large baskets, where the best effect is desired in a short time, several of these plants of different kinds could be used for the margin, with other plants in the center

Growing House Plants in Moss.—In one of the Swiss villages nearly all the inhabitants are engaged in watch making. They work in large rooms, which, being abundantly lighted and well warmed, allow the workmen to cultivate plants that, on account of the uncertainty and rigor of the climate, cannot be grown in the open air. The president of one of the local horticultural societies in Switzerland gives an account of the great success with which plants are cultivated in moss in these watch factories. One great advantage in the use of moss is the readiness with which plants may be grouped in large vases and boxes. In France a "fertilized moss" is sold, but ordinary moss, with occasional application of liquid fertilizers, will answer as well. Ordinary sphagnum, or peat moss, such as is used by florists in packing, may be employed, but the writer prefers the moss which grows in sheets upon rocks, and around the trunks of trees at their base. Wire baskets lined with this moss are used, as are jardinieres of metal, glazed pottery, etc., taking care to provide sufficient drainage. The liquid fertilizer used on these house plants should be without unpleasant odor; weak guano water, solutions of nitrate of soda, or sulphate of ammonia may be employed, and very fine flour of bone may be mixed with the moss.

Dutch Honeysuckle in the House.—An English writer gives the following, which suggests a way in which hardy wood-climbers might be made available for window decoration in winter or early spring:

"Some years ago, as I was passing through a room used only occasionally, I perceived an odor of fresh flowers that surprised me, as none were ever kept there. On raising the curtain of the east window, I saw that a branch of Dutch honeysuckle had found its way between the two sashes at one corner, while growing in the summer, and had extended itself quite across the window; and on the branch inside there were three or four clusters of well-developed flowers, with the usual accompaniment of leaves, while on the main bush outside there was not a leaf to be seen. The flowers inside were just as beautiful and fragrant as if they had waited until the natural time of blooming. Since then I have tried the experiment purposely, and always with the same good result." A heavy covering of the ground over the roots of the plants with leaves, and sufficient protection of the stem outside, would allow this method to be practiced in quite severe climates.

Some New Plants Offered by German Florists.
—Among the new plants offered by German florists, we take occasion to note the following:

Megarrhiza Californica, Fig. 1, is a new and very rapid growing member of the Cucurbitaceæ family, of the same elegant habit and handsome appearance as Pilogyne suaris, but of much larger dimensions, the stems often attaining a length of twenty to thirty feet in one season.

MEGARRHIZA CALIFORNICA.—FIG. 1.

The beautiful, glossy, silvery leaves, about three to six inches in diameter, bear short scattered hairs, the small white sterile flowers appearing in slender racemes, while the fertile ones grow singly, and are somewhat larger; the oblong shaped fruits, about two inches long, are densely covered with stout, pungent spines, similar to those of the Cucurbitaceæ introduced up to the present time, being of about the same size and form as a broad bean, and germinating as easily and surely as pumpkin seeds. The plant becomes fully developed when grown as an annual, but it can also be cultivated as a perennial, as it produces long and large tuberous roots.

BROMUS PATULUS NANUS.—FIG. 2.

Bromus Patulus Nanus, Fig. 2, is quite a new form of this very valuable ornamental grass, differing from the original species, not only in its lower growth, but far more in its much more graceful, thinner and shorter panicles. By comparing a panicle of Bromus patulus with the one shown in natural size in the figure, the superiority of the above-named sort may easily be noticed. This variety has already been cultivated for several years, and has proved perfectly true from seed. It represents a valuable addition to the assortment of ornamental grasses grown on an extensive scale for bleaching purposes or dry grass bouquets.

RHYNCHOCARPA GLOMERATA.—FIG. 3.

Rhynchocarpa Glomerata, Fig. 3, is a charming and interesting climbing member of the same family, from Brazil, growing twelve to fifteen feet in height. Its branching habit and thickly-set, abundant foliage make it especially well adapted for covering arbors and fences, or for garnishing festoons. The whitish flowers, as is mostly the case in this tribe of plants, are not very conspicuous, but the deeply-cut, five-lobed leaves, together with the numerous hazle-nut-like fruits appearing in dense clusters, render this plant one of the most attractive climbers for outdoor culture. To judge by the tuberous-like root it may be treated as a perennial, but it succeeds well in any warm border as an annual.

Begonia Davisii, Fig. 4, is a beautiful free-flowering new tuberous-rooted species of dwarf habit. The flowers are of the brightest scarlet imaginable, standing well out of the foliage, as the illustration shows plainly. Undoubtedly it is one of the finest introductions among the tuberous-rooted class.

A Sponge Garden.—A hanging garden of sponge is one of the latest novelties in gardening. Take a white sponge of large size, and sow it full of rice, oats and wheat. Then place it for a week or ten days in a shallow dish, in which a little water is constantly kept, and as the sponge will absorb the moisture, the seeds will begin to

BEGONIA DAVISII.—FIG. 4.

sprout before many days. When this has fairly taken place, the sponge may be suspended by means of cords from a hook in the top of the window, where a little sun will enter. It will thus become a mass of green, and can be kept wet by merely immersing it in a bowl of water,

An Ivy Screen.—The old Celtic word for cord is *Hedra*, hence the generic name of the true ivies, in allusion to their cord-like stems. The most common species is the *Hedra helix,* native of various parts of Britain, and from which many varieties have been produced. Old ruins of castles and churches, as well as the sacred temples of a later day, are often half concealed with the deep green leaves of ivy. In our climate these plants do not succeed as well in the open air as in some portions of Europe; still, when planted in a half shady position on the north side of the wall, the hardy species will thrive most luxuriantly, as may be seen by examining some of the old specimens in our Eastern cities.

The ivies are especially valuable for covering rock work, either natural or artificial, particularly when it is located in a cool, shady place, where few other plants will thrive. Within the past few years our florists have paid far more attention to the cultivation of ivy than formerly, and great numbers of plants are sold every year for hanging baskets and similar ornaments. Among the many fine climbers grown as house plants, there are few that succeed as well as the hardy ivies, for they require very little care, not being very sensitive to cold, and thrive better in shade than when exposed to the direct rays of the sun.

AN IVY SCREEN.

The ivies are also very readily propagated by cuttings made from almost any portion of the stem, whether old or young, and they will strike root in almost any kind of soil, clay, loam, peat, or sand, although a mixture of the last two is preferable to the former. It must not, however, be supposed that because ivy will grow in a poor soil, that it does not prefer one that is rich; and if a strong growth is desired, generous treatment must be given.

Many beautiful ornaments may be made with these plants, and one of the most unique as well as useful, is the ivy as shown in the illustration. Such a screen cannot be made in a few days, but requires time, care and patience. Provide a strong box of the length required for the screen, and fill it with silver-sand, peat, or leaf mold, adding a small quantity of soil scraped up in the barnyard. Some old pieces of bricks broken up finely may be placed in the bottom before the soil is put in; then fill up to within an inch of the top. Plant either well-rooted slips or cuttings, and then give water whenever required, but do not keep the soil constantly soaked. When the plants begin to grow, carefully tie them to slender stakes until they are three feet high, and then put up the frame for the screen, which should be of wire, painted green, and of any design to suit the fancy or purse of the owner. As the plants grow, the small shoots may be drawn through the meshes of wire and interlaced, until both sides of the screen become a solid wall of "Ivy green."

We know that our lady readers will readily appreciate this hint, and know just where to place such a screen to produce the most desirable effect in a room, as well as how to keep the leaves free from dust, so that they will show to the best advantage. If a solid wall of green is considered too dark and gloomy, some of the variegated sorts may be intermingled with the plain leaved, but unless carefully tended and watched they will often appear sickly and wither away.

A Living Vase.—This process of ornamenting vases is by no means new; but, as the thing is still far from being common, and as it may give some one a new idea by which to help beautify the home, we have deemed it worth while to give a representation of it so as to show the result, and to indicate the means employed to obtain it, which are most simple. Though any kind

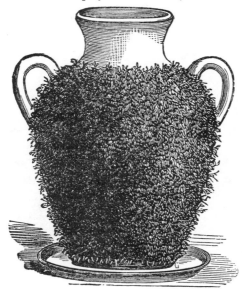

A LIVING VASE.

of vases can be used indiscriminately, those in unglazed terracotta are preferable, being porous. In such vessels the water with which the vase is filled percolates constantly through the sides and moistens the plants which are fixed on its surface. This kind of vase is, however, not indispensable, for we can ornament all kinds, whether in glass or metal. In the latter case it is necessary to prepare the surface so as to convert it into a sort of soil, which it really represents—an operation which is easily managed by the aid of a piece of cloth or flannel which is fixed by means of a little packthread or thin iron or brass wire. This being understood, the means employed to grow the seed must next be described.

If a porous vase be used it is filled with water or, better still, left in a pail of water to soak. After a lapse of 24 hours, when the water has thoroughly saturated the vase, it is laid on its side, and the seed sprinkled slightly over the surface, taking care to turn the vase in different directions, in order that the whole surface may be well covered with seed. This operation terminated, the vase is placed in a dark closet for some time, and, if possible, under a glass frame, so as to preserve humidity and facilitate germination. When the plants are developed, and in case they get detached from the vase, they are secured by passing round, in different directions, a little packthread or fine wire, which soon disappears under the vegetation.

If a non-porous vase, after having well soaked the cloth which covers it, the seed is sown upon it and the same care is given it as has already been indicated. When a porous vase is used it should be kept constantly full, as it is the water filtering slowly through it that feeds the plants which cover the sides. If that be insufficient to insure vigorous growth, the vase must be watered, taking care to pour the water cautiously, so as not to detach the plants. If glazed or metal vases be used, glass bottles, for instance, they must be constantly watered; the water should be poured from the top over all, so that, in descending, it wets all parts of the cloth, which should always be damp. Whenever the plants droop they must be refreshed by watering them carefully. The vase should stand in a saucer or plate.

The seeds used should be very fine, and especially light and of easy and quick germination. The common garden cress is most suitable from its great rapidity of growth, the easy and very quick germination of its seeds, and also on account of the little nourishment the plant requires; but it has several drawbacks; first, it has a tendency to sink more or less, then to have gaps, to show flowers very quickly and then to wither away. The common ryegrass is also suitable, but experiments with other seeds may be made. We ought to multiply and vary the experiments until satisfactory results are obtained. The following kinds of plants might prove suitable: Crested Dog's-tail Grass, White Clover, Yellow Clover (*Meduago lupulina*), Flax, but particularly the Timothy Grass (*Phleum pratense*), which appears to be singularly appropriate for this mode of ornamentation. Let our readers experiment.

How to Grow Smilax.—Smilax is an exceedingly graceful vine, with glossy, green-ribbed leaves, and is now more extensively used than any other plant for decorating parlors, the hair, and for trimming dresses. With a little care it can be grown successfully as a house plant. The vine does not require the full sun, but will grow well in a partially shaded situation. It can be trained on a small thread across the window or around the pictures. Grown from both seeds and bulbs. Pot the bulbs as soon as received, watering but little until you see signs of growth. They grow very rapidly and should always have strings to twine on. Give plenty of fresh air, but be careful and not let a direct draft of cold air blow upon the vines, as they are very tender when young. Give them a warm place and they will amply repay all care. When growth is complete the foliage will turn yellow. Then gradually withhold water and allow the bulbs to dry. They then can be put in some cool, dry place. After they have been in this dormant state six or eight weeks they will begin to show signs of life, and then are ready for another season's growth.

Ferns in the House.—I should like to say to the person who wishes to know what ferns can be grown in the house, that I have had for three winters, in a furnace heated parlor, very handsome plants of Aspidium molle and Adiantum cuneatum; and I have a friend who has Pteris tremula, looking as well as it could in a greenhouse. I also know that Pteris hastata does well in the house; so does the Japanese climbing fern and Lygodium scandons. All require to be kept comfortably warm, not too wet, and seldom sprinkled—just often enough to keep them clean. I have found that wetting the foliage often causes it to turn black.

To Keep Geraniums through the Winter.—Those who have no place in their greenhouses for geraniums, etc., will do well to put them in a window with a south aspect, carefully covering the pots with a little straw or moss, in order to prevent the frost from hurting the roots. Or take them from the pots and hang them up by the roots in a dark place, where the frost cannot touch them; if planted again in the spring they will shoot and flourish remarkably well.

Wardian Cases.—An illustration of a Wardian case is herewith given. A bed or box of well-drained soil, with a (cheap or costly) glass case over it, comprise a Wardian case. The sides should be of glass, else the plants will "spinder up." Take a common table frame, with the top of the table off; nail on boards on the bottom of the frame, line the whole with zinc, fill with earth (or set the plants in the case in pots), and over it put a case made of glass—common window glass will answer. Any glazier can make one at little cost. It may be made of any shape and height desirable. There should be a door or sliding pane in it, so as to gain ready access to the plants. In the center of the bed should be a hole for drainage, over which a plant saucer should be inverted. Fill the bottom or the bed for an inch or two with broken charcoal.

The case may be filled with plants in spring or autumn. If in spring, the ferns may be gathered from the woods, and will grow all summer. It is a

better time to make selections than late in the fall. Plants in a Wardian case are not so likely to freeze with the same degree of cold in a room as unprotected house plants; but the room should be kept warm, nevertheless. The plants in a Wardian case require less care than plants in a room. Drench the soil well when the planting is done, and they will require watering but once or twice a month. They will need ventilation by removing the sliding pane or opening the door of the case occasionally, when the moisture on the glass seems in excess, so as to obscure the glass.

Not only ferns and mosses, but wintergreens, princess pine, partridge

A WARDIAN CASE.

berry, the trailing arbutus, and scores of other pretty wood-plants, can be grown and arranged with rock and shell work, to suit the fancy and please the eye. We are astonished that these cases are not more common in the homes of the people.

Fresh-Blown Flowers in Winter.—Choose some of the most perfect buds of the flowers you wish to preserve, such as are latest in blooming and are ready to open; cut them off with a pair of scissors, leaving to each, if possible, a piece of stem about three inches long; cover the end of the stem immediately with sealing wax, and when the buds are a little shrunk and wrinkled wrap each of them up separately in a piece of paper, perfectly clean and dry; then lock them up in a dry box or drawer, and they will keep without corrupting. In winter, or at any time, when you would have the flowers blow, take the buds at night and cut off the end of the stem sealed with wax, and put the buds into water wherein a little nitre of salt has been diffused; the next day you will have the pleasure of seeing the buds open and expand themselves, and the flowers display their most lovely colors and breathe their agreeable odors.

Parlor Ornament.—We saw, in the parlor of a friend, a very beautiful conceit. It is, of course, the fancy of a lady, and consists of the burr of a pine tree placed in a wine glass half full or water, and from between the different layers of the burr are shooting forth green blades—bright, beautiful, refreshing. For a little thing, we have seen nothing that so pleased us by its beauty and novelty. And the secret is this: The burr was found dried and open; the different circles were sprinkled with grass-seed, and it was placed in a wine glass with water in as above. In a few days the moisture and nourishment gave the burr life and health, the different circles closed and buried within themselves the grass-seed, and a few days more gave to the seed also life, sprout and growth, and now a pyramid of living green, beautifully relieved by the somber hue of the burr, is the result—as pretty and novel a parlor ornament as we have for a long while seen. We do not know whether the idea was original with the lady, but we do know that its success is beautiful.

Arranging Bouquets.—The art of arranging bouquets is very simple. Having collected the flowers to be used on a tray, all the superfluous leaves should be stripped from the stems, and by placing the flowers side by side, you can easily see the order in which they can be most advantageously displayed. A very pretty hand bouquet can be made by taking a small, straight stick, not over a quarter of an inch in diameter, tie a string to the top of it, and begin by fastening on a few delicate flowers, or one large, handsome one, for the center-piece, winding the string about each stem as you add the flowers and leaves to the bouquet. Always place the flowers with the shortest stems at the top, preserving all those with long stems for the base, and finish off the bouquet with a fringe of finely cut foliage. Then cut all the stems evenly, wrap damp cotton around them, and cover the stems with a paper cut in pretty lace designs. In making bouquets from garden flowers, such as are most easy to procure, the flowers can be arranged flatly, and a background made from sprays of evergreen.

A Cheap Plant Stand.—We made a very effective plant stand for our front yard last summer in the following manner: A cedar stake, two or three inches in diameter, was driven into the ground so as to stand firmly, and of the required height, a small piece of board nailed across the top, and another piece, a little larger, nailed over this, so as to make a substantial base, and a cheese box nailed to this. Then we filled the box half full by putting in a couple of inches of sand and sphagnum over it. The whole was then covered with pendent lichen, and the box filled with plants in pots, tall ones in the center and smaller one around them, with trailing plants to hang over the sides. It was shaded by trees during the hotter portions of the day, and such plants as gleechoma, alyssum, ivy, etc., succeeded finely by merely pressing a handful of sphagnum around the base of cuttings and pressing them into the spaces between the pots.

A Fern Paradise at Home.—It is not only the poor who have to live in gardenless dwellings and look out from sunless windows. The mansions of the rich, and thousands of houses of the well-to-do and of the middle classes are necessarily in great cities placed where the sun cannot exert his charming life-giving influence. Many a window of a grand house looks out upon nothing but brick walls, which tower up high, and blot out the sun's rays. The occupants of these houses are often bound by the exigencies of business to make their homes for weary months in these shadowy dwelling places. Why then do they not bring the beautiful ferns into requisition?

What exquisite grace would be shed over every room in a house if every available space were occupied by the feathery fronds of those beautiful plants! On tables and side boards, on mantel pieces and on window sills; hanging from window rods, on the landing of the stairs, in the hall, in the bedroom—everywhere in fact.

We give an illustration of a cane stand lined with zinc and filled with ferns and begonias, which might be bought for a dollar or two, and which would not be out of place in the most elegant apartment.

House Plants.—Contrive some cover over them at sweeping time. This may be, for plants on shelves, a curtain of some light material; if on a table, an upright post or stick set in a hole in the middle of the table, to hold up the center of a spread of some kind; or contrive some method of using old newspapers. Let this covering remain until the dust has completely settled. All smooth-leaved plants, especially ivy, camelias, cape jessamine, and the like, should have their leaves washed with a soft sponge—a rag will answer—on both sides, with tepid water, at least once a week. It will be found much less trouble

STAND FOR FERNS.

than one would suppose, and the increased beauty of the foliage will lead to its repetition. Rough-leaved plants, such as geraniums, and many others, cannot be washed to advantage. Set these in a bath tub, or in a sink, and give their leaves a good drenching by using a garden syringe or a watering-pot with fine holes, holding it up high so that the water will fall with force upon the leaves. Be sure that the water is not too cold, as it would tend to check the growth.

To Preserve Scarlet Geraniums through the Winter.—Take them out of the borders in autumn, before they have received any injury from frost, and let this be done on a dry day. Shake off all the earth from their roots, and suspend them, with their heads downward, in a cellar or dark room, where they will be free from frost. The leaves and shoots will become yellow and sickly; but when potted about the end of May, and exposed to a gentle heat, they will recover and vegetate luxuriantly. The old plants, stripped of their leaves, may also be packed closely in sand; and in this way if kept free from frost, they will shoot out from the roots, and may be repotted in the spring.

Manure for Bulbs.—An ounce of nitrate of soda dissolved in four gallons of water is a quick and good stimulant for bulbs, to be applied twice a week after the pots are filled with roots, and the flower spikes are fairly visible. A large handful of soot, or about a pint, tied up in a piece of old canvas, and immersed in the same quantity of water for a day or two, will furnish a safe and excellent stimulant; also good and safe is a quarter of a pound of cow manure mixed in a large garden pot of water, and used as required. Any of these stimulants will do good, or the whole of them applied alternately will benefit bulbs that need more sustenance than the soil affords.

TRELLIS FOR PLANTS.

Trellis for Plants.— With a little slightly-galvanized wire any one can make the little iron trellis shown in our illustration on this page, in a very neat manner—and it will look much neater and prove handier and more graceful than the painted stick trellises which are so common.

How to Grow the Pansy.—The pansy delights in a cool, rich loam; the richer, the larger will be the flowers, in a partially shaded situation. It never flourishes as well during the hot days of July and August as later in the season. Young plants, from seeds sown early in the spring, if the bed be very rich, will come into handsome bloom during the latter part of June. All the first blossoms should be picked off that the plant may first become robust. Even with the old plants, the great secret of keeping them in constant bloom is to pick off the blossoms early and constantly, since it weakens the plant more to ripen one seed-pod than to yield a dozen flowers.

Autumn Sowing of Flower Seeds.—Persons say that the finest flowers they ever had of certain annuals were from "volunteer" plants from self-grown seeds. The real reason for their superiority is not due to the manner, but to the time of sowing. Seeds are "self-grown" soon after they are ripe, and the superiority of the plants from these suggests autumn sowing. The annual flowers classed as "hardy" should as a general thing, if practicable, be sown in autumn. Larkspurs and pansies are incomparably finer when thus sown. Clarkia, whitlavia, gilia, and nearly all the rest of the California annual, to give the best results, should be sown in autumn.

To Repot Plants.—Shake the old earth from the plants after they commence to grow in spring, then pot them into smaller pots than those just occupied; as the plants make fresh growth and fill these pots with roots, repot into those of a size larger, and so on until the plants are in their flowering pots. By adopting this plan the plants are supplied with fresh soil from time to time, and not kept growing on from year to year in the same soil, which soon becomes exhausted. The above remarks apply more particularly to such plants as fuchsias, pelargoniums, etc.

Treatment of English Ivy.—The use of the English ivy cannot be too strongly recommended as a decoration in our rooms during the winter season. A lady noted for the beauty and freshness of her ivies was asked the secret of her success, which was simply putting a small piece of beefsteak at the roots of the plants every spring and fall. It is also said that to lightly rub each leaf on both sides with sweet oil will preserve a fresh, vigorous appearance of ivies, in spite of furnace heat and gas, usually so injurious to all house plants. These simple measures are well worth trying.

How to Make Moss Baskets.—Very beautiful baskets for holding flowers can be made of the longer and more feathery kind of mosses. A light frame, of any shape you like, should be made with wire and covered with common pasteboard or calico, and the moss, which should first be well picked over and cleansed from any bits of dirt or dead leaves which may be hanging about it, gathered into little tufts, and sewed with a coarse needle and thread to the covering so as to clothe it thickly with a close and compact coating, taking care that the points of the moss are all outward. A long handle, made in the same manner, should be attached to the basket, and a tin or other vessel, filled with either wet sand or water, placed within to hold the flowers. By dipping the whole structure into water once in three or four days, its verdure and elasticity will be fully preserved, and a block of wood about an inch thick, and stained black or green, if placed under the basket, will prevent all risk of damage to the table from moisture.

Carnations from Cuttings.—Carnations are easily rooted from slips. Take off the small side shoots when about two inches long. If your plants are in pots, plant them around the edge, pressing the soil very firmly about the portion inserted. Do not water them only when the parent plant requires it. If they are cultivated in the ground, plant them in the same bed, taking the same precaution to make the earth compact about the slips, so they will not dry up instead of rooting. If the ground is slightly moist, it is enough for them, but if very dry sprinkle occasionally.

Gypsy Fern Case.—This fern case consists of three bars crossed at the top and fastened into a triangular base. A basket is suspended from the center of the case, and the base is decorated with shells, acorns or corals. The best method of making this case is to have the base first made of wood, then lined with zinc. The sides should hold glass neatly filled into the bars, thus inclosing the plants from the outer air. The height should be about three feet, and width of base two feet on each side. Any florist can supply ferns for such a structure. Choose only the smaller growing sorts, and avoid those which branch widely. No household elegancy is more desirable than a tasteful fernery, well taken care of.

Fuchsias Among Roses.—A London florist had some of his standard roses killed by the late spring frosts, but having some large fuchsia plants, they were used to fill up the "ugly gaps," and the result was a pleasant surprise. They stood the rough weather well, and vied with the roses as to quantity of bloom. He says: "If all is well we shall use fuchsias more extensively next season."

Treatment of Callas.—For blooming callas, writes a lady, I use the soil from the hennery, and on cold mornings I pour hot water in the saucers; I have had a bloom from every bulb. As my fuchsias never grew very large, I put in fresh soil and then used some fine manure from the hennery, and before spring it covered the window, with every shoot in full bloom.

Frozen Plants.—Whenever house-plants are accidentally frozen, they should be placed in a dark place and then sprinkled with cold water. Geraniums, fuchsias, and similar kinds of plants, may often be saved if care is given in thawing them out, even if frozen quite hard. The same rule applies to dormant plants, such as grape vines and trees that become frozen while being carried from one section of the country to another. If packages of plants are received in this condition they should be placed in a cellar and then sprinkled with cold water, and allowed to remain undisturbed until thawed. Burying in the earth will answer equally as well, although seldom convenient in cold weather. Hardy plants, when well packed in damp moss, seldom receive any injury from frost.

Potting and Watering Plants.—Plants cultivated in the house often suffer from being put into pots very much too large for them. The mass of soil, which is quite out of proportion to their needs, by frequent watering, soon gets into such a sour and sodden condition, that the roots rot away completely and the plant dies. Even when the amount of soil is not greater than the plant needs, it is quite an easy matter to give too much water to succulents, such as the cactus family, the agaves, crassulas, and others of like habit. In fact, these plants, when at rest, as most of them are during winter, need scarcely a drop of water.

Covering for Tender Plants.—A horticultural writer says: I always disliked the looks of clumsy straw and matting coverings for plants. It made the garden look so mean that I thought I would try another plan. I had read that evergreen boughs were the best thing with which to cover pansies and any tender plants, so I thought I would try it on tender roses and such things, and I never had such success. I believe there is something beneficial in the balsamine odor of the leaves, the plants look so nice—almost like summer.

A Novel House Plant.—The common cranberry is a most attractive plant when properly cultivated in pots, and can endure a great deal of neglect which would be fatal to other plants. It only needs to be kept cool and moist. A compost of muck and sand is the proper material for potting it in. Although usually regarded as aquatic in its nature, it will not do to have the soil saturated with water. What it requires, is that water shall be within reach of its roots, and that the soil shall be one through which water can rise readily by capillary attraction.

Crystallizing Grasses.—A lady asks for directions for crystallizing grasses. The following is a good recipe: Dissolve in a quart of hot water all the alum you can by heating and stirring—it may be a pound, it may be twenty ounces. Have the grasses divided into small bunches, tied. When the solution begins to cool, dip in the grasses, holding them there five minutes, three minutes, two or one minute, according to the size of crystals you wish. The cooler the solution the quicker the crystals form. A glass jar is convenient for heating the alum, as one can see through the glass when the crystals are forming, and know when to take them out. Do not let the grass touch the side of the jar. Place an old plate under the bottom to prevent the glass breaking.

A Home-Made Flower Stand.—A very pretty flower stand can be made out of a table, a bucket, and a half a dozen old tin cans. Place the bucket in the center of the table. Punch several holes in the bottom of each can, and screw them firmly to the table by screws in the holes.

Arches of stout wire may be made across the top of the cans. For ferns planted in the cans, which require a great deal of water, cover the top of the table with a shallow pan to catch the drip. Other plants should only have the soil kept damp. Geraniums are fine for winter blooming, as are also coleus, fuchsias, and petunias. Some kind of a vine should be planted in each of the corner cans. Trailing plants produce a good effect.

The Acorn.—If an acorn be suspended by a piece of thread within half an inch of the surface of some water contained in a hyacinth glass, and so permitted to remain without being disturbed, it will, in a few months, burst, and throw a root into the water, and shoot upward its straight and tapering stem, with beautiful little green leaves. A young oak tree growing in this way on the mantel-shelf of a room is a very elegant and interesting object. I have seen several oak trees, and also a chestnut tree, thus growing, but all of them, however, have died after a few months, probably owing to the water not being changed sufficiently often to afford them the necessary quantity of nourishment from the matter contained in it.

Moving Plants.—In the fall those plants that are to be taken to the house to serve as window plants for the winter, should be looked after before the season arrives for their removal. If, with a sharp spade, each plant is cut around, so as to leave a ball of earth the right size for the pot, and then allowed to remain two or three weeks, young fibrous roots will form; when the plant, with the ball of earth attached is lifted, it will scarcely experience any check.

To Keep a Bouquet Fresh.—To keep a bouquet fresh for a number of days, sprinkle lightly with fresh water, then put it into a vessel containing soapsuds, which nutrify the roots and keep the flowers as bright as new. Take the bouquet out of the suds every morning and lay it sideways, the stalk entering first into the water. Keep it there a moment, then take it out and sprinkle the flowers lightly by the hand with water. Replace it in the soapsuds, and it will bloom as fresh as when first gathered. The soapsuds need changing every other day.

Watering Plants.—The following directions for watering house plants during the winter will assist those having care of them in keeping them in a healthy condition: Take carbonate of ammonia four parts; nitrate of potash (saltpetre) two parts; pulverize and mix well. Put one drachm (one-eighth of an ounce) of this powder into a gallon of rain water. Use this for watering plants. Give them a good sunlight and not too much heat, and plants will keep green and fresh.

Flowers kept in a warm room should be watered with tepid water. Very cold water is apt to freeze the roots.

Starting Plants.—Boxes in windows is an excellent way of starting plants for early setting, though it must necessarily be on a small scale. For a small garden a good supply may thus be procured: In sowing the seeds, avoid putting them in too deep; a half inch is ample for all, and a less depth is better for the small seeds. Press the soil closely around the seed.

Steam Baths for Geraniums.—Geraniums and similar plants are greatly benefitted during winter if given a steam bath once a week. To do this place them above the bath after filling it with hot water. Close the doors and windows and let the flowers remain there for an hour or two. Another good method is to place the flowers in the kitchen on wash day, where the steam arising from the clothes will benefit them.

Plant Fertilizers.—Two or three ounces of guano to a gallon of water is a proper proportion for house plants. Keep the mixture well stirred, as the guano, not being actually dissolved by the water, settles to the bottom. Save the soot that falls from the chimneys when they are cleaned. A pint of soot to a pailful of water will make a liquid manure of the greatest value for flower beds and plants of all kinds.

Cut Back the Geraniums.—But few persons cut them back enough. If the stalks are cut back to within two or three inches of the surface of the ground, numerous healthy side shoots will put out and grow vigorously.

The Amaryllis.—If any one has an amaryillis she will find it will blossom more freely if the dirt is kept away from the top of the bulb. An amaryllis should have plenty of water.

First, be careful! Many of the cures cited in this chapter sound as dangerous as the diseases. I'm no healer but I'll counsel that simpler and milder is better. Don't do anything rash. Understand the principles behind what you do for yourself or allow to be done to you for health. Better to do nothing and to concentrate on passing through a problem than to take a 'cure' that will add to your problems. This pertains to medications which hide the symptoms but leave the cause of the problem untouched.

This chapter presents a long list of diseases, deficiencies, and problems. Illness may have held a larger place in Victorian life; death and mourning certainly did. In 1888 people tended to treat themselves and their families more. Now, with our centralized hospitals full of miraculous equipment and highly specialized personnel, we find it hard to understand a situation in which people lived days away from doctors and hospital care was almost unheard of. People treated themselves in their homes with the help of patent medicines, homeopaths, pharmacists and the family doctor. Only when the American Medical Association was formed (to fight what doctors saw as quackery but others see as viable alternative forms of health care) did medicine and health standards take on some uniformity in the U.S. Now, herbal healers, midwives and homeopaths are practically illegal in many states.

If you are interested in your body and in maintaining a good general level of health, there are many books and disciplines to choose from. Many of the books report one individual's success with a particular regimen. What has worked for one person, however, may not work the same way for another person, another metabolism. Be wary of systems which explain everyone's problems in terms of a single element. One of the best books about the body is *Our Bodies, Our Selves* by the Boston Womens Health Collective (NY: Simon & Schuster, 1976).

The role of diet in healthiness has drawn much attention over the years. You may want to look into the virtues of vegetarianism; Adele Davis' whole, naturally complementary foods; George Oshawa's macrobiotics; Robert Rodale's organic foods; fasting; raw foods; and various other dietary patterns. The right diet is a highly individual choice, but it may be a choice you want to make, rather than letting the average supermarket decide for you.

For centuries people have observed the curing properties of herbs. Sometimes their medical efficacy can be proved, sometimes not. Jethro Kloss' *Back To Eden* (Santa Barbara, Ca.: Woodbridge Press, 1975) sums up much of the available herbal knowledge. Mildred Fielder's *Plant Medicine and Folklore* (NY: Winchester Press, 1975) is helpful, readable and illustrated with good drawings and photographs.

After years of research in the indigenous medicine of Vermont, Dr. D.C. Jarvis wrote *Folk Medicine* (NY: Henry Holt & Co., 1958). The book details what he learned from talking to and observing his patients, the ways they treated themselves. He takes their practices seriously. The book deals with what can be learned from the way animals cure themselves, what children know about sickness, folk medicines such as kelp, castor oil, corn oil, honey, lemon and vinegar. *Folk Medicine* is an unpretensious approach to an overlooked field.

For people interested in self-diagnosis, or in understanding what the doctor's talking about, or in greater knowledge of the workings of the body, I recommend the purchase of a good medical encyclopedia such as *Symptoms, The Complete Medical Home Encyclopedia* (NY: Thomas Y. Crowell Pub. Co., 1976). Written by a team of doctors, it clarifies the technical medical language, summarizes what's known about the body and contains good prophylactic advice.

THE HOME PHYSICIAN.

Preventives of Malaria.—Scarcely a section of our beautiful country is free from malarial disease in some of its forms. Many localities formerly free from malaria have recently been visited by this insidious foe of humanity. Two reasons are given for this result: First, the ponds and swamps have been dried up, and the lower forms of organic matter have been exposed to the air, and second, wells and springs have become so low that the water is very impure, and no doubt its use produces an unhealthy state of the human body.

If the use of impure water alone were the cause of malarial difficulties the remedy would be simple, namely, to substitute pure water instead, if it could be had, or by filtration and other means, purify what was at hand.

The malarial influence arising from swamps or marshes can be only counteracted by ærating the soil and thus getting rid of the lower organisms resident there. By means of drainage the sour soil water is carried off, the air enters and decay is completed—the poison is destroyed and a more healthful condition ensues.

But there are vast stretches of country where these means cannot be employed, and other methods must be provided. It is now pretty well proven by actual plantings in California of the blue gum tree, or Eucalyptus of Australia, that by its use over a sufficient area the malarial tendencies can be counteracted. Unfortunately, by actual test, we find that the *Eucalyptus Globosa* will not endure the cold of this section of the Union.

What then can we employ? Professor Maury, before our late internecine war, proved at the Washington Observatory that extensive plantations of the common sunflower will, during its growing season, counteract malaria. These can be grown all over our States, and should be extensively tried.

The common willow, being a coarse feeder and rapid grower, revelling in wet and swampy land, has also been **commended** as one of the very best agents for the destruction of malarial germs. Its roots spread widely through the soil, while its leafage is simply enormous in proportion to its woody development. The three sorts of willow grow with great rapidity, but more immediate effects may be produced by planting sprouts of the osier or basket willow thickly all over the whole of a wet or swampy surface soil.

This would be a remunerative product aside from its destruction of malaria. The plan is worthy of trial.

Pneumonia.—It will be remembered that in old age the lungs are much shriveled, less elastic, and can not be fully inflated; the air cells are dilated to about twice their size, many of the capillaries are obliterated, the breathing is more feeble and shallow, and the power to get rid of carbonic acid is greatly diminished.

Hence pneumonia (inflammation of the lungs) is not only one of the most common diseases of old age, but the most fatal—over three-fourths (some say nine-tenths) of the aged dying with it. The main work of the lungs is done by the air-cells, the tiny laboratories in which the smaller branches of the air-tubes terminate, as the branches of a tree terminate in the leaves. Now it is these that are the seat of pneumonia.

In the first stage of the disease they become—in some part of the lungs —filled with a sticky fluid, exuded frcm the blood vessels; in the second stage this fluid becomes solid; in the third it changes to pus. If the pus is absorbed—which is seldom the case in the old—the person may recover, but only after months of convalesence. If it result in gangrene (mortification), the gangrene may form numerous small abscesses through an entire lung.

In the aged the disease seldom commences with well-defined symptoms. In about one-half the cases there is simply a chill or a pain in the side. In most of the other cases the main symptom is a feeling of exhaustion. If there is already chronic bronchitis or asthma, the person may merely feel a little tired, and suddenly die.

Though most persons cough, there is for a time no expectoration. When it appears it is at first scanty, gray and frothy; then yellow, and at length reddish and sticky. Patients seldom complain of pain or difficulty of breathing.

The more common exciting cause is cold, especially dry, sharp. Nine-tenths of all cases occur between November and May. During this period the aged cannot be too carefully protected from exposure. They should constantly wear flannel.

About all that can be done for the patient is to stimulate him with drinks, nourish him with concentrated fluid food, and secure him absolute rest.

Antidotes for Poisons.—(1) The most dangerous of the vegetable poisons are the hemlocks (including the hemlock dropwort, water hemlock, and the common hemlock), fool's parsley, monkshood, foxglove, black helle-bore, or Christmas rose, buck-bran, henbane, thorn apple, and deadly night-shade. In a case of vegetable poisoning, says *Knowledge*, "emetics (the sulphate of zinc, if procurable) should be used at once, the back of the throat tickled with a feather, and copious draughts of tepid water taken to excite and promote vomiting. Where these measures fail, the stomach-pump must be used. Neither ipecacuanha nor tartar emetic should be used to cause vomiting, as during the nausea they produce before vomiting is excited the poison is more readily absorbed. Vinegar must not be given until the poisonous matter has been removed; but afterward it may be given in doses of a wineglassful, one part vinegar to two parts water, once every two hours in mild cases, but oftener—to half hourly doses—in cases of greater severity. Where there is stupor, the patient should be kept walking about, and if the stupor is great cold water may be dashed over the head and chest. Strong coffee may be used where the narcotic effect of the poisoning is very marked. It is all-important that in cases of vegetable poisoning a medical man should be sent for at once."

(2) If a person swallow any poison whatever, or has fallen into convul-sions from having overloaded the stomach, an instantaneous remedy, more efficient and applicable in a larger number of cases than any half a dozen medicines we can think of, is a heaping teaspoonful of common salt and as much ground mustard, stirred rapidly in a teacup of water, warm or cold, and swallowed instantly. It is scarcely down before it begins to come up, bringing with it the remaining contents of the stomach; and lest there be any remnant of poison, however small, let the white of an egg, or a teacup

of strong coffee be swallowed as soon as the stomach is quiet. These very common articles nullify a larger number of virulent poisons than any medicines in the shops.

(3) Great quantities of Paris green are used during some seasons of the year, and as accidents may happen, it is well to know the antidote for the poison. Paris green owes its deadly properties to arsenic, as does London purple. Should either of these be taken into the stomach, let the person drink copious draughts of milk, or raw eggs beaten up, and as soon as possible give an emetic, mustard is as good as anything, and keep up the action of vomiting by giving milk between the paroxysms of vomiting. When the stomach no longer rejects what is swallowed, give a good dose of castor oil.

(4) It cannot be too generally known that the ordinary calcined magnesia, mixed with water, is considered a certain antidote to numerous poisons, especially those of metallic origin, such as arsenic, corrosive sublimate, sulphate of zinc, etc. In cases of this deplorable kind, two or three teaspoonfuls of magnesia, mixed with water, should be at once administered, which, in all probability, will save the patient until the doctor comes.

(5) Hundreds of lives have been saved by a knowledge of this simple receipt. A large teaspoonful of made mustard mixed in a tumbler of warm water, and swallowed as soon as possible; it acts as an instant emetic, sufficiently powerful to remove all that is lodged in the stomach.

(6) A standing antidote for poison by dew, poison-oak, ivy, etc., is to take a handful of quicklime, dissolve in water, let it stand half an hour, then paint the poisoned parts with it. Three or four applications will never fail to cure the most aggravated cases.

(7) The only safe and immediate remedy within the reach of a non-professional, in case of poisoning with prussic acid, is to pour a stream of cold water, from an elevation, upon the head and spine of the patient.

(8) If a person has taken an over-dose of laudanum, very strong coffee is a specific antidote. Keep the patient on his feet and keep him walking. Sleep is fatal under such circumstances.

Dangers of Childhood.—Childhood is the period during which the foundations of the physical structure are laid. It ends, at the age of about fourteen, with the completion of the permanent teeth. It is characterized by almost absolute dependence on the parents, and therefore the responsibility rests upon them whether the foundations of the superstructure shall be good or bad, and, indeed, whether there shall be any superstructure! The fact that one-half of all who are born die within this period, while multitudes of adults find, when it is too late, fatal defects in the very groundwork of their constitutions, is a fearful witness against the competency of most parents for the care of children. What farmer would employ a hand that let one-half of all his calves, colts and lambs die? In the matter of food, if milk fails the mother, how few mothers know what to give the child! How few know that many of the compounds sold as "Infants' food" contain no food whatever! and that cow's milk, harmful when taken alone, is generally safe with a certain proportion of lime water! How few mothers know that too protracted nursing will result in "rickets?" That overfeeding all through childhood is a prolific source of disease? and that, in case of most bowel complaints, a spare diet for a few days is better than all medicines? In our climate, where the mercury ranges through 140 degrees and often varies between the extremes suddenly and violently, how little do mothers realize the importance of aiding nature, with clothing and food, so that the internal temperature is held steadily at 98 degrees? Do you know that a change of half a dozen degrees of the internal temperature, either way, is almost sure death? The great mortality of children in summer is due mainly to heat. An abundance of woolen clothing alone can guard against the effects of the violent changes in the climate of the autumn and winter and spring. How few are aware that the infectious diseases which so ravage childhood are caused by careless exposure to the contagion, or, if aware, act accordingly?

Nervousness.—This unhealthy state of system depends upon general debility. It is often inherited from birth, and as often brought on by excess of sedentary occupation, overstrained employment of the brain, mental emotion, dissipation and excess. The nerves consist of a structure of fibers or cords passing through the entire body, branching off from, and having a connection with each other, and finally centers on the brain. They are the organs of feeling and sensation of every kind, and through them the mind operates upon the body. It is obvious, therefore, that what is termed the "nervous system" has an important part in the bodily functions; and upon them not only much of the health, but happiness, depends.

Treatment.—The cure of nervous complaints lies rather in moral than in medical treatment. For although much good may be effected by tonics, such as bark, quinine, etc., there is far more benefit to be derived from attention to diet and regimen. In such cases, solid food should preponderate over liquid, and the indulgence in warm and relaxing fluids should be especially avoided; plain and nourishing meat, as beef or mutton, a steak or chop, together with half a pint of bitter ale or stout, forming the best dinner. Cocoa is preferable to tea; vegetables should be but sparingly eaten. Sedentary pursuits should be cast aside as much as possible, but where they are compulsory, every spare moment should be devoted to outdoor employment and brisk exercise. Early bedtime and early rising will prove beneficial, and the use of the cold shower bath is excellent. Gymnastic exercises, fencing, horse-riding, rowing, dancing, and other pursuits which call forth the energies, serve also to brace and invigorate the nervous system. It will also be as well to mingle with society, frequent public assemblies and amusements, and thus dispel that morbid desire for seclusion and quietude which, if indulged in to excess, renders a person unfitted for intercourse with mankind, and materially interferes with advancement in life.

Measles.—Measles are an acute inflammation of the skin, internal and external, combined with an infectious fever.

Symptoms.—Chills, succeeded by great heat, languor, and drowsiness, pains in the head, back and limbs, quick pulse, soreness of throat, thirst, nausea and vomiting, a dry cough, and high colored urine. These symptoms increase in violence for four days. The eyes are inflamed and weak, and the nose pours forth a watery secretion, with frequent sneezing. There is considerable inflammation in the larynx, windpipe, and bronchial tubes, with soreness of the breast and hoarseness. About the fourth day the skin is covered with a breaking out which produces heat and itching, and is red in spots, upon the face first, gradually spreading over the whole body. It goes off in the same way, from the face first and then from the body, and the hoarseness and other symptoms decline with it; at last the outside skin peels off in scales.

Treatment.—In a mild form, nothing is required but a light diet, slightly acid drinks, and flax seed or slippery elm tea. Warm herb teas, and frequent sponge baths with tepid water, serve to allay the fever; care should be taken not to let the patient take cold. If the fever is very high, and prevents the rash coming out, a slight dose of salts; or a nauseating dose of ipecac, lobelia, or hive syrup should be given, and followed by teaspoonful doses of compound tincture of Virginia snake-root until the fever is allayed. If the patient from any derangement takes on a low typhoid type of fever, and the rash does not come out until the seventh day, and is then of a dark and livid color, tonics and stimulants must be given, and the expectoration promoted by some suitable remedy. The room should be kept dark to protect the inflamed eyes. As long as the fever remains the patient should be kept in bed. Exposure may cause pneumonia, which, in other words, is acute inflammation of the lungs. Keep in the room as long as the cough lasts. There is always danger of the lungs being left in an inflamed state after the measles, unless the greatest care is taken not to suffer the patient to take cold.

Should there be much pain, and a severe cough, this must be treated as a separate disease, with other remedies.

Rheumatism.—(1) Dr. Ebrards, of Nimes, states that he has for many years treated all his cases of sciatica and neuralgic pains with an improvised apparatus consisting merely of a flat-iron and vinegar, two things that will be found in every house. The iron is heated until sufficiently hot to vaporize the vinegar, and is then covered with some woolen fabric, which is moistened with vinegar, and the apparatus is applied at once to the painful spot. The application may be repeated two or three times a day. Dr. Ebrard states that, as a rule, the pain disappears in twenty-four hours, and recovery ensues at once.

(2) Take cucumbers, when full grown, and put them into a pot with a little salt; then put the pot over a slow fire, where it should remain for about an hour; then take the cucumbers and press them, the juice from which must be put into bottles, corked up tight, and placed in the cellar, where they should remain for about a week; then wet a flannel rag with the liquid, and apply it to the parts affected.

(3) Half ounce of strongest camphorated spirit, one ounce spirits of turpentine, one raw egg, half pint best vinegar. Well mix the whole, and keep it closely corked. To be rubbed in three or four times a day. For rheumatism in the head, or face-ache, rub all over the back of the head and neck, as well as the part which is the immediate seat of pain.

(4) Dr. Bonnett, of Graulbet, France, recommends and prescribes for chronic rheumatism the use of the essential oil of turpentine by friction. He used it himself with perfect success, having almost instantaneously got rid of rheumatic pains in both knees and in the left shoulder.

(5) A very simple remedy for rheumatism of the extremities, and one that very often gives great relief is, to take a large piece of thick flannel, sprinkle it well with finely pulverized sulphur, and then bind snugly about the limb, with the sulphur next the skin.

(6) For sciatic rheumatism the following is recommended: Two drachms iodide potassium, four ounces cinnamon water. Mix. Take a teaspoonful three times a day before eating. It is also excellent for dyspepsia.

(7) Tincture of gum Guaicum, ten to fifteen drops, three times a day. I have never known it to fail in making a cure, except in cases of long standing, when it will afford great relief.

Toothache.—(1) Bi-carbonate of soda as a remedy for toothache, has been used very successfully. It was first introduced to the public by Dr. Duckworth, of St. Bartholomew's Hospital, London, who resorted to it when chloroform, carbolic acid, and everything else had failed. His recipe is to soak small pieces of cotton in a solution of thirty grains of bi-carbonate of soda to one fluid ounce of water, and insert the cotton in the tooth. Dr. Duckworth is of the opinion that very frequently the pain is due to the contact of acid saliva with the decayed tooth; and therefore, it is important, in cases of toothache, first to determine whether the saliva had an acid reaction. If this be the case, then a simple alkaline application, as above stated, is the most efficacious means of cure.

(2) The worst toothache, or neuralgia coming from the teeth, may be speedily ended by the application of a small bit of clean cotton saturated in a strong solution of ammonia to the defective tooth. Sometimes the application causes nervous laughter, but the pain has disappeared.

(3) If the tooth contains a cavity which can be easily reached, fill it with sugar of lead. Allow it to remain a few minutes, then wash it out with warm water, being careful to remove all of it. This is the most prompt relief for toothache—save the forceps with which we are familiar.

(4) Put a piece of quicklime, as big as a walnut, in a pint of water in a bottle. Clean the teeth with a little of it every morning, rinsing the mouth with clean water afterward. If the teeth are good, it will preserve them, and keep away the toothache; if the teeth are gone, it will harden the gums, so that they will masticate crusts and all.

(5) Take alum, reduce to an impalpable powder, 2 drachms; nitrous spirits of ether, 7 drachms. Mix and apply them to the tooth. This is said to be an infallible cure for all kinds of toothache (unless the disease is connected with rheumatism).

(6) Steep a piece of coarse brown paper in cold vinegar, then grate ginger on it, and apply to the side of the face affected; the application to be made at bedtime, and kept on during the whole of the night.

(7) One ounce alcohol, two drachms cayenne pepper, one ounce kerosene oil; mix, and let stand twenty-four hours—a sure cure.

Wounds.—(1) A wound produced by a sharp cutting instrument will heal without trouble when the edges are nicely brought together, and left so, without putting on any salve, provided the access of air is shut off and the person possesses a good constitution. If the wound is produced by a rusty nail, or a similar cause, so as to be jagged, it will soon become very inflamed, and in such a case it is recommended to smoke such a wound with burning wool or woolen cloth. Twenty minutes in the smoke of wool will take the pain out of the worst wound, and if repeated once or twice will allay the worst case of inflammation arising from a wound.

(2) The best simple remedy for surface wounds, such as cuts, abrasion of the skin, etc., is charcoal. Take a large coal from the fire, pulverize it, apply it to the wound, and cover the whole with a rag. The charcoal absorbs the fluid secreted by the wound, and lays the foundation of the scab; it also prevents the rag from irritating the flesh, and is an antiseptic.

(3) Without waiting for it to stop bleeding, press the edges of the lacerated flesh together, and apply immediately a plaster made of soot and cream, binding it firmly on, not to be removed till healed, without cleanliness requires it. Then put another of the same on, without delay, not allowing exposure to the air any more than possible to prevent.

(4) It is not generally known that the leaves of geranium are an excellent application for cuts, where the skin is rubbed off, and other wounds of that kind. One or two leaves must be bruised and applied to the part, and the wound will be cicatrized in a short time.

(5) There is nothing better for a cut than powdered resin. Get a few cents' worth, pound it until it is quite fine, put it in a cast-off spice box, with perforated top, then you can easily sift it on the cut. Put a soft cloth around the injured member, and wet it with water once in a while; it will prevent inflammation or soreness.

(6) When a nail or pin has been run into the foot, instantly bind on a rind of salt pork, and keep quiet till the wound is well. The lockjaw is often caused by such wounds, if neglected.

(7) It is a wise plan to keep a cup of alum water always convenient, so that sudden cuts or bruises can be bound up in a cloth wet in it. If treated thus they will heal quickly.

Sprains and Bruises.—(1) The best treatment of sprains and bruises is the application of water, of such temperature as is most agreeable. The degree of temperature varies with the temperature of the weather and the vigor of the circulation. In a hot day use cool or cold water. If the circulation is low use warm water. The bruised or sprained parts may be immersed in a pail of water, and gently pressed or manipulated with the hand or soft cloth for ten or fifteen minutes, or even longer in severe cases, after which wrap up the parts in cloths wet in cold water, and keep quiet. This treatment keeps down the inflammation, and in nine cases out of ten proves a speedy cure. The liniments and filthy ointments so much used for sprains do not compare with this simple treatment in efficacy.

(2) Take one part blue clay and two parts vinegar, and make into a paste, and bind on at night with a wet towel. One application is generally sufficient.

(3) Make pounded resin into a paste with fresh butter, lay it on the sprained part and bind it up.

Weak and Inflamed Eyes.—(1) Borax, half drachm; camphor water, three ounces. The above simple prescription is in common use by the highest medical authorities. It makes a wash unexcelled for the treatment of inflammation of the eyes. In using it lean the head back and drop three drops in the corner of each, and then open the eyes and let it work in. Use it as often as the eyes feel badly.

(2) When the eyes become inflamed from any cause, do not rub them at all—such irritation is dangerous—but bathe them in tepid milk and water, keep the bowels open by some gentle medicine and eat little meat. The eyes are very sensitive to the state of the stomach. Avoid the glare of strong light.

(3) Bathe your eyes night and morning in a tolerably strong solution of salt and water. We have known some remarkable cures effected by this simple remedy. After bathing the eyes daily for about a week, intermit a day or two, and then resume the daily bathing, and so on till your eyes get strong again.

(4) Take rose leaves, the more the better, and put them into a little water; then boil; after this strain it into a bottle and cork it tight. You will find this liquid very beneficial in removing redness and weakness from the eyes,

(5) Cut a slice of stale bread as thin as possible; toast both sides well, but don't burn; when cold, lay in cold spring or ice water; put between a piece of old linen and apply, changing when it gets warm.

(6) Take half an ounce of Golden Seal (you will find it at the drug stores), pour one-half pint boiling water upon it and let it cool. Bathe the eyes with a linen rag dipped in this, each night on going to bed, and you will soon effect a cure.

(7) Three or five grains of alum dissolved in half a pint of water, and applied to the eyes whenever they are weak or inflamed.

(8) Scrape a raw potato; use as a poultice; or slippery elm. Bathe with warm water or rose water.

Dust in the Eye.—(1) If a cinder or bit of dust gets into the eye do not rub the eyeball; that only irritates it. If the intruder is beneath the upper eyelid, lift the upper lid with the thumb and finger of the right hand, and with the forefinger of the left hand raise upward the under eyelid while you pull down over it the upper lid. This will seldom fail to remove the cinder, the soft skin and eyelashes taking it off without injuring the eyeball.

(2) A small camel's-hair brush, dipped in water and passed over the ball of the eye on raising the lid. The operation requires no skill, takes but a moment, and instantly removes any cinder or particle of dust or dirt, without inflaming the eye.

(3) To remove specks of dirt from the eye, immerse it in cold water, then roll and wink it rapidly, still keeping it in the water, till the desired result is accomplished. In cases of slight inflammation or dryness of the eye, this bath has a good effect. Use tepid, slightly salted water, instead of the cold.

(4) A celebrated oculist in Utrecht recommends, in all cases where dirt, lime, or specks get into the eyes, that the sufferer have pure olive oil poured in until everything of a hurtful nature is removed. The remedy is quite painless, and never fails to remove all foreign substances.

Sore Throat.—(1) An exchange thinks that salt and water, a large table-spoonful of salt to half a tumbler of water, used as a gargle for sore throat just before meal time, is an excellent remedy for such complaint. A little red pepper should be added if the salt water does not prove successful. Red pepper, honey or sugar, and sharp vinegar, simmered together, and then tempered with water so as not to be too strong, is a good remedy easily obtained.

(2) Sometimes a sore throat can be cured by the following simple recipe: Soak in water a small piece of bread and mix with it a pinch of cayenne pepper; roll it up in the form of a pill and swallow it. Usually in three hours the patient will be relieved of all pain. In aggravated cases a second dose may be requisite.

(3) If you have a sore throat, slight or serious, a piece of camphor-gum as large as a pea, kept in the mouth until dissolved, will give relief and ofttimes cure. It is said on good authority, if the gum is used in season, you will never have diphtheria—it is a good preventive.

(4) A gargle of salt and vinegar, with a little cayenne pepper, will do more to disperse soreness of the throat than any other remedy of which we have heard. It stimulates the glands, promotes free secretion, and will sometimes cure in a few hours.

(5) One ounce of best Peruvian bark, two wineglassfuls of honey, burnt

alum the size of two walnuts, borax the size of a shellbark. Mix these in-gredients in a quart of water, and then stew them until reduced to a pint. Shake the mixture previous to using it.

(6) An excellent remedy for sore throat is brewers' yeast and honey—four tablespoonfuls of the first and one teaspoonful of the latter. Mix in a cup, and gargle the throat two or three times an hour.

(7) Chlorate of potash dissolved in water is a standard remedy for sore throat, particularly when the throat feels raw.

(8) Use a gargle of a goblet half full of water, with a teaspoonful of common baking soda dissolved in it.

Dieting for Health.—This has sent many a one to the grave, and will send many more, because it is done injudiciously or ignorantly. One man omits his dinner by a herculean effort, and thinking he has accomplished wonders, expects wonderful results; but by the time supper is ready, he feels as hungry as a dog, and eats like one—fast, furious and long. Next day he is worse, and "don't believe in dieting" for the remainder of life.

Others set out to starve themselves into health, until the system is reduced so low that it has no power of resuscitation, and the man dies.

To diet wisely, does not imply a total abstinence from all food, but the taking of just enough, or of a quality adapted to the nature of the case. Loose bowels weaken very rapidly—total abstinence from all food increases the debility. In this case, food should be taken which, while it tends to arrest the disease, imparts nutriment and strength to the system. In this case, rest on a bed, and eating boiled rice, after it has been parched like coffee, will cure three cases out of four of common diarrhœa in a day or two.

Others think that, in order to diet effectually, it is all important to do without meat, but allow themselves the widest liberty in all else. But in many cases, dyspeptic conditions of the system particularly, the course ought to be reversed, because meat is converted into nutriment, with the expenditure of less stomach power than vegetables, while a given amount of work does three times as much good, gives three times as much nutriment and strength as vegetable food would.

Scald Head.—This appearance is the result of a bad state of the system —bad blood—the humors affecting the head often in consequence of neglect of cleanliness, or too rough combing or brushing of the head. There are cases in which wet cloths applied to the head, wet in arnica and water (four parts of water to one of arnica), may soon remove the difficulty if there is not too much of impurity in the system seeking an escape in this way.

Such a child should be much in the open air, be regular in taking food, eat the simplest kinds—the less the better of grease, salt, and the sweets generally. The parts may be bathed in arnica, glycerine or sweet oil, to protect them from the irritation of the air, etc.

In specially stubborn cases, it is well to produce an irritation in another part of the body, by the mustard or blister plaster, diverting it from the head, since the head is more likely to be attacked than most parts of the body. Its appearance is not a misfortune, but the location is not the best.

By no means use any sugar of lead or anything like it—an active poison—and do not attempt to "dry it up," or suddenly cure it, since there is always danger of driving it to some internal organ, some unsafe place; it is safer to do nothing, allowing nature to care for it, than to do wrong. It is not best to "dabble" with unknown remedies—poisons—or to listen to all told you by your neighbors, who may know nothing of the matter, though they may have had many children, which fact never gives intelligence.

Medical Qualities of Lemons.—A good deal has been said about the healthfulness of lemons. The latest advice is how to use them so that they will do the most good, as follows: Most people know the benefit of lemonade before breakfast, but few know that it is more than doubled by taking another at night also. The way to get the better of the bilious system without blue pills or quinine is to take the juice of one, two or three lemons, as appetite craves, in as much ice water as makes it pleasant to drink without sugar before going to bed. In the morning, on rising, at least half an hour before breakfast, take the juice of one lemon in a goblet of water. This will clear the system of humor and bile with efficiency, without any of the weakening effects of calomel or congress water. People should not irritate the stomach by eating lemons clear; the powerful acid of the juice, which is always most corrosive, invariably produces inflammation after a while, but properly diluted, so that it does not burn or draw the throat, it does its medical work without harm, and, when the stomach is clear of food, has abundant opportunity to work over the system thoroughly, says a medical authority.

Whooping Cough.—(1) Dr. Grath, of Vienna, proposes a singular treatment for this distressing ailment, which will doubtless receive careful consideration from the medical profession. He states that by placing twenty drops of the oil of turpentine on a handkerchief, holding it before the face, and taking about forty deep inspirations, to be repeated thrice daily, marked relief, succeeded in cases of laryngeal catarrh by speedy cure, is the result. Being called in to attend an infant of fifteen months in the convulsive stage, he instructed the child's mother to hold a cloth moistened, as already described, before it when awake, and to drop the oil upon its pillow when asleep. In this instance the remedy in its effect was most beneficial. The frequency and severity of the attacks sensibly decreased in the course of twenty-four hours, and by proper support by the help of stimulants, improvement was rapid.

(2) Dissolve a scruple of salt of tartar in a gill of water; add to it ten grains of cochineal; sweeten it with sugar. Give to an infant the fourth part of a tablespoonful four times a day; two years old, half a tablespoonful; from four years, a tablespoonful. This has been a very successful mixture.

(3) The following is regarded as an excellent remedy: Pure carbonate of potassa, one scruple; cochineal, one grain. Dissolve in six ounces of water sweetened with sugar. Dose for a child four or five years old, one teaspoonful three times a day, to be taken before meals.

(4) The inhalation of air charged with ammonia vapors, as a remedy for whooping cough, has been tried in France with success. One of the methods of application employed is boiling strong ammonia in the room where the patient is.

(5) Pound best black resin very fine, and give as much as will lie on a cent in a little moist sugar three times a day, commencing before breakfast in the morning. I have known it to cure the most obstinate cases of whooping cough in three weeks.

(6) An excellent cure for whooping cough, and one that I have seen tried in several instances with entire success, is simply this: Steep a handful of

chestnut leaves in a pint of boiling water; sweeten, cool, and give as a common drink five or six times a day.

Neuralgia. — (1) A very simple relief for neuralgia is to boil a small
handful of lobelia in half a pint of water till the strength is out of the herb,
then strain it off and add a teaspoonful of fine salt. Wring cloths out of the
liquid as hot as possible, and spread over the part affected. It acts like a
charm. Change the cloths as soon as cold till the pain is all gone; then
cover the place with a soft dry covering till perspiration is over, to prevent
taking cold. Rheumatism can often be relieved by application to the painful
parts, of cloths wet in a weak solution of sal soda water. If there is inflammation in the joints the cure is very quick. The wash should be lukewarm.

(2) Procure a half-ounce of the oil of peppermint, and, with a camels'
hair brush, paint the parts of the face where the pain is felt. We have
found it an excellent application in all forms of pain in the face. A drop
applied to the cavity of an aching tooth, and confined there with a pellet of
cotton, will arrest the pain.

(3) A noted cure for neuralgia is hot vinegar vaporized. Heat a flatiron
sufficiently hot to vaporize the vinegar, cover this with some woolen material,
which is moistened with vinegar, and the apparatus is then applied at once
to the painful spot. The application may be repeated until the pain disappears.

(4) Have a flannel cap made to fasten under the chin; wear three nights;
let three nights pass, then put on again if necessary. For neuralgia in eyebrows, bind a strip of flannel around the head; rub the teeth with equal
parts of salt and alum, pulverized, on a soft, wet bit of linen.

(5) Squeeze the juice of a good-sized lemon into a tumbler of water, and
every half hour take two or three mouthfuls of this liquid. If relief is not
experienced within twenty-four hours, continue the remedy. In slight cases
the above has often proved an effectual cure.

(6) Many cases of neuralgia have been cured by the common field thistle.
The leaves are macerated and used on the parts affected as a poultice, while
a small quantity of the leaves are made a tea of, and a small wine of the
decoction is taken as a drink before each meal.

(7) A simple remedy for neuralgia is horseradish. Grate and mix it in
vinegar, the same as for table purposes, and apply to the temple when the
face or the head is affected, or the wrist when the pain is in the arm or
shoulder.

(8) Half a drachm of sal-ammoniac in one ounce of camphor water, to be
taken a teaspoonful at a dose, and the dose repeated several times, at
intervals of five minutes, if the pain be not relieved at once.

(9) Persons troubled with neuralgia will find this a cure, if they try it.
Two drops of laudanum in half teaspoonful of warm water and dropped into
the ears; it will give immediate relief.

(10) It is said that the fumes of sugar snuffed up the nose will cure
ordinary cases of neuralgia. Put a small quantity of sugar on a hot shovel
and try it as directed.

Earache. — (1) As soon as any soreness is felt in the ear—which feeling
always precedes the regular ache—let three or four drops of tincture of
arnica be poured in, and then the orifice filled with a little cotton to exclude
the air, and in a short time the uneasiness is forgotten. If the arnica is not
resorted to until there is actual pain, the cure may not be so speedy, but it

is just as certain. If one application of the arnica does not effect a cure, it will be necessary to repeat it, it may be, several times.

(2) Persons will find relief for earache by putting in a spoon two or three drops of sweet oil, or, better still, almond oil, the same of molasses and laudanum, warming it altogether. Absorb some of the mixture in cotton wool; put it in the ear, with a piece of wool outside to keep out the cold air, repeating the thing if necessary. A roast onion heart dipped in this and surrounded with the cotton is also often very efficacious.

(3) The most effectual remedy has been a small clove of garlic, steeped for a few minutes in warm salad oil, and put into the ear rolled up in muslin or thin linen. In some time the garlic is reduced to a pulp, and having accomplished its object should be replaced with cotton to prevent the patient getting cold.

(4) To cure earache take a bit of cotton batting, put upon it a pinch of black pepper, gather it up and tie it, dip in sweet oil and insert into the ear. Put a flannel bandage over the head and keep it warm. It will give immediate relief.

(5) Dissolve assafœtida in water; warm a few drops and drop in the ear, then cork the ear with cotton.

Worms.—Some members of the profession still cling with bull-dog tenacity to the opinion that worms do not affect the health of children, and that they are natural to them. The latter may or may not be true, but when they accumulate in the intestines, they produce the same disturbance that any foreign, indigestible substance would do. We find the picking of the nose, swollen lower eye-lids, restlessness in sleep, groaning, gritting teeth, starting, and lastly, spasms.

Worms kill more children than teething; and when you find the above symptoms with a strawberry tongue and a fever, which will attack several times daily, going off as frequently in cold sweats, you can swear that you have a case of worms, and had as well prepare and attack them.

Now as to the best means of getting rid of them. I use the fluid extract of senna and spigelia in teaspoonful doses for patients of eight or ten years of age, and less in proportion, night and morning, for three nights and days, following this up each morning with a good dose of castor oil, provided the senna and spigelia does not act. Then wait three days, and again institute the same proceedings, and for the same length of time.

This treatment is for the lumbric oid. For the oxyuris, or "thread worm," I use any bitter infusion by enema, sulph. quinine, followed by an enema of common salt and milk—warm water half an hour afterward, which will destroy and expel them.

The symptoms of the presence of the worm are the same as the former, with the exception that in the latter you will find the sufferer scratching the anus. If every practitioner will use these he will be gratified by the restoration to immediate health of many a little sufferer, who would otherwise linger in sickness for many months and perhaps eventually die.

Warts.—(1) A much safer remedy for warts than nitrate of silver is sal-ammoniac. Get a piece about the size of a walnut; moisten the warts, and rub the sal-ammoniac well on them every night and morning, and in about a fortnight they will probably disappear. If not, do not despair, but continue the process till they are gone.

(2) The best treatment of warts is to pare the dry and hard skin from

their tops, and then touch them with the smallest drop of strong acetic acid, taking care that the acid does not run off the wart upon the neighboring skin; for if it does, it will occasion inflammation and much pain. If this is continued once or twice daily, with regularity, paring the surface of the wart occasionally, when it gets hard and dry, the wart will be soon effectually cured.

(3) Take half an ounce of sulphur; half an ounce of alcohol, 95 per cent.; put into an ounce phial, shake them well together, and apply freely once or twice a day for two or three weeks. By the end of this time, or a month at the most, the warts will be gone.

(4) Dissolve as much common washing-soda as the water will take up; wash the warts with this for a minute or two, and let them dry without wiping. Keep the water in a bottle, and repeat the washing often, and it will take away the largest warts.

(5) Oil of cinnamon dropped on warts three or four times a day will cause their disappearance, however hard, large, or dense they may be. The application gives no pain nor causes suppuration.

(6) The bark of the willow tree, burnt to ashes, applied to the parts, will remove all warts or excrescences on any part of the body.

Burns and Scalds.—(1) Mix common kitchen whitening with sweet oil, or, if sweet oil is not at hand, with water. Plaster the whole of the burn and some inches beyond it, all round, with the above, after mixing it to the consistency of common paste, and lay it on an eighth, or rather more, of an inch in thickness. It acts like a charm; the most agonizing pain is in a few minutes stilled. Take care to keep the mixture moist by the application, from time to time, of fresh oil or fresh water, and at night wrap the whole part affected in gutta-percha or flannel, to keep the moisture from evaporating. The patient will, in all probability, unless the flesh be much injured and the burn a very bad one, sleep soundly.

(2) For burns and scalds nothing is more soothing than the white of an egg, which may be poured over the wound. It is softer as a varnish for a burn than collodion, and being always at hand can be applied immediately. It is also more cooling than the sweet oil and cotton which was formerly supposed to be the surest application to allay the smarting pain. It is the contact with the air which gives the extreme discomfort experienced from the ordinary accident of this kind, and anything which excludes the air and prevents inflammation is the thing to be applied.

(3) The following is one of the best applications we know of in cases of burns or scalds, more especially where a large surface is denuded of the skin: Take one drachm of finely-powdered alum, and mix thoroughly with the whites of two eggs and one teacup of fresh lard; spread on a cloth, and apply to the parts burned. It gives almost instant relief from pain, and, by excluding the air, prevents inflammatory action The application should be changed at least once a day.

(4) Common baking soda—the bicarbonate—has been found to cure burns or scalds, affording immediate relief when it is promptly applied. For a dry burn, the soda should be made into paste with water. For a scald of wet burned surface, the powdered soda (or borax will do as well) should be dusted on.

(5) It is said that charcoal is a sure cure for burns. By laying a small piece of cold charcoal on the burn, the pain subsides immediately. By leaving the charcoal on for an hour the wound is healed, as has been demonstrated on several occasions.

(6) **For** burns sweet oil and cotton are the standard remedies. If they are not at hand sprinkle the burned part with flour and wrap loosely with a soft cloth. Don't remove the dressing until the inflammation subsides, as it will break the new skin that is forming.

(7) One ounce of pulverized borax, one quart of boiling water, half ounce of pulverized alum. Shake up well and bottle. Wrap the burn up in soft linen, and keep constantly wet with the solution. Do not remove the linen until the burn is cured.

(8) Soak a piece of linen rag in linseed oil, suspend it from the tongs over a saucer, and ignite the lower end; the oil which drops from it, while consuming, should be applied, when cold, with a feather, to the burn or scald.

(9) Smear the scorched surface with glycerine, by means of a feather, then apply cotton wadding; lastly, cover with oil-silk. This treatment has been very successful in cases of recent occurrence.

(10) The true physiological way of treating burns and scalds is at once to exclude the air, with cotton batting, flour, scraped potato or anything that is handiest.

Headache.—(1) All ships sailing in hot climates carry a supply of limes, whose acid juice is a remedy for biliousness. Dr. Haire says he has cured many victims of sick headache with the following simple prescription: When the first symptoms of a headache appear, take a teaspoonful of lemon juice, clear, fifteen minutes before each meal, and the same dose at bedtime. Follow this up until all symptoms are past, taking no other medicines, and you will soon be freed from your periodical nuisance. Sick headache is the signal of distress which the stomach puts up to inform us that there is an over alkaline condition of its fluids—that it needs a natural acid to restore the battery to its normal working condition. Lemonade without sugar, plain lemon juice and water, is a grateful and medicinal beverage for a person of bilious habit, allaying feverishness and promoting sleep and appetite. Some who cannot afford to be sick may be willing to make a conscientious trial of the above remedy, which is neither patented nor costly. To make it a sovereign remedy it will in most cases need the help of a reform in diet, or a let-up from work and care—one or both. In other words, the same causes will be apt to reproduce the effect—as the pinching boot will recreate corns where they have been removed.

(2) A new remedy for headache has been found by Dr. Haley, an Australian physician, who says that for some years past he has found minimum doses of iodide of potassium of great service in frontal headache; that is, a heavy, dull headache, situated over the brow, and accompanied by languor, chilliness and a feeling of general discomfort, with distaste for food, which sometimes approaches to nausea, can be completely removed by a two grain dose dissolved in half a wineglassful of water, and this quietly sipped, the whole quantity being taken in about ten minutes. In many cases, he adds, the effect of these small doses has been simply wonderful, as, for instance, a person, who a quarter of an hour ago was feeling most miserable, and refused all food, wishing only for quietness, would now take a good meal and resume his wonted cheerfulness. If this cure of Dr. Haley's is in reality a practical one, he will merit, for the discovery, the gratitude of suffering millions.

(3) Dr. Lauder Brunton says: "The administration of a brisk purgative, or small doses of Epsom salts, thrice a day, is a most effectual remedy for

frontal headache when combined with constipation; but if the bowels be regular, the morbid processes on which it depends seem to be checked, and the headache removed even more effectually by nitro-hydrochloric acid, or by alkalies, given before meals. If the headache is immediately above the eyebrows, the acid is best; but if it be a little higher up, just where the hair begins, the alkalies appear to me to be the more effectual. At the same time that the headache is removed, the feelings of sleepiness and weariness, which frequently lead the patients to complain that they rise up more tired than they lie down, generally disappear."

(4) Dr. Hall states that sick headache is the result of eating too much and exercising too little. Nine times in ten the cause is in the fact that the stomach was not able to digest the food last introduced into it, either from its having been unsuitable, or excessive in quantity. A diet of bread and butter with ripe fruits or berries, with moderate, continuous exercise in the open air, sufficient to keep up a gentle perspiration, would cure almost every case in a short time. Two teaspoonfuls of powdered charcoal in a half glass of water, and drank, generally gives instant relief.

(5) Put a handful of salt into a quart of water, add one ounce of spirits of hartshorn, and half an ounce of camphorated spirits of wine. Put them quickly into a bottle, and cork tightly to prevent the escape of the spirits. Soak a piece of rag with the mixture, and apply it to the head; wet the rag afresh as soon as it gets heated.

(6) A mixture of ice and salt, in proportion of one to one-half, applied to the head, frequently gives instant relief from acute headache. It should be tied up in a small linen cloth, like a pad, and held as near as possible to the seat of the pain.

(7) For sick headache, induced by bilious derangement, steep five cents' worth of senna and camomile flowers in a little water, to make strong decoction, and take. It has been tried successfully in various cases.

(8) Coarse brown paper soaked in vinegar and placed on the forehead is good for a sick headache. If the eyelids are gently bathed in cool water the pain in the head is generally allayed.

(9) Nervous headache is said to be instantly relieved by shampooing the head with a quart of cold water in which a dessertspoonful of soda has been dissolved.

Offensive Breath.—(1) From six to ten drops of the concentrated solution of chloride of soda, in a wineglassful of pure spring water, taken immediately after the ablutions of the morning are completed, will sweeten the breath, by disinfecting the stomach, which far from being injured will be benefitted by the medicine. If necessary, this may be repeated in the middle of the day. In some cases the odor arising from carious teeth is combined with that of the stomach. If the mouth is well rinsed with a teaspoonful of the solution of the chloride in a tumbler of water, the bad odor of the teeth will be removed.

(2) To correct the odor of decayed teeth, two or three drops of a solution of permanganate of potassa may be used in a glass of water as a wash, or a few drops of the solution may be put into the cavity of the tooth on a small piece of cotton. A good remedy for a bad breath, arising from a foul stomach, is charcoal powder in teaspoonful doses—a dose every other morning before breakfast for two or three weeks, if necessary.

(3) Bad breath from catarrh, foul stomach, or bad teeth, may be temporarily relieved by diluting a little bromo chloralum with eight or ten parts

of water, and using it as a gargle, and swallowing a few drops before going out. A pint of bromo chloralum costs fifty cents, but a small vial full will last a long time.

(4) Take eight drops of muriatic acid, in half a tumbler of spring water, and add a little lemon peel or juice to suit the palate. Let this mixture be taken three times a day for some weeks, and, if found beneficial, then use it occasionally.

(5) The best treatment in regard to offensive breath is the use of powdered charcoal, two or three tablespoonfuls per week, taken in a glass of water before retiring for the night.

To Stop Bleeding.—(1) If a man is wounded so that the blood flows, that flow is either regular, or by jets or spurts. If it flows regularly, a vein has been wounded, and a string should be bound tightly around below the wounded part, that is, beyond it from the heart. If the blood comes out by leaps or jets, an artery has been severed, and the person may bleed to death in a few minutes; to prevent which apply the cord above the wound, that is, between the wound and the heart. In case a string or cord is not at hand, tie the two opposite corners of a handkerchief around the limb, put a stick between and turn it round until the handkerchief is twisted sufficiently tight to stop the bleeding, and keep it so until a physician can be had.

(2) It is said that bleeding from a wound, on man or beast, may be stopped by a mixture of wheat flour and common salt, in equal parts, bound on with a cloth. If the bleeding be profuse, use a large quantity, say from one to three pints. It may be left on for hours or even days, if necessary. The person who gave us this receipt says: "In this manner I saved the life of a horse which was bleeding from a wounded artery; the bleeding ceased in five minutes after the application."

(3) Blood may be made to cease to flow as follows: Take fine dust of tea and bind it close to the wound; at all times accessible and easily to be obtained. After the blood has ceased to flow, laudanum may be advantageously applied to the wound. Due regard to these instructions would save agitation of mind, and running for the surgeon, who would, probably, make no better prescription if he were present.

(4) Powdered rosin is the best thing to stop bleeding from cuts. After the powder is sprinkled on, wrap the wound with a soft cotton cloth. As soon as the wound begins to feel feverish, keep the cloth wet with cold water.

(5) For internal bleeding put the patient in bed with the head slightly raised, keep the room cool, and give frequently a swallow of the coldest water or a pellet of ice.

(6) For bleeding, take linen or other rags, burn to charcoal and put it in the wound, and no more blood will come.

(7) For bleeding at the cavity of an extracted tooth, pack the alveolus fully and firmly with cotton wet with alum water.

Children's Falls.—A child rolls down the stairs, or falls from a height, and in either case strikes its head with force. What shall be done till the doctor comes? We would give the following directions, as nearly as possible in the order in which they should be adopted. Raise the child gently in the arms, and carrying to the nearest sofa or bed, place him on it—unless crying loudly, when he can be soothed quickest in his mother's arms. All the clothing should be loosened, especially about the neck, to afford the freest circulation of the blood to and from the head. To equalize the circulation and prevent inflammations the head should be kept cool and the extremities warm. Cooling lotions of arnica or witch hazel and water or simply water should be applied to the head on thin cloths, well wrung out so as not to wet the pillows and bed-clothes. Not more than two or four thicknesses of linen should be used, because thick cloths prevent evaporation, and what was intended to cool the head acts as a poultice and makes the head hotter. Ice and cold water should not be used unless the head be very hot, as it is believed children have been killed by the application of pounded ice to the head.

Bottles of hot water or hot irons are all that is necessary, besides the bed-clothing, to heat the extremities. All applications of mustard and other irritants possess no advantage over these, and have the disadvantage of disturbing the sufferer. Should the patient's face be very pale, and signs of fainting appear, camphor or ammonia should be applied to the nostrils, and a little brandy or wine be given.

Then the room should be made as quiet as possible and every means used to invite " Nature's sweet restorer," sleep. We know the popular idea is that patients suffering from any injury to the head should be kept awake by all means; and it is mainly to combat this erroneous notion that we are prompted to write out these directions.

No injury—or degree of injury—of the head contraindicates the sufferer's sleeping. In fact positive harm may be done in trying to prevent sleep. Rest is what the brain and blood vessels want more than any other thing; and, if not allowed, what would have passed off in a few hours or days may be prolonged into inflammation, with all its dangerous consequences.

Of course the air of the room should be kept pure—windows and doors open if the weather permit—and the presence of persons not absolutely necessary forbidden.

Cancer.—(1) The following is said to be a sure cure for cancer: A piece of sticking plaster is put over the cancer, with a circular piece cut out of the center, a little larger than the cancer, so that the cancer and a small circular rim of healthy skin next to it is exposed. Then a plaster, made of chloride of zinc, blood root and wheat flour, is spread on a piece of muslin, the size of this circular opening, and applied to the cancer for twenty-four hours. On removing it, the cancer will be found burned into, and appear of the color and hardness of an old shoe sole, and the circular rim outside of it will appear white and parboiled, as if scalded by hot steam. The wound is now dressed, and the outside rim soon separates, and the cancer comes out in a hard lump, and the place heals up. The plaster kills the cancer, so that it sloughs like dead flesh, and never grows again. The remedy was discovered by Dr. King, of London, and has been used by him for several years with unfailing success, and not a case has been known of the reappearance of the cancer when this remedy has been applied.

(2) An old Indian cancer doctor in Oregon pronounces this a sure cure: Take common wood sorrel, bruise it on brass, spread it in the form of a poultice, and apply as long as the patient can bear; then apply bread and milk poultice until the patient can bear the wood sorrel again. Continue this until the cancer is drawn out by the roots.

(3) Take the blossoms of red clover and make tea of them, and drink freely. It will cure cancer in the stomach as well as on the surface.

Consumption.—(1) A correspondent in Canada writes this interesting and, perhaps, useful letter to *Chambers' Journal*: "Noticing an extract from the *World of Science*, in which a physician strongly recommends hot water in place of tea or coffee as a stimulant for the use of those requiring to study late at night, I would like to give my experience of it as a beneficial agent in consumption: Mrs. ——, one of a family a number of whose members had died of consumption, was, after severe exposure to a snow storm, seized with a serious cough and expectoration, accompanied with a loss of flesh. Examination by a physician showed that one lung was seriously affected. She was wholly confined to her room, and everything that medical attendance and loving care could do to mitigate her suffering was done, but ineffectually. The depressing night sweats continued, together with loss of rest from repeated fits of coughing. Losing all faith in medicine some six months ago, its use was wholly abandoned and the use of nourishing diet only continued. About ten weeks ago the patient's attention was directed to a newspaper paragraph recommending hot water as a remedy for consumption. Feeling that little harm could ensue from its use, she determined to test it. At the moment of retiring a large tumbler of hot water, in which the juice of a lemon had been mixed to free it from nausea, was taken. In a few moments a glow of warmth would pervade the lungs, chest, etc., quickly followed by the most refreshing sleep, which would be unbroken by any cough, and the patient would awake in the morning rested and strengthened. A few days ago she was seized with a fit of coughing, during which was coughed up into her mouth a small stone about the size of a pea—formed of sulphate of lime, I believe, and usually considered a symptom of the healing of a cavity in the lung."

(2) A correspondent writes as follows about the flower of a well-known plant: "I have discovered a remedy for consumption. It has cured a number of cases after they had commenced bleeding at the lungs and the hectic flush was already on the cheek. After trying this remedy to my own satisfaction, I have thought that philanthropy required that I should let it be known to the world. It is common mullen, steeped strongly and sweetened with coffee sugar, and drank freely. Young or old plants are good, dried in the shade and kept in clean bags. The medicine must be continued from three to six months, according to the nature of the disease. It is very good for the blood vessels also. It strengthens and builds up the system instead of taking away the strength. It makes good blood and takes inflammation away from the lungs."

(3) English physicians recommend the free use of lemons for consumption. It has long been known that they are excellent in the cure of rheumatism, and, fortunately, they are both cheap and grateful to the palate. A little sugar only should be used with them, and a dozen a day are none too many.

Felons.—(1) Felons, which are usually termed "Whitlow" by physicians, we believe, are a very painful and often very serious affection of the fingers, generally of the last joints, and often near or involving the nails. As the fingers are much exposed to bruises, felons are quite common among those who constantly use their hands at hard work. If allowed to continue until matter (pus) forms, and the periosteum or bone sheathing is affected, lancing is necessary; but if taken in time, a simple application of copal varnish, covering it with a bandage, is highly recommended. If the varnish becomes dry and unpleasantly hard, a little fresh varnish may be applied from time to time. When a cure is effected, the varnish is easily removed by rubbing into it a little lard and washing with soap and water. Dr. A. B. Isham details, in *Medical News*, a number of cases of its application with uniform success, where formations of pus had not previously occurred. In two cases there were apparently a combination of the " run-around " with a felon, and in all of them there was swelling, redness, heat, and great pain. He suggests the use of copal varnish for felons, run arounds, boils, and any local acute inflammations of external parts.

(2) Take the root of the plant known as dragon root, Jack-in-the-pulpit, or Indian turnip, either green or dry; grate about one-half a teaspoonful into four tablespoonfuls of sweet milk; simmer gently a few minutes, then thicken with bread crumbs, and apply as hot as possible. This can be heated again two or three times, adding a little milk each time. If the felon is just starting, this will drive it back; if somewhat advanced will draw it out quickly and gently. It is well to put a little tallow on the poultice, especially after opening, to prevent sticking. This same poultice is good for a carbuncle or anything rising.

(3) Many persons are liable to extreme suffering from felons on the finger. The following prescription is recommended as a cure for the distressing ailment: Take common rock salt, such as is used for salting down pork or beef, dry it in an oven, then pound it fine and mix with spirits of turpentine in equal parts. Put it on a rag and wrap it around the part affected, and as it gets dry put on more, and in twenty-four hours you are cured—the felon is dead.

(4) The following directions carefully observed, will prevent those circular and osseous abominations, known as felons. As soon as the disease is felt, put directly over the spot, a fly blister, about the size of your thumb nail, and let it remain for six hours, at the expiration of which time, directly under the surface of the blister, may be seen the felon, which can instantly be taken out with the point of a needle or lancet.

(5) At first great relief is obtained by soaking the part in half a gill of strong vinegar, in which has been dissolved one tablespoonful of saleratus. Use it as hot as it can be borne, and repeat as often as the pain returns. A thimbleful of unslacked lime and soft soap has cured some cases in a few hours. If matter forms, it had better be poulticed and lanced, or it will be painful from two to six weeks.

(6) As soon as it makes its appearance apply a poultice, of equal parts of saltpeter and brimstone, mix with sufficient lard to make a paste, and renew as soon as it gets dry. A few applications will effect a cure.

Dyspepsia.—(1) We have seen dyspeptics who suffered untold torments with almost every kind of food; no liquid could be taken without suffering; bread became a burning acid; meat and milk were solid liquid fires; and we have seen their torments pass away, and their hunger relieved by living on the white of eggs which have been boiled in bubbling water for thirty minutes. At the end of a week we have given the half yelk of the egg with the white, and upon this diet alone, without food of any kind, we have seen them begin to gain flesh and strength, and quiet, refreshing sleep. After weeks of this treatment they have been able, with care, to begin upon other food. And all this without taking medicine. Hard-boiled eggs are not half so bad as half-boiled ones, and ten times as easy to digest as raw eggs, even in egg-nog.

(2) Milk and lime water is said to prove beneficial in dyspepsia and

weakness of the stomach. The way to make the lime water is simply to procure a few lumps of unslaked lime, put the lime in a fruit can, add water until it is slaked and of the consistency of thin cream; the lime settles, and leaves the pure and clear lime water at the top. A goblet of cow's milk may have six or eight teaspoonfuls of lime water added with good effect. Great care should be taken not to get the lime water too strong; pour off without disturbing the precipitated lime. Sickness of the stomach is promptly relieved by a teacupful of warm water with a teaspoonful of soda dissolved in it. If it brings the offending matter up, all the better.

(3) Dr. Nichols, who has made a series of dietetic experiments on himself, has arrived at the conclusion that, if the stomach is allowed to rest, any case of dyspepsia may be cured; that the diet question was at the root of all diseases; that pure blood can only be made from pure food, and that, if the drink of a nation were pure and free from stimulating qualities, and the food was also pure, the result would be pure health.

(4) In mild cases take one teaspoonful sweet oil, after eating, three times a day. In severe forms take a dessertspoonful. This followed up has cured cases where doctors have given them up. Ye who suffer from this dread disease, don't fail to try it; surely it can't hurt you.

(5) Burn alum until the moisture in it is evaporated, then take as much as you can put on a dime, about half an hour before eating. Three or four days probably will answer; but take it until cured.

Dysentery.—(1) Dysentery, or inflammation of the great intestine, prevails in the autumnal season more particularly, and in low-lying and marshy districts. It occasionally occurs also as an epidemic in overcrowded institutions and unhealthy localities. Treatment: Dysentery attacks those soonest whose blood is impoverished and whose vital powers are generally depressed from some cause—a fact which suggests a building-up plan of treatment. Although dysentery commences in the great intestine, the liver soon becomes secondarily affected, and it, therefore, behooves the patient to be very cautious as to the amount of stimulation he subjects himself to; malt liquors and spirits are not permissable. His food, too, must be of the lightest kind. The following medicines will be found most useful: Castor-oil mixture: Take of castor-oil, six drachms; compound powder of tragacanth, one ounce; cinnamon water, six ounces. Take a sixth part three times a day. The nitric acid mixture: Take of dilute nitric acid, two drachms; spirit of chloroform, two drachms; tincture of opium, half a drachm; peppermint water, six ounces. Take two tablespoonfuls every four hours. With either of the above mixtures a powder containing three grains of ipecacuanha and six grains of sugar may be taken every night and morning. Ipecacuanha becomes an invaluable medicine in dysentery, by virtue of the specific power it exerts on all mucous membranes in causing increased action of their mucous follicles; and thus it is that it gives so much relief to the dysenteric patient, in whom the dry and, perhaps, ulcerated surface of the intestine is soothed and lubricated by an increased flow of mucus.

(2) The egg is considered one of the best of remedies for dysentery. Beaten up slightly, with or without sugar, and swallowed at a gulp, it tends, by its emollient qualities, to lessen the inflammation of the stomach and intestine, and, by forming a transient coating on these organs, to enable nature to resume her healthful sway over a diseased body. Two, or at most three eggs per day, would be all that is required in ordinary cases, and since egg is not merely medicine but food as well, the lighter the diet otherwise

and the quieter the patient is kept the more certain and rapid is the recovery.

(3) Take one pint of best wine vinegar, and add half a pound of best loaf sugar. Simmer them together in a pewter vessel, with a pewter top. Let the patient drink this during the day—a small quantity at a time—either clear, or diluted with water.

Diphtheria.—(1) Dr. Chenery, of Boston, has lately discovered that hyposulphite of soda is the specific remedy against diphtheria, that so much dreaded ailment, which of late years has carried off many valuable lives. He reports a very large number of cases saved by the use of this remedy. The dose of the hyposulphite is from five to fifteen grains or more in syrup, every two to four hours, according to age and circumstances. It can do no harm, but if too much is given it will purge; as much as the patient can bear without purging is a good rule in the severer cases. The solution or mixture can be used in doses of five drops to half a drachm in milk. The amount for thorough stimulation is greater than can be taken in water. The doctor usually gives it in such doses as can be easily taken in milk, using milk besides as a food for small children. One fact, however, needs to be borne in mind, namely, the hyposulphite prevents the digestion of milk, and it should not be given in less than an hour after taking the medicine. They may be used alternately, however, without interference, in sufficiently frequent doses.

(2) The treatment consists in thoroughly swabbing the back of the mouth and throat with a wash made thus: Table salt, two drachms; black pepper, golden seal, nitrate of potash, alum, one drachm each. Mix and pulverize, put into a teacup half full of water, stir well, and then fill up with good vinegar. Use every half hour, one, two, and four hours, as recovery progresses. The patient may swallow a little each time. Apply one ounce each of spirits of turpentine, sweet oil, and aqua ammonia, mixed, every hour, to the whole of the throat, and to the breast bone every four hours, keeping flannel to the part.

(3) A correspondent writes that he has used the following remedy for diphtheria in a great many hard cases, and in not one has it failed to effect a cure. It is as follows: Procure some pitch tar—not gas tar—put a little on a hot iron, invert funnel over the smoke, and let the patient inhale as much as he can for a few minutes five or six times a day. During the intervals let the patient have small pieces of ice to keep as near the root of the tongue as possible.

(4) In France lemon juice is in high repute as a remedy for diphtheria. As a local application it is preferred to chlorate of potash, nitrate of silver, perchloride of iron, alum or lime water. It is used by dipping a little plug of cotton wool twisted around a wire in the juice, and pressing it against the diseased surface four or five times daily.

(5) A gargle of sulphur and water has been used with much success in cases of diphtheria. Let the patient swallow a little of the mixture. Or, when you discover that your throat is a little sore, bind a strip of flannel around the throat, wet in camphor, and gargle salt and vinegar occasionally.

(6) Take a common tobacco pipe, place a live coal within the bowl, drop a little tar upon the coal, and let the patient draw smoke into the mouth, and discharge it through the nostrils. The remedy is safe and simple, and should be tried whenever occasion may require

Croup.—There are various remedies for this enemy in the nursery. As in other diseases, prevention is better than cure. Children liable to croup should not play out of doors after three o'clock in the afternoon. If a woolen shawl is closely pinned around the neck of the patient when the first symptoms of croup appear the attack may be diminished in power. The child struggling for breath naturally throws its arms out of bed to breathe through its pores, and thus takes more cold and increases its trouble. Bi-chromate of potassa in minute doses—as much as will rest on the point of a penknife—given every half hour till relief is obtained, is the best remedy we have ever tried. Mustard plasters on the ankles, wrist and chest will draw the blood from the throat and relieve it, cloths wrung from hot water and placed about the chest and throat and wrapped with flannel, give relief. A teaspoonful of alum pulverized and mixed with twice its quantity of sugar, to make it palatable, will give almost instant help. Another remedy is the following: Take equal parts of soda or saleratus and syrup or molasses; mix and give a teaspoonful for a child two years, larger doses for older children, smaller for nursing babies. Repeat the doses at short intervals until the phlegm is all thrown up, and upon each recurrence of the symptoms. Or, grate a raw onion, strain out the juice, and to two parts of the juice put one part of castor oil; keep it well corked in a bottle, shake well, give one teaspoonful once in two or three hours. Or, take two parts sweet lard and six parts pulverized sugar, mix thoroughly, and give a teaspoonful every fifteen minutes until relief is obtained. Among the many remedies given we hope that one or more may be available to every mother who needs aid in this matter.

Diarrhœa.—(1) It is said the small plant commonly known by the name rupturewort, made into tea, and drank frequently, is a sure cure for diarrhœa. Rupturewort grows in nearly every open lot, and along the roads. It is a small plant, throwing out a number of shoots in a horizontal direction, and lying close to the ground, something similar to the manner of the pusleyweed, and bears a small, dark green leaf, with an oblong, purple spot in the center. When the stem is broken, a white milky substance will ooze from the wound. It is very palatable, and infants take it as readily as any drink. This is an old Indian cure, and may be relied on. The botanical name of this plant is *Euphrobia Maculata*.

(2) Blackberry cordial is said to be almost a specific for summer complaint or diarrhœa. From a teaspoonful to a wineglass is to be taken, according to the age of the patient, until relieved. Following is a recipe for making blackberry cordial: To two quarts of juice add one pound of white sugar; half ounce nutmeg, half ounce cinnamon, pulverized; half ounce cloves, pulverized. Boil all together for a short time, and when cold add a pint of brandy.

(3) Take Indian corn, roasted and ground in the manner of coffee, or coarse meal browned, and boil in a sufficient quantity of water to produce a strong liquid, like coffee, and drink a teacupful warm, two or three times a day. One day's practice, it is said, will ordinarily effect a cure.

(4) The ingredients are: Sulphate of morphia, one grain; Glauber salts, quarter of an ounce; water, two ounces. Dose: A teaspoonful twice a day. If attended with much pain and looseness, administer this medicine every two hours.

(5) A strong solution of bicarbonate of soda (baking soda) taken frequently is a reliable remedy for diarrhœa troubles, particularly those arising from acidity of the stomach.

Corns.—(1) For soft corns soak the feet well in hot water before going to bed, then pare down the corn, and, after having just moistened it, rub a little lunar caustic on the corn and just around the edge, till it turns light gray. By the next morning it will be black, and when the burnt skin peels off it will leave no vestige of the corn underneath. Of course, the corn is liable to return, but not for some length of time. Or, scrape a bit of common chalk, and put a pinch of the powder on the corn at night, binding a piece of linen round. Repeat this for a few days, when the corn will come off in little scales.

(2) Take quarter cup of strong vinegar, crumb finely into it some bread. Let stand half an hour, or until it softens into a good poultice. Then apply, on retiring at night. In the morning the soreness will be gone and the corn can be picked out. If the corn is a very obstinate one, it may require two or more applications to effect a cure.

(3) To cure corns, take a lemon, cut a piece of it off, then nick it so as to let in the toe with the corn. Tie this on at night so that it cannot move, and you will find the next morning that, with a blunt knife, the corn will come away to a great extent. Two or three applications will effect a thorough cure.

(4) For soft corns dip a piece of linen cloth in turpentine and wrap it around the toe on which the corn is situated, night and morning. The relief will be immediate, and, after a few days, the corn will disappear.

(5) Soft corns can be cured by this corn salve: Boil tobacco down to an extract, then mix with it a quantity of white pitch pine, and apply it to the corn, renewing it once a week until the corn disappears.

(6) Boil a potato in its skin, and after it is boiled take the skin and put the inside of it to the corn, and leave it on for about twelve hours; at the end of that period the corn will be nearly cured.

(7) Macerate the tender leaves of ivy in strong vinegar for eight or ten days, then apply to the corns by means of cloths or lint saturated with the liquor. In a few days the corns will drop off.

Liquor Appetite.—(1) Dr. Unger insists that the following remedy will cure the cravings of the worst drunkard in the land: Take one pound of best, fresh, quill red Peruvian bark, powder it, and soak it in one pint of diluted alcohol. Afterward strain and evaporate it down to half a pint. Directions for its use: Dose—a teaspoonful every three hours the first and second day, and occasionally moisten the tongue between the doses. It acts like quinine, and the patient can tell by a headache if he is getting too much. The third day take as previous, but reduce the dose to one-half teaspoonful. Afterward reduce the dose to fifteen drops, and then down to ten, then down to five drops. To make a cure it takes from five to fifteen days, and in extreme cases thirty days. Seven days are about the average in which a cure can be effected.

(2) At a festival of one of our reformatory institutions, a gentleman is reported to have said: "I overcame the appetite for liquor by a recipe given to me by old Dr. Hatfield, one of those good old physicians who do not have a percentage from a neighboring druggist. The prescription is simply an orange every morning half an hour before breakfast. 'Take that,' said the doctor, 'and you will want neither liquor nor medicine.' I have done so regularly, and find that liquor has become repulsive. The taste of the orange is in the saliva of my tongue; and it would be as well to mix water

and oil as rum with my taste." The recipe is simple, and has the recommendation that it can do no harm if it does no good.

(3) The following recipe has been found efficacious in a great many cases: Sulphate of iron, five grains; peppermint water, eleven drachms; spirits of nutmeg, one drachm. This preparation acts as a tonic and stimulant, and so partially supplies the place of the accustomed liquor, and prevents the absolute physical and moral prostration that often follows a sudden breaking off from the use of stimulating drinks. It is to be taken in quantities equal to an ordinary drachm, and as often as the desire for a drachm returns.

Coughs and Colds.—(1) An old-fashioned remedy for a cold: A warm " stew," getting into bed with covering well tucked in, hot bricks to feet, and drinking abundantly of hot teas until there is a dripping perspiration, to be kept up an hour or two or more until the system is relieved, and then to cool off very gradually in the course of another hour, is derisively styled " an old woman's remedy "; but for all that it will break up any cold taken within thirty-six hours; it will promptly relieve many of the most painful forms of sudden disease, with the advantage of being without danger, gives no shock to the system, nor wastes its strength.

(2) Borax has proved a most effective remedy in certain forms of colds. In sudden hoarseness or loss of voice in public speakers or singers, from colds, relief for an hour or so may be obtained by slowly dissolving, and partially swallowing, a lump of borax the size of a garden pea, or about three or four grains held in the mouth for ten or fifteen minutes before speaking or singing. This produces a profuse secretion of saliva, or " watering " of the mouth and throat, just as wetting brings back the missing notes to a flute when it is too dry.

(3) The following remedy, communicated by a Russian, as the usual mode of getting rid of those complaints in that part of Russia from whence he came, is simple, and we can, from experience, also vouch for its efficacy. It is no other than a strong tea of elder flowers, sweetened with honey, either fresh or dried. A basin of this tea is to be drank as hot as possible, after the person is warm in bed; it produces a strong perspiration, and a slight cold or cough yields to it immediately, but the most stubborn requires two or three repetitions.

(4) To a pint and a half of water, add two large poppy-heads, and two large lemons. Boil them till they are soft, press the lemons into the water, strain the liquor, and add half a drachm of saffron, and half a pound of brown sugar-candy, pounded. Boil all together till the sugar-candy is dissolved; stir the whole till you perceive it will jelly; strain it a second time, and take the seeds from the poppies.

(5) Put five cents' worth of pine pitch into a pint of water. Let it simmer until the water is well impregnated with the flavor. Dip out the gum which remains undissolved and add honey enough to sweeten and make a thick syrup. Strain this and bottle. Dose, a teaspoonful four or five times a day, according to the severity of the cough. It will afford speedy relief.

(6) Take two ounces of balm of gilead buds, the freshest you can procure, and boil them very slowly in a quart of water. Let it simmer down to one pint, then strain it, and then add one pound of honey in comb, with the juice of three lemons. Let them all boil together until the wax in the honey is dissolved. This has been known to cure a cough of long standing.

(7) Melt some resin at night on going to bed, and let the smoke from it

fill the room. Inhaling the smoke heals the inflammation, and sleep is often produced when one could not sleep before for much coughing. Presevere until a cure is effected. A change for the better should be felt within a week.

(8) For colds, coughs, croup, or lung fever, take lard or sweet oil, two parts; coal oil, two parts; spirits of camphor, one part; spirits of turpentine, one part; saturate flannel and apply to the throat and chest warm.

Cold in the Head.—(1) This may sometimes be cured by inhaling through the nose the emanations of ammonia contained in a smelling bottle. If the sense of the smell is completely obliterated, the bottle should be kept under the nose until the pungency of the volatile alkali is felt. The bottle is then removed, but only to be reapplied after a minute; the second application, however, should not be long, that the patient may bear it. This easy operation being repeated seven or eight times in the course of five minutes, but always very rapidly, except the first time, the nostrils become free, the sense of smell is restored, and the secretion of the irritating mucous is stopped. This remedy is said to be peculiarly advantageous to singers.

(2) A cold in the head can be cured at once, if taken care of at the very beginning. Dissolve a tablespoonful of borax in a pint of hot water; let it stand until it becomes tepid; snuff some up the nostrils two or three times during the day, or use the dry, powdered borax like snuff, taking a pinch as often as required. At night have a handkerchief saturated with spirits of camphor, place it near the nostrils so as to inhale the fumes while sleeping.

(3) A hot lemonade is one of the best remedies in the world for a cold. It acts promptly and effectually, and has no unpleasant after effects. One lemon properly squeezed, cut in slices, put with sugar, and covered with half a pint of boiling water. Drink just before going to bed, and do not expose yourself on the following day. This remedy will ward off an attack of chills and fever if used properly.

(4) When one has a bad cold and the nose is closed up so that he cannot breathe through it, relief may be found instantly by putting a little camphor and water in the center of the hand and snuffing it up the nose. It is a great relief.

Catarrh.—(1) Ordinary cases of catarrh can be cured by snuffing up the nose a little table salt three or four times a day; but many cases of this troublesome complaint are caused by inability of the liver to perform its function properly. In such cases there is often a too alkaline condition of the blood. If persons thus afflicted will squeeze the juice of a good-sized lemon into a half-tumbler of water, and drink it without sugar just before dinner, they will, if they live abstemiously, be surprised to see how soon the catarrhal difficulty will diminish. When it fails to do so, it may be considered as due to other causes.

(2) The catarrh, writes a correspondent, can be cured by a daily use of raw onions as an article of food; at the same time use a snuff made of white sugar, laundry starch, and burned alum, pulverized and mixed in equal quantities—to be used the same as other snuff.

(3) A most unfailing remedy for catarrh is to smoke crushed cubeb berries in a clay pipe and swallow the smoke. They can be procured at any drug store, at a moderate cost. Try it.

(4) Put one tablespoonful of iode-bromide of calcium comp. into a tea-cupful of warm water. Snuff it up the nose night and morning. It is very cleansing and healing.

(5) Burn a piece of alum on the stove until it becomes a white powder, and use it as a snuff, and it will cure catarrh and is a good remedy for cold in the head.

(6) Take one pint of whiskey, and add two ounces of sulphur; shake it up and take a tablespoonful three mornings, then miss three; so proceed until taken up.

Scarlet Fever.—(1) Mr. Robert Christie, a San Francisco journalist, suggests a remedy for the scarlet fever which he avers has invariably proved successful. It is very simple, and lies within the reach of those whose limited means preclude them from employing the services of a physician. It is this: Take an onion, and cut it in halves; cut out a portion of the center, and into the cavity put a spoonful of saffron; put the pieces together, then wrap in cloth and bake in an oven until the onion is cooked so that the juice will run freely, then squeeze out all the juice, and give the patient a tea-spoonful, at the same time rubbing the chest and throat with goose grease or rancid bacon, if there is any cough or soreness in the throat. In a short time the fever will break out in an eruption all over the body. All that is then necessary is to keep the patient warm, and protected from draught, and recovery is certain. Mr. Christie says he has been employing this remedy for many years, and never knew it to fail, when proper care was taken of the patient after its application. One family, in which there were five children down with the disease at one time, recently, used this simple remedy upon his telling them of it, and every one of the little ones recovered in a short time.

(2) An eminent physician says he cures ninety-nine out of every hundred cases of scarlet fever, by giving the patient warm lemonade with gum arabic dissolved in it. A cloth wrung out in hot water and laid upon the stomach, should be removed as rapidly as it becomes cool.

Ivy Poisoning.—(1) Dr. Benjamin Edson, of Brooklyn, has had much experience with cases of poisoning by poison ivy, *Rhus Toxicodendron*. He is familiar with alkali and other washes usually employed in their treatment and considers them of little, if any, value. He has treated some severe cases, he states in the *Medical Record*, with fluid extract of gelsemium with uniformly the best results. As most of our readers know, gelsemium is the yellow jessamine of the South. The extract was employed in a wash made by mixing together a half drachm of carbolic acid, two drachms of the fluid extract of gelsemium, one-half ounce of glycerine and four ounces of water. With this cloths were kept moistened and applied to the parts affected. Two drops of the fluid extract of gelsemium was also given internally every three hours. Some cases were also treated with the same mixture with the carbolic acid omitted, and these yielded no less promptly than the others.

(2) Bathe the parts affected with sweet spirits of niter. If the blisters are broken so that the niter be allowed to penetrate the cuticle, more than a single application is rarely necessary, and even where it is only applied to the surface of the skin three or four times a day, there is rarely a trace of the poison left next morning.

(3) A wash made from the spotted alder is recommended for ivy poison-

ing. Also the shop water of a blacksmith's trough as a sure cure for poison ivy, and dogwood and strong salt and water as an antidote for the poisoning of sumach.

Nose Bleed.—(1) Snuffing up powdered alum will generally control troublesome bleeding from the nose. It will also almost always stop excessive hemorrhage from a cavity caused by the extraction of a tooth, by being placed in it.

(2) The best remedy for bleeding at the nose, as given by Dr. Gleason in one of his lectures, is in the vigorous motion of the jaws, as if in the act of mastication. In the case of a child, a wad of paper should be placed in its mouth, and the child should be instructed to chew it hard. It is the motion of the jaws that stops the flow of blood. This remedy is so very simple that many will feel inclined to laugh at it, but it has never been known to fail in a single instance, even in very severe cases.

(3) Lint, dipped in the nettle juice and put up the nostril, has been known to stay the bleeding of the nose when all other remedies have failed; fourteen or fifteen of the seeds, ground into powder and taken daily, will cure the swelling of the neck, known by the name of *goitre*, without in any way injuring the general health.

(4) Bleeding from the nose may be stopped by pressing the nostrils together for some minutes. Ice applied to the bridge of the nose or nape of the neck; snuffing up into the nostrils ice-water, vinegar, or gum-arabic powder, are all of them available means to check the effusion.

Baldness.—(1) A gentleman who had lost nearly all his hair after a very severe attack of fever, consulted a French physician of great reputed success as a hair restorer. The prescription given him was a drachm of homeopathic tincture of phosphorus to one ounce of castor oil; the bare spot he rubbed two times weekly, for half an hour each time, after the skin of the head had been thoroughly cleansed with warm water without soap. The treatment was faithfully carried out about six months; the hair soon began to grow, and, in a year from the time of following the doctor's advice, his head was as thoroughly covered as ever, the new hair being about two shades darker than the old.

(2) In two ounces of spirits of wine steep two drachms of cantharides (pulverized) for a fortnight or three weeks, shaking it repeatedly during that time. Then filter it, and rub up one-tenth of the tincture so procured, with nine-tenths of cold hog's lard. Scent it with a few drops of any kind of perfume, and rub it well into the head every morning and evening.

(3) Hair, removed by fevers and other sickness, is made to grow by washing the scalp with a strong decoction of sage leaves once or twice a day.

Small Pox.—(1) The following remedy for this loathsome disease is very simple, and on the authority of a surgeon of the British army of China, it is said to be a thorough cure, even in extreme cases: When the preceding fever is at its height, and just before the eruption appears, the chest is rubbed with croton oil and tartaric ointment. This causes the whole eruption to appear on that part of the body, to the relief of the rest. It also secures a full and complete eruption, and thus prevents the disease from attacking the internal organs.

(2) The following will cure not only small pox, but also scarlet fever. It is harmless when taken by a person in health: Sulphate of zinc, one grain; foxglove (digitalis), one grain; half a teaspoonful of sugar; mix with two

tablespoonfuls of water. When thoroughly mixed add four ounces of water. Take a spoonful every hour. Either disease will disappear in twelve hours. For a child, smaller doses, according to the age. If countries would compel their physicians to use this there would be no need of a pest house.

(3) "I am willing to risk my reputation as a public man," wrote Edward Hine to the *Liverpool Mercury*, "if the worst case of small pox cannot be cured in three days, simply by the use of cream of tartar. One ounce of cream of tartar, dissolved in a pint of water, drank at intervals when cold, is a certain never-failing remedy. It has cured thousands, never leaves a mark, never causes blindness, and avoids tedious lingering."

Sleeplessness.—(1) Nervous persons, who are troubled with wakefulness and excitability, usually have a strong tendency of blood to the brain, with cold extremities. The pressure of the blood on the brain keeps it in a stimulated, or wakeful state, and the pulsations in the head are often painful. Let such rise and chafe the body and extremities with a brush or towel, or rub smartly with the hands, to promote circulation, and withdraw the excessive amount of blood from the brain, and they will fall asleep in a few moments. A cold bath, or a sponge bath and rubbing, or a good run, or rapid walk in the open air, or going up or down stairs a few times just before retiring, will aid in equalizing circulation and promoting sleep. These rules are simple and easy of application, in castle or cabin.

(2) A little English work, "Sleep and How to obtain it," says that insomnia is not so dangerous as is commonly supposed, for the author knows an eminent man of letters who has suffered from it for many years without injury. When a man begins to dream of his work he may know that he is under too great a mental strain. The author's plan of inducing sleep is to reckon up friends and acquaintances whose name begins with a certain letter.

(3) If troubled with wakefulness on retiring to bed, eat three or four small onions; they will act as a gentle and soothing narcotic. Onions are also excellent to eat when one is much exposed to cold.

Ringworm.—(1) Oil of paper made by burning a sheet of ordinary writing paper upon a plate, will cure a ringworm, which is caused by contagion or some impurity in the blood; the oil will be seen after the paper is burned in the form of a yellow spot; this applied with the finger twice a day will in a very short time cure the worst of ringworms.

(2) Tincture of iodine, painted over a ringworm, for three or four days in succession, will entirely cure it in a few days. It stains the skin considerably whenever it is applied, and this is the only objection to it. Those who object to this need not use it; they may keep the ringworm. The stain goes off in a few days.

(3) Heat a shovel to a bright red, cover it with grains of Indian corn, press them with a cold flat iron. They will burn to a coal and exude an oil on the surface of the flat iron, with which rub the ring, and after one or two applications it will gradually disappear.

(4) Make a curd by mixing alum and the white of an egg over a fire until it is the consistency of pomatum; spread over the ringworm. One or two applications should effect a cure.

(5) Simple cerate, one pound; dilated sulphuric acid, one-quarter of a pound. Mix and apply.

(6) To   part of sulphuric acid add sixteen parts of water. Use a brush or feather, and apply it to the parts night and morning. If the solution prove too strong, add a little more water. If the irritation is excessive, apply a little glycerine. Avoid the use of soap.

Chilblains.—(1) Slice raw potatoes, with the skins on, and sprinkle over them a little salt, and as soon as the liquid therefrom settles in the bottom of the dish, wash with it the chilblains; one application is all that is necessary.

(2) An unfailing remedy for chilblains: A solution of thirty grains of permanganate of potassa in an ounce of pure water, to be applied thoroughly with brush or swab, or in the form of a poultice.

(3) Rub the part affected with brandy and salt, which hardens the feet at the same time that it removes the inflammation. Sometimes a third application cures the most obstinate chilblains.

(4) To relieve the intense itching of frosted feet, dissolve a lump of alum in a little water, and bathe the part with it, warming it before the fire. One or two applications is sure to give relief.

(5) Put the hands and feet once a week into hot water, in which two or three handfuls of common salt have been thrown. This is a certain preventive as well as a cure.

(6) In the evening, before retiring, take salt and vinegar made as hot as can be borne on the parts affected; bathe with a small cloth, and do so until cured.

(7) Mix together one ounce of turpentine and three-eighths of an ounce of oil of sassafras. Apply the solution morning and evening.

Costiveness.—(1) Bread and milk, though excellent for children in general, is not as good food for a costive child as bread made of corn-meal or graham flour. Wheat bread is not good for a very costive child. When medicine becomes necessary, a teaspoonful of magnesia dissolved in sweetened milk or water, and given morning and night, until the bowels become regular, is usually sufficient. Purgatives should be carefully avoided, except for a disordered stomach, and then they become necessary. Well-ventilated sleeping-rooms, and frequent bathing, go further than most people suppose, toward keeping the body in a healthy condition. To mothers who nurse their infants, we say, if the mother is regular, the child will be, and the reverse. Therefore, instead of dosing a child with medicine, let her diet for the evil, and save her little one much suffering. A lady correspondent some time since wrote us: "I have used, with much benefit, the herb known as thoroughwort, prepared by putting the dried herb in water and letting it stand until it becomes bitter. A portion drank before each meal, has proved the best remedy for costiveness I ever used."

(2) Common charcoal is highly recommended for costiveness. It may be taken either in tea or tablespoonful, or even larger doses, according to the exigencies of the case, mixed with molasses, repeating it as often as necessary. Bathe the bowels with pepper and vinegar. Or take two ounces of rhubarb, add one ounce of rust of iron, infuse in one quart of wine. Half a wineglassful every morning. Or take pulverized blood-root, one drachm; pulverized rhubarb, one drachm; Castile soap, two scruples. Mix and roll into thirty-two pills. Take one morning and night. By following these directions it may perhaps save you from a severe attack of piles, or some other kindred disease.

Cholera Morbus.—(1) The following is the recipe for the celebrated "Sun Cholera Mixture": Take equal parts of tincture of opium, tincture of capsicum, rhubarb, peppermint, and camphor, and mix. Dose from fifteen to twenty drops in four tablespoonfuls of water. Repeat the dose every half hour till relieved. This is also an excellent remedy for any ordinary laxity of the bowels, or summer complaint. In that case one dose, as above prescribed, twice in every 24 hours, will suffice for a cure, if taken in time.

(2) For cholera morbus, take black pepper and grind it tolerably fine. Then put in a glass a tablespoonful of this and a tablespoonful of salt, and fill about half full with warm water, then fill up the glass with good cider vinegar, and stir it up. Now take one tablespoonful, and then wait a little and take another, and keep on stirring and using it while the vomiting lasts. If one glass does not cure, try another.

(3) (Said to be a certain cure).—The ingredients are: One glassful of West India rum, one glassful of molasses, one glassful of spring water, and three tablespoonfuls of ginger. Mix them altogether and take it. It is said to afford immediate relief.

To Restore the Drowning.—The rules that ought to be observed in treating a person rescued from the water are few and simple. Dr. H. R. Silvester's methods of restoring the apparently dead or drowned—which have been approved by the royal medical and chirurgical society—are practical, easily understood, and are in accordance with common sense. The one important point to be aimed at is, of course, the restoration of breathing, and the efforts to accomplish this should be persevered in until the arrival of medical assistance, or until the pulse and breath have ceased for at least an hour. Cleanse the mouth and nostrils; open the mouth; draw forward the patient's tongue with a handkerchief, and keep it forward; remove all tight clothing from about the neck and chest. As to the patient's position, place him on his back on a flat surface, inclined a little from the feet upward; raise and support the head and shoulders on a small, firm cushion or folded article of dress placed under the shoulder blades. Then grasp the arms just above the elbows, and draw the arms gently and steadily upward, until they meet above the head (this is for the purpose of drawing air into the lungs); and keep the arms in that position for two seconds. Then turn down the patient's arms, and press them gently and firmly for two seconds against the sides of the chest (with the object of pressing air out of the lungs; pressure on the breast bone will aid this). Repeat these measures alternately, deliberately and perseveringly, fifteen times in a minute, until a spontaneous effort to respire is perceived, upon which cease to imitate the movements of breathing, and proceed to induce circulation and warmth. This may be done by wrapping the patient in dry blankets and rubbing the limbs upward, firmly and energetically. Promote the warmth of the body by the application of hot flannels, bottles of hot water, etc., to the pit of the stomach, the arm-pits, and to the soles of the feet. Warm clothing may generally be obtained from a bystander. On the restoration of life, stimulants should be given, and a disposition to sleep encouraged.

Bright's Disease.—Dr. Alex. De Borra, of Crystal Springs, N. Y., writes that, after years of practical test of the milk diet for Bright's disease, he has a long list of cases in which he has made perfect cures. Great care is taken to get absolutely pure skimmed milk, from healthy and well-fed cows, and no other food of any kind is given after the patient can bear five pints of milk a day. Up to this point, and until the stomach is able to take care of so much, is found to be the most trying period in this treatment, but no other medicine is given, and hand and hair-glove rubbing is daily administered.

Another correspondent takes exception to the claim made that no drug of any therapeutic value in that disease has yet been discovered. In support of his assertion he sends us a recipe which he claims has effected a cure in Bright's disease, as well as in dropsy, in every case in which it has been tried during the last fifteen years. He recommends the drinking of an infusion of the dry pods of the common white soup bean or corn bean. When the latter cannot be readily obtained, the pods of the "snap short" bean will answer, and even the Lima bean, though the latter is of inferior strength. The recipe is as follows: "Take a double handful of the pods to three quarts of water; boil slowly for three hours until it is reduced to three pints. Use no drink of any kind but this, the patient drinking as much as he conveniently can; it may be taken either hot or cold."

Hot Water as a Remedy.—There is no remedy of such general application and none so easily attainable as water, and yet nine persons in ten will pass by it in an emergency to seek for something of far less efficacy.

There are but few cases of illness where water should not occupy the highest place as a remedial agent.

A strip of flannel or a napkin folded lengthwise and dipped in hot water and wrung out and then applied around the neck of a child that has the croup will usually bring relief in ten minutes.

A towel folded several times and dipped in hot water and quickly wrung and applied over the seat of the pain in toothache or neuralgia will generally afford prompt relief. This treatment in colic works like magic. I have seen cases that have resisted other treatment for hours yield to this in ten minutes. There is nothing that will so promptly cut short a congestion of the lungs, sore throat or rheumatism as hot water when applied promptly and thoroughly.

Pieces of cotton batting dipped in hot water and kept applied to old sores or new cuts, bruises and sprains, is the treatment now generally adopted in hospitals. I have seen a sprained ankle cured in an hour by showering it with hot water, poured from a height of three feet.

Tepid water acts promptly as an emetic, and hot water taken freely half an hour before bedtime is the best of cathartics in the case of constipation, while it has a most soothing effect on the stomach and bowels. This treatment continued for a few months, with proper attention to diet, will cure any curable case of dyspepsia.

To Remove Superfluous Hairs.—Some few hairs will frequently grow where they are not wanted, and are often difficult to get rid of Close shaving and cutting strengthens them and increases their number; the only plan is to pull them out individually with a pair of tweezers, and afterward to dress the part two or three times a day in the following manner: Wash it first with warm, soft water, but do not use soap; then apply with a piece of soft rag, immediately after the washing, a lotion of milk of roses, made according to the following directions, and rub the skin gently till it is dry with a warm, soft cloth: Beat four ounces of sweet almonds in a mortar to a paste with half an ounce of white sugar; then work in, in small quantities, eight ounces of rosewater; strain the emulsion through muslin, put the liquid into a bottle, return the residuum to the mortar, pound it again, and add half an ounce of sugar and eight ounces of rosewater; then strain again, and repeat the process a third time. This will give thirty-two ounces of fluid, to which add twenty grains of bichloride of mercury dissolved in two ounces of alcohol. Shake the whole for five minutes, and the lotion will be ready for use.

Convulsions.—Dr. Williamson reports an interesting and remarkable case in which he saved the life of an infant in convulsions by the use of chloroform. He commenced the use of it at nine o'clock one evening, at which period the child was rapidly sinking, numerous remedies having been already tried without effect. He dropped half a drachm of chloroform into a thin muslin handkerchief, and held it about an inch from the infant's face. In about two minutes the convulsions gave way, and the child fell into a sleep. By slightly releasing the child from the influence of the chloroform, he was able to administer food by which the child was nourished and strengthened. The chloroform was continually administered in the manner described, from Friday evening at nine o'clock until Monday morning at nine. This treatment lasted sixty hours, and sixteen ounces of chloroform were used. Dr. Williamson says he has no doubt that the chloroform was instrumental in saving the infant's life; and that no injurious effects, however trivial, from the treatment adopted, have subsequently appeared.

Mumps.—This disease, most common among children, begins with soreness and stiffness in the side of the neck. Soon a swelling of the parotid gland takes place, which is painful and continues to increase for four or five days, sometimes making it difficult to swallow, or open the mouth. The swelling sometimes comes on one side at a time, but commonly upon both. There is often heat and sometimes fever, with a dry skin, quick pulse, furred tongue, constipated bowels, and scanty and high-colored urine. The disease is contagious.

Treatment.—Keep the face and neck warm, and avoid taking cold. Drink warm herb teas, and if the symptoms are severe, four to six grains of Dover's powder; or if there is costiveness, a slight physic, and observe a very simple diet. If the disease is aggravated by taking cold, and is very severe, or is translated to other glands, physic must be used freely, leeches applied to the swelling, or cooling poultices. Sweating must be resorted to in this case.

To Ascertain the State of the Lungs.—Draw in as much breath as you conveniently can, then count as long as possible in a slow and audible voice without drawing in more breath. The number of seconds must be carefully noted. In a consumptive the time does not exceed ten, and is frequently less than six seconds; in pleurisy and pneumonia it ranges from nine to four seconds. When the lungs are sound the time will range as high as from twenty to thirty-five seconds. To expand the lungs, go into the air, stand erect, throw back the head and shoulders, and draw in the air through the nostrils as much as possible. After having then filled the lungs, raise your arms, still extended, and suck in the air. When you have thus forced the arms backward, with the chest open, change the process by which you draw in your breath, till the lungs are emptied. Go through the process several times a day and it will enlarge the chest, give the lungs better play, and serve very much to ward off consumption.

Hysterics.—This complaint is confined chiefly to females. A fit of hysterics is generally the result of some natural and immediate cause, and until this is discovered and removed, the patient will always be subject to these fits. When a person is seized with a fit the dress should be loosened, fresh air admitted, cold water dashed in the face, and salts or singed feathers applied to the nostrils. If consciousness does not then return, a draught of sal-volatile and water should be given, and if the patient be still insensible, the temples and the nape of the neck should be rubbed with brandy. When hysterics can be traced to impaired natural action, equal portions of pennyroyal and wormwood should be steeped in boiling water, and suffered to simmer by the fire until the virtue of the herbs is extracted. It should then be allowed to cool, and half a pint be taken twice or thrice a day, succeeded on each occasion by a compound asafœtida pill, until the desired relief is afforded.

Colic.—(1) For the violent internal agony termed colic, take a teaspoonful of salt in a pint of water; drink and go to bed. It is one of the speediest remedies known. It will revive a person who seems almost dead from a heavy fall.

(2) Phares's method of treating colic consists in inversion—simply in turning the patient upside down. Colic of several days' duration has been relieved by this means in a few minutes.

(3) Dr. Tepliashin has recommended a thin stream of cold water from a teapot lifted from one to one and a half feet from the abdomen, in cases of colic. He has seen it relieve pain when opium and morphia had failed.

(4) A loaf of bread, hot from the oven, broken in two, and half of it placed upon the bowels, and the other half opposite it upon the back, will relieve colic from whatever cause almost immediately.

The Earliest Sign of Consumption.—A quick pulse and a short breath, continuing for weeks together, is the great alarm bell of forming consumption; if these symptoms are attended with a gradual falling off in flesh, in the course of months, there is no rational ground for doubt, although the hack of a cough may never have been heard. Under such circumstances, there ought not to be an hour's delay in taking competent medical advice.

The vast mass of consumptives die, not far from the ages of twenty-five; and this, in connection with another fact, that consumption is several years in running its course, suggests one of the most important practical conclusions yet announced, to wit:

In the large majority of cases, the seeds of consumption are sown between the ages of sixteen and twenty-one years, when the steadily excited pulse and the easily accelerated breathing, may readily be detected by an intelligent and observant parent, and should be regarded as the knell of death, if not arrested, and yet it is easily, and uniformly done, for the spirometer will demonstrate the early danger, and the educated physician will be at no loss to mark out the remedy.

The quick pulse and short breath go together; rather " easily put out of breath," is the more common and appropriate expression.

Sciatica.—An English officer, who served with distinction in the war with Napoleon, was once laid up in a small village in France, with a severe attack of sciatica. It so happened that at that time, a tinman was being employed at the hotel where he lodged, and that this tinman, having been himself a soldier, took an interest in the officer's case, and gave him the cure which in this instance succeeded immediately and forever, and which

I am about to set down. It is at any rate so simple as to be worth a trial: Take a moderate size potato, rather large than small, and boil it in one quart of water. Foment the part affected with the water in which the potato has been boiled as hot as it can be borne at night before going to bed; then crush the potato and put it on the affected part as a poultice. Wear this all night and in the morning heat the water, which should have been preserved, over again, and again foment the part with it as hot as can be borne. This treatment must be persevered with for several days. It occasionally requires to be continued for as much as two or three weeks, but in the shorter or longer time it has never yet failed to be successful.

Biliousness.—If the victims of this diseased condition will exercise due care, they need not ransack creation for " anti-bilious pills." The bile does not belong in the stomach, but reaches there in consequence of improper food, too much of the oily, as butter, pork, lard, etc. The bile is nature's grand cathartic medicine, passing from the liver in a direction to indicate that it is to pass on into the bowels, there to perform its important mission. When the liver is overtaxed by too much labor, or by the presence of too much greasy food, digestion is impaired and the whole system becomes out of order.

If one would avoid biliousness, let him fast, passing over one or more meals. As soon as the " mouth tastes bad," the tongue is coated, the appetite flags— the best possible evidence that too much food has been taken— thus allowing nature to rally, the accumulated food to pass off, and the system be relieved. In nine cases out of ten, this fasting will remove the difficulty, save a fit of sickness, and cheat the doctor. Any quack nostrum that will do as much as fasting, would yield a fortune to the inventor. Many of them, however, if not most, increase disease, rather than improve health.

Hints About Glasses.—Persons finding their eyes becoming dry and itching on reading, as well as those who find it necessary to place an object nearer than fourteen inches from their faces to read, need spectacles. Persons under forty years of age should not wear glasses until the accommodating power of the eyes has been suspended and the exact state of refraction determined by a competent ophthalmic surgeon. The spectacle glasses sold by peddlers and by jewelers generally are hurtful to the eyes of those who read much, as the lenses are made of inferior sheet glass and not symmetrically ground. No matter how perfectly the lenses may be made, unless they are mounted in a suitable frame and properly placed before the eye, discomfort will arise from their prolonged use.

Persons holding objects too near the face endanger the safety of their eyes, and incur the risk of becoming near sighted.

The near sighted eye is an unsound eye, and should be fully corrected with a glass, notwithstanding the fact it may need no aid for reading. The proper time to begin wearing glasses is just as soon as the eyes tire on being subjected to prolonged use.

Nettle Rash.—This disease takes its name from its being attended by an eruption similar to what is produced by the stinging of nettles. The causes of this complaint are by no means obvious; but it seems to proceed either from the perspiration being checked, or from some irritating matter in the stomach. In all cases there prevails considerable itching and some heat in the parts affected; and in some constitutions a slight degree of fever either precedes or attends the eruption. Its duration seldom exceeds three or four days.

In some cases nettle rash is accompanied with large wheals or bumps, which appear of a solid nature, without any cavity or head, containing either water or other fluid.

Half a teaspoonful of magnesia, and the same quantity of cream of tartar mixed in half a teacupful of milk, an hour before breakfast, and repeated as required, will be found very efficacious.

Coffee and Typhoid Fever.—Dr. Guillasse, of the French navy, in a recent paper on typhoid fever, speaks of the great benefit which has been derived from the use of coffee. He has found that no sooner have the patients taken a few tablespoonfuls of it than their features become relaxed and they come to their senses; next day the improvement is such as to leave no doubt that the article is just the specific needed. Under its influence the stupor is dispelled and the patient rouses from the state of somnolency in which he has been since the invasion of the disease; soon, all the functions take their natural course, and he enters upon convalescence. Dr. Guillasse gives to an adult two or three tablespoonfuls of strong black coffee every two or three hours, alternated with one or two teaspoonfuls of claret or Burgundy wine—a little lemonade or citrate of magnesia to be taken daily; after a while quinine.

Ingrowing Toe Nails.—As this is a very painful malady, it may be worth a great deal to some of our readers to know that the trouble is not with the nail, but with the flesh, which gets pushed upon it, thereby becoming inflamed, and the inflammation and swelling are kept up by the presence of the nail, which then acts as a foreign body. To cure it, take the neighboring toe—which, by the way, is really the offender—and with it press the swollen flesh down and away from the nail, then bind the two firmly together with adhesive strips, which may be had at any drug store. If the strips get loose, and the flesh slips up on the nail again, readjust the toes and put on fresh plaster until the flesh rehabituates itself to its former place.

Abscess.—In some particulars an abscess resembles a large boil. There is an inflammatory condition, with heat, pain, and swelling. The result of this inflammation is the discharge of degenerated matter or pus. They may be opened as soon as pulsation is detected, the same as boils, or the operation may be delayed until by using hot water compresses, flax seed poultice, bread and hot milk poultice, they come to a point or head. The matter or pus should be completely discharged by gentle pressure, and the cavity freely washed out by injecting a mixture of one part carbolic acid and twenty of warm water, and pressure exerted by a bandage, when healing will rapidly take place.

Blistered Hands or Feet.—When the hands are blistered from rowing or the feet from walking or other causes, be careful not to allow the blisters to break, if possible. Some persons are in the habit, by means of a needle and piece of worsted, of placing a seton into blisters to draw off the water; but in our opinion this is a great mistake and retards the healing. Bathe the blisters frequently in warm water, or if they are very severe, make a salve of tallow, dropped from a lighted candle into a little gin and worked up to a proper consistence, and on going to bed cover the blisters with this salve and place a piece of clean soft rag over them.

Stammering.—No stammering person ever found any difficulty in singing. The reason of this is, that by observing the measure of the music—by keeping time—the organs of speech are kept in such position that enunciation is easy. Apply the same rule to reading or speech, and the same result will follow. Let the stammerer take a sentence, say this one—"Leander swam the Hellespont," and pronounce it by syllables, scan it, keeping time with his finger if necessary, letting each syllable occupy the same time, thus, Le-an-der-swam-the-Hel-les-pont, and he will not stammer. Pronounce slowly at first, then faster, but still keeping time; keeping time with words instead of syllables. Practice this in reading and conversation until the habit is broken up. Perseverance and attention is all that is necessary to perform a perfect cure.

Hemorrhage.—(1) Hemorrhage of the lungs can be instantly cured by throwing into the mouth of the patient, from a vial, one or two teaspoonfuls of chloroform, according to the severeness of the attack. It will give instant relief to the greatest suffering, and stop the most severe case of bleeding of the lungs.

(2) To stop hemorrhage of the lungs, cord the thighs, and arms above the elbow, with small, strong cords tightly drawn and tied. It will stop the flow of blood almost instantly, as it has done for the writer many times. It was recommended by a physician of experience.

(3) Spitting or vomiting of blood may be stopped by sage juice mixed with a little honey. Take three teaspoonfuls, and repeat, if necessary, in about fifteen minutes.

(4) Hemorrhages of the lungs or stomach are promptly checked by small doses of salt. The patient should be kept as quiet as possible.

Asthma.—(1) The asthma, writes a correspondent, may be relieved, if not cured, by the following treatment: "Buy of the druggist five cents' worth of saltpeter, and get also a sheet or two of grayish paper, which druggists have, thick like the common brown paper. Dissolve the saltpeter in half a pint of rain water, and saturate strips of the paper in the water, and dry it in pans or on plates. Now roll them up like lamp lighters. When a paroxysm comes on, light one and inhale the fumes. If necessary throw a cloth or shawl over the head. If the saltpeter is very strong it may fuse a little. If the paper described cannot be got, brown paper may be used instead, but the smoke of the former is purer."

(2) The following mixture is recommended as a relief for the asthmatic: Two ounces of the best honey, and one ounce of castor oil mixed. A teaspoonful to be taken night and morning. I have tried the foregoing with the best effect.

Hydrophobia.—(1) Elecampane is a plant well known to most persons, and is to be found in many of our gardens. Immediately after being bitten, take one ounce of the root of the plant, the green root is perhaps preferable, but the dried will answer, and may be found in our drug stores, slice or bruise, put in a pint of fresh milk, boil down to half a pint, strain, and when cold drink it, fasting at least six hours afterward. The next morning repeat the dose prepared as the last, and this will be sufficient. It is recommended that after each dose nothing be eaten for at least six hours.

(2) The following is said to be a cure for hydrophobia: Take two tablespoonfuls of fresh chloride of lime, mix it with one-half pint of water, and with this wash keep the wound constantly bathed and frequently renewed.

The chloride gas possesses the power of decomposing the tremendous poison, and renders mild and harmless that venom against whose resistless attack the artillery of medical science has been so long directed in vain. It is necessary to add that this wash must be applied as soon as possible.

Scrofula.—(1) Yellow dock root has proved very useful in scrofula. It is given in powder or decoction. Two ounces of the fresh root bruised, or one ounce of the dried, may be boiled in a pint of water, of which two fluid ounces may be given at a dose, and repeated as the stomach will bear. The root has also been applied externally in the shape of ointment, cataplasm, and decoction, to the cutaneous eruptions and ulcerations for which it has been used internally. The powdered root is also recommended as a dentifrice, especially when the gums are spongy. There is no doubt that in a great many cases the disease is inherited; some contend that it is so in all cases. It shows itself in various forms—as hip-disease, white swelling, rickets, salt rheum, etc. Persons affected by it are subject to swelling of the glands, particularly those of the neck.

(2) A tea made of ripe, dried whortleberries, and drank in place of water, is a sure and speedy cure for scrofula difficulties, however bad.

Sickness of Stomach.—(1) The following drink for relieving sickness of the stomach was introduced by Dr. Halahan, and is said to be very palatable and agreeable: "Beat up one egg very well, say for twenty minutes; then add fresh milk, one pint; water, one pint; sugar, to make it palatable; boil, and let it cool; drink when cold. If it becomes curds and whey it is useless.

(2) Salts of tartar, thirty grains; oil of mint, six drops; powdered gum arabic, eighth of an ounce; powdered loaf sugar, eighth of an ounce; water, six ounces. A tablespoonful of this mixture is a dose.

(3) Sickness of the stomach is most promptly relieved by drinking a teacupful of hot soda and water. If it brings all the offending matter up all the better.

Bronchitis.—(1) Get from the druggist's a little good wood creosote. Put two drops of it into a bottle holding a pint or so. Pour in a little more than half a pint of clear water, and shake it well; shake well always before using it. Take a mouthful of this, throw the head back, gargle it some time in the throat, and then swallow it. Repeat this every two hours, more or less, so as to use up the liquid within twenty-four hours. For each subsequent twenty-four hours, use three drops of the creosote in three to four gills of water. This three drops a day may be continued as long as any bronchitis appears. Two to four days is usually enough, though it may be continued indefinitely without harm.

(2) A simple, but oftentimes efficacious remedy, is this. It may afford relief: Syrup of tolu, one ounce; syrup of squills, half an ounce; wine of ipecac, two drachms; paregoric, three drachms; mucilage of gum arabic, one and a half ounces. Mix. Take a teaspoonful three times a day.

(3) A simple recipe, which affords relief in ordinary cases of bronchitis, is to occasionally suck a small piece of common saltpetre as you would candy, and swallow the juice. If the case be severe, medical advice should be had without delay.

Lockjaw.—(1) If any person is threatened or taken with lockjaw from injuries of the arms, legs or feet, do not wait for a doctor, but put the part injured in the following preparation: Put hot wood ashes into water as warm as can be borne; if the injured part cannot be put into water, then wet thick folded cloths in the water and apply them to the part as soon as possible, and at the same time bathe the backbone from the neck down with some laxative stimulant—say cayenne pepper and water, or mustard and water (good vinegar is better than water); it should be as hot as the patient can bear it. Don't hesitate; go to work and do it, and don't stop until the jaws will come open. No person need die of lockjaw if these directions are followed.

(2) The following is said to be a positive cure: Let any one who has an attack of the lockjaw take a small quantity of spirits of turpentine, warm it and pour it on the wound, no matter where the wound is or what is its nature. Relief will follow in less than one minute. Turpentine is also a sovereign remedy for croup. Saturate a piece of flannel with it and place on to the throat, chest, and, in severe cases, three to five drops, on a lump of sugar may be taken internally.

Erysipelas.—(1) We have found sour milk, buttermilk, or whey therefrom, an excellent remedy to apply for the erysipelas as a wash. Also to apply glycerine twice or three times a day; it has a soothing effect. We have many times applied the milk hot, and found it allayed the inflammation better than cold applications, and far less troublesome than poultices.

(2) Erysipelas is of two kinds—one affecting principally the skin, the other the whole system. In mild cases, affecting the skin only, lemonade made from the fresh fruit helps the patient very much, being, in addition, very grateful to the palate.

(3) As a local application, slippery elm has been found efficacious. Make a mucilage of it, and apply it warm on cloths to the face. Sometimes common flour, dusted on the inflamed parts, will afford relief.

(4) One pint of sweet milk and a handful of pokeberry roots. This is a sure cure.

(5) Make a poultice of cranberries, and apply to the face.

Hoarseness.—(1) Horseradish will afford instantaneous relief in most obstinate cases of hoarseness. The root, of course, possesses the most virtue, though the leaves are good till they dry, when they lose their strength. The root is best when it is green. The person who will use it freely just before beginning to speak, will not be troubled with hoarseness. Boiled down and sweetened into a thick syrup, will give relief in the severest cases.

(2) Take a small quantity of dry, powdered borax, place it on the tongue, let it slowly dissolve and run down the throat. It is also good to keep the throat moist at night and prevent coughing.

(3) Hoarseness and tickling in the throat are best relieved by the gargle of the white of an egg beaten to a froth in half a glass of warmed, sweetened water.

Chills and Fever.—(1) One-half ounce spirits nitre, one-half ounce tincture pepper, thirty-five grains quinine, one pint of brandy. Take a wineglassful three times a day, one-half hour before meals. If for a child, give only half the quantity.

(2) If you have chills and fever, express the juice of three large lemons and drink it down. Continue so to do every other day until the disease is broken. We have known this treatment to cure when quinine had no effect.

(3) The following is said to be a remedy for fever and ague: Twenty-four grains of quinine, two drachms of elixir of vitriol, twenty-two large tablespoonfuls of rain water. Dose, take each half hour through the day until taken up.

(4) Dissolve fifteen grains of citric acid in a cup of hot coffee, and drink it just before the chill attacks you. It has been known to cure the worst cases of this disease.

Dropsy.—(1) Take one pint of bruised mustard seed, two handfuls of bruised horseradish root, eight ounces of lignumvitæ chips, and four ounces of bruised Indian hemp root. Put all the ingredients in seven quarts of cider, and let it simmer over a slow fire until it is reduced to four quarts. Strain the decoction, and take a wineglassful four times a day for a few days, increasing the dose to a small teacupful three times a day. After which use tonic medicines. This remedy has cured cases of dropsy in one week's time which has baffled the skill of many eminent physicians. For children the dose should be smaller.

(2) The ingredients are: Acetate of squills, one ounce; nitrate of potash, sixty grains; water, five ounces. Dose: A tablespoonful every two hours.

(3) It is said that a tea made of chestnut leaves, and drank in the place of water, will cure the most obstinate case of dropsy in a few days.

Bunions.—(1) Let fall a stream of very warm water from a teakettle, at the highest elevation from which the patient can bear the water to fall directly on the apex of the swelling; continue this once a day for a short time and a cure will be effected, providing you desist from wearing short shoes. The greater the elevation of the kettle, the more effectual the remedy.

(2) It is said that the following is a good bunion remedy: Use pulverized saltpetre and sweet oil; obtain at the druggist's five or six cents' worth of saltpetre, put into a bottle with sufficient olive oil to nearly dissolve it; shake up well, and rub the inflamed joints night and morning, and more frequently if painful. This is a well-tried remedy.

(3) When the bunion is painful, put three or four leeches on the joint of the toe, and do not disturb them till they drop off; then bathe the bunions twice a day in fresh cream, and afterward renounce tight boots. Of course this remedy will not remove the swelling of the bone.

Fits.—(1) When these are brought on by indigestion, place the child in a warm bath immediately, give warm water, or a lobelia emetic, rub the skin briskly, etc., to get up an action. In brain disease the warm water is equally useful. In fact, unless the fit is constitutional, the warm bath will relieve the patient by drawing the blood to the surface.

(2) Fits can be instantly cured by throwing a spoonful of fine salt as far back into the mouth of the patient as possible, just as the fit comes on.

Dandruff.—(1) A preparation of one ounce of sulphur and one quart of water, repeatedly agitated during intervals of a few hours, and the head saturated every morning with the clear liquid, will, in a few weeks, remove every trace of dandruff from the scalp, and the hair will soon become soft and glossy.

(2) There is no simpler or better remedy for this vegetatious appearance (caused by dryness of the skin) than a wash of camphor and borax—an ounce of each put into a pint and a half of cold water; and afterward rub a little pure oil into the scalp.

Scurf.—A lump of fresh quicklime the size of a walnut, dropped into a pint of water and allowed to stand all night, the water being then poured off from the sediment and mixed with a quarter of a pint of the best vinegar, forms the best wash for scurf in the head. It is to be applied to the roots of the hair.

(2) Half a pint of rose-water, and one ounce of spirits of wine mixed together. Part the hair as much as possible, and apply the mixture with a piece of flannel.

Quinsy.—(1) Our cure is tar spread on the throat and quite up under the ears. Cover with a cloth and go to sleep and wake up well. Only a brown stain will remain; it is easily washed off with castile soap. It is a sure relief. It is our opinion that in cases of incipient scarlet fever or diphtheria this is the remedy. It looks reasonable if it brings sure relief in quinsy, which it does.

(2) A teacupful of red sage leaves to one quart of water, boil ten minutes, add four tablespoonfuls of vinegar, and sweeten with honey. In the first stage of the disease, it might be used as a gargle, and then to rinse the mouth; it should be used warm. It will be found invaluable.

To Prevent Hydrophobia.—(1) The bites of mad dogs have been rendered harmless by immediately cauterizing the wound with a saturated solution of carbolic acid, and keeping it constantly wet with a weaker solution of the same, at the same time giving the patient, according to age, from two to six drops of the spirits of ammonia in water, every two hours for twelve or fourteen hours. The wound is not allowed to dry for an instant for three or four days.

(2) Take immediately warm vinegar, or tepid water, and wash the wound very clean; then dry it, and pour upon the wound a few drops of muriatic acid. Mineral acids destroy the poison of the saliva, and its evil effect is neutralized.

Heartburn.—(1) Relief will be obtained by using the following mixture, which has been much recommended: Juice of one orange, water, and lump sugar to flavor; and in proportion to the acidity of the orange, about half a teaspoonful of bi-carbonate of soda. Dissolve the sugar in the water, add the orange-juice, then put in the soda. Stir, and drink while effervescing.

(2) A small piece of chalk put in a pitcher of water, without imparting any taste whatever to the same, will exercise a corrective effect upon the stomachs of those who are troubled with acidity or heartburn, as it is called.

Inflammatory Rheumatism.—(1) Sulphur and saltpeter, of each one ounce; gum guaiacum, one-fourth ounce; colchicum root, or seed, and nutmegs, of each one-fourth ounce; all to be pulverized and mixed with simple syrup, or molasses, two ounces. Dose: One teaspoonful every two hours until it moves the bowels rather freely; then three or four times daily until cured.

(2) Half an ounce of pulverized saltpetre put in a half a pint of sweet oil; bathe the parts affected, and a sound cure will speedily be effected.

Stye on the Eyelid.—(1) Put a teaspoonful of tea in a small bag; pour on it just enough boiling water to moisten it; then put it on the eye pretty warm. Keep it on all night, and in the morning the stye will most likely be gone; if not, a second application is sure to remove it.

(2) Ice will check at first; if they do not suppurate quickly, apply warm poultices of bread and milk; prick them and apply citrine ointment.

(3) Dip a feather in the white of an egg, and pass it along the edge of the eyelids.

To Purify the Blood.—(1) A well-known physician says that he considers the following prescription for purifying the blood as the best he has ever used: One ounce yellow dock, one-half ounce horseradish, one quart hard cider. Dose, one wineglassful four times a day.

(2) Mix half an ounce sulphate of magnesia with one pint water. Dose, a wineglassful three times a day. This can be used in the place of iron tonic, or in connection with it.

For Liver Complaint.—(1) Twenty grains of extract of dandelion, divided into four pills, and to be taken four times a day; it acts on the liver, and is also a tonic for debilitated persons.

(2) A cup of fresh buttermilk every day is said to be a cure for liver complaint.

Cramps.—A correspondent gives the following directions for the relief of cramps: When the cramp is in the calf of the leg, draw up the foot strongly toward the shin bone, and in a few seconds the cramp will disappear. When they are in the thighs or arms, tie a towel, cord, or handkerchief around the limb, just above the cramped part, and then rub this part with the naked hand alone, or using some stimulating liniment like spirits of camphor or red-peppered whiskey. The preparation may also be rubbed upon the neck when cramps attack this part. Cramps in the stomach may be checked by first strongly rubbing and kneading over the stomach, and then rubbing upon and around the pit of the stomach a mixture of equal parts of sweet oil or linseed oil, essence of peppermint, laudanum, and spirits of camphor.

Petroleum in Pulmonary Diseases.—A partial investigation has been made of the alleged utility of this article in affections of the chest. The petroleum of Pennsylvania and Virginia was first experimented upon—a very safe substance, for even considerable quantities, when swallowed by error, have caused only a little nausea. It is found that in chronic bronchitis, with abundant expectoration, it rapidly diminishes the amount of secretion and the paroxysms of coughing, and in simple bronchitis rapid amelioration has been obtained. Its employment in phthisis has been continued for too short a time, as yet, to allow of any judgment being formed as to its efficiency, beyond that it diminishes the expectoration, which also loses its purulent character. The petroleum is customarily taken in doses of a teaspoonful before each meal, and, after the first day, any nausea which it may excite in some persons disappears.

Corpulence.—For those people whose fleshiness is a matter of solicitude, whether because it is uncomfortable or unfashionable, the following diet is proposed by Dr. George Johnson: May eat—Lean mutton and beef, veal and lamb, soups not thickened, beef tea and broth; poultry, game, fish, and eggs; bread in moderation, greens, cresses, lettuce, etc., green peas, cabbage, cauliflower, onions; fresh fruit without sugar. May not eat—Fat meat, bacon or ham, butter, cream, sugar, potatoes, carrots, parsnips, rice, sago, tapioca, macaroni, custard, pastry and puddings, sweet cakes. May drink—Tea, coffee, cocoa from nibs, with milk, but no sugar; dry wines in moderation without sugar; light bitter beer, soda and seltzer water. May not drink—Milk, except sparingly; porter and stout, sweet ales, sweet wines. As a rule, alcoholic liquors should be taken sparingly, and never without food.

Salt in Intermittent Fever.—Take a handful of table salt and roast in a clean oven with moderate heat till it is brown- the color of roasted coffee. Dose for an adult, a soupspoonful dissolved in a glass of warm water; take at once. When the fever appears at intervals of two, three, or four days, the remedy should be taken fasting on the morning of the day following the fever. To overcome the thirst, a very little water should be taken through a straw. During the forty-eight hours which follow the taking of the salt, the appetite should be satisfied with chicken and beef broth only; it is especially necessary to observe a severe diet and avoid taking cold. The remedy is very simple and harmless, and has never been known to fail where it has been given trial.

Colic in Infants.—Infants are very subject to colic from overfeeding, too early feeding, constipation, and many other causes. They often suffer terribly from these pains, tossing about, drawing up their legs, and screaming vehemently. *Treatment.*—When it arises from costiveness, a teaspoonful or tablespoonful of castor oil will often remove the defect, and at or about the same time give three drops of essence of peppermint or spearmint, in a little sweetened water. A very little saleratus often gives relief, and paregoric in two to five-drop doses every hour, will give relief. Hot flannels applied over the bowels and stomach are useful, and often the infant can be greatly relieved by laying it upon the belly on the knee, trotting it and gently tapping its back; this must be done cautiously, for if unsuccessful it might increase the pains.

How People Get Sick.—Eating too much and too fast; swallowing imperfectly masticated food; using too much fluid at meals; drinking poisonous whiskey and other intoxicating drinks; repeatedly using poison as medicines; keeping late hours at night, and sleeping late in the morning; wearing clothing too tight; wearing thin shoes; neglecting to wash the body sufficiently to keep the pores open; exchanging the warm clothes worn in a warm room during the day for costumes and exposure incident to evening parties; compressing the stomach to gratify a vain and foolish passion for dress; keeping up constant excitement; fretting the mind with borrowed troubles; swallowing quack nostrums for every imaginary ill; taking meals at irregular intervals, etc.

Taking Cold.—When a person begins to shiver, the blood is receding from the surface; congestion, to a greater or less extent has taken place, and the patient has already taken cold, to be followed by fever, inflammation of the lungs, neuralgia, rheumatism, etc. All these evils can be avoided and the cold expelled by walking, or in some exercise that will produce a prompt and decided reaction in the system. The exercise should be sufficient to produce perspiration. If you are so situated that you can get a glass of hot water to drink, it will materially aid the perspiration, and in every way assist nature in her efforts to remove the cold. This course followed, your cold is at an end, and whatever disease it would ultimate in is avoided, your sufferings are prevented and your doctor's bills saved.

Relief for the Feet.—Every woman who is obliged to stand at the ironing table for hours during July and August, finds that her feet are prolific sources of suffering. Even if she is wise enough to wear thick soled shoes, she will find her lot a hard one. One little thing can be done to relieve her somewhat. Take an old comforter, or part of one, fold it in just as many thicknesses as is possible to make it soft, and yet perfectly easy to stand on. Her feet will be cooler, and when she is through with her work she will not have the stinging and burning sensation which is as hard to bear as pain is. It is a good plan to have a good supply of holders, so that she can change them often.

Sunstroke.—As soon as you reach your patient take hold of him or her and carry or drag him or her into the shade. Place the body in a sitting posture, the back against a wall, with the feet and legs resting upon the sidewalk and extending in front of the body. Get ice water and a bottle of some strong essence of ginger. Pour the ice water over the head, copiously; never mind the clothes. Then pour two or three tablespoonfuls of ginger in about half a tumbler of water, and make the patient swallow it quickly. Keep the head cool by using a little of the ice water, and in case there is not much of a glow on the body give more ginger. If this recipe is promptly used and fully carried out in every case the Board of Health will never have a death to record from this cause. It is no experiment or quack remedy. It costs but a few cents and a half-hour or an hour's time. Ginger is by far the best to use, and where it cannot be had quickly two or three good drinks of brandy will answer.

Knock-Knees.—A correspondent says: " I commenced the practice of placing a small book between my knees, and tying a handkerchief tight round my ankles. This I did two or three times a day, increasing the substance at every fresh trial, until I could hold a brick with ease breadthways. When I first commenced this practice I was as badly knock-kneed as possible; but now I am as straight as any one. I likewise made it a practice of lying on my back in bed, with my legs crossed and my knees fixed tightly together. This, I believe, did me a great deal of good."

Indigestion.—I have been troubled for years with indigestion, sick headache, and constipation, writes a lady, and have been greatly helped by dropping all remedies and drinking a coffeecupful of as warm water as can be drank comfortably, the first thing on rising and just before retiring, always on an empty stomach. It will cause an unpleasant feeling at first, but persevere and you will be surprised at the benefit received. If the kidneys are at fault, drink water blood warm.

Jaundice.—Red iodide of mercury, seven grains; iodide of potassium, nine grains; distilled water, one ounce; mix. Commence by giving six drops three or four times a day, increasing one drop a day until twelve or fifteen drops are given at a dose. Give in a little water, immediately after meals. If it causes a griping sensation in the bowels, and fullness in the head, when you get up to twelve or fifteen drops, go back to six drops, and up again as before.

Gout.—Take hot vinegar, and put into it all the table salt which it will dissolve, and bathe the parts affected with a soft piece of flannel. Rub in with the hand and dry the foot, etc., by the fire. Repeat this operation four times in twenty-four hours, fifteen minutes each time, for four days; then twice a day for the same period; then once, and follow this rule whenever the symptoms show themselves at any future time.

Sore Nipples.—Pour boiling water on nutgalls (oak bark if galls cannot be obtained), and when cold, strain it off, and bathe the parts with it, or dip the cloth in the tea, and apply it; or twenty grains of tannin may be dissolved in an ounce of water, and applied. The application of a few drops of collodion to the raw surface is highly recommended. It forms, when dry, a perfect coating over the diseased surface.

Preventive of Seasickness.—The following remedy, preventive of seasickness, is recommended by Prof. E. Tourgee, of Boston, manager of tourist excursions. It was tried by himself and family, five in all, who had suffered from sea-sickness on every former voyage across the Atlantic, and in each case it proved entirely successful, and produced no unfavorable results. Dissolve one ounce of bromide of sodium in four ounces of water. Take one teaspoonful three times a day before eating. Begin taking the above three days before starting on the ocean voyage.

Prickly Heat.—Prickly heat is a very common and troublesome disease. The most effectual treatment for it that we know of is a powder composed of one part of oxide of zinc, three parts of oxide of magnesia, and sixteen parts of sublimate of sulphur. Place the powder on a plate and press a damp sponge on it. Rub the body with the sponge, to which the particles of powder have adhered, and continue the application for fifteen minutes, then wash the parts clean of the adhering particles. Repeat twice or three times every twenty-four hours.

Ulcers.—Here is a receipt that will cure any sore on man or beast that has ulcerated. Take two and one-half drachms blue stone, four drachms alum, six drachms loaf sugar, one drachm sugar of lead, one tablespoonful honey. Put all into a bottle, put in one pint of vinegar, shake it three or four times a day, until they are dissolved, and it is ready for use. Pour some of it out and add water when you first apply to any sore, as it makes it smart at the first application; apply three times a day.

Nursing Children.—Mothers who nurse their children should bear in mind that what they eat at such a time is of great importance, both to themselves and to the children. The very best article of food that they can avail themselves of is oatmeal mush or gruel, which is always delicious when properly cooked. The oatmeal furnishes the earthy phosphates and materials out of which good milk is made, so that the mother's own structures are not drawn upon, and her teeth are saved from decay.

Anodyne for Painful Menstruation.—Extract of stramonium and sulphate of quinine, each sixteen grains; macrotin, eight grains; morcrotin, eight grains; morphine, one grain; make into eight pills. Dose, one pill, repeating once or twice only, forty or fifty minutes apart, if the pain does not subside before this time. Pain must subside under the use of this pill, and costiveness is not increased.

To Prevent Contagion.—Impregnation of the atmosphere of a sick chamber when the patient is ill of diphtheria, measles, scarlet fever, or of any allied disease, with the odor of a mixture of equal parts of turpentine and carbolic acid, is recommended by a celebrated physician. Half a teaspoonful of mixture will be enough at a time, if it is put into a kettle of water kept near the boiling point. The odor gives some relief to the sufferer, and and tends to prevent the spread of the malady.

Salt Rheum.—Take half a pound of swamp sassafras-bark and boil it, in enough fresh water to cover it, for the space of half an hour. Take off the water, and thoroughly wash the part affected. Add hog's lard to some of the water, and simmer it over a moderate fire until the water is evaporated; anoint the part affected, continuing the washing and anointing four days. A cure is generally certain.

Simple Disinfectant.—The following is a refreshing disinfectant for a sick-room, or any room that has an unpleasant aroma pervading it: Put some fresh ground coffee in a saucer, and in the center place a small piece of camphor gum, which light with a match. As the gum burns allow sufficient coffee to consume with it. The perfume is very pleasant and healthful —being far superior to pastiles and very much cheaper.

To Protect the Lungs from Dust.—In farm labor one has often to encounter a hurtful amount of dust. A simple and cheap protection from such an annoyance is to get a piece of sponge large enough to cover the nostrils and mouth, hollow it out on one side with a pair of scissors, to fit the face, attach a string to each side and tie it on. First wet it well, and squeeze out most of the water. Repeat this whenever the sponge becomes dry. All the dust will be caught in the damp cavities, and it is easily washed out.

Fainting.—Fainting is caused by the blood leaving the brain. Place the patient flat and allow the head to be lower than the body. Sprinkle cold water on the face. Hartshorn may be held near the nose, not to it. A half teaspoonful of aromatic spirits of ammonia, in a wineglassful of water, will tend to revive the patient. If the symptoms recur, send for a physician.

Bee Stings.—Take a pinch in the fingers of common salt, put on the place stung and dissolve with water, rub with the finger. If not relieved in one minute wet the place with aqua ammonia. Care should be taken not to get the ammonia into the eye. I have used this remedy for several years and it has never failed with me. It has always arrested the poison and prevented swelling.

Cramp in the Leg.—A garter applied tightly round the limb affected will, in most cases, speedily remove the complaint. When it is more obstinate, a brick should be heated, wrapped in a flannel bag, and placed at the foot of the bed, against which the person troubled may place his feet. No remedy, however, is equal to that of diligent and long-continued friction.

Boils.—These should be brought to a head by warm poultices of camomile flowers, or boiled white lily root, or onion root by fermentation with hot water, or by stimulating plasters. When ripe they should be destroyed by a needle or lancet; but this should not be attempted until they are fully proved.

Pulmonary Complaints.—When an effusion of blood from the lungs takes place, a prompt and infallible resource might readily be provided, so as to meet the occasion with a safe and decided effect. From twenty to thirty-five drops of the spirits of turpentine in a glass of water will produce an instantaneous collapse of the mouth of the blood vessel. It is also asserted that, in the above case, a tumblerful of strong gin-toddy, or gin and water, will have the same effect.

Tobacco Antidote.—Buy two ounces or more of gentian root, coarsely ground. Take as much of it after each meal, or oftener, as amounts to a common quid of "fine-cut." Chew it slowly and swallow the juice. Continue this a few weeks, and you will conquer the insatiable appetite for tobacco, which injures both mind and body, and from which thousands struggle to be free, but give up in despair.

Ice for Teething Children.—The pain of teething may be almost done away, and the health of the child benefited by giving it fine splinters of ice, picked off with a pin, to melt in its mouth. The instant quiet which succeeds hours of fretfulness is the best witness to this magic remedy.

Odor from Perspiration.—The unpleasant odor produced by perspiration is frequently the source of vexation to persons who are subject to it. Nothing is simpler than to remove this odor. Put two tablespoonfuls of spirits of ammonia (hartshorn) in a basin of water, and wash. This leaves the skin clean and fresh. The wash is perfectly harmless and very cheap.

Swelled Feet and Ankles.—Take plantain leaves (which can be found in almost any grass-plot, and in our public parks); wilt them by putting separately between the hands; cover the swollen parts with them, and keep in place by wrapping the limb with rags or a towel on going to bed at night, or keep them on during the day if not obliged to be upon the feet. A cure will be speedily effected.

Acid Stomach.—A little magnesia and water will sometimes correct the acidity of a child's stomach, and render unnecessary any stronger medicine. Powder a teaspoonful of magnesia, and put it in half a glass of water; it will not dissolve, of course, but will mix with the water so that an infant can swallow it. Give a teaspoonful of this three times a day until indications warrant you in discontinuing it.

Diet During Diarrhœa.—Tea without milk, and very little sugar; mutton and chicken broths, or beef tea, thickened with a little flour or arrowroot; boiled rice, tapioca, sago; rice-water or toast-water to drink. If the attack is severe, or of long continuance, the patient must be kept in bed. The feet must be kept warm, and the covering to suit the feelings of the patient.

To Prevent Sunstroke.—Sunstroke is prevented by wearing a silk handkerchief in the crown of the hat, or green leaves, or a wet cloth of any kind; but, during an attack, warm water should be instantly poured on the head, or rags dipped in the water and renewed every minute. The reason is two-fold—the scalp is dry and hot, and the warm water not only removes the dryness but carries off the extra heat with great rapidity by evaporation.

To Ascertain Fractures.—Fractures of the ribs may be ascertained by placing the tips of two or three fingers on the spot where the pain is, and desiring the patient to cough. If a rib be broken, a grating sensation will be felt. All that is necessary is to pass a broad bandage round the chest so tight as to prevent the motion of the ribs in breathing, and to observe a low diet.

Removing Substances from the Ear.—Take a horse-hair about six inches long, and double it so as to make a loop at one end. Introduce this loop as deeply as possible into the auditory canal, and twist it gently around. After one or two turns, according to the originator of the plan, the foreign body is drawn out with the loop. The method is ingenious, and at all events causes little pain, and can do no harm.

Deficiency of Wax in the Ear.—Deafness is sometimes the consequence of a morbidly dry state of the inner passages of the ear. In such cases, introduce a bit of cotton wool dipped in an equal mixture of oil of turpentine and oil of almonds, or in the liniment of carbonate of ammonia.

Snake Bites.—Turpentine is said to be a sure cure for a bite of a snake. It should be put in a bottle, and the mouth being placed over the spot, the liquid brought directly in contact with the wound by inverting the bottle, which should be held there until relief is obtained. A complete alleviation of pain has been known to ensue in less than a quarter of an hour. An important discovery.

Sore Eyes.—Get the roots of linwood (some call it bass-wood), wash and scrape the outer bark clean, then scrape the inner bark very fine, filling a tumbler about one-third full. Then fill the tumbler nearly full of rain-water. It will, in a little while, thicken like jelly. Now take a thin, soft cloth, the thinner the better, put some of the mucilage between two pieces and place it upon the eyes. It is very soothing.

Laxatives.—Infusions of Epsom salts and senna are often taken as laxatives, or opening medicines. It is a well known fact that a teaspoonful of salts in a tumbler of cold water, if drunk before breakfast, is as effectual a dose as the usual ounce. Senna, too, if steeped in cold water, is equally efficacious, and free from the nauseous bitter taste which it has when infused in boiling water.

To Prevent Gray Hair.—To check premature grayness, the head should be well brushed morning and night, with a brush hard enough to irritate the skin somewhat. The bristles should be far enough apart to brush through the hair, as it were, rather than over it. Oil, rather than pomade, should be used. Common sweet oil, scented with bergamot, can be recommended.

Cholera Infantum.—For cholera infantum, the whites of two eggs, well beaten; then mix with water; add one teaspoonful of orange flower water and a little sugar; a tablespoonful every hour. It will, says an authority, cure the worst case of cholera infantum, the egg coating the bowels.

Treatment for Fever.—If the patient has a burning fever, take an earthen wash-bowl, fill two-thirds full of tepid water, in which put one tablespoonful of common baking soda; then bathe the face, body, and limbs freely with it and wipe dry. This treatment for fever was learned from one of our best physicians.

Blood Blister.—When a finger is bruised so as to cause a blood-blister under the nail, it should immediately be drilled with a knife or other sharp-pointed instrument, and the blood allowed to escape. This affords instant relief to an injury which may otherwise become exceedingly painful.

A Vapor Bath.—A vapor bath may easily be prepared at home. Place a pail of hot water under a cane-bottomed chair, or if you have not one, put a narrow piece of board across the pail; on this the patient should sit for half an hour, covered by a blanket reaching to the floor, so as to keep in the steam.

Ventilation.—The best way to admit pure air in the night (where windows are the only mode of ventilation) is to open the sleeping-room into a hall where there is an open window in order to avoid the draught. A window with a small opening at the top and bottom ventilates more than one with one opening only.

A Cheap and Simple Way to Disinfect a Room.—Heat a common iron fire-shovel hot, but not quite red hot, and pour an ounce of carbolic acid fluid on it. The fumes will penetrate the room everywhere and cleanse the air of its impurities. This should be repeated daily so long as it is necessary.

Deafness.—Put a tablespoonful of bay-salt into nearly half a pint of cold spring water; and after it has steeped therein for twenty-four hours, now and then shaking the phial, pour a small teaspoonful in the ear most affected, nightly, when in bed, for seven or eight successive nights.

Tetter.—Procure some strawberry leaves, and lay the outside, or woolly side of the leaf on the parts affected. They must be laid on very thick, and be changed occasionally. They will draw out inflammation, and cure the disease.

Stiff Neck.—Apply over the place affected a piece of black oil-cloth with the right side to the skin, then tie up the neck with a thick handkerchief. In a short time the part will grow moist, and, by leaving thus twelve hours, the pain will be removed.

Food for a Young Child.—If a very young child has to be fed, take the top crust of good, sweet home-made bread; soak it in cold water half an hour, and then boil twenty minutes; cover tight; then beat with a fork until smooth and sweet. This will agree with the stomach better than anything else.

Piles.—The ingredients are: Two tablespoonfuls of tar, eight tablespoonfuls of lard, not heaped. First wash the parts effected with castile soap and water, and then apply the ointment. The ointment should be used once or twice each day.

Cramp, in Bathing.—For the cure of the cramp when swimming, Dr. Franklin recommends a vigorous and violent shock to the part affected, by suddenly and forcibly stretching out the leg, which should be darted out of the water into the air if possible.

Spasms.—To cure this distressing form of malady, take two pennyworth of camphor, and infuse it in one pint of brandy. Let it stand forty-eight hours, and then it is fit for use. When the attack comes on, take one teaspoonful in a wineglass of water.

Gum-Boil, or Weakness of the Gums.—Take of acetate of morphia, two grains; tincture of myrrh, six drachms; tincture of krameria, one ounce; spirits of lavender, three ounces and a half. Let a lotion be made.

Choking.—To prevent choking, break an egg into a cup and give it to the person choking, to swallow. The white of the egg seems to catch around the obstacle and remove it. If one egg does not answer the purpose, try another. The white is all that is necessary.

Scrofulous Sore Eyes.—Take blue violets, which are growing wild in most places, dig them up, top and root, wash clean, dry them and make a tea; drink several times a day, wetting the eyes each time, and it will soon cure.

Weak Ankles.—Bathing them in wine-lees will strengthen them; frequent bathing in salt and water—four ounces of salt to one quart of water—is also beneficial. Skating moderately indulged in, will be attended by good results.

Hot Milk as a Stimulant.—If any one is fatigued, the best restorative is hot milk, a tumbler of the beverage as hot as can be sipped. This is far more of a restorative than any alcoholic drink.

Cold Feet.—Cold feet are the precursors of consumption. To escape them, warm your feet well in the morning, and covering the sole with a piece of common paper, carefully draw on the sock, and then the boot or shoe.

Drink in Cases of Fever.—There is no more refreshing drink in cases of fever than weak green tea, with lemon juice added instead of milk. It may be taken either cold or hot, but the latter is preferable.

Frozen Limbs.—Dissolve from one quarter to half a pound of alum in a gallon of warm water, and immerse the feet or hands in it when frozen, for ten or fifteen minutes, and a cure will be effected.

Foreign Bodies in the Throat.—"Foreign bodies lodged in the throat can be removed," says Dr. Beveridge, a British naval surgeon, "by forcibly blowing into the ear." The plan is so easily tried and so harmless that we suggest its use.

Hiccough.—Hiccough effects some persons very persistently, and where a simpler remedy does not check it, a half teaspoonful of nitre in a half tumbler of water is recommended as an instantaneous remedy.

Cankers.—Those whitish-looking specks which appear on the inside of the cheeks and lips, may be easily removed by touching them with burnt alum.

Enlarged Neck.—To cure enlarged neck, take two tablespoonfuls of salt, two of borax and two of alum, dissolve in two of water and apply three times a day for three weeks.

A Prompt Emetic.—The ingredients are: Tartar emetic, one grain; powdered ipecac, twenty grains. Take the above in a wineglassful of sweetened water.

Swelled Feet.—For swelled feet a good remedy will be found in bathing them in vinegar and water.

THE TOILET--Update

Concerns for cosmetics and cleanliness have changed over the last ninety years. I know few people who've attempted to remove their freckles with lemon juice; being tanned is now as fashionable as pale, clear skin was then. If you want to stain your hair, there are easier preparations than walnut juice. Most people are now less concerned with scents, essences, pomades and powders than with simple cleanliness.

Some of the recipes which are of lasting interest are those for cold cream, tooth powder, soap and shampoo. These seem to me to be good basic recipes, though I'm surprised that the list of toothpowders does not include the simplest formula: baking soda and salt.

Some other money-savers not mentioned here are: shaving with cake soap, mug, and brush; using witch hazel for after-shave (also for cuts, bites, burns); alum solution as styptic, mouth wash made from salt, water and peppermint extract; alum and water or cornstarch and baking soda for a wet or dry deodorant. These materials may be prepared at home and will be fully as effective as the expensive, commercial brands found at the drug store.

A heavy application of cocoa butter has been successful in treating sunburn, both stopping the pain and saving the burned skin.

Several age-old problems are discussed in this chapter: loss of hair and pimples. I cannot conceive of applying the concoctions the *Cyclopaedia* recommends to my hair; hair or its lack has been shown to be a genetic matter. If you want to know how your hair will go, observe your mother's father. I've never known of a case in which balding was reversed. For pimples, most doctors suggest avoiding oily foods and regular, strenuous face-washing. Conscientious cleanliness is of greater value than any patent medicine. Borax is an excellent cleaning agent when mixed in the wash water.

THE TOILET.

Tooth Powder.—(1) Dissolve two ounces of borax in three pints of boiling water, and before it is cold, add one teaspoonful of the spirits of camphor, and bottle for use. A tablespoonful of this mixture, mixed with an equal quantity of tepid water, and applied daily with a soft brush, preserves and beautifies the teeth, extirpates all tartarous adhesion, arrests decay, induces healthy action of the gums, and makes the teeth pearly white.

(2) The dark colored substance which collects on neglected teeth cannot be removed with a brush and water. Pulverized charcoal will take it off, but this scratches the enamel and leads to decay of the tooth. A better substance is pumice stone in powder. Dip a pine stick into it, and scour the teeth. After this treatment the daily use of the tooth brush and tepid water will be sufficient.

(3) A good way to clean teeth is to dip the brush in water, rub it over genuine white castile soap, then dip it in prepared chalk. A lady says: "I have been complimented upon the whiteness of my teeth, which were originally anything but white. I have used the soap constantly for two or three years, and the chalk for the last year. There is no danger of scratching the teeth, as the chalk is prepared, but with a good stiff brush and the soap, is as effectual as soap and sand on a floor.

(4) Mix six ounces of the tincture of Peruvian bark with half an ounce of sal-ammoniac. Shake it well before using. Take a spoonful and hold it near the teeth; then with a finger dipped into it, rub the gums and teeth, which must afterward be washed with warm water. This tincture cures the toothache, preserves the teeth and gums, and makes them adhere to each other.

(5) Prepared chalk, one pound; camphor, one or two drachms. The camphor must be finely powdered, by moistening it with a little spirits of wine, and then intimately mixed with the chalk.

(6) Ingredients: Powdered charcoal, four ounces; powdered yellow bark, two ounces; powdered myrrh, one ounce; orris root, half an ounce.

(7) Ten cents' worth ground chalk, five cents' worth orris root, five cents' worth myrrh, one teaspoonful powdered castile soap. Mix all well together.

(8) A mixture of honey with the purest charcoal will prove an admirable cleanser.

Freckles.—(1) Freckles are easily removed by the following treatment, but the directions must be followed regularly: Five grains corrosive sublimate, two ounces alcohol, four ounces water. Apply two or three times during the day. At night use the following ointment: One ounce of white wax, one teacupful of nice white lard, lump of camphor the size of a chestnut, one teaspoonful glycerine. Put the wax and camphor in a tin to melt, crumbling the camphor; when melted, add the other ingredients. Stir thoroughly, and pour into molds which have been dipped in water.

This recipe will be found to remove pimples as well as tan and freckles.

(2) A good freckle lotion for the cure of freckles, tan, or sun-burned face or hands is made thus: Take half a pound of clear ox-gall, half a drachm each of camphor and burned alum, one drachm of borax, two ounces of rock salt, and the same of rock candy. This should be mixed and shaken well several times a day for three weeks, until the gall becomes transparent; then strain it very carefully through filtering paper, which may be had of the druggist. Apply to the face during the day, and wash off at night.

(3) Wash in fresh buttermilk every morning, and rinse the face in tepid water; then use a soft towel. Freckles may also be removed by applying to the face a solution of nitre and water. Another good wash for freckles is made by dissolving three grains of borax in five drachms each of rose water and orange flower water. There are many remedies for freckles, but there is none that will banish them entirely.

(4) Take one ounce of lemon juice, a quarter of a drachm of powdered borax, and half a drachm of sugar. Mix and let them stand in a glass bottle for a few days, then rub it on the face and hands night and morning. Two tablespoonfuls of lemon juice would equal an ounce.

(5) Rectified spirits of wine, one ounce; water, eight ounces; half an ounce of orange flower water, or one ounce of rose water; diluted muriatic acid, a teaspoonful. Mix. To be used after washing.

(6) Take grated horseradish and put in very sour milk. Let it stand four hours; then wash the face night and morning.

To Prevent the Hair Falling Off.—(1) When the hair, after being naturally luxuriant, begins to grow thin, without actually coming out in particles, use the following receipt: Take of extract of yellow Peruvian bark, fifteen grains; extract of rhatany root, eight grains; extract of burdock root and oil of nutmegs (mixed), of each, two drachms; camphor dissolved with spirits of wine, fifteen grains; beef marrow, two ounces; best olive oil, one ounce; citron juice, half a drachm; aromatic essential oil, as much as is sufficient to render it fragrant; mix, and make into an ointment. Two drachms of bergamot and a few drops of attar of roses would suffice. This is to be used every morning.

(2) Onions must be rubbed frequently on the part. The stimulating powers of this vegetable are of essential service in restoring the tone of the skin, and assisting the capillary vessels in sending forth new hair; but it is not *infallible*. Should it succeed, however, the growth of these new hairs may be assisted by the oil of myrtleberries, the repute of which, perhaps, is greater than its real efficiency. These applications are cheap and harmless, even where they do no good; a character which cannot be said of the numerous quack remedies that meet the eye in every direction.

(3) To prevent hair from falling out or turning gray, take a teacupful of dried sage, and boil it in a quart of soft water for twenty minutes. Strain it off and add a piece of borax the size of an English walnut; pulverize the borax. Put the sage tea, when cool, into a quart bottle; add the borax; shake well together, and keep in a cool place. Brush the hair thoroughly and rub the wash well on the head with the hand. Then, after a good hard rubbing, brush the hair well before the fire so it will become dry.

(4) Put equal quantities of rum and sweet oil into a bottle, and, before using, shake them well together. This mixture should he applied with a

soft brush to the roots of the hair every night; it should be tried for a month at the least, before any improvement can be expected.

(5) Put one pound of unadulterated honey into a still, with three handfuls of the tendrils of vine and the same quantity of rosemary tops. Distill as cool and as slowly as possible. The liquor may be allowed to drop till it tastes sour.

(6) To prevent the hair from falling out apply once a week a wash made of one quart of boiling water, one ounce of pulverized borax and half an ounce of powdered camphor. Rub on with a sponge or a piece of flannel.

(7) Take a piece of saltpetre the size of a hickory nut, and put in a quart of water, and wet the head daily.

To Soften the Hands.—(1) To soften the hands, fill a wash-basin half full of fine, white sand and soap suds as hot as can be borne. Wash the hands in this five minutes at the time, washing and rubbing them in the sand. The best is the flint sand, or the white, powdered quartz sold for filters. It may be used repeatedly by pouring the water away after each washing, and adding fresh to keep it from blowing about. Rinse in warm lather of fine soap, and, after drying, rub them with dry bran or cornmeal. Dust them, and finish with rubbing cold cream well into the skin. This effectually removes the roughness caused by housework, and should be used every day, first removing ink or vegetable stains with acid.

(2) Soap is an indispensable article for cleansing hands, but it often leaves the skin rough; cracks on the hands come, and soap is often unpleasant. Use honey, rub it on when the skin is dry; moisten a little, rub harder, use a little more water; finally wash thoroughly and your hands will be as clean as though the strongest soap were used, and no cracks or roughness will annoy you.

(3) Keep a dish of Indian meal on the toilet stand near the soap, and rub the meal freely on the hands after soaping them for washing. It will surprise you, if you have not tried it, to find how it will cleanse and soften the skin, and prevent chapping.

(4) Before retiring take a large pair of gloves and spread mutton tallow inside, also all over the hands. Wear the gloves all night, and wash the hands with olive oil and white castile soap the next morning.

(5) After cleansing the hands with soap, rub them well with oatmeal while still wet. Honey is also very good, used in the same way as lemon-juice, well rubbed in at night.

To Whiten the Hands.—(1) Keep some oatmeal on the washstand, and, as often as the hands are washed, rub a little oatmeal over them; then rinse it off, and, when dry, put on a little bit of pomade, made as follows: Take about five cents' worth each of white wax, spermaceti, and powdered camphor, and olive oil enough to make it the thickness of soap; put it in a gallipot, and let it stand in an oven to melt; mix it up, and, when cold, it will be found very good for the hands. Gloves, worn either in the day or night, will help to keep the hands white.

(2) A cake of brown Windsor soap scraped into thin flakes, and then mixed with a tablespoonful of eau de cologne, and a tablespoonful of lemon juice, is said to make a useful preparation for this purpose. There is nothing injurious to the skin in the composition. When the soap has been thoroughly blended with the lemon juice and eau de cologne, it should be pressed into a mold—one made of cardboard in the form of a small

box, the size of a cake of soap, will answer the purpose—and allowed to dry before it is used.

(3) Half an ounce of white wax, half an ounce of spermaceti, quarter of an ounce of powdered camphor. Mix them with as much olive oil as will form them into a very stiff paste, and use as often as you wash your hands.

(4) Mixtures of two parts of glycerine, one part ammonia, and a little rose water whiten and soften the hands.

Pimples.—(1) It requires self-denial to get rid of pimples, for persons troubled with them will persist in eating fat meats and other articles of food calculated to produce them. Avoid the use of rich gravies, or pastry, or anything of the kind in excess. Take all the out-door exercise you can and never indulge in a late supper. Retire at a reasonable hour, and rise early in the morning. Sulphur to purify the blood may be taken three times a week—a thimbleful in a glass of milk before breakfast. It takes some time for the sulphur to do its work, therefore persevere in its use till the humors, or pimples, or blotches, disappear. Avoid getting wet while taking the sulphur.

(2) Try this recipe: Wash the face twice a day in warm water, and rub dry with a coarse towel. Then with a soft towel rub in a lotion made of two ounces of white brandy, one ounce of cologne, and one half ounce of liquor potassa. Persons subject to skin eruptions should avoid very salt or fat food. A dose of Epsom salts occasionally might prove beneficial.

(3) Wash the face in a dilution of carbolic acid, allowing one teaspoonful to a pint of water. This is an excellent and purifying lotion, and may be used on the most delicate skins. Be careful about letting this wash get into the eyes.

(4) Oil of sweet almonds, one ounce; fluid potash, one drachm. Shake well together, and then add rose water, one ounce; pure water, six ounces. Mix. Rub the pimples or blotches for some minutes with a rough towel, and then dab them with the lotion.

(5) Dissolve one ounce of borax, and sponge the face with it every night. When there are insects, rub on flour of sulphur, dry, after washing, rub well and wipe dry; use plenty of castile soap.

(6) Dilute corrosive sublimate with oil of almonds. A few days' application will remove them.

Cosmetics.—(1) Oatmeal may be used for beautifying the complexion in this way: Take a small quantity of meal and pour sufficient cold water over it to make a thin paste; then strain through a fine sieve and bathe the face with the liquid, leaving it to dry upon the skin. This preparation renders the complexion very soft and white.

(2) Take an ordinary milk pan, and fill it with the white flowers of the elderberry bush. The flowers should be covered with boiling water, placed out-of-doors in the sun for about three days, strained off, and bottled. The liquid should be of a dark mahogany color. It is an excellent lotion to remove sunburn and freckles.

(3) Squeeze a little lemon juice on a soft, wet rag, and pass the rag over the face a number of times before retiring at night. Repeat the operation as often during the following day as you find it convenient, allowing the juice of the lemon to dry on the face. In a week or so you will experience great benefit.

(4) Glycerine and lemon juice make a very good toilet article for improv-

ing the complexion. Mix before applying it. A convenient way of using these articles is to pour a little of the glycerine into the palm of the hand, then squeeze out a few drops of lemon, rub together, and apply to the face.

(5) Take half a cup of water, and add to it a tablespoonful of glycerine. Add to this a tablespoonful of alcohol and a teaspoonful of cologne. Apply with a sponge or a soft cotton cloth.

(6) An infusion of horseradish and milk, as a correspondent informs us, will make a most excellent, harmless, and effective cosmetic. It is certainly very easily tried.

(7) Melt one pound of soft soap over a slow fire, with half a pint of sweet oil, and add a teacupful of fine sand. Stir the mixture together until cold.

(8) Use a teaspoonful of powdered borax every morning in the basin of water, when washing the face or hands; also use it when taking a bath.

Sunburn.—(1) Take two drachms of borax, one drachm of Roman alum, one drachm of camphor, half an ounce of sugar-candy, one pound of ox-gall; mix and stir well for ten minutes or so, and repeat this stirring three or four times a day for a fortnight, till it appears clear and transparent. Strain through blotting paper, and bottle up for use. It is said that strawberries rubbed over the face at night will remove freckles and sunburn.

(2) Wash the face at night with either sour milk or buttermilk, and in the morning with weak bran tea and a little eau-de cologne. This will soften the skin and remove the redness, and will also make it less liable to burn again with exposure to the sun. Bathing the face several times in the day with elder flower water and a few drops of eau-de-cologne is very efficacious.

(3) Put two spoonfuls of sweet cream into half a pint of new milk; squeeze into it the juice of a lemon, add half a glass of genuine French brandy, a little alum and loaf sugar; boil the whole, skim it well, and, when cold, it is fit for use.

Pomade for the Hair.—(1) Ingredients: one quarter pound of lard; two pennyworth of castor oil; scent. Mode: Let the lard be unsalted; beat it up well; then add the castor oil, and mix thoroughly together with a knife, adding a few drops of any scent that may be preferred. Put the pomatum into pots, which keep well covered to prevent it turning rancid.

(2) A flask of salad oil, one and a half ounces of spermaceti, half ounce of white wax; scent as desired. Cut up the white wax and spermaceti into small pieces, and put them into the oven to melt with a small quantity of the oil. When the lumps have disappeared, and all the ingredients are thoroughly amalgamated, pour in the remainder of the oil and the scent, and stir with a spoon until cold.

(3) Three ounces of olive oil, three quarters of a drachm of oil of almonds, two drachms of palm oil, half an ounce of white wax, a quarter of a pound of lard, and three quarters of a drachm of essence of bergamot. This pomade is excellent for strengthening the hair, promoting the growth of whiskers and moustaches, and preventing baldness.

(4) Take one ounce of spermaceti, one ounce of castor oil, four ounces of olive oil, and two pennyworth of bergamot, and melt them together in a pot placed in boiling water, stirring the mixture all the while; when thoroughly mixed, pour the mixture into pots while hot.

The Teeth.—The teeth need brushing at least before going to bed every night, and are better for being cleansed after each meal. Tartar can be removed by using pumice stone reduced to powder, rubbing it on the teeth with a bit of soft wood made into a brush. Where the gums are sensitive, there is nothing better than the chalk and myrrh dentifrice. Where the top of a tooth is very sensitive, wet a bit of chalk and lay it on under the lip. Where the breath is offensive the mouth should be rinsed with water in which an atom of permanganate of potash has been dissolved; just enough should be used to make the water pink. Take care not to swallow any, as it is a poison. Crooked teeth in children can often be straightened, without applying to a dentist, if the parents watch the teeth when coming through, and several times a day press the crooked one into position. Of course where the arch of the mouth is defective, the upper teeth protruding over the under lip, or the under jaw projects, the services of a skillful dentist will be required. It is only after the permanent teeth arrive that such operations are performed.

Toilet Powder.—Just think of it, one of the most deadly poisons known —used because of its cheapness, to add weight to an article applied solely to the delicate skins of women and children. Fearful and incurable skin diseases upon children to whom it has been applied to prevent chafing, led to the discovery. It is safe to discard *all French* toilet powder. Safe preparations are put up in this country, but each mother can make her own, because the best are only perfumed starch. Starch, made perfectly dry, and sifted through the finest sieve, may be used, or a few drops of any desired perfume may be mixed with it. Those who have lavender or other aromatic flowers can fold them in thin paper, and place these with layers of starch, in a box, renewing the flowers every few days, until the starch has absorbed sufficient perfume. The starch will take up a little moisture from the flowers, and it is best to let it be exposed to the sun, until quite dry, and then if at all lumpy, be sifted again.

Rose Bandoline for the Hair.—Of gum tragacanth, six ounces, or one and one-half ounces; of rose water, one gallon, or two pints; of attar of roses, one-half ounce, or one drachm; steep the gum in the water for a day or so; as it swells or forms a gelatinous mass, it must from time to time be well agitated. After about forty-eight hours' maceration, it is then to be squeezed through a coarse, clean linen cloth, and again left to stand for a few days; then pass it through the cloth a second time, to insure uniformity of consistency; when this is the case, the attar of roses is to be thoroughly incorporated. Almond bandoline is made precisely as the above, scenting with a quarter of an ounce of attar of almonds in place of the roses.

Eruptions on the Face.—Dissolve an ounce of borax in a quart of water, and apply this with a fine sponge every evening before going to bed. This will smooth the skin when the eruptions do not proceed from an insect working under the cuticle. Many persons' faces are disfigured by red eruptions caused by a small creature working under the skin. A very excellent remedy is to take the flour of sulphur and rub it on the face dry, after washing it in the morning. Rub it well with the fingers, and then wipe it off with a dry towel. There are many who are not a little ashamed of their faces, who can be cured if they follow these directions.

Chapped Hands.—(1) To cure chapped hands, take common starch and rub it into a fine, smooth powder, put it in a clean tin box, and every time the hands are removed from dish water or hot suds, rinse them carefully in clean water, and while they are damp, rub a pinch of starch over them, covering the whole surface.

(2) Melt spermaceti, one drachm, with almond oil, one ounce; and add powdered camphor, one drachm. It will be improved by adding a couple of drachms of glycerine, using as much less of the almond oil.

(3) One-half ounce of glycerine with same amount of alcohol. Mix, and add four ounces of rose water. Bottle, and shake well. An excellent remedy for rough or chapped hands.

To Sweeten the Breath.—From six to ten drops of the concentrated solution of chloride of soda in a wineglassful of spring water, taken immediately after the ablutions of the morning are completed, will sweeten the breath by disinfecting the stomach, which, far from being injured, will be benefitted by the medicine. If necessary, this may be repeated in the middle of the day. In some cases the odor from carious teeth is combined with that of the stomach. If the mouth is well rinsed with a teaspoonful of the chloride in a tumbler of water, the bad odor of the teeth will be removed.

Bay Rum.—Saturate one-quarter pound of carbonate of magnesia with oil of bay; pulverize the magnesia, place it in a filter, and pour water through it until the desired quantity is obtained, then add alcohol. The quantity of water and alcohol employed depends on the desired strength and quantity of the bay rum. Another: Oil of bay, ten fluid drachms; oil of pimento, one fluid drachm; acetic ether, two fluid drachms; alcohol, three gallons; water, two and a half gallons. Mix, and after two weeks' repose, filter.

Otto of Roses.—Fill a large glazed earthen jar with rose leaves, carefully separated from the cups; pour upon them spring water, just sufficient to cover them, and set the jar with its contents in the sun for two or three days, taking it under cover at night. At the end of the third or fourth day, small particles of yellow oil will be seen floating on the surface of the water, and which, in the course of a week, will have increased to a thin scum. The scum is the otto of roses; take it up with a little cotton tied to the end of a stick, and squeeze it into a phial.

Essence from Flowers.—Procure a quantity of the petals of any flowers which have an agreeable fragrance; card thin layers of cotton, which dip into the finest Florence or Lucca oil; sprinkle a small quantity of fine salt on the flowers alternately until an earthen vessel or wide-mouthed glass bottle is full. Tie the top close with a bladder, then lay the vessel in a south aspect to the heat of the sun, and in fifteen days, when uncovered, a fragrant oil may be squeezed away, leaving a whole mass quite equal to the high-priced essences.

To Curl the Hair.—There is no preparation which will make naturally straight hair assume a permanent curl. The following will keep the hair in curl for a short time: Take borax, two ounces; gum arabic, one drachm; and hot water, not boiling, one quart; stir, and, as soon as the ingredients are dissolved, add three tablespoonfuls of strong spirits of camphor. On retiring to rest, wet the hair with the above liquid, and roll in twists of paper as usual. Do not disturb the hair until morning, when untwist and form into ringlets.

Black Spots on the Face—The black spots on the face are not always what are called flesh worms. What are mistaken for them are produced in this way: The skin may be coarse, and the ducts, being large, collect the perspiration, which hardens and blackens, and hence the common supposition of there being grubs or maggots in the skin. The remedy is simple. Clean the part affected by squeezing out the substance that is lodged, and then use a lotion of diluted spirits of wine several times a day, until the blotches have disappeared. If they are really flesh worms take something to purify your blood—sulphur or sarsaparilla.

Moth Patches.—(1) It is said that the drinking of hard cider—two or three glasses per day—will remove moth spots. At least, so writes a correspondent who has tried it with success. While drinking the cider let tea and coffee alone.

(2) Moth patches may be removed from the face by the following remedy: Into a pint bottle of rum put a tablespoonful of flour of sulphur. Apply this to the patches once a day, and they will disappear in two or three weeks.

(3) Bathe the face two or three times a day in borax water; a teaspoonful of powdered borax in a basin of warm water.

Cold Cream.—This is a simple and cooling ointment, exceedingly serviceable for rough or chapped hands, or for keeping the skin soft. It is very easily made. Take half an ounce of white wax, and put it into a small basin, with two ounces of almond oil. When quite melted add two ounces of rose water. This must be done very slowly, little by little, and, as you pour it in, beat the mixture smartly with a fork to make the water incorporate. When all is incorporated, the cold cream is complete, and you may pour it into jars for future use.

Scent Powder.—A good receipt for scent powder to be used for wardrobes, boxes, etc., far finer than any mixture sold at the shops, is the following: Coriander, orris root, rose leaves, and aromatic calamus, each one ounce; lavender flowers, ten ounces; rhodium, one-fourth of a drachm; musk, five grains. These are to be mixed and reduced to a coarse powder. This scents clothes as if fragrant flowers had been pressed in their folds.

Walnut Hair Dye.—The simplest form is the expressed juice of the bark or shell of green walnuts. To preserve this juice, a little rectified spirits may be added to it, with a few bruised cloves, and the whole digested together, with occasional agitation for a week or fortnight, when the clear portion is decanted, and, if necessary, filtered. Sometimes, only a little common salt is added to preserve the juice. It should be kept in a cool place.

Lavender Water.—Best English lavender, four drachms; oil of cloves, half a drachm; musk, five grains; best spirits of wine, six ounces; water, one ounce. Mix the oil of lavender with a little spirit first, then add the other ingredients, and let it stand, being kept well corked for at least two months before it is used, shaking it frequently.

To Increase the Growth of Hair.—Take of mutton suet, one pound; best white wax, four ounces; essences of bergamot and lemon, of each, three drachms; oils of lavender and thyme, of each, one drachm. Mix the suet and wax over a gentle fire and then add the perfumes.

To Thicken the Hair.—One quart of white wine, one handful of rosemary flowers, one-half pound of honey, one-quarter pint of oil of sweet almonds. Mix the rosemary and honey with the wine, distill them together, then add the oil of sweet almonds and shake well. When using it, pour a little into a cup, warm it, and rub it into the roots of the hair.

Crimping Hair.—To make the hair stay in crimp, take five cents' worth of gum arabic and add to it just enough boiling water to dissolve it. When dissolved, add enough alcohol to make it rather thin. Let this stand all night and then bottle it to prevent the alcohol from evaporating. This put on the hair at night, after it is done up in papers or pins, will make it stay in crimp the hottest day, and is perfectly harmless.

The Nails.—Great attention should be paid to keeping the nails in good order. They should be brushed at least twice a day, and the skin round the lower part should be kept down by rubbing with a soft towel. The sides of the nails need clipping about once in a week. If they become stained, wash them well with soap, and after rinsing off the soap well, brush them with lemon juice.

Toilet Soap.—Take two pounds of pure beef tallow, two pounds of sal soda, one pound of salt, one ounce of gum camphor, one ounce of oil of bergamot, one ounce of borax; boil slowly an hour; stir often, let it stand till cold, then warm it over, so it will run easily, and turn into cups or molds, dipped in cold water. This is very nice for all toilet purposes, and is greatly improved by age.

Almond Paste.—Take of bleached almonds four ounces, and the white of one egg; beat the almonds to a smooth paste in a mortar, then add the white of egg, and enough rose water, mixed with one-half its weight of spirits of wine, to give the proper consistence. This paste is used as a cosmetic, to beautify the complexion, and is also a remedy for chapped hands, etc.

Hair Wash.—Take one ounce of borax, half an ounce of camphor powder—these ingredients fine—and dissolve them in one quart of boiling water. When cool, the solution will be ready for use. Damp the hair frequently. This wash is said not only to cleanse and beautify, but to strengthen the hair, preserve the color and prevent baldness.

To Make Eau de Cologne.—Rectified spirits of wine, four pints; oil of bergamot, one ounce; oil of lemon, half an ounce; oil of rosemary, half a drachm; oil of neroli, three-quarters of a drachm; oil of English lavender, one drachm; oil of oranges, one drachm. Mix well, and then filter. If these proportions are too large, smaller ones may be used.

Care of the Hair.—To keep the hair healthy, keep the head clean. Brush the scalp well with a stiff brush while dry. Then wash with castile soap, and rub into the roots, bay rum, brandy, or camphor water. This done twice a month will prove beneficial. Brush the scalp thoroughly twice a week. Dampen the hair with soft water at the toilet, and do not use oil.

Pearl Water for the Complexion.—Take castile soap, one pound; water, one gallon. Dissolve; then add alcohol, one quart; oil of rosemary and oil of lavender, of each two drachms. Mix well.

Fresh Milk of Roses.—Two and one-half pints of rose water, one-half pint of rosemary water, two ounces of tincture of storax, two ounces of tincture of benzoin, one-half ounce of esprit de rose. First mix the rose water and rosemary water, and then add the other ingredients. This is a useful wash for the complexion.

Violet Powder.—Wheat starch, six parts by weight; orris root powder, two. Having reduced the starch to an impalpable powder, mix thoroughly with the orris root, and then perfume with otto of lemon, otto of bergamot, and otto of cloves, using twice as much of the lemon as either of the other ottos.

Perfume for Handkerchiefs.—Oil of lavender, three fluid drachms; oil of bergamot, three fluid drachms; extract of ambergris, six minims; camphor, one grain; spirits of wine, one pint. To be well shaken every day for a fortnight, and then filtered.

Bouquet de la Reine.—Take one ounce of essence of bergamot, three drachms of English oil of lavender, half a drachm of oil of cloves, half a drachm of aromatic vinegar, six grains of musk, and one pint and a half of rectified spirits of wine. Distill.

Oil of Roses for the Hair.—Olive oil, one quart; otto of roses, one drachm; oil of rosemary, one drachm; mix. It may be colored by steeping a little alkanet root in the oil (with heat) before scenting it. It strengthens and beautifies the hair.

Shampooing Liquid.—An excellent shampoo is made of salts of tartar, white castile soap, bay rum and lukewarm water. The salts will remove all dandruff, the soap will soften the hair and clean it thoroughly, and the bay rum will prevent taking cold.

Hair Restorative.—A good hair restorative may be made of boxwood leaves, of which take a handful and put into one pint of boiling water; digest for an hour, simmer ten minutes, and then strain. In applying it to the hair rub it well into the roots.

Lip Salve.—Melt a lump of sugar in one and a half tablespoonfuls of rose water; mix it with two tablespoonfuls of sweet oil, a piece of spermaceti half as large as an English walnut; simmer the whole, and turn it into boxes.

Wash for the Hair.—The best wash we know for cleansing and softening the hair is an egg beaten up, and rubbed well into the hair, and afterward washed out with several washes of warm water.

Cure for Chapped Lips.—Dissolve a lump of beeswax in a small quantity of sweet oil—over a candle—let it cool, and it will be ready for use. Rubbing it warm on the lips two or three times will effect a cure.

New fabrics, new soaps and detergents, new washers and driers make a new wash-day. Would anyone enjoy returning to the day-long, boiling water and mechanical wringer style of wash-day? What about the starching and ironing? The special handling for special fibers?

Most clothing now is relatively colorfast, non-shrinking, and no-iron. Few people have to worry about washing delicate laces, muslins, lawns, linens, silks or woolens. If you should have such materials in antique clothing, this chapter furnishes some good instructions for carefully washing them.

Little clothing is now made of pure natural fibers. Most is a mixture of natural fibers and manmade fibers such as dacron. Dacron is wrinkle-resistant. Clothing may also be made no-iron by the treatment of its fibers. These clothes cannot be ironed but, to obtain best results, they should be removed from the wash before spin cycles and hung out to drip dry. I can't stand no-iron clothing. The no-iron process gives them, to my touch, an irritating texture. I choose clothing from denim, flannel, corduroy and, when I can find them, pure cottons.

Washing, especially with bleaches, weakens fibers. The life of the cloth is diminished with each bleaching. Driers are very hard on fabrics; their intense heat shrinks and damages the fibers. Drying on an outdoor line gives clothes a clean, fresh smell and they last longer. To get your white clothing whiter without chlorine bleach, spread the clothes on the grass to dry. Oxygen from the grass will help to whiten the cloth.

Of the commercially available detergents, I like Boraxo and Arm & Hammer the best. Ivory and Duz are soaps; they require softer water. Amway products, sold by agents in the area, are highly concentrated, easily soluble and biodegradable. You may also wish, especially in the summer months, to add borax or baking soda to the wash. They keep damp clothes from souring and improve the soap's efficiency. Good bluing is hard to get now so people who want to blue their white clothing may wish to use the recipe in this chapter. Be careful of the very poisonous oxalic acid.

Making soap is quite easy. You can buy a can of lye, or you can make lye by boiling hardwood ashes and skimming the lye off the top. The best soaps are made from tallow (sheep and cow fat), lard (swine fat), olive oil or other vegetable oils. Fats can be clarified and cleaned by boiling. About six pounds of fat at 120-130° and a 13 oz. can of lye dissolved in 5 cups of cold water and heated to 90-95° will make about ten pounds of soap. Be careful about temperatures and never use aluminum pots for this process. After stirring the mixture for half an hour, let it set in a mold with wax paper in the bottom. A couple days setting should harden the soap enough so that it can be cut into convenient-sized bars. By grating the soap and adding about 1 part of borax (for sudsing) to 9 parts of soap, you can make very good soap flakes. Soap will absorb the odor of your favorite flowers, or oils such as sassafras, lavender, lemon or almond can be added directly to the mixture. Homemade soaps have the advantage of being mild, making use of fats you'd otherwise throw out, and containing none of the phosphates, caustic sodas, and other additives that make detergents dangerous to the environment. They're fun to make.

THE LAUNDRY.

A Washing Machine.—The opinion is now becoming general that the proper way to wash clothes is to alternately fill them with water and press it out, avoiding friction as much as possible. We herewith present a description of a machine for this purpose. The figure is a sectional view. *A* is a cylinder two feet in diameter, made of any suitable material. In the middle of the cylinder will be seen a stationary cylinder head, *B*, which is perforated with holes. *C C* are two movable pistons, working watertight in the cylinder—both of them fastened rigidly to the rod *D*. On the top part of the rod is a rack, which gears into the pinion *E*, worked by the crank *F*. The operation is as follows: The upper piston is raised above the top of the cylinder, and the clothes to be washed are placed therein, with a sufficient quantity of soap and water. On depressing the piston by means of the crank, the upper piston presses all the water out of the clothes, passing through the cylinder head *B*, thence following the lower piston to the bottom of the cylinder. Thus all the water is squeezed out of the clothes. On reversing the direction of the crank the pistons rise, and the lower one forces the water through the stationary head again into the clothes. It is thus depressed and raised alternately, soaking and squeezing the water out of the clothes. A stop-cock should be placed in the side of the cylinder to let off the water when not required.

Washing Lace Curtains.—There are many ways of doing this work; those which are bleached by the use of many of the bleaching powders make the lace beautifully clear and white, but usually injure the fabric; and when possible it is much safer to have them done up at home. The prevailing impression has been that there was some peculiar mystery in bleaching lace of any kind; that the process was tedious and very intricate, and if not done by a professional cleaner the lace was in imminent danger of destruction.

It is not so at all. Once understood, the work is as simple as any washing. Shake all the dust out of the lace curtains when taken down, but be gentle about it to avoid tearing. The shaking will remove the greater part of the loose dirt. Then spread them across two lines near together in the clothes yard, and brush them softly with a clean feather duster. When all has been brushed off, put them, one at a time, into a tub half full of milk-warm water and add two tablespoonfuls of liquid ammonia. Let it remain ten or fifteen minutes, turning it over carefully every minute or two, and squeezing with the hands. This through the ammonia will loosen all the dirt, after which squeeze out gently but as dry as can be done without breaking the meshes. Have ready another tub of tepid water with some more ammonia, and put the curtain into that immediately. Let it soak while the next curtain is taken through the same process as the first, and so on until all the curtains have been taken through at least three waters, or till the water looks clear, squeezing and washing the curtains with the hands as the work goes on. Ammonia in the two first waters is sufficient, and if not very gray and smoky, it will only be needed in the first.

After taking the curtains through the three waters many starch and blue them, and, without any soap or scalding, prepare to stretch them and pin in shape. But we prefer to put them into a bag, or coarse pillow-case, and scald in clean soapsuds (not very strong) for a few minutes. The suds should be made of very pure soap, and the water, when they are first put in only tepid; then just bring to a boiling heat. While the curtains are scalding prepare two tubs of clean water—one to rinse the curtains when they are taken from the boiler, and the other for the last rinsing. This should be blued; and the starch requires to be blued quite deeply, as, when hung up against the light, lace does not appear blue. The blued water and starch should be strained, that no mote of bluing may escape to settle on the curtains.

Take the curtains from the boiler when slightly scalded, rinse thoroughly, but with a gentle hand, till all the suds are out, then wring or squeeze out, and put through the bluing-water, wring out from that, and prepare to stretch, and pin out smoothly to the original length and width. This must be done when just taken from the water, as lace cannot be stretched when dry. The whole process of washing, scalding, rinsing and stretching should be done as expeditiously as consistent with thorough work, for no other cotton material shrinks so easily.

Many pin a clean sheet on to a carpet, in an unoccupied airy room, and pin the curtains on to the sheet. Every point and scallop should be pulled out and pinned on to the sheet evenly. But that is a very hard way for any one who finds stooping and bending over painful; and we don't think the lace looks as clear, because when pinned on to a carpet there can be no free circulation of air from underneath.

It is easier, and in every way better, to keep on hand four strips of thin boards, about three inches wide, made very similar to quilting-frames, with holes at suitable distances, to increase or diminish the length and breadth to suit the size of the curtains, and strong wooden pins put through the holes to fasten the frames strongly together. Tack, closely, strips of cloth, selvedge edge out, or wide tape, the whole length of the bars. Then place them on chairs so that they will stand firm and steady—out-doors, on a still, bright, sunny day—and pin or baste the curtains to the tape, pulling out and fastening every point in the lace.

Before wetting the curtains do not forget to measure them in length and breath, and mark the measure on the frame they are to be dried on. When washed they must be fastened at both ends first, and then stretched to match this measure. It takes but a little time to dry curtains thus stretched in the sun, and if well rinsed, free from soap, several curtains may be stretched out at the same time. This is a great saving of time; but we always fear the lace will not look as clear as if dried separately. But we have never tried that way. We, however, hear it approved by those who have.

Instead of nailing tape or strips of cloth to the " frame," small-sized galvanized tenter hooks are often driven into the frame on all four sides, and the lace or muslin curtains are caught on to these hooks and thus stretched out to dry. We do not like this so well as basting the curtains to the tape. We fancy the lace will be more injured on the hooks than it could be if sewed on. Lace should never be ironed. It costs but very little to make these bars, and they will last a life-time if carefully put away when not in use; and the curtains can be made to look quite as well as if done up in a French laundry, and will last much longer. It costs every year twice the expense of this frame to hire curtains done up.

Convenient Clothes Bars.—The bars are two inches wide by one inch thick. Four bars are three feet eleven inches long, and four are one foot eleven inches. The rods are dressed out one inch square, and of the following lengths: Four rods four feet long; two rods four feet two inches long; two rods three feet ten inches long; one rod four feet three inches long for the center, to project three inches at one end; another rod for the top four feet four inches long and to project two inches in order to receive the piece shown in the engraving to regulate the height. It can be shut so as to not occupy

more than a foot in width, or spread so as to hang a washing on. A three-fourth inch auger should be used in making. Any one who can use a plane or auger can make them.

To Wash Blankets.—Take half a cake of soap, cut it into small pieces and dissolve it thoroughly in hot water. Pour this into enough cold water to cover the blankets; add two ounces of borax (pulverized dissolves most readily),

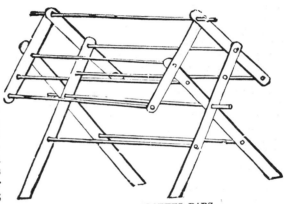

CONVENIENT CLOTHES BARS.

and put your blankets to soak all night. In the morning take them out and squeeze most of the water out of them and rinse thoroughly in cold water, in which a little borax has been dissolved; put them through a second rinsing water and then through the bluing water. Do not wring or squeeze them this time, but hang them up to drain and dry. The easiest way is to take them, while in the last water, out under the clothes line, as it is not convenient to carry them when full of water. It is best not to double them over the line, but hang by one end or side. Of course you want a sunny day for drying them nicely, and if you put in to soak at night and the next day is stormy, it will not hurt them to soak longer. If the wool is very greasy, use more soap and borax. Fine flannels and baby's crocheted skirts and sacques are nice when washed in this way, and if you use cold water they will not shrink. Vary the proportions of soap and borax to suit the quantity of water. I would not advise you to wash colored goods in this way, as they might fade.

Washing Fluid.—(1) Take one pound of sal soda and half a pound of unslacked lime, and put them in a gallon of water; boil twenty minutes, let it stand till cool, then drain off and put in a small jug or jar; soak your dirty clothes over night, or until they are wet through, then wring them and rub on plenty of soap, and in one boiler of clothes well covered with water, add a teacupful of the washing fluid; boil half an hour briskly, then wash them thoroughly with suds; rinse, and your clothes will look better than by the old way of washing twice before boiling. This is an invaluable receipt, and it should be tried by every woman who would save time and labor.

(2) For washing alpaca, camel's hair, and other woolen goods, and for removing marks made on furniture, carpets, rugs, etc.: Four ounces ammonia, four ounces white castile soap, two ounces alcohol, two ounces glycerine, two ounces ether. Cut the soap fine, dissolve in one quart of water over the fire; add four quarts of water. When nearly cold, add the other ingredients. This will make nearly eight quarts. It must be put in a bottle and stoppered tight. It will keep good any length of time.

(3) An excellent washing fluid and one that will not injure the finest fabric is made of one bar of Russian soap cut up fine, one tablespoonful of kerosene oil, a half cupful of washing soda and one gallon of water. The night before washday, put your clothes to soak in warm water. In the morning boil the fluid twenty minutes, add whatever cold water is required, for washing the clothes, put in the clothes and boil one-half hour; they are then ready to rinse and starch.

(4) Any one who will take a tablespoonful of kerosene to a gallon of water, along with a small quantity of common yellow soap, brought to a boiling heat, will find a chemical compound which makes clothes as white as snow with very little labor. They are first soaked in warm water as long as convenient, and then boiled in the mixture half an hour, when the dirt wrings out readily. No odor of the oil remains, and the clothes are perfectly clean.

(5) Add one pound of unslacked lime to three gallons of soft, boiling water. Let it settle and pour off. Then add three pounds of washing-soda, and mix with the lime-water. When dissolved, use a large wineglassful to each pailful of water. Add one gill of soft-soap to a pailful of water.

(6) To make washing fluid, take half a pound of sal soda, quarter of a pound of borax, dissolved in one gallon of hot water; let it settle; pour off in bottles. One gill of this mixture with a pint of soft soap, or half a bar of soap dissolved in hot water, is enough for a washing.

(7) Put one pound of saltpeter into a gallon of water, and keep it in a corked jug; two tablespoonfuls for a pint of soap. Soak, wash, and boil as usual. This bleaches the clothes beautifully without injuring the fabric.

To Wash Flannel.—Cut up what soap may be needed and dissolve in a skillet of boiling water. Let it stand on the stove and simmer till every particle is dissolved. Never rub soap on the flannel, or allow a bit to settle on them. Nothing " fulls " flannel so badly as rubbing soap on it, or letting bits of it settle on the cloth. A place on which a bit of soap has lodged or been rubbed will have a different shade from the rest when dried, making the whole garment look spotted.

Take a small tub not quite half full of scalding hot or boiling water. Into this pour enough of the dissolved soap to make a rich suds, also some ammonia, a teaspoonful and a half to ten or twelve quarts of suds is a fair proportion. Stir this and the soap into the hot water till it is all thoroughly incorporated. Then put in the flannels. Two or three articles are enough to soak at one time. Press them well under the water, but turn them over in the suds occasionally while soaking. Let them remain in the water till it is cool enough to put the hands in without discomfort. While washing keep a good quantity of water at boiling heat on the range for rinsing purposes, and to keep the suds as hot as it can be used. Before one piece is washed and ready to be wrung out fill a small tub half full of clear hot water. Into this stir a little more "bluing" than would be used for cotton or linen. Shake out each piece as soon as washed, quickly, and throw at once into the hot rinsing water.

Rub the flannel as little as possible, but draw it repeatedly through the hands, squeezing rather than rubbing. Harsh rubbing thickens and injures the fabric. Never wring with a wringer, as the pressure mats the nap down so closely as to destroy all the soft, fleecy look of good flannel. Wring with the hands as dry as possible, then rinse and wring out again; and when as dry as it can be made by hand, snap out, stretch and pull out into the true shape; dry in the open air, if possible. Bring in when not quite dry, roll up a short time, and iron while still a little damp, so that each part can be more readily brought into shape. Pressing, when ironing, is better for the flannel than rubbing. It does not make the fabric feel so hard and wiry.

Scarlet flannel is poisonous to some skins if used before washing, and as one is not always sure how one may be affected by it, it is safer to give it a scald in hot water with a little soap—not enough to make a strong suds. Let it stand and soak a few minutes, then wring out and treat like other flannels.

Clothes Sprinkler.—Sprinkling clothes previous to ironing by dipping our hand in a vessel of water and flirting it over the out-spread garment is, to say the least, performed in a very inefficient manner, for the clothes are unequally dampened. Conse-

CLOTHES SPRINKLER.

quently, in ironing, some portions of the cloth are quite dry, while other parts are quite too damp. A sprinkler made of tin in the form shown, with its lower part perforated with minute holes, is, when desired for use, placed in a vessel of water; by its own gravity it fills with water; after the sprinkling of each garment it is placed in the vessel to again fill. Old dipper handles properly perforated serve an excellent purpose. This arrangement can also be used in watering delicate plants, sprinkling the carpet, etc.

To Wash Lace.—Washing valuable lace should be a labor of love; time and patience are important requisites to do it well, and it comes especially within the province of the gentlewoman who possesses it. A long wooden board, say two yards by one, will be necessary for deep flounces. For smaller pieces, one yard by half a yard will do, but the larger size is prefer-able, as several pieces can be done on it at the same time. The board must be covered with thick flannel, and slightly stuffed to form a thick cushion. A good supply of fine, long lace pins, with small round heads, will be re-quired, as well as an ivory punch or an ivory knitting-needle, with a round point, a lobster's claw or a dog's tooth. Before washing, the yellow stains sometimes observable in old lace should be removed by placing the discol-ored portion on a hot iron, covered with linen moistened with a solution of oxalic acid; the lace should afterward be steeped in luke-warm water. Tepid water expels the starch or stiffening, hot water shrinks the thread, while cold water sets the dirt. Having well soaked the lace, wash it in a lather of purest white soap and luke-warm water. This must be done with great delicacy of touch, and rubbing must not be attempted; it must be merely dabbed or patted, and pressed between the hands gently to and fro in the water. When the dirt is well out rinse it several times in lukewarm water, and if any stiffness is required pass it through water just sweetened with the finest white sugar candy. In drying, the moisture must be expelled by gentle pressure; hand wringing must never be resorted to for any of the finer kinds of lace.

Doing up Men's Linen.—Many a husband easy to please in all other respects, has had his weekly grumble over " the way this collar sets," or " how this bosom bulges out!" And many a housewife has tried again and again to remedy these faults. A lady explains the difficulty in the following language:

Some time ago my husband used to complain that his linen collars did not set nicely in front. There was always a fullness, which in the case of standing collars was particularly trying to a man who felt a good deal of pride in the dressing of his neck, as it spoiled the effect of his cravat, and often left a gap for the display of either the collar band of the shirt or a half inch of bare skin. While talking with a practical shirtmaker one day, he mentioned his annoyance, and inquired if there was any means of relieving it.

" Yes," answered the man, " the fault lies with your laundress. While doing up your collars she stretches them the wrong way. Damp linen is very pliable, and a good pull will alter a fourteen-inch collar in the twinkling of an eye. She ought to stretch them crosswise, and not lengthwise. Then, in straightening out your shirt bosom, she makes another mistake of the same sort. They also ought to be polished crosswise instead of lengthwise, particularly in the neighborhood of the neck. A lengthwise pull draws the front of the neckband up somewhere directly under your chin, where it was never meant to go, and of course that spoils the set of your collars. With the front of your neckband an inch too high, and your collar an inch too long, you have a most undesirable combination."

The speaker was right. As soon as my husband ordered the necessary changes to be made in the methods of our laundry, a wonderful difference manifested itself in the appearance of that most important part of his clad anatomy, the neck. Let me commend the shirtmaker's hint to other distressed women.

How to Gloss Linen.—Inquiry is frequently made respecting the mode of putting a gloss on linen collars and shirt fronts, like that of new linen. This gloss, or enamel, as it is sometimes called, is produced mainly by friction with a warm iron, and may be put on linen by almost any person. The linen to be glazed receives as much strong starch as it is possible to charge it with, then it is dried. To each pound of starch a piece of sperm or white wax, about the size of a walnut, is usually added. When ready to be ironed, the linen is laid upon the table and moistened very lightly on the surface with a clean wet cloth. It is then ironed in the usual way with a flat-iron, and is ready for the glossing operation. For this purpose a peculiar heavy flat-iron, rounded at the bottom, as bright as a mirror, is used. It is pressed firmly upon the linen and rubbed with much force, and this frictional action puts on the gloss. " Elbow grease " is the principal secret connected with the art of glossing linen.

Washing Made Easy.—To save your linen and your labor pour on half a pound of soda two quarts of boiling water, in an earthenware pan; take half a pound of soap, shred fine, put it into a saucepan with two quarts of cold water, stand it on a fire till it boils, and when perfectly dissolved add it to the former. Mix it well, and then let it stand till cold, when it has the appearance of a strong jelly. Let your linen be soaked in water, the seams and any other dirty part rubbed in the usual way, and remain till the following morning. Get your wash boiler ready, and add to the water about a pint basin full. When lukewarm put in your linen and allow it to boil twenty minutes. Rinse it in the usual way, and that is all which is necessary to get it clean and keep it in good color. The above recipe is invaluable to housekeepers. Give it a trial.

Washing Clothes Without Fading.—Wash and peel Irish potatoes, and then grate them into cold water. Saturate the articles to be washed in this potato water, and they can then be washed with soap without any running of the color. I have taken oil out of carpets saturated with this potato water, when simple cold water would make the color run ruinously; have set the color in figured black muslins, in colored merinos, in ribbons and other silk goods. Often the potato water cleanses sufficiently without the use of soap, but the latter is necessary where there is any grease. In such cases (without soap) I take the grated potato itself and rub the goods with a flannel rag. In woolen goods it is necessary to strain the water, else the particles will adhere, but this is not necessary on goods from which they can be well shaken.

A French Way of Washing Clothes.—A system of washing clothes has been introduced in some French towns which is worthy of special mention. Its economy is so great as to greatly reduce the cost. This is the process: Two pounds of soap are reduced with a little water to a pulp, which having been slightly heated, is cooled in ten gallons of water, to which is added one spoonful of turpentine oil and two of ammonia; then the mixture is agitated. The water is kept at a temperature which may be borne by the hand. In this solution the white clothes are put and left there for two hours before washing them with soap, taking care, in the meantime, to cover the tub. The solution may be warmed again and used once more, but it will be necessary to add a half a spoonful of turpentine oil and another spoonful of ammonia. Once washed with soap, the clothes are put in hot water, and the blue is applied.

This process, it is obvious, saves much labor, much time and fuel, while it gives the clothes a whiteness much superior to that obtained by any other process, and the destructive use of the wash-board is not necessary to clean the clothes from impurities.

Bluing.—Bluing made from the following recipe has been in constant use in many families for several years. It does not injure even the finest clothes, and the cost is trifling compared with any other bluing. The quantity here noted has been known to last a family of six persons a year: Get one ounce of oxalic acid, one ounce of Chinese or Prussian blue (either will do), one quart of soft water. Put in a bottle and shake it well for two or three days after mixing it; after this do not shake it at all. If any of it settles to the bottom you can fill the bottle after using the first water. If when you buy it, it is not powdered, ask the druggist to powder it in a mortar for you. Unless the Chinese or Prussian blue is pure it will not be a success;

it will precipitate and make the clothes spotted. Ask the druggist to warrant it, for if it is all right it is unequaled by any bluing in the market, and it is a matter of great economy to use it; the quantity mentioned costing only about twenty cents.

To Wash Shetland Shawls.—Make a thin lather of boiled soap and water; plunge the shawl in this, and gently strip it through the hand. It must never be rubbed or wrung. When clean, rinse through water without any soap, hang it up for about a minute, shake it gently by each side alternately, pin it out on a sheet exactly square, and if the shawl be of a fine texture it should be lightly sewed down to the sheet by the top of the fringe to prevent it running up; then go over the whole fringe, drawing each thread separate, and laying it straight out. If these directions are carefully attended to the shawls may be washed many times, and each time appear as well as when new. They should never be put into the hands of any but those who are accustomed to wash lace.

Washing Hosiery.—Stockings that are stained or troublesome to clean are improved by being stretched out on a board and scrubbed with a hand-brush. Colored stockings ought to be rinsed quickly and well, and opened by pulling them on the hands on each side, and holding them thus until the toe is reached, then letting them fall, and pinning them by the top and side to the line. Woolen stockings are kept from shrinking if dried on a wooden shape of the right size. These are easily made from shingles of thin boards.

To Wash Colored Cottons.—Boil two quarts of bran in water for half an hour, let it cool, then strain it, and mix the liquor with the water in which the things are to be washed. They will only require rinsing, as the bran will stiffen them sufficiently. For colored muslins, rice-water is very good, as it helps to preserve the color; but, although it makes white muslins clear, it sometimes gives them a yellow tinge. When used it should previously be boiled in the proportion of one pound of rice to one gallon of water. No soap is required.

New Mixture Used in Washing Clothes.—In Berlin, Prussia, the washerwomen use a mixture of two ounces of spirits of turpentine and one quarter ounce of spirits of sal-ammoniac, well mixed together. This mixture is put into a bucket of warm water, in which half a pound of soap has dissolved. Into this mixture the clothes are immersed during the night and the next day washed. The most dirty cloth is perfectly freed from all dirt, and after two rinsings in pure water, the cloth has not the least smell of the turpentine. The cloth does not require so much rubbing, and fine linen is much longer preserved by it.

Whitening Yellow Flannels.—Flannel that has become yellow from being badly washed can be whitened by soaking it for two or three hours in a lather made of one quarter of a pound of curd soap, two tablespoonfuls powdered borax and two tablespoonfuls of carbonate of ammonia, dissolved in five or six gallons of water. Boil the soap in small shavings in water till dissolved, then add to it the other ingredients. Let the flannel lie in it until it looks whiter, then squeeze and press it, and rinse in bluing water, and hang in the hot sun to dry. Iron while it is still damp.

Hints for the Laundry.—If you wish your white clothes to look clear and pure white, always have ready a kettle of boiling water and scald them thoroughly before putting them in the last rinse-water. Clothes washed ever so clean will look dingy if soapy water is allowed to dry into them. Scalding removes the suds. Prints should be washed out a piece at a time in warm water, rinsed, and hung to dry immediately. But very few colors will bear soaking in hot soapsuds. If you want your flannels to full, wash them in *hot* water, rub well upon a board, using plenty of soap, and rinse in *cold* water. This rule never fails.

To Take Mildew from Clothes.—Mix soft soap with powdered starch, half as much salt, and the juice of a lemon; lay it on the part with a brush; let it lay on the grass, day and night, till the stain comes out. Iron molds may be removed by the salt of lemons. Many stains may be removed by dipping the linen in sour buttermilk, and then drying it in a hot sun; wash it in cold water; repeat this three or four times. Stains, caused by acids, may be removed by tying some pearlash up in the stained part; scrape some soap in cold, soft water, and boil the linen till the stain is gone.

Gum Arabic Starch.—Take two ounces fine white gum arabic and pound it to a powder; next put it into a pitcher and pour on it a pint or more of boiling water, according to the degree of strength you require, and then having covered it, let it stand all night. In the morning pour it carefully from the dregs into a clean bottle; cork and keep it for use. A tablespoonful of gum water stirred into a pint of starch that has been made in the usual manner will give to lawns (either white or printed) a look of newness to which nothing else can restore them after washing.

For Washing Black or Navy Blue Linens, Percales, Etc.—Take two potatoes grated into tepid soft water (first having peeled and washed them), into which put a teaspoonful of ammonia. Wash the goods in this and rinse in cold blue water. Starch will not be needed, and if at all practicable, they should be dried and ironed on the wrong side. It is said that an infusion of hay will preserve the colors of buff linens; an infusion of bran will do the same for brown linens and prints.

To Bleach Linen.—Mix common bleaching powder in the proportion of one pound to a gallon of water; stir it occasionally for three days, let it settle, and pour it off clear. Then make a lye of one pound of soda to one gallon of boiling soft water, in which soak the linen for twelve hours, and boil it half an hour; next soak in the bleaching liquor, made as above; and lastly, wash it in the usual manner. Discolored linen or muslin may be restored by putting a portion of bleaching liquor into the tub wherein the articles are soaking.

To Wash Lawns.—Boil two quarts of wheat bran in six quarts or more of water half an hour. Strain through a coarse towel, and mix in the water in which the muslin is to be washed. Use no soap, if you can help it, and no starch. Rinse lightly in clean water. This preparation both cleanses and stiffens the lawn. If you can, conveniently, take out all the gathers. The skirt should always be ripped from the waist. According to Marion Harland these are best directions.

Hints to Ironers.—Garments to be ironed in cold starch should be immediately dipped in boiling water, and ironed as soon as starched. You will, in this way, have no trouble with flats sticking to the cloth. Another good way is to wet the starch with weak cold suds made from white soap.

Washing Woolens.—If you do not wish to have white woolens shrink when washed, make a good suds of hard soap, and wash the flannels in it. Do not rub woolens like cotton cloth, but simply squeeze them between the hands, or slightly pound them with a clothes pounder. The suds used should be strong, and the woolens should be rinsed in warm water. By rubbing flannels on a board, and rinsing them in cold water, they soon become very thick.

Scorched Linen.—Peel and slice two onions; extract the juice by pounding and squeezing; add to the juice half an ounce of cut fine white soap, two ounces of fuller's earth, and half a pint of vinegar; boil all together. When cool, spread it over the scorched linen and let it dry on; then wash and boil out the linen, and the spots will disappear, unless burned so badly as to break the thread.

To Whiten Linen.—Stains occasioned by fruit, iron rust, and other similar causes, may be removed by applying to the parts injured a weak solution of the chloride of lime—the cloth having been well washed—or of soda, oxalic acid, or salts of lemon, in warm water. The parts subjected to this operation should be subsequently well rinsed in soft clear warm water, without soap, and be immediately dried in the sun.

To Prevent Streaking.—Do not let your laundress or washerwoman put clothes into the bluing water until they have been well shaken; if tossed in while folded, as they come through the wringer they are almost certain to be streaked with bluing, and although after repeated washings these streaks will come out, every one knows how aggravating it is to use napkins or handkerchiefs that show traces of careless washing.

Washing Merinos and Silk.—The following directions for washing merinos, lambswool and silk under-clothing may be useful: Use one pound of dissolved soap in four gallons of warm water, in which well rinse the articles to be washed, drawing them repeatedly through the hand, wring them as dry as possible to remove the soap; rinse them again briskly in clean, lukewarm water; wring and stretch them to their proper shape, and dry in open air if possible.

To Wash a Muslin Dress.—Make a good lather, and wash the muslin in cold water, never putting it into warm water, even to rinse it. If the muslin is green, add a wineglassful of vinegar to the water in which it is rinsed; if lilac, the same quantity of ammonia. For black and white muslins, use a small quantity of sugar of lead.

To Remove Rust from Linen.—Dissolve an ounce of oxalic acid in a pint of water, apply liberally to the spots of iron rust, then expose them to the sun's rays for half a day. The same will remove ink stains, but in either case it must have the *first* chance—that is, before soap suds or any other application. Label the bottle *poison!*

To Wash a Cambric Handkerchief.—To wash a fine cambric handkerchief, embroidered in colored silks, so that the colors do not run, the secret is to wash in a soap lather very quickly, wring thoroughly and then iron, so that it dries at once. There should be no soaking, and the embroidered corner should be kept out of the water as much as possible. A little alum in the water will make the process more sure.

To Prevent Spotting.—A teaspoonful of black pepper will prevent gray or buff linens from spotting, if stirred into the first water in which they are washed. It will also prevent the colors running, when washing black or colored cambrics or muslins, and the water is not injured by it, but just as soft as before the pepper was put in.

To Prevent Lumps in Starch.—To keep flour starch from lumping, mix the flour with water first, then remove the boiling water from the fire for a minute before stirring in the mixture, or it will cook into lumps before it reaches the bottom. It is well to remember this in making gruel, corn-starch, etc.

Iron Rust.—Iron rust, it is said, may be removed by tying a little cream of tartar in the stained spot before putting the cloth to boil. If this does not succeed, thicken lemon juice with equal parts of salt and starch, add some soft soap, apply the mixture to the cloth, and lay it in the hot sun. Renew the application several times.

To Make Potato Starch.—Grate six medium-sized potatoes and mix thoroughly with one gallon of water; strain through a coarse towel, let settle, drain off the water, and turn on another gallon of clear water, and let settle again; drain again, put in an earthen dish, and set in a warm place (not too warm) to dry. Use same as corn-starch for starching clothes.

Towels Should be Thoroughly Dried.—Many persons iron towels, fold them and put them away before they are thoroughly dry. This is an error, and sometimes leads to results not expected. In their damp condition there is a mold which forms on them called oidium, one variety of which causes numerous skin diseases.

To Save Soap.—The addition of three-quarters of an ounce of borax to a pound of soap, melted in without boiling, makes a saving of one-half in the cost of soap, and three-fourths the labor of washing, and improves the whiteness of the fabrics; besides, the usual caustic effect is removed, and the hands are left with a peculiar soft and silky feeling, leaving nothing more to be desired by the most ambitious washerwoman.

To Whiten Yellow Linen. Linen garments which have become yellow from time, may be whitened by being boiled in a lather made of milk and pure white soap, a pound of the latter to a gallon of the former. After the boiling process the linen should be twice rinsed, a little blue being added to the last water used.

Alum in Starch.—For starching muslins, ginghams, and calicoes, dissolve a piece of alum the size of a shellbark, for every pint of starch, and add to it. By so doing the colors will keep bright for a long time, which is very desirable when dresses must be often washed, and the cost is but a trifle.

To Prevent Calico from Fading.—To render the colors of cotton fabric permanent, dissolve three gills of salt in four quarts of water; put the calico in while hot, and leave it till cold; it will not fade by subsequent washing.

To Prevent the Iron from Sticking.—A spoonful of kerosene oil put into cold starch will prevent the iron from sticking.

To Restore Faded Blue Stockings.—Pale blue stockings which have faded can have the color restored by dipping into hot water in which common bluing has been poured and some lumps of alum are dissolved. Old white stockings can be colored in this way and do a good deal of service.

To Wash Colored Table Linen.—To wash colored table linen use tepid water, with a little powdered borax; wash quickly, using but little soap, and rinse in tepid water containing boiled starch; dry in the shade, and when almost dry, iron.

To Cleanse Black Cashm :e.—To clean black cashmere, wash in hot suds in which a little borax has been placed. Rinse in bluing water—very blue—and iron while damp. If carefully done the material will look equal to new.

To Clean Rusty Flat-Irons.—Beeswax and salt will make your rusty flat-irons as clean and as smooth as glass. Tie a lump of wax in a rag and keep it for that purpose. When the irons are hot, rub them first with the wax rag, then scour them with a paper or cloth sprinkled with salt.

To Clean White Worsted Goods.—For cleansing white worsted hoods, and clouds, or nubias, rub them thoroughly with wheat flour, then shake well, to remove the flour, and they will have all the clear, airy appearance of new.

To Iron a Calico Dress.—Never iron a calico dress on the right side; if ironed smoothly on the wrong side there will be no danger of white spots and gloss, which gives a new dress "done up" for the first time the appearance of a time-worn garment.

For Taking Out Scorch.—If a shirt bosom or any other article has been scorched in ironing, lay it where bright sun will fall directly on it. It will take it entirely out.

HINTS AND HELPS--Update

Here we have advice about canaries and walnut furniture polish, uses for old newspapers, how to beat an egg--in short all things specific and general, serious and frivolous. I am determined, someday, to try those recipes for making an Aeolian Harp and a handy, cheap barometer.

I would like to give some hints and helps of my own. Use plenty of hot water, taken internally in the form of tea or soup, or externally, in a tub of hot water with some salt added. Both ways will cure much of what ails you.

HINTS AND HELPS.

For the Removal of Stains and Spots.—The following methods of removing spots and stains from clothing are given on the authority of high chemical and textile authorities. They are believed to be trustworthy:

Matter Adhering Mechanically.—Beating, brushing and currents of water, either on the upper or under side.

Gum, Sugar, Jelly, etc.—Simply washing with water at a hand heat.

Grease.—White goods, wash with soap or alkaline lyes. Colored cottons, wash with lukewarm soap lyes. Colored woolens, the same or ammonia. Silks, absorb the grease with French chalk or fuller's earth, and dissolve away with benzine or ether.

Oil Colors, Varnish, and Resins.—On white or colored linens, cottons or woolens, use rectified oil of turpentine, alcohol, lye and soap. On silks, use benzine, ether and mild soap, very cautiously.

Stearine.—In all cases, use strong, pure alcohol.

Vegetable Colors, Fruit, Red Wine and Red Ink.—On white goods, sulphur fumes or chlorine water. Colored cottons and woolens, wash with lukewarm soap-lye or ammonia. Silk, the same, but more cautiously.

Alizarine Inks.—White goods, tartaric acid, the more concentrated the older the spots are. On colored cottons and woolens, and on silks, dilute tartaric acid should be applied cautiously.

Blood and Albuminoid Matters.—Steeping in lukewarm water. If pepsin or the juice of Carica papaya can be procured, the spots are first softened with lukewarm water, and then either of these substances is applied.

Iron Spots and Black Ink.—White goods, hot oxalic acid, dilute muriatic acid, with little fragments of tin. On fast dyed cottons and woolens, citric acid cautiously and repeatedly applied. Silks, impossible.

Lime and Alkalies.—White goods, simple washing. Colored cottons, woolens and silks are moistened, and very dilute citric acid is applied with the finger end.

Acids, Vinegar, Sour Wine, Must, Sour Fruits.—White goods, simple washing, followed up by chlorine water if a fruit color accompanies the acid. Colored cottons, woolens and silks are very carefully moistened with dilute ammonia, with the finger end. (In case of delicate colors, it will be found preferable to make some prepared chalk into a thin paste with water, and apply it to the spots.)

Tannin from Chestnuts, Green Walnuts, etc., or Leather.—White goods, hot chlorine water and concentrated tartaric acid. Colored cottons, woolens, and silks, apply dilute chlorine water cautiously to the spot, washing it away, and reapplying it several times.

Tar, Cart-wheel Grease, Mixtures of Fat, Resin, Carbon and Acetic Acid.—On white goods, soap and oil turpentine, alternating with streams of water. Colored cottons and woolens, rub in with lard, let lie, soap, let lie again, and treat alternating with oil of turpentine and water. Silks the same, more carefully, using benzine instead of oil of turpentine.

Scorching.—White goods, rub well with linen rags, dipped in chlorine water. Colored cottons, re-dye if possible; in woolen, raise a fresh surface. Silks, no remedy.

Coloring Recipes.—In using the following recipes remember that the goods should always be wet in hot soapsuds before they are put into the dye. Be very careful to have the materials thoroughly dissolved and keep the dye hot, constantly stirring the goods, lifting them up to the air and turning them over.

Brown.—For five pounds of goods allow one pound of catechu and two ounces of alum, dissolved in sufficient hot water to wet the goods. Put this in a brass kettle or tin boiler on the stove, and when it is boiling hot put in the goods and remove it from the stove. Have ready four ounces of bi-chromate of potash dissolved in hot water in a wooden pail. Drain the goods from the catechu and dip them into the bi-chromate of potash, then back into the catechu again. Proceed in this way, dipping into each alternately until the required shade is produced. This colors a nice brown on cotton, woolen, or silk.

Blue (on cotton).—Dissolve four ounces of copperas in three or four gallons of water. Soak the goods thoroughly in this, and then drain and transfer to a solution of two ounces of prussiate of potash in the same quantity of water. Lift the goods from this and put them to drain, then add to the prussiate of potash solution one-half ounce of oil of vitriol, being careful to pour in a few drops only at a time; stir thoroughly, return the goods, and as soon as of the desired shade rinse them in clear water and dry. This will color five pounds.

Yellow (on cotton).—For five pounds of goods, dissolve one pound of sugar of lead in enough water to thoroughly saturate the goods, and one-half pound of bi-chromate of potash in the same quantity of water in a separate vessel. Dip the goods well, and drain in each alternately until the desired shade is secured, then rinse and dry. If an orange is desired, dip the yellow rags into strong, hot lime water before rinsing.

Green (on cotton).—First color blue, and then proceed as in yellow.

Turkey Red (on cotton).—For four pounds of cloth, take one pound of sumac in enough soft water to cover the cloth in a tub, soak over night, wring out and rinse in soft water. Take two ounces of muriate of tin in clear soft water, put in the cloth and let it remain fifteen minutes. Put three pounds of bur wood in cold soft water, in a boiler on a stove, and nearly boil, then partly cool, then put in the cloth and boil one hour. Take out the cloth and add to the water in the boiler one ounce of oil of vitriol, put in the cloth and boil fifteen minutes. Rinse in cold water.

Dark Brown.—For dark brown, four ounces of blue vitriol, two pounds of cutch, and six ounces of bi-chromate of potash. This is for ten pounds of cloth. Put the cutch in an iron kettle, in cold water enough to cover the cloth, heat until dissolved, dissolve the vitriol, and add it to the dye, put in the cloth and scald it an hour or more. Wring it from the dye, dissolve the bi-chromate of potash in boiling water in brass, and put in the cloth for fifteen minutes.

Canary (on cotton).—Take one-half pound of sugar of lead, and dissolve it in hot water. Dissolve one-fourth pound of bi-chromate of potash in cold water in a wooden vessel. Dip the goods first in the lead water, then in the potash, so continuing until the color suits. This quantity will color five pounds of rags,

Several Ways to Clean and Polish Brass or Copper.—1. First remove all the stains, by rubbing the brass with a flannel dipped in vinegar; then polish with a leather and dry rotten-stone.

2. Rub the surface of the metal with rotten-stone and sweet oil, then rub off with a piece of cotton flannel, and polish with a piece of soft leather. A solution of oxalic acid rubbed over brass soon removes the tarnish, rendering the metal bright. The acid must be washed off with water, and the brass rubbed with whiting and soft leather. A mixture of muriatic acid and alum dissolved in water imparts a golden color to brass articles that are steeped in it for a few seconds.

3. Brass ornaments should be first washed with a strong lye made of rock alum, in the proportion of one ounce of alum to a pint of water. When dry, rub with leather and fine tripoli. This will give to brass the brilliancy of gold.

4. Copper utensils or brass articles may be as thoroughly cleaned and look as bright by washing them with a solution of salt and vinegar as by using oxalic acid, and the advantage of running no risk of poisoning either children or careless persons. Use as much salt as the vinegar will dissolve, and apply with a woolen rag, rubbing vigorously, then polish with pulverized chalk, and the article will look like new, with little labor, as the acid of the vinegar is very efficient in removing all stains from either copper or brass.

5. The quickest and easiest way to brighten copper or brass, is to wet a cloth in a strong solution of oxalic acid, and rub till it is clear, then dip a dry flannel into tripoli or prepared chalk, and rub it well.

6. A good paste for cleaning brass may be made by mixing one part oxalic acid and six parts rotten stone, with equal parts of train oil and spirits of turpentine, making a thick paste of the whole.

7. Clean brass with a solution made by dissolving one tablespoonful oxalic acid and two tablespoonfuls tripoli in a half pint of soft water. Apply with a woolen rag, and after a few minutes wipe dry and polish.

8. Wash with warm water to remove grease, then rub with a mixture of rotten-stone, soft soap, and oil of turpentine, mixed to the consistence of stiff putty. The stone should be powdered very fine and sifted; and a quantity of the mixture may be made sufficient to last for a long time. A little of the above mixture should be mixed with water, rubbed over the metal, then rubbed briskly with a dry, clean rag or leather, and a beautiful polish will be obtained.

Protection Against Moths.—In May the clothes-moth begins to fly about our rooms. It is a small, light, buff-colored " miller," dainty and beautiful on close inspection. Its highest mission seems to be to teach us to set our affections only upon incorruptible treasures which "moth and rust cannot destroy." But it is necessary to keep a sharp lookout for the safety of our furs and flannels, and we must wage war upon it. In the first place we must carefully put away everything we can, upon which it will lay its eggs. If we pack away our furs and flannels early in May, before the moth has begun to lay its eggs, and leave them in boxes and bags so tight that the flying moth cannot squeeze in, no further precaution is necessary. Clean paper bags are recommended for this purpose—those used for flour and meal bags. They should be without holes or opening anywhere. These bags, when filled and closed firmly, may be put away on closet shelves or in loose boxes, without danger to their contents, so far as moths are concerned.

without need of camphor or other strong odors to drive moths away. **Furs** are usually sold in boxes in which they may be kept. Beat them well when you finally put them away for the season. If you delay putting them away until June, examine the furs well, and shake and beat them very thoroughly, in order that any moth eggs that may possibly have been laid in them may be thoroughly removed or killed. Furs sealed up early in May need no camphor or tobacco or other preventive. Muff and tippet boxes should be tied up securely in bags, or made safe by mending holes and pasting a strip of paper around the juncture of the cover with the box below, so as to close all openings. Woolen garments must not hang in closets through the summer, in parts of the country where moths abound. They should be packed away in tight trunks or boxes, or sealed up in bags. Woolen blankets must be well shaken and carefully put away, unless they are in daily use. Early in June the larvæ of the moth begin their ravages, and then, unless you dwell in places where moths are not found, look sharp, or you will find some precious thing that you have forgotten—some good coat unused for a few weeks, or the woolen cover of a neglected piano, already more or less riddled by the voracious moths. It is their nature to eat until they have grown strong enough to retire from the eating business, and go into the chrysalis condition.

Some things cannot be well packed away in tight boxes and bags, and among these it is well to scatter small lumps of camphor or clippings of Russia leather. Some use tobacco, though I think camphor is usually preferred. It is said that powdered black pepper, scattered under the edge of carpets, will preserve them from attacks.

Several Ways to Destroy Ants.—Put red pepper in the places the ants frequent the most, and scrub the shelves or drawers with strong carbolic soap.

A small bag of sulphur kept in a drawer or cupboard, or saucers of olive tar set where they are, will drive them away.

A string wet in kerosene oil and tied around sugar barrels, lard cans, preserves, etc., is said to keep away ants. The string should be wet with the oil every few days.

Ants may be driven away by putting Scotch snuff wherever they are in the habit of going for food,

A small spray of wormwood if placed on buttery shelves, will, it is said, destroy or drive away ants.

Persons who are troubled with ants in their houses may get rid of them by rubbing the shelves with gum camphor. Two applications will be sufficient, with a week intervening.

A strong solution of carbolic acid and water, poured into holes, kills all the ants it touches, and the survivors immediately take themselves off.

Ants that frequent houses or gardens may be destroyed by taking flour of brimstone half a pound, and potash four ounces; and set them in an iron or earthen pan over the fire until dissolved and united; afterward beat them to a powder, and infuse a little of this powder in water—and wherever you sprinkle it the ants will die or leave the place.

Red ants may be banished from a pantry or store-room by strewing the shelves with a small quantity of cloves, either whole or ground. We use the former, as not being so likely to get in the food placed upon the shelves. The cloves should be renewed occasionally, as after a time they lose their strength and decay.

To Make an Æolian Harp.—This instrument, when placed in a window in a draft of air, produces the most pleasing music. We here give directions whereby any one may construct one for himself: Length, thirty-two inches by six inches; depth, one and three-quarter inches. The strings are attached to the small hooks at the end, corresponding to the pegs. The strings must be about the thickness of the first string of the violin. These strings answer well, but if too expensive the small gut used by whip manufacturers may be used. The bottom plank of the harp should be oak, three-quarters of an inch thick, length three feet, breadth ten inches. The bridges may be any sonorous wood (but steel will give the best sound), half an inch in height, cut angular to a blunt point. They must not be flattened down, but must be made to fit very flat to the bottom board, or it will jar and never play well. This is the great defect in all harps made by amateurs. The ends of the harps should be oak, one inch thick, and must be fixed very firmly to the bottom board, but not with metal screws or glue; and in these the pins are fixed for tightening the strings. Use fiddle pins, half at each end. The top should be half an inch thick, and sycamore wood is the best, and may be polished; it should be very slightly fastened on, for it has to be removed every time to tune. Common catgut does nearly as well as German. Get as thick a string as you can for one side, and a thin one for the other; then graduate them from the thick to the thin, so as not to have two alike. They are in general tuned to treble C, but it is preferable to tune to low C, and then each string an octave higher. This is easily altered, if desirable. The instrument must be very strong in all respects, for the strings exert almost incredible strength. The position for placing the harp at the window to be with the upper surface inclined towards the draft of air.

Staining Woods.—*Rosewood.*—Boil eight ounces of logwood in three pints of water until reduced to half; apply it boiling hot two or three times, letting it dry each time. Put in the streaks with a camel's hair brush dipped in a solution of copperas and verdigris in a decoction of logwood.

Light Mahogany.—Brush over the surface with diluted nitrous acid, and when dry apply with a soft brush the following: Four ounces of dragon's blood, one ounce of carbonate of soda, three pints of alcohol. Let it stand in a warm place, shake it frequently and then strain.

To Stain Musical Instruments.—Boil one pound of ground Brazil wood in three quarts of water for one hour; strain it, then add half an ounce of cochineal; boil a half hour longer. This makes a crimson stain.

Ebony.—Wash the wood several times with a solution of sulphate of iron; let it dry, then apply a hot decoction of logwood and nutgalls. When dry wipe it with a wet sponge; and when dry again polish it with linseed oil.

Black Walnut.—Pine may be stained to represent black walnut in the following manner: Put pulverized asphaltum into a bowl with about twice its bulk of turpentine and set where it is warm, shaking from time to time until dissolved; then strain and apply with either a cloth or a stiff brush. Try a little first, and if the stain be too dark, thin it with turpentine. If desirable to bring out the grain still more, give a coat of boiled oil and turpentine. When the wood is thoroughly dry, polish with a mixture of two parts shellac varnish and one part boiled oil. Apply by putting a few drops at a time on a cloth and rubbing briskly over the wood.

Oak.—A very fair oak stain may be produced by equal parts of potash and pearlash, say two ounces of each to about a quart of water. Keep it corked up in a bottle, and it is always ready for use; if it strikes **too** deep a color, add more water.

Staining with Iodine.—Wood may acquire an oak, walnut, or cherry tree color by staining it with ordinary tincture of iodine diluted with spirit until the exact shade is obtained. While shellac must be added to the iodine solution if the stain is to be made permanent, or the wood after the stain is applied may be French polished. The iodine may be laid on with a rag or a brush.

Purple.—Boil a pound of chip logwood in three quarts of water for an hour; then add four ounces of alum.

Blue.—Boil four parts of alum with eighty-five parts of water.

Hanging Wall Paper.—There are many housekeepers who have one or more rooms they would like to re-paper, but are kept from doing as much of this kind of work as they would like on account of the expense of getting a professional paper-hanger to put the paper on. Any one who takes the pains to notice, can soon learn to put on paper as well as the best paper-hanger. In the first place, you can often find among the cheap papers one or more lots that look just as well, and are of as good quality as the more expensive ones. When you have got your paper home, trim off the edge on the right side, as it is better for an inexperienced hand to commence at the left side of a door or window, and go toward the left. When you are ready to begin, make your paste with boiling water, and let it boil about as long as common starch, and it should be no thicker than starch after it is cold Let it cool and strain it through a common salt sack to take out the lumps. Then take a piece of washing soda as large as a walnut with the hull off, dissolve it in water, and put it in the paste and you need not use any glue or anything else whatever. Let an assistant hold the paper up to the wall, so that it will match with the piece already on, and cut it off the right length, always half an inch short, as it will stretch that much. Lay the paper wrong side up on a large table; let your help hold one end while you put on the paste quickly and evenly with a whitewash brush. Be sure to get every part covered. Take hold of the upper end, while your assistant takes the lower end, fasten it at the top, then sweep it down with a soft broom or brush, pick all windy places with a pin, and pat gently with a soft cloth. If it should become fast at the bottom too soon for the rest, pull it out carefully from the wall and replace it again. Paper put on with washing soda in the paste will not crack and come loose on greasy walls, as it often does without it. Try this plan, and your rooms will look nice and new with but little expense.

Table Etiquette.—There is nothing so disagreeable as careless and untidy table-manners; and to acquire graceful and pleasing habits while eating, sometimes takes years of practice. But it can be done; we see everywhere ladies and gentlemen, and sometimes children, who show their good breeding by their conduct at the table. To begin to make yourselves like these, the first thing to do is to sit down and think how you really behave at the table. Are your hands and nails, and face clean, and hair brushed back smoothly? Do you seat yourself quietly, and remember to put on your napkin? Do you sometimes put your knife in your mouth, instead of a fork or spoon? Do you pour your tea in your saucer, instead of drinking from the cup? How do you pass your plate, if you are to be helped a second time? The best way is to hold your knife or fork in your hand, and then it will not fall on the cloth.

Then about passing articles of food: Do you reach over another person's plate, or stand up to reach something not near at hand, and knock over a glass or cruet in the attempt? Do you eat fast and loud, and put large pieces in your mouth, or speak with food unchewed, or pick your teeth? Oh, I hope none of these, for any one of them would make you appear impolite and uncultivated. And then you remember not to whisper, yawn, or stretch, or touch the hair, or blow the nose. If it is necessary to use your handkerchief, do it so quietly that no one will notice it; but this should be done before you come to the table. And if there are bones, cherry pits, and things that cannot be swallowed, do not spit them on the plate, but put them on your spoon, and then on your plate.

Will you think of these hints the next time you sit down to your dinner, and avoid them? And remember that courtesy at the table is as indispensable as away from it, and if you practice it at home, you will not have to put it on when you are away, it will be so natural and easy for you.

To Can Corn, Beans, Etc.—After stripping off the husks and picking off the silk, slice off carefully about half or two-thirds of the corn, with a sharp knife; then, with the back of the blade, press or scrape off that part of the kernels left on the cob. This prevents cutting of the cob. Fill the can about one-third, and with the small end of a potato masher, or other stick, gently pack it down; put in more corn and pack again, and continue until the can is full to the very top. Put on the rubber, and screw the top on very tight. Put some cloth, hay or straw in the bottom of the wash boiler and on it set (or lay) the filled cans. Fill the boiler with cold water, being careful to cover the cans with it; set over the fire, and boil for three hours or more. Do not fear that the cans will burst, even if very tightly screwed down. When you take them out, try if it is possible to screw the cover on more securely. After the jars are cool, wrap each one in paper, and set away in the dark. This is essential. This process succeeds perfectly, absolutely without a failure. Succotash is put up in the same way, and so are green beans and string beans. Peas you cannot pack—shake down very closely- put on rubbers, screw on cover, and boil in the same manner as directed for the corn. They will shrink in the can—corn will not if packed hard.

Furniture Polish.—(1) Take beeswax and turpentine in the proportion of two ounces of the former to half a pint of the latter. Put the turpentine in a tin basin and cut the beeswax in small pieces and put in, then put in the oven when not very hot, so it (the wax) will gradually melt; stir it constantly. Apply to the furniture with a piece of woolen rag (a piece of broadcloth is best for the purpose), and have another piece to rub with. Don't be afraid to use plenty of "elbow grease."

(2) One-third of spirits of wine, one-third of vinegar and one-third of sweet oil; or rather more of the last. Shake the bottle well daily for three weeks; it is then fit for use, but the longer it is kept the better it is. The furniture must be rubbed till the polish is dry. Use every two or three months, and rub the furniture over daily when dusted. For dining-room tables and sideboards, use it every week; it makes them beautifully bright.

(3) If you wish one of the simplest and best, get a pint bottle and fill it with equal parts of boiled linseed oil and kerosene oil; any druggist has the former; mix and apply with a flannel, and rub dry with a second flannel.

It will remove all scratches and white marks made by bruising. Destroy the rags or keep in open sight, as oiled cloths have been known to ignite spontaneously.

(4) Into one pint of linseed oil put half a pound of treacle and a glass of gin; then, stirring well, apply sparingly with a linen rag, and if rubbed until quite dry with linen cloths, this mixture will produce a splendid gloss. Eating tables should be covered with oilcloth or baize, to prevent staining, and be instantly rubbed when the dishes are removed.

(5) Make a mixture of three parts of linseed oil and one part spirits of turpentine. It not only covers the disfigured surface, but restores wood to its original color, and leaves a lustre on the surface. Put on with a woolen cloth, and when dry rub down with woolen.

(6) A nice furniture polish is made by mixing boiling linseed oil and white varnish, using one-fourth varnish to three-fourths of the oil. Apply with a flannel, rubbing thoroughly, and afterwards rubbing with dry flannel or chamois skin.

(7) Equal quantities of common wax, white wax, white soap, in the proportion of one ounce of each to pint water. Cut the above ingredients fine, and dissolve over a fire until well mingled.

A Very Cheap Bed Covering.—The *American Agriculturist* says: Many years ago, in one of the severe winters when there was much hardship among the poor, a city paper suggested that old newspapers, spread over the bed, would form an excellent substitute for blankets and coverlets. This brought upon the journal a great deal of harmless ridicule from other papers, but it brought comfort to many a poor family. In the matter of bed-clothing, especially, we are apt to associate warmth with weight, and do not consider that there is no warmth in the coverings themselves, but that they merely prevent the heat of the body from passing off. Whatever is a poor conductor of heat will make a warm covering. Paper itself is a poor conductor, but still poorer are the thin layers of air that are confined when two or three newspapers are laid upon one another. A few newspapers laid over the bed will keep one much warmer than some of the heavy, close woven blankets. We do not propose newspapers as a substitute for blankets and comforters, but it is one of those makeshifts that it is well to know. In traveling one may, by the aid of a few papers, secure a comfortable rest in a thinly-clad bed, and if we cannot afford to give a destitute family a blanket or a comforter, we may show them how to increase the usefulness of their thin coverings by stitching a few layers of newspapers between them. It may be well to remind those who grow window plants that, by removing them away from the window and arranging a cover of newspapers over them, they may be preserved from harm in severely cold nights. With the plants as with ourselves, it is not so much that cold comes in as that the heat goes off, and often a slight protection will prevent the escape of heat.

What an Old Housekeeper has Learned.—"Never too old to learn," and here are a few of the things we have learned at our house:

That ripe cucumbers make a good sweet pickle.

That a piece of cork is better than cloth for applying brick to knives.

That clabbered milk is better than water for freshening salt fish.

That people who chew plenty of good beef and eschew pork are sensible.

That apples which take a long while to bake, should have a little water in the pan.

That salt pork will be nearly as nice as fresh, if soaked in sweet milk and water, equal parts.

That if we wish to prolong our lives we should always put one day between washing and ironing.

That liver should be thrown into boiling water after being sliced thin and then fried in lard or dripping.

That pie crust will not be soggy if it is brushed over with the white of an egg before the fruit is put in.

That half a cup of vinegar in the water will make an old fowl cook nearly as quick as a young one, and does not injure the flavor in the least.

That a tough beefsteak may be made eatable by mincing it pretty fine with a chopping-knife and cooking quickly in a pot with a close cover, to prevent the steam from escaping.

To Keep Apples.—1. Having selected the best fruit, wipe it perfectly dry with a fine cloth, then take a jar of suitable size, the inside of which is thoroughly coated with cement, and having placed a layer of fine sand perfectly dry at the bottom, place thereon a layer of the fruit—apples or pears, as the case may be—but not so close as to touch each other, and then a layer of sand; and in this way proceed till the vessel is full. Over the upper layer of fruit a thick stratum of sand may be spread and lightly pressed down with the hands. In this manner choice fruit perfectly ripe may be kept for almost any length of time, if the jar be placed in a situation free from moisture.

2. Take fine dry sawdust, preferably that made by a circular saw from well seasoned hard wood, and place a thick layer on bottom of a barrel. Then place a layer of apples, not close together and not close to staves of the barrel. Put sawdust liberally over and around, and proceed until a bushel and a half, or less, are so packed in each barrel. They are to be kept in a cool place.

The Best Kind of Beds.—Do you sleep upon a feather bed? We hope not. Years ago a feather bed was supposed to be an important part of a housekeeping outfit. If you have a feather bed, put it in the spare room, lock the door, and loose the key. A curled-hair mattress of the best quality makes one of the most desirable couches, but curled hair is expensive and all cannot afford it. The next best thing, indeed, almost as good, is afforded by that plant, so dear to every American farmer—Indian corn. Whoever grows corn, need not lack for the most comfortable of beds. We are aware that ticks are sold filled with husks with the stem part left on. A bed of this kind is not the kind of husk bed we have in mind. To make the very best possible husk bed, save the husks from the green corn as it is daily used. The husks are coarse, and should be slit. An old-fashioned hatchet, where there is such an implement, answers well, but a substitute can be made by driving a few large nails through a board, and filing them sharp. Drawing the husks across these will slit them into shreds an inch or less wide. An old carving fork may be used to slit the husks. Then put them to dry in a garret or some airy loft. If the green-corn season is past, then, at the regular husking of the field crop, secure a stock for mattresses. Reject the weather-worn outer husks, taking only the thin, papery ones.

Artificial Gold.—This is a new metallic alloy which is now very extensively used in France as a substitute for gold. Pure copper, one hundred parts; zinc, or, preferably, tin, seventeen parts; magnesia, six parts; sal-ammoniac, three-sixths parts; quick-lime, one-eighth part; tartar of commerce, nine parts, are mixed as follows: The copper is melted first, and the magnesia, sal-ammoniac, lime and tartar are then added separately, and by degrees, in the form of powder; the whole is now briskly stirred for about half an hour, so as to mix thoroughly; and then the zinc is added in small grains by throwing it on the surface, and stirring until it is entirely fused; the crucible is then covered, and the fusion maintained for about thirty-five minutes. The surface is then skimmed, and the alloy is ready for casting. It has a fine grain, is malleable, and takes a splendid polish. It does not corrode readily, and for many purposes is an excellent substitute for gold. When tarnished, its brilliancy can be restored by a little acidulated water. If tin be employed instead of zinc, the alloy will be more brilliant.

To Dye Feathers.—*Black.*—Immerse for two or three days in a bath, at first hot, of logwood, eight parts, and copperas or acetate of iron, one part.

Blue.—With the indigo vat.

Brown.—By using any of the brown dyes for silk or woolen.

Crimson.—A mordant of alum, followed by a hot bath of Brazil wood, afterwards by a weak dye of cudbear.

Pink or Rose.—With saf-flower, or lemon juice.

Plum.—With the red dye, followed by an alkaline bath.

Red.—A mordant of alum, followed by a bath of Brazil-wood.

Yellow.—A mordant of alum, followed by a bath of turmeric or weld.

Green.—Take of verdigris and verditer, of each one ounce; gum water, one pint; mix them well and dip the feathers (they having been first soaked in hot water) into the said mixture.

Purple.—Use lake and indigo.

Carnation.—Vermilion and smalt. Thin gum or starch water should be used in dyeing feathers.

To Wash and Curl Feathers.—Wash in warm soap-suds and rinse in water a very little blued, if the feather is white, then let the wind dry it. When the curl has come out by washing the feather or getting it damp, place a hot flat-iron so that you can hold the feather just above it while curling. Take a bone or silver knife and draw the fibers of the feather between the thumb and the dull edge of the knife, taking not more than three fibers at a time, beginning at the point of the feather and curling one-half the other way. The hot iron makes the curl more durable. After a little practice, one can make them look as well as new feathers. When swans' down becomes soiled it can be washed and look as well as new. Tack strips on a piece of muslin and wash in warm water with white soap, then rinse and hang in the wind to dry. Rip from the muslin and rub carefully between the fingers to soften the leather.

To Clean Furs.—For dark furs: warm a quantity of new bran in a pan, taking care that it does not burn, to prevent which it must be briskly stirred. When well warmed, rub it thoroughly into the fur with the hand. Repeat this two or three times, then shake the fur, and give it another sharp brushing until free from dust. For white furs: lay them on a table, and rub well with bran made moist with warm water; rub until quite dry, and afterward with dry bran. The wet bran should be put on with flannel, then dry with book muslin. Light furs, in addition to the above, should be well rubbed with magnesia or a piece of book muslin, after the bran process, against the way of the fur. Soiled white fur can be nicely cleaned by rubbing it thoroughly in white flour. It should then be hung out of doors for about thirty minutes. Repeat the process several times, and the fur will be equal to new.

An Home-made Refrigerator.—Nearly all housekeepers who are not able to obtain a refrigerator, keep their ice wrapped up in bits of old carpeting or some non-conducting material, which wastes the ice, and affords no help in preserving food. To them these directions may offer attractions: Take two large wooden boxes—dry goods boxes for instance—select the second one about a couple of inches smaller on all sides, and bore a one-inch hole in both, correspondingly to give drainage and ventilation. Perhaps a couple of holes would do better. Fill up the space under the boxes with powdered charcoal or coal ashes. Put the inner box in place and fill up all the spaces with the same. Sawdust might do if nothing better is procurable, yet it is apt to become musty. Fix on the lids to both boxes to fit tightly, with iron hinges (leather ones can be substituted), and fasten with straps of leather, or a lock and key. Put shelves on each side of the inner box by means of cleats. Leave a place in the center for the ice. This is a rough refrigerator, to be sure, but far better than none. A zinc lining, or one of felting, would improve the inner box. A rack made of lathing can be laid at the bottom for the ice to rest upon. Legs can be added to the outer box by putting pieces of wood at each corner, and the drainage and ventilation will be improved; and an ingenious man can make an excellent ice box in this way.

Cleaning Carpets.—In all our own experiments we have found nothing so safe and serviceable as bran slightly moistened—only very slightly—just sufficient to hold the particles together. In this case it is not necessary to stop and clean the broom every few minutes. Sweeping the carpet after the bran has been sprinkled over it not only cleans the carpet and gathers all the dirt into the bran, but keeps the broom clean at the same time. If too much dampened, aside from injuring the carpet it makes the work harder, because the bran becomes very heavy if very damp. The bran should be sifted evenly over the floor, and then the room swept as usual. The bran scours and cleanses the whole fabric, very little dust is made while sweeping with it, and scarcely any settles on furniture, pictures, etc., after the work is accomplished, because every particle of dirt, thread, bits of paper or lint is gathered up into the mass of bran that is being moved over the floor, and so thoroughly incorporated with it that it will not be easily separated. Carpets swept in this way retain very little dust, as will be plainly demonstrated whenever they are taken up to be shaken.

Hints on Cake Baking.—When cakes are made without yeast or eggs, soda and powder being the substitutes, they require quick baking in a moderately hot oven, and should be drawn directly when they are done, or they get dry and tasteless. For a plain cake, made with one pound of flour, etc., the time to be allowed in baking would be from forty to fifty minutes, at the outside not more than an hour. Yeast cakes take longer—say from ten to fifteen minutes—and will bear to be left in the oven rather over the time without much injury. Very rich cakes, in which butter and eggs predominate, take, of course, a much longer time to cook; pound cake taking from an hour and a half to two hours, and bride cake three and a half. On no account should the oven be too hot when the cakes are put in—that is, not hot enough to brown at once; if so, in five minutes the whole outside will be burned, and the interior will stand little chance of being cooked. The old plan of feeling the handle of the oven door to test the heat, is not always successful; it is better to sprinkle a little flour inside, and shut the door for about three minutes; if at the end of that time it is of a rich light brown, the cake may be put in; but if burned, the heat must first be lessened.

Household Conveniences.—There are many little contrivances which add much to the comfort of the household, and cost but little money. A little forethought often saves time and labor. A calico curtain tacked over the wheel of the sewing machine, protects the operator's dress from grease. A small wadded quilt made and kept especially to cover the bread when it is set to rise, is much nicer and more cleanly than the old coats and shawls which perform that duty in too many households.

Mothers with several little children who attend school, will save time and money by securely fastening each child's glove to its coat by strong tapes. A small table provided with a support which reaches to the floor and steadies it, will be found very useful in a crowded kitchen. It should be attached to the wall by hinges, and when not in use can be folded up, thus leaving the space it occupied for other purposes. It can be used for dish washing, is a capital place to mold the bread, or to iron upon. A large dining-table may be made in the same way, only it must be fastened up against the wall and secured by a button or bolt.

Mending Rubber Boots.—Procure some pure gum, which can be bought at any wholesale rubber house, or you can have your druggist order it for you at a cost of about five cents per ounce. At the same time order patching, and it is well to have two thicknesses for mending different goods. Put an ounce or two of gum into three or four times its bulk of benzine, cork tightly and allow it to stand four or five days, when it will be dissolved. Wet the boots with benzine for an inch or more around the hole and scrape with a knife; repeat this wetting with benzine and scraping several times until thoroughly cleaned, and a new surface exposed. Wet the cloth side of the patching with benzine and give one light scraping, then apply with a knife a good coating of the dissolved rubber, both to the boot and patch, and allow it to dry until it will not stick to your fingers, then apply the two surfaces and press or lightly hammer into as perfect compact as possible, and set away for a day or two, if possible, before using. If you do not succeed it will not be the fault of the process.

Upholstering Old Cane Chairs.—When the cane seat of a chair is broken, it may be made as good as new, or better, by upholstering it at home. After removing the superfluous bits of cane, cover the space with matting formed of three-inch wide canvas belting woven together. Tack it temporarily in place. After placing over this some coarse muslin, draw both smooth, and secure at the edge with twine, making use of the perforations. Remove the tacks, turn the raw edge over toward the center and baste it down. Arrange the curled hair and wool, or whatever you propose to use for stuffing, and keep it in position by basting over it a piece of muslin. Then carefully fit the rep, pin it in different places until you are certain it is in perfect shape, and tack it permanently, following, of course, the tracing made for the cane. Cover the edge with galloon to match the rep, using tiny ornamental tacks, and tie with an upholsterer's needle in as many places as is desirable, leaving a button on the upper side. When the back of the chair is to be repaired, a facing must be tacked on the outside,

Canning Fruit.—Those housekeepers who have not been successful in their attempts at this work will find the following a most excellent recipe: Place the fruit in either a granite, iron, or porcelain kettle; never use common iron, brass or tin for this purpose. Allow it to boil for about five minutes. Have the jars in readiness, and standing in a vessel of warm water, so that they may be heated gradually. Just before filling the jar with fruit, dip a towel in boiling water and wrap it around the jar, and tuck the corners under the bottom for the jar to rest upon. Fill the jar quickly, and when full thrust a knife to the bottom and stir it around several times, and the air bubbles will rise to the top. Seal as tight as possible, and stand the jar on the top in a moderately cool place. In a few hours turn the jar up, and try to seal tighter, standing it again on the top. Continue this several times, or until the cover is tightly screwed on. Stand the jars in a cool, dark place in the cellar, looking at them occasionally for a few days. For several years the above has been my method of canning, and I know from experience that all varieties of fruits and vegetables can be canned with perfect success in this way.

To Exterminate Bedbugs.—(1) Shut the windows tight, leave all clothing in its place, and open trunks and drawers. Put a thick layer of ashes into the iron kettle, on which place the live coals. Have no obstacles between yourself and the open door. Put a handful of sulphur on the coals, and immediately close the room, leaving it undisturbed for several hours. When opened, the room and contents can be aired, and the odor will soon be gone. It is rarely that a second fumigation is necessary. Burn sulphur in rooms where there are moths.

(2) Take two ounces of quicksilver and the whites of two eggs, and so on in this ratio for a larger or smaller quantity. Beat the quicksilver and the whites together until they unite and become a froth. With a feather then apply the compound thus formed to the crevices and holes in your bedsteads. This done twice in a year will prove effectual.

(3) Blue ointment and kerosene, mixed in equal proportions and applied to bedsteads, is an unfailing bug remedy, and a coat of whitewash is ditto for a log house.

To Determine the Quality of Silk.—The following directions for detecting the spurious from the genuine article in black silk will be found useful: Take ten fibres of the filling in any silk, and if on breaking they show a feathery, dry, and lack luster condition, discoloring the fingers in handling, you may at once be sure of the presence of dye and artificial weighting. Or take a small portion of the fibres between the thumb and forefinger and very gently roll them over and over, and you will soon detect the gum, mineral, soap, and other ingredients of the one, and the absence of them in the other. A simple but effective test of purity is to burn a small quantity of the fibres; pure silk will instantly crisp, leaving only a pure charcoal; heavily dyed silk will smolder, leaving a yellow, greasy ash. If, on the contrary, you cannot break the ten strands, and they are of a natural luster and brilliancy, and fail to discolor the fingers at the point of contact, you may be well assured that you have a pure silk, that is honest in its make and durable in its wear.

To Prevent Silverware from Tarnishing.—Solid silverware, as well as plated goods, grows dark and tarnished in a very short time when exposed to the air, and even when put away in a dark place. This is especially the case where hard coal is used in the house or neighborhood, as the sulphur in the coal, liberated by heat, is sure to stain all the silverware within reach. This annoying tarnishing can be entirely prevented by painting the silverware with a soft brush dipped in alcohol in which some collodion has been dissolved. The liquid dries immediately and forms a thin, transparent and absolutely invisible coating upon the silver, which completely protects it from all effects of the atmosphere, etc. It can be removed at any time by dipping the article in hot water. This recipe has been in use for some time in the large establishments at London, where most of the goods in the show cases are protected in this manner.

A Handy and Cheap Barometer.—One that answers the purpose of indicating the approach of fair or foul weather, can be made as follows: Take an eight-ounce bottle, the glass being clear and white, and put into it six ounces of the highest colored whiskey to be obtained, and put into it all the gum-camphor it will dissolve, and a little more. Set in some convenient place. On the approach of rain or bad weather the camphor will settle toward the bottom of the bottle; the heavier the rain, or the more sultry the weather, the closer the camphor will settle to the bottom. Fair weather is indicated by the feather-like appearance of the camphor, which rises and floats in the liquid. If alcohol is used, it must be diluted so that it will not be stronger than the whiskey, for if it is, so much of the camphor will be held in solution that the atmosphere will have no perceptible effect upon it.

French Polish.—Many will be glad to know how the fine origina. polish of furniture may be restored, especially in the case of such articles as pianos, fancy tables, cabinets, lacquered ware, etc., which have become tarnished by use. Make a polish by putting half an ounce of shellac, the same quantity of gumlac and a quarter of an ounce of gum sandarac into a pint of spirits of wine. Put them all together in a stone bottle near the fire, shaking it very often. As soon as the gums are dissolved it is ready for use. Now make a roller of woolen rags—soft old broadcloth will do nicely—put a little of the polish on it, and also a few drops of linseed oil. Rub the surface to be polished with this, going round and round, over a small space at a time, until it begins to be quite smooth. Then finish by a second rubbing with spirits of wine and more of the polish, and your furniture will have a brilliant luster, equal to new.

How to Make a Hammock.—A comfortable, inexpensive hammock is thus made: Bring your old flour barrel from the cellar or store-room, knock it to pieces, clean, and paint the staves. Procure a rope four times the length, each place where it is to be suspended, and in size a little larger than a clothes-line. Now halve the rope, double each piece in the middle, and commencing two yards or so from the end, weave it over and under each stave about three inches from the end of each one, which will bring the rope crossed between each; do both sides the same and your hammock is complete.

Fruit Stains.—In the season of fruits, the napkins used at the table, and often the handkerchiefs and other articles, will become stained. Those who have access to a good drug store can procure a bottle of Javelle water. If the stains are wet with this before the articles are put into the wash, they will be completely removed. Those who cannot get Javelle water can make a solution of chloride of lime. Four ounces of the chloride of lime is to be put into a quart of water, in a bottle, and after thorough shaking allow the dregs to settle. The clear liquid will remove the stains as readily as Javelle water, but, in using this, one precaution must be observed. Be careful to thoroughly rinse the article to which this solution has been applied, in clear water, before bringing it in contact with soap. When Javelle water is used, this precaution is not necessary; but with the chloride of lime liquid it is, or the articles will be harsh and stiff.

How to Clean Marble-top Furniture.—It may be of some value to housekeepers who have marble-top furniture to know that the common solution of gum arabic is an excellent absorbent, and will remove dirt, etc., from the marble. The method of applying is as follows: Brush the dust off the piece to be cleaned, then apply with a brush a good coat of gum arabic, about the consistency of thick office mucilage, expose it to the sun or dry wind, or both. In a short time it will crack and peel off. If all the gum should not peel off, wash it with clean water and a clean cloth. Of course if the first application does not have the desired effect, it should be applied again. Another method of cleaning marble is to make a paste with soft soap and whiting, wash the marble with it, and then leave a coat of paste upon it for two or three days. Afterward wash off with warm (not hot) water and soap.

How to Dress a Fowl Properly.—In a large majority of households, poultry is thought to be sufficiently cleansed when thoroughly washed, and rinsed, in cold water, often after the fowl is cut up ready for cooking, thus seriously injuring the flavor of the meat. The proper method is to scald, pick, and singe the fowl as usual, and then to soap the fowl thoroughly, with the hand or a cloth, rubbing it well. You will be surprised to find so much impurity in the soapsuds, in which the fowl has been washed. Use two or three rinsing waters and immerse in pure cold water for a few moments. Drain and wipe dry. The skin of the fowl is now delicately clean, and if placed beside a fowl, dressed in the ordinary way, a vast difference is observed in favor of the clean fowl; be very particular to remove the entrails, crop, and gall, without disturbing their contents, and one slight rinsing is sufficient, and the delicate flavor preserved.

Discolorations from Matches.—What neat housekeeper is not annoyed when she sees on the spotless woodwork of her door or windows those long dark scratches which reveal that some one has tried to light a match by drawing it across the paint? Now this is sometimes our experience, for servants will be forgetful or careless, and the tell-tale scratches greet our eyes in most unlooked-for quarters. But we have found a remedy for the marks, which, as every one knows, quite defy soap and water. Cut a sour orange or lemon in half, apply the cut half to the marks, rubbing for a moment quite hard; then wash off with a clean rag, dipped first in water to moisten it, and then in whiting. Rub well with this rag, dry thoroughly, and nine times out of ten the ugly mark will vanish. Of course, sometimes they are burned in so deeply that they cannot be quite eradicated. All finger-marks on painted walls, etc., should be rubbed off with a little damp whiting in the same way, and never washed with soapsuds, which destroys the paint.

Preserving Glassware.—Almost every drawing-room nowadays has a lamp of some rich design upon the center-table, and to careful housekeepers it is a vexed problem how to keep lamp chimneys from cracking. The *Diamond* is a Leipsic journal devoted to glass matters, and from that we clip the following bit of useful information: "Place your tumblers, chimneys or vessels which you desire to keep from cracking, in a pot filled with cold water and a little cooking salt; allow the mixture to boil well over a fire, and then cool slowly. Glass treated in this way is said not to crack, even if exposed to very sudden changes of temperature. Chimneys become very durable by this process, which may also be extended to crockery, stone-ware, porcelain, etc. The process is simply one of annealing, and the slower the process, especially the cooling portion of it, the more effective will be the work."

A Good Cement.—A good cement for mending almost anything may be made by mixing together litharge and glycerine to the consistency of thick cream or fresh putty. This cement is useful for mending stone jars or any coarse earthenware, stopping leaks in seams of tin pans, wash-boilers, cracks and holes in iron kettles, etc. Holes an inch in diameter in kettles can be filled and used the same for years in boiling water and feed. It also may be used to fasten on lamp-tops, to tighten loose nuts, to secure bolts whose nuts are lost, to tighten loose joints of wood or iron, loose boxes in wagon hubs, and in a great many other ways. In all cases the articles mended should not be used until the cement is hardened, which will require from one day to a week, according to the quantity used. This cement will resist the action of water, hot or cold, acids, and almost any degree of heat.

The Best Known Receipt for Corning Beef.—Cut the beef in small pieces, leaving out the large bones, pack solid in a six-gallon crock with a weight on top. Pour over the beef boiling-hot brine made as follows: Two gallons of water, three pounds of salt, one ounce of saltpetre, a pound of sugar and two large spoonfuls of baking soda. After two weeks, heat and skim the brine, and repeat the process whenever you think necessary, but never put the brine on hot after the first time. If the weather is hot you can add a handful of salt and soda at any time, and like all pickling be sure the brine covers the beef. If packed in a barrel, a large cloth should be securely tied over it in summer, to secure its contents from flies. The nicest vessel to put it into is a half barrel earthen jar.

The Use of a Broom.—As simple as the advice may seem, but very few people handle a broom properly, although they are accustomed to sweep more or less every day of their lives. There is science in handling a broom, as well as in many other kinds of labor. Always draw your broom, by lean-ing the handle forward, because the position of the broom will take the dirt along more gently; it will sweep cleaner; it will not wear out the carpet so fast. Your broom will be kept in proper shape and not half so much dust will be raised to be afterward wiped from your furniture. Most careless sweepers thrust their broom forward of them in a sort of a digging way, with the handle inclining towards them. This way you will find breaks your broom, flirts up more dust, and makes the sweeping much more laborious.

To Render Leather Waterproof.—(1) This simple and effectual rem-edy is nothing more than a little beeswax and mutton suet, warmed in a pipkin until in a liquid state. Then rub some of it lightly over the edges of the sole where the stitches are, which will repel the wet, and not in the least prevent the blacking from having the usual effect.

(2) Gum copal varnish applied to soles of boots and shoes, and repeated as it dries until the pores are filled and the surface shines like polished mahogany, will make the sole waterproof, and it lasts three times longer for the application.

A Good Paste.—To make a paste that will keep, take of wheat flour, one ounce; powdered alum, one-half drachm; water sufficient, or eight ounces; oil of cloves, or wintergreen, three or four drops. Rub the flour and the alum with water to the consistence of milk; place this over a moderate fire and stir constantly until the paste drops from the wooden paddle in jelly-like flakes and has the appearance of starch. While the mass is still hot, add the essential oil and pour the paste into an earthenware pot or open jar. In the course of about an hour a crust forms on the top; pour gently on this an inch of water, more or less. When some paste is wanted, decant the water, take out the quantity needed and put some water again on the remainder, repeating the operation each time. Paste may be kept in this way for months, and will never be troubled with flies.

To Wash Graining.—Use clear, warm water, no soap, a clean, white cloth. Wash only a small place at a time, and wipe dry with another clean, white cloth. Do not wet more space than can be dried immediately with the dry cloth, as graining must not be left to dry in the atmosphere. It must be rubbed dry; hence the necessity of white, dry cloths. If the graining has been neglected, or soiled with greasy fingers, or specked by summer growth or flies, a little hard soap may be necessary in the first water, but must be speedily rinsed off in clear water and wiped dry. But, if possible, avoid the use of soap, as it deadens the varnish, however carefully handled, and on no account must any soap be rubbed on the cloth.

To Make a Cheap Telephone.—Take a wooden tooth-powder box and make a hole of about the size of a half crown in the lid and the bottom. Take a disk of tinned iron, such as can be had from a preserved meat tin, and place it on the outside of the bottom of the box, and fix the cover on the other side of it. Then take a small bar-magne , place on one end a small cotton or silk reel, and round the reel wind some iron wire, leaving the ends loose. Fix one end of the magnet near, as near as possible without touching, to the disk, and then one part of the telephone is complete. A similar arrangement is needed for the other end. With this one can converse at a distance of about one hundred yards.

Mosquito Remedy.—To clear a sleeping-room of mosquitoes, take a piece of paper rolled around a lead-pencil to form a case, and fill this with very dry Pyrethrum powder (Persian insect powder), putting in a little at a time, and pressing it down with the pencil. This cartridge, or cigarette, may be set in a cup of sand to hold it erect. An hour before going to bed the room is to be closed, and one of these cartridges burned. A single cartridge will answer for a small room, but for a large one two are required. Those who have tried this find that it effectually disposes of the mosquitoes.

To Prevent Fruit Jars Breaking.—Canning fruit is hot enough work without any hot water or hot jars around. Instead of this, wrap the jars with a towel saturated with cold water, and pour in your hot fruit. Any one who has not tried it will naturally say: "That is the sure way to break jars." I would say, just try one jar and see. We have canned hundreds of jars.

one and two quarts, and have never broken one in filling. I can't explain why, but simply know that it is the fact.

To Cleanse Woodwork. —Save the tea leaves for a few days, then steep them in a tin pail or pan for half an hour, strain through a sieve and use the tea to wash all varnished paint. It requires very little "elbow polish," as the tea acts as a strong detergent, cleansing the paint from all impurities, and making the varnish equal to new. It cleans window sashes and oil cloths; indeed, any varnished surface is improved by its application. It washes window panes and mirrors much better than water, and is excellent for cleaning black walnut picture and looking-glass frames. It will not do to wash unvarnished paint with it. Take a small quantity on a damp flannel, rub lightly over the surface, and you will be surprised at its effects.

To Clean Silver Plate. —Hartshorn is one of the best possible ingredients for plate-powder in daily use. It leaves on the silver a deep, dark polish, and is less hurtful than any other article. To wash plate carefully is first to remove all the grease from it, and this can be done with the use of warm water and soap. The water should be as nearly hot as the hand can bear it. Then mix as much hartshorn powder as will be required into a thick paste with cold water. Smear this lightly over the plate with a piece of soft rag, and leave it for some little time to dry. When perfectly dry, brush it off quite clean with a soft plate-brush, and polish the plate with a dry leather. If the plate be very dirty or much tarnished, spirits of wine will be found to answer better than water for mixing the paste.

To Clean Velvet. —Velvet requires very careful manipulation, as it loses its fine appearance if wrung or pressed when it is wet. To remove dust, strew very fine dry sand upon the velvet, and brush in the direction of the lines until all the sand is removed. The brush must be a new one. To remove dirt, dissolve ox gall in *nearly* boiling water, and add some spirits of wine; dip a soft brush in this solution and brush the dirt out of the velvet. It may require repeated brushing. After this, hang the velvet up carefully to dry. For finishing, apply a weak solution of gum, by means of a sponge, to the reverse side of the velvet.

Canning Sweet Corn. —The "Oneida Community" preserves sweet corn by cutting the corn raw into tin cans; then fill with cold water even with the top of the corn; solder up the can, pricking a small hole in the cover; solder that also. Boil the cans and contents in boiling water two and a half hours; then with a hot iron open the small hole and let the gas blow out, after which solder up and boil again two and a half hours and set away for use. Peas, string beans, and lima beans can be put up in this same manner, and they certainly pay for the trouble of putting up. Every family should have a soldering apparatus, as it would pay for itself in a very short time, and save many trips to the tinner's.

To Remove Grease from Carpets. —The following mixture is recommended for taking grease out of carpets: Aqua ammonia, two ounces; soft water, one quart; saltpetre, one teaspoonful; shaving soap, one ounce, finely scraped. Mix well, shake and let it stand a few hours or days, before using, to dissolve the soap. When used pour on enough to cover any grease or oil that has been spilled, sponging and rubbing well and applying again if necessary; then wash off with clear cold water. It is a good mixture to have in the house for many things; is sure death to bed bugs if put in the crevices which they inhabit; will remove paint where oil was used in mixing it, and will not injure the finest fabrics.

To Polish Black Walnut.—To give black walnut a fine polish, so as to resemble rich old wood, apply a coat of shellac varnish, and then rub it with a smooth piece of pumice stone until dry. Another coat may be given, and the rubbing repeated. After this, a coat of polish, made of linseed oil, beeswax, and turpentine may be well rubbed in with a dauber, made of a piece of sponge tightly wrapped in a piece of fine flannel several times folded, and moistened with the polish. If this work is not fine enough, it may be smoothed with the finest sandpaper, and the rubbing repeated. In the course of time the walnut becomes very dark and rich in color, and in every way is superior to that which has been varnished.

To Clean Britannia Metal.—(1) Rub the article with a piece of flannel moistened with sweet oil; then apply a little pounded rotten-stone or polishing paste with the finger till the polish is produced, then wash the article with soap and hot water, and when dry, rub with soft wash leather, and a little fine whiting.

(2) To clean britannia metal, use finely powdered whiting, two tablespoonfuls of sweet oil and a little yellow soap. Mix with spirits of wine to a cream. Rub on with a sponge, wipe off with a soft cloth and polish with a chamois skin.

Care of Clothes.—Spots of grease may be removed from colored silks by putting on them raw starch made into a paste with water. Dust is best removed from silk by a soft flannel, from velvet with a brush made specially for the purpose. If hats and bonnets when taken from the head are brushed and put away in boxes and covered up, instead of being laid down anywhere, they will last fresh a long time. Shawls and all articles that may be folded should be folded when taken from the person in their original creases and laid away. Cloaks should be hung up in place, gloves pulled out lengthwise, wrapped in tissue paper and laid away, laces smoothed out and folded, if requisite, so that they will come out of the box new and fresh when needed again. A strip of old black broadcloth four or five inches wide, rolled up tightly and sewed to keep the roll in place, is better than a sponge or cloth for cleansing black or dark colored clothes. Whatever lint comes from it in rubbing is black and does not show.

Cleaning Black Silk.—One of the things "not generally known," at least in this country, is the Parisian method of cleaning black silk; the *modus operandi* is very simple, and the result infinitely superior to that achieved in any other manner. The silk must be thoroughly brushed and wiped with a cloth, then laid flat on a board or table, and well sponged with hot coffee, thoroughly freed from sediment by being strained through muslin. The silk is sponged on the side intended to show; it is allowed to become partially dry, and then ironed on the wrong side. The coffee removes every particle of grease, and restores the brilliancy of silk without imparting to it either the shiny appearance or crackly and papery stiffness obtained by beer or, indeed, any other liquid. The silk really appears thickened by the process, and this good effect is permanent. Our readers who will experimentalize on an apron or cravat will never again try any other method.

How to Clean Wall Paper.—Take off the dust with a soft oil. With a little flour and water make a lump of very stiff dough, and rub the wall gently downward, taking the length of the arm at each stroke, and in this way go round the room. As the dough becomes dirty, cut the soiled part off. In the second round commence the stroke a little above where the last one ended, and be very careful not to cross the paper or to go up again. Ordinary papers cleaned in this way will look fresh and bright, and almost as good as new. Some papers, however—and these most expensive ones—will not clean nicely; and, in order to ascertain whether a paper can be cleaned, it is best to try it in some obscure corner, which will not be noticed if the result is unsatisfactory. If there be any broken places in the wall, fill them up with a mixture of equal parts of plaster-of-paris and silver-sand, made into a paste, with a little water; then cover the place with a little piece of paper like the rest, if it can be had.

To Make Fruit Extracts, Etc.—Good alcohol, one quart; oil of lemon, two ounces. Break and bruise the peel of four lemons, and add to them alcohol for a few days, then filter. For currants, peaches, raspberries, pine-apples, strawberries, blackberries, etc., take alcohol and water half and half, and pour over the fruit, entirely covering it, and let it stand for a few days. For essence of cinnamon, nutmeg, mace, vanilla, etc., pulverize either article thoroughly, and put about two ounces of the resulting powder to each pint of reduced alcohol, agitate the mixture frequently for two weeks, then filter and color as desired.

To Renovate Carpets.—To one pail of warm water add one pint of ox-gall; dip a soaped flannel into the mixture, and rub well the surface of the carpet, piece by piece, rinsing it as you proceed with clean, cold water, taking care not to make the carpet too wet, and finish off by rubbing with a dry coarse cloth. The carpet, of course, must be well beaten before it is operated upon. This process is simply and surprisingly effective in renovating the colors. The only drawback is the effluvium given off by the gall; but this is soon remedied by exposure to the air, or by opening the windows if the carpet be laid down.

Extempore Shade for Reading Lamps.—An additional shade can sometimes be used with comfort, and is made in a moment, as follows: Take a half sheet of letter paper, or any somewhat similar piece of stiffish paper, turn down about an inch and a half of one side of it, and emphasize the turn by a scrape with thumb nail or paper cutter. Then open the turned strip part way and set the strip under the front edge of the shade of the lamp, between the shade and the frame on which it rests. The rest of the sheet is to stand up in front of the shade. The hold of the bent paper will keep the sheet against the glass shade, and the paper agreeably modifies the effect of the light on the eyes, without keeping any of it from the table.

To Preserve Hams from Flies.—The best way to preserve hams from flies is, as soon as they are smoked, to wrap them in two old newspapers, first with one end and again with another, and tie the ends of the paper or paste them down. Let the string to hang them up by come through the paper, being very careful that the hole shall only be large enough to let the string through. No insect can get through paper. Woolens and furs can be kept perfectly in the same way, being careful that the egg of the moth is not previously deposited.

Gilding Without a Battery.—Clean the silver or other article to be gilded with a brush and a little ammonia water, until it is evenly bright and shows no tarnish. Take a small piece of gold and dissolve it in about four times its volume of metallic mercury, which will be accomplished in a few minutes, forming an amalgam. Put a little of the amalgam on a piece of dry cloth, rub it on the article to be gilded. Then place on a stone in a furnace, and heat to the beginning of redness. After cooling, it must be cleaned with a brush and a little cream of tartar, and a beautiful and permanent gilding will be found.

Fluid for Soldering and Tinning.—The following compounds are useful for soldering or tinning: Tin—one part muriatic acid, with as much zinc as it will dissolve; add two parts of water and some sal ammoniac. Brass and copper—one pound muriatic acid, four ounces zinc, five ounces sal ammoniac. Zinc—one pound muriatic acid, and two ounces sal ammoniac, with all the zinc it will dissolve, and three pints of water. Iron—one pound of muriatic acid, six ounces sperm tallow, four ounces sal ammoniac. Gold and silver—one pound muriatic acid, eight ounces sperm tallow, and eight ounces sal ammoniac.

To Keep Cheese from Mold.—Dissolve a spoonful of bruised pepper, two teaspoonfuls of salt, and the same quantity of boracic acid in a quarter of a pint of brandy for a few days; then filter the fluid through a cloth and dilute with an equal quantity of water. Some of the preparation is introduced into the cracks of the cheese by means of a feather, or better with a small glass syringe. If places which have been nibbled by mice are rubbed with the liquid no mold will form. It will put " jumpers " to flight.

Grease on Kitchen Floors.—With the greatest care the housewife will occasionally spill a little grease on the kitchen floor. When possible, the best thing is immediately to pour over it cold water, and prevent it penetrating the wood. Scrape off all that is possible, rub thickly with soap, and wash off with boiling water. When dry, fold thicknesses of brown wrapping paper, lay over the spot, and place on it a hot smoothing iron; this will draw much of the grease into the paper; then wash again with soap and hot water. T' i; will take out so much of the spot that it will hardly be noticed if daily washed off as it draws out of the wood, for every particle has to come out at the top of the boards, and the more persistently one works at it, the sooner it will disappear.

To Clean Gloves.—The following is recommended as the best mode of cleaning gloves: Mix one-fourth ounce carbonate of ammonia, one-fourth ounce fluid chloroform, one-fourth ounce sulphuric ether, one quart distilled benzine. Pour out a small quantity in a saucer, put on the gloves, and wash as if washing the hands, changing solution until gloves are clean; take off, squeeze them, replace on hands, and with a clean cloth rub fingers, etc., until they are dry and perfectly fitted to the hand This cleaner is also an excellent clothes, ribbon and silk cleaner; is perfectly harmless to the most delicate tints. Apply with a soft sponge, rubbing gently until spots disappear; care must be taken not to use it near fire, as the benzine is very inflammable.

To Cure Meats.—For curing beef, pork, mutton, and hams, the following recipe is good: To one gallon of water take one and a half pounds of salt, one-... pound of sugar, one-half ounce each of saltpetre and potash. In this ratio the pickle can be increased to any quantity desired. Let these be boiled together until all the dirt from the sugar rises to the top and is skimmed off. Then throw it into a tub to cool, and when cold, pour it over your beef or pork. The meat must be well covered with pickle, and should not be put down for at least two days after killing, during which time it should be sprinkled with powdered saltpetre, which removes all the surface blood, etc., leaving the meat fresh and clean.

Cement for Fastening Instruments in Handles.—A material for fastening knives or forks into their handles, when they have become loosened by use, is a much needed article. The best cement for this purpose consists of one pound of colophony (purchasable at the druggist's), and eight ounces of sulphur, which are to be melted together and either kept in bars or reduced to powder. One part of the powder is to be mixed with half a part of iron filings, fine sand, or brickdust, and the cavity of the handle is then to be filled with this mixture. The stem of the knife or fork is then to be heated and inserted into the cavity; and when cold it will be found fixed in its place with great tenacity.

Glue which will Unite even Polished Steel.—A Turkish receipt for a cement used to fasten diamonds and other precious stones to metallic surfaces, and which is said to strongly unite even surfaces of polished steel, although exposed to moisture, is as follows: Dissolve five or six bits of gum mastic, each of the size of a large pea, in as much spirits of wine as will suffice to render it liquid. In another vessel dissolve in brandy as much isinglass, previously softened in water, as will make a two-ounce phial of strong glue, adding two bits of gum ammoniac, which must be rubbed until dissolved. Then mix the whole with heat. Keep in a phial closely stopped. When it is to be used set the phial in boiling water.

Glycerine Leather Polish.—Mix intimately together three or four pounds of lamp-black and a half pound of burned bones with five pounds of glycerine and five pounds of syrup. Then gently warm two and three-quarter ounces of gutta-percha in an iron or copper kettle until it flows easily, add ten ounces of olive oil, and when completely dissolved, one ounce of stearine. This solution, while still warm, is poured into the former and well mixed. Then add five ounces of gum senegal dissolved in one and a half pounds of water, and a half ounce of lavender or other oils to flavor it. For use it is diluted with three or four parts of water. It gives a fine polish, is free from acid, and the glycerine keeps the leather soft and pliable.

French Polish Dressing for Leather.—Mix two pints best vinegar with one pint soft water; stir into it a quarter pound of glue, broken up, half a pound logwood chips, one quarter ounce finely-powdered indigo, one-quarter ounce of the best soft soap, one-quarter ounce of isinglass; put the mixture over the fire and let it boil ten minutes or more; then strain, bottle and cork. When cold, it is fit for use. Apply with a sponge.

To Clean Black Lace.—Ladies who have rolls of old lace put by may want to make it fresh again by a simple process. Make some green tea, and, while it is boiling hot, hold the lace over it so that it is completely steamed, pulling it well out with the hand during the process, and at once iron it between paper.

Jet Black Varnish.—To make a jet black varnish that can be used for furniture or for small wood-handles, that will make them smooth and shining and hard and solid, so that they will not get dim by handling or lose their gloss, take of asphaltum, three ounces; boiled oil, four quarts; burnt umber, eight ounces, and enough oil of turpentine to thin. The three first must be mixed by the aid of heat, and the turpentine gradually added (out of doors and away from fire) before the mixture has cooled. The work (dry) is given several coats, each being hardened in a japanner's oven. The last coat may be rubbed down, first with tripoli applied on a soft cloth, then with a few drops of oil.

How to Fit Keys Into Locks.—When it is not convenient to take locks apart in the event of keys being lost, stolen, or missing, when you wish to fit a new key, take a lighted match or candle and smoke the new key in the flame, introduce it carefully into the keyhole, press it firmly against the opposing wards of the lock, withdraw it, and the indentations in the smoked part of the key will show you exactly where to file.

To Clean Kid Gloves.—To clean kid gloves, have ready a little new milk in one saucer, and a piece of brown soap in another, and a clean cloth or towel, folded three or four times. On the cloth spread out the gloves smooth and neat. Take a piece of flannel, dip it in the milk, then rub off a good quantity of soap to the wetted flannel, and commence to rub the glove toward the fingers, holding it firmly with the left hand. Continue the process until the glove, if white, looks of a dingy yellow, though clean; if colored, until it looks dark and spoiled. Lay it to dry, and the operator will soon be gratified to see that the old glove looks nearly new. It will be soft, glossy, smooth and elastic.

Remedy for Flies.—An Irish clergyman, Rev. George Meares Drought, believes that he has discovered a remedy against the plague of flies—and a very simple and pleasant one—namely: a window-garden of geraniums and calceolarias. He says that he had for a long time been congratulating himself on his exemption from the plague of flies from which his neighbors suffered, when, at length, in preparing for removal, he sent away his window-box of geraniums and calceolarias to his new residence. Immediately, his room was as full of flies as that of any of his neighbors, and so he found out that it was his window-garden which saved him.

A Cement Withstanding Heat and Moisture.—Pure white lead, or zinc-white, ground in oil, and used very thick, is an excellent cement for mending broken crockeryware; but it takes a very long time to harden. It is well to put the mended object in some store-room, and not to look after it for several weeks, or even months. It will then be found so firmly united that, if ever again broken, it will not part on the line of the former fracture.

To Clean Hair Brushes and Combs.—Dissolve a piece of soda in some hot water, allowing a piece the size of a walnut to a quart of water. Put the water into a basin, and after combing out the hair from the brushes, dip them, bristles downward, into the water and out again, keeping the backs and handles as free from the water as possible. Repeat this until the bristles look clean, then rinse the brushes in a little cold water; shake them well, and wipe the handles and backs with a towel, but not the bristles, and set the brushes to dry in the sun or near the fire, but take care not to put them too close to it. Wiping the bristles of a brush makes them soft, as does soap.

Uses of Paper.—Rubbing with paper is a much nicer way of keeping a teakettle, coffeepot and teapot bright and clean than the old way of washing them in suds. Rubbing with paper is also the best way of polishing knives, tinware and spoons; they shine like new silver. For polishing mirrors, windows, lamp chimneys, etc., paper is better than dry cloth. Preserves and pickles keep much better if brown paper, instead of cloth, is tied over the jar. Canned fruit is not so apt to mold if a piece of writing paper cut to fit the can, is laid directly on the fruit. Paper is much better to put under a carpet than straw. It is warmer, thinner, and makes less noise when one walks on it.

Stain for Floors.—The best, cheapest and only permanent stain for floors is permanganate of potash. You can get it at any drug store. Mix about one-quarter ounce to a quart of water. Apply freely and quickly to a dry floor with a brush so as to not stain your hands. Repeat the process if a very dark color is desired. When dry, oil with burnt linseed oil or beeswax and turpentine. You cannot wash this color out, as it actually stains the wood. When applying this at first, for a few moments the color is bright magenta; but this at once changes to a dark, permanent brown. This makes a very cheap stain.

Dish Wiping.—The following is an arrangement for wiping dishes that saves half the risk, while the dishes look nicer and brighter: The only outlay required is a half-bushel basket. Set this either in the sink or in a pan. Wash the dishes as usual, and put them in a tin pan or pail. Pour boiling water over them, rinse them thoroughly, then set them up edgewise in the basket, so as to drain. The heat will dry them perfectly, and not a streak or particle of lint is to be seen. Five minutes will leave them perfectly dry. No one who tries it once will be likely to go back to the old way.

Grease Spots on Clothes.—Grease or paint spots in clothes are easily removed by oil of turpentine, or a hot iron pressed on the place over coarse brown paper, after scraping all that can be got off with a blunt knife. Stains may be removed from light-colored clothes, such as drabs, buffs, or whites, with fuller's earth; but this is apt to take the color out of dark clothes. It should be dissolved in a little boiling water, put on the spot when hot, held to the fire to dry, and then brushed out. Pitch is removed, first, by rubbing the place over with grease or oil, and then taking out the oil by the application of spirits of turpentine.

Lamp Explosions.—Many of these may be prevented by trimming the wick daily. When burned for several evenings without trimming, the wick becomes black, clogged, and incapable of supplying the oil clearly and uniformly, and the chimneys are sometimes filled with flame and smoke, to the embarrassment and alarm of those present. Some explosions would be prevented by never blowing out the lamp down the chimney; for if the wick happens to be too small, the flame may be driven down into the oil. The best way is to turn it down with the button until extinguished.

To Destroy Insect Pests.—It is an undisputed fact that if powdered borax is scattered freely where the cockroach has found a hiding place, it will not only prevent its remaining, but will destroy it. In the dark and sometimes damp closets, under sinks and wash basins, they sometimes make their appearance, and it is a good practice to once or twice a year scatter a little of this powder in such places. Nothing but persistent care, and absolute and unvarying neatness about closets, cupboards, and cellar stairs will prevent insects of various kinds from finding agreeable homes.

To Bleach a Straw Bonnet.—First scrub the bonnet well with yellow soap and a brush dipped in clean water; after this, put into a box a saucer containing burning sulphur; it must remain there a short time, and as soon as it is removed, the bonnet must be placed in the box and well covered up, so that the sulphuric atmosphere may whiten it; next dissolve a little oxalic acid in boiling water. Wash all over the bonnet with a small paint brush; put it into a pail of cold water, and let it remain half an hour; then hang it out to dry; it must afterward be stiffened with gelatine, dried again, and then pressed into shape.

The Care of Towels.—Never put a new towel in the wash until you have overcast the fringed edge. The use of this is obvious the moment one is told of it, though a dozen towels might be worn out before one would discover it. If, when towels are washed, the fringe is shaken well before they are hung up to dry, the fresh appearance will be preserved for a long time. If vigorously shaken, that is all that is necessary; otherwise it is best to have the laundress whip the fringe over the clean back of a kitchen chair. This is much better than any combing process. Besides, it does not wear the fringe so much.

To Exterminate Rats and Mice.—Mix powdered *nux vomica* with oatmeal, and lay it in their haunts, observing proper precaution to prevent accidents. Another method is to mix oatmeal with a little powdered phosphorus. In respect to rats, another way is to mix arsenic and lard together, and spread it on bread, and push a piece into every rat hole; or some small pieces of sponge may be fried in dripping or honey, and strewed about for them to eat. Or half a pint of plaster of Paris, mixed with one pint of oatmeal, with prove equally fatal to them.

Sharpening a Razor.—It has long been known that the simplest method of sharpening a razor is to put it for half an hour in water to which one-twentieth of its weight of muriatic or sulphuric acid has been added, then lightly wipe it off, and after a few hours set it on a hone. The acid here supplies the place of a whetstone by corroding the whole surface uniformly, so that nothing further than a smooth polish is necessary. The process never injures good blades, while badly hardened ones are frequently improved by it, although the cause of this improvement remains unexplained.

Frosting Glass.—The frosty appearance of glass, which we often see where it is desired to keep out the sun, or "man's observing eye," is done by using a paint composed as follows: Sugar of lead, well ground in oil, applied as other paint; then pounded, while fresh, with a wad of batting held between the thumb and finger; after which, it is allowed to partially dry; then, with a straight-edge laid upon the sash, you run along by the side of it a stick sharpened to the width of line you wish to appear in the diamonds, figures, or squares, into which you choose to lay it off.

Mucilage.—A very superior quality of mucilage is made by dissolving clear glue in equal volumes of water and strong vinegar, and adding one-fourth of an equal quantity of alcohol, and a small quantity of a solution of alum in water. The action of the vinegar is also due to the acetic acid which it contains. This prevents the glue from glutinizing by cooling; but the same result may be accomplished by adding a small quantity of nitric acid. Some of the preparations offered for sale are merely boiled starch or flour, mixed with nitric acid to prevent the glutinizing.

Care of Umbrellas.—Most persons, when they come in from the rain, put their umbrellas in the rack with the handle upward. They should put it downward, because when the handle is upward the water runs down inside to the place where the ribs are joined to the handle, and cannot get out, but stays, rotting the cloth and rusting the metal until slowly dried away. The wire securing the ribs soon rusts and breaks. If placed the other end up the water readily runs off, and the umbrella dries almost immediately.

To Restore the Color of Carpets.—A tablespoonful of ammonia in one gallon of warm water will often restore the color of carpets, even if injured by acid or alkali. If a ceiling has been whitewashed with the carpet down, and a few drops should fall, this will remove it. Or, after the carpet is well beaten and brushed, scour with oxgall, which will not only extract grease, but freshen the colors. One pint of gall in three gallons of warm water will do for a large carpet. Table and floor oilcloths may be thus washed. The suds left from a wash, when ammonia is used, even if almost cold, cleanses floor cloths well.

How to Keep Fresh Meat.—Perhaps all our readers are not aware that steak (pork and beef), sausages, puddings, etc., can be kept fresh the year round, by frying and seasoning when fresh, the same as for the table, packing down in crocks or lard cans, and pouring hot lard over them, covering about an inch. When needed, scrape off the lard, and heat through. This is valuable information to farmers and others, who kill and dispose of a portion at a low rate. It is impossible to detect any difference between the preserved and the recently prepared.

To Bore Holes in Glass.—Any sharp steel will cut glass with great facility when kept freely wet with camphor dissolved in turpentine. A drill may be used, or even the hand alone. A hole may be readily enlarged by a round file. The ragged edges of glass may also be thus smoothed with a flat file. Flat window glass can be readily sawed by a watch-spring saw, by the aid of this solution. In short, the most brittle glass can be wrought almost as easily as wood, by the use of drilling tools kept constantly moist with camphorized oil of turpentine.

Ink on Books.—To remove ink-stains from a book, first wash the paper with warm water, using a camel's hair pencil for the purpose. By this means the surface ink is got rid of. The paper must now be wetted with a solution of oxalate of potash, or, better still, oxalic acid, in the proportion of one ounce to half a pint of water. The ink stains will immediately disappear. Finally, again wash the stained place with clean water, and dry it with white blotting paper.

To Restore a Cane Chair Bottom.—Turn the chair bottom upward, and with hot water and sponge wash the cane work well, so that it is well soaked; should it be dirty, use soap; let it dry in the air, and it will be as tight and firm as new, provided none of the canes are broken.

A Valuable Discovery.—It is said that a lady in Springfield, Mass., has been making some interesting experiments in putting up canned goods without cooking. Heating the fruit tends more or less to the injury of the flavor, and the lady referred to has found that by filling the cans with fruit, and then with pure cold water, and allowing them to stand until all the confined air has escaped, the fruit will, if then sealed perfectly, keep indefinitely, without change or loss of original flavor.

To Clean Plush.—That plush may be cleaned is a fact of interest; children's plush coats that have become soiled on the front can be softly and delicately sponged with a little borax and water, without injury; a teaspoonful of powdered borax to nearly a quart of water is the proper proportion; use a very soft sponge—and, by the way, a sponge may be softened by boiling it in clear water; then take it out and rinse it in several waters; if not softened sufficiently, repeat the boiling and rinsing process.

Bottling Fruit.—Have ready some dry glass bottles, wide-mouthed and clean. Burn a match in each to exhaust the air; place the fruit quickly in each; cork with soft bungs or corks, and put in a cool oven; let them remain until the fruit has shrunken one-fourth. Take out the bottles; beat the corks well in and cover them with melted rosin. If the fruit has been picked dry, and is quite sound, it will keep for months in a cool, dry place, and retain all the flavor.

To Remove Stains from the Hands, Etc.—Dampen the hands first in water, then rub them with tartaric acid or salt of lemons, as you would with soap; rinse them and rub them dry. Tartaric acid or salt of lemons will quickly remove stains from white muslins or linens. Put less than half a teaspoonful in water; wet the stain with it, and lay it in the sun for an hour; wet it once or twice with cold water during the time; if this does not quite remove it, repeat the acid water and lay it in the sun.

Waterproof Blacking.—Dissolve an ounce of borax in water, and in this dissolve gum shellac until it is the consistency of thin paste; add lampblack to color. This makes a cheap and excellent blacking for boots, giving them the polish of new leather. The shellac makes the boots or shoes almost entirely waterproof. Camphor dissolved in alcohol added to the blacking makes the leather more pliable and keeps it from cracking. This is sold at 50 cents for a small bottle. By making it yourself $1 will buy materials for a gallon.

To Renovate Black Cloth.—Clean the cloth from grease and dirt with the following mixture thoroughly dissolved: Aqua ammonia, two ounces; soft water, one quart; saltpeter, one teaspoonful; shaving soap, in shavings, one ounce. Then when dry, make a strong decoction of logwood by boiling the extract in a gallon of soft water; strain, and when cool add two ounces of gum arabic; apply evenly with a sponge over the surface and hang in the shade. When thoroughly dry brush the nap down smooth and it will look as well as new. Keep the liquid tightly corked in a bottle.

To Determine if Fruit Cans are Air Tight.—A lady writes: "Do you wish to know," said a man of science to me recently, "how to know that your fruit can is certainly air tight?" I was that moment contemplating a can which had a little neck on the upper edge, and it was hard to judge whether the rubber would effectually keep the air out. The man lighted a bit of paper, put it into the can, slipped the rubber ring over, and put the glass cover on. The burning paper exhausted the air, and behold the cover was with difficulty removed.

Cleaning Lamp Chimneys.—Most people, in cleaning lamp chimneys, use either a brush made of bristles twisted into a wire, or a rag on the point of scissors. Both of these are bad; for without great care the wire or scissors will scratch the glass as a diamond does, which under the expansive power of heat soon breaks, as all scratched glass will. If you want a neat little thing that costs nothing, and will save half your glass, tie a piece of sponge the size of your chimney to a pine stick.

Filling for Cracks in Floors.—A very complete filling for open cracks in floors may be made by thoroughly soaking newspapers in a paste made of one pound of flour, three quarts of water and a tablespoonful of alum, thoroughly boiled and mixed; make the final mixture about as thick as putty, a kind of paper putty, and it will harden like papier mache.

Painting and Kalsomining Walls.—Before paint or kalsomine is applied to walls every crevice should be filled with plaster or cement. For the kalsomine put a quarter of a pound of white glue in cold water over night, and heat gradually in the morning until dissolved. Mix eight pounds of whiting with hot water, add the dissolved glue and stir together, adding warm water until about the consistency of thick cream. Use a kalsomine brush, and finish as you go along. If skim milk is used instead of water, the glue may be omitted.

Marine Glue.—This glue resists the action of water, both hot and cold, and most of the acids and alkalies. It is made in the following manner: Take of gum shellac three parts, and of caoutchouc, or India rubber, one part by weight. Dissolve the shellac and rubber in separate vessels, in ether, free from alcohol, applying a gentle heat. When thoroughly dissolved, mix the two solutions, and keep in a bottle tightly corked. Pieces of wood, leather, or other substances, joined together by it, will part at any other point than the joint thus made. If the glue be thinned by the admixture of ether, and applied as a varnish to leather, along the seams where it is sewed together, it renders the joint or seam water tight, and almost impossible to separate.

Artificial Honey.—Take ten pounds of Havana sugar, and three pounds of water, and forty grains of cream tartar, and ten drops of essence of peppermint, and three pounds of honey. First dissolve the sugar in the water over a slow fire, and take off the scum arising therefrom; then dissolve the cream tartar in a little warm water, and add with some stirring; then add the honey heated to a boiling pitch; then add the essence of peppermint, stir a few moments, and let stand until cold, when it will be ready for use.

Cement to Mend China.—Take a very thick solution of gum arabic, and stir into it plaster of Paris, until the mixture is of proper consistency. Apply it with a brush to the fractional edges of the chinaware, and stick them together. In a few days it will be impossible to break the article in the same place. The whiteness of the cement renders it doubly valuable.

How to Cut Glass.—It is not generally known that glass may be cut, under water, with a strong pair of scissors. If a round or oval be required, take a piece of common window-glass, draw the shape upon it in a black line; sink it with your left hand under water as deep as you can without interfering with the view of the line, and with your right use the scissors to cut away what is not required.

Polish for Boots and Shoes.—Mix together two pints of the best vinegar, and one pint of water; stir into a quarter of a pound of glue, broken up, half a pound of logwood chips and a quarter of an ounce of isinglass. Put the mixture over the fire and let it boil ten or fifteen minutes. Then strain the liquid, and bottle and cork it. When cold it is fit for use. The polish should be applied with a clean sponge.

To Keep Furs in Summer.—Furs or woolens may be kept safely from moths during the summer by brushing thoroughly, so as to eradicate all the moth eggs; then wrap them up in newspaper so that every part is covered entirely. This is unfailing if the clothes or furs be well brushed beforehand. Some think gum camphor put with them is desirable, but I have used only the newspaper, and never had any trouble unless the moths were there when wrapped up in it.

To Make Tough Beef Tender.—Those who have worn down their teeth in masticating old, tough beef, will find that carbonate of soda will remedy the evil. Cut the steaks, the day before using, into slices about two inches thick, rub over them a small quantity of soda—wash off next morning—cut it into suitable thicknesses, and cook. The same process will answer for fowls, legs of mutton, etc. Try it, all who love delicious, tender dishes of meat.

To Clean Ostrich Feathers.— White or light tinted ones can be laid on a plate and scrubbed gently with a toothbrush, in warm soap suds, then well shaken out and well dried either by the hot sun or a good fire. At first the feather will have a most discouraging appearance, and a novice is apt to think it perfectly spoiled. But after it is perfectly dry it should be carefully curled with a penknife or scissors' blade, and it will recover all its former plumy softness.

How to Clean Oil Cloths.—To *ruin* them, clean them with hot water or soap suds, and leave them half wiped, and they will look very bright while wet, but very dingy and dirty when dry, and will soon crack and peel off. But if you wish to *preserve* them, and have them look new and nice, wash them with soft flannel and luke-warm water, and wipe perfectly dry. If you want them to look extra nice, after they are dry, drop a few spoonfuls of milk over them, and rub with a dry cloth.

Cement for Kerosene Oil Lamps.—The cement commonly used for fastening the tops on kerosene lamps is plaster of Paris, which is porous and quickly penetrated by the kerosene. Another cement which has not this defect is made with three parts of rosin, one of caustic soda, and five of water. This composition is mixed with half its weight of plaster of Paris. It sets firmly in about three quarters of an hour, and is said to have great adhesive power, not permeable to kerosene, a low conductor of heat, and but superficially attacked by water.

A Labor-Saving Invention.—A labor saving invention is to have one long cake tin divided in the middle. When making cake put half the quantity in one end of the tin. Add to the remainder spices, raisins, etc., according to taste, and put in the other end of the tin. This saves time in making and baking. The result will be two kinds of cake for the basket, and if the family is small, one is less likely to have dry cake on hand than if two large cakes are made at the same time.

To Prevent Woodenware from Cracking.—Wooden bowls and other ware of this sort, as well as all cross sections from tree trunks, and short logs cut for various purposes, are very apt to split while seasoning. To prevent this completely, the pores of the wood should be well filled with linseed, or some other oxidizing oil, while it is yet green, and before it begins to show any signs of cracking or checking. This will completely obviate this inconvenience.

Sweeping.—In sweeping carpets, use wet newspaper wrung nearly dry and torn into pieces. The paper collects the dust, but does not soil the carpet. A carpet, particularly a dark carpet, often looks dusty when it does not need sweeping; wring out a sponge quite dry in water (a few drops of ammonia helps brighten the color), and wipe off the dust from the carpet. This saves much labor in sweeping.

To Clean an Oily Vessel.—To clean a vessel that has contained kerosene oil, wash the vessel with thin milk of lime, which forms an emulsion with the petroleum, and removes all traces of it. By washing a second time with milk of lime and a very small quantity of chloride of lime, and allowing the liquid to remain in the vessel about an hour, and then washing it with cold water, the smell may be removed. If the milk of lime be used warm instead of cold, the operation is rendered much shorter.

Smoky Chimneys.—Trouble with smoky chimneys caused by their being used for two or more stoves may be averted in most cases by inserting vertically in the flue a piece of sheet iron, dividing the flue in the center for about two feet above the point where each pipe enters, turning the bottom of the sheet iron under the pipe, so as to shut it completely off from the part of the flue below it.

Cleansing Sofa Coverings.—If the covers of sofas and chairs are dirty, they may be cleansed without being removed, by first washing them over with warm water and soap rubbed over them with a flannel; then, before they are dry, sponge them over with a strong solution of salt and water, in which a small quantity of gall has been mixed. The windows of the room should be opened, so as to secure a perfect drying, and the colors and the freshness of the articles will be restored.

Home Made Baking Powder.—Take by weight six parts of bicarbonate of soda to five parts of tartaric acid, which being much purer than cream of tartar, is greatly to be preferred. Get the ingredients in this proportion from a reliable wholesale druggist. See that they are perfectly dry, roll the lumps out, mix thoroughly together, bottle tightly, and keep in a dry place. This has been used for months with much satisfaction.

To Exterminate Fleas.—Take half a pound of Persian insect powder, half pound powdered borax, one ounce oil cedar, quarter ounce oil of pennyroyal properly put up by a druggist; close the room tight, sprinkle this powder on carpet, furniture, and beds, and keep closed over day or night; then open all windows and air thoroughly, and in twenty-four hours there will be no fleas, flies, or mosquitoes left; the rooms can then be swept and dusted. This applies nearly as well to roaches and water-bugs.

To Clean Corsets.—A lady correspondent writes: "Take out the steels at front and sides, then scrub them thoroughly with tepid or cold lather of white castile soap, using a very small scrubbing brush; do not lay them in water. When quite clean, let cold water run on them freely, to rinse out the soap thoroughly. Dry, without ironing (after pulling lengthwise until they are straight and shapely), in a cool place.

To Preserve Cut Flowers.—A bouquet of freshly cut flowers may be preserved alive for a long time by placing them in a glass or vase with fresh water in which a little charcoal has been steeped, or a small piece of camphor dissolved. The vase should be set upon a plate or dish, and covered with a bell glass, around the edges of which, when it comes in contact with the plate, a little water should be poured to exclude the air.

To Clean Looking Glasses.—Keep for this purpose a piece of sponge, a cloth, and a silk handkerchief, all entirely free from dirt, as the least grit will scratch the fine surface of the glass. First sponge it with a little spirits of wine, or gin and water, so as to clean off all spots; then dust over it powder-blue, tied in muslin, rub it lightly and quickly off with the cloth, and finish by rubbing it with the silk handkerchief. Be careful not to rub the edges of the frame.

To Clean Gilt Jewelry.—Take half a pint of boiling water, or a little less, and put it in a clean oil flask. To this add one ounce of cyanide of potassium; shake the flask and the cyanide will dissolve. When the liquid is cold, add half a fluid ounce of liquor ammonia, and one fluid ounce of rectified alcohol. Shake the mixture together, and it will be ready for use. All kinds of discolored gilt articles may be rendered bright by brushing them with the above-mentioned liquid.

Paste for Cleaning Knives.—Make a mixture one part emery and three parts crocus martis, in very fine powder. Mix them to a thick paste with a little lard or sweet oil. Have your knife-board covered with a thick buff leather. Spread this paste on your leather to about the thickness of a quarter of a dollar. Rub your knives in it, and it will make them much sharper and brighter, and will wear them out less than the common method of cleaning them with brickdust on a bare board.

A Burning Chimney.—A burning chimney, when the soot has been lighted by a fire in the fireplace, can be extinguished by shutting all the doors in the room, so as to prevent any current of air up the chimney; then, by throwing a few handfuls of common fine salt upon the fire in the grate or on the hearth, the fire in the chimney will be immediately extinguished. In burning the salt, muriatic-acid gas is evolved, which is a prompt extinguisher of fire.

To Purify a Room.—Set a pitcher of water in the apartment, and in a few hours it will have absorbed all the respired gases in the room, the air of which will have become purer, but the water utterly filthy. The colder the water is, the greater the capacity to contain these gases. At ordinary temperature a pail of water will absorb a pint of carbonic acid gas and several pints of ammonia. The capacity is nearly doubled by reducing the water to the temperature of ice. Hence, water kept in a room awhile is unfit for use. For the same reason, water from a pump should always be pumped out in the morning before any of it be used.

Bread-Making.—A correspondent writes as follows: "I have lately adopted a new way in bread making, which has given me the best satisfaction. Make a hole in the middle of your pan of flour, pour in the required amount of yeast and milk, and cover it over slightly with dry flour. If this is done at night, you will find in the morning a light foamy mass which I stir down once or twice before kneading for the bread tins. I think the bread nicer for the ingredients being mixed so slowly.

To Purify Water.—A tablespoonful of pulverized alum sprinkled into a hogshead of water (the water stirred at the same time) will, after a few hours, by precipitating to the bottom the impure particles, so purify it, that it will be found to possess nearly all the freshness and clearness of the finest spring water. A pailful, containing four gallons, may be thoroughly purified by a single teaspoonful of the alum.

Save Your Sugar.—All housekeepers should know that sugar boiled with an acid, if it be but three minutes, will be converted into glucose, which is the form of sugar found in sweet apples. One pound of sugar has as much sweetening power as two and a quarter pounds of glucose. In other words, one pound of sugar stirred into the fruit after it is cooked, and while yet warm, will make the fruit as sweet as two and a quarter pounds added while the fruit is boiling.

To Make Shell Frames.—The part of the frame that is to be ornamented with shells must be covered thickly with fresh putty; press the shell down into the putty nearly or quite to the top edge of the shell; form flowers or any fancy design; then carefully cut away any of the superfluous putty that remains, using a sharp pen-knife; if any should unavoidably show, it can be colored pink or white; let the frame remain in a flat position until the putty hardens.

To Restore the Pile of Velvet.—Stretch the velvet out tightly, and remove all dust from the surface with a clean brush; afterward, well clean it with a piece of black flannel, slightly moistened with Florence oil. Then lay a wet cloth over a hot iron, and place it under the velvet, allowing the steam to pass through it, at the same time brushing the pile of the velvet till restored as required. Should any fluff remain on the surface of the velvet, remove it by brushing with a handful of crape.

A Simple Insecticide.—Hot alum water is the best insect destroyer known. Put the alum into hot water and let it boil till it is all dissolved; then apply the solution hot with a brush to all cracks, closets, bedsteads, and other places, where any insects are found. Ants, bedbugs, cockroaches and creeping things are killed by it; while it has no danger of poisoning the family or injuring the property.

To Remove Grease.—Aqua ammonia, two ounces; soft water, one quart; saltpeter, one teaspoonful; shaving soap in shavings, one ounce; mix together; dissolve the soap well, and any grease or dirt that cannot be removed with this preparation, nothing else need be tried for it.

Mending Glass.—For mending valuable glass objects which would be disfigured by common cement, chrome cement may be used. This is a mixture of five parts gelatine to one of a solution of acid chromate of lime. The broken edges are covered with this, pressed together and exposed to sunlight, the effect of the latter being to render the compound insoluble even in boiling water.

To Improve Pine Work.—Pine work brushed two or three times with a strong boiling decoction of logwood chips, and varnished with a solution of shellac in alcohol, appears almost like mahogany, both in color and hardness. After washing with decoction of logwood and drying thoroughly, it should receive two coats of varnish. Then carefully sandpaper and polish, and give a final coat of shellac varnish.

Ink from Carpets.—To remove freshly-spilt ink from carpets, first take up as much as possible of the ink with a teaspoon. Then pour cold sweet milk upon the spot and take up as before, pouring on milk until at last it becomes only slightly tinged with black; then wash with cold water, and absorb with a cloth without too much rubbing.

Black Ink.—To make jet black ink, that is shiny and glistening when applied, dissolve in one-half pint of soft water, three-eighths ounce of potassium bichromate, and add sixty ounces of logwood extract dissolved in one gallon of water; then dissolve in one gallon of water, by continued boiling, borax six ounces, shellac one and one-half ounces. Mix all together while warm and add ammonia three ounces.

Fastening Fruit Jars.—Very many housekeepers are greatly annoyed by the opening of their fruit jars after they have been carefully sealed. The difficulty arises from the fact that the rubber bands furnished with them are so hard, have so little rubber in them, that they do not yield to compression, and hence do not become tight. Boiling the bands before using is said to obviate the difficulty.

To Color Stockings Blue.—To color stockings a delicate blue, use bluing. Put into warm water till the right shade, dip the stocking in and set with salt and water. Very handsome pink of a delicate shade may be made by using rose aniline. Make a very little dye and weaken to the right shade; it would be better to dissolve the aniline in a bottle and shade by adding till the right shade is obtained. Those are pretty set with warm alum water.

To Clean Japanned Waiters.—Rub on with a sponge a little white soap and some warm water, and wash quite clean. Never use hot water, as it will cause the Japan to peel. Wipe dry, sprinkle a little flour over it; let it rest awhile, and then rub it with a soft dry cloth, and finish with a soft piece of old silk.

Moths in Carpets.—If the moths have begun to eat your carpet, take the tacks out, turn it back a half yard all around the room, wash the boards with a saturated solution of camphor, putting it on with a brush (a paint brush is good), then lay the carpet back in its proper place, and put over it a towel wrung out of water and camphor, and iron it thoroughly with a real hot iron so as to steam it through and through, and this will kill the insects and all their larvæ.

To Clean Steel Articles.—Polished steel articles, if rubbed every morning with leather, will not become dull or rusty; but if rust has been suffered to gather, it must be immediately removed by covering the steel with sweet oil, and allowing it to remain on for two days; then sprinkle it over with finely-powdered unslaked lime, and rub it with polishing leather.

A Useful Table for Housewives.—Flour—One pound is one quart. Meal—One pound and two ounces are one quart. Butter—One pound is one quart. Powdered white sugar—one pound and one ounce is a quart. Ten eggs are a pound. A common tumbler holds half a pint. A teacup is a gill.

Crystallized Chimney Ornaments.—Select a crooked twig of white or black thorn; wrap some loose wool or cotton around the branches, and tie it on with worsted. Suspend this in a basin or deep jar. Dissolve two pounds of alum in a quart of boiling water, and pour it over the twig. Allow it to stand twelve hours. Wire baskets may be covered in the same way.

To Restore Color.—When color on a fabric has been accidentally or otherwise destroyed by acid, ammonia is applied to neutralize the same, after which an application of chloroform will, in almost all cases, restore the original color. The application of ammonia is common, but that of chloroform is but little known.

Cleaning Wooden Floors.—The dirtiest of floors may be rendered beautifully clean by the following process: First scrub with sand, then rub with a lye of caustic soda, using a stiff brush, and rinse off with warm water. Just before the floor is dry, moisten with dilute hydrochloric acid, and then with a thin paste of bleaching powder (hypochlorite of lime). Let this remain over night, and wash in the morning.

To Remove Stains from Broadcloth.—Take one ounce of pipe-clay that has been ground fine, and mix it with twelve drops of alcohol, and the same quantity of spirits of turpentine. Moisten a little of this mixture with alcohol, and rub it on the spots. Let it remain till dry, then rub it off with a woolen cloth, and the spots will disappear.

To Dye Furs.—Any dye that will color wool will color furs. In buying furs, examine the density and length of the down next the skin: this can easily be done by blowing briskly against the set of the fur; if it is very close and dense, it is all right, but if it opens easy and exposes much of the skin, reject it.

How to Preserve Shoe Soles.—Melt together tallow and common resin, in the proportion of two parts of the former to one of the latter, and apply the preparation, hot, to the soles of the boots or shoes—as much of it as the latter will absorb. One farmer declares that this recipe alone has been worth more than five dollars.

To Take Stains from Marble.—Make a mixture of one ounce of soda, a piece of stone lime the size of a walnut, quarter of a pound of whiting and the same amount of soft soap; boil these together ten minutes, and then put the mixture on the marble while hot; leave this on twenty-four hours, then wash off with clean, warm water. Polish first with soft flannel and then with chamois skin.

To Clean Marble.—Mix powdered chalk with pumice stone, each one part with two parts of common soda, into a paste with water, and rub it thoroughly on the marble; or mix quicklime and strong soap lye to consistency of milk, and lay it on the marble for twenty-four hours; in both cases wash off thoroughly with soap and water.

To Purify Butter.—The French purify their butter by melting it in pots plunged into water heated to nearly boiling point; and sometimes they mix a pure brine with the melting butter, whereby they flavor the subsidence of the coagulated caseine and other impurities. The supernatant clear butter should be drawn or poured off, and rapidly cooled.

To Mount Chromos.—Take unbleached muslin and stretch it over a wooden strainer; next dampen the back of the picture with paste, and lay it on the canvas; then with a dry rag rub well the back of the canvas to prevent blistering. If you use card or pasteboard, simply dampen the back of the picture with paste and lay it on the board, taking care that it is smoothly laid on.

How to Keep Cider Sweet.—The cider after it comes from the press is allowed to stand until the pomace settles. It is then put into a clean vessel over a fire, and brought to a boil—in the meantime skimming off the scum as it rises. It is then put into small kegs or bottles, and tightly corked or sealed. By this process cider may be kept sweet for years.

Excellent Paste Blacking.—Half a pound of ivory black, half a pound of molasses, half an ounce of powdered alum, one drachm of turpentine, one ounce of sulphuric acid, two ounces of raw linseed oil. The ivory black and molasses must first be mixed together until thoroughly incorporated; then add the rest of the ingredients. It keeps best in a bladder.

To Color Floors Walnut Tint.—Apply with paint brush or rag raw linseed oil, mixed with burnt umber. When dry, apply a coat of boiled linseed oil without color. The quantity of umber depends upon the wood, some requiring much more color to make a given tint. A small quantity of the mixture well rubbed in, has the best effect and dries sooner.

To Improve Pens.—When a pen has been used until it appears to be spoiled, place it over a flame (a gaslight for instance) for, say, a quarter of a minute, then dip it into water, and it will be again fit for use. A new pen, which is found too hard to write with, will become softer by being thus heated.

Vinegar.—A cheap and wholesome article of vinegar may be made of water, molasses and yeast, say twenty-five gallons of water, four of molasses, and one of yeast. This, when it ferments, will yield very good vinegar. A fair imitation of white wine vinegar may be made of mashed raisins and water kept in a warm place for a month.

Sponges.—After long use sponges are liable to smell very badly unless carefully cleaned every day. By rubbing a fresh lemon thoroughly into the sponge and then rinsing it several times in lukewarm water it will become as sweet as when new.

To Renovate the Tops of Kid Boots.—Defaced kid boots will be greatly improved by being rubbed *well* with a mixture of cream and ink.

To Preserve Bright Grates or Fire Irons from Rust.—Make strong paste of fresh lime and water, and with a fine brush smear it as thickly as possible over all the polished surface requiring preservation. By this simple means, all the grates and fire irons in an empty house may be kept for months free from harm, without further care or attention.

Simple Disinfectant.—Cut two or three good-sized onions in halves, and place them on a plate on the floor; they absorb noxious effluvia, etc., in the sick room, in an incredibly short space of time, and are greatly to be preferred to perfumery for the same purpose. They should be changed every six hours.

To Whiten Porcelain Saucepans.—Have the pans half filled with hot water; throw in a tablespoonful of pulverized borax, and let it boil. If this does not remove all the stains, soap a cloth and sprinkle on plenty of pulverized borax. Scour them well.

To Take Grease from Paper.—Gently warm the part containing the grease, and apply blotting-paper so as to extract as much as possible. Boil some clear essential oil of turpentine, and apply it to the warm paper with a soft, clean brush. A little rectified spirits of wine should be put on afterward.

To Set Colors.—Salt or beef's gall in the water helps to set black. A tablespoonful of spirits of turpentine to a gallon of water sets most blues, and alum is very efficacious in setting green. Black or very dark calicoes should be stiffened with gum arabic—five cents' worth is enough for a dress. If, however, starch is used, the garment should be turned wrong side out.

To Clean Ribbons.—Take one tablespoonful of brandy, one of soft soap, and one of molasses. Mix thoroughly together; place the ribbon upon a smooth board, and apply the mixture with a soft brush; after which rinse in cold water, and roll up in a cloth until nearly dry. Iron with a flat-iron, not too hot.

Copying-Ink.—Take two gallons of rain water and put into it one-quarter pound of gum arabic, one-quarter pound clean copperas, three-quarters pound nutgalls pulverized. Mix and shake occasionally for ten days, and strain. If needed sooner, let it steep in an iron kettle until the required strength is obtained.

To Cleanse Gilt Frames.—Take sufficient flour of sulphur to give a golden tinge to one and one-half pints of water; boil in this water four or five onions, strain, and when cold wash with soft brush any part that requires restoring; when dry it will come out as good as new.

Paste for Removing Grease from Silk.—Rub together fine French chalk and lavender to the consistence of a thin paste, and apply thoroughly to the spots with the fingers; place a sheet of brown or blotting-paper above and below the silk, and smooth it with a moderately-heated iron. The French chalk may then be removed by brushing.

To Purify Vessels.—All sorts of vessels and utensils may be purified from long retained smells of every kind in the easiest and most perfect manner, by rinsing them out well with charcoal powder after the grosser impurities have been scoured off with sand and water.

Glycerine Cement.—A cement, said to be capable of use where resistance to the action of both water and heat is required, is composed by mixing ordinary glycerine with dry litharge, so as to constitute a tough paste. For uniting the joints of steam-pipes, and other similar applications, this preparation is said to be very satisfactory.

A Candle to Burn all Night.—When, as in a case of sickness, a dull light is wished, or when matches are mislaid, put powdered salt on the candle till it reaches the black part of the wick. In this way a mild and steady light may be kept throughout the night by a small piece of candle.

To Clean White Kid Shoes.—White kid shoes can be cleaned by dipping a perfectly clean white flannel cloth in a little ammonia, and then rubbing the cloth over a cake of white soap; after doing this, rub the kid gently, and the soiled places will be white again. As the flannel becomes soiled, change for a clean one.

To Clean White Goods.—The following volatile soap will remove paint, grease spots, etc., and restore the purity of color of white goods: Four tablespoonfuls of spirits of hartshorn; four tablespoonfuls of alcohol, and a tablespoonful of salt. Shake the whole well together in a bottle and apply with a sponge.

To Restore Kid Gloves.—To restore old kid gloves, make a thick mucilage by boiling a handful of flaxseed; add a little dissolved soap; then when the mixture cools, with a piece of white flannel wipe the gloves, previously fitted to the hand. Use only enough of the cleaner to take off the dirt, without wetting through the glove.

Taking Up a Carpet.—On taking up a carpet, remove it carefully, then apply wet (not too wet) sawdust plentifully again and again. The floor will scarcely need washing, and you will be surprised at the absence of smothering dirt, and I am sure will use no other method in future.

To Prevent Rust in Tinware.—An easy and effectual plan to keep tinware from rusting consists in rubbing the new vessel inside and out with fresh lard or butter; then placing in the oven and keeping hot for several hours. The heat must not be so great as to melt the solder; still it is essential that the tin be kept very warm.

To Render Fruit Jars Air Tight.—When canning fruit have a cup of flour paste ready; if your rubbers are old, or the zinc rings or covers are bent a little, you may still make them air tight with the paste. If you are at all doubtful about the condition of your can it is a good notion to use the paste.

To Preserve Green Peas for Winter Use.—Gather the peas when plentiful, shell them; then wash and scald them in hot water. When thoroughly drained, put them into bottles, and fill up each bottle with a strong brine; at the top of the bottle pour a thin layer of salad oil. Cork and seal the bottles, which must be quite full and kept upright.

Liquid Glue.—Liquid glue may be made by dissolving glue in strong, hot vinegar, and adding one-fourth as much alcohol and a little alum. This will keep any length of time when placed in a closely stopped bottle, and will mend horn, wood and mother-of-pearl.

To Crystallize Windows.—Windows are crystallized, or made to imitate ground glass, by dissolving epsom salts in hot beer or a weak solution of gum arabic. You can make any pattern or border you please by cutting out a design on a sheet of pasteboard, and rubbing the design with a damp cloth.

To Take Grease out of Velvet.—Get some turpentine from the oil-shop, and pour it over the place that is greasy; rub it till quite dry with a piece of clean flannel. If the grease be not removed, repeat the application, and when done brush the place well, and hang the garment up in the open air to take away the smell.

To Freshen Black Lace.—Lay it on a clean table, sponge it all over with a weak solution of borax, about an even teaspoonful, or less, to a pint of warm water. Use a piece of old black silk, or black kid glove is better, to sponge with. While damp cover with a piece of black silk or cloth, and iron.

To Remove Grease from a Stove Hearth.—When oil or any other grease has been dropped on a stove hearth, immediately cover the place with very hot ashes. After a while clear away the ashes, and if the grease has not quite disappeared, repeat the process.

Waterproof Coating for Cotton or Linen.—Boiled linseed oil, containing about an ounce of the oxide of manganese, or litharge, to the quart, will make an excellent waterproof coating for cotton or linen cloth. Put on several coats with a brush, and allow each to dry perfectly.

Indelible Marking Ink.—Nitrate of silver, two drachms; distilled water three ounces. Dissolve. Moisten the spot to be marked with a concentrated solution of carbonate of potassa, to which a little gum water must be added. When the spot has become dry, write upon it with the solution of nitrate of silver.

Canaries.—The parasites which affect these pretty feathered pets may be got rid of by merely placing a clean white cloth over the cage at night. In the morning it will be covered with very minute red spots, almost invisible without a microscope. These are the vermin so annoying and so fatal to the birds.

To Improve Stove Polish.—Stove luster, when mixed with turpentine, and applied in the usual manner, is blacker, more glossy, and more durable than when mixed with any other liquid. The turpentine prevents rust, and when put on an old rusty stove will make it look as well as new.

To Remove Paint from a Wall.—If you intend papering a painted wall, you must first get off the paint, otherwise the paper will not stick. To do this, mix in a bucket with warm water a sufficient quantity of pearlash, or potash, so as to make a strong solution. Dip a brush into this, and with it scour off all the paint, finishing with cold water and a flannel.

To Brighten Jewelry.—It is possible, if not probable, that you do not know how to brighten gold or silver jewelry, if tarnished. Very well, then, brush it with an old tooth brush wet with soap suds, and place in sawdust to dry. Some ladies keep their jewelry in sawdust. The jewelers use this method.

To Prevent Rust.—A composition that will effectually prevent iron, steel, etc., from rusting. Mix with fat oil varnish four-fifths of well rectified spirits of turpentine. Apply this varnish with a sponge, and the articles will retain their metallic brilliancy, and not be liable to rust.

To Clean Black Veils.—Pass them through a warm liquor of bullock's gall and water; rinse in cold water; then take a small piece of glue, pour boiling water on it, and pass the veil through it; clap it, and frame to dry. Instead of framing, it may be fastened with drawing-pins closely fixed upon a very clean paste, or drawing-board.

To Sharpen Scissors.—Take a coarse sewing needle and hold it firmly between the thumb and forefinger of the left hand; then take the scissors in your right hand, and cut them smoothly and quickly from hand to point. The dullest scissors, unless they are entirely worn out, can soon be sharpened in this way.

Ink Stains on Furniture.—Ink stains on mahogany or black walnut furniture may be removed by touching the stains with a feather wet in a solution of nitre and water, eight drops to a spoonful of water. As soon as the spots disappear rub the place *at once* with a cloth wet in cold water. If the ink stains then remain, repeat, making the solution stronger.

Kerosene Fires.—It ought to be more generally known that wheat flour is probably the best possible article to throw over a fire caused by the spilling and igniting of kerosene. It ought to be known, because flour is always within convenient reach.

Use of Lemon Leaves.—Lemon seeds, if planted and treated as house plants, will make pretty little shrubs. The leaves can then be used for flavoring. Tie a few in a cloth and drop in apple sauce when boiling and nearly done. It is a cheap essence.

Unpleasant Odor from Cabbage.—The reason why cabbage emits such a disagreeable smell when boiling is because the process dissolves the essential oil. The water should be changed when the cabbage is half-boiled, and it will thus acquire a greater sweetness.

Glazed Whitewash.—Take two gallons of water, one pound and a half of rice, and one pound of moist sugar. Let the mixture boil until the rice is quite dissolved, and then thicken it to the consistence of whitewash with finely-powdered lime. This whitewash has a pretty satiny look, and does nicely for the inside of bird cages, as well as for commoner purposes.

Mold on Jelly.—If the paper which is put over jelly be dipped in the white of an egg, it will when dry be tight and firm, and keep the fruit from molding with much more certainty than if it is dipped in alcohol or brandy. The paper which is laid next the fruit is meant, not that which is tied or pasted over the glass.

Positive Cure for Water Bugs.—To a kettleful of water add a cupful of washing soda. Let it come to a boil; after which pour it down the water pipes, commencing at the top of the house. Repeat the operation once or twice and you will have destroyed 99 per cent. of the bugs, which breed inside the pipes during the month of September. The few remaining in the room can be reached with insect powder.

To Remove Tar from the Hands.—We recommend rubbing the hands with the outside of fresh orange or lemon peel, and wiping dry immediately. It is astonishing what a small piece will clean. The volatile oils in the skins dissolve the tar, so that it can be wiped off.

Drying Fruits.—Families of farmers engaged in drying fruits are reminded that the solar heat is not sufficiently intense to destroy insect eggs that may have been deposited in the fruit when green, or in the process of drying. If put in a moderately warm oven for ten minutes all parasites and their eggs would be destroyed. In countries where fruits are extensively dried the treatment is practiced generally.

Cement for Glass, Crockery, Etc.—Four pounds of white glue, one and a half pounds of dry white lead, half a pound of isinglass, one gallon of soft water, one quart of alcohol, one-half pint of white varnish. Dissolve the glue and isinglass in the water by gentle heat if preferred, stir in the lead, put the alcohol in the varnish, and mix the whole together.

Care of Lamp Chimneys.—After the lamps are filled and the chimneys washed and put on the shelf, take pieces of newspaper and roll in the form of a chimney and slip over chimney and lamp. It will protect from dust and flies, and when the lamps are lighted one will be rewarded by finding them as clear and bright as when first put in order.

Care of Flour.—Flour is like butter; it absorbs smells readily. It should not be kept in a place where there are onions, fish, vegetables decaying, or other odorous substances, nor in a damp room or cellar. Keep it in a cool, dry, airy room, where not exposed to a freezing temperature, nor to one above 70 degrees, and always sift before using.

Mites in Cheese.—Cheese kept in a cool larder or cellar, with a cloth rung out of clean cold water constantly upon it will never have mites in it, or if it has, this will soon destroy them, and also greatly improve the cheese, keeping it always moist.

To Clean Glass.—For cleaning glass a newspaper is one of the best articles to use. The chemical operation of some of the ingredients of printing ink gives a beautiful polish. Slightly moisten a piece of paper, roll it up and rub the glass; then take a dry, soft piece and repeat the process. No lint will remain, as is the case when cloth is used.

Cleaning Hats.—White fur or light beaver hats can be nicely cleaned with salt and Indian meal. Take about equal proportions of each, place it in a pan and heat it in the oven until it is as hot as can be handled. Lay the fur on a clean cloth and rub gently with the salt and meal until the dirt is removed, then shake it thoroughly.

To Improve Pickles.—Grape leaves are recommended to put on top of pickles to keep them sharp and free from mold. Fresh green grape leaves are better than flannel cloths. They should be rinsed in pure water and then drained quite dry, and laid over every piece in the jar. They should be changed once a week.

To Clean Smoky Ceilings.—Ceilings that have been smoked by a kerosene lamp should be washed off with soda water. Grained wood should be washed with cold tea.

To Remove Marks from Tables.—Hot dishes sometimes leave whitish marks on varnished tables, when set, as they should not be, carelessly upon them. For removing them, pour some lamp-oil on the spot, and rub it hard with a soft cloth. Pour on a little spirits, and rub it dry with another cloth, and the whole mark will disappear, leaving the table as bright as before.

To Soften Water.—Hard waters are rendered very soft and pure, rivaling distilled water, by merely boiling a two-ounce vial, say, in a kettleful of water. The carbonate of lime and any impurities will be found adhering to the vial. The water boils very much quicker at the same time.

To Remove Bruises from Furniture.—Wet the bruised spots with warm weather. Soak a piece of brown paper of several thicknesses in warm water, and lay over the place. Then apply a warm flat-iron until the moisture is gone. Repeat the process if needful, and the bruises will disappear.

Celebrated Recipe for Silver Wash.—One ounce of nitric acid, one ten cent piece, and one ounce of quicksilver. Put in an open glass vessel, and let it stand until dissolved; then add one pint of water, and it is ready for use. Make it into a powder by adding whiting, and it may be used on brass, copper, German silver, etc.

To Blacken Stoves.—Those who are troubled to blacken their kitchen stoves in winter, on account of keeping a constant fire, try my plan of adding about a teaspoonful of sugar to a teacupful of mixed blacking. You can use this when the stove is quite hot, and the sugar causes the blacking to adhere to the stove.

Damp Closets.—For a damp closet or cupboard, which is liable to cause mildew, place in it a saucer full of quicklime, and it will not only absorb all apparent dampness, but sweeten and disinfect the place. Renew the lime once a fortnight, or as often as it becomes slaked.

New Kettles.—The best way to prepare a new iron kettle for use is to fill it with clean potato parings; boil them for an hour or more, then wash the kettle with hot water, wipe it dry, and rub it with a little lard; repeat the rubbing for half a dozen times after using. In this way you will prevent rust and all the annoyances liable to occur in the use of a new kettle.

To Clean White Knitted Garments.—Take those not needing washing, being only slightly soiled, place them in a pillow-case one at a time, sprinkle flour through it, and shake well, until it looks as bright as new. Borax is excellent to wash flannels with, dissolved in luke warm water.

To Improve and Preserve Butter.—Take two parts good salt, one part sugar, one-half part saltpetre; mix well together, and use one ounce for every pound of butter, thoroughly worked into it. It makes the butter rich, good color, and prevents bitterness. It will keep good for two or three years. Let it stand a month before it is used, and keep it closely covered.

To Keep Cranberries all Winter.—Put them in a cool room, where there is no danger of freezing, and either spread out on a cloth or so as to give each berry light and air; or, which is a sure way, put them in a barrel under water.

For Oiling Walnut Furniture.—Raw linseed oil rubbed with a flannel cloth, then polish with dry flannel; be careful not to put too much on.

To Whiten Linen Garments. —Linen garments which have become yellow from time, may be whitened by being boiled in a lather made of milk and pure white soap, a pound of the latter to a gallon of the former. After the boiling process the linen should be twice. rinsed, a little bluing being added to the last water used.

To Eradicate Vermin. —It is said that common sulphur will kill or drive away the little fish-shaped, silvery pest which infests our pantry. Sprinkle the sulphur freely about, and the place will soon be cleared of the vermin.

How to Smooth Ribbons. —Take a moderately hot flat-iron on the ironing-board, then place the ribbon on the left side of the iron, and pull it carefully through underneath the iron. If the ribbon is not pulled too fast, and the iron is the right warmth, this will be found to be a much better way than simply rubbing the iron over the ribbon.

To Get Rid of Flies. —The following is better than fly paper: Take half a teaspoonful of black pepper in powder, one teaspoonful of brown sugar, and one teaspoonful of cream; mix them well together and place them in a room, on a plate, where the flies are troublesome, and they will soon disappear.

To Take the Woody Taste Out of a Wooden Pail. —Fill the pail with boiling hot water; let it remain until cold, then empty it, and dissolve some soda in lukewarm water, adding a little lime to it, and wash the inside well with the solution; after that scald with hot water and rinse well.

To Prevent Iron from Rusting. —Warm the iron until you cannot bear your hand on it without burning yourself. Then rub it with new and clean white wax. Put it again to the fire till it has soaked in the wax. When done rub it over with a piece of serge. This prevents the iron from rusting afterwards.

To Revive Withered Flowers. —Plunge the stems into boiling water, and by the time the water is cold, the flowers will revive. The ends of the stalks should then be cut off, and the flowers should be put to stand in cold water, and they will keep fresh for several days.

To Remove Putty from Glass. —Dip a small brush in nitric or muriatic acid, and with it paint over the dry putty that adheres to the broken glasses and frames of the windows. After an hour's interval the putty will have become so soft as to be easily removed.

To Clean Fine Toothed Combs. —Clean a fine-toothed comb by putting a piece of rather coarse sewing silk through the arm of a chair, or fastening it in some way at a convenient height. Hold the two ends of the thread and press the comb upon it, rubbing briskly, letting the silk penetrate all the spaces.

Baking Griddle Cakes Without Grease. —If you wish to do away with the use of grease on the griddle for baking cakes, have the ordinary iron griddle ground smooth on a grindstone and rubbed off with a piece of fine sand paper wrapped round a block of wood. This is much better than a soapstone griddle.

Preserving Fruit.—Dr. Kedzie says: In cooking acid fruits housekeepers unwittingly waste a good part of the sugar. Anxious to get the fullest effect of the sugar upon the small fruits, they boil the two together, and thus convert most of the cane sugar into grape sugar. Several years ago my assistant in chemistry tested this matter by placing one hundred parts of ripe gooseberries in a stewpan with water to cover them, added twenty-five parts of sugar and cooked the fruit. A second portion of the same berries was cooked without sugar, and after the fruit was partially cooked the twenty-five parts of sugar added, and when this sugar had dissolved both samples of cooked fruit were analyzed, when one-half the sugar in the first batch was converted into glucose, and only one-tenth of the cane sugar in the second batch was thus changed. If the gooseberries had been green the results would have been more striking. If very acid fruits, like currants and cranberries, are rapidly cooked by boiling and then set to cool for a few minutes and the sugar added, a fine jelly-like mass will be found when the sauce is cold, very different from the watery mess so often seen. In making preserves the same principles hold good for the most part, though preserves are more apt to work or ferment if sugar is not cooked with the fruit. In this case it is better to steam the fruit till it is so tender that a straw may penetrate it, then put the fruit into cans, add the sugar, and seal up at once. Three pounds of sugar for four pounds of fruit will be ample.

How to Preserve Feathers.—The disposal and management of the feathers is a thing that calls for attention. As soon as a fowl is killed, and while yet warm, let it be carefully plucked. Separate the large wing-feathers; put the others into small paper bags previously prepared. Put these bags into an oven and let them remain about half an hour; take them out, repeat the process two or three times, then keep the feathers in a dry place till required. The oven must not be too hot. Care must be taken to free the feathers of any skin or flesh that may adhere to them while being plucked, or they will be tainted. The hard quilly portion of the larger feathers must be cut off with a pair of scissors. The wing and tail feathers may be stripped and added to the others. Previous to putting them in the oven, some recommend that the feathers should be put loosely into a dry tub or basket and shaken up daily, so that all may in turn be exposed to the air. Others recommend, as an easier plan, merely to suspend the bag from the ceiling of a warm kitchen, or on the wall behind a fire-place, where it is practicable. In this case they will take longer to dry. Feathers can be quickly and effectually dried and cleaned by the agency of steam; but it is rather an expensive method, and the thrifty henwife will doubtless prefer having the produce of her own yard prepared under her own eye and by her own directions.

Putting Away Winter Clothing.—Housewives when about to put away their heavy winter clothing should select one closet in the house in which to hang the dresses, overcoats, and heavy jackets. The clothes should be hung on a line in the yard on a sunny day and well aired and beaten. The closet should be thoroughly washed and sprinkled with good black pepper and insect powder. Then hang the garments up and close the door. They will keep all summer, but more pepper should be put in every month. Furs should have the same treatment, and after being thoroughly sprinkled with black pepper, should be put in newspapers so that no air may get at them. Every opening in the paper must be sealed. This process of wrapping in newspapers is said to insure safety against moths, as they cannot cut through the printer's ink without dying; but it is wise to sprinkle the garment with pepper unless one intends to take it out during the warm weather.

To Keep Lamp Chimneys from Cracking.—The following recipe for keeping lamp chimneys from cracking is taken from a Leipzig journal devoted to the glass interest. Place your tumblers, chimneys or vessels which you desire to keep from cracking, in a pot filled with cold water, add a little cooking salt, allow the mixture to boil well over a fire, and then cool slowly. Glass treated in this way is said not to crack even if exposed to very sudden changes of temperature. Chimneys are said to become very durable by this process, which may also be extended to crockery, stoneware, porcelain, etc. The process is simply one of annealing, and the slower the process, especially the cooling portion of it, the more effective will be the work.

Care of Velvet.—How to brush velvet is a thing, easy as it seems, not known to everybody. The whole secret lies in the management of the brush. Take a hat brush that is not too soft, but has the bristles elastic, and that will return at once to their original state after being pressed aside. Hold this firmly under the palm of the hand, in the direction of the arm, and with the bristles downward; and pressing them first gently into the substance of the velvet, then twist around the arm, hand, and brush altogether as on an axis, without moving them forward or backward. The foreign matters will be drawn up and flirted out of the flock without injury to the substance of the velvet; and the brush must be lifted up and placed in a similar manner over every part required to be brushed. By this means velvet will be improved instead of deteriorated; and will last for years.

Housekeeper's Weights and Measures.—Two gills make half a pint. Two pints make one quart. Four quarts make one gallon. Half a gallon is a quarter of a peck. Two gallons make one peck. Four gallons make half a bushel. Eight gallons make one bushel. About sixty drops of any thin liquid will fill a common-sized teaspoon. Four tablespoons, or one-half a gill, will fill a common-sized wine-glass. Four wine-glasses will fill a half-pint measure, a common tumbler, or a large coffee-cup. Ten eggs usually weigh one pound before they are broken. A tablespoonful of salt weighs one ounce.

Cleaning Matting.—To clean and freshen old matting, rub it with a cloth wet in salt water, being careful not to allow any drops of water to dry in the matting, as they will leave spots difficult to remove. Heavy, varnished furniture should never rest directly upon the matting, for even good varnish, becoming soft in warm weather, will stain the straw. Matting may be turned if the loose ends of the cords are threaded in a large needle and drawn through to the other side.

To Remove Coffee or Milk Stains.—The use of glycerine is recommended for this purpose. The silk, woolen, or other fabric is painted over with glycerine, then washed with a clean linen rag dipped in lukewarm rain water, until clean. It is afterwards pressed on the wrong side with a moderately warm iron as long as it seems damp. The most delicate colors are unaffected by this treatment.

To Mend Cracks in a Wall.—Mend cracks in a wall with plaster of Paris mixed with cold water to a very soft paste. Wet but little at a time, as it hardens rapidly, and cannot be used again. Apply with a knife blade. If the plaster is not convenient, fill cracks with stiff flour paste, cover with a strip of white muslin, and whitewash over. Old, cracked closets look wonderfully well after this treatment.

To Keep Milk.—If milk is brought just to the boiling point, then poured immediately into cans and sealed air tight, it will keep indefinitely. As the air is expelled by boiling, the milk keeps just as canned goods do. If glass jars are used they must be heated so that the boiling milk will not break them. Many families keep but one cow, and this plan will enable them to have milk during the weeks that she is dry.

To Preserve Steel Pens.—A simple mode of preventing ink from damaging metallic pens, is to throw either into the inkstand or the bottle in which the ink is kept, a few nails, broken bits of steel pens (not tarnished) or any other pieces of iron not rusted. The corrosive action of the acid contained in the ink is expended on the iron introduced.

To Destroy Clinkers in a Stove.—Clinkers will accumulate on fire brick. Empty the stove or grate of coals and ashes; while hot, throw in two or three quarts of oyster shells, or a less quantity of salt, then cleave off the clinkers.

To Clean Damask Curtains.—If crimson, wash well with ordinary soap and water, then rinse in clean cold water, wring through a wringing-machine, and hang in the open air to dry. If the curtains are green, use gall instead of soap. Silk trimmings must be removed, as they cannot be cleaned.

Hard Soap.—Six pounds sal-soda, four pounds unslacked lime, twenty-four quarts rain-water. Put all on the fire, and boil, then set off and let settle. Drain off and put over the fire with six pounds clear grease, and one-half pound rosin. Boil until it begins to thicken, throw in a couple handfuls of salt. Let cool and cut.

To Clean Tea and Coffee Pots.—Discolored tea and coffee pots may be cleaned by filling them with water in which two or three tablespoonfuls of wood ashes have been placed, and letting it boil up, then wash thoroughly with hot soapsuds, and rinse.

Ink on Clothing.—To extract ink from cotton, silk, or woolen goods, dip the spots in spirits of turpentine, and let it remain for several hours; then rub thoroughly between the hands, and it will all disappear without changing either the color or texture of the fabric.

Volatile Soap, for Removing Paint, Etc.—Four tablespoonfuls of spirits of hartshorn, four tablespoonfuls of alcohol, and a tablespoonful of salt. Shake the whole well together in a bottle, and apply with a sponge or brush.

To Clean Lamps.—Oil lamps sometimes burn dimly because of their becoming incrusted inside with the settling from the oil. Take soapsuds and fill the lamp about one-third full; then put in a little coarse sand and shake vigorously. Every particle of the settling will soon be removed.

To Clean Tinware.—An experienced housekeeper says the best thing for cleaning tinware is common soda. She gives the following directions: Dampen a cloth and dip in soda and rub the ware briskly, after which wipe dry. Any blackened ware can be made to look as well as new.

To Revive a Mattress.—When mattresses get hard and bunchy, rip them, take the hair out, pull it thoroughly by hand, let it lie a day or two to air, wash the tick, lay it in as lightly and evenly as possible, and catch it down as before. Thus prepared they will be as good as new.

Removing Iodine Stains.—To remove iodine stains from linen, dip the stained portion in cold water, and then hold over the fire until dry, repeating the operation until the stain is removed.

How to Give Finish to Woolen Articles.—Hold the article over boiling water. When it is thoroughly dampened, fold in good shape and put under a linen press. This process gives them a flat, even and smooth appearance.

To Perfume Linen.—Rose leaves, dried in the shade, or at about four feet from a stove, one pound; cloves, caraway seeds, and allspice, of each one ounce—pound in a mortar, or grind in a mill; dried salt, a quarter of a pound; mix all together, and put into muslin bags.

To Clean Gold.—Powder some whiting, and make it into a moist paste with some sal-volatile. Cover over the gold ornaments and surface with a soft brush; let it dry, and then brush it off with a moderately hard brush.

To Restore the Color of Silks.—When the color of silks has been destroyed by any strong acid, it may be restored by carefully wetting the spot with a strong soap lather, to which a little saleratus has been added. When the color has been taken out by fruit stains ammonia will restore it.

To Exterminate Cockroaches.—Borax is a very good cockroach exterminator. Take some pieces of board, spread them over with molasses, only sufficient to make the borax when sprinkled upon it stick, and place the boards in their haunts.

To Clean Carpets.—Carpets may be cleaned without taking up by sprinkling them over with moist tea leaves and sweeping well. Then sprinkle Fuller's earth very thickly over the grease spots, cover them with a sheet of brown paper and iron with a warm smoothing iron until the spots disappear.

To Prevent Wooden Bowls from Cracking.—Either pour sweet, hot lard in them, or immerse in cold water, bring to the boiling point, boil an hour longer, then let the water cool gradually, when the bowl may be taken out.

To Perfume Clothes.—Cloves, in coarse powder, one ounce; cassia, one ounce; lavender flowers, one ounce; lemon peel, one ounce. Mix and put them into little bags, and place them where the clothes are kept, or wrap the clothes around them. They will keep off insects.

To Re-color Hair.—Get one yard of seal brown or black common cambric. Put in cold water and boil till the color is well out, then add the switch and boil slowly two hours. Dry, and if not dark enough, repeat.

To Clean a Chimney.—To clean a chimney, place a piece of zinc on the live coals in the stove. The vapor produced by the zinc will carry off the soot by chemical decomposition. Those who have tried the process claim that it will work every time.

To Remove a Screw Rusted in the Wood.—Heat a poker in the fire red-hot, and put it on the top of a screw for a minute or two; then take the screw-driver, and you will easily get it out, if you do it whilst it is warm.

To Clean Articles Made of White Zephyr.—Put in flour of magnesia, changing often, shake off the flour and hang in the open air a short time.

Improvement in Chandeliers.—To renew a dusty and discolored chandelier, apply a mixture of bronze powder and copal varnish. The druggist where they are purchased will tell you in what proportion they should be mixed.

Crust in Kettles.—This is formed by every sort of water except rain water. A simple mode of prevention is to place a large marble in the kettle, which, by attracting the mineral particles in the water, will keep the inside free.

Jelly Molds.—Jelly molds should be greased with cold butter. When you wish to remove the jelly or pudding, plunge the mold into hot water, remove quickly, and the contents will come out in perfect form and without any trouble.

To Clean Old Lamp-Burners.—Wash them in ashes and water, and they will come out bright as new. Many times a burner is condemned because the light is poor, when, having clogged up with sediment, the wick is at fault.

To Give a Stove a Fine Brilliant Appearance.—A teaspoonful of pulverized alum mixed with stove polish will give the stove a fine lustre, which will be quite permanent.

To Improve Beefsteak.—A tablespoonful of strong coffee put in the gravy of melted butter, pepper and salt to be poured over beefsteak, imparts a delicious flavor to gravy and meat. It makes the gravy a rich brown.

Care of a Coffee Pot.—A carelessly kept coffee pot will impart a rank flavor to the strongest infusion of the best Java. Wash the coffee pot thoroughly every day, and twice a week boil borax water in it for fifteen minutes.

To Remove Stains from Tableware.—A little saleratus rubbed on with the finger or a bit or linen, will remove stains from cups and other articles of tableware. It will also remove spots from marbleized oilcloths, and many stains from tin ware.

To Beat Eggs Quickly.—To beat the whites of eggs quickly put in a pinch of salt. The cooler the eggs the quicker they will froth. Salt cools and also freshens them.

Airing Feather Beds.—Never sun feather beds. Air them thoroughly on a windy day in a cool place. The sun draws the oil, and gives the feathers a rancid smell.

To Clean Diamonds.—To clean diamonds nicely, wash in soap-suds, rinse in alcohol, and dry in sawdust; then brush with a soft brush, and polish with fine tissue paper.

Straw Matting.—A thin coat of varnish applied to straw matting will make it much more durable and keep the matting looking fresh and new. White varnish should be used on white matting.

To Stop Mouse-Holes.—Stop mouse-holes with plugs of common hard soap, and you will do it effectually. Rats, roaches and ants will not disregard it.

To Take Rust Out of Steel.—Cover the steel with sweet oil, well rubbed in. In forty-eight hours rub with finely powdered, unslaked lime until the rust disappears.

To Restore the Color of Black Kid Boots.—Take a small quantity of good black ink, mix it with the white of an egg, and apply it to the boots with a soft sponge.

Finger Marks on Mirrors.—For washing finger marks from looking-glasses or windows, put a few drops of spirits of ammonia on a moist rag, and make quick work of removing them.

To Keep Seeds From the Depredations of Mice.—Mix some pieces of camphor with them. Camphor placed in trunks or drawers will prevent mice from doing them injury.

To Clean Zinc.—A good way to clean zinc is to rub it with a piece of cotton cloth dipped in kerosene; afterward rub it with a dry cotton cloth, and it will be as bright as when new.

To Imitate Ground Glass.—A ready way of imitating ground glass is by dissolving Epsom salts in ale (don't use this as a beverage) and applying with a brush; as it dries it crystallizes.

For Rusty Stove Pipe.—Rub with linseed oil, a little goes a good way; build a slow fire at first till it dries. Oil in the spring to prevent it from rusting.

Finger Marks on a Piano.—To remove finger-marks on a highly polished piano, wipe with a cloth wet in pure *cold* water. It does not injure in the slightest if wiped dry, and restores the new look at once.

To Sweeten Rancid Lard.—Heat the lard, and when melted slice three or four pared potatoes; continue heating until the slices (which should be quite thin) are well browned.

To Improve Tin Kettles.—Kerosene will make tin kettles as bright as new. Saturate a woolen rag and rub with it. It will also remove stains from clean varnished furniture.

To Whiten Ivory.—Discolored ivory may be whitened by rubbing it with a paste composed of burnt pumice stone and water, and then place it under glass in the sun.

To Pack Canned Goods.—Pack canned fruits in saw-dust. This material will certainly help to keep the cans cool in summer and prevent freezing in winter.

INDEX.